JESUS, THE GOSPELS, AND CINEMATIC IMAGINATION

Jesus, the Gospels, and Cinematic Imagination

Introducing Jesus Movies, Christ Films, and the Messiah in Motion

RICHARD WALSH AND JEFFREY L. STALEY

t&tclark
LONDON • NEW YORK • OXFORD • NEW DELHI • SYDNEY

T&T CLARK
Bloomsbury Publishing Plc
50 Bedford Square, London, WC1B 3DP, UK
1385 Broadway, New York, NY 10018, USA
29 Earlsfort Terrace, Dublin 2, Ireland

BLOOMSBURY, T&T CLARK and the T&T Clark logo are trademarks
of Bloomsbury Publishing Plc

First published in Great Britain 2022

Copyright © Richard Walsh and Jeffrey L. Staley, 2022

Richard Walsh and Jeffrey L. Staley have asserted their right under the Copyright,
Designs and Patents Act, 1988, to be identified as Authors of this work.

Cover design by Charlotte James
Image courtesy Ronald Grant Film Archive/Mary Evans
Picture Library Image vectors © designer29 / iStock

All rights reserved. No part of this publication may be reproduced or transmitted
in any form or by any means, electronic or mechanical, including photocopying,
recording, or any information storage or retrieval system, without prior permission
in writing from the publishers.

Bloomsbury Publishing Plc does not have any control over, or responsibility for, any
third-party websites referred to or in this book. All internet addresses given in this
book were correct at the time of going to press. The author and publisher regret
any inconvenience caused if addresses have changed or sites have ceased to exist,
but can accept no responsibility for any such changes.

A catalogue record for this book is available from the British Library.
Library of Congress Cataloging-in-Publication Data
Names: Walsh, Richard G., author. | Staley, Jeffrey Lloyd, 1951- author.
Title: Jesus, the gospels, and cinematic imagination : introducing Jesus movies, Christ films,
and the Messiah in motion / Richard Walsh and Jeffrey L. Staley.
Description: London, UK ; New York, NY, USA : T&T Clark, 2021. | Includes bibliographical
references and index. | Summary: "Richard Walsh and Jeffrey Staley introduce the full history
and phenomenon of Jesus movies. Beginning with an introduction to the prevalent themes
in cinematic depictions of Jesus and messiah figures, they survey over twenty of the most
influential and distinctive individual films"– Provided by publisher.
Identifiers: LCCN 2021005419 (print) | LCCN 2021005420 (ebook) | ISBN 9780567693839 (hb) |
ISBN 9780567693846 (pb) | ISBN 9780567693853 (epdf) | ISBN 9780567693877 (epub)
Subjects: LCSH: Jesus Christ–In motion pictures.
Classification: LCC PN1995.9.J4 W35 2021 (print) | LCC PN1995.9.J4
(ebook) | DDC 791.43/638232–dc23
LC record available at https://lccn.loc.gov/2021005419
LC ebook record available at https://lccn.loc.gov/2021005420

ISBN:	HB:	978-0-5676-9383-9
	PB:	978-0-5676-9384-6
	ePDF:	978-0-5676-9385-3
	ePUB:	978-0-5676-9387-7

Typeset by Integra Software Services Pvt. Ltd.

To find out more about our authors and books visit www.bloomsbury.com
and sign up for our newsletters.

CONTENTS

List of Figures		vii
Introduction: Digitalizing Jesus		1
1	*La vie du Christ* or *La naissance, la vie et la mort du Christ* (The Birth, the Life, and Death of Christ) Alice Guy, **1906**	17
2	*La vie et passion de notre seigneur Jésus Christ* (The Life and Passion of Jesus Christ) Ferdinand Zecca, **1907**	27
3	*From the Manger to the Cross* Sidney Olcott, **1912**	36
4	*Intolerance: Love's Struggle throughout the Ages* D. W. Griffith, **1916**	47
5	*The King of Kings* Cecil B. DeMille, **1927**	59
6	*King of Kings* Nicholas Ray, **1961**	74
7	*Il vangelo secondo Matteo* (The Gospel According to St. Matthew) Pier Paolo Pasolini, **1964**	90
8	*The Greatest Story Ever Told* George Stevens, **1965**	105
9	*Godspell* David Greene, **1973**	121
10	*Jesus Christ Superstar* Norman Jewison, **1973**	133
11	*Il messia* (The Messiah) Roberto Rossellini, **1975**	147
12	*Jesus of Nazareth* Franco Zeffirelli, **1977**	164
13	*Monty Python's Life of Brian* Terry Jones, **1979**	184
14	*The Jesus Film* John Krish and Peter Sykes, **1979**	197
15	*The Last Temptation of Christ* Martin Scorsese, **1988**	213
16	*Jésus de Montréal* Denys Arcand, **1989**	229
17	*Jesus* Roger Young, **1999**	243

18	*The Miracle Maker* Derek W. Hayes and Stanislav Sokolov, **2000**	257
19	*The Gospel of John* Philip Saville, **2003**	268
20	*The Passion of the Christ* Mel Gibson, **2004**	280
21	*Son of Man* Mark Dornford-May, **2006**	298
22	*Mary Magdalene* Garth Davis, **2018**	309

A Gospels Harmony of Select Jesus Films — 321

References — 355
Film Index — 373
Topic Index — 376

FIGURES

1.1	Veronica holds the true image in *La vie du Christ*	20
2.1	The transfigured Christ in *La vie et passion de notre seigneur Jésus Christ*	30
3.1	The cruciform shadow auguring the cross in *From the Manger to the Cross*	40
4.1	The heavenly cross that ends all war in *Intolerance*	51
5.1	The blind girl (and audience) sees Jesus for the first time in *The King of Kings*	64
6.1	One of several extreme closeups of Jesus's striking blue eyes in *King of Kings*	79
7.1	Jesus rejects his mother in *Il vangelo secondo Matteo*	95
8.1	Jesus prays outside Lazarus's tomb in *The Greatest Story Ever Told*	108
9.1	The red ribbon, chain-link fence crucifixion in *Godspell*	125
10.1	Magdalene comforts Jesus as Judas looks on in *Jesus Christ Superstar*	137
11.1	While working on a winnowing fork, Jesus teaches his village gospel in *Il messia*	152
12.1	Jesus reconciles fiery Peter and tax collector Matthew in *Jesus of Nazareth*	171
13.1	Brian prompts his "followers" to think for themselves in *Monty Python's Life of Brian*	186
14.1	Jesus, Peter, and others walk past four crosses in *The Jesus Film*	204
15.1	Jesus asleep on Judas's chest in *The Last Temptation of Christ*	218
16.1	Mireille holds Daniel in a pietà beneath Pascal's "head" in *Jésus de Montréal*	234
17.1	Jesus roughhousing with his disciples in *Jesus*	248
18.1	Tamar reaches out, Ben-Hur style, to comfort Jesus in *The Miracle Maker*	261
19.1	Digitalizing the apostolic witness (book) in *The Gospel of John*	273
20.1	Mary, as co-sufferer, listens for her child's groans in *The Passion of the Christ*	287
21.1	Jesus crucified in protest above Khayelitsha in *Son of Man*	302
22.1	Jesus anoints Mary's eyes in *Mary Magdalene*	313

Introduction: Digitalizing Jesus

Jesus films came into existence with (celluloid) film itself and have continued into the digital age. Various streaming platforms make Jesus films increasingly available and DVDs an antiquated technology.[1] That transition, along with significant scholarly work on Jesus films, has led to this complete revision of *Jesus, the Gospels, and Cinematic Imagination: A Handbook to Jesus on DVD* (2007).

This edition introduces twenty-two Jesus films (with passing comments about numerous others), chosen for their importance in the tradition, availability, and diversity.[2] The films represent early and recent exemplars; they display different theologies and ideologies (or different stances vis-à-vis the Jesus tradition); they focus on different aspects of the "Jesus story"; they characterize differently; and they hide and call attention to both the camera and interpretation. They appear in such diverse forms that they defy simple generic classification. Even "Jesus film" names some incorrectly—for some purposes.[3]

JESUS FILMS: DIVERSITY AND FAMILY CHARACTERISTICS

Most think of Jesus films as historical epics like *The King of Kings* (1927), *King of Kings* (1961), *The Greatest Story Ever Told* (1965), *Jesus of Nazareth* (1979, although a television miniseries), and *The Passion of the Christ* (2004). The earliest Jesus films, however, marketed themselves as filmed passion plays (e.g., *The Höritz Passion Play* 1897; *The Passion Play of Oberammergau* 1898).[4] This approach allowed filmmakers to deflect charges of irreverence onto the play/director (see Gaudreault 2016). Despite their "antique look," the films were not attempting historical reconstruction; they presented a Jesus of (if not in) worship/tradition.[5] Viewed from the perspective of later "Jesus histories," they are Jesus relocations, situating Jesus in the (eternal) present.[6]

Soon, passion films—rather than filmed plays—became the norm (e.g., *La vie du Christ* 1906; *La vie et passion de notre seigneur Jésus Christ* 1907). Ever since, passion films (e.g., *The Passion of the Christ* 2004) and filmed passions (*The Lawton Story* 1949; *Celui qui doit mourir* [He Who Must Die 1957]; *Jesus Christ Superstar* 1973; *Jésus de Montréal* 1989; and *Jesus Town USA* 2014) have been fixtures in the tradition. Filmed passions relocate Jesus to their own times (and to Christ figures)—not to worship—to the extent they focus on their Jesus actors' lives outside the passion play.[7] Adele Reinhartz describes such films as "the passion in present tense" and sees them as a subset of a larger group placing Jesus alongside a contemporary story (2013a: 116–25; cf. *Intolerance* 1916). Other films forego

"Jesus" for contemporary figures seen by others, or themselves, as Jesuses or Christs or messiahs (perhaps, *Godspell* 1973; *Son of Man* 2006; certainly, *The Ruling Class* 1972; *The Favour, the Watch, and the Very Big Fish* 1991). According to Reinhold Zwick (2018), such "second comings" are the preferred German Jesus since *Der Galiläer* (1921, a passion film sometimes marketed as a filmed play) and *I.N.R.I.* (1923, which paired Jesus with a contemporary story).[8]

Early Jesus silents were spectacles, not stories. They offered the passion (or something else, e.g., the exotic holy land or color) as something to behold. All early cinema was a "cinema of attractions," until it developed the visual techniques to "tell" stories (Gunning 1986; 1994: 10–30). Jesus cinema simply developed visual storytelling codes more slowly (Keil 1992; Shepherd 2016b: 271–6).[9] Even *Golgotha* (1935), the earliest Jesus "talkie," is still a passion spectacle (Shepherd 2016b: 276–80) as is, for that matter, *The Passion of the Christ*, which Mel Gibson wanted to release without subtitles.[10] The passion is so important to Jesus films that *Son of Man* "resurrects" its dead protagonist to crucify his corpse on a hill above Khayelitsha, and Christ-figure film enthusiasts fixate on cruciform deaths as telltale signs of "hidden" Christs.

Early cinematic Jesuses were icons, talismans, christeners, and/or triumphant crosses. Story developed in Jesus adjacents, films focusing on those alongside Jesus—including, among Jesus silents, *La vie du Christ*'s omnipresent women; Judas (*Le Baiser de Judas* [The Kiss of Judas 1909]); Barabbas (*The Shadow of Nazareth* 1913); the protagonists in *Intolerance*'s developed modern and Babylonian stories; and, in its most developed form, the protagonist of *Ben-Hur: A Tale of the Christ* (1925) (see Shepherd 2016b: 271–6).

As *Ben-Hur* indicates, such films often move beyond the gospels' supporting casts (including collated protagonists like Tamar in *The Miracle Maker* 2000 and minor characters like *Greatest Story*'s Lazarus or *The Gospel of John*'s [2003] Leading Pharisee) to inventions based on previous plays or novels (like Ben-Hur)[11] or characters created de novo (like *King of Kings*' Lucius). These can all easily be Christ figures. *The Passion of the Christ*'s Simon of Cyrene, for example, literally creates a Christ bearer.

Such characters provide novelty. They also hallow the iconic Christ by providing surrounding stories of conversion (e.g., Magdalene) and degradation (e.g., Judas; Walsh 2003: 33). Even the Jesus epics, utilizing their longer running times, often shift focus to the surrounding cast.[12] They enrich Jesus's demonic and elite opposition (particularly Caiaphas, Antipas, and Pilate), various Jesus supporters (like Jesus's mother, Magdalene, and Judas), and the apostles (especially *Jesus of Nazareth*). They also create entirely new characters (e.g., Lucius, the Dark Hermit, Sorak, and Zerah).

The protagonist in *Monty Python's Life of Brian* (1979) is different. He bears the wrong name, yet is too close and too far from Jesus (perhaps, both Jesus and not-Jesus) to be Jesus adjacent. Instead, he suggests other Jesuses and messiahs (or, simply, exposes the workings of Christian discourse; cf. Stracci in *La ricotta* 1963).

Matt Page argues that Jesus adjacents are particularly prominent in Italian cinema (2021: 129, 134–6). Given Italian involvement in international television productions (see Chapter 12), Jesus adjacents are also prominent in (international) television, for example, in the *Friends of Jesus* or *Close to Jesus* series (with films on Joseph, Magdalene, Judas, and Thomas 2000–1), marketed in the United States as part of TNT's *The Bible Collection*. Perhaps, the success of *Jesus of Nazareth*, which lavished attention on Jesus's supporting cast, had some influence on these productions.

Jesus histories arrived only after filmmakers trekked through filmed passions, passion films, Jesus adjacents, and Christ figures. Further, the earliest histories differed from the later epics. *From the Manger to the Cross* (1912) and *Christus* (1916) capitalized on audience interest in travel, the Holy Land, lecture/magic lantern shows, and the exotic (Orientalism) by marketing their travelogue's "on location" filming. Although not shot on location, both *Intolerance* and *The King of Kings* also capitalized on Orientalizing spectacles (Babylon and Magdalene's palace, respectively). Kevin McGeough (2021) argues that Jesus histories, even the epics, always depend on such Orientalizing and on creating comfortable, expected visuals.[13]

For Robert Rosenstone, cinematic "histories" are all of this nature. At least, he argues that cinematic histories aim at lavish recreations of expected settings and, with famous (Oliver Stone) exceptions, at faithfulness to the popular memory of well-known events and persons (e.g., Jesus's nonviolence, love command, and cross), while fictionalizing wildly in plot and character (e.g., Jesus adjacents). The historical Jesus epics then are cinematic, not academic, histories.[14]

Thus, the well-known Jesus epics are only one type of Jesus histories. Travelogues preceded them and after the epic heyday, a historical "look" migrated into other forms: for example, the rock opera *Jesus Christ Superstar*; television (e.g., *Jesus of Nazareth*; *Jesus* 1999); visual translations (*The Jesus Film* 1979; *The Gospel of John*); other Jesuses (*Life of Brian*); and stop motion puppetry (*The Miracle Maker*). *Jesus Christ Superstar*, *Gospel Road* (1973), and *The Jesus Film* reprise the early travelogues by touting their "on location" filming. The greatest evidence of history's eventual centrality in Jesus films, however, is the fact that even those challenging the tradition often work in/with "histories": for example, *Il vangelo secondo Matteo* (1964); *Jesus Christ Superstar*; *Il messia* (1975); *Life of Brian*; and *The Last Temptation of Christ* (1988).[15]

While relocated Jesuses highlight their contemporizing and interpretation (cf. also Pasolini's analogical *Il vangelo*), Jesus histories obscure their own modernizing and interpretation. Challenging/alternative "histories" are, of course, an exception to this rule. The risen Jesus's appearances above a modern city in *The King of Kings*' finale and in modern dress among modern children in *Jesus* (1999) are notable exceptions, but these final transparencies are inconsistent with the films' general surreptitiousness. By contrast, *Jesus Christ Superstar*'s modern dress and "ruins" locations, as well as its modern interruptions (e.g., jets), are more jarring because it is striving to make its Jesus interpretation obvious.

Ironically, Jesus histories also relocate Jesus to the present because history is a modern or contemporary construct (see nn6–7). In fact, compared to filmed passions and passion films, Jesus histories are double relocations. First, they place their Jesuses in cinematic histories, not worship or Christian art. Second, their histories reflect modern questions and concerns (see Forshey 1992: 83–121; Babington and Evans 1993: 91–168; Walsh 2003: 173–85; Humphries-Brooks 2006; Reinhartz 2013a: 57–82). Such Jesus histories fulfill mythic functions for their audiences[16] by locating the audience's issues and virtues in this important founding (Jesus) moment and by enshrining the audience as "the end" of its inevitable history (see Walsh 2018a). Not surprisingly, since the silent era, most Jesus films have opted for this "look."

The Jesus epic ended (before Gibson revived it), but Jesus histories and Jesus films' mythic use did not. The end of Jesus epics coincided, roughly speaking, with the end of the Christian metanarrative's dominance in Canada and the United States (having ended previously in Western Europe). Consequently, Jesus films targeted smaller markets (e.g., visual translations) and experimented with different genres (e.g., *Godspell*; *Jesus Christ Superstar*), POVs (e.g., Jesus adjacents), and ideologies (e.g., *Il vangelo*; *Il messia*; *Son of Man*).

Many have seen these experiments as attacks on traditional Jesus Christs (e.g., *Last Temptation*). Speaking about Jesus fictions, Robert Detweiler argues instead that matters have moved not from tract to parody (or to irony or antichrist [see Ziolkowski 1972: 270–98]), but simply beyond Christian metanarratives' control (Detweiler 1964: 112–13, 120–1). "Jesus" and "Christ" and "messiah" have become endlessly plastic symbols. Their meaning, if any, comes from new myths, ideologies, and fictions. They have been appropriated, rather than merely adapted (using Sanders's terminology [2006: 1–41]). Using more classic biblical critical terminology, they have either been remythologized or turned into parables vis-à-vis the Jesus tradition (e.g., *Jesus Christ Superstar*; *Life of Brian*; *Jésus de Montréal*)[17]—even as more traditional (e.g., *The Passion of the Christ*; visual translations) and non-Eurocentric Jesuses have proliferated (see Chapter 21).

Jésus de Montréal nicely reflects this bewildering pluralism. In roughly sequential order, the film's viewer sees a traditional passion play Jesus, various Jesuses as its protagonist Daniel researches a new passion play, a "Deep Throat" scholar's "critical" Jesus, statues and other iconic Jesuses, Jesuses created by the troupe's different acting styles, the radically new, historical Jesus of Daniel's passion play, and finally Daniel himself as Christ or "son of man" figure.

One can no longer assume that Jesuses/messiahs bear Christian meanings. They may be traditional; they may be antichrists; they may be rejecting Christian discourse; or they may not even know Christian discourse. "Messiahs" are particularly ambiguous as the term has come to signify destructive, obsessive fanatics in popular culture.[18] "Jesus" is a more certain connection to Jesus traditions, but even it does not always mean "as it should" (see, e.g., Bruno Dumont's *La vie de Jésus* 1997).

Long ago, Theodore Ziolkowski proposed a helpful, fivefold taxonomy of Jesus fictions: (1) fictional histories/biographies (including the gospels); (2) Jesus redivivus (relocations); (3) imitatio Christi; (4) pseudonyms of Christ; and (5) fictional transfigurations of Jesus (1972: 3–29).[19] If one thinks about Jesus cinema in these terms, one can see similar types/transformations. They are listed here roughly in the order they appeared:

1 filmed passions and passion films (Jesus relocations [from the perspective of Jesus histories]);
2 Jesus adjacents (and/or Christ figures, including those deliberately imitating Christ);
3 historical Jesus cinema (travelogues, epics, television, etc.);

4 other genres (experimental [e.g., musicals] or directed to specific audiences [e.g., visual translations]);
5 other relocations (e.g., Zwick's "second comings"); and
6 other Jesuses/messiahs (Christ figures and antichrists, parables, and even "un-Christs").

With less certainty, given the types' diversity, one might also claim that (centrist?) Jesus films share certain "family characteristics":[20]

1 he shall be called "Jesus" (the name's iconic significance);
2 worship/reverence/hagiography (Christian art);
3 passion spectacle;
4 high ("gnostic") Christology (Jesus as icon or talisman);
5 harmonizing gospel hermeneutic (relying most heavily on John);
6 surrounding stories of conversion and degradation;
7 cinematic history (Orientalism); and
8 apolitical, individualistic religion (emphasis on nonviolence, love).

Family characteristics establish fuzzy—not precise—definitional boundaries. Further, from the very beginning, filmmakers pushed at—or did not recognize—these boundaries. Again, with the demise of Christian metanarratives, these characteristics have become far less definitive. Films that push too hard against them, however, run the risk of not being "Jesus films" (see Walsh 2016c: 504–5; 2017a: 94–6).

STRUCTURE OF THE BOOK

This introduction to Jesus films begins at its end with "A Gospels Harmony of Select Jesus Films" (and at each chapter's end—with the time/DVD chapter location of film incidents) because the authors first approached Jesus films from academic readings of the gospels. The volume's "introductory" matter arose gradually as the authors spent more time with film. Accordingly, this revision is more cinema-centric than its precursor, as is evident in the more detailed readings of plot, authority, cultural location, and director. Further, this revision discusses four more films than the 2007 work: *La vie du Christ*; *Il messia*; *Son of Man*; and *Mary Magdalene*. These additions help ameliorate the tradition's overwhelming patriarchy and Eurocentrism.

The four tables in this chapter catalogue the chapters' major topics, facilitating the selective use of films or topics. Each chapter begins with an interpretative plot summary and notes about the film's Jesus and other memorable characters. Table 0.1 summarizes those discussions. For reasons of space, all four tables list the films by their directors.

A further word on "secondary" characters is necessary.[21] Women are particularly important in *La vie du Christ*, *Il messia*, *Son of Man*, and *Mary Magdalene*. Not surprisingly, the Syrophoenician woman who critically instructs Jesus is remarkably rare (see *Jesus*

Table 0.1 Plot summaries and memorable characters.

Film	Plot	Jesus	Other characters
Guy	Women around Jesus	Women's Jesus	Supporting women Veronica
Zecca	Film miracles	Transfigured Christ	Angels
Olcott	Gospel on location	Stranger in exotic lands	Dark Judas Composite Magdalene
Griffith	Jesus as footnote	Icon, talisman	Christ figures Innocent victims
DeMille	Suffer little children	Ethereal, avuncular	Mark; Caiaphas Magdalene; Judas
Ray	Messiah of peace ~~war~~	American youth ~~Rebel~~	Lucius; Judas; Mary
Pasolini	Sword for the people	Gramscian intellectual	Suffering people/Mary
Stevens	Jesus in the West	Light of the world Son of West	Lazarus; Dark Hermit
Greene	Clowning the gospel	Clown	Troupe; Christ figures
Jewison	Rocking the gospel	Job-Jesus	Job-Judas; Magdalene
Rossellini	Philosopher king	Ideal king	Mary; the village
Zeffirelli	Whose Jesus?	Of Nazareth Blasphemer or Christ? Commodity	Mary; Magdalene Apostles; Zerah
Jones	~~Messiah;~~ naughty boy	Epic Christ	Brian the unchrist Ordinary bunglers
Krish	Road to salvation	Transfigured Christ	Peter; Magdalene
Scorsese	Quest for God	Introspective searcher	Judas; Magdalene
Arcand	Becoming son of man	Multiple Jesuses Radical historical Jesus	Christ figures Son of man
Young	Human, for love	Kenotic Christ Laughing, happy Jesus	Supportive parents Livio Pilate; Satan Magdalene
Hayes	Little child leads	Lofty, but for children Resurrected Jesus	Tamar; Magdalene Judas
Saville	Digitalizing the word	I am that I am	Beloved Disciple Magdalene Lead Pharisee Head Guard

Gibson	Sorrowful mysteries	Sacrificed "meat" "Rising" action hero	Mary; Magdalene John Simon; Pilate Satan; Caiaphas Judas
Dornford-May	This is my world	Steve Biko-Jesus Jesus of color	Satan; Mary; Peter Judas Slaughtered children
Davis	Woman's POV	Divine Christ Women's Jesus	Magdalene; Peter Judas

1999; visual translations), although Magdalene has a similar role in *Mary Magdalene*. Perhaps because of screenwriter Gene Gauntier, *From the Manger to the Cross* omits the "disreputable" women in Jesus's ministry (Salome, the Samaritan woman, and the woman taken in adultery). Finally, women are Daniel/Jesus's true disciples in *Jésus de Montréal*.

Mary figures prominently because of the nativity[22] and because of her Roman Catholic roles as intercessor/co-sufferer/co-redeemer. She dominates *Il messia* and *Son of Man*.[23] In the former, she is co-leader in Jesus's ministry, and the film follows her Via Dolorosa (not Jesus's). She also figures prominently on the Via Dolorosa in *The King of Kings* and *The Passion of the Christ*.[24] Mary knows Jesus's destiny better than he in *From the Manger to the Cross*, *King of Kings*, *Il messia*, and *Son of Man*. She is Jesus's mentor in the last two films and in *Jesus* (1999). She disciples Magdalene in *King of Kings*, *Jesus of Nazareth*, and *Jesus* (1999). She is also a prominent intercessor in *The King of Kings* and *The Passion of the Christ*. The pietà is quite common, and Mary is almost always the Stabat Mater (even in *Jésus de Montréal*), but *Il vangelo*, *Il messia*, and *The Passion of the Christ* emphasize her suffering passion. She leads the post-Jesus community in *Jesus* (1999) and *Son of Man*. *Il messia* ends with a shot of her from within Jesus's tomb. By contrast, Joseph is most important in *La vie et passion de notre seigneur Jésus Christ*, *Jesus of Nazareth*, and *Jesus* (1999) (see also *Il vangelo*'s peasant Joseph).

Magdalene is significant in film because of the tradition of her dramatic conversion and because of modern interest in female disciples.[25] *Last Temptation*, perhaps the most patriarchal Jesus movie, gives her life of prostitution the most screen time (see also *Jesus of Nazareth*; *Jesus* 1999).[26] Further, it makes her the hero's "domestic" temptation. *The King of Kings* and *Miracle Maker* provide her most dramatic exorcisms, while *Mary Magdalene* denies her possession as calumny. She is frequently the woman taken in adultery (*King of Kings*; *Greatest Story*; *Jesus Christ Superstar* [in song lyrics]; *Il messia*; *Last Temptation*; *The Passion of the Christ*; *Son of Man*) and, even more often, Luke's disreputable anointer (*La vie et passion de notre seigneur Jésus Christ*; *From the Manger to the Cross*; *Greatest Story*; *Jesus Christ Superstar*; *Jesus of Nazareth*; *The Jesus Film*; *Jésus de Montréal*; *Miracle Maker*; and *Son of Man*). Usurping his mother, she is Jesus's chief comfort in *Jesus Christ Superstar* and *Mary Magdalene*. She is also Jesus's true disciple in *Greatest Story*, *Jésus de Montréal*,

Jesus (1999), *The Gospel of John,* and *Mary Magdalene. Jesus* (1999) and *Mary Magdalene* reject gender as a discipleship criterion. Patriarchy banishes her, however, from leadership in *Jesus of Nazareth* and *Mary Magdalene.*

Judas is significant for anti-Semitic reasons, as Jesus's destiny (cf. the Baptist),[27] and as degradation's astounding example.[28] As Jesus's chief disciple, Judas dominates *Jesus Christ Superstar* and *Last Temptation.* Some movies depict the mysterious (*Greatest Story*), greedy (*From the Manger to the Cross; The King of Kings*), or demonic gospel traitors (*The Jesus Film; The Passion of the Christ*). Lost innocence explains Judas's behavior in *Jesus of Nazareth* (a duped intellectual)[29] and *Son of Man* (child abuse). Despite his political language, the Judas in *Jesus Christ Superstar* grapples extensively with his (Christian/celebrity) fate. *From the Manger to the Cross* and *The Gospel of John* (among others) consign him to darkness; *The King of Kings* to the abyss; but *The Passion of the Christ* presents, most horribly, his demonic possession and "descent into hell."[30] *Son of Man*'s Judas is the most determined traitor, repeatedly struggling to "get" video evidence on Jesus. More modern, understandable Judases occur as movies provide Judas with political agendas, whether revolutionary (*King of Kings; Last Temptation; Jesus* 1999; *Miracle Maker*) or as negotiators (*Jesus Christ Superstar; Jesus of Nazareth*). Judas is Jesus's destiny (or the inescapable "story") in *Godspell, Jesus Christ Superstar,* and *Last Temptation. Last Temptation*'s buddy, without whom Jesus could not accomplish his destiny, and Mary's only friend among the revolutionary disciples in *Mary Magdalene* are the most sympathetic Judases.

Jesus's community is most important in *La vie du Christ, Godspell, Il messia, Son of Man,* and *Mary Magdalene* (and strikingly unimportant in *Il vangelo*).[31] *Jesus of Nazareth* develops the traditional apostles most fully.[32] Its Peter represents the apostolic institution, and *Mary Magdalene*'s Peter is the patriarchal institution. He is the model of evangelical conversion in *The Jesus Film* (cf. *The Passion of the Christ*'s Simon of Cyrene). He is a giant (a rock?) in *The King of Kings,* but dumb as a rock (so Judas says) in *Last Temptation.* He is intertwined with Judas/betrayal in *Il vangelo, Jesus Christ Superstar, Jesus of Nazareth, Jesus* (1999), and *The Passion of the Christ* (see Telford 2005). Peter names all the disciples "Judases"—and forgiven—in *Jesus of Nazareth.* He is Jesus's personal portrait (graffiti) artist in *Son of Man.* The apostles provide connections with the film/Jesus for the (Christian) audience, as do *The King of Kings*' Mark and *Miracle Maker*'s Tamar. Judas provides access for "outsiders" as do *King of King*'s Lucius and *Greatest Story*'s Lazarus.

The epics (and *Jesus of Nazareth; Jesus* 1999) give the most time to Jesus's elite opposition. Fortress Jerusalem (*Greatest Story*) and walled Jerusalem (*Il messia*) are visually ominous, but so, too, is the ideological opposition *Il vangelo* creates (particularly in the visualization of the Baptist and Mt. 23). Satan is most visible in *The King of Kings, Greatest Story* (Dark Hermit), *Jesus* (1999), *The Passion of the Christ,* and *Son of Man.* The most villainous (and anti-Semitic) Caiaphases are in *The King of Kings* (a greedy spider), *Jesus Christ Superstar* (vulture), and *The Passion of the Christ* (Satan).[33] While duped by Pilate, the most noble Caiaphas appears in *Jesus* (1999). Film often invents characters to shift villainy away from gospel characters, if not to mitigate anti-Semitism (e.g., Sorak in *Greatest Story*; Zerah in *Jesus of Nazareth*; Livio in *Jesus* 1999; Asher in *Miracle Maker*).[34]

The beleaguered gospel Pilates mean that most cinematic Pilates are noble law-and-order figures, forced by circumstances (or Jews) into Jesus's crucifixion. Despite knowing Josephus's vicious Pilate, *The Jesus Film* defaults to Luke's portrayal. By contrast, *King of Kings* and *Last Temptation*'s Pilates never declare Jesus innocent. *Jesus of Nazareth* and *Jesus*'s (1999) Pilates sentence Jesus to death without blaming the Jews.[35] The most callous, cynical Pilates are in *King of Kings*, *Last Temptation*, *Jésus de Montréal*, and *Jesus* (1999).[36] *The Passion of the Christ* offers the most complex Romans—ranging from the animalistic (Eastern) brutes gleefully torturing Jesus, to the law-and-order officers appalled at such actions (Pilate and Abenader), and including apparent converts (Claudia, Cassius, and Abenader). Pilate is the most human figure in *The Passion of the Christ* (cf. *King of Kings*' Lucius). Herod Antipas is always villainous (most so in *Greatest Story*) and often "foppish" (e.g., *Jesus Christ Superstar*; *Jesus of Nazareth*; *The Passion of the Christ*).

Table 0.2 summarizes the chapters' next two subsections: memorable visuals and key authority/scripture. While the transfiguration seldom appears, the cinematic Jesus, like the Johannine, is always transfigured. He appears out of light and/or disappears into light. Until the experimental period, he is always above or beyond the action. Accordingly, shots from above (particularly prone [e.g., *Last Temptation*] or in judgment [e.g., *King of Kings*]) carry great weight. Cross foreshadowings and the crucifixion are ubiquitous. Characters stand in awe (sometimes even in horrified rigor). Villains lurk on the frame's edges. Children (of the kingdom) are de rigueur.

Tissot and Doré biblical illustrations, and other nineteenth-century Orientalizings, linger. The emphasis on the light entering the world makes dark and shadows (of the cross) equally important. Rembrandt and Caravaggio obviously contribute. Bosch faces—or just the people (in *Il vangelo*)—are memorable, although "beautiful" Euro-American Jesuses and celebrities are more common.

Table 0.2 Memorable visuals and key authority/scripture.

Film	Visuals	Authority	Scripture
Guy	Veronica's image	Angelic intertitles	Lk. 8:2-3
Zecca	Transfigured Christ	Editing miracles	Transfiguration story
Olcott	Cruciform shadow	Location; Tissot	Scripture intertitles Johannine "I ams"
Griffith	Mother rocking Cross spectacle	Spectacle; Editing	Harmony editing
DeMille	Blind girl sees Jesus Passion-earthquake	Spectacle of light DeMillish miracles	"New KJV" intertitles DeMille's gospel
Ray	Closeup of blue eyes Red-robed Romans/Jesus	Voiceover; Lucius	Sermon spectacle "Liberal" Sermon
Pasolini	Closeups of angry Jesus Closeups of the people	Pasolini's camera Music	Mt. 10:34

Stevens	Western landscapes "Frames" Celebrity cameos	West or church? Prophecy (Mic. 5:2)	John
Greene	Faded Superman t-shirt Carrying cruciform Jesus	Alternative reality Comedy, music	Sung Matthew Lukan Matthew Prodigal Son
Jewison	Judas and Negev ruins Jesus/Judas transfigured	Questions Story as destiny	Jesus's anointings
Rossellini	Zoom of working village	Neutral aesthetic	Mary's village gospel Luke
Zeffirelli	Synagogue Torah readings Unblinking Christ Celebrity cameos	Zoom "inside" Supersessionism	Luke-Acts Johannine "I ams"
Jones	Song and dance crosses	Epic Jesus Individual freedom Comedy	Mk 13:5-6, 21-22
Krish	Earth from heaven Empty crosses	Evangelical paratext *Jesus of Nazareth*	Evangelical Luke Lk. 18:10-14
Scorsese	Tormented Jesus from above Intimate Jesus and Judas	Kazantzakis Interior voiceovers Jesus films	Eccentric gospel events Mk 3:21-35
Arcand	Crushed by the cross Cruciform, organs harvested	"Liberal values" Stations of the Cross	Death-of-God Mark Mk 15:34 Mk 3:28; 8:29-31
Young	Violence in Jesus's name Playful Jesus Modern children's embrace	*Jesus of Nazareth* *Last Temptation* Free choice	Miracles Phil. 2:5-11
Hayes	Cel animated inside views Tamar's Ben-Hur scene	Inside views Children's Jesus	Lk. 8:40-56 Luke
Saville	Jesus in sunlight Jesus's intimate touches Digital Beloved Disciple	Harmony camera Narrator Flashbacks	Jn 3:16 Harmonized John
Gibson	Rise/crushing snake's head Rise during scourging Bloody Christ and Mary Teardrop judgments	Passion devotion Action hero *The King of Kings*	Isa. 53 Johannine cross
Dornford-May	Slaughtered children Red-ribbon crucifixion	Chester Mysteries The disappeared *Il vangelo*; *Godspell*	Music Johannine cross Son of Man
Davis	Freediving women POV of prone Mary Jesus anoints Mary's eyes Mary's gaze at dying Jesus	Jesus films Mary's POV	Gospel of Mary Open your eyes Born of water

Locations become characters: Olcott and Krish's Holy Land; Stevens's American West; Pasolini, Gibson, and Davis's southern Italy (which becomes almost a second Holy Land); Rossellini, Zeffirelli, Jones, and Scorsese's North Africa; Greene's empty New York City; Jewison's Negev ruins; Arcand's Montréal; and Dornford-May's Khayelitsha.

While the 2007 edition highlighted film's conversation with scripture, this edition spends more time on authoritative film techniques and Jesus film tradition.[37] Intertitles (scriptural or not) and voiceovers have immeasurable impact. Lighting, editing, and "spectacle" create miracles. Sometimes location (e.g., Olcott; Stevens; Dornford-May) or music (e.g., Pasolini; Green; Jewison; Scorsese; Arcand; Dornford-May) almost overwhelms. Sometimes directors simply imprint their own authoritative, aesthetic style (Griffith's spectacle and crosscutting; DeMille's spectacle, sleaze, and sentimentality; Pasolini's abrupt editing, closeups, and contamination of styles; Rossellini's "neutral" aesthetic; Scorsese's interior views and suffering POVs; and Gibson's ground-level POVs).[38] When "inside views" occur, they carry great weight (Zeffirelli; Scorsese; Hayes).

Within Jesus films, *The King of Kings* is most influential (see Staley 2018). *Il vangelo* dominates films with artistic or political aspirations. *Jesus Christ Superstar* and *Last Temptation* linger in other films, if only because other filmmakers strive to answer them. *Jesus of Nazareth* has had a significant impact upon television and visual translation films.[39]

"A Gospels Harmony of Select Jesus Films" tracks the appearances of important gospel incidents. However, as a harmonizing approach dominates the tradition, the gospel parallel that is most important to a particular film scene requires more detailed study. Material unique to other gospels regularly crops up even in visual translations. Although not covered here (see Chapter 19), the Lumo Gospels often use the same visuals to illustrate (supposed) gospel parallels with surprising results.

Among the individual gospels, John has pride of place.[40] Matthew is, however, obviously important for *Il vangelo* (along with John) and *Godspell* (along with Luke). Luke is important to *King of Kings* ("history"), *Il messia* (the lowly), *Jesus of Nazareth* (supersessionism), and *The Jesus Film* (although a Johannine or evangelical Luke). Mark is the least important gospel, having a major impact only on *Jésus de Montréal*. *The Gospel of Mary* is particularly important (versus patriarchy) to *Mary Magdalene*.

Table 0.3 summarizes the chapters' next two subsections (Cultural Location and Genre constitute one subsection). In terms of cultural location, women are important in early film and in *Mary Magdalene*, but their differing cultural locations make the films "mean" differently. So, too, do the films of the Progressive Era, the Cold War, the exploratory 1960s, the 1980s return to conservatism, postcolonialism, and post-9/11's revived imperialism. As Jesus films typically support the cultural dominant (act mythically), revolutionary or non-dominant (or non-Euro-American) forays are particularly noteworthy (e.g., *Il vangelo*; *Life of Brian*; *Jésus de Montréal*; *Son of Man*; Chapter 21).[41]

Genre is this work's most idiosyncratic section. This introduction provides the context for the volume's use of "genre" (see n3) by naming various "Jesus film" genres. The chapters' "genre" discussions locate the films within Jesus films in terms of their contributions to that tradition, and in terms of their ideologies. Genres are ideological claims and constructions of "reality";[42] therefore, genre speaks to whether these films (1) do history (i.e., present the

Table 0.3 Cultural location, genre (or film issue), and director.

Film	Cultural location	Genre	Director
Guy	Victorian era to new woman	Tableau aesthetic	Comedy Gender construction
Zecca	Early cinema	Exhibitor's cut Stencil-coloring	Naturalism Féeries
Olcott	Victorian piety	Travelogue	On location
Griffith	Progressive era	US epic	Visual syntax Cinema as art *Birth of a Nation*
DeMille	Mass media for immigrants	Hays Code	Biblical epic Biblical trilogy
Ray	Liberal discontent with Empire	Deform epic	Rebels, misfits *Rebel Without a Cause*
Pasolini	Art-house; Marxism	Reject epic Analogy	Unconsumable film *La ricotta*
Stevens	Subjective individualism	Epic undone	Director Oscars *Shane*
Greene	Counterculture; youth	Relocated Jesus Vaudeville *Parable*	Church to Broadway
Jewison	Critique celebrity and consumer culture	Rock opera Passion play	Social problem films *In the Heat of the Night*
Rossellini	European art/ideology film	Populist Pasolini Educational film	*Roma città aperta* Grand Historical Project
Zeffirelli	Validating institutions: church/capitalism	TV miniseries Commercials	Opera *Brother Sun, Sister Moon*
Jones	Anti-establishment comedy	Parody/parable	*Flying Circus* *M. Python & Holy Grail*
Krish	Protestant evangelicalism	Visual translation	Filmed Bible Project New Media Luke
Scorsese	Rejection of epic/cultural gnosticism	Inverting epic	POV of riven heroes *Mean Streets*; *Silence*
Arcand	Post-Quiet Revolution Consumerism Post colonial (vs. United States)	Filmed passion Parable	Documentary critiques *Déclin empire américain*
Young	International family TV	TV Bibles	TV miniseries *Moses*, *Paul*, *Red Tent*
Hayes	Children's animation Stop action puppetry	Children's Bible	Watts's *Lion Bible* Hayes's *Testament*

Saville	Evangelism; TEV	Visual translation	Filmed plays
Gibson	Post-9/11 imperialism	Epic horror Action hero	Suffering action hero *Braveheart*
Dornford-May	Postcolonialism	Relocated Jesus Global Jesus	Dimpho di Kopane *Yiimimangaliso*
Davis	Equality of women	Jesus adjacent	*Lion*

[gospel] truth; e.g., Jesus histories and visual translations); (2) do "history" (i.e., overtly "construct"; e.g., Jesus relocations), or (3) do fiction (i.e., consciously raise interpretative issues; e.g., Jesus parables/parodies). Finally, comments on genre (reality/ideology) lead back to films' cultural locations and thus to whether a film functions mythically or in a more critical fashion (see, e.g., the various twists on the epic Jesus).

The discussion of directors deals with film more generally, asking specifically how a director's Jesus film fits into that director's larger body of work. While various films are brought into the conversation, some of the key non-Jesus films (or genres) appear in Table 0.3. As some directors are less influential, this section sometimes includes discussion of producers (e.g., Samuel Bronston; John Heyman) or scriptwriters (e.g., Gene Gauntier). The chapters also note the actors playing Jesus, and some of the other key roles, with reference to their other important work—although primarily in endnotes.

Table 0.4 discusses the chapters' final content section (before the identification of DVD extras and time/DVD locations of film incidents). While not every chapter has a section on problematic issues, it occurs at times to highlight persistent problems in the tradition: for example, patriarchy; Orientalism; anti-Semitism; Eurocentrism; ideology/interpretation; and commodification.

Extensive endnotes suggest other Jesuses, possibilities, and stories—all supported, at least, in an introductory fashion by the References. That scholarly paraphernalia points to the most important Jesus film scholarship, both generally (see n1) and with reference to the film discussed. Such paraphernalia calls attention to the inevitability of interpretation and, hopefully, provides a foundation for the discussion of yet other Jesus films of all sorts.

Table 0.4 Problematic issue.

Film	Problematic issue
Guy	Patriarchy, androcentrism
Zecca	Seeing and believing
Olcott	Orientalism
Griffith	Anti-Semitism
DeMille	
Ray	American beauty
Pasolini	Owning interpretations
Stevens	

Greene	Visualizing the sacred
Jewison	Celebrity
Rossellini	
Zeffirelli	Jesus commodified
Jones	(Making) messiahs
Krish	Gospel truth
Scorsese	Gnosticisms
Arcand	Jesuses
Young	
Hayes	
Saville	
Gibson	Violence
Dornford-May	Global Jesuses
Davis	

NOTES

1 Space limitations prevent a detailed review of Jesus film scholarship. Each chapter's endnotes and citations suggest further research possibilities on its specific film. Important broad works include Kinnard and Davis (1992) (Jesus films' novelty and immediate reception); Forshey (1992), Babington and Evans (1993), and Reinhartz (2013a) (epics as modern "identity" constructions); Kreitzer (1993; 2002) (films as new POVs on gospel incidents); Baugh (1997) (film-informed, theological reading of Jesus and Christ-figure films); Zwick (1997) (literary comparisons with the gospels); Tatum (2013) (historical-critical discussions); Stern, Jefford, and DeBona (1999) (cultural and theological insights); Walsh (2003) (literary readings of paired films and gospels; comments on US mythology); Humphries-Brooks (2006) (construction of American cinematic heroes; cf. also Prothero 2003); Reinhartz (2007) (biopics); Staley and Walsh (2007) (introduction to eighteen films); Malone (2012) (theological appraisal); Shepherd (2013; 2016b) (silents); and Lindvall (2007) and Lindvall and Quicke (2011) (church films). For non-Hollywood Jesus films, see Chapter 21. For diverse scholarly approaches, see the essays in Walsh (2018e; 2021c).

2 *Il messia* is difficult to obtain (with English subtitles), but its numerous innovations demand its inclusion.

3 Rick Altman argues that genres depend on the purposes of those who name, package, store, serve, or consume them. Genre is thus a contested, evolving construct—defined by institutions to meet their needs (1999: 98–9, 179, 214–15). For a discussion of *Le tout nouveau testament* (2015) as "Jesus film" from this perspective, see Vander Stichele (2021). On Jesus and Christ films as "fuzzy" categories, see Walsh (2003: 29–39; 2013a: 192–4).

4 According to David Shepherd, the earliest Jesus film was a (five-minute) passion play staged for filming (*Passion du Christ* 1897; 2016b: 3–4). On these early films, see Cosandey, Gaudreault, and Gunning (1992), Shepherd (2013: chaps. 1–2; 2016b: 1–14), and Gaudreault (2016).

5   Visual translations have some similarities with filmed plays (or texts). See Chapter 19.
6   "Relocation," if it implies an essential or original Jesus, is problematic. It is better, outside of worship and devotion, to think of Jesus as a (malleable) sign or unit of Christian (or other) discourse.
7   "Relocate" is less problematic here because the sign/name "Jesus" belongs to the "present" only in worship, mass media, or academic discourse.
8   See Zwick (2016) and Shepherd (2018: 132–6).
9   Jesus films have successfully marketed technological innovations, but the tradition evinces a "stylistic retardation" (Keil 1992) when seen through the lens of *La ricotta* (1963), *Life of Brian*, or *South Park*'s "The Passion of the Jew" (2004).
10 Films that "look away from" or minimize the passion require interpretation. See, e.g., the Jesus adjacents (e.g., the recent *Histoire de Judas* 2015 and *Mary Magdalene* 2018) or the striking example of such among Jesus films—*Il messia*.
11 On the Ben-Hur "franchise," see Ryan and Shamir (2016) and Kreitzer (2018). *Quo Vadis* is the comparable franchise, but its Roman persecution setting likely suggests Christ-figure cinema to most. See Scodel and Bettenworth (2009) and Walsh (2016d: 508–11).
12 The turn to other characters even in the epics suggests that Jesus cinema is always, already Jesus adjacent. Charles Keil famously said of early Jesus films that Jesus is "the structuring absence within his own story" (1992: 114), and others have extended that appraisal to cover the tradition (see Walsh 2003: 33–9; 2016a). Worshipful reverence and high Christologies play a significant role in this character retardation. Consequently, many prefer Christ-figure films (see Baugh 1997: 3, 109–12).
13 McGeough (2021) sees nineteenth-century theater and art (historical and landscape) as influential. The Tissot Bible is also a major influence.
14 See Moore (2018). Barnes Tatum laments film's failure to offer a historical Jesus (2013: 304–10). See also Reinhartz (2007: 21–40). *Monty Python's Life of Brian* and *Jésus de Montréal* reflect on the academic and cinematic construction of history.
15 The "radical" historical Jesus in *Jésus de Montréal*'s modernized passion play also deserves mention.
16 This description uses "myth," as in comparative religion, to depict community's master narratives, metanarratives, originating stories, charters, commonsense, etc.
17 These parables call attention to the semiotics of Christ figuring.
18 Significant work on cinematic Christ figures includes, among others, Hurley (1981), Malone (1988), Baugh (1997), Kozlovic (2004), Deacy (2006), and Reinhartz (2009; 2013a: 148–74). For critique of Christ-figure interpretations, see Deacy (2006). On the Christ-figure status of Jesus films' Jesuses, see Walsh (2003: 29–39; 2013a: 192–4). For attempts to think about non-Christian "messiahs," see Seesengood and Walsh (2018), Seesengood (2021), and Walsh (2021a).
19 For other attempts to explore/organize Jesus fictions, see Detweiler (1964), Swindell (2010: 176–203), and Crook (2011).
20 For more detailed discussion of these family characteristics, see Walsh (2016c; 2017a).
21 Reinhartz (2007) helpfully collects information on many characters.
22 Note especially *Jesus of Nazareth*'s first hour.
23 *Il vangelo* has the most convincing peasant girl Mary. In the passion, Pasolini's own mother plays the Stabat Mater.
24 Veronica is most important in *La vie du Christ* and *The Passion of the Christ*.

25 On Magdalene in film, see Chapter 22.
26 *The Gospel of John* suggests prostitution with her red clothing.
27 Like prophecy, the Baptist represents Jesus's (divine destiny), perhaps most obviously in *King of Kings*, *Greatest Story*, and *Godspell*. By contrast, he is the failure that *Jésus de Montréal's* Daniel/Jesus surpasses.
28 On Judas in film, see Walsh (2006; 2010). For more "positive" assessments, see Paffenroth (2001) and Hebron (2016b).
29 *Il messia's* Judas is an intellectual, a Torah scribe; however, his motives for betrayal are not clear.
30 *The Passion of the Christ*, however, builds on *Il vangelo* and *Jesus Christ Superstar's* "run to suicide" images.
31 These films are less Jesus-centric than the tradition's norm.
32 On the apostles in film, see Walsh (2016d).
33 On Caiaphas in film, see Reinhartz (2007: 213–25).
34 Jesus films sometimes present a divided Sanhedrin (e.g., *Greatest Story*; *Jesus of Nazareth*; *Jesus* 1999) or voices for Jesus in the crowd at the Roman trial to ameliorate anti-Semitism.
35 An *Intolerance* intertitle says Pilate ordered Jesus crucified, but the film hardly evades Jesus silents' rampant anti-Semitism. *The Jesus Film* features disdainful Pilate's slow-motion toss of the judgment scroll.
36 *Life of Brian* mocks Pilate as an amusing, bumbling bureaucrat, but he orders the crucifixions.
37 Individual chapters make copious comparisons to other Jesus films.
38 See also Director discussions.
39 For responses from different religious traditions, see Tatum (2013).
40 See Walsh (2018c). See Walsh (2021b) for an appraisal of the various gospels' influence on Jesus films.
41 On Jesus films as mythic or parabolic (from a US perspective), see Walsh (2003: 173–85). All "revolutionary" films are anti-mythic, parabolic, or remythologizing.
42 For a discussion of genre and reality, see Aichele (1985).

1

La vie du Christ or *La naissance, la vie et la mort du Christ* (The Birth, the Life, and Death of Christ)

Alice Guy, director, Gaumont, 1906

PLOT SUMMARY: THE WOMEN AROUND JESUS

Alice Guy's film is a series of twenty-five scenes (listed in DVD). While harmonizing material from all the gospels, the film's episodic nature and passion focus resemble Mark. In fact, Guy's film emphasizes the passion (nineteen scenes) even more than Mark. Her Palm Sunday scene, which begins the passion, appears a little after the nine-minute mark in the thirty-three-minute film. By contrast, the same incident does not appear in Mark until Mk 11:7-10 (cf. its similar placements in Mt. 27:7-9; Lk. 19:35-38; Jn 12:12-19). Similarly, while Mark devotes little more than a verse to the Via Dolorosa (Mk 15:20b-21; cf. the similar treatments in Mt. 27:31b-32; Lk. 23:26-32; Jn 19:17),[1] Guy's film devotes more scenes to the way to the cross than to either the nativity (three) or the ministry (three). Given the cross's importance in Western Christianity and the Stations of the Cross (and thus the Via Dolorosa) in Roman Catholic Christianity, this passion focus is not surprising.[2] After all, passion plays were Jesus films' immediate artistic forerunners, and the first Jesus films were filmed passion plays, not "historical" treatments of Jesus (see Shepherd 2013: 11–34; Gaudreault 2016).

Intertitles, held by three girls dressed as angels, introduce the twenty-five scenes (all capitalized in this discussion). Except for the Sleep of Jesus, Jesus Falls the First Time, and Saint Veronica, the intertitles refer to recognizable gospel moments. However, only the Ecce Homo (Jn 19:5) intertitle "quotes" scripture. An accompanying lecturer, a commonplace in the exhibition of early biblical silents, may have supplied biblical/gospel quotations.[3]

Most scenes are single shots. Saint Veronica is a notable exception, with its cut-in of Veronica holding up the true icon (see also the Resurrection). Aspiring to a "historical look," Guy carefully stages each scene's mise-en-scène,[4] often relying on the notes and watercolors of James Tissot's illustrated *The Life of Our Savior Jesus Christ* for scene construction and costuming (particularly in the triumph, trial, and Via Dolorosa scenes, and in the presence of women in the latter).[5] Her insistence on "natural" acting[6] makes her film more "realistic" than other early silents (Foster 2013).

She was Alice Guy when she directed this film. She later married and became Alice Guy Blaché.

Guy's reliance on Tissot, as well as the passion play tradition's influence, renders her film a series of tableaux vivants. But, unlike the deposition tableau mocked by *La ricotta* (1963), Guy's tableaux are vibrant. Her scenes have action and depth. Characters enter and exit throughout individual scenes (see the Miracle of Jairus's Daughter). Action takes place in the foreground, background, and margins.

Consequently, Jesus is not always the center of attention.[7] Several other families seek entry at the inn before the holy family arrives. Jesus enters the Miracle of Jairus's Daughter and Palm Sunday late. During the Miracle of Jairus's Daughter, Jesus eventually takes center stage, but the scene focuses on the family's post-miracle celebration. The daughter never approaches Jesus, although other women worship Jesus in the left foreground. In Palm Sunday, a wall hides much of Jesus's triumph while women and children prepare his way.

Jesus is frequently lost in the crowd or at the back of a scene. In the Denial of St Peter, Peter sits in the middle of the frame at a charcoal fire. As the action ensues, one catches various glimpses of Jesus through archways in the rear as Jesus passes and repasses on his way to his Roman trial. The focus is on the anguished Peter seeing Jesus, and Jesus seeing Peter's denials. At times, in the Via Dolorosa scenes, Jesus is lost in the crowd or dwarfed, sometimes rendered unseeable, by his gigantic cross. In the Crucifixion, soldiers drop Jesus onto the cross and nail him to it. But the focus is the crowd in the foreground that, like the audience, has come to see Jesus's death.

By contrast, the Jesus film tradition makes Jesus the static center of a scene's composition, and Guy's film sometimes follows this pattern too (e.g., in the Nativity, the Sleep of Jesus, the Samaritan, Mary Magdalene, the Last Supper, the Agony, and Descending from the Cross). Guy's Jesus, however, is typically in motion—whether carried by others (Arrival in Bethlehem, the Descent from the Cross, and Committed to the Tomb), led passively to trial and suffering (Judas's Betrayal, Jesus before Caiphus [sic], the Denial of St Peter, Jesus before Pontius Pilate, the Torment, and the various Via Dolorosa scenes), or moving under his own volition (the Miracle of Jairus's Daughter, Palm Sunday, the Olive Garden, the Night Watch, and Judas's Betrayal).

Guy's Jesus is "passer-by" (Mk 6:48; Gospel of Thomas 42) and the film is a ritualistic/ imperial procession. In this, the film echoes Luke's travel narrative, where Jesus "sets his face" to go to Jerusalem (Lk. 9:51). The treks to Bethlehem and to the tomb bookend the film, but the lengthy Via Dolorosa scenes also bespeak procession. These processional stretches, as well as the fact that Jesus often enters scenes late, make the camera wait for Jesus (particularly in Climbing Golgotha).

The film pauses, as it processes, for the spectacle of the child in the manger (emphasized by the Sleep of Jesus), the risen Jesus, Veronica's true image (see Figure 1.1),[8] and most importantly (the spectacle of everyone gathering to see) Jesus's agony on the cross. A previous scene confirms the cross's centrality as Jesus "climbs Golgotha" with a cross so large that it dwarfs and obscures him.[9] Similarly, at the Last Supper, the (three female) angels suddenly present Jesus transfigured, already attired (in loincloth) for the cross.

One of Guy's striking innovations vis-à-vis the gospels and other early Jesus silents is the Sleep of Jesus. The incident stands in the place of the slaughter of the innocents (although no European film had yet presented that scene; Shepherd 2016a: 62) and stresses Jesus's angelic protection and amusement (by an angelic choir). The angels who appear at the Last Supper and in the Olive Garden are different. They foreshadow and facilitate Jesus's crucifixion.

These angels, and the angelic intertitles, represent the (preordained) story that everyone knows. Despite the attention these special-effect angels draw, Guy adds angels to the gospels only at the supper. The resurrected Jesus who appears and disappears in the empty tomb (following the order of Mk 16:6: "he is risen, he is not here") is another special effect highlight.

While critics often remark on Guy's realism (see Foster 2013), the angels and Jesus's transfigurations indicate her equal fascination with the supernatural. She displays no post-Enlightenment leeriness of miracle. For Guy, if one could pull back the curtain of the everyday, one would see angels everywhere.

In contrast, the ubiquitous women gesture at the everyday, the household, or even the real(istic). In the Jesus film tradition, Guy's film stands out because of these women.[10] While women are always present in nativities, it is rare for the magi to have (exotic) women with them. It is even rarer for Jesus's entire ministry to consist only of acts with women—the Samaritan woman, Jairus's daughter, and Magdalene. In the passion, women are absent only from the Last Supper, the Olive Garden, the Night Watch, and the Bearing of the Cross.[11] They and children are quite troublingly present in Jesus before Caiphus and in the Torment.

Clearly, Guy's Jesus belongs to these women. They press forward to be with him while men constantly push them away in the trials, on the Via Dolorosa, at the cross, and at the tomb.[12] Even in the film's first scene, a Roman soldier rudely sends a weeping, exhausted Mary from the street,[13] and the public ministry ends with men dismissing Magdalene from the house where she seeks Jesus.[14]

Film often invents characters not in the gospels. And Guy adds women to the Jesus story so liberally that the film almost becomes a Jesus adjacent film. But, perhaps, these women simply realize the story hinted at by Lk. 8:2-3.[15]

MEMORABLE CHARACTERS

1 The women who support Jesus and establish his community.
2 The angels who protect, amuse, and worship Jesus, but who also "call" him to his sufferings as well as presenting the film (as revelation) to the audience.
3 Jesus as passer-by.

MEMORABLE VISUALS

1 Medium shot of Veronica holding out the cloth with the true image for a worshiping woman and the audience to see (see Figure 1.1). This shot may be a synecdoche of the film.[16]

Figure 1.1 Veronica holds the true image in *La vie du Christ*, directed by Alice Guy, Gaumont, 1906. All rights reserved.

2. Angels miraculously appearing and disappearing in the Sleep of Jesus and the Last Supper.
3. Pilate's wife (standing next to him on a balcony) trying to stop Jesus's mocking and scourging.
4. Jesus processing toward the camera on the Via Dolorosa, particularly the long shot of Jesus or of the huge, oversized cross moving toward, passing by, and moving away from the camera in Climbing Golgotha. The sequence includes a sweeping pan shot.

KEY AUTHORITY/SCRIPTURE

1. The angelic intertitles are the film's key (female) voice/authority, along with Veronica's true image, which she extends to the audience as if on a white sheet, like those exhibitors used to display films.
2. The film quotes scripture rarely, but the film's key scripture is Lk. 8:2-3, because of the ubiquitous presence of women who stand with and serve Jesus.

CULTURAL LOCATION/GENRE: EARLY CINEMA

Early cinema had limited storytelling techniques. Accordingly, most filmmakers favored histrionic, pantomime acting. Guy deviates from this style by demanding "natural" acting.[17] Further, Leon Gaumont entrusted Guy with exploring the possibilities of narrative film at his studio in opposition to the Lumière brother's famous "actualities" (e.g., workers leaving a factory or a train arriving in a station). Accordingly, Guy is at the forefront of narrative film.[18]

Nonetheless, early cinema was largely a cinema of attractions.[19] Given Guy's sparing use of intertitles and her tableau style, her Jesus film clearly belongs to this era.[20] Filmmakers were attracted to what they could "show," and, with Jesus films, this was the passion. After all, churches prominently displayed crosses or crucifixes.[21]

While early silent films were quite short, Guy's Jesus film is twice the length of any other Gaumont production of 1906. It was a lavish, expensive production with over a hundred extras and some location shots. Guy liked to use outdoor locations, and she filmed the garden scenes and Climbing Golgotha outside Paris in the forest of Fontainebleau. She was one of the first directors to "shop" for locations and sometimes created stories to utilize those locations (Williams 1992: 56). Although Zecca's Jesus film soon surpassed it in popularity, Guy's film was the biggest hit in French film to that time, Gaumont's blockbuster, and harbinger of the later Jesus epics.

Finally, Guy was the first female film director and the head of all Gaumont's production from 1905 until she left with her husband to handle Gaumont's US operations and then to form their own film company (Solax in 1910). Women's prominence in her film reflects both her own business experiences and a culture that was moving from Victorian ideals of woman as the angel of the household to the progressive New Woman (see Foster 2013). Guy's film(s) reflects tensions between these two ideals (see Problematic Issue or, e.g., her own *Les Résultats du féminisme* [The Consequences of Feminism 1906], remade in 1912 as *In the Year 2000*). Unfortunately, cinema's early openness to female leadership was soon left behind, particularly by the monied, male hierarchies policing the US film industry (see Foster 2013).

DIRECTOR

Alice Guy made hundreds of films for Gaumont and Solax. Only three were known to be extant at the time of her death, but Gaumont released sixty-four previously unknown Guy films in 2008. Her films are often slapstick comedies (particularly her early shorts) or comedies of marriage,[22] but some, like her Jesus film, are "miracle films" combining realism with the fantastic/miraculous (see also *La Fée aux Choux*; *La Noël el de M. la cure* [The Parish Priest's Christmas 1906]).[23] In the former, new babies are found in a cabbage patch, as in French folklore. In the latter, when a priest cannot collect enough money for a Christmas baby, children lead the parishioners to the altar to pray; the altar's statue of Mary comes to life and hands a baby to suddenly appearing angels, who hand the baby to the worshipers, who place it in the crèche.

Children are also important in *Falling Leaves* (1912). In this film, a doctor predicts the death of Trixie's older consumptive sister before the last leaf falls, so Trixie ties leaves to their branches. This film's finale, however, is romantic, not miraculous. A young doctor sees Trixie's "prayerful" leaf intervention and comes to the sister's rescue with a new serum—and flowers. In short, "a child shall lead them," as is also often the case in scenes in *La vie du Christ*.

These films, like *La vie du Christ*, reflect the cultural transition from the Victorian era to that of the New Woman. Guy's marriage comedies, her subsequent films starring Vinnie Burns as a female action hero (e.g., *Two Little Rangers* 1912; *Greater Love Hath No Man* 1913; *Dick Whittington and His Cat* 1913), and her cross-dressing comedies (e.g., *Cupid and the Comet* 1911; *Officer Henderson* 1913) foreground gender's construction (see McMahan 2002: 206–41). In *Les Résultats du féminisme*, men care for children and do housework, and women bully these men and leave the house for work or drink. Perhaps, reflecting the era's transitional nature, the film's end abruptly restores traditional gender roles. In this conjunction, *La vie du Christ* seems an even more feminized portrait of Jesus as at the film's end Jesus belongs—even if he is no longer present—with women in the tomb's interior.[24]

PROBLEMATIC ISSUE: PATRIARCHY AND ANDROCENTRISM

While Guy's *La vie du Christ* is a breath of fresh air among patriarchal Jesus films, it remains somewhat problematic. For instance, Guy, following Tissot, troublingly names the sinful, anointing woman (Lk. 7:36-50) Magdalene, even though Luke does not. In fact, one of the ministry's other two prominent women, the Samaritan woman (Jn 4:1-42), also has a suspect reputation. The combination of these women with the nativity's Mary veers quite close to the Madonna-Whore dynamic long derided by feminists.

The other prominent woman in the ministry is Jairus's unnamed wife. Further, women's absence (except for the angels) from the Last Supper and the garden scenes (until after Jesus's arrest) may also suggest an enclave of male privilege. The women publicly celebrating Jesus in his triumph, defending him at trial, and supporting him on the Via Dolorosa do bring women out of the (female) house into the public world (of men). Nonetheless, because Jesus belongs to the women and angels (another world) and is rejected by men (as there are no resurrection appearances to human characters), the film remains close to an old private/female versus public/male dichotomy.

Further, Guy's Jesus is the suffering Christ, and Guy's women, who stand with him, are repeatedly "abused." Does Guy's film ask women to accept their suffering—at the hands of men—for Christ? If so, is this Jesus film as haunting as 1 Pet. 2-3, which holds forth Jesus's suffering as exemplary for wives and slaves?

Hopefully, the female angel intertitles and Veronica's true image tell a different story of a Jesus that is not conceived androcentrically, of a Jesus that disappears into a community of women, the (Roman) men having moved on to other things. If so, Lk. 8:2-3 may indeed finally be more important than 1 Pet. 2-3.[25]

GAUMONT VIDEO 2008. KINO INTERNATIONAL, 33 MINUTES, 2009[26]

DVD Extras

Sixty-four of Alice Guy's films are arranged chronologically from 1897 to 1907 in this three-hour and forty-five-minute DVD.

Intertitles

Title, 0:00

1 Arrival in Bethlehem (Lk. 2:1-6), 0:39
2 Nativity and Arrival of the Magi, 2:18
   Shepherds arrive (Lk. 2:8-20), 2:18
   The three magi arrive (Mt. 2:1-12), 3:25
3 The Sleep of Jesus, 4:19
4 The Samaritan [Woman] (Jn 4:1-42), 5:48
5 The Miracle of Jairus's Daughter (Mk 5:21-43 pars.), 6:38
6 Mary Magdalene Washes the Feet of Jesus (Lk. 7:36-50), 8:13
7 Palm Sunday (Mk 11:1-10 pars), 9:17
8 The Last Supper (Mk 14:17-31 pars), 10:06
9 The Olive Garden (Mk 14:32-40), 11:32
10 The Night Watch, 12:26
11 Judas's Betrayal (Mk 14:41-52 pars), 13:00
12 Jesus before Caiphus [sic] (Mk 14:53-15:1 pars), 14:01
13 The Denial of St Peter, 16:02
14 Jesus before Pontius Pilate (Mk 15:2-20), 17:37
   Barabbas, 18:24
   A pitcher for Pilate's handwashing, 18:47
15 The Torment, 19:15
   Pilate's wife, Claudia, enters the balcony, 19:33
   Jesus stripped, 19:43
   Claudia gestures to Pilate to stop Jesus's scourging (Mk 15:15-20 pars), 20:12
   Jesus mocked as king, as Pilate quarrels with Claudia, 20:35
16 Ecce Homo, 20:49
17 The Bearing of the Cross (Mk 15:20-22 pars), 21:10
   A Black man (Simon of Cyrene?) lifts the (full) cross (Mk 15:21 pars), 21:18

18 Jesus Falls the First Time, 21:49

    Jesus falls, and a woman tries to pick up the cross, 22:35

    The sorrowing mother comforts Jesus three times, 22:46

        John, the Beloved Disciple, pulls her away

19 Saint Veronica, 23:34

    The true image, 25:15

20 Climbing Golgotha, 25:26

21 The Crucifixion, 27:29

    Nailing to the cross (Mk 15:25-27 pars), 28:16

    Sorrowful women (Mk 15:29-33 pars), 28:34

22 The Agony, 28:37

    Spear thrust (Jn 19:31-37), 29:10

23 Descending from the Cross (Mk 15:42-46 pars), 29:32

    Magdalene and another woman unwrap the shroud, 30:03

    The sorrowing mother comforted by John, the Beloved Disciple, 30:46

24 Committed to the Tomb (Mk 15:46-47), 31:03

25 The Resurrection, 31:57

    Four angels appear to lift off the sarcophagus's lid (Mk 16:1-8 pars), 32:14

    Jesus, in white robes, appears above the sarcophagus, 32:29

    The guards fall to the ground (Mt. 27:62-66; 28:4, 11-15)

    Jesus opens his robes and begins to ascend (Lk. 24:50-52; Acts 1:6-11), 32:35

    Ten women worship at the empty sarcophagus, 33:23

Music Credits, 33:28

NOTES

1. Luke's treatment is the longest and includes the "daughters of Jerusalem."
2. See Chapter 20 for discussion of the Stations on the Cross, with reference to *The Passion of the Christ* (2004).
3. Both Gaumont and Pathé, the company producing Ferdinand Zecca's film, created lecture books for their films. See Shepherd (2013: 11–34).
4. The Jesus film tradition relies upon Orientalizing nineteenth-century art and archaeology for costuming and mise-en-scène. See the discussion in Chapter 3 and McGeough (2021).
5. See Shepherd (2016a: 60–1, 66–8). In 2009, the Brooklyn Museum exhibited Tissot's *Life of Christ* (October 23, 2009 through January 17, 2010), in concert with a Whitney Museum of Art's Retrospective on Alice Guy Blaché: Cinema Pioneer (November 6, 2009, through

January 24, 2010), in recognition of how indebted Guy's film is to Tissot. For the Brooklyn Tissot watercolors, see Dolkart (2009). For the Whitney exhibition, see Simon (2009b).

6 Pamela B. Green's 2018 documentary about Guy is accordingly entitled *Be Natural: The Untold Story of Alice Guy-Blaché*.
7 "Instead of being centered on the figure of Christ, with all the other performers drifting into the background, Guy constructs a living world in which all the participants are equally important to the gaze of the camera" (Foster 2013).
8 David Shepherd claims this is a POV shot (2016a: 71–4), although it does not have the final shot that later became standard: shot of person who sees, shot of what they see, shot of person who saw again.
9 John Wright, the film editor for Mel Gibson's *The Passion of the Christ*, speaks of that film's enormous cross as "its own character" (see Chapter 20, DVD Extras). Cf. *The Gospel of Peter*'s walking, talking cross.
10 Women are active participants with Jesus in *Il messia* (1975), *Son of Man* (2006), and *Mary Magdalene* (2018).
11 The women's absence from the first three might suggest an inner circle of male privilege. Female angels are, however, present at the Last Supper and the Olive Garden.
12 For a summary of female acceptance of Jesus and male resistance of both women and Jesus, see Shepherd (2016a: 70–1). Shepherd notes that women also receive more attention (than in the gospels) in both Tissot and Anne Katherine Emmerich, upon whom Tissot depended.
13 Note that the miraculous birth follows, despite this Roman hostility. Further, while mounted Romans send Mary rudely away and lead Jesus to crucifixion, the resurrection frightens the Romans and sends them fleeing. While a frightened Roman guard appears in Mt. 28:4, it is more intriguing to read Guy's frightened men vis-à-vis Mark's frightened women (Mk 16:8) and the film as rewriting Mark's frightened women finale.
14 Does Jesus's treatment of Magdalene precipitate his arrest?
15 See Shepherd (2016a: 70). Gwendolyn Foster (2013) asserts more boldly that "this life of Christ is told through the eyes of the girl angels who guide us through the story … This is a life of Christ told not only from the point of view of these angels, but a tale that is *performed* and *enacted* by women and children throughout the entire narrative" (Foster's emphasis).
16 This shot is the film's only medium "closeup."
17 A sign emblazoned with "Be Natural" hung in her Solax studio. See Simon (2009a: 18).
18 Some claim her first film, *La Fée aux Choux* (The Cabbage Fairy 1896, remade as *Sage-femme de première classe* [Midwife to the Upper Classes 1902]), was the first narrative film. While Alison McMahan disputes this assertion, she places Guy at narrative film's inception (2002: 1–42).
19 See Gunning (1986; 1994: 10–30). Shepherd notes that silent Jesus films tend to either spectacle (the passion, color, the exotic holy land, the magi's star, or Egypt) or narrative. The latter, however, tends to appear only in Jesus adjacents, like *Ben-Hur* (2016b: 271–80).
20 Diana Foster (2014) states that intertitles first appeared in film in 1903.
21 Matt Page (2017b), relying on David Bordwell (2017), notes some features of Guy's camera that move away from the tableau style.
22 Alan Williams says that Guy should be judged by her comedies, not her dramas. He claims her finest French comedy is *Le Matelas alcoolique* (The Drunken Mattress 1906) and her best American film is *Dick Whittington and His Cat* (1913) (2009: 41, 43). McMahan concurs, saying the latter is the best example of Guy's preferred type of film, a fantasy period piece, relying on fairy tales or art, with elaborate sets and costumes and child heroes (2002: 165).

23 McMahan claims she made one to two such films a year at Gaumont, but very few survive (2002: 98–9). In America, these became forgiveness films, although they sometimes still end with a secular pietà (2002: 108, 125–7).
24 The Victorian age often constructed religion as an affair of women.
25 McMahan argues that Guy's cross-dressing comedies, and their "behavioral transvestism," address a female audience and render gender fluid (2002: 206–41). Shepherd similarly claims that the Veronica scene bespeaks an address to women (2016a: 70–4).
26 The DVD's English intertitles were added in 2009.

2

La vie et passion de notre seigneur Jésus Christ (The Life and Passion of Jesus Christ)

Ferdinand Zecca, director, Pathé, 1907

PLOT SUMMARY: FILM MIRACLES

Zecca's film is an episodic display of Jesus's life from the annunciation to his enthronement at God's right hand. The Pathé catalogue offered the 1907 film for sale as a whole or in four parts (rather than selling individual scenes as they had with previous Jesus films): the nativity; the childhood; the public ministry; and the passion (Boillat and Robert 2016: 51 n24). Thirty-five red intertitles, capitalized in this discussion, punctuate the tableaux vivants and display two trademark Pathé roosters.[1] Like Guy's, Zecca's intertitles simply introduce the (one-shot) scene (or sequence; e.g., in The Nativity and Adoration of the Wise Men; The Flight into Egypt; and The Holy Family at Nazareth). The nativity and childhood have nine intertitles; the ministry has nine; and the passion has seventeen. The intertitles do not quote scripture, although most refer to recognizable gospel episodes. An angelic choir does, however, display a Lk. 2:14 banner in The Wonderful Star, and Moses holds tablets in The Transfiguration.

The passion begins after the twenty-four-minute mark of the approximately forty-four-minute film, and the film devotes approximately fourteen minutes to the nativity and childhood, so it has a Lukan or Matthean aura.[2] The first three intertitles refer to Lukan material and the next four to Matthean, with a return to another Lukan scene after an invented sequence (The Holy Family at Nazareth). John's gospel is important during the ministry (The Wedding Feast, Jesus and the Woman of Samaria, and The Raising of Lazarus), but the ministry begins and ends with Synoptic material (Baptizing Christ, The Transfiguration). Nevertheless, the overall film has a Johannine cast (see Key Authority).

Zecca's individual scenes are flatter than Guy's, and his film a better example of the tableau aesthetic than Guy's (Boillat and Robert 2016: 39). The processions are less developed and the action more centripetal. If Jesus is not at the center of the action or at the front of the screen, he soon will be (e.g., The Raising of Lazarus; Jesus Given over to the People). If Jesus is at the back of the action, then the other characters, in a carefully choreographed movement, will step to the sides to funnel the audience's gaze directly to Jesus (e.g., Jesus Driving Out the Money-Changers from the Temple; The Last Supper). The film's movement then is simply about creating the right tableau or "pregnant moment" (Boillat and Robert 2016: 39) before the characters disperse to form the next tableau. Not surprisingly, characters act histrionically and for the camera, not with other actors.

While Tissot's Bible is a key influence on Guy's costuming and mise-en-scène, Zecca'a film (particularly the 1902–5 version[s]) depends more heavily on Gustav Doré's biblical engravings for costuming, exaggerated theatrical postures (like Jesus pointing heavenward even as a boy in the temple), and stage-like spaces.[3] Given Guy's influence on Zecca's 1907 film, the influence of both Doré and Tissot (or Guy) can be seen in the 1907 version (see Friesen 2016: 87–92).

A concern for "realism" is most obvious in the elaborate backdrops, for which Pathé sets were famous.[4] Elsewhere, Zecca's focus is almost always on the iconic, the spectacular, and the miraculous. The use of color, achieved through a patented Pathé stenciling process, is still striking (e.g., in bright yellow angel wings, nimbuses, and the star vis-à-vis pastel costuming and black and white or even blue-wash scenes).

Through superimposition, angels appear and disappear (e.g., in The Annunciation;[5] The Wonderful Star; The Flight into Egypt; Jesus on the Mount of Olives; The Resurrection; and The Ascension). An angelic choir appears more than once, but the most spectacular instance is the heavenly choir (in The Wonderful Star) holding an inscribed banner, "Gloria in excelsis deo" (Lk. 2:14; see also The Flight into Egypt and The Ascension). An armed female angel appears to protect Jesus and confuse his enemies—the slaughter of the innocents having already begun—in The Flight into Egypt and The Resurrection. Intriguingly, the angels—particularly the angel of The Annunciation and the armed female angel—have halos seemingly constructed from film reels.

Superimposition also allows the sudden appearance of a bright yellow star in The Wonderful Star and The Nativity and Adoration of the Wise Men. The star provides a sense of divine plotting connecting several nativity scenes. Superimposition allows the heavenly dove to appear at the baptism, Jesus to be transfigured with Moses and Elijah, and Jesus to rise from the waters (Walking on the Waters) and from the tomb.

Film editing makes these miracles possible and credible, as the film produces them before its audience's eyes. The Image DVD chapter for Jesus's ministry, which also includes his youthful appearance in the temple, is quite appropriately entitled "Miracles." After all, except for Mary Magdalene at the Feet of Jesus (Lk. 7:36-50) and Jesus and the Woman of Samaria, every episode in the ministry is miraculous.[6] After the baptism, Jesus's public ministry opens with the wedding at Cana, where the water-become-wine jars are front and center. The raising of Jairus's daughter occurs after Jesus has walked through a desperate crowd and healed a blind man and a lame man. The girl's raising occurs immediately after Jesus enters the room, and she immediately rises and bows to worship Jesus at the front center of the screen, as does Lazarus after his resurrection. In what is a relatively rare cinematic scene, Jesus walks upon the waters alone, and then, in the next scene, walks on the waters again toward some disciples in a boat (The Wonderful Draught of Fishes).

The miraculous catch presumably depends upon Lk. 5:1-11, but because Jesus does not walk on the water in that pericope, Zecca's film outdoes the miraculous gospels. The miracle at Cana functions similarly, with the audience at "center stage" for the event, even though it is unclear in Jn 2:1-11 when the miracle occurs or who knows of it. In all these miracle sequences, cinema's technological power is, at least, as obvious as Jesus's power (see Problematic Issue). Thus, in Christ Walks on the Waters, after an establishing shot of ocean waves, a superimposed Jesus rises from these waves and walks toward the camera.

Only the audience sees this miracle, so the scene/film becomes a cinematic hierophany. The resurrection is similar. After superimposed angels remove the sarcophagus's lid, a superimposed Jesus rises from it in triumph, scattering the Roman guard in fear. As in Guy's film, these Romans and the audience are the cinematic miracle's only witnesses.[7] Medium cut-in closeups of the Ecce Homo-Jesus and of Veronica holding the true image, both against a white screen backdrop suitable for projecting a film, indicate a similarly revelatory cinema.

These miracles, as well as the tableau aesthetic and the reliance on Doré, create an incredibly iconic Christ. Jesus is at his most human when his mother holds a fully nude baby aloft. The *Lion King*-like scene, however, follows the baby's sudden, miraculous superimposed appearance in the manger (cf. the baby floating through a shaft of light toward Mary's womb in various Medieval and Renaissance paintings).[8] Consequently, the baby's humanity hardly disrupts the iconicity. The film's Johannine or Doré Christ is always pointing heavenward to indicate his authority and, given the nativity, his otherworldly origins.

Zecca's Jesus is the Johannine revealer from above (if not a more gnostic figure).[9] He appears suddenly in the crib, and he rises, levitating out of his sarcophagus, before ascending (returning) to the right hand of God.[10] The risings from the waters and at the transfiguration (see Figure 2.1) succinctly visualize Zecca's Christ.[11] Jesus enters the transfiguration scene with three disciples. They stay behind, kneeling in worship, as he walks back atop a small rise. Suddenly, his entire upper body is superimposed within a gold nimbus as his clothes turn brilliantly white and Moses and Elijah appear beside him.[12] Like the Johannine Christ, however, Zecca's Christ is always transfigured. Accordingly, Zecca's film ends with the audience watching the film and looking into heaven.

The passion is less miraculous, although lightning and darkness attend Jesus's crucifixion as in the Synoptic Gospels. Notably, Zecca replaces Guy's dichotomy in which women are "for" and men are "against" Jesus[13] with an anti-Semitic contrast in which Roman soldiers "protect" Jesus from an angry Jewish mob. The Jesus Given over to the People intertitle expresses the point succinctly (cf. Mt. 27:24-25).[14] Further, after the scourging, a Jew from the crowd rams the crown of thorns onto Jesus's head and other Jews mock him with a robe (in contrast to the gospels' mocking Roman soldiers). During the Ecce Homo scene, soldiers try vainly to keep the people away as a Jew drags Jesus forward and throws him to the ground at center screen. Jewish people even drag the cross to Jesus. As Jesus proceeds along the Via Dolorosa, the crowd, including women, gestures angrily at him. This antiSemitism, an evil omen for later Jesus films, stems not only from the gospels' passions but also from this film's see-believe ideology (see Problematic Issue).

MEMORABLE CHARACTERS

1 The always-transfigured Christ (see Figure 2.1). He "wears" this glory from his first miraculous appearance in the manger, through the walking on the waters, to the resurrection/ascension.
2 The angels, who like Jesus, miraculously appear and disappear.
3 The passion's angry Jewish crowd, from whom the Roman soldiers protect Jesus.

MEMORABLE VISUALS

1. The baby Jesus's miraculous appearance in the manger, and Mary holding him aloft for adoration in a naked, full frontal view.
2. The sword-wielding, female angel who protects the vanishing holy family from Herod's soldiers and who reappears at the empty tomb.
3. Jesus's rise from the waters to walk upon the sea.
4. The transfigured Christ (see Figure 2.1).
5. Jesus's rise from the sarcophagus and ascension to God's right hand on a cloud swing.

KEY AUTHORITY/SCRIPTURE

1. The camera and editing produce miracles (angels, the star, the heavenly dove, the transfigured Christ, and God himself), authorizing and hallowing the film. The medium closeups of the Ecce Homo and Veronica's true image on white screens also configure the film itself as hierophany. What one sees, one must believe.

Figure 2.1 The transfigured Christ in *La vie et passion de notre seigneur Jésus Christ*, directed by Ferdinand Zecca, Pathé, 1907. All rights reserved.

2   Other than "Ecce Homo," the clearest gospel citation is the angels' "Gloria in excelsis deo" banner (Lk. 2:14).

3   Given the editing miracles, the Synoptic Gospels' transfiguration narratives are the film's key scripture.

CULTURAL LOCATION/GENRE: THE EXHIBITOR'S CUT

In early cinema, producers sold films or film scenes, rather than renting them to exhibitors. The rental period began around 1910, with multi-reel fictional narratives. Guy's and Zecca's films both belong to the exhibitor period. The relative autonomy of tableaux vivants also contributed to diversity. Further, producers regularly marketed new scenes for old films. An exhibitor could also splice disparate films together, and exhibitors certainly decided whether (and what) music and lectures would accompany a film. Searching for an original film then is almost as "utopian" as searching for an original gospel (see Boillat and Robert 2016: 25–6).

Pathé was adept at managing its Jesus film's longevity by advertising new editions both as innovative in some small way and as continuing their tradition. Alain Boillat and Valentine Robert identify four major movements in Pathé's *La vie et passion de notre seigneur Jésus Christ* tradition: (1) 1899, sixteen tableaux; (2) 1902, twenty-eight tableaux; (3) 1907, thirty-seven tableaux (no longer sold separately, but in four sets); (4) 1913, forty-three tableaux (also sold in four groups) (2016: 51 n24). Zecca directed the 1902 version, but Pathé advertised additional scenes, which were shot from 1902 to 1905 and directed by Lucien Nonquet. Pathé released both black- and- white and color versions of films, and Dwight Friesen has demonstrated that the 1907 film existed in at least two versions with different scene compositions (2016: 78–80).

While the Image Entertainment DVD packaging claims to be the 1905 version, recent scholarly analysis has determined this DVD (and current streaming versions) to be nearest to the 1907 "movement" (see Boillat and Robert 2016: 31; Friesen 2016). Not incidentally, the 1907 film was the most successful Jesus film in the US marketplace until *From the Manger to the Cross* (1912), and the most seen film in the United States in 1907.[15]

DIRECTOR

The French film historian, George Sadoul, claims that a Lumière tendency (photography; actualities) and a Méliès tendency (theater) marked French film from its inception. While one can push this point too far, Gaumont's films reflect the Lumière trend, with Pathé's nearer to Méliès's theatrics and tricks (Williams 2009: 37–8). The rival companies produced their two Jesus films competitively, expecting their differing studio styles (e.g., Gaumont/Guy's tendency to shoot on location; Pathé/Zecca's preference for sets with elaborate backdrops) to appeal to their distinctive audiences (Gaumont's restraint appealing to the upper middle class, and Pathé's showmanship to the petty bourgeoisie). Gaumont/Guy's Jesus film is new and, therefore, shorter and more integrated, while Pathé/Zecca added tableaux to an existing Jesus film (tradition), which is, therefore, longer and less integrated (Williams 2009: 38–41).[16]

While Guy innovated in subject matter and mise-en-scène, Zecca, in his career, used the camera more innovatively (Williams 2009: 40).[17] Whether one thinks of Zecca as an artist or not, Williams claims, "probably no other person in the history of cinema contributed as much or as fast to its evolution as did Ferdinand Zecca" (1992: 45). Zecca did so because he relentlessly stole and adapted material from competitors like Gaumont, as well as from various media. His and Charles Pathé's success formula prized innovation: "Try everything, then try it all again; stick with what works, but never let a fixed way of doing things get in the way of borrowing from your competition" (Williams 1992: 44).

Scholars see Zecca's dramatic and "naturalist" films as his greatest successes. Like Émile Zola's literature, this cinema explored the tragic destinies of the everyday life of the lower classes and criminals in terms of melodramatic emotion, not the political causes of crime and sordid conditions (Williams 1992: 45–6; Abel 1994: 96–101). Zecca's early *Histoire d'un crime* (1901) is a notable example. Based on an exhibit of the same name at the Musée Grévin, *Histoire d'un crime* portrays a murder and the murderer's execution. Despite the naturalist "grit," the film's highlight is the emotional, flashback projection on the murderer's cell wall (a film) of his original fall into crime (cf. his Jesus film's editing miracles).

Zecca, however, believed that cinema's future lay with the féeries (Moen 2013: 40), like those made famous by Georges Méliès (e.g., *Cendrillon* [Cinderella 1889] or *Le voyage dans la lune* [A Trip to the Moon 1902]).[18] Zecca was quite proud of his *Sept châteaux du diable* (Seven Castles of the Devil 1901). To move fairy tales, magic tricks, or wondrous transformations from stage to film, Méliès developed most of the camera's optical effects: "substitution splicing (by which he could simulate sudden appearances, disappearances, and transformations), superimposition through multiple exposures, matting several images together into different parts of a single frame, dissolves, and so on" (Williams 1992: 36). Zecca's editorial miracles followed in Méliès's footsteps or worked within what Kristian Moen calls a cinema of transformations (2013: 39).

Alan Williams claims that Guy's film respects Christianity as a cultural tradition while Zecca's film is the work of a "master showman." His resurrection scene, in particular, "might as well have been directed by Georges Méliès—or by a previous incarnation of Busby Berkeley. The word 'kitsch' is hard to avoid in describing it" (Williams 2009: 40). The elaborate colorizing of many scenes added to the film's spectacle, which, unlike the editing, was a genuine innovation. Segundo de Chomon developed a patented stencil-coloring process for Pathé that allowed the use of different colors in the same scene.[19] Some think de Chomon important enough to be considered Zecca's co-director.

PROBLEMATIC ISSUE: SEEING AND BELIEVING

In an important article, Méliès argued that cinema had produced four different "views" (or world constructions): natural (e.g., Lumière actualities); scientific (made through cinematic technologies that heighten perception); composed subject (actors perform an action); and transformation (or fantastic), which he claimed to have invented (Moen 2013: 50–8). Of transformation, Méliès said that filmmaking is "a profession in which everything, even the seemingly impossible, is realized, and the most fanciful dreams are given the semblance of reality. Finally, needless to say, one must absolutely realize the impossible, since one photographs it and renders it visible" (cited in Moen 2013: 53). It also renders incredulity virtually impossible.

One sees the miracles and the transfigured Christ, and believes. What one believes in, however, may be the cinematic hierophany—film's valorizing of itself and its technological, consumer capitalist society.[20] Such spectacle may render the audience passive and mute.[21] Significantly, the gospels are less sanguine about the equivalence between seeing and believing (see, e.g., Jn 6:26, 64-65; 20:29; Staley 2021).

IMAGE ENTERTAINMENT DVD, 44 MINUTES, 2003
DVD Extras

This film is on the same DVD with Olcott's *From the Manger to the Cross* (1912). Italicizing indicates the film's intertitles.

DVD Chapters

1 Main title: The Annunciation

    The Annunciation (Lk. 1:26-38), 0:20

    The Arrival of Joseph and Mary in Bethlehem (Lk. 2:1-6), 1:29

2 *The Wonderful Star*, 2:39

    Following the Star, 4:05

    The Nativity and Adoration of the Wise Men (Mt. 2:1-12), 4:41

    The Massacre of the Innocents (Mt. 2:16-18), 6:52

    The Flight into Egypt (Mt. 2:13-15), 7:30

    The Holy Family at Nazareth, 12:03

3 Miracles, 13:54

    Jesus and the Doctors (Lk. 2:41-50), 13:55

    Baptizing Christ (Mk 1:9-11 pars), 14:41

    The Wedding Feast (Jn 2:1-11), 15:26

    Mary Magdalene at the Feet of Jesus (Lk. 7:36-50), 16:49

    Jesus and the Woman of Samaria (Jn 4:1-42), 17:56

    Raising of the Daughter of Jairus (Mk 5:21-43 pars), 18:58

    Christ Walks on the Waters (Mk 6:45-52), 20:23

    The Wonderful Draught of Fishes (LK. 5:1-11), 21:01

        Jesus again walks on water, 21:24

    The Raising of Lazarus (Jn 11:1-46), 22:16

    The Transfiguration (Mk 9:2-8 pars), 23:38

       Entering Jerusalem (Mk 11:1-10 pars), 24:33

       Jesus Driving out the Money-Changers from the Temple (Mk 11:15-19 pars), 25:16

4 The Last Days, 26:17

       The Last Supper (Mk 14:17-31 pars), 26:19

       Jesus on the Mount of Olives. The Kiss of Judas (Mk 14:32-52 pars), 27:22

       Jesus before Caiaphas (Mk 14:53-15:1 pars), 29:13

       Peter Denies Christ, 29:59

       Jesus before Pilate (Mk 15:2-20 pars), 30:30

       The Scourging; the Crowning with Thorns (Mk 15:15-20 pars), 31:33

       Jesus Given over to the People, 32:45

            "Ecce Homo," 33:06

            Pilate washes his hands (Mt. 27:24-25)

5 The Crucifixion, 34:13

       Jesus Falls under the Weight of the Cross (Mk 15:20-22 pars), 34:15

            Veronica's veil

       Calvary, 35:25

       Christ Put on the Cross (Mk 15:25-27), 36:43

            Mary grieves at the foot of the cross

       Agony and Death of Christ, 38:25

            The Roman who pierces Jesus's side recognizes him as "Son of God" (Jn 19:31-37; Mk 15:39 pars)

       Jesus Taken from the Cross (Mk 15:42-46 pars), 39:15

       Jesus Put into the Tomb (Mk 15:46-47 pars), 40:32

6 The Resurrection and Ascension, 41:13

       The Resurrection (Mk 16:1-8 pars), 41:13

            Angels lift off the stone; Jesus rises from the grave

            The Roman guards see Jesus first (Mt. 27:62-66; 28:4, 11-15)

       The Ascension (Lk. 24:50-52; Acts 1:6-11), 42:31

            Jesus, seated at the right hand of God in glory

7 End Credits, 44:06

NOTES

1 Pathé introduced its trademark rooster to discourage piracy. Most scenes, with the notable exception of Peter's denial, also have a white rooster painted somewhere within them. See Friesen (2016: 92, 96 n49).

2   The film devotes more time, proportionally, to the nativity/childhood than do Matthew and Luke: fourteen of forty-four minutes compared to two of Luke's twenty-four chapters and two of Matthew's twenty-eight.
3   See Doré ([1859] 2014). Boillat and Robert claim that Zecca's slender palm trees and tall, oriental-style buildings stem from Doré, as do the Last Supper's colonnades, and that the Wedding Feast and the Resurrection reproduce Doré illustrations exactly (2016: 39–41).
4   Williams says Pathé's set designers are the film's true authors (1992: 56).
5   Gabriel's appearance is quite dramatic: on clouds and with a cross halo (perhaps the earliest cross foreshadowing in Jesus cinema).
6   Zecca replicates all three of Guy's ministry episodes.
7   The resurrection, relatively rare in Jesus films, appears in both Guy and Zecca. *Il vangelo secondo Matteo* (1964) shows the stone blown away from the tomb.
8   Friesen traces this visualization to the *Protoevangelium of James*, in which the baby Jesus emerges from a cloud and blinding light (2016: 93).
9   On film's tendency to gnostic Christs, see Stern, Jefford, and DeBona (1999: 291–5).
10 When God does (rarely) appear in film, it is typically in comedies. See Burnette-Bletsch (2016c).
11 Perhaps the decision to end the ministry with the transfiguration reflects Luke's (9:31) structure.
12 The transfiguration is relatively rare in film, but it appears in *The Jesus Film* (1979).
13 Some think that Zecca deliberately restores the role of men to correct Guy. See Shepherd (2016a: 62, 64–6) and Friesen (2016: 91). He does privilege men in comparable scenes. For example, in Guy, Mary watches over the sleeping Jesus while it is Joseph in Zecca. Similarly, Jairus plays a more prominent role in Zecca while Guy emphasizes the unnamed wife. Finally, men prepare the way for Jesus in Zecca's Palm Sunday while it is women and children in Guy. Zecca even includes a scene where Jesus works with Joseph who teaches him carpentry.
14 See *Il vangelo*; *Il messia* (1975); and *The Passion of the Christ* (2004). For the more recent history of Mt. 27:25, see *Shoah 1985 Part 1 First Era* 3.45:28-4.04:00 (https://www.youtube.com/watch?v=_n7_gSUVCwc).
15 See Shepherd (2013: chap. 3) and Abel (1999: 60–4). Richard Abel discusses the construction of an American (nationalistic) cinema vis-à-vis Pathé films' US popularity.
16 Some claim that Guy's film revised an earlier Jesus film (1899) that she did for Gaumont. Alison McMahan (2002: 28–9) and David Shepherd (2013: chap. 2, n13) think the previous Gaumont film was George Hatot's, made originally for the Lumières, and later marketed by both Gaumont and Pathé.
17 His Jesus film is not a good example of this. It does include a few lateral pans (e.g., in The Nativity and Adoration of the Wise Men; The Holy Family at Nazareth; and Raising of the Daughter of Jairus) (Williams 2009: 40).
18 On the cinematic féeries, see Abel (1994: 61–87, 278–97) and Moen (2013: 39–73). Méliès also filmed the short *Le Christ marchant sur les flots* (Christ Walking on the Water 1899). Perhaps this accounts for the inclusion of a similar scene, relatively rare in Jesus cinema, in Zecca and Olcott's films.
19 Gaumont simply tinted various frames in one color.
20 Many have written about film's tendency to hallow itself and its culture in terms of the mythic support of, and propagation of, the cultural status quo.
21 These reflections are about cinema's surreptitious ideological or mythological power, not a denial that audiences can and do respond actively and differently to film.

3

From the Manger to the Cross

Sidney Olcott, director, Kalem, 1912

PLOT SUMMARY: THE GOSPEL ON LOCATION

This, the first feature-length Jesus film (five reels), has three roughly equal parts: birth and early life; public ministry; and last days. Consequently, Olcott gives more time proportionally to Jesus's public ministry than Guy or Zecca do.

Opening intertitles declare the film was shot "on location." Contemporary audiences also likely noticed the film's heavy dependence upon the Tissot Bible. Both helped establish the film's "authenticity" (see Cultural Location).[1]

Now, however, the reliance on Tissot detracts dramatically. The film simply marches from the manger to the cross—the title provides the narrative continuity—through one Tissot tableau after another. Valentine Robert counts almost twenty exact Tissot replicas (2019: 72; cf. Staley 2013a: 99–100). Almost everything takes place before a static camera in wide (or long) shots (a few pans occur). As Charles Keil observes, the film is retrograde compared to contemporary cinema.[2] The storytelling is ponderous.

The slowness stems partly from an innovation that Olcott makes. Guy and Zecca use intertitles sparingly to "establish" tableaux. Olcott uses ten "chapter" intertitles similarly (listed in italics in DVD), but he also deploys over 100 scripture intertitles.[3]

The chapter intertitles use artwork (reminiscent of Tissot) as a background. The scripture intertitles appear against a black billboard (a placard or scroll?) with the film's title as an unfurled banner above the citation. The penultimate intertitle differs: moving clouds, a darkening sky, and a falling building visualize Matthew's crucifixion earthquake.

The scripture intertitles cite and quote, usually abbreviating, a KJV gospel passage. The quotations "establish" shots.[4] Sometimes they quote Jesus to Christological effect (e.g., Jn 8:58; 18:6). Sometimes they are incorrect, presumably because of typographical errors.[5]

Sometimes, however, the "errors" reveal gospel harmonizing. For example, the film cites Matthew for the blind man healed at Jericho, but has only one man healed (as in Mark) while Matthew has two.[6] The film cites Matthew for the complaint about the anointing's waste of money, but shows Judas "voicing" this complaint (only in Jn 12:4-6). Again, the film quotes Lk. 22:41 before the torch-bearing party comes to arrest Jesus, when only John mentions this detail.

Vitagraph bought Kalem in 1917 and re-released the film in 1919. The latter, discussed here, is the one commonly available today.

This harmonizing probably also lies behind the tactic of switching from one gospel to another for no apparent reason (e.g., moving from Mk 4:1 to Mt. 14:25, from Lk. 19:37 to Mt. 21:9, and from Lk. 22:41 to Mt. 31:46[sic]). This maneuver creates certain peculiarities when, for example, the film cites the textually suspect Lk. 22:19b-20, rather than the more textually certain Synoptic parallels, or in the film's heavy reliance on Luke's crucifixion, when that gospel's passion portrayal does not easily lead to the final scriptural intertitle, Jn 3:16.

The intertitles' onscreen time matters far more. They are there for much longer than it takes to read them, and the film often multiplies scripture's screen time by having different title cards when one would suffice (e.g., Lk. 1:28a then 1:28b; Jn 1:23a then Jn 1:23b; and Jn 1:36a then 1:36b).[7] The intertitles make the film even more episodic than its predecessors and the gospels. These intertitles visualize the gospel text itself, rendering the KJV, like the cinematic Christ, a sacred talisman.[8] The film thus becomes a precursor of later visual "translations" (e.g., *The Jesus Film* 1979; *The Gospel of John* 2003; see Walsh 2021b).

Following Tissot in both instances, Mary wears Arab peasant clothing and carries a jar of water into her house and, yet, is dressed as a nun during the annunciation. Unlike its precursors, however, the film does not visualize Gabriel or include his message. A bright light (a theater device used to represent angels or even Jesus) and Mary's awed response signify the angel.[9] Olcott never includes any angels nor any gospel scenes asserting Jesus's otherworldly identity: the baptism, exorcisms,[10] the transfiguration, the centurion's confession, nor the resurrection. The contrast with Zecca's final apotheosis is astounding.

Instead, as in *Il vangelo* (1964), the audience sees Joseph see Mary (not visibly pregnant) before his angelic dream. Joseph also sees only a bright light, but he and the audience hear (or read) the angelic message (Mt. 1:20-21). That the boy Jesus "shall save his people from their sins" is the film's first description of Jesus's salvific significance (cf. the citations opening the ministry [Jn 1:36] and ending the film [Jn 3:16]).[11]

The star, shepherds, wise men, and manger-adoration typical of Christmas pageants follow—but in a restrained style. Olcott gives a great deal of screen time to an incredibly morose Herod,[12] but he does not include the slaughter of the innocents. He shows instead the holy family's quiet, nocturnal flight, focusing on the location and using it to effect for the first time with shots before the pyramids and the Sphinx (with Joseph mirroring the sphinx's pose).

In addition to the twelve-year-old Jesus in the temple, extended to show the parents' worries about their lost son, Olcott creates two memorable childhood scenes. In the first, Mary reads from a scroll to Jesus (who wears a yarmulke) while Joseph watches from the background, working a piece of wood, and stopping to listen. The film implies that Mary is Jesus's teacher, if not divine providence's voice. She certainly carries more weight than the temple's scribes do. In the second invented and perhaps most famous scene, Olcott's carpenter boy walks toward the camera and into the light carrying a board across his shoulders so that it creates a cruciform shadow (see Figure 3.1). In the background, Mary covers her mouth in angst, clearly seeing the shadow's portent.[13]

The Baptist's identification of Jesus as the Lamb of God opens the public ministry (Jn 1:36), as Jesus walks (unidentifiably) on the distant horizon.[14] When Jesus calls fisherman to follow him, the audience (as disciples) sees the adult Jesus (Robert Henderson-Bland) recognizably for the first time.[15] While Olcott includes more teaching scenes than does Guy or Zecca, he specifies only two Johannine "I ams" (8:58; 18:6; including neither parables nor the Sermon on the Mount).

Jesus's ministry is a series of miracles, accomplished by Jesus's waving hand or touch or by someone touching Jesus or his robe. In addition to "off-hand" healings as Jesus passes through a crowd (blind; demoniac; leper) and as he teaches in the temple (Mt. 21:14), the film devotes significant time to the turning of water into wine, the healing of the paralytic lowered through a roof, the raising of the widow's son at Nain, Jesus's walking upon the water, Lazarus's resurrection, and the healing of a blind man at Jericho.[16]

Like Guy, Olcott, presumably with Gene Gauntier's guidance, gives women considerable attention. The film includes two anointings: the first visualizing Lk. 7:36-50, and the second representing the other gospels' Bethany anointing.[17] The first anointer wears a headscarf and the second does not, but both seem to be played by the same actress, credited as Magdalene (Alice Hollister).[18] What is certain is that Magdalene is also Mary, the sister of Martha, in a reenactment of Lk. 10:38-42 and in the depiction of Lazarus's resurrection. In the passion, the women are noticeable at the cross, which they watch at first from afar (Lk. 23:49).[19] Significantly, Olcott does not include the "disreputable" women scenes: for example, Salome, the Samaritan woman, and the woman taken in adultery.[20]

The nativity's Herod, the leaders' attempt to stone Jesus because of his blasphemous "I am" (Jn 8:58-59), and Judas's anger at the anointing waste introduce conflict and prepare for Jesus's passion. Judas's anger provides the turning point.

The triumphal entry uses the Jerusalem location to advantage by filming the procession from behind as it descends the Mount of Olives and heads toward Jerusalem on the horizon. More healings, the temple cleansing (in Henderson-Bland's most dramatic moment), and darkly clad Judas (Robert G. Vignola) haggling over the betrayal price (cf. Tissot), follow in quick succession. The haggling scene is crosscut with Jesus sitting alone on the mountain and worriedly pondering Jerusalem. The scenes end with Judas facing the camera in horror and fear, seemingly recognizing his betrayal, while the religious leaders smirk in the background.[21]

In the extensive upper room material, which includes a rare cinematic instance of the foot washing, Jesus identifies his betrayer when Judas greedily grabs the "sop" from Jesus (Jn 13:26) and turns away to eat while facing the camera (on the viewer's side of the table).[22] When Jesus stands imperially, Judas reacts as if horrified. Reluctantly, he gathers his sandals and leaves. As Jesus shares communion with his remaining disciples, Olcott cuts to Judas scurrying down a dark street and disappearing into the shadows. The scene ends with a black screen.

In Gethsemane, Judas brings the soldiers by lamplight (Jn 18:3). After the kiss, Judas and the soldiers fall back in revelatory awe before Jesus's "I am" (Jn 18:6). Olcott completes Judas's story—the repentance and hanging (Mt. 27:3-10)—with Judas and the leaders reacting differently yet again. Judas throws the money and himself to the ground in anguish and prayer while the leaders shake with laughter in the background. After fleeing down dark streets again, Judas is last seen, as a dark shadow, hanging from a tree.

In Jesus's Roman trial, Jesus stands bound as Pilate moves between Jesus and the accusing religious leaders inside and the murderous crowd that Pilate repeatedly addresses from a balcony.[23] Pilate sends Jesus away to Herod (Lk. 23:8-11), where Jesus is beaten and mocked, and then away again for a brutal scourging (based on Tissot). Pilate then presents the bloody man (Ecce Homo; Jn 19:5) to the crowd, which still demands Jesus's crucifixion. While the film does not cite Mt. 27:24, Pilate washes his hands and gives Jesus over to more mockery (by soldiers who dump trash on his head) and crucifixion.

Olcott films the Via Dolorosa on location, with the Ecce Homo arch in the background, as Jesus carries a T-shaped cross and soldiers whip him. Jesus falls three times on the Via Dolorosa; the second and third falls include incidents with Mary and Simon, but not Veronica.

The audience first sees Golgotha from behind the women watching from afar (cf. the distant shot of the Lamb of God). Then, in a long shot, the audience sees soldiers straddle a writhing Jesus, nail him to the cross, and hoist the (now traditionally shaped) cross into position. The cross is so tall that one can barely make out Jesus's feet as soldiers gamble beneath it. One does see, however, the crucified Christ in a long shot as he promises the good thief paradise and as he takes a Roman soldier's sponge. One sees the cross from behind, as Mary and Magdalene clutch the cross. John stands nearby. After a "moving" intertitle depicting darkness and earthquake, the film's final visual is a long shot of Jesus dying on the cross.

A fade to black leads to the final scripture intertitle: Jn 3:16. The closing art intertitle displays wise men following the star, perhaps suggesting that the wise still seek him. Notably, there is no Easter morning.

MEMORABLE CHARACTERS

1. Jesus is an ethereal, supernatural figure. He is notably Johannine (see Key Scripture). He causes miracles by touch or with the wave of his hand. While he indicates his compassion with his left hand upon his heart, he faces the camera instead of the healed, turning the miracles into hierophanies, or Johannine signs.
2. Olcott develops Judas psychologically more than the gospels or previous films do (see, however, n21).
3. Other than Jesus and Judas, Mary, Magdalene (a composite of various gospel Marys), and John have the most screen time. One of them is often "with" Jesus. Olcott even includes Magdalene in the Last Supper at the screen's front right (Hebron 2016a: 552 n8).

MEMORABLE VISUALS

1. The boy Jesus carries a piece of wood and forms a cruciform shadow (see Figure 3.1).
2. Judas haggles about the betrayal price with the priests.

Figure 3.1 The cruciform shadow auguring the cross in *From the Manger to the Cross*, directed by Sidney Olcott, Kalem, 1912. All rights reserved.

3 Judas's dark clothing during the last days, which stands in dramatic contrast to Jesus's white attire; as well as Judas's disappearance into shadows and a black screen; his arrival with a torch in the garden; and his final hanging shadow.

4 Jesus writhing in pain as he is nailed to the cross.

5 The "moving" intertitle depicting the cross's darkness and earthquake.

6 The absence of a resurrection scene.

KEY AUTHORITY/SCRIPTURE

1 The "on location" effect.
2 The Tissot Bible reproductions.
3 The Johannine intertitles that depict Jesus's identity (Jn 1:36; 3:16; 8:58; 18:6).
4 While the film never cites Jn 1:5, that text captures the lighting and color contrasts distinguishing Jesus (light/white) and Judas (shadows/black).

CULTURAL LOCATION/GENRE: VICTORIAN WOMEN, TISSOT'S BIBLE, AND TRAVELOGUE

From the Manger to the Cross was Kalem's most popular, profitable film. Its success depended upon the audience's growing curiosity about exotic peoples and places. Accordingly, the second intertitle markets the film as travelogue: "With scenes filmed at Jerusalem, Bethlehem and other authentic locations in Palestine."[24] By the late nineteenth century, international travel had become more accessible to upper middle-class Europeans and Americans, but most people relied on touring lecturers' descriptions of exotic adventures or the traveling exhibitions of "uncivilized heathens from distant lands," presented by church mission societies or city museums.

Appealing to this interest, the film packages a traditional Christmas pageant and passion play as travelogue, as is most evident in location shots of Mary and Joseph in front of the Sphinx and pyramids of Egypt; the triumphal "entry" toward Jerusalem; Jesus praying on the mountain overlooking Jerusalem; and in such details as the goatskin flask used to fill the purification water jars at the wedding at Cana and the Turkish rugs on display when Judas is betraying Jesus to the Jerusalem priests. The details are often "Orientalizing" (see Problematic Issue).

"On location" also implies a claim to (historical) authenticity. In this appeal, Olcott's film is a harbinger of the Jesus histories eventually dominating Jesus cinema. The film's authenticity, however, also relies on its heavy dependence upon the Tissot Bible (see Reynolds 1992; Robert 2019). Frank Marion, one of the Kalem owners, specifically instructed Olcott to use the Tissot Bible in constructing the film. James Tissot had himself traveled in the Holy Land twice in the 1880s sketching and photographing scenes and people. This work became the basis for his famous, popular watercolors illustrating the life of Jesus. James Gardner, a contemporary minister, said, "To look upon these pictures … is to come as near to the living Christ's life as is permitted anyone living in this modern world" (in Staley 2013a: 99). Tissot's illustrations were famous in published forms and in various exhibitions, sometimes appearing in the very places that also showed Guy and Olcott's films (see Robert 2019: 75).

The film also represents an important period in the history of religious film—and of film in general—in its presentation of Jesus as one who visually reflects the domestic (late Victorian) piety of early-twentieth-century American religion. Olcott includes almost as many women as Guy does, but with less complexity. The portrayal of women at Jesus's feet marks Jesus as a domestic, feminized figure. He belongs to women, and they and religion belong to the home. Nonetheless, women are among the few characters that Jesus looks at directly, and Mary and Magdalene are among the film's most important characters. In fact, Mary (Magdalene) and Martha have the one scene that slightly challenges the Jesus movement's domesticity and femininity (Lk. 10:38-42).[25]

DIRECTOR

While beginning his career as an actor, Sidney Olcott became a prolific, successful director working for Kalem in 1907 and for Famous Players-Lasky (later Paramount) from 1915 to

1927. For Kalem, Olcott directed at least one one-reel film a week. Today, he is famous for directing the one-reel *Ben Hur* of 1907 (also written by Gauntier) because the Lew Wallace estate sued Kalem for copyright violation. The successful lawsuit forever changed film's accessibility to material. While briefly charting the trajectory of Wallace's novel, *Ben Hur* focuses on the chariot race (omitting all the novel's Jesus scenes).

At Kalem, Olcott and his players, including Gene Gauntier (the Kalem Girl and Olcott's frequent screenwriter), shot several films on location. The first of these were shot in Ireland to appeal to the US Irish population, and then were followed by films in the exotic (Orientalized) Mediterranean, often using Egyptian locales to great effect.

Olcott did not plan a Jesus film until Gene Gauntier, whom some consider Olcott's assistant director, presented him with the idea. Like Pasolini later (*Sopralluoghi in Palestina per il vangelo secondo Matteo* [On Location in Palestine 1965]), Olcott also shot a documentary of the Holy Land, *Jerusalem in the Time of Christ* (1908). Among other sites, the film depicts the traditional Mount of Temptation and the traditional site of Jesus's baptism at the Jordan River near Jericho.

PROBLEMATIC ISSUE: ORIENTALISM

In *Orientalism* ([1978] 1994), Edward Said founded the postcolonial critique of "Orientalism." He claimed that Europe and the United States have falsely reified and essentialized the identity of the Oriental (Arab, Muslim) to advance European and US aims (imperialism). In short, the West defines the East as other than itself to subject the East. In contrast to the West, the East is primitive, irrational, violent, despotic, feminine, and so forth. Both exotic and dangerous, the East needs the rational West's control.

Orientalism is endemic to the Bible's academic study—in archeology, philology, and history, and its founding texts—because the discipline came into being during the nineteenth-century heyday of the Orientalizing European empires. A reliance on the Tissot Bible as well as Victorian theater and art (landscapes) for "historically realistic" visuals also inscribed Orientalism deeply into Jesus films (see Shepherd 2013: 145). In fact, Kevin McGeough (2021) argues that Jesus films still rely on Orientalizing nineteenth-century art and archeology.

In Jesus films, Jesus's Orientalized other is primitive, irrational, and violent. The angry crowd that Pilate strives, but fails, to control is perhaps Olcott's premier example of this Orientalized other—an "othering" that most subsequent Jesus films replicate.[26] Other examples include Olcott's contrast between a light/white Jesus and dark/black Judas, and the smirking, uncontrollably laughing religious leaders.[27]

Orientalism also includes—the "so white" Jesuses of the film tradition. In *From the Manger to Cross*, the actor playing Jesus (and all other significant actors) is not only white but also comfortably imperial (both British and Johannine). While the Victorian Christ is feminine, Henderson-Bland imagines Jesus as the "Lion of Judah," who properly subdues Oriental corruption and irrationality in the temple cleansing.[28] That all this is what Olcott's audiences—and those of later Jesus films—expected to see is precisely the issue.

IMAGE ENTERTAINMENT DVD, 71 MINUTES, 2003
DVD Extras

The Image Entertainment DVD with *The Life and Passion of Jesus Christ* (1907) includes this film and a four-page insert entitled: *Filming "From the Manger to the Cross" The First Moving Picture of the Life of Christ Made in the Land Where He Lived and Died*. The insert was "condensed from a 1927 reminiscence by a major player and scenarist of the film." Italicizing indicates the film's ten-chapter intertitles.

DVD Chapters

1 Main Title: The Infancy of Christ
> *The Annunciation and the Infancy of Christ*, 1:01
> And the virgin's name was Mary" (Lk. 1:27-28), 1:27
> "And Joseph also went up" (Lk. 2:4-10), 4:30
> "There came wise men" (Mt. 2:1-12), 7:36
>> Burning frankincense (Mt. 2:11), 12:05
> *The Flight into Egypt* (Mt. 2:13), 13:17

2 *The Period of Youth*, 15:29
> "And he arose ... and came into the land of Israel" (Mt. 2:19-23), 15:34
> Carpenter boy Jesus (shadow of a cross), 21:25

3 The Calling and Miracles, 21:33
> *After Years of Silent Preparation: Heralded by John the Baptist* (Jn 1:23, 36), 21:35
> *The Calling of the disciples* (Mt. 4:18-21), 23:23
> *The Beginning of miracles*, 25:23
>> Wedding at Cana (Jn 2:1-7), 26:25
>> Cleansing a leper (Mk 1:40), 28:24
>> Healing the paralytic (Mk 2:2-11), 29:08
>> Raising the widow's son (Lk. 7:12-14), 31:31
>> Anointing woman (Lk. 7:37-50), 32:30

4 *Scenes in the Ministry*, 33:45
> Walking on the water (Mt. 14:25), 34:21
> "And they laid the sick in the streets" (Mk 6:56), 34:34
> Mary and Martha (Lk. 10:38-42), 35:15
> Raising of Lazarus (Jn 11:1-48), 37:57
> Healing blind Bartimaeus (Mt. 20:34), 42:16
> Anointing in Bethany (Mt. 26:1-12), 42:55

5 *Last Days in the Life of Jesus*, 45:11

    Triumphal entry to Jerusalem (Lk. 19:37), 45:18

    Cleansing the temple (Mt. 21:12), 46:27

    On the Mount of Olives (Lk. 21:37), 48:58

    Judas plans the betrayal (Mk 14:10), 49:34

6 *The Last Supper*, 51:19

    Washing the disciples' feet (Jn 13:5), 51:28

    The first communion (Lk. 22:19-20), 54:08

7 *The Crucifixion and Death*, 55:50

    Going to the Mount of Olives (Mt. 26:47), 56:01

        "Betrayer is at hand!" (Mt.26:46), 57:55

        "I am he" (Jn 18:6), 58:33

        Peter cuts off the high priest's servant's ear

    Judas repents and hangs himself (Mt. 27:3-5), 58:59

    Jesus led to Pontius Pilate (Mt. 27:2), 1.00:01

    Herod's men mock Jesus (Lk. 23:11), 1.01:12

    Jesus scourged (Jn 19:1), 1.02:10

    "Behold the man" (Jn 19:5-6), 1.02:52

    Crown of thorns (Mt. 27:31), 1.04:06

    Led away to be crucified (Mt. 27:31; Jn 19:17), 1.04:45

    Simon of Cyrene (Mk 15:21), 1.05:51

    Women watch from afar (Lk. 23:49), 1.06:26

    Crucified (Mk 15:25), 1.06:57

        The penitent thief (Lk. 23:42-43), 1.07:48

        "I thirst" (Jn 19:28), 1.08:12

        His mother grieves (Jn 19:25), 1.08:40

        Earthquake

    "For God so loved the world" (Jn 3:16), 1.09:52

8 End Credits 1.10:08

NOTES

1. Art historian Cyrille Sciama claims that Tissot seems to be behind the film's camera (in Robert 2019: 72).
2. See Keil (1992). Robert notes that Olcott's film is retrograde compared to Tissot's Bible, which employed multiple perspectives (including Jesus's) to depict the crucifixion (2019: 73).
3. Gauntier (1927) says she chose the scripture citations in the editing process.

4   They sometimes follow the visual upon which they comment. For example, one sees the Baptist preaching before the citation of Jn 1:23.
5   For example, Mt. 2:3 should be 2:13 (in The Flight to Egypt); Jn 11:40 should be 11:39; Mk 20:29 should be Mt. 20:29; Mt. 26:47 should be 26:30; Mt. 31:46 should be 26:46; and Mt. 28:51 should be 27:51. Perhaps, Jn 18:6 should also be 18:5, as 18:5 is Jesus's direct speech.
6   Olcott's *Jerusalem in the Time of Christ* has two blind men healed.
7   The film does not cite a and b sections of verses, but it often quotes only a passage's beginning or end.
8   For attempts to categorize the different ways in which the Bible appears on screen, see Reinhartz (2003: 184–8), Burnette-Bletsch (2016b), and Walsh (2018b: 3–4).
9   Theatrical versions of *Ben Hur* represented Jesus on stage with a blue light. Marion wanted Jesus depicted similarly, but Olcott and Gauntier presented their onscreen Jesus as a fait accompli. See Gauntier (1927) and Kramer (2017).
10 See Tatum (2013: 26, 29) and Kramer (2017). One exorcism happens, but "off-hand" in the healings in the crowd (Mt. 4:23).
11 Hebron claims that Gauntier wanted to present a human Jesus (2016a: 550). That desire might explain the "missing" angels and resurrection scene. The film's first proposed title was *Jesus of Nazareth*, but it could not be copyrighted. Robert Henderson-Bland's portrayal of "Christus," however, is of a magisterial Johannine Christ. He introduced himself to Olcott as Jesus Christ, saying he would play himself and announcing a vision had told him he was God's chosen son (Gauntier 1927; Foster 2000: 229; Staley 2013a: 100).
12 Herod also figures prominently in Olcott's *Jerusalem in the Time of Christ* (1908).
13 As the film's scriptwriter, Gene Gauntier, plays the Virgin Mary, she has more than biblical foreknowledge. On Gauntier, see Hebron (2016a: 547–53).
14 Cf. the shepherd walking on the hill under the cross in *Jesus Christ Superstar* (1973).
15 Staley observes that Henderson-Bland resembles Tissot's Christ (2013a: 100). Henderson-Bland was a respected English stage actor. As n11 indicates, he gave himself wholly to the role of Christus, trying to portray him as the "Lion of Judah," not a meek shepherd (Tatum 2013: 29). He wrote two memoirs about his role as Jesus.
16 Olcott plays a healed blind man.
17 The woman anoints both Jesus's head (Matthew and Mark) and feet (John).
18 The cast played multiple roles. Hollister played the femme fatale in *The Vampire* (1913), directed by Robert G. Vignola, who plays Judas here. Vignola, a former theater actor, became a Kalem fixture, sometimes serving as Olcott's assistant. He later became a successful silent film director.
19 While Olcott places this shot before the crucifixion, the Synoptic Gospels refer to these women after Jesus's death. Mary, Magdalene, and the Beloved Disciple are at the foot of the cross in Jn 19:25-27, providing the basis for art and film's well-known tableau. Olcott eventually includes this shot as well.
20 His earlier *Jerusalem in the Time of Christ* depicts the woman taken in adultery and names her Magdalene.
21 Armand Bour's *Le Baiser de Judas* (1908) is a significant precursor here, showing great interest in Judas's psychology. See Shepherd (2013: chap. 4).
22 The seating follows Tissot. Cinema favors the Da Vinci arrangement.
23 The omission of a Jewish trial hardly mitigates the film's anti-Semitism, given the portrayal of the Jewish priests, who point accusingly during Pilate's questioning of Jesus, and the murderous people demanding Jesus's execution.

24 The marketing of *Christus* (1916) also touted on-location shooting. For *Christus*, however, Egypt is most important. Its Jesus even teaches there. See Pucci (2016). *Christus* also relies on the Tissot Bible. See Robert (2019).
25 That the beardless, feminine Beloved Disciple is also often with Jesus also demarcates a feminine, domestic space.
26 Olcott's *Jerusalem in the Time of Christ* is more blatantly Orientalist in its depiction of Jerusalem's exotic decadence and villainy.
27 Clearly, such depictions are also anti-Semitic, for which the Jesus film tradition is infamous (see Walsh 2018c). Said speaks of Orientalism, not anti-Semitism (even though anti-Semitism would encompass prejudice against Arabs) because he imagines modern Israel as part of the imperial West.
28 Cf. the Orientalizing depiction of the courtesan Magdalene and her submission to the paternalistic Jesus opening *The King of Kings* (1927), which notably ends with Jesus risen over a (Western) industrialized city.

4

Intolerance: Love's Struggle throughout the Ages

D. W. Griffith, director, Wark/Triangle, 1916

PLOT SUMMARY: JESUS AS "THEMATIC FOOTNOTE"

Intolerance's spectacle surpasses previous epics, including D. W. Griffith's own *Judith of Bethulia* (1914) and *The Birth of a Nation* (1915). The film answers *The Birth of a Nation*'s critics by reviewing "love's struggle through the ages" against (religious) "intolerance." The film crosscuts repeatedly between four stories from different times (tinted differently) as if the stories were occurring simultaneously. In order of appearance, they are: (1) *The Mother and the Law*,[1] a modern romance about the Boy and the Dear One who suffer because of meddling, reforming "Uplifters" (tinted amber); (2) Jesus fragments, focusing on Jesus as a victim of the Pharisee's intolerance (tinted blue); (3) the sixteenth-century Medici massacre of the Huguenots (tinted sepia);[2] and (4) *The Fall of Babylon* to Cyrus because of Bel priests' betrayal (tinted gray-green).

Each story concerns threats to the nuclear family. While nick-of-time rescues often save Griffith families (including his first film *The Adventures of Dollee* 1908; see O'Dell 1970: 50–2), three of *Intolerance*'s stories end badly.[3] While the mother (or Jesus) takes precedence over "Law," mother/love is always under threat. Thirty shots of a mother (Lillian Gish) rocking a cradle—with the three fates ominously in the background—reiterate this point.[4]

Less than ten minutes into the film, Griffith crosscuts from the female Uplifters ("Modern Pharisees"), whose reforms put people out of work, to hypocrites "among the Pharisees," who interrupt the people's work with prayers (Lk. 18:9–14). The crosscut establishes the film's ideological message.[5] Such crosscuts vilify the modern Uplifters, ancient Pharisees, the Medici, and the priests of Bel and venerate the innocent Boy, the Dear One, Jesus, the Huguenot Brown Eyes, the Babylonian Mountain Girl, Belshazzar, and Princess Beloved (see Walsh 2016d).

These innocent "Christ figures" intrigue Griffith more than Jesus does,[6] who appears in only seven episodes,[7] comprising about twelve minutes of the three-hour plus film:[8]

1 (The unseen) Jesus's introduction as the greatest enemy of intolerance, juxtaposed with a Pharisee's hypocritical prayer.
2 The wedding at Cana.
3 The woman taken in adultery.

4 Jesus surrounded by little children with a title card, "Suffer little children."
5 The Via Dolorosa.
6 Three crosses at Calvary.
7 A cross of light.

The first Jesus segment sets the film's ideological tone, pairing the Pharisees with the modern Uplifters. A factory owner supports their reforms by cutting his workers' pay,[9] which leads to a strike, strike-ending violence, and flight to the city—including the Boy (Robert Harron) and the Dear One (Mae Marsh). Lacking work, the Boy joins a gang, but his growing love for the Dear One gradually saves him. When the Dear One's father dies, the Boy comforts and courts her in scenes, which are crosscut with the wedding at Cana.

Similarly, Jesus is "the Comforter out of Nazareth." After a shot of the Cana bride and groom celebrating, an intertitle commands harmlessness like a dove (Mt. 10:6), and Jesus (Howard Gaye)[10] appears on screen for the first time. He walks among doves to the festivities, while Pharisees, in phylacteries, frown. A "scorned and rejected of men" intertitle (Isa. 53:3) summarizes their hostility, which Griffith emphasizes by superimposing a black cross on Jesus as he changes the water into wine. Thereafter, Jesus watches from the festivities' background, without participating.

Griffith cuts to the Huguenot Brown Eyes' (Marjery Wilson) engagement and then to the Boy and the Dear One's. The modern Uplifters, "hypocrites of another age," rise to power, and Griffith returns to the Pharisees' denunciation of Jesus as a glutton, friend of sinners, and winebibber (Mt. 11:19). Jesus feasts with the people (refusing wine). Previous scriptural intertitles have had a (commandment's) tablet backdrop, but subsequent intertitles do not, as Jesus visually takes the Pharisees' place by sitting where they did.

Following Moses's law, the Pharisees demand a verdict on the (unnamed) woman taken in adultery. However, when Jesus exhorts them about their own sins, they withdraw, leaving one large stone before Jesus and the woman. While never coming too close to her, Jesus forgives and sends her away. Also dismissed, the Pharisees never reappear in the film.

Looking (ironically) for Christ's modern example, Griffith returns to the closing of various "sin centers" and prostitute arrests, which simply create a black market for vice. Framed by his former crime boss for theft, the Boy goes to prison. After a sequence about the Babylonian Bel priests' treason, the Dear One falls ill. When the reformers learn she procured an illegal remedy (alcohol) for her cold and has had a man visitor (a kindly neighbor dropping off food), they take her baby away.

After a closeup of her baby's empty bootie, Griffith crosscuts to a "Jesus welcoming the children" tableau, garnished with an intertitle, "Suffer little children." The citation omits a "the" after "suffer" (from Mk 10:14 KJV), so that the text seals children's fate, rather than inviting them to Jesus. The adaptation matches the scene with the modern story, where the baby has been taken to an orphanage. Interestingly, contemporary Christian orphanages often had this scripture hanging on their walls.

Here, as elsewhere, Griffith reduces the Jesus story to tableaux,[11] but these tableaux are not the film's focus. They function like the Old Testament tableaux in the previous passion play/cinema tradition (see Shepherd 2013: chap. 1). They are analogues, interpretive foils, or "thematic footnotes" (Tatum 2013: 37–8) for the other more important stories.[12]

Nonetheless, these first Jesus fragments—the wedding, the woman taken in adultery, and Jesus among the children—constitute an embryonic version of Griffith's threatened/restored families. Read so, the adulterous woman threatens the family implied by the wedding, and the children restore it. The genderless Jesus defends heterosexual monogamy and loves women and children (see Runions 2010). Jesus thereby becomes a Griffith character, defending the family.[13]

The film's first act ends with Catherine de Medici, "that old serpent," plotting the Huguenots' extermination and with Belshazzar (Alfred Paget) repelling Cyrus's (first) attack on Babylon. The next Jesus fragment is almost an hour away. The film concentrates instead on the spectacle of Babylon's siege, the orgiastic spectacle of Belshazzar and Princess Beloved's (Seena Owen) wedding, the treasonous Bel priests, the Huguenot massacre, and the (second) framing of the Boy for his former crime boss's murder.

Only after the innocent Boy is judged guilty does Griffith return to the Jesus story with an intertitle applying to both Jesus and the Boy, announcing the people's verdict, "Let him be crucified." After a glimpse of Jesus on the Via Dolorosa, a judge sentences the Boy to hanging until "dead, dead, dead" (cf. Cyrus's exhortation during the siege to "kill, kill, kill"). Repeated cuts during the Boy's sentencing to the suffering Dear One, now wearing a hooded cloak, suggest the Stabat Mater.

Amid various cuts to the Mountain Girl's (Constance Talmadge) futile race to warn Belshazzar, the Huguenot and Brown Eyes' family's massacre, and the Boy's friends' attempts to obtain him a pardon, the Boy crosses himself and takes his last sacrament. He does not actually take the wafer, however, until after a second depiction of Jesus's Via Dolorosa. The crosscutting intertwines the two innocent deaths.[14]

In a whirlwind fourteen minutes involving rapid cuts between the various stories, Prosper Latour races through Paris but fails to save Brown Eyes and her family; the Mountain Girl arrives too late to warn Belshazzar and avert Babylon's doom; and friends of the Boy seek a last-minute pardon while three men prepare to cut the threads preventing his hanging (cf. the three fates). Finally, as the Boy walks to the gallows, *Intolerance* segues to Calvary's three crosses, seen from afar. A crowd sways ritualistically in the foreground in a spectacle of intolerance (so Shepherd 2013: chap. 6).[15]

While this shot is only seconds long, it is one of the longer shots in the helter-skelter finale and, thus, creates the tableau aesthetics' "pause." Griffith then cuts back to the modern story's happy ending. The Boy's friends arrive with a pardon, and, as the recovered priest hovers nearby, the Boy and Dear One are reunited in a scene that looks like a wedding.

The Kino version cuts to the final coda, but the Killiam version includes a scene reuniting the couple with their baby, and another cut to the spectacle of passion intolerance. Then the frame's upper left-hand section (where the crosses are in the distance) explodes into light, ushering in the final coda where heaven descends to end war, prisons become flowery fields, and guns become flowerpots. Love triumphs as a heavenly cross of light connects the heavenly and earthly worlds (see Figure 4.1), and as the mother rocks the cradle (now filled with flowers), one last time.

Not counting this coda, the Jesus story makes up less than two minutes of *Intolerance*'s second act. Further, despite the coda's suggestions about the cross's ultimate victory, Griffith's cross does not seem salvific, particularly in the Kino version (see Tatum 2013: 45). At least, Griffith establishes no causal connection between Jesus's story and the modern couple's last-minute rescue. Further, Jesus is not personally important. He appears less often than his story does, and the cross and love ultimately replace him (in the superimposed cross at the wedding at Cana and the finale's two crosses of light; see Figure 4.1). While those are rather traditional substitutions, the notion that Jesus is an apostle of religious tolerance, like Belshazzar, reflects Griffith's particular vision.

Jesus is merely one victim of intolerance, and *Intolerance* uses Jesus to Christ figure all suffering innocents from the fall of Babylon to the apocalypse.[16] The Boy, whose trial and gallows are interchangeable with Jesus's, is the most obvious Christ figure. Both also have their own Via Dolorosa, and Griffith uses the Eucharist to further connect their sufferings. In fact, given Jesus's minimal deployment, Griffith's Boy is more Christlike than Jesus is. At least, the Boy overshadows Jesus and transforms Jesus into a Griffith-character, a martyr of intolerance.

Belshazzar, who chooses love (Ishtar and Princess Beloved) over the Bel priests, is the film's other developed Christ figure (see Shepherd 2013: chap. 6). Belshazzar is also an apostle of religious tolerance and, like Jesus, saves women (the Mountain Girl) from degradation. This scene occurs slightly before those depicting the Boy and Jesus as comforters. Later, the jealous older priests betray Belshazzar to Cyrus, choosing empire (law and order) over love. Crosscuts parallel Belshazzar's last meal with the Boy's communion and Jesus's Via Dolorosa.[17]

This interpretation of innocent Belshazzar/Babylon and villainous Cyrus inverts the ethical characterization of its biblical, artistic, and cinematic precursors (see Shepherd 2013: chap. 6). It fits Griffith's theme, however, and along with the film's concentration on the spectacular Babylonian siege and orgy, it allows Griffith to hallow "Babylon" and his spectacle/film. Thus, Babylon symbolizes the film industry's fate (Hollywood) at the hands of reforming censors.[18]

MEMORABLE CHARACTERS

1 The Christ-figured (criminal) Boy and Belshazzar.
2 Jesus is an omen (of innocent victims); a christener of innocents, the family, and film; and a talisman of sacred power (the cross's apocalyptic victory) (see Walsh 2016a).[19] Griffith's Jesus thus forecasts the cinematic Jesus's future, in which Jesus materializes the sacred, serves as ethical lodestone, augurs innocent sacrifice and victims, and guarantees righteous victory. The cinematic Jesus is an emblem of nonviolent love, his conquering cross, and, sometimes, merely his name. He is a vanishing act around which swirl other, more interesting stories.

MEMORABLE VISUALS

1 Mother rocking the cradle, with the three fates in the background.
2 The shadow cross superimposed on Jesus at the wedding at Cana.
3 The heavenly cross of light that ends war (see Figure 4.1).

KEY AUTHORITY/SCRIPTURE

1 Spectacle is the film's key authority, hallowing Babylon and film.
2 The harmonizing crosscutting is the other major authority. The presentation of four different stories "as one" resembles gospel harmonizing. Both share certain aesthetic effects, the most important of which is the sense that the harmony reveals an idea, truth, or gospel above history's chaotic diversity, forecasting the direction of that chaos to guarantee the imperial deification of those who see this truth (see Walsh 2016d: 55–63).[20]
3 Although the film never quotes the passages, posing Jesus versus the hypocritical Pharisees relies ultimately upon Mt. 5-7; 23. Jesus is also the comforter, the friend of sinners (cf. Mt. 11:19; Jn 7:53–8:11).

Figure 4.1 The heavenly cross that ends all war in *Intolerance*, directed by D. W. Griffith, Wark/Triangle, 1916. All rights reserved.

CULTURAL LOCATION/GENRE: US EPIC

Griffith helped make feature films acceptable as middle-class and family entertainment (see Gunning 1994: 85–90). He campaigned relentlessly to have film accepted as an art form and was tireless in his fight against censorship. He is the first great, and first artistic American director, and stands at the forefront of a uniquely American cinema.[21]

Gilles Deleuze claims Griffith films provide the first examples of US cinema's endlessly repeated story of the revolutionary "birth of a nation-civilization" (cf. Wood 1989). Embryonically present in *Judith of Bethulia*, where a small community defends itself against a greedy, foreign empire, it appears full-blown in *The Birth of a Nation*, which rewrites "the North" as the imperial threat and "the South" as the "real" United States. This repeated story probably also partly accounts for Griffith's ethical inversion of the typically good Cyrus and evil Belshazzar.[22] In US cinema's typically "monumental" view of history, everything prefigures the United States (Deleuze 1997: 31, 141–51). And, as the United States is the end of history, no substantive critique of it is possible.

For Sergei Eisenstein, Griffith's films incarnate two aspects of the early-twentieth-century United States. On one hand, his rapid crosscutting reflects industrial (and cinematic) developments. On the other, his closeups and themes celebrate the family and small-town United States (1949: 196–200). The Progressive Era's changes and conflicts, caused by urbanization, industrialization, immigration, and reform movements, are everywhere in Griffith, but Eisenstein finds no revolutionary solutions.[23] Instead, Griffith's parallel montages (crosscutting) copy Charles Dickens's "dualistic picture of the world, running in two parallel lines of poor and rich toward some hypothetical [or apocalyptic] reconciliation" (1949: 235).[24] For Eisenstein, Griffith simply accepted Dickens's Victorian sentiments (1949: 206–34). Even his greatest films remain moralistic melodramas.

Perhaps, this "conservatism" accounts for Griffith's negative portrayal of the Uplifters, who share the social concerns (white slavery, alcoholism, etc.) of white, middle-class Protestant women's groups like purity leagues and the *Woman's Christian Temperance Union*. Griffith's Jesus addresses none of the pressing social issues of the era directly. Instead, *Intolerance* is a plea for individual liberty (and the nuclear family) versus oppressive institutions and reforms, seemingly equating imperialism and Puritanism.[25]

Griffith's exaltation of pacifism was untimely. The film opened in New York City in September 1916. The United States entered the First World War in April 1917. Griffith claimed *Intolerance*'s economic failure depended to a large extent on the disjoint between its message and the United States' new wartime situation (Drew 1986: 123).[26]

DIRECTOR

Griffith did not invent the closeup or crosscutting, but he and his cameraman Billy Bitzer were at the forefront of using such techniques to create narrative film's visual syntax while at Biograph (1908–13).[27] Griffith forsook the theater spectator's perspective by moving the camera back to suggest a far larger "world" (and even mounting it on a train to follow action) and forward (closeup) to focus on an object or character to show the character's reactions, emotions, or thoughts. Chase scenes, at which Griffith excelled, created a sense that various shots captured only part of a larger space (Gunning 1994: 66), and crosscutting virtually pinned spectators into the film as narratees who needed to unite and interpret various spaces presented by the unseen, omniscient camera's selection and shaping (narrating) (1994: 66, 206). The result is the visual "narrator system" that eventually dominated film (1994: 10–30, 289–97).

While chase scenes were cinematic staples, Griffith's desire for "cinematic art" led him to film literary classics (like *After Many Years* 1908, a version of Tennyson's *Enoch Arden*) and pushed him to two-reel films like *Massacre* (1912), which Lewis Jacobs calls the first American spectacle ([1939] 1967: 114]). Two-reel films eventually led to the four-reel *Judith of Bethulia* (made in 1913; released in 1914).

Judith includes huge sets in the massive siege of Bethulia's walls and in Holofernes's (Henry B. Walthall) tent, which is large enough for the Orientalizing spectacle of a bevy of dancing girls. Griffith humanizes the spectacle with closeups, particularly in repeated shots of a young woman (Lillian Gish) with a starving baby, and by cutting to Naomi (Mae Marsh) and Nathan (Robert Harron), young lovers imperiled by larger forces. These shots also justify the righteous violence to come. The heroine Judith (Blanche Sweet) leaves her prayers and her starving people to go to Holofernes's tent, risking her life and her honor "to do a thing which shall go through all generations." The seduction titillates almost as much as Holofernes's beheading. Despite being enamored of Holofernes, Judith chooses duty and people over her own (romantic) feelings.

Seen in hindsight, all these elements make *Judith* a prototypical biblical epic.[28] Griffith's two great films, *The Birth of a Nation* and *Intolerance*, refine the pattern: epic scale; focalization on romantic couples (humanizing the epic scale); crosscutting to build suspense. Twelve reels in length and with an enormous two-dollar admission charge, *The Birth of a Nation* made more money than any film until *Gone with the Wind* (1939).[29] Griffith focuses on the romantic relationships that develop when the sons of the Northern (Austin) Stoneman family visit the Southern (Doctor) Cameron family's plantation before the war. Amid massive battle scenes, still praised by critics for their choreography and editing, Griffith highlights the death of two Cameron sons and one Stoneman son, and Ben Cameron's (Henry B. Walthall) heroic charge at Petersburg, which climaxes when he plugs a canon with the rebel flag. While Elsie Stoneman (Lillian Gish) nurtures him in a prison hospital, Lincoln's pardon saves him.

After Lincoln's assassination, vengeful Northerners subject the South to reconstruction, the depiction of which begins with a Christ-figuring intertitle: "The agony which the South endured that a nation might be born." This second act is vilely racist and depends upon Thomas Dixon's *The Clansman* (the film's original name).[30]

Reconstruction-era Blacks are children (or subhuman beasts)[31] unfit for self-rule and dupes of self-serving Northerners like Austin Stoneman.[32] The white South is another Griffith-style innocent sufferer. White fears about miscegenation dominate and lead ultimately to the salvific KKK's creation.[33] When Flora Cameron (Mae Marsh) leaps to her death rather than submit to the freedman Gus's amorous pursuit, the KKK, born in her blood, retaliates by murdering Gus.

Bearing a fiery cross, the Christ-figured KKK rides to two last-minute deliverances (crosscut and accompanied by "The Ride of the Valkyrie"). The KKK saves Elsie from the mulatto Silas Lynch's lechery and the remnants of the Cameron family, Phil Stoneman (Elmer Clifton), and two former Union soldiers from the Black militia.[34] The deliverances lead to a victorious KKK parade, carefully monitored (whites only) elections, and the double honeymoon of Margaret Cameron (Miriam Cooper) and Phil Stoneman, and Elsie Stoneman and Ben Cameron. The United States is born as a white paradise, which is apparently equivalent to Christ's peaceful earthly kingdom, established in a final fantastic vision (cf. *Intolerance*'s apocalyptic coda).[35]

The two films' similarities raise important questions about Griffith's vision. While preaching tolerance, both films have their own imperial codas. Further, Griffith's Jesus is troublingly white, American, and intolerant.

PROBLEMATIC ISSUE: ANTI-SEMITISM

Given the Jews' portrayals in the gospel passion narratives, the passion play tradition, and other Christian art, Jesus films inevitably skate on the edge of anti-Semitism.[36] To avoid this moral pitfall, many directors use Jewish religious leaders as on-set advisors, as Griffith did, and pay attention to Jewish focus group's responses to reports about or previews of their films, as Griffith did.

Nonetheless, Griffith's choice to follow Matthew (although citing Luke) in framing the Pharisees as Jesus's intolerant opposition certainly plays into and along with anti-Semitic attitudes (see Reinhartz 2007: 204–6). That Griffith posts an intertitle restricting the opposition to some hypocrites among the Pharisees hardly mitigates his antagonistic visuals. Nor does it matter that the Pharisees cease to appear after the woman taken in adultery scene, as they have already been established as the hostile source of Jesus's fate (through the intertitle citing Isa. 53:3).

Moreover, the Pharisees stand for the law, which opposes the titular mother, rejects the people's innocent pleasures (Mt. 11:19), and condemns the innocent Boy. Jesus and the Mother/Dear One, of course, represent love. The polarization reflects melodramatic tropes, but also smacks of Marcionism.

Further, while the Pharisees are not present in the passion's brief scenes, Griffith clearly continues the tradition of Zecca and Olcott (see also *Der Galiläer* 1921) by intensifying the crazed, Jewish mob's murderous opposition to Jesus. While Griffith did omit scenes he shot that showed Jews actually crucifying Jesus (Tatum 2013: 44), Jews still heap abuse on Jesus on the Via Dolorosa and, more importantly, form a swaying sea of intolerance dominating the crucifixion scene (see Shepherd 2013: chap. 6). Finally, while the film does not include the blood curse of Mt. 27:25 (*Der Galiläer* presents it three times), an intertitle cites the people's demand for Jesus's crucifixion (Mt. 27:22-23), although it presents the biblical citation as Pilate's decision (Tatum 2013: 42).

That mere Jesus fragments could convey so much anti-Semitism is troubling. In fact, whether interpretation deems a Jesus film anti-Semitic or not, the whole tradition betrays supersessionist, if not anti-Semitic structures: (1) the presentation of Jesus as a stranger from afar alien to or in opposition to his Jewish context; (2) the presentation of Jesus as the light of an otherwise dark world; (3) the notion that only those who belong to the dark (evil) could fail to comprehend his divinity (see Olcott's Judas); and (4) the presentation of Jesus's cross as victorious over his enemies (e.g., the cross of light in the Killiam version, blasting the sea of Jewish people, or the cross of light rising out of the broken menorah in *The King of Kings*' [1927] shattered temple).

KINO VIDEO, 197 MINUTES, 2002
DVD Extras

"The Real Story of *Intolerance*," by Henry Stephen Gordon. Excerpted from *Photoplay Magazine*, October 1915 (one-page insert).
Special Features:

> Introduction by Orson Welles
>
> Excerpt of *The Last Days of Pompeii* (1913), an Italian epic inspiring Griffith
>
> Excerpt of *Cabiria* (1914), inspiring Griffith's Babylon's scale and design
>
> Excerpt of *The Fall of Babylon*'s alternate ending in which the Mountain Girl lives happily with the Rhapsode
>
> Pamphlets
>
> About the Score
>
> The Book: The text used as an intertitle background, providing a summary of the film's structure and ideology

DVD chapters (Jesus segments only)

3. Jerusalem the Golden City, 8:40-11:39
    Prayer of the Pharisee (Lk. 18:9-14), 10:04
9. The Love Temple, 50:47
10. The Hopeful Geranium, 53:50
11. Wedding in Galilee (Jn 2:1-11), 1.01:56-1.06:20
    "Be ye harmless as doves" (Mt. 10:16)
        (Shadow of a cross over Jesus as he turns water to wine.)
12. The Dear One's Vow, 1.08:42
13. Cast the First Stone (Mt. 11:19; Jn 7:53-8:11), 1.13:28-1.16:15
14. The Results of Reform, 1.16:18
15. Winds of War, 1.24:26
16. Modern Motherhood, 1.30:15
    "Suffer little children" (Mk 10:14), 1.36:58-1.37:19
24. The Verdicts, 2.34:09
    "Let him be crucified" (Mt. 27:22-23), 2.34:13-2.34:49
        On the Via Dolorosa (Mk 15:20-22 pars)

27. The Massacre, 2.52:06
    Via Dolorosa continued, 2.56:37–2.57:00
29. On the Gallows, 3.10:41
    Long shot of Calvary (Mk 15:37, 40-41 pars), 3.11:21–3.12:00
30. Epilogue, 3.14:37
    Angelic Hosts, 3.15:22
    With a cloudy cross, 3.16:28

NOTES

1 Griffith was working on this romance when other spectacles motivated him "to go bigger." The first and fourth stories have titles because they were released in 1919 as separate features to recoup some of *Intolerance*'s losses.
2 This massacre was the pre-Holocaust symbol of horrendous massacres (Drew 1986: 36).
3 In the 1919 version, the Babylonian story ends differently. The Mountain Girl recovers and leaves Babylon with the Rhapsode.
4 An intertitle citing Walt Whitman's "Out of the Cradle, Endlessly Rocking" sometimes accompanies this shot. Whitman's poem hallows the art (film) that sings for lost love in the face of death (censorship). A book, named *Intolerance*, serves as a backdrop for some intertitles and claims intolerance is the common human story. Sergei Eisenstein calls the rocking woman the film's chief metaphor (1949: 205, 231–41).
5 The film's message is simple: Do not be intolerant. Do not meddle in that which is not your business, specifically Mr. Griffith's right to make his films. In response to *The Birth of a Nation*'s critics, Griffith wrote a pamphlet, *The Rise and Fall of Free Speech in America*, which includes a (thirteen times) repeated refrain: "Intolerance is the root of all censorship." Griffith lists twelve crimes of intolerance/censorship, including the crucifixion and, climactically, motion picture censorship, Christ-figuring Griffith himself ([1915] 1967). See Kino DVD Extras. The egotism is overwhelming, but Griffith saw cinema as potentially salvific. See Walsh (2016a).
6 Several silents combine a Jesus/biblical story with a modern analogue: for example, *Civilization* (1916); *I.N.R.I.* (1923); *The Ten Commandments* (1923); and *Leaves from Satan's Book* (1921). The last is a fourfold story, like Griffith's, but the film presents each story in its entirety before moving on, rather than crosscutting. Cf. also *Restitution* (1918).
7 Adele Reinhartz says the film originally had thirty cuts to the Judean story (2007: 206).
8 The film exists today in multiple versions. The discussion here deals with the Kino DVD version, transferred from various 35 mm prints, the film's most popular "cut." The Killiam Show Version, transferred from a third-generation 16 mm print, has a shorter running time, but includes more material (because the Kino version was transferred at a slower frame rate). The Killiam Version is available as an Image DVD and online at the Internet Archive (https://archive.org/details/Intolerance). Griffith constantly recut his films (e.g., he created two independent films out of *Intolerance*) and even traveled for some time with the roadshow version of *Intolerance*, adapting it for each showing. See Merritt (1990).
9 Miss Jenkins, the factory owner's sister, leads the reformers, symbolized by three additional spinsters. Their number echoes the three fates.
10 Howard Gaye also plays Cardinal de Lorraine in the Huguenot story. He plays Robert E. Lee in *The Birth of a Nation* and Jesus again in *Restitution*, a film he also directed. See n6.

11 Richard Schickel describes the Jesus material as three tableaux—the wedding at Cana, the woman taken in adultery, and the crucifixion (1996: 314).
12 Cf. Pasolini's different attempt at analogy in *Il vangelo secondo Matteo* (1964).
13 *Son of Man* (2006) depicts Jesus similarly. See Walsh (2013a: 198–200).
14 Paul O'Dell claims that, despite abrupt cuts, the second story "carries on the momentum," and the stories so directly parallel one another that "the effect is almost never jumpy or irritating" (1970: 47). In short, it is hard to distinguish the Boy from Jesus from Belshazzar, etc.
15 In previous Jesus cinema, the Jewish people help precipitate Jesus's crucifixion.
16 W. M. Drew notices the heterodoxy involved in comparing Jesus's suffering to that of others (1986: 35).
17 As David Shepherd notes, the orgy is for the audience; Belshazzar has eyes only for the Princess Beloved (2013: chap. 6).
18 Erin Runions claims Babylon's positive portrayal celebrates film (2010: 146). Babylon has certainly become a symbol of Hollywood. Griffith shot the Babylonian story last, having to wait for the huge, expensive set to be built on Sunset Boulevard. It was the first huge exterior built in Hollywood and stood as a symbol of Hollywood near the intersection of Sunset and Hollywood for years. See Schickel (1996: 309–16). The Hollywood and Highland Center, built in 2001, includes a three-story courtyard with two pillars with elephants atop them replicating part of Griffith's Babylon set. The site was once the home of the Hollywood Hotel and of Grauman's Chinese Theater, and it remains the site of the Hollywood Walk of Fame. See Merritt (1979: 13).
19 The "bootie" signifying the mother's lost child is an example of Griffith's ability to create "tokens" (see Eisenstein 1949: 210). So, too, is Griffith's Jesus (cross) talisman.
20 Griffith appeals to his arduous attempt to create a historically accurate story by placing footnotes, citing source material, into some of his intertitles.
21 Others were certainly involved. See Abel (1999) for how fears about Pathé's influence led to a more nationalistic American cinema. Shepherd notes that Italian film's (Cines) influence in the United States increased as French film's (Gaumont and Pathé) waned (2013: chap. 6). On Cinecittà and biblical film, see Page (2021).
22 For Griffith's own "progressive," pro-individual, anti-imperial views, see Drew (1986: 139–65). If one sees the family as the nation's microcosm, the pattern already appears in *The Adventures of Dollee*.
23 On montage as the key to a film's "idea," see Eisenstein (1949: 234) and Deleuze (1997: 29–55).
24 Griffith claimed his crosscutting style came from Dickens's novels. Eisenstein was disappointed by the "revolutionary" failure of Griffith's *A Corner in Wheat* (1909).
25 See Drew (1986: 139–40, 161, 165). Drew labels the attitudes reflected in Griffith's films "Jeffersonian democracy."
26 Others point to the film's complexity and length as well as the huge expense incurred by *Intolerance*'s roadshow version. Griffith insisted theaters have special decorations and a full orchestra. On differing perspectives on war and pacifism in Jesus films before and after the First World War, see Shepherd (2018).
27 Tom Gunning argues that an ad Griffith placed when he left Biograph, coupled with Jacobs's description of Griffith's work in an influential history of American film ([1939] 1967), created the legend that Griffith pioneered the closeup and crosscutting (1994: 6, 32–3). Most now credit much of the pioneering camera work to Griffith's "career-long" (from 1908)

photographer (e.g., closing scenes with a fade out or iris; using lighting and the camera to create mood; and matte photography).

28 Shepherd finds these traits, particularly the love story, in *Quo Vadis* (1913), which he claims influenced Griffith (2013: chap. 6).

29 It is Griffith's most famous film and appeared on the American Film Institute's 1998 list of 100 best American films. *Intolerance* has now replaced *The Birth of a Nation* in critics' estimation. It was on the 2007 AFI list while *The Birth of a Nation* was not.

30 Another intertitle claims that the film "is not meant to reflect on any race or people of today." But those words hardly counter the images that follow.

31 Griffith used white characters in blackface for most of the prominent Black and mulatto roles. The NAACP challenged the film's racist ideology and historical mistakes when it was released.

32 Stoneman fictionalizes Thaddeus Stevens. The contrast between Griffith's Stoneman and Steven Spielberg's Stevens (*Lincoln* [2012]) illustrates shifts in US attitudes toward race, as does Nate Parker's *The Birth of a Nation* (2016), whose title indicates it responds to Griffith's film.

33 Reportedly, KKK recruiters still use the film to evangelize. Clips from the film (and from *Gone with the Wind*) occur in the black-and-white PSA white supremacist rant by Dr. Kennebrew Beauregard opening Spike Lee's *BlacKkKlansman* (2018).

34 The KKK riders look like something from a Sir Walter Scott romance, a genre beloved by those who bemoaned the South's fate. Griffith's father was a Confederate officer who regaled the young Griffith with romantic tales of the South.

35 A troubling, fantastic scene intercedes between the two, with a supernatural rider wielding a sword and lording it over worshipers to his right and a field of the slain to his left in what may be the single most concise visual of the American Jesus ever created.

36 For helpful overviews, see Reinhartz (2007: 197–227; 2012; 2016). One of the most anti-Semitic Jesus movies is *Der Galiläer* (Reinhartz 2007: 239, 248–50; Zwick 2016).

5

The King of Kings

Cecil B. DeMille, director, DeMille Pictures, 1927

PLOT SUMMARY: SUFFER LITTLE CHILDREN

The tableau aesthetic dominating Jesus silents pushes them toward spectacle. *The King of Kings* is a spectacle of light, with Jesus appearing for the first time out of light to a healed blind girl (Jn 12:46) and then in the Easter scenes as light breaking out of the tomb and through the upper room's closed door. Many intertitles near the beginning have a background with a sunrise breaking behind a dark hill. Cecil B. DeMille's Jesus always radiates, but the opening and closing color sequences, along with the crucifixion earthquake, are the most spectacular moments.

Other silents created narratives by focusing on stories around Jesus (e.g., *Quo Vadis?* 1913; *Ben-Hur* 1925), or by making biblical precursors serve interpretatively for modern stories (e.g., *Intolerance* 1916; *The Ten Commandments* 1923). DeMille almost makes Jesus into a cinematic story,[1] but the narrative weight eventually falls elsewhere.[2]

The film opens in two-strip Technicolor in Magdalene's opulent, Orientalized villa. Scantily clad, she lounges full length among exotic animals and wealthy, effeminate old men.[3] She mockingly dominates these men, but her lover Judas has left her for "a carpenter from Nazareth." Betting her suitors her wiles can blind any man, Mary zooms off to retrieve Judas in her chariot pulled by four zebras—followed by Nubian slaves.

DeMille implies a titillating romantic triangle in which Mary loves Judas and saves him from homosexual ruin.[4] DeMille intended this opening to shock critics of biblical films and then surprise them by turning, from what this introduction teases, to what he wants them to see: his paternalistic gospel in which Mary loves Jesus and Jesus loves all (the little children of the world) (1959. 275).[5]

Accordingly, DeMille breaks abruptly to black-and-white shots of the poor and sick crowded around a house with Jesus inside (the intertitles' backgrounds have hands reaching toward the light).[6] Color only returns at the resurrection. Ambitious Judas[7] maneuvers to use King Jesus to gain power, Roman soldiers laze in the sun, Caiaphas's spies (a temple guard, scribe, and Pharisee) watch jealously, and a little blind girl gropes futilely for Jesus.[8] A young lame boy, the future author of the Gospel of Mark, announces that Jesus has healed

---

This synopsis describes the full-length, roadshow version. The *Criterion Collection* DVD also includes the shorter 1928 general release version (112 minutes). For some of the significant materials not in the shorter 1928 version, see nn 23, 25, 30, 31, and 36. The film was the first shown at Grauman's Chinese Theatre. It was re-released in 1931 with synchronized music.

him.[9] Mark (Michael D. Moore) follows Jesus throughout the film, seeing many things not in the Gospel of Mark.[10] Mark throws aside his useless crutch,[11] which accidentally strikes the Pharisee spy,[12] who then threatens Mark before Big Peter[13] saves him.

After introducing the disciples (except Matthew), the film follows the fumbling blind girl whom Mark leads to Mary's weaving loom.[14] Mary brings the girl to her son as the Sabbath begins. The girl kneels and prays, saying she has never seen the light.[15] A shaft of light penetrates the dark screen; an intertitle quotes Jn 12:46 (without citation); light envelopes the girl; she sees a hazy nimbus; then she—and the audience—finally sees Jesus emerge from this nimbus (see Figure 5.1).[16]

Finally, haughty Magdalene arrives. Visibly repulsed by the needy, she forces her way inside the house, but Jesus does not quail before her as she expects. Instead, his gaze transfixes her, and he cleanses her of the seven deadly sins (citing Mt. 8:3).[17] Superimposed Magdalenes/sins leave her, with emphasis upon the film's chief sins—lust, greed, and pride. Peter paraphrases the narrator's words in Lk. 8:2. Overcome with shame, Magdalene wraps herself like a nun and kneels at Jesus's feet (as instrumental music indicates the pure in heart see God).

This lengthy introduction (almost thirty minutes) weaves together three miracles to portray Jesus's ministry as miraculously salvific.[18] DeMille invents two (those of the blind girl and Mark [although not shown]) and turns a Lukan report about the Magdalene's exorcism into special-effects drama. Later, DeMille creates a fishing miracle out of Jesus's words (Mt. 17:27) and turns Jesus's writing in the sand into special-effects Hebrew accusations (with English translations). Other DeMillish miracles occur in the passion. The only gospel miracle relatively un-DeMilled is Lazarus's resurrection,[19] although even there, Jesus glows DeMillishly. The handling of the miracles highlights (DeMille's) film's miraculous, spectacular nature (see Shepherd 2013: chap. 9).

Other than those of the Magdalene and Lazarus, the most important, redemptive miracles are the healing of lame Mark and of the blind girl, which arguably transform John's healings of a lame man (Jn 5) and a blind man (Jn 9) into children's stories. The miracles' early location helps introduce the film as DeMille's children's gospel. If Alice Guy's Jesus is for women, DeMille's paternalistic Jesus is for children.[20] Even when Jesus sets his face to go to Jerusalem (Lk. 9:51), he dallies with children and "heals," in another DeMille invention, a little girl's broken (soldier) doll. When Judas objects,[21] he becomes the dark, adult doppelgänger of the kingdom's children (Mk 10:14-15). Mark, as he is present throughout the film, particularly represents the childlike faith for which DeMille is nostalgic.

The film's first (sin to salvation) narrative sequence began with an intertitle stating that Magdalene "laughed alike at God and man"; the second begins more ominously: "The chief priests and the scribes sought to destroy him" (Lk. 19:47; intertitles here have scroll backgrounds). The section's narrative thread is Caiaphas's three attempts to trap Jesus. Appropriately, Caiaphas sits at a huge desk with spider artwork and a bag of money, which he smirkingly counts, for he "cared more for revenue than religion."[22] He is the film's chief villain, and yet another DeMille invention.[23]

In his first trap, Caiaphas sends spies and Roman soldiers to ensnare Jesus with a question about paying imperial taxes, sure that Jesus's response will alienate either the Romans or the people. DeMille connects the temple tax story (Mt. 17:24-27), turned into a fishing miracle, with Jesus's "Render unto Caesar" saying (Mt. 22:15-22), Judas's empty money bag (Jn 12:6), Matthew's call (Mt. 9:9),[24] Judas's failure to heal the "lunatic" boy (Mt. 17:14-19), and the demon-possessed man's cry, "I know who you are, the Holy One of God" (Mk 1:24).[25] After the healing, Jesus relaxes in the lunatic boy's father's carpentry shop, nostalgically planing a large timber, until the boy's mother pulls aside a cloth, revealing the timber to be a Roman cross.[26] This foreshadowing directs Jesus to Jerusalem (an intertitle says the cross shadows Jesus; cf. Lk. 9:51), although he pauses to dally with children, "heal" a doll, and resurrect Lazarus.

In Jerusalem, an angry Caiaphas sets his second trap, ordering the temple guard and the Pharisee spy to take the woman taken in adultery (not Magdalene) to Jesus so that Jesus's own words might lead the people to stone him.[27] The trap fails when Jesus steps imperially between the prone woman and the mob, already raising stones, and dispels the mob by writing their sins in the sand. Jesus then cleanses the temple courtyard, which an intertitle describes as Caiaphas's corrupt, profitable market—without ever striking anyone with the leather thong wrapped around his hand.

After Jesus turns away Caiaphas and the guard who fails to arrest him (citing Jn 2:19), palm-waving people enter Jerusalem, triumphantly acclaiming Jesus. Jesus vanishes before Judas can place a makeshift crown upon him. Inside the temple, a black-clad Satan, standing villainously behind Jesus, offers him worldly kingdoms. Jesus, holding one of the lambs loosed in his temple act, rejects this temptation by declaring that his kingdom is not of this world (Jn 18:36) and then leads the people in the Lord's Prayer.

Caiaphas hatches his third trap by threatening to remand Judas to the Romans. Panic-stricken Judas, with "all hope of earthly kingdom gone," agrees to betray Jesus's secret place of prayer (the intertitle has a cross in a nimbus of light background). Jesus's passion has begun, and dominates this film as it does most Jesus silents. Not surprisingly, DeMille adds distinctive touches.

First, although Judas's betrayal headlines the passion (in an intertitle),[28] Caiaphas dominates, counting coins for the disturbed Judas. And after the arrest, Caiaphas leads a rope-bound Jesus slowly upstairs to the Sanhedrin, mocking Jesus about his absent disciples. Meanwhile, Peter betrays Jesus in the courtyard below,[29] while a pulled curtain leaves the audience outside the Jewish trial. Despite the large Roman eagle behind Pilate, Caiaphas motivates the action at the Roman trial (the intertitles have eagle backgrounds), reading charges against Jesus from a scroll and trapping Pilate adroitly.[30] Caiaphas's spies scatter Jesus's friends and bribe rogues to call for Jesus's crucifixion.[31] After Pilate releases Barabbas, Caiaphas, standing behind Pilate (as the tempting Satan stood behind Jesus),[32] says, "Crucify him" (words spoken by the mob in Mk 15:14). When Pilate declares himself innocent, Caiaphas happily agrees to see "to it" (replacing the infamous Mt. 27:25). When Judas appears in the Roman court (not the temple) to repent, Caiaphas ruthlessly asks why "they" would care (Mt. 27:4). Thereafter, Caiaphas "sees to it," following the cross on the Via Dolorosa and standing beneath the cross, mocking Jesus to come down (taking over the words of Mt. 27:42).

In a second innovative touch, DeMille embellishes the spectacle. The camera lingers on the chalice after the group leaves the supper, transfiguring it with light. The tomb and the door of the upper room also glow with light. Divine light also lifts Jesus out of his anguish in the garden.³³ Finally, in a shot that matches Jesus's first appearance out of light, a single ray of heavenly light breaks the darkness at the cross (creating a Rembrandt-like effect).³⁴ The light returns after Mary prays, "Give us back the light" (cf. the blind girl's prayer). The resurrection, in color, follows. There is no burial scene.

DeMille's film is far more miraculous than the gospels—it shows the resurrection. In fact, miracles punctuate the passion. Not only does Jesus heal the temple guard's ear in the garden, but also a roomful of sick people on the Via Dolorosa—simply by passing them.

Most of Jesus's suffering (except for that in the garden) takes place offscreen or at a distance. A curtain hides the scourging, until it is pulled back and the audience sees the tormented Judas watching. Further, Jesus's cross is raised from afar, behind Judas's own hanging tree.³⁵ DeMille's camera focuses at least as much on Judas's hanging as it does Jesus's crucifixion.³⁶ It is almost as if Judas and Jesus's enemies suffer more than he does. In contrast to Mt. 27:3-10, Judas dies after Jesus.

As in *The Passion of the Christ* (2004), the passion's true spectacle is the devastating judgments that befall Jesus's oppressors.³⁷ After Jesus's death in darkness and thunderstorm, an earthquake splits the earth (Mt. 27:51). The earthquake consumes one of Caiaphas's spies, spectators, and Judas and his tree. The holy trio at the cross is safe, with Magdalene clinging to the cross. The earthquake also spares Caiaphas who returns to the temple to pray. After lightning strikes the temple veil and destroys the menorah (from which a cross of light rises), Caiaphas (like Judas before him) repents, "I alone am guilty."³⁸

In a third innovative touch, the children's gospel continues when DeMille's Jesus addresses his disciples as "little children" (Jn 13:33-34) at the last supper. Judas is seated beside Jesus, but as in the "suffer little children" scene, he outs himself from the "kingdom" group when he cannot partake of the bread and wine.³⁹ Even on the Via Dolorosa, Jesus blesses a baby. More importantly, Mark remains ubiquitous. He is in the garden fighting on Jesus's behalf. When the guard takes Jesus away, Mark and Judas are left to watch, representing, respectively, the kingdom's children and those left outside. In one of the film's most memorable scenes, Mark shames Simon⁴⁰ into bearing Jesus's cross by saying he would do so if he were so big and strong.⁴¹ Finally, in the final upper room scene, Jesus lovingly embraces Mark, as he did the little blind girl in his first film appearance.

The return of color in the resurrection scene recalls the film's beginning and thus reinforces the film and Magdalene's sin-to-salvation story. The soldiers flee after light flows from the tomb's stone so only the audience sees the stone roll away and the resurrected, transfigured Jesus's emergence (cf. the audience's first sighting of Jesus with the healed blind girl). Amidst a flurry of white doves, recalling Mary's first film appearance and the blind girl's healing (although doves appear elsewhere), Jesus appears first to his mother and then to Magdalene.

In a black-and-white scene, a cross on the closed door to the upper room glows with light before Jesus steps through to comfort his disciples (John 10:9). Mark, Thomas, and the Marys soon arrive to complete the joyous reunion. As Jesus sends his witnesses to the nations, everyone else fades away and Jesus rises in glowing cruciform. A modern, industrialized city appears behind and below him. "Lo I am with you always" (Mt. 28:20) appears over this visual as the film ends.

MEMORABLE CHARACTERS

1 Jesus is the spectacular light of the world, radiating through the film. He is also a paternalistic Christ "for the children," holding children in his first and last scenes. He is a feminized, Victorian Christ (Babington and Evans 1993: 122). But DeMille wanted a "manly Christ" (1959: 276), so Jesus does have some heroic moments: he faces down the wanton Magdalene; he presses on to Jerusalem despite the shadow of the cross; he agrees to drink the cup despite his overwhelming anxiety; he faces trials the giant Peter cannot; and he bears a cross the larger Simon has difficulty lifting.

2 DeMille's gospel/kingdom is for children—including the blind girl, the girl with the broken doll, the disciples (Jn 13:33-34), but primarily Mark—and the saved, including Magdalene, who clings to the cross as the film becomes a "disaster movie" (Tatum 2013: 54). She also provides DeMille's standard seductive woman (lust) and his oft-repeated sin-to-salvation story.

3 The film's three deadly sins are lust (Magdalene), greed (Caiaphas), and pride (ambitious Judas). Judas's pride eventually makes him Caiaphas's pawn. He fails to heal the lunatic boy, joins Satan in trying to crown Jesus, and will not suffer the kingdom's children. Much of Jesus's physical suffering is shot from Judas's POV and emphasizes its debilitating psychological effects on him. His fall into the abyss is the climactic moment.

4 Caiaphas is greed, master of the corrupt temple trade, and (in the 1927 version) cares more for revenue than religion. Spider-like, he plots to trap Jesus and eventually seduces Pilate to listen to the bribed mob. Like Judas, he does have a repentance scene (dealing innovatively with the infamous Mt. 27:25).

MEMORABLE VISUALS

1 Magdalene's Orientalized villa and her exorcism/conversion.
2 Jesus introduced through the healed blind girl's POV, Jesus films' first complete A/B/A' POV shot and first medium closeup of Jesus (see Figure 5.1).
3 Jesus working on a Roman cross.
4 Jesus "healing" a child's broken (soldier) doll.
5 Jesus, holding a lamb, rejecting worldly kingdoms.
6 Medium closeup, low-angle shot of Jesus's cross scraping across the ground, with a dog and people's feet walking around it.
7 Supporting shafts of light in the garden and piercing the dark at the cross.
8 Passion-earthquake-judgment spectacle.
9 Jesus's resurrection appearances out of light and his luminous ascension over a modern city.

Figure 5.1 The blind girl (and audience) sees Jesus for the first time in *The King of Kings*, directed by Cecil B. DeMille, DeMille Pictures, 1927. All rights reserved.

KEY AUTHORITY/SCRIPTURE

1 Opening intertitles claim the film fulfills Jesus's commandment to take his message to the nations. The final resurrection scene, including a similar command and Jesus's ascension over a modern, industrialized city, visually reiterates the intertitle/command and indicates the command's authoritative nature.

2 The film asserts its independent authority through its spectacle of light, as well as with its distribution of reward and punishment in the spectacular earthquake/crucifixion and in the return to color in the resurrection scene.

3 DeMille's "new KJV" intertitles authorize his gospel emphases, character innovations, and narrative sequencing.[42] DeMille adds gospel citations in places other than their gospel locations. He changes the speaker and/or the person addressed (see Westbrook 2016). He shortens and edits, and he sometimes adds language to the source cited.[43] Generally, he quotes Jesus, but no one else, carefully (Stern, Jefford, and DeBona 1999: 36). He also uses the archaic KJV style for non-gospel speeches and narrative description. All this creates a "Gospel effect."[44] Notably, Jesus's first and last speeches have no gospel citations (although they come from Jn 12:46; Mt. 28:20). They are DeMille's gospel.

CULTURAL LOCATION/GENRE: GOSPELING THE MIDDLE CLASS (SPECTACLE)

According to the 1920 US census, for the first time more people lived in metropolitan areas (towns with populations over 2500) than in rural areas. Immigration was at its height, and large cities like New York and Chicago had foreign-born populations of over 50 percent. DeMille's portrayal of Jesus's activity in "cities" with large crowds of begging children and desperately needy adults would have resonated deeply with his viewing audiences.

Before 1920, DeMille had become the United States' most successful director. If Griffith is US film's early auteur, DeMille is the mass entertainer and at the forefront of cinema's role in producing massified culture (Stern, Jefford, and Debona 1999: 49).[45] DeMille's Jesus stands with the people versus corrupt, decadent wealth (Humphries-Brooks 2006: 11–2, 20). Where Griffith indicts contemporary America for various failings, DeMille provides an easily consumable, sentimentalized Jesus, welcoming most with open arms. The film has none of Jesus's infamously "hard sayings" about wealth, the family, and so forth.

As the opening Magdalene scene indicates, DeMille realizes he needs to attract an audience, and he uses sensational sexuality to do so. He had developed the latter's deployment in romantic comedies in the era of the New Woman and as the Jazz Age opened (*The Cheat* 1915; *Male and Female* 1919; *Why Change Your Wife* 1920; *The Affairs of Anatol* 1921).[46] He had even given Joan of Arc a torrid romance (*Joan the Woman* 1916).

The film industry, however, was struggling with censorship. In 1915, the Supreme Court had decided free speech did not extend to film. In 1922, after a series of films (including some of DeMille's) were found morally suspect and various public relations debacles involving filmmakers occurred, major studios asked William H. Hays to rehabilitate film's reputation.[47] In 1925, Hays distributed a formula of "dos and don'ts," a version of which major studios adopted in the form of the Hays Code (or the Motion Picture Production Code) in 1930 and began enforcing in 1934 (until 1968).[48]

DeMille's biblical epics, *The Ten Commandments* (1923) and *The King of Kings*, were ahead of the game. They combined the vulgar and sensational with a sin-salvation story that policed attractive immoral scenarios with middle-class piety and morality. Titillating sexual fantasies, like Magdalene, are eventually domesticated (see also *The Sign of the Cross* 1932).[49] DeMille's forte then is the sexualized biblical epic (see *Samson and Delilah* 1949). This epic, of course, is packaged in and as a spectacle of light and, at the cross, melodrama.

DIRECTOR

DeMille made five popular and financially successful biblical epics: *The Ten Commandments* (1923); *The King of Kings*; *The Sign of The Cross*; *Samson and Delilah*; and *The Ten Commandments* (1956). The third and fourth are the most DeMillish, with the third supplying the memorable DeMille elements: bathtubs, lions, and orgies. The last is still seen annually on television and is his most famous film. In it, DeMille himself introduces the film to explain its Cold War significance. This quintessentially American film is, in DeMille's own words, "the story of the birth of freedom" whose theme "is whether men are to be ruled by God's law or whether they are to be ruled by the whims of a dictator .... are men the property of the state or are they free souls under God. This same battle continues throughout the world today." In the finale, Moses (Charlton Heston), in a Statue of Liberty pose, intones, "Go, proclaim liberty to all lands."[50]

The first three films form a Christian trilogy (DeMille 1959: 305–6), stretching from the Old Testament to the early church. *The Ten Commandments* (1923) opens with a cinematic Exodus climaxing with the Sinai orgy (Exod. 32), focusing on a sexually flagrant Miriam. DeMille then shifts to the modern tale of moral John and immoral Dan, and their respective fates. Dan cynically violates each of the commandments and worships (the) gold(en calf), but eventually shipwrecks his life on the commandments when the church he built with shoddy materials collapses and kills his pious mother (holding his dying mother, he sees the tablets on the wall). Literally, his boat (*Defiance*) shipwrecks on a mountain that looks like the Paramount and Sinai mountains. John, a carpenter, ultimately rescues Mary, the girl who turned bad with Dan, healing her from what she thinks is leprosy (Miriam and another Orientalized femme fatale are also lepers) by reading the story of Jesus's cleansing of a similar woman (the audience sees a woman at Jesus's feet). John closes the film by telling Mary that "it's gone in the light."[51]

DeMille's *The Sign of the Cross* depicts the sadomasochistic spectacle of Nero's persecutions and imperial Rome's decadence.[52] Nero's wife, Poppaea (Claudette Colbert), lolls in a famously revealing milk bath. She loves the playboy Prefect of Rome, Marcus Superbus (Frederic March). In the course of his Christian-hunting duties, however, Marcus falls in love with the Christian Mercia (Elissa Landi). He refuses to turn her over for execution, and a jealous rival, Tigellinus (Ian Keith), seeks to undo him through this misstep. Desperate, Marcus takes Mercia to an orgy in his home, hoping to convert her to his decadent lifestyle. One of his many women seduces Mercia with a sensual dance. While Marcus leers, Christians march by on their way to death, singing hymns. Redeemed by song, Mercia asks Marcus to return her to the arena. In the finale, Marcus joins faithful Mercia, marching upstairs with her to death in the arena (cf. *The Robe*'s [1953] finale). Morality trumps titillation; the film's last shot is a cross formed of light on the closed door leading to the arena (cf. *The King of Kings*'s resurrection door).

Clearly, the themes of these biblical epics reflect the DeMille gospel seen in *The King of Kings*.

CRITERION DVD, 155 MINUTES, 2004

Special-edition, double-disk set. Disk one (1927) 155 minutes; Disk two (1928) 112 minutes. Disk one: Black and white and color; Disk two: Black and white only. Silent. New musical scores commissioned by *Criterion* for each version.

DVD Extras

The King of Kings (thirty-six-page booklet)
    "Showman of Piety," by Peter Matthews

"The King of Kings," by Robert S. Birchard

"Hollywood Moves to the Holy Land," by Grace Kingsley

"The Screen as a Religious Teacher," by Cecil B. DeMille

DVD Extras (Disk 1)
- Supplements
  - Opening Night
    - Newspaper Ads
    - Stills
    - Telegrams
  - Original Program
  - Press Book
  - Blessings from the Clergy
    - (Roman Catholic, Protestant denominations, and a Jew, a Muslim, and a Buddhist)
  - Trailers

The Score
- About Sosin

DVD Extras (Disk 2)
- Supplements
  - Scenes from the making of *The King of Kings*
    - Behind the Scenes (out takes, etc.)
      - Jeanie Macpherson, who wrote the screenplay, is on set for much of the filming
    - Stills Gallery
  - Sketches by Dan Sayre Groesbeck
  - Portraits by W. M. Mortensen
- The Scores
  - Original 1928 Score by Hugo Riesenfeld
  - Alternate 2004 Score by Timothy J. Tikker

DVD Chapters (Disk 1, 1927)

Scripture references for individual scenes appear in canonical order, not in the order of onscreen appearance.

1 Opening Credits
2 Prologue, 1:14
3 The House of Magdalene, 1:52
4 "Take me to Him" (film shifts from color to black and white), 8:32
    Healed Mark (Mk 2:12), 10:26

Peter first appears, 12:16
5 Jesus the Great Physician, 13:47
    Disciples named—except for Matthew, 13:50
    Mary, with doves, 14:50
    A Sabbath healing (of a blind girl) (Mk 3:2), 15:20-20:37
        First view of Jesus (through the girl's healed eyes), 18:44
        Jesus's and Judas's response (Lk. 8:39), 19:45-20:37
6 Seven Deadly Sins, 20:38
    Magdalene cleansed of seven deadly sins (Mt. 8:3; Lk. 8:2; Mt. 5:8), 22:15-26:45
7 House of Caiaphas, 26:47
    Spider art, 27:10, 28:21 (see also 52:24)
    Caiaphas's tax plan to catch Jesus involves tax-collector Matthew, 29:22
8 Judas Fails to Heal (the lunatic), 30:22
9 "Follow me, Matthew," 35:16
    Tribute to Caesar (coin in the fish's mouth) (Mt. 17:24-27)
    "Is it lawful to give tribute?" (Mt. 22:17-21)
    "Matthew—follow me!" (Mt. 9:9)
    Jesus the carpenter stares at suddenly unveiled cross, 41:35
10 "Suffer little children," 42:46
    Children pick olives; Judas objects to children's presence (Mk 10:14)
    Jesus fixes a child's broken doll, 44:22-45:36
11 The Tomb of Lazarus, 45:37
12 The Adulteress, 52:06
    Caiaphas decides to use woman taken in adultery as a trap
13 At the Temple, 54:30
    Animals slaughtered, 55:16
    The adulteress (Lk. 18:11; Jn 8:1-11), 55:45
14 Den of Thieves, 1.01:10
    Caiaphas face to face with Jesus (Mt. 21:23), 1.05:00
15 "He is our King," 1.06:12
    People enter with hosannas; Judas finds a "crown"
    Satan tempts Jesus (Mt. 4:8-9; Lk. 4:8), 1.08:48
    A lamb in the temple, 1.10:53
16 Thirty Pieces of Silver, 1.11:14
    A kingdom not of this world (Jn 18:36), 1.12:30

Thirty pieces of silver (Mt. 26:14-15; Mk 14:2), 1.13:42

17 The Last Supper, 1.15:28
  (Mt. 20:28; 26:22, 27-28; Lk. 22:19, 21, 33-34; Jn 13:27, 33-34; 16:33)
  Jesus's mother is outside the door
  The dove and the glowing chalice, 1.25:20

18 The Garden of Gethsemane, 1.25:50
  (Mt. 26:36-38, 40-42, 48-49, 52, 55; Lk. 22:42-44, 48; Jn 17:1-4; 18:18)
  Mark fights off the bad guys; Matthew takes notes

19 Peter Denies Jesus, 1.35:12
  (Mt. 26:57-58, 71-72; Mk 14:71; Jn 18:19, 25-26)
  Sanhedrin behind a closed curtain, 1.39:46

20 Hall of Judgment, 1.40:00
  Caiaphas brings Jesus to Pilate (Mt. 27:20; Lk. 23:2-3, 14-22; Jn 18:37-38; 19:10, 12)
  Pilate's wife (Mt. 27:19), 1.45:16

21 The Crown of Thorns, 1.47:38
  Roman scourging; Judas watches

22 "Crucify him!" 1.51:46
  Barabbas and Jesus are brought before Pilate, 1.52:54
  "Behold the man" (Mt. 27:22; Lk. 23:18; Jn 18:39; 19:5), 1.53:47
  Caiaphas says, "Crucify him" (Mk 15:14; Jn 19:6, 15), 1.55:25
    Magdalene defends Jesus, 1.56:58
  Pilate washes his hands (Mt. 27:24), 1.58:52
  Judas returns the thirty pieces to Caiaphas (Mt. 27:4), 1.59:33

23 The Way of the Cross, 2.01:26
  The disciples watch Jesus pass by from inside the upper room, 2.03:32
  Mary and John in the street, 2.03:57
  Jesus heals a lame man (watching from a room), 2.04:25
  Simon and Mark (Mk 15:21), 2.05:05

24 Calvary, 2.07:53
  Caiaphas mocks, 2.10:40
  Jesus's last words (Lk. 23:34, 39-43), 2.11:56
    Mary comforts the mother of the unrepentant thief, 2.14:05–2.15:18

25 God's Wrath, 2.15:19
  "It is finished" (Lk. 23:46; Jn 19:30), 2.17:00

Judas hangs himself, 2.17:37

A crow sits on Gestas's cross, 2.18:49

The Beloved Disciple, 2.19:00

Earthquake (Mt. 27:51), 2.19:09

    Judas's hanging body falls into the abyss, 2.20:07

    The Roman centurion; spear thrust (Mk 15:39; Jn 19:34), 2.20:18

    Temple veil split (Mt. 27:5), 2.20:53

        Caiaphas says, "I alone am guilty!" 2.21:15

    A cross rises from the broken menorah, 2.21:17

26 The Resurrection, 2.22:42 (shot in color until 2.29:25)

Roman guards witness the glowing stone

Magdalene and Mary come to the tomb (white doves), 2.25:55

    Both see Jesus separately

    Jesus appear out of cross-light in the upper room (Mk 16:15, 17-18; Lk. 24:39; Jn 20:19; 21:15-17, 28-29), 2.29:25

    Mark bursts into the room, 2.31:26

    Thomas, Mary, and Magdalene arrive

    Ascension over a modern city, 2.36:25

NOTES

1. DeMille claims he simply transferred the gospels to a new medium (1959: 267, 284). The credits, however, name Jeannie MacPherson the scriptwriter. She began her film career as an actress for Griffith, directed one film (*The Tarantula* 1913), but is famous for her thirty-two DeMille scripts. She also had a longtime affair with him, reportedly sanctioned by DeMille's wife (Gaines n.d.).
2. DeMille's film is an example of Jesus films' dominant pattern: "stories of conversion and degradation swirling around his [Jesus's] structuring absence" (Walsh 2003: 33-9; following Keil 1992: 114).
3. Ziegfeld Follies girl Jacqueline Logan plays the Magdalene.
4. On this romantic triangle, see Paul von Heyse's 1901 German play, which also presents the passion from Mary's perspective (cf. the POV of *Mary Magdalene* 2018). Mrs. Harrison Grey Fiske, whose husband led the public outcry against Salmi Morse's passion in 1880 (shuttered in San Francisco in 1879), and who was one of the premiere Broadway actresses of the early twentieth-century, directed and starred in a 1902-3 Broadway version (Bial 2015: 54-7). See also Edgar Saltus's 1891 novel, *Mary Magdalen*, as well as the films, *Mary Magdalene* (1919) and *Giuda* (1919) (see Shepherd 2013, chap. 9), and more recently, *Jesus Christ Superstar* (1973) and *The Last Temptation of Christ* (1988).
5. Jesuit priest Daniel Lord, the film's Roman Catholic advisor, recalls that DeMille shot 2500 feet of this "DeMillish romance" before realizing that Christ's love for mankind was the only

romance necessary (Shepherd 2013: chap. 9). DeMille chose not to include a sensual kiss and a scene suggesting Magdalene was Judas's mistress (see Walsh 1996: 53).

6 The shift from the rich courtesan, filmed in color, to the poor and sick, filmed in black and white, like the introduction of the villainous Caiaphas's counting money, creates a dichotomy between the evil rich and the people/Jesus. See Cultural Location.
7 Joseph Schildkraut, the son of the actor playing Caiaphas, plays Judas. Famous for film villains, he won an Oscar for his role as Captain Alfred Dreyfus in *The Life of Emile Zola* (1937). He also played Nicodemus in *The Greatest Story Ever Told* (1965).
8 Galilee exteriors were shot in 1926 on Santa Catalina Island.
9 Child evangelists were quite popular in the 1920s. The fifteen-year-old Pentecostal evangelist Uldine Utley had been preaching for four years to crowds of thousands before this film's release (Robinson 2013).
10 He witnesses the blind girl's healing, the exorcism of the "lunatic" spirit, Lazarus's resurrection, Jesus's response to the adulterous woman, the triumph, the agony in the garden, the Via Dolorosa, and Jesus's final resurrection appearance and ascension.
11 While an intertitle cites Mk 2:1 for the crowded house scene, Mark's healing replaces that of the Markan paralytic (2:1-12). The Markan scene does begin a lengthy controversy sequence (2:1–3:6, 20-35), which DeMille's spies echo faintly. DeMille's cinematography draws heavily upon *From the Manger to the Cross* (1912) (25:36).
12 DeMille creates the character by inserting him into many scenes and by giving him actions or words that belong to others or to narration in the gospels. Cf. the creation of the Leading Pharisee in *The Gospel of John* (2003) as well as Mark and Caiaphas here.
13 Ernest Torrence, famous for silent film villains like Captain Hook, plays the gentile giant.
14 Dorothy Cumming, in her thirties, plays Mary. The actor playing her son was in his fifties.
15 DeMille satisfies both Protestant and Roman Catholic audiences by having Mark (the gospel) and Mary (the intercessor) bring the girl to Jesus. See also the children's reports of the famous Marian apparitions in Fatima, Portugal, in 1917. The sequence (perhaps the entire film) is quite Markan. Cf. the two healings of the blind (8:22-26; 10:46-52) bookending Mark's central teaching section, which presents Jesus as the Christ who dies as a matter known only through revelation.
16 This POV shot and other intimate medium closeups of Jesus are striking compared to earlier Jesus films. DeMille pioneered the use of a newly developed small camera (Eyemo) to capture the shots, which offer the spectator a religious encounter (so Stern, Jefford, and DeBona 1999: 53–4). The avuncular H. B. Warner plays Jesus. Warner is best known for the bumbling druggist, Mr. Gower, in *It's a Wonderful Life* (1946). He also played himself, in a card game, in *Sunset Blvd.* (1950) in which DeMille also appears as himself, directing a biblical epic.
17 Jesus's Matthean words address a leper.
18 The film's small amount of teaching emphasizes Jesus's Johannine identity (cf. *From the Manger to the Cross*).
19 The other "gospel" miracle is the healing of the lunatic boy (Mt. 17:14-21), but the film "DeMilles" it by making Judas the sole example of "un-faith" and by making it part of the suddenly revealed cross sequence. The Synoptic Gospels also pair the failed exorcism with a passion prediction.
20 Bruce Babington and Peter Evans argue that a child's perception of "father" lies under the film (1993: 121) and that DeMille produces Christ in his own image as a patriarchal storyteller

(1993: 118). DeMille says his biblical films were born as he listened to his father read the Bible to him as a child (1959: 31).

21 Jesus reprimands Judas with words addressing all the disciples in Mk 10:14. The villains in *The Greatest Story Ever Told* (1965) and in *Son of Man* (2006) dismiss reports about Jesus as (mere) children's stories.

22 Rudolph Schildkraut, famous in German theater and film, plays Caiaphas. His most famous role was as Shylock.

23 DeMille creates Caiaphas as he did the Pharisee spy. Because of pre-release complaints about anti-Semitism, DeMille made Caiaphas the film's chief villain, having him, for example, confess to his solitary guilt for Jesus's death. Nonetheless, the crushed temple scene is highly supersessionist as a cross of light emerges out of a menorah smashed by lightning. DeMille never admitted the anti-Semitism, still claiming to be shocked by Jewish opposition to the film in his autobiography (1959: 282–4). As Caiaphas's visual depiction reprises medieval anti-Semitic caricatures of the greedy Jew, Stephenson Humphries-Brook's observation is more prescient: "In the image vocabulary of *The King of Kings*, the latent message is that Jesus and his disciples are white, Anglo-Saxon, American Protestants who share the values of hardworking pious American Protestants. Their opponents and crucifiers are rich and Jewish" (2006: 16). David Shepherd notes that the 1928 version tones down some anti-Semitic scenes (the scourging; the crucifixion; the trial before Pilate) and replaces Caiaphas's defamatory, introductory intertitle with one saying he was appointed by Rome and was Jesus's archenemy (2013: chap. 9).

24 In some subsequent scenes (e.g., in the garden and in the resurrection's upper room), Matthew is writing (or caring for Mark).

25 The 1928 version omits this entire sequence.

26 Cf. *Last Temptation*'s cross-making Jesus and *From the Manger to the Cross*'s carpentry-shop cross-foreshadowing.

27 This sequence is also innovative. DeMille "DeMilles" the woman taken in adultery, the temple cleansing, the people's (not Jesus's) triumph, the wilderness attempt to crown Jesus, Jesus's (relocated) wilderness temptation, Jesus's (reset) kingdom not of this world saying, and the (reset) Lord's Prayer.

28 Dialogue intertitles are more common than in previous Jesus silents (Westbrook 2016: 268).

29 Peter catches Jesus's eye only at the scene's tragic end.

30 Pilate's wife Claudia asks him to have nothing to do with this innocent man. She does not appear in the 1928 version.

31 One man refuses, saying, "You cannot bribe me, a Jew, to cry for the blood of an innocent brother!" Before the Pharisee spy shouts her down as a harlot, Magdalene defends Jesus: "His only crime hath been to heal your sick, and raise your dead! Save Him—ye may, yourselves, need mercy!" The 1928 film omits this sequence.

32 Judas also stands behind Jesus in the garden before his betraying kiss, creating a visual connection between Satan, Caiaphas, and Judas.

33 Cf. Luke's supportive angel (22:43). DeMille also deploys Luke's bloody sweat (22:44). Plays and films (see, e.g., Olcott) often replace angels with light.

34 Marketing touted the similarity of various scenes' lighting to Rembrandt's art.

35 The distance is particularly striking given the camera's earlier intimacy with Jesus.

36 Meanwhile, Jesus asks God to forgive them (Lk. 23:34) and promises paradise to the good thief (Lk. 23:43). Jesus looks fondly on his mother, but does not entrust her to the beloved disciple (Jn 19:26-27). He says "It is finished" (Jn 19:30 is not cited) and entrusts his spirit

into God's hands (Lk. 23:46). He does not utter the cry of derelicion (Mk 15:34). Instead, the accompanying music is "Nearer My God to Thee." In a DeMille invention, Mary comforts the mother of the bad thief (omitted in the 1928 version).

37 DeMille toys with the spectacle of battle in the garden between Jesus's disciples and the cohort coming to arrest him. *King of Kings* (1961) overwhelms the Jesus story with epic battles.
38 The Roman centurion makes the obligatory confession. The resurrection defeats the Roman soldiers, including the centurion who tries to kneel in prayer before another soldier pulls him away.
39 No women are present for this supper. Mary sits outside watching the door. A visibly moved Judas passes her on his way to gather the arrest party. When Jesus leaves, his mother begs him to return to Nazareth.
40 The credits name him Simon. As the film intertitles do not name him, Vivian Westbrook claims he is an "everyman" (2016: 267). She thinks the six sets of hands, raising the cross for Jesus to bear before the Via Dolorosa, function similarly, "signifying collective guilt" (2016: 266). William Boyd plays Simon. While he began his film career as a DeMille extra, he became famous playing Hop-a-Long Cassidy in multiple films and Saturday morning television.
41 This scene is another Markan moment, as its basic teaching calls Jesus's followers to take up their own crosses (e.g., 8:34).
42 Each of these intertitles has its own interpretative, artistic background (some are noted in the text).
43 For example, DeMille claims that Mark 15:1 says Pilate alone had authority to sentence to death, and that Matthew 27:20 says Caiaphas instructed his spies to bribe the crowd.
44 DeMille also relies on several gospel texts that biblical critics see as textually uncertain: for example, Jn 7:53-8:11; Lk. 22:19b; 22:44; 23:44; Mk 16:15, 17-18.
45 The enormous interior of the Jewish temple and Pilate's magnificent Roman eagle likely reminded some movie-goers of the huge bronze eagle in the seven-floor atrium of Wanamaker's Philadelphia Department store (see Kirk 2018: 161–4, 189).
46 Babington and Evans claim DeMille's comedies reflect the transition from Victorian values to consumer culture, while his biblical epics maintain older gendered, ethical stereotypes about women (1993: 113–7).
47 DeMille had the major actors in *The King of Kings* sign contracts with morals clauses.
48 The text of the code is available online: https://productioncode.dhwritings.com/multipleframes_productioncode.php.
49 Critics often refer to such films as last-reel salvations.
50 As always, DeMille combines the moralizing with salacious scenes. See, for example, the pairing of the spectacular giving of the law with the decadent orgy below.
51 For more discussion, see Shepherd (2013, chap. 8) and Walsh (2016a).
52 The film reprises an 1895 play by Wilson Barrett and an earlier 1914 film. Some refer to *The Sign of the Cross* as the left-hand version of *Quo Vadis*.

6

King of Kings

Nicholas Ray, director, MGM, 1961

PLOT SUMMARY: A MESSIAH OF PEACE

As the "talkie" era began, filmmakers re-released some Jesus silents with synchronized sound. The first genuine Jesus "talkie" was Julien Duvivier's *Golgotha* (aka *Ecce Homo* 1935). The film focuses on the political machinations during Jesus's last days in Jerusalem, where Jewish authorities quarrel rancorously about Jesus (who is often difficult to see, e.g., in the triumphal entry), and where Judas's POV is often privileged. The camera comes closest to Jesus at the Last Supper and after his arrest. At the Roman trial, huge Jewish crowds overwhelm Pilate,[1] who, despite Claudia's extensive pleadings, washes his hands and gives in to the Jews.[2]

After DeMille, the biblical epic pushed Jesus even farther off the screen.[3] Hollywood studios' "sword and sandal" spectacles like *Quo Vadis* (1951), *Salome* (1953), *The Robe* (1953), and *Ben-Hur* (1959)[4] present Jesus as a bit character or extra (sometimes uncredited).[5] He appears, if at all, from behind, from afar, obscured in some way, or as a voice/memory.

In contrast, Nicholas Ray's *King of Kings* returns Jesus to striking visual centrality—offering, among other things, extreme closeups of Jesus's startlingly blue eyes in 70 mm and brilliant Technicolor (see Figure 6.1).[6] Nonetheless, as in the epics (and the era's lesser-known Jesus films), larger political issues frame Jesus. The "times" (and epic tropes) overwhelm Jesus (Forshey 1992: 88).

King of Kings starts with Rome's brutal colonization of the Jews and Pompey's triumphal entry, not Jesus's. Orson Welles's heavy-handed voiceover accompanies the visuals,[7] conjuring Holocaust memories (Jews fall into pyres) and navigating Cold War fears about tyranny's threat to freedom and Arab threats to modern Israel. Orientalizing narration depicts maleficent Herod (Grégoire Aslan) as an Arab "of the Bedouin tribe" and says the Romans appointed him because no Jew was sufficiently villainous. Clearly, the film moves away from Jewish responsibility for Jesus's fate.[8]

The images and voiceover feature sheep for the slaughter, forests of crosses, and the Jews' messianic hopes. The voiceover is hardly triumphant (contrast *Quo Vadis*'s "victorious" opening voiceover). The film's trailer says that Jesus's story "comes out of the shadows" of ruthless power and idolatry, but Jesus remains largely in the shadows[9] on the political story's margins.

Passing quickly through an out-of-place nativity pageant, the film emphasizes the Roman taxation that brings the holy family to Bethlehem[10] and Herod's slaughter of the innocents.¹¹ Ray extends the brief gospel scene into a sequence by adding Herod's anguished ("self-crucified") death, Herod Antipas's (Frank Thring)¹² callous succession (taking "murder as his crown"), and a scene in Nazareth (not the Jerusalem temple) twelve years later. Lucius, a Roman centurion (Ron Rendell) who reluctantly led Herod's "slaughter of the innocents," comes to Nazareth checking tax rolls. Lucius, the film's chief witness to the Jesus story,¹³ interviews Mary (Siobhán McKenna)¹⁴ about her twelve-year-old son, born in Bethlehem. As tension mounts, he finally tells her to register Jesus.

Twenty years later, John (Robert Ryan)¹⁵ baptizes at the Jordan. But the story veers to Lucius and Antipas (accompanied by Herodias [Rita Gam] and the vicious Salome [Brigid Bazlen]) as they ride past to meet ambitious Pilate ([Hurd Hatfield] accompanied by Claudia [Viveca Lindfors]).¹⁶ In true epic fashion, 10,000 Jewish rebels, or freedom fighters, wait in the hills for Pilate's arriving army. The camera looks down on Barabbas (Harry Guardino)¹⁷ and his lieutenant Judas (Rip Torn,¹⁸ not identified), as they attack. If not for Lucius's propitious arrival (including hand-to-hand combat with Barabbas), the Jewish guerrillas would have been victorious.¹⁹

Barabbas escapes, and the film presents Jesus's baptism (thirty-three minutes in). After a *Ben-Hur*-like moment with a gourd ladle, the Baptist meets the adult Jesus (Jeffrey Hunter).²⁰ The subjective camera puts the audience intimately between the two, cutting to closeups of their faces and extreme closeups of their eyes. Then Jesus is gone, without an earthly or heavenly word spoken. A conversation takes place later that night between John and Mary. (John, the future disciple, is also there.) Mary, the film's voice of destiny, says her son will take his message to Jerusalem when it is time (cf. her earlier conversations with a camel driver and with Lucius).

Alone in the wilderness with disembodied voices (Satan and Welles),²¹ Jesus faces the temptations which "create" him.²² In the climax, he says, "You shall not force me to put the Lord my God to the proof" (Lk. 4:12). This wilderness lesson explains Jesus's later passivity and provides the standard by which Judas fails.

While Jesus slowly gathers his disciples, the film concentrates on the elite's interaction with the Baptist who rails against the idolatry of the Roman standards in the temple. As the elite dine, the Baptist harangues the incestuous Herodians from the street below. Goaded into action by Pilate, Herodias, and Salome's taunts, Antipas has Lucius arrest John.

The narrator (with accompanying brief, shadowy visuals) and Judas report Jesus's miraculous activity and popularity. Judas finds Barabbas hiding in Jerusalem, and they discuss using the prophet Jesus to lead a revolt.²³ Judas and Barabbas find Jesus passing through the streets, teaching his disciples en route to the Baptist (Mk 8:36; Mt. 13:36-43, with references to the Son of Man). A stone-bearing crowd chases the "woman taken in adultery" (Carmen Sevilla as Magdalene) down the street, and, in his most active moment, Jesus faces down the crowd—with Barabbas wrenching a stone from the lone "innocent's" hand. Barabbas flees into the shadows (to hide from approaching Romans), and Judas looks puzzledly at his own stone. Welles comments that Judas will have to decide "whether to run with Barabbas, the messiah of war ... or walk with Jesus the new messiah of peace."

The film stays with Jesus as he meets privately with Lucius, telling him he cannot understand the freedom offered John because Lucius "places faith in nothing but his sword." Lucius warns Jesus he will be merciless, if Jesus breaks Caesar's law, despite having "favored your mother once before." As Jesus stands, moonlit in the cell window, a chained John crawls up an inclined wall to grasp the silent Jesus's outstretched hand/blessing as the theme music swells.[24]

After reports from Welles (with visuals of Jesus hugging a madman into submission) and from Lucius (who has never seen a miracle) to the political elite,[25] the Baptist asks Lucius to send a message asking Jesus if he is the one "foretold, or are we to expect another?" (cf. Lk. 7:19). Meanwhile, Salome dances salaciously for the Baptist's head.[26] Trapped by his lust and need to prove his kingly power, Antipas accedes to her request. The Baptist hears Jesus's voiceover answer to his question (Lk. 7:22, 24-28) before his offscreen execution.

Antipas dithers about Jesus being the Baptist resurrected and Caiaphas refuses to offer advice, so Pilate sends Lucius to spy on Jesus's upcoming Sermon.[27] Caring only for Roman peace and taxes, Pilate instructs Lucius to act immediately if he hears anything treasonous (cf. Lucius's earlier warning to Jesus).

In the spectacular Sermon,[28] Jesus emerges briefly "out of the [political] shadows" (the Sermon is about twelve minutes long). The Sermon's words and visuals depict Jesus as hoped-for messiah (answering the opening voiceover and the Baptist's query). Like the Roman soldiers, Jesus now wears a red robe (for the first time). Despite the visual comparison, Jesus's notion of power/politics/kings differs dramatically from Rome's. Further, near the Sermon's beginning, a shepherd leads his flock on the hillside. The shot echoes the prologue's scattered, slaughtered sheep (and presages those of Passover). Appropriately, Jesus identifies himself as the good shepherd who lays down his life for his sheep (Jn 10:11).[29]

Even without considering other scattered teaching, the Sermon devotes more time to Jesus's teaching than does any previous Jesus film.[30] The camera looks up and frames him against a brilliant blue sky (with swelling theme music) before he walks down among the people, who include most of the film's significant characters (Mary, Magdalene, Judas, Barabbas, Caiaphas, Lucius, Claudia, and the disciples). Jesus teaches by responding to questions, and the camera cuts between Jesus and his interlocutors, inserting the audience into the conversation.[31]

Loosely following the structure of Mt. 5-7 (without the legal and ritual antitheses or the parabolic ending) or Lk. 6:20-49, the Sermon draws liberally from all the gospels (see DVD Chapters). It locates the Kingdom of God within (Lk. 17:21), emphasizing service and loving one's enemies. Repeating the spiritual wisdom gleaned in the wilderness (Lk. 4:12), Jesus refuses to be tested (cf. Lk. 11:16) and refuses to test God by asking God to remove the Romans. He glosses this innovatively, as the camera finds Lucius in the crowd: "The Romans are conquerors; to conquer them would make you no different than they."[32] The Sermon ends with the Golden Rule and the Lord's Prayer (and swelling theme music).

Jesus withdraws, Barabbas dismisses the Sermon as (mere) "words," and Lucius reports to Pilate Jesus's message of "peace, love, and the brotherhood of man" [sic]. Welles observes that even the Twelve want a conquering messiah, so Jesus teaches them love and peace in the wilderness and sends them out by twos, promising to meet them in Jerusalem. Ominously, Barabbas forges arms and plans to time his revolt with Jesus's arrival.

After the intermission, the atheistic Lucius and the political elite discuss possible revolt. Understanding his fate more clearly than he, Mary accompanies Jesus to Jerusalem. Jesus arrives in triumph as Welles notes, "the city prepared for the Passover killing of the lambs." Instead of cleansing the temple, Jesus enters it to preach peace (one supposes; the camera stays outside). Outside, superior Roman forces slaughter Barabbas's men when they revolt. Foregoing Jesus's "do not test God" wisdom, an anguished Judas decides to betray Jesus to force him to overthrow the Romans.[33]

Jesus eats the Last Supper at a Y-shaped table (Ray wanted it to resemble a broken cross). It is a Seder—complete with references to bitter herbs. Jesus dismisses Judas to his "task" with Caiaphas,[34] speaks of laying down his life for his friends (Jn 15:12-13),[35] and recites Jewish blessings extolling God as king of the world. The last resonates strikingly with the film's concern with different notions of power.

Jesus suffers more visibly than at any other point in an anguished Gethsemane scene (recalling his wilderness temptations), and Judas betrays him with a kiss. Peter denies him while Jesus watches from Caiaphas's courtyard. Omitting a Jewish trial, the film offers a low-key Roman one. Jesus stands waiting, with bowed head, just off a red carpet as Pilate and Lucius stride down it. No group of Jewish leaders or "mob" is in view. Pilate/Rome cares only about sedition (kingdom claims). When Jesus, still with bowed head, refuses to answer, Pilate appoints Lucius his advocate. After the opposing "lawyers" argue their cases, Jesus finally asserts his kingdom is of God and that he came to bear witness to the (one) truth. To Pilate's famous query, Jesus responds: "Be true to God."[36]

Pilate sends the Nazarene to Antipas who still wonders if Jesus is the Baptist returned. When Jesus will do no miracles, Antipas clothes him in a red robe, mocks him as a fake king, and sends him back to Pilate.[37]

Pilate considers Jesus a threat to Roman power because he is different (continuing the contrast between Jesus's "power" and that of others) and dangerous because he influences even Caesar's daughter.[38] Jesus's scourging is offscreen, and the audience sees Judas watching it, who runs into a cross as he tries to leave. He faints with blood on his hands.

As Jesus carries his cross, Lucius releases Barabbas because "his followers yelled loudest." Barabbas and Judas separately watch the Via Dolorosa from the city rooftops.[39] On Golgotha, a shot of Barabbas and Judas recalls their pose in their first film appearance. Barabbas wonders why "that man would die in my place." Placed on top of the cross, the camera looks "down" on Jesus as he is laid upon it and as it is raised to show Mary beneath Jesus's bloody feet.[40] Judas walks dejectedly away, stopping to pick up a stone—reproducing the scene where he first met Jesus and Magdalene.

The three traditional crosses appear in a long shot, with several T-shaped crosses behind them, recalling the prologue's forest of crosses. Clearly, Jesus has not liberated his people. In a postmortem storm, however, Claudia (Caesar's daughter) and Lucius kneel, looking up at the dead Jesus against a darkening sky. Then, Lucius finally answers the question Welles posed for Judas: "He [not Barabbas] is truly the Christ."

When Barabbas finally leaves Golgotha, he finds Judas's corpse hanging from a tree. The limb breaks, and Barabbas holds Judas in a bleak pietà. Welles narrates the deposition, which includes the traditional pietà (under the cross's shadow), and burial.

On Easter morning, Jesus appears to Magdalene (still) waiting at the tomb. Welles reports other appearances, and then the audience sees the eleven at the Sea of Galilee. An offscreen Jesus commissions his witnesses as a shadow crosses the fishing net on the beach, forming the film's final shot—the shadow of the cross.

MEMORABLE CHARACTERS

1 Lucius is the film's "witness" to Jesus and its most innovative, complex character. A cynical, atheistic political realist, he is the film's good Roman (secular American). Last seen at the cross, he declares Jesus the Christ, although whether that is a Christian confession is not clear (see Cultural Location).

2 This human Jesus recalls the liberal Christ of nineteenth-century Protestant historical criticism, preaching "peace, love, and the brotherhood of man" [sic]. Despite various suggestive film asides, his death is not salvific. Larger political forces crush him, rendering his teaching (politically) irrelevant.

3 Mary, Jesus's middle-aged mother (the actress was thirty-eight), is wisdom/destiny, knowing Jesus's future better than he and explaining him to the Baptist and Magdalene.

4 The Herodians and Pilate are, respectively, the corrupt local and ambitious imperial powers. Concerned only for his own advancement, Pilate is viler than previous Pilates (cf. Pilate in *The Last Temptation of Christ* 1988). Notably, he never declares Jesus "innocent."

5 The Baptist's preaching in the temple, arrest in Jerusalem, and execution make him Jesus's forerunner. His subplot dominates the film's first seventy-five minutes.

6 The revolutionary subplot of Jesus Barabbas (Mt. 27:16-17) and Judas dominates the film's Jerusalem. Barabbas is Jesus of Nazareth's messianic/political foil. The Thomas DeQuincey Judas fails by trying to prove (test/force) Jesus as supernatural deliverer (contra Lk. 4:12).

MEMORABLE VISUALS

1 The forest of crosses in the prologue (with corpses rolled into pyres) and at Golgotha.
2 Jesus's blue eyes in extreme closeup (see Figure 6.1).
3 Judas staring at the uncast stone in the adulteress scene and on Golgotha.
4 Jesus's shadow (most significantly in the last scene).
5 Tracking Jesus through the crowd at the Sermon.
6 Salome's dance (with a jeweled ornament in her navel to satisfy the Hays Code).
7 Jesus "talking" with the imprisoned Baptist.
8 Jesus with bowed head before Pilate and Lucius.

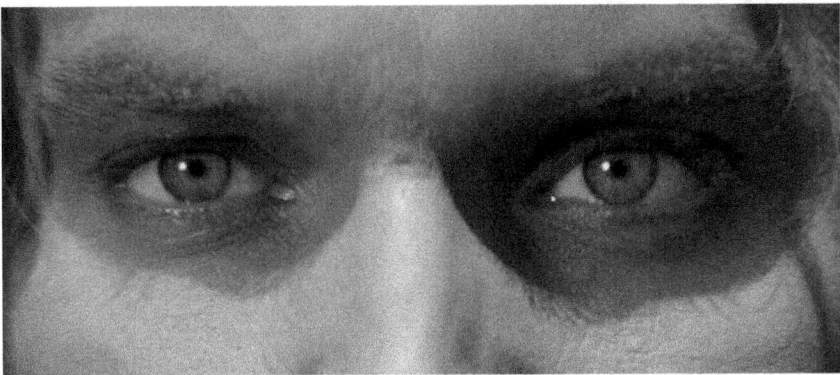

Figure 6.1 One of several extreme closeups of Jesus's striking blue eyes in *King of Kings* directed by Nicholas Ray, MGM, 1961. All rights reserved.

KEY AUTHORITY/SCRIPTURE

1 The wide-screen (70 mm) and Technicolor visuals, along with Orson Welles's voiceover narration (replacing the silents' scriptural titles), are the film's chief authority.

2 Lucius's reports and narrative comments, with his presence in important scenes, provide the film's authoritative witness.

3 Various passages setting forth Jesus as a different messiah than Barabbas, with a different conception of power than that of the elite—particularly in rejecting testing/proving God (Lk. 4:12) and in the "liberal" Sermon—provide the film's chief scriptural authority.

CULTURAL LOCATION/GENRE: SWORD AND SANDAL SPECTACLE

US biblical epics had their heyday in the 1950s. They celebrated American values (e.g., freedom and individualism) as vocal Cold War rhetoric. In that context, Samuel Bronston began producing epic films in Spain as a cheaper alternative to Hollywood. Bronston worked with a group of regulars, including Philip Yordan, scriptwriter, and Miklós Rózsa, composer (for *King of Kings*). Notable productions include *John Paul Jones* (1959), *King of Kings* (1961), *El Cid* (1961), *55 Days at Peking* (1963, also directed by Ray), *The Fall of the Roman Empire* (1964), and *Circus World* (aka *The Magnificent Showman* 1964). These productions share many characteristics: excellent photography, well-choreographed battle scenes, spectacles, over-long, rambling narratives, and banal dialogue (see Vallance 1994). *King of Kings* was successful enough that Bronston began constructing a huge studio in Las Rozas. *El Cid* was also financially successful (and the most critically favored Bronston epic). The expensive studio and other film failures led, however, to Bronston's financial bankruptcy (see Vallance 1994; Zagarac 2008).

In a savage, contemporary review, Moira Walsh said that the film equated Christianity and the American way of life, asking viewers to "take up our credit card" and follow (1961: 74). By contrast, Barnes Tatum sees the pacifist film (Jesus) as being as much out of its place/time as was Griffith's *Intolerance*. The film appeared in October 1961 between the Bay of Pigs (April 1961) and the Cuban missile crisis (October 1962) (2013: 90; cf. Humphries-Brooks 2006: 36-7).

Further, Ray himself was known for social problem films (see Director) and hardly saw his era as anything like the TV sitcoms of the time (e.g., *Father Knows Best* 1954-60; see Stern, Jefford, and DeBona 1999: 82-7).[41] The United States was beset not only by Cold War and imperial politics but also by racial issues. Rosa Parks was arrested in December 1955. The Greensboro, NC, Woolworth's lunch counter incident took place in February 1960. Freedom Riders began in May 1961.

The US empire maintained itself only by violence. Empire disturbed the leftist Ray, so he focused on imperial oppression and rediscovered a Jesus whose shadow haunts empire. Jesus's teaching is, at best, irrelevant for the empire.[42] He is no earthly king. Thereby, Ray deformed the biblical epic (see Walsh 2003: 136-9).

Lucius is key. He is the noblest Roman (American) of them all, without whom Rome could not stand, as Pilate observes. He has also, like Roy Batty in *Blade Runner* (1982), "seen things"—but not miracles, so he cannot believe in God (empire's ultimate authority). He has also done things for corrupt, ambitious politicians. He has sacrificed the innocent.[43] Moreover, while Lucius esteems Jesus over Barabbas (cf. his words when releasing Barabbas), he watches while the empire crucifies Jesus. Despite his cross confession, it is not clear whether it is a conversion, a recognition of nobility, a hope for another kind of power, or simply the jaded exhaustion of one tired of war and imperial politics—as he does not reappear in the film.[44]

The Robe's (1953) story of the centurion at the cross is a clearer conversion. More importantly, Romans' conversion to Christianity is a standard biblical epic pattern (see Walsh 2018a). Such epics feature the birth of Christian (read American) Empire. Perhaps, the ambiguity here most clearly indicates Ray's deformation of this genre and his discontent with (Christian) empire.[45]

DIRECTOR

Nicholas Ray was involved with the New Deal's Federal Theater Project (1935-9), which was defunded by the House Un-American Activities Committee for supporting integration and communism. In the 1950s, Howard Hughes's support kept Ray from being blacklisted. Ray was a left-leaning liberal with empathy for rebels, social misfits, and even criminals. Arguably, the tragic story (or biopic) of the individual in conflict with institutions is Ray's cinematic pattern (Andrew 1991: 81). Certainly, he deals with isolated, alienated figures—admirable failures with just a glimmer of hope (Stern, Jefford, and DeBona 1999: 90).[46] Accordingly, the Baptist, Barabbas, and Judas are more important in *King of Kings* than is Jesus.

Ray's important early films were film noirs or social problem films: for example, *They Live by Night* (1949), a prototype for films about young criminal lovers on the run, *Knock on Any Door* (1949), *In a Lonely Place* (1950), and *On Dangerous Ground* (1951). Such films explore the post-war United States' underside and expose the 1950s of TV sitcoms as an advertising campaign designed to sell appliances (Stern, Jefford, and DeBona 1999: 83). These films and *King of Kings* are early forms of *Pleasantville* (1999), with more bite.

As many of Ray's misfits are young people, Ray explores how little a father often knows (Stern, Jefford, and DeBona 1999: 84). Ray's most famous version of the alienated adolescent is *Rebel Without a Cause* (1955), which some say "invented" the American teenager. Publicly drunk, Jim Stark (James Dean), the new kid in town, meets two other troubled youths, Judy (Natalie Wood) and Plato (Sal Mineo), at the police station. Jim quickly runs afoul of Buzz, Judy's boyfriend, and finds himself in an afternoon knife fight and an evening "chicken run." When Buzz dies accidentally in the race, Jim, Judy, and Plato seek refuge from Buzz's murderous gang in a deserted mansion where they pretend to be the happy family they desire. When the gang finds Plato there, he seeks refuge in a nearby planetarium. Although Jim talks Plato out of the standoff, the police shoot and kill Plato as he comes out of the planetarium holding an unloaded gun.

Ray's Jesus is, like Jim Stark, quite youthful.[47] In fact, a review in *Time Magazine* pejoratively dubbed the film, "I Was a Teen-Age Jesus" (cited in Forshey 1992: 89). The film fits the emerging youth culture of the 1960s and American social anxieties about young people. Unlike Jim, however, Ray's Jesus is unusually submissive to his (divine) father (as well as to father surrogates like Lucius and Pilate). Accordingly, *King of Kings* has a mythic serenity that *Rebel Without a Cause* never attains. Like Jim, Jesus provides a surrogate family for his disciples in tumultuous times. But it is Ray's Judas, who is the alienated figure struggling to find a father figure (between Barabbas and Jesus), that resonates most strongly with Ray's *Rebel Without a Cause*. In fact, Judas is another version of Ray's Plato.[48]

PROBLEMATIC ISSUE: AN AMERICAN BEAUTY?

Bruce Babington and Peter Evans observe that Ray's cinema, and biblical epics generally, explores notions of ideal masculinity (1993: 133–8, 227–37). The most popular twentieth-century US portrait of Jesus was Warner Salman's *Head of Christ* (see anonymous 2015; Blum and Harvey 2012: 208–11). Jeffrey Hunter, and most cinematic Jesuses since, strongly resembles this image. The cinematic Jesus is an American beauty, enfranchising people who look like this and relegating others to inferiority.[49]

Historians know that a first-century Jew would hardly have looked like H. B. Warner, Jeffrey Hunter, Ted Neeley, Robert Powell, or Jim Caviezel.[50] In 2002, *Popular Mechanics* published a digital reconstruction of a first-century Galilean based on forensic anthropology (see Fillon 2020). The cinematic actor/Jesus who comes closest to the forensic recreation is Selva Rasalingam in the Lumo Project's visual translation of the four gospels (2014–16; see Taylor 2017).[51] In Hollywood's "American Beauty" context, any cinematic Jesus produced outside the cultural dominant of Western Europe and the United States is a helpful reminder of cultural relativity and imperial politics (see Chapter 21).[52]

WARNER HOME VIDEO, 168 MINUTES, 2003

DVD Extras

Cast and Crew
The Camera's Window to the World (3:57 minutes)
    Planning for the Sermon
King of Kings—Impressive Premiere on Two Coasts (1:45 minutes)
King of Kings: Egyptian Theater Premiere, Hollywood, CA (1:09 minutes)
Theatrical Trailer (1:39 minutes)
Languages
    Spoken: English, French
    Subtitles: English, French, Spanish

DVD Chapters

(Lucius's appearances are in italics)

1 Overture

2 Credits, 3:47

3 Fallen Jerusalem, 6:12

4 Herod's Forests, 10:50

    Jewish rebellions, forests of crosses, 12:14

5 A Bethlehem Stable, 12:53

6 Crown of Murder, 16:02

    (*Lucius in charge of*) slaughter of innocents (Mt. 2:16-18), 16:50

7 The Census, 20:50

    (*Lucius meets*) twelve-year-old Jesus in Nazareth

8 Pontius Pilate, 23:11

    Twenty years later, Barabbas the zealot (and unnamed Judas)

    The Baptist, 26:55

        (*Lucius sees John*)

9 Ambushing the Romans, 28:33

10 John Meets Jesus, 33:00

    John the Baptist meets Mary—"He is without sin"

11 Desert Temptation, 36:48

12 Fisher of Men, 41:16

> John's disciples, John and Andrew, follow Jesus, 41:26
>
> Simon, "who shall be called Peter," 42:05

13 Voice of an Agitator, 43:09

> Tiberius's plaques in Jerusalem (*Lucius* and Pilate)

14 John Imprisoned [*Lucius arrests*], 48:06

15 Healer at Work, 51:58

16 Uncast Stone, 54:48

> Two messiahs for Judas—one of peace, one of war

17 Familiar Face, 59:47

> Jesus, wanting to see John the Baptist, meets *Lucius*

18 Blessing through Bars, 1.02:18

19 Madman and Magdalene, 1.04:01

> Magdalene meets Mary the mother of Jesus, 1.05:35

20 So It Is Reported, 1.07:52

21 John's Request, 1.10:38

> *Lucius visits John the Baptist in prison* (Lk. 7:19)

22 Whatever Salome Wants, 1.12:30

23 Salome's Dance, 1.15:29

24 Head on a Platter, 1.17:41

25 Message to John, 1.19:50

> (Lk. 7:22, 24-28)

26 A Great Multitude, 1.21:51

> *Pilate tells Lucius to go hear Jesus's Sermon*

27 Sermon on the Mount 1.25:09

> *Beatitudes* (Lk. 6:20; Mt. 5:5-7, 4, 8-10)
>
> Testing question (cf. Lk. 11:16)
>
> Beatitudes (cont.) (Lk. 6:22)
>
> Kingdom within (Lk. 17:21), 1.27:42
>
> Inherit eternal life? (cf. Lk. 10:25-29), 1.27:57
>
> Messiah? (Jn 10:11), 1.28:35
>
> Fulfill law and prophets (Mt. 5:17)
>
> Love your enemies (Lk. 6:27; Mt. 5:46)
>
> Why eat with sinners? (Mt. 9:12-13 pars.), 1.29:14

      Cannot serve two masters (Mt. 6:24; Lk. 16:13), 1.29:37

      Be not anxious (Mt. 6:25-28)

      Heavy-laden (Mt. 11:28), 1.30:50

      Son of Man comes to serve (Mt. 20:28; Mk 10:45, but without "ransom"), 1.31:15

      Service (Mt. 20:26-27; Mk 10:43-44)

      From Satan? (Mk 3:24; Lk. 11:18; Mk 3:23b), 1.31:36

      Son of God? (Jn 10:37-38, but without "Father in me"), 1.32:06

      Ask God to destroy Romans; do not tempt God (Mt. 4:7; Lk. 4:12), 1.32:28

          Shot of Lucius

      Faith of mustard seed (Mt. 17:20-21), 1.32:44

      Judge not (Mt. 7:1-3, 5), 1.33:04

      Do not give holy to dogs (Mt. 7:6)

      Ask and receive (Mt. 7:7-11)

      Golden rule (Mt. 7:12, although he says "law of the prophets")

28 The Lord's Prayer (Mt. 6:9-13), 1.35:05

29 Reactions, 1.37:44

      Lucius reports peace/love Sermon to Pilate/Herod

30 Jesus and the Apostles, 1.39:16

      Jesus's task to keep his disciples from the doubting cities

      "Receive without payment" (Mt. 10:8, 16-23), 1.41:13

31 Fire and Water, 1.41:54

      Lucius uncovers Barabbas's weapons "factory"

32 Intermission, 1.45:30

33 Entr'acte, 1.46:15

34 Eyes toward Jerusalem, 1.50:35

      Lucius and Pilate: The work of Barabbas and Jesus

      Jesus and his (prescient) mother, 1.51:56

35 Entry into the City, 1.53:28

36 To the Slaughter, 1.55:58

37 "I [Judas] will force His hand," 2.01:02

38 The Last Supper, 2.02:49

      Judas leaves before the Eucharist

39 Garden Torment, 2.08:38

      Judas at Caiaphas's house, 2.08:42

      Judas, the Temple police, and the Romans, 2.12:10

40 Betrayed and Denied, 2.13:00

41 On Trial, 2.16:16

> "He has been judged by Caiaphas; guilty on two counts," 2.16:58

> *Lucius as Jesus's advocate*

42 "What is truth?" 2.20:52

43 Still Made of Clay, 2.22:25

44 Scourged and Crowned, 2.25:41

45 Free Men, 2.28:27

> *Lucius asks Barabbas if he knows Jesus, releasing him*

46 Procession to Calvary, 2.32:05

> (Silence; there are no shouting crowds)

47 Crucifixion, 2.35:27

> Judas and Barabbas watch

48 "It is finished," 2.38:36

49 Bodies Claimed, 2.41:00

> *Lucius and Claudia kneel: "He is truly the Christ"*

> Barabbas finds Judas's hanging body

50 "He is risen," 2.44:31

51 With You Always, 2.46:33

52 Exit Music, 2.48:39

NOTES

1. The French star Jean Gabin played Pilate while the relatively unknown Robert Le Vignan played Jesus (Baugh 1997: 13). Le Vignan was an outspoken anti-Semite, fascist, and a Nazi collaborator who was imprisoned and then fled the country after the war.
2. See Kinnard and Davis (1992: 56–7), Page (2005), and Hebron (2016b: 81–91). For reflections on Jesus's silence in this "talkie," see Shepherd (2016b: 276–8).
3. The first US "talkie" was *The Lawton Story* (1949), an extremely low-budget roadshow production of a passion play presented in Lawton, OK, since 1926. The film shows play preparations, the play itself, and a sentimental tale in which a young girl leads her evil uncle to faith by convincing him to see the play. See Kinnard and Davis (1992: 62–5) and Hall (2018). *Jesus Town USA* (2014) is a more recent, less pious take on the Lawton passion.

   Rev. James K. Friedrich created Cathedral Films in 1939 to produce religious films. See *Gospel Films Archives* (n.d.), Lindvall and Quicke (2011: 34–40), and Suit (2017). Friedrich's Jesus films include *The Great Commandment* (1939), *The Living Christ Series* (1951, NBC miniseries), *I Beheld His Glory* (1953, a TV movie constructed from passion material in the miniseries), and *Day of Triumph* (1954, Century Films). Light sometimes represents Jesus, who does not otherwise appear in *Great Commandment*. The director (Irving Pichel) "voices" Jesus. The Good Samaritan parable leads the Zealot Joel to forego his plan to force Jesus into revolt and to embrace his "brother," the Roman soldier Longinus (converted at the cross). Robert Wilson played Jesus in the other productions, with Lowell Gilmore taking the role of Pilate. In *I Beheld His Glory*, Cornelius, the centurion at the cross, tells the Jesus story in flashback and converts after hearing Thomas's resurrection message.

While it opens with a striking medium shot of Jesus teaching (the sower parable), *Day of Triumph* is also primarily a flashback, but from the Zealot Zadok (Lee J. Cobb, receiving top billing) and Andrew the disciple. The film anticipates Ray's political machinations. Zadok, the true Zealot mastermind, has long-range plans for freedom, but Judas stumbles onto an opportunity when Zadok offhandedly says Caiaphas would never arrest Jesus, because it would lead to revolt. Accordingly, Judas arranges the arrest, but Zadok's men's demand for Barabbas (a relatively insignificant character) dashes Judas's hopes. As the film ends, Zadok reflects on Zealot failures and wonders if universal spiritual salvation might be a loftier goal. The resurrected Jesus appears, settling the issue. See Kinnard and Davis (1992: 95–8), Friedrich (n.d.), Hebron (2016b: 99–103), Page (2017a), and Suit (2017: 143–63).

4   Three biblical epics were the highest grossing films of individual years: *Quo Vadis* (1951), *The Ten Commandments* (1956), and *Ben-Hur* (1959). The last two were also in the decade's top ten.
5   *Hail, Caesar!* (2016) mocks Jesus's epic marginality by having a studio gofer ask the actor playing Jesus on the cross (seen only from behind) if he is a principal or an extra.
6   The 70 mm makes the film's width greater than its height.
7   MGM added the voiceovers, written by Ray Bradbury, after Ray lost editorial control of the film (Andrew 1991: 181–2). If one watches Jesus films chronologically, the intertitles' absence is palpable. Welles's narration, however, is as intrusive, authoritative, "scriptural," disruptive, and dominating. No character speaks until Joseph requests a room (13:44 minutes in). Welles's famous voice sets scenes, notes the passage of time, explains ancient customs, reports scientifically troubling miracles, gives inside views (e.g., that Judas must decide between two messiahs; even the twelve wanted revolution), defines Judas's betrayal as his testing of God (contrasted with the prayerful, obedient Jesus in Gethsemane), and ends the story by reporting (all but one) resurrection appearances (Walsh 2003: 126).
8   The Herodians (and later Pilate) replace DeMille's Caiaphas as villains. John Farrow, who wrote the film's original script (titled *Son of Man*), and was also to direct, claimed that he left the project because producer Samuel Bronston wished to "whitewash" the Jews. Ray also claimed he wanted to avoid anti-Semitism (Kreidel 1977: 190). The film omits many gospel anti-Semitisms: for example, the Sermon's antitheses; most controversy pericopes; the temple cleansing; the Sanhedrin trial; and oracles about Jerusalem's destruction. Given the film's plot, the reduction of the mob's choice of Barabbas to Lucius's report is perhaps most significant. Accordingly, neither Pilate's handwashing nor the blood curse (Mt. 27:25) appears.
9   The film reduces most miracles to reports by Lucius or Welles. Ray does offer an extreme closeup of Jesus's eyes during the healing of a blind man. Jesus's shadow dominates Welles's "time of miracles" narration and his resurrection appearance in the final Sea of Galilee scene.
10 Only Luke mentions Roman taxation in the nativity (2:1-5) and in the charge against Jesus before Pilate (23:2).
11 Only *Son of Man* (2006) makes this gospel incident as thematically significant.
12 Thring played Pilate in *Ben-Hur* (1959).
13 Lucius fulfills narrative functions like those of the voiceovers. See n7 above. Lucius is the audience's guide into the Herodian and Roman scenes, where he explains Jewish customs

and Roman law and order, assesses threats to Rome, and relates the Jesus story to the elite. He is present in most of the film's important Jesus scenes (for a list, see DVD Chapters). He has private conversations with almost every important film character, often expressing what seem the film's own evaluative standards. As the film has so many connections with the Gospel of Luke (e.g., locating Jesus in history, focusing on the Jews' tragedy [or suffering], and presenting a non-salvific passion [see Walsh 2003: 121–46]), it is tempting to associate Lucius with Luke. Also note the concern for witnesses in Luke (e.g., 1:1-4; 23:49; 24:48; Acts 1:8, 21-22). Lucius improves on the non-witness Luke by being an eyewitness.

14 Her most famous role was as the protagonist in a stage version of Shaw's *Saint Joan*.
15 Ryan is famous for playing tortured souls and angry villains. He won an Oscar for Best Supporting Actor in his role as the anti-Semitic murderer in *Crossfire* (1947). He also appeared in several other Ray films, including *Born to Be Bad* (1950), *Flying Leathernecks* (1951), and *On Dangerous Ground* (1961).
16 All three women have larger roles than in previous Jesus films, except for Salome films. See Vander Stichele (2018).
17 He is known primarily for playing brash, tough "guys," particularly on television.
18 A relative newcomer at the time he played Judas, Torn was later nominated six times for an Emmy for his role on HBO's *The Larry Sanders Show* (winning once).
19 Gerald Forshey says Barabbas's character depends upon Lk. 23:19 (1992: 88), but it also depends on US cinema's repeated story of the revolutionary establishment of a free society. See Wood (1989) and Deleuze (1997: 31, 141–51).
20 Hunter had early success and then a revival with his role in *The Searchers* (1956). He also starred alongside Robert Wagner in Ray's *The True Story of Jesse James* (1957). Most remember him for his matinee idol looks. Bronston cast Hunter as Jesus because of his eyes. See Forshey (1992: 89).
21 In scenes like these and in other long shots, the 70 mm is quite effective. The film also uses barren Spanish landscapes effectively.
22 Babington and Evans say the film follows the Hollywood biopic pattern: self-recognition, ordeal, triumph/tragedy (1993: 128). While the voiceover says Jesus "brought his soul forth in the [cinematic?] light to be … known," it is an incredibly brief, almost thematically empty scene for its biopic function. Contrast the more effective Gethsemane "self-recognition" scene that begins *The Passion of the Christ* (2004). On the biopic, see Custen (1992). On the Jesus biopic, see Reinhartz (2007).
23 The revolutionary Judas comes ultimately from Thomas de Quincey (and certain German precursors). See Walsh (2010: 67–9, 113–16, 142–4). While hinted at by DeMille, the Judas of *Day of Triumph* is a clearer precursor of Ray's. See n3.
24 The music takes the place of any audible blessing from Jesus. It swells at the end of almost every scene. Miklós Rózsa composed the music, utilizing a seventy-four-piece symphony orchestra. He also created the music for *Quo Vadis* and *Ben-Hur*, winning one of his Oscars for the latter.
25 Antipas and Claudia wonder if such reports could be true, but Pilate thinks them ridiculous nonsense. In another innovative scene, Magdalene (not yet named), like the Baptist before her, comes to Mary to understand Jesus. Mary, the intercessor, welcomes her with her son's story of lost sheep (Mt. 18:12-14).
26 In contrast to the fates of DeMille's Magdalene and the protagonist of William Dieterle's 1953 *Salome* (Rita Hayworth), this titillation does not lead to salvation.

27 People traipse through the Holy Land to learn about Jesus in *Ben-Hur* (1925), *The Robe* (1953), and *Risen* (2016; cf. *Gospel Road* 1973). Lucius's skepticism makes him precursor of historical critics, as is the Jew Pilate blackmails into spying on Jesus in Theissen (1987).

28 The filmmakers advertised that it took more than a month to prepare and shoot the Sermon, with eighty-one separate setups and twenty-one days of shooting. A long dolly shot required more than 160 feet of track on a fifty-eight-degree mountain slope (Forshey 1992: 91). Extras swelled Jesus's audience to 7,000 people. Ray imagined a twenty- to thirty-minute Sermon, but lost editorial control (Baugh 1997: 21, 243 n24).

29 Cf. Jesus walking in the distance as *From the Manger to the Cross*'s (1912) Baptist identifies the lamb of God and the post-crucifixion shepherd passing under the cross in *Jesus Christ Superstar* (1973). Shepherd is an important biblical image for both God and (Davidic) king. The Sermon, which Welles introduces by saying the "flocks" came to hear "and be healed," is more salvific than is Jesus's death.

30 Jesus's teaching is also quite prominent in the little-known *The Great Commandment*. See n3 above.

31 It resembles a modern press conference (Baugh 1997: 21).

32 Ray uses the camera interpretatively by offering different shots of Jesus (cf. the Sermon in *Il vangelo* 1964) and by highlighting particular people in the crowd at appropriate moments.

33 As this scene takes place two plus hours into the film, *King of Kings* gives far less time proportionally to the passion than previous Jesus films.

34 As Judas leaves, Welles comments that Judas wishes to prove (test) the Messiah.

35 The Supper teaching includes a reference to bloodshed for the remission of sins (Mt. 26:28). Further, when Lucius frees Barabbas, he tells him to go look at the one who dies for him.

36 At a Roman trial, these words are dangerously close to the Zealot motto: "No king but God."

37 Jesus's appearances in red (like the Romans) constitute Ray's distinctive Jesus: the Sermon and his sufferings. Only the wilderness trial rivals these scenes in importance.

38 At various points, Caiaphas, Pilate, and Lucius remark that Jesus is different.

39 The Via Dolorosa includes the traditional elements, including Veronica and her veil—although the "true icon" does not appear.

40 Except for "I thirst," the film repeats Jesus's traditional last words, including the cry of desolation (Mk 15:34; Mt. 27:46). The cross's violence, like that of John's beheading and Jesus's scourging, is largely offscreen, in keeping with Hays Code guidelines.

41 Ray's cinema is off-center, not quite fitting generic expectations (Kreidel 1977: 28, 43–59). See, for example, *Johnny Guitar* (1954), in which women play roles usually reserved for men.

42 The subjectivizing of religion in the United States fosters Jesus's political irrelevance. Ray and his Jesus may be discontent with empire, but they are not prophetically or apocalyptically opposed to it. The film includes none of Jesus's difficult sayings or actions. Contrast *Il vangelo*'s Jesus's prophetic critique of empire/institution.

43 Hauntingly, Adolf Eichmann's Jerusalem trial began in April 1961.

44 Compare the equally ambiguous end of *Barabbas* (1962). See Walsh (2008a).

45 Such ambiguity is often a big-budget picture strategy to allow different types of viewers to be comfortable with the film. However, Kraemer asks whether the film's relative lack of success meant that it was dealing with uncomfortable issues (2013: 171). Intriguingly, Kinnard and Davis say the film looks better now than when it was released (1992: 133).

46 French filmmakers and Martin Scorsese greatly admire Ray's cinema. Arguably, Scorsese's Jesus is more representative of most Ray protagonists than Ray's own Jesus is.

47 Babington and Evans succinctly say that, with respect to DeMille, Ray's film performs "a double act of transgressive oedipal intertextuality": secular filial Hunter succeeds pious fatherly Warner (1993: 138).

48 Given her extreme youth, Salome is another troubled teenager, and the Herodian family rivals any dysfunctional family in *Rebel Without a Cause*.

49 Critics typically say that cultures conceive the beautiful and Jesus after their own image (Pelikan 1985) and that Jesus images tend to enforce the cultural dominant (Graybill 2018). Edward Blum and Paul Harvey, however, use the story of the September 1963 white supremacist bombing of the Sixteenth Street Baptist Church in Birmingham, Alabama, to hold together their more complicated "racial" Christ-imaging. The bombing killed four young girls and left a hole in the stained-glass representation of a comforting, white Christ, long acceptable to the congregation. Children in Wales collected money to replace the glass, resulting in the representation of a Black Christ in the *Wales Window for Alabama*. During his presidency, President Obama visited the church to meditate before the glass and the portraits of the four young martyrs (2012: 1–5, 23–4, 276–7). Movie buffs will remember another complicated site: Walter Salman's *Head of Christ* hangs behind the pulpit in the interracial, poor church established in *The Apostle* (1997; Blum and Harvey 2012: 256–9). One could also complicate the beautiful American Jesus if one pursued ideas in *American Beauty* (1999), where death and a plastic bag are as beautiful as traditional American Dream images.

50 To quote Cassidy, who Christ figures the protagonist in *The Wrestler* (2008): they "have the same hair …. Sacrificial ram." The hair has connections to the American teenager and counterculture that follows Ray.

51 See also Fiorenzo Mattu who plays Jesus in *Su Re* (2012; available only in Sardinian and Italian). Lloyd Baugh (2018) discusses *Su Re* in terms of Isa. 53:2-3.

52 On these alternative cinematic Jesuses, see Friesen (2008), Bakker (2009; 2013), the articles in Walsh, Staley, and Reinhartz (2013), and Zwick (2021).

7

Il vangelo secondo Matteo (The Gospel According to St. Matthew)

Pier Paolo Pasolini, director, Arco Films, 1964

PLOT SUMMARY: A SWORD FOR THE PEOPLE

Those accustomed to the Hollywood or Cinecittà biblical epic find themselves in unfamiliar territory: black-and-white photography, not rich Technicolor, and the percussive, vibrant "Gloria" from the Missa Luba, set in the musical styles of the Congo.[1] Bach and Mozart follow, but so do American blues.[2] Pasolini shot the film primarily in southern Italy's[3] countryside and villages, casting locals and some of his intellectual, artistic friends[4] rather than professional actors.[5] The camera and editing are jarring (the Hollywood style hides both). Because of these features, some contemporary reviewers described the film as representing a local village pageant, not a historical reproduction (see Kinnard and Davis 1992: 166).

Pasolini described his film as "analogical" (Stack 1969: 78–82). Instead of recreating a "past" that reflects the present, analogy brings something from the past jarringly into the present, revealing similarities and differences.[6] (Pasolini often filmed "the classics" to this end.) In this case, the past is Matthew's gospel, which Pasolini brings into the present, eschewing Hollywood subplots and invented characters.[7] He strove to translate "Matthew" into images. Christian art and music are, however, everywhere. Pasolini prided himself on "contamination," a mixture or pastiche of film and music styles. For Pasolini, the film was not just "Matthew," but Matthew plus 2,000 years of church history (Stack 1969: 82–7).[8] While he began filming with a "sacred style" that he had used to Christ figure sub-proletariat characters in his first two films (*Accattone* 1961; *Mamma Roma* 1962), he turned eventually to something documentary-like or neorealistic (Stack 1969: 83–4).[9] Anticipating his famous desire for a "cinema of poetry," Pasolini sought visuals reflecting Matthew's own violent, elliptical style to present a Christ that "radically contradicts the appearance and shape that life assumes for modern man: a gray orgy of cynicism, irony, brutality, compromise and conformism" (in Greene 1990: 73; see also Testa 1994: 197). Accordingly, Pasolini's Jesus is often in frontal closeup; confrontational, rather than conversational. He is a violent, social critic—the most John-the-Baptist-like Jesus in Jesus film. He brings a sword (Mt. 10:34)[10]—the verse Pasolini says inspired the film (in Testa 1994: 208 n39).

After the credits (accompanied by music), the film opens in silence, with closeups of a peasant girl and an older man. A long shot follows. The first visibly pregnant Mary (unidentified) in film stands in front of an unfinished archway. Joseph (unidentified) walks away, down a rocky road to a nearby village. With sounds of children playing nearby, he falls asleep against a wall. A white-clad adolescent female angel appears, speaking Mt. 1:20-21. The "Gloria" returns, and Joseph walks back down the long, rocky road to Mary as the narrator recites Mt.1:23/Isa. 7:14. After several closeups cutting between Mary and Joseph, they both smile, but never speak.

An abrupt cut segues to the wise men riding into a noisy village and meeting with a smiling, perfidious Herod. Later, as they descend a hill toward the holy family, Odetta's rendering of "Sometimes I Feel Like a Motherless Child" (an African American spiritual popular during the Civil Rights Movement) is heard. Smiling children are everywhere. As the wise men leave, the adolescent angel sends them another way, warning Joseph to flee to Egypt. As children watch them depart, the narrator recites Mt. 2:15/Hos. 11:1. Herod's guards rush downhill, brandishing swords. Swords flail; soldiers grab and throw women and babies; bodies roll downhill and litter the ground (one in bloody closeup) in the most gruesome film slaughter of the innocents to its time. The narrator recites Mt. 2:18/Jer. 31:25, and Sergei Prokofiev's score for Sergei Eisenstein's *Alexander Nevsky* (1938) plays in the background. Herod's death scene follows (lasting over a minute—although Matthew conveys this in one subordinate clause), seemingly just recompense. After Herod's death, the peasant angel sends the holy family to Nazareth.

Following Matthew closely, Pasolini pans up the rocky Jordan to John baptizing. Again, the background music is "Sometimes I Feel Like a Motherless Child." John calls the people and religious leaders, passing on the hill above, to repent (3:2, 7-10). Suddenly, the adult Jesus (Enrique Irazoqui)[11] appears in closeup, wearing a black headscarf. (The background music is Mozart's *Maurerische Trauermusik in C minor*.) Kneeling for baptism, Jesus looks heavenward, and the camera pulls back to a long shot from the heavens. The narrator provides the heavenly voice. An abrupt cut leads to Jesus praying (orant style) in the wilderness and being tempted by a richly dressed Satan (in black).

Matthew moves to Jesus's ministry with a subordinate clause indicating the Baptist's arrest. Pasolini's longer scene visualizes the uncompromising social critic's fate. The Baptist languishes in a dark prison, a glimmer of light touching his face, as the narrator recites Mt. 4:16/Isa. 9:2. Suddenly, Jesus tramps through the countryside, demanding repentance (4:17) from peasants he meets by happenstance on the road.

Smiling, Jesus calls fisherman to his work (the Red Army choir performs "Oh You, Wide Steppe" in the background). Now, Pasolini freely rearranges Matthew to emphasize a "to the work/revolt" message. After a call of the disciples (with closeups), Jesus strides before them, turning around to instruct them, as they and the camera race to follow. Jesus's teaching focuses on their peasant work (9:27-28; omitting the more religious 10:1-15) and on society's opposition to them (10:16-20, 22, 28-31, 34-37, 39). Unlike Matthew, which begins Jesus's teaching with blessings, Pasolini's angrier Jesus warns of suffering. (Mozart's *Maurerische Trauermusik in C minor*, from the baptism, returns as background.) A closeup of Jesus's angry face accompanies the crucial Mt. 10:34.

Jesus walks, always ahead and sometimes looking back. He kneels in prayer in front of a tower full of sick and possessed, apparently healing them all (their cries grow silent) and then heals a leper who approaches him (8:2-4). A cut away from the leper and a cut back to the healed man accomplish the miracle, which is accompanied by the Missa Luba's "Gloria."

Finally, Jesus delivers the Sermon a-walking (not on the Mount). At the beginning and end, people follow, but the bulk of the Sermon comes from a lonely, isolated, talking-head Jesus caught in full frontal closeup—in at least twelve different scenes with different clothing, lighting, background, and sound: (1) 5:3-12; (2) 7:9-12; (3) 5:17; (4) 5:13-15; (5) 6:19-20, 24; (6) 6:3-4; (7) 5:38-39, 43-45; (8) 7:1-3; (9) 6:7-13; (10) 6:25-34; (11) 7:13-14; (12) 11:25-30. This Sermon stresses God's provision, the demand for kingdom allegiance, love of enemies, and the hope for the people's liberation.[12] In the finale, Jesus holds a child as he offers peasants a different yoke.

The authorities, who consider Jesus demonic, plot to kill him (12:1-14, 23-34). But God's servant (angrily reciting 12:18/Isa. 42:1-3 as he walks away from the leaders) provides miraculously for the people: healing a lame man (Blind Willie Johnson singing "Dark was the Night, Cold was the Ground" in the background); feeding the 5,000 (14:15-21); and walking on water (14:22-31).[13] The parables (Mt. 13) are conspicuously absent.

While visibly happy with children (whom Pasolini adds lavishly to scenes) and responding kindly to the Baptist's question (11:4-24), Jesus is increasingly confrontational. He refuses to provide signs, dismisses all those not with him, pronounces judgments on cities, dismisses his family (with a closeup of Pasolini's mother in the role of Mary; see Figure 7.1) and hometown in favor of those who do God's will, and sends away the rich and other would-be disciples.

Ominously, Antipas dispatches the Baptist after a jacks-playing Salome nonchalantly asks for his head during an elaborate party. The rulers and wealthy are callous. The people and social critics are disposable—if noticed. The film's first part ends with Jesus's sadness about the Baptist's fate: the dead must bury the dead; Jesus himself has no place (8:20, 22).

The films second part opens with the narrator pronouncing judgment upon "the city" (cf. Isa. 14:31). Peter makes his confession, Jesus names him the church's rock,[14] and Jesus, always walking ahead, turns back toward "Satan" to make two rapid predictions of his passion (16:21; 17:22-23). The transfiguration is absent. Children surround the smiling Jesus as he speaks of children and the kingdom, humility, and forgiveness (18:3-8, 12-14, 21-22).[15]

The tone changes abruptly as Jesus looks down on Jerusalem and predicts his passion a third time (20:18-29), and changes abruptly again when he enters the city (with two animals, ambient crowd noise, smiling children's voices, and the Missa Luba "Gloria" again). Religious leaders watch from a balcony as Jesus cleanses the temple— represented by a building's courtyard (21:15-16). Even though Jesus retires to a house outside the city, the confrontation continues. He prays over the city and angrily curses a fig tree, which withers immediately (as Judas notes). Then Jesus is in the courtyard again for the Mt. 21-22 controversies with the leaders (except for 22:41-46) and judgmental parables (except for 22:1-13).

Pasolini's Jesus offers his second great sermon (Mt. 23), the negative form of the Sermon (on the Mount) and the only Matthean teaching section used in its entirety. Jesus's audience is more visible than Jesus is, as Pasolini films from the back of the crowd—sometimes so far away that Jesus's words seem a voiceover. Pasolini breaks Jesus's harangue against the leaders (cf. the Baptist's tirade in 3:7-20) into three scenes (23:1-12, 13-24, 25-39) marked by increasing police presence and street tumult. A medium shot of Jesus accompanies the sermon's sorrowful end (including 24:2, where Jesus looks back at the city from the road below). The background music is the Russian folk song, "You Fell Victim." Omitting the rest of Mt. 24-25, Pasolini cuts immediately to the leaders' murderous plot (26:4-5).[16]

A cut to the withered fig tree leads to a cut revealing a peasant woman anointing Jesus's head, which provokes Judas's protestations (harmonizing 26:6-13 with Jn 12:3-8). Judas runs immediately to the priests where closeups capture his smiling betrayal.

At the supper, Judas dips to eat before Jesus's betrayal prediction. He also eats the broken bread (but does not drink the wine onscreen). The background music is the "Kol Nidre."[17] As they leave the room, Jesus predicts Peter's denial (accompanied by Bach's "Erbarme dich, mein Gott"). In the garden, Jesus paces restlessly (as Pasolini alternates between silences, ambient noise, and a whistling reprise of Salome's dance music, uniting Jesus with the Baptist yet again). When the guard arrives, Jesus rushes to stop his disciples' resistance (accompanied by Bach's "Wir setzen uns mit Tränen"). Although he is under arrest, Jesus leads the guard to Caiaphas as Peter follows.

Pasolini shoots the Jewish trial (in the temple courtyard) cinema verité style, from the back of the crowd, with a handheld camera. Heads sometimes obscure the camera's view, which is more invested in Peter's denial than in Jesus's silence and confession. As Jesus is beaten, Pasolini offers a striking closeup of Peter's eyes, then leaves Jesus to his fate, following Peter's weeping departure and sobbing collapse in the streets (Bach's "Erbarme dich, mein Gott" returns). Then, Pasolini cuts to Judas watching Jesus from the crowd, as Caiaphas orders Jesus's death and sends him to Pilate. After another closeup (with "Dark was the Night, Cold was the Ground" as background), Judas throws the blood money at the priests' feet and then runs along a hillside, disrobing as he runs. Finally, he hangs himself from another leafless tree, wearing only a loincloth.[18]

Pasolini also shoots the very brief Roman trial cinema verité. The handheld camera moves from extremely long shots of Jesus to medium shots and closeups of Mary and John (with several closeups of John's eyes). Interestingly, Pilate never asks whether Jesus is the king of the Jews.[19] An offscreen speaker delivers the heinous blood curse (27:25).

After mockery by partially clad soldiers, Jesus carries his cross, already inscribed with INRI. Pasolini focuses here and at the cross on John and Mary's sufferings (another Johannine element). At times, one sees the cross bobbing through the crowd as if through waves. An extreme long shot catches Jesus ascending the hill with one thief already crucified and another being laid upon his cross. As the audience hears hammering and screaming, a camera from the top of the hill shows Jesus's group approaching. After Jesus's cross is raised, Pasolini cuts between long shots of Jesus and closeups of Mary's contorted face, and a medium shot of her supported by two other women (a cruciform).[20] After a closeup of Jesus's face, the screen fades to black, and the narrator recites Isa. 6:9-10. The cry of desolation follows. When Jesus screams, an earthquake destroys the city. The centurion's confession is noticeably absent. A final closeup shows Jesus's slumped head (the background music is Mozart's *Maurerische Trauermusik in C minor*, echoing its use in the baptism and missionary discourse).

The deposition and burial[21] also feature Mary's suffering (as well as several shots of boys and young men at the tomb). When Mary and others bring flowers to the tomb, the tomb blows open as the Missa Luba "Gloria" erupts again (and continues until the film's end). In another echo of the opening, the adolescent, peasant, white-clad angel appears, now with the resurrection message to a smiling Mary in closeup (not Magdalene). As at the beginning of Jesus's ministry, peasant farmers run, carrying farm implements and children, as Jesus now teaches them (and his disciples) in voiceover (28:18-20). A final closeup of Jesus accompanies 28:20b.

MEMORABLE CHARACTERS

1 Pasolini's Jesus is angrier and more confrontational than any previous cinematic Jesus. An aloof Gramscian intellectual/artist providing the people with a revolutionary myth,[22] he is young, meticulously groomed, and clean; unlike the peasants and poor attracted to him.

2 The people/disciples are hardly distinct characters. The children are joyful, but the populist leaders are angry, and the people suffer. During the passion, Pasolini prioritizes the suffering of Mary in particular, as well as that of Peter, Judas, and John; the move maintains Stabat Mater traditions while shifting the focus from Jesus's unique, atoning suffering to the people's suffering at the hands of society (cf. *Intolerance* 1916).

MEMORABLE VISUALS

1 Peasant Joseph and (pregnant) Mary.
2 Slaughter of the innocents and Herod's prolonged death.
3 Closeups of Jesus's angry, confrontational face as he turns back to talk while walking away.
4 Medium shots of Jesus smiling with children.
5 Barren trees.
6 Jesus lost from view, from the back of the crowd, during his harangue against the rulers and in his trials.
7 The religious leaders' medieval headgear (see n16).
8 The lingering closeups of handsome young men, whose beauty contrasts strikingly with the plain, aged women, leads critics to speak of the phallocentric camera (see Viano 1993: 11–16; Baugh 1997: 101; Maggi 2009).

Figure 7.1 Jesus rejects his mother in *Il vangelo secondo Matteo,* directed by Pier Paolo Pasolini, Arco Films, 1964. All rights reserved.

KEY AUTHORITY/SCRIPTURE

1 Pasolini's unique visuals, abrupt editing, and eclectic musical choices give the film a compelling aesthetic authority.

2 The narrator, who recites biblical quotations (especially the black-screen voiceover of Isa. 6:9-10 at the cross) and delivers the baptism's heavenly voice, has an authority like the silents' intertitles or Orson Welles in *King of Kings* (1961).

3 Repeated closeups of Jesus's confrontational, uncompromising face provide gravitas. Pasolini's Matthew is Gramscian—at least Pasolini's "translation" attempts to counter the hegemony of the people's daily lives.[23] Pasolini rewrites the Matthean ministry so that Jesus calls workers into increasing conflict with the authorities (9:27-28; 10:16-20, 22, 28-31, 34-37, 39) while enjoining them to find succor in traditional spirituality (the Sermon ends with 11:25-30). Abandoning Matthew's "five teaching sections" structure (5-7; 10; 13; 18; 24-25),[24] Pasolini moves part of Mt. 10 forward; fragments and rearranges Mt. 5-7; utilizes about half of Mt. 18; and takes only one verse from Mt. 24-25. He also omits most of Matthew's miracles. His focus is the sword (Mt. 10:34), which his Jesus takes to the Jerusalem authorities (using almost all of Mt. 21-22) and which climaxes with street preaching (Mt. 23). The passion (of one provoking such unrest) is more understandable than that of any other cinema Jesus, so Matthew's passion narrative follows (Mt. 26-27) with minor modifications. The return of the film's first song, the Missa Luba "Gloria" in the finale, expresses the ongoing hope for the people's liberation.

CULTURAL LOCATION/GENRE: ART HOUSE CINEMA

Feeling that Marxism had failed to liberate the Italian people, Pasolini made *Il vangelo* to reinvigorate Marxism with the new Catholicism of Pope John Paul XXIII, to whom he dedicated the film. Pasolini's neorealist treatment, from a believer's perspective of his new national-popular myth (Stack 1969: 82, 86), allowed the Roman Catholic Church to embrace the film (see Tatum 2013: 120–2).[25] A 1995 Vatican list of the best films included *Il vangelo*—the only Jesus film on the list. While critical reviews at the time were mixed, religious academics still often describe Pasolini's film as the best Jesus film ever produced. Pasolini's angry, social reformer Jesus—who criticizes society but does not actually induce social reform—mirrors some academics' own perceived role in society.

In Italy and France, the film fit into a rich history of cinematic experimentation and pointedly ideological films.[26] In the United States, the film premiered at a 1966 benefit for the Msgr. William Kelly School. Thereafter, it was seen in art houses and on college campuses. Supreme Court decisions disallowing studio monopolies of production-distribution (1948) and granting freedom of speech rights to cinema (1952) were factors allowing a small but growing audience access to art (usually "foreign") films. This college-educated, café cultural niche, bored with "factory" films, received Pasolini as they did the more popular Ingmar Bergman. *Il vangelo* was (difficult) art, not entertainment (see Stern, Jefford, and DeBona 1999: 114–18).

DIRECTOR

Pasolini's early films (*Accattone*, *Mamma Roma*) depict the desperate, downward spiral of the urban marginal (and the false hope of petit bourgeoisie life). Death is a fait accompli from the beginning, but Pasolini depicts these lives "reverentially," Christ figuring Accattone (beggar, scrounger) and Ettore with Christian icons and music. Dante, *St Matthew's Passion*, angels, and death dreams dominate *Accattone*. At one point, Ettore, the son of the prostitute protagonist (Anna Magnani) in *Mamma Roma*, lies ill in his prison bed in a pose resembling Mantegna's *Lamentation of Christ* (1480). The contamination of style and content provokes.

This contamination reaches its height in *La ricotta*, Pasolini's short included in *Ro. Go.Pa.G.* (including shorts directed by Rossellini, Godard, and Gregoretti [1963]). In *La ricotta*, a parodic "Pasolini" (Orson Welles) directs the filming of a Hollywood-style passion play in bright, expensive color. The bored actors are hardly pious. Pasolini's camera catches them in almost orgiastic scenes. Two men dance the twist in front of the crucifixion. The filming of a "Mannerist" deposition tableau (cf. Pontormo; Rosso Fiorentino) degenerates from a staid sterility into profanity. The story of the Hollywoodish epic's filming is in black and white and concentrates on a local peasant, Stracci (Rags), who plays the good thief crucified with Christ and is constantly abused by the richer crew members. By chance, Stracci finally gets enough to eat and gorges himself on ricotta. After taking his place on the cross for filming (with requisite thunderstorm), Stracci dies of indigestion—unnoticed—while the crew discusses technical issues. When he fails to supply his scripted line, the director wryly observes that Stracci had to die to be noticed.

La ricotta's shift from sentimentalizing Hollywood epic color to black-and-white Stracci presages *Il vangelo*'s similar aesthetic shifts. Further, *Il vangelo*'s Jesus is, in some ways, an intellectual version of Stracci. Of course, *Il vangelo* is far more hopeful than *La ricotta*—perhaps the most hopeful film in Pasolini's oeuvre.

After *Il vangelo*, Pasolini lost faith in the people's revolution as Italian consumerism increased. *Uccellacci e uccellini* (The Hawks and the Sparrows 1966), about two "innocents" (played by famous Italian comic actor Totò and Ninetto Davilo, Pasolini's lover), marks this turning point (Greene 1990: 80–9). A talking crow, representing leftist (revolutionary) intellectual views, accompanies the duo and eventually tells them a parable about two medieval Franciscans who try to teach hawks and sparrows to love one another, before the predictable end of that project. After a brief news report on the funeral of the long-time leader of the Italian Communist Party, the innocents eat the crow. Neither Christianity nor Marxism seems a viable alternative any longer.[27]

Thereafter, Pasolini, nostalgic for impossible innocence, turned to the exploration (and escape) of mythic pasts (Nowell-Smith 1977: 12). His mythological quartet includes *Edipo re* (1967), *Teorema* (1968), *Porcile* (1969), and *Medea* (1969). *Teorema*, for example, portrays a bourgeoisie family's destruction by a mysterious stranger's (Terence Stamp) arrival, (sexual) love, and departure. The film ends with the father wandering the wilderness (the same location as *Il vangelo*'s temptation scene) and screaming in despair.[28] Matters are similar in the Trilogy of Life: *Il Decameron* (1971); *I racconti di Canterbury* (1972); and *Il fiore delle Mille u una Notte* (1974). Seen by many as escapes to exotic pasts/ places, these films made Pasolini more mainstream and then angrier and more pessimistic. His last film, for which he may be most famous today, *Salò o le 120 giornate di Sodoma*, cinematizes the Marquis de Sade's dark, violent work. Sometimes considered horror, the film displays the abuses, rapes, and murders perpetuated by fascist libertines (and those they hire). It reflects Pasolini's ideal of a cinema "unconsumable" by bourgeois society (see Greene 1990: 139; Schwartz 1992: 631–41; Maggi 2009).[29]

PROBLEMATIC ISSUE: OWNING INTERPRETATIONS

In George Stevens's *The Greatest Story Ever Told* (1965), Jesus belongs to the church. The film begins and ends in a church apse. While extremely aware that the gospel belongs to the church, Pasolini felt institutional religion held no liberating possibilities (from bourgeois society).[30] At the time he made *Il vangelo*, Pasolini thought that liberation might lie among the marginal, so he removes the gospel from the church and from the four-gospel harmony governing its interpretation to return it to the people. The result disrupts the natural and the (assumed) true, raising the issue of (gospel) interpretation. Something similar happens for a different audience when Pasolini abandons Hollywood and Cinecittà conventions. What does Matthew mean outside those accustomed, familiar boundaries (see Aichele 2002; Walsh 2003: 101–9)? To whom does it belong? What does Matthew look like when translated by an atheist, homosexual, Marxist intellectual and artist? Such questions, of course, belong to ideological or political criticism, all of which trace their origins ultimately to Marx, Nietzsche, and Freud—a trio important to Pasolini (see Viano 1993).

WATERBEARER FILMS, 142 MINUTES, 2003

Widescreen. Italian with English subtitles. No English dubbed track. No DVD Chapters.

DVD Extras

Pier Paolo Pasolini: A Filmmaker's Life, thirty minutes, English. Documentary. Includes some of Pasolini's reflections on the making of *Il vangelo.*
  On *The Gospel of Matthew,* 12:50–14:50
  On religious experience and the power of the Catholic Church in Italy, 21:15–24:10
  On his fascination with the Italian peasantry, 26:00–27:00
  Credits, 27:58

DVD Segments

Wherever possible, DVD segment titles reflect those of the *HarperCollins Study Bible* (NRSV).
Segments 13–15 and 17–26 are indented to demarcate Matthew's Sermons.

(Gospel of John motifs are in italics)

1 Jesus the Messiah's Birth (1:18), 3:04
2 Wise Men's Visit (2:1), 6:40
3 Escape to Egypt (2:13), 14:55
4 Massacre of the Infants (2:16), 17:20
5 Return to Nazareth (2:19), 20:00
6 The Baptist's Proclamation (3:1), 22:47
   John (the youngest disciple) is there, as is his brother James, 23:41
7 Jesus's Baptism (3:13), 26:25
8 Jesus's Temptation (4:1), 28:35
9 Jesus Begins His Galilean Ministry (4:12), 32:00
   John the Baptist in prison, 32:03
   "Repent for the kingdom of heaven is at hand" (4:17), 33:37
10 Jesus Calls the First Disciples (4:18), 33:55
11 Harvest Is Great, the Laborers Few (9:35), 35:45
12 Twelve Apostles (10:1), 36:00
    13 Coming Persecutions (10:16)
    14 Have No Fear (10:26)
    15 Cost of Discipleship (10:34), 38:35
16 Jesus Cleanses a Leper (8:1), 38:44

17 Beatitudes (5:1), 41:35
18 Instructions on Conduct and Prayer (7:7)
19 Fulfilling the Law and the Prophets (5:17)
20 Salt and Light (5:13)
21 Orientation to God (6:19)
22 Piety That God Rewards (6:1)
23 Jesus's Teaching Alters the Law (5:38)
24 Instructions on Conduct and Prayer (7:1)
25 Piety That God Rewards (6:5)
26 Orientation to God (6:25)
27 Jesus as Wisdom's Spokesperson (11:25)
28 Plucking Grain on the Sabbath (12:1), 48:00
Judas keeps the money bag
29 Man with a Withered Hand (12:10), 50:02
30 God's Chosen Servant (12:15)
31 Man with the Withered Hand [again] (12:14), 51:50
32 Feeding the Five Thousand (14:13), 52:07
33 Jesus Walks on the Water (14:22), 54:20
34 Messengers from John the Baptist (11:2), 55:47
35 Woes to Unrepentant Cities (11:20), 58:52
36 Sign of Jonah (12:38), 1.00:00
37 Jesus's True Kindred (12:46), 1.00:46
38 Rejection of Jesus at Nazareth (13:54), 1.02:34
Mary is there; Jesus sheds a tear
39 Rich Young Man (19:16), 1.05:20
40 Jesus Blesses Little Children (19:13), 1.07:17
Jesus picks up a child (perhaps the first time he touches anyone in the film)
Judas tells children to "leave him in peace"
41 Death of John the Baptist (14:1), 1.07:55
Salome, her mother, and the dance, 1.08:40
Jesus has a tear on his cheek when he hears of John's death
42 Jesus's Would-be Followers (8:18), 1.13:00

Part Two, 1.14:15

43 The Narrow and the Wide Gates (7:13)
44 Peter's Declaration about Jesus (16:13), 1.14:50
45 Christ Foretells His Death and Resurrection (16:21), 1.16:11

46 Jesus Again Foretells His Death and Resurrection (17:22), 1.17:10
47 True Greatness (18:1), 1.17:23
   Pasolini's lover, Ninetto Davoli, teases a little boy with a straw hat (1.17:23)
48 "If your hand or foot offend you" (5:29-30)
49 Parable of the Lost Sheep (18:10), 1.18:45
50 Forgiveness (18:21), 1.19:07
51 Jesus Again Foretells His Death and Resurrection (17:22), 1.20:00
52 Triumphal Entry (21:1), 1.20:50
   Lots of children!
53 Jesus Cleanses the Temple (21:12), 1.24:19
   Followed by children into the temple, shouting "Hosanna!"
54 Jesus Curses the Fig Tree (21:18), 1.26:14
55 Authority of Jesus Challenged (21:23), 1.29:00
56 Parable of the Two Sons (21:28), 1.29:55
57 Parable of the Wicked Tenants (21:33), 1.30:44
58 Parable of the Wedding Banquet (22:1)
   No parable, just "few are chosen" (22:14), 1.32:15
59 Question about Paying Taxes (22:15), 1.32:50
60 On the Resurrection of the Dead (22:23), 1.33:40
61 Greatest Commandment (22:34), 1.34:54
   Roman soldiers are in the scene, 1.35:11
62 Jesus Denounces Scribes and Pharisees (23:1), 1.35:26
   Jesus's words start a riot
63 Lament over Jerusalem (23:37), 1.40:50
64 Destruction of the Temple Foretold (24:1), 1.41:50
65 Plot to Kill Jesus (26:1), 1.42:00
   Another view of the withered fig tree (21:19), 1.42:50
66 Anointing at Bethany (26:6), 1.43:00
   John (the "Beloved Disciple") is next to Jesus, on his right
   Judas is the disciple who challenges the "waste"
67 Judas Agrees to Betray Jesus (26:14), 1.45:45
68 Passover with the Disciples (26:20), 1.46:20
69 Institution of the Lord's Supper (26:26), 1.47:25
70 Peter's Denial Foretold (26:30), 1.48:56
   John is beside Jesus as the disciples leave the "upper room"

71 Jesus Prays in Gethsemane (26:36), 1.49:50
Jesus hugs John

72 Jesus's Betrayal and Arrest (26:47), 1.53:38
Lights in the upper left corner of screen (Jn 18:3), 1.53:47-52
Jesus runs back to stop his disciples from drawing swords, 1.54:06
Judas hugs Jesus (but *without a visible kiss,* cf. Jn 18:5), 1.54:22
Peter follows from a distance

73 Jesus before the High Priest (26:57), 1.56:25
Guilty of blasphemy, Jesus should die
Jesus is beaten on the way to Pilate, 1.57:57

74 Peter's Denial of Jesus (26:69), 1.57:58

75 Jesus Brought before Pilate (27:1) 1.59:50
Three men bound, ready to go to Pilate, 2.00:04

76 Judas's Suicide (27:3), 2:01:05

77 Pilate Questions Jesus (27:11), 2.02:33
Mother Mary looks on and hugs John (the other disciple) (cf. Jn 18:15-16)
Mary tries to hold John back as he goes into Pilate's chamber
"His blood be on our children!" (27:25), 2.04:08

78 Soldiers Mock Jesus (27:27), 2.04:15
John and Mary follow to Calvary

79 Jesus's Crucifixion (27:32), 2.06:48
Camera focuses on another being victim being nailed
INRI placard (Latin only) above the cross (Jn 19:19), 2.08:58
John and the three Marys watch Jesus being crucified

80 Jesus's Death (27:45), 2.10:00
Black screen; quotation of Isa. 6:9-10 (13:14-15)

81 Burial of Jesus (27:57), 2.12:01
John, the three Marys, and two others (Joseph of Arimathea? Nicodemus?) watch deposition

82 Guard at the Tomb (27:62), 2.14:11

83 Resurrection of Jesus (28:1), 2.14:35
Three Marys, *Peter,* and *John* are there when the stone is rolled away.

84 Commissioning of the Disciples (28:16), 2.15:55
Ninetto Davoli is in the film's final scene

85 Credits, 2.16:19

NOTES

1. Father Guido Haazen, director of a school in the Belgian Congo, organized a male choir, eventually named Les Troubadors du Roi Baudoin, and developed the Missa Luba by improvising traditional song forms. It was performed in Africa (1958) and thereafter (and recorded) in Europe.
2. For the identification of the extradiegetic music, see Martellozzo (2019) and Baugh (2021). After the "Gloria," the chorus ending Bach's *St Matthew Passion*, "Wir setzen uns mit Tränen," occurs. Pasolini used the *St Matthew Passion*, which sets Mt. 26-27 to music, throughout *Accattone* to Christ figure the pimp protagonist.
3. For a list of locations, see Baugh (1997: 98). Pasolini toured Israel for shooting locations and decided he could not film there. He documented his experience in *Sopralluoghi in Palestinia per il vangelo secondo Matteo* (On Location in Palestine 1965). Pasolini turned to the people of his homeland in southern Italy for something sacred but lost in modern, urban experience. See Stack (1969: 9, 23–5), Greene (1990: 21–52), and Baugh (2021).
4. For example, Giorgio Agamben played Philip and Enzo Sicillano played Simon.
5. *Il figlio dell'uomo* (The Son of Man 1954) anticipates Pasolini on many of these points: documentary style, black-and-white photography, outdoor locations, and a non-professional, proletariat cast. See Viano (1993: 136) and Page (2021: 130–2). Pasolini's nonprofessional actors and lingering closeups indicate Carl Theodor Dreyer and Robert Bresson's influence.
6. Pasolini wrote a script to bring St Paul's words into conflict analogically with Pasolini's present, setting the story in various modern cities including Rome, Paris, and New York. For an English translation, see Pasolini (2014). For discussion, see Walsh (2019) and Marchal and Seesengood (2019).
7. Pasolini claimed he was in Assisi for a meeting hosted by the Pro Civitate Christiana, an organization dedicated to connecting the gospel and works of culture, when he was trapped by the pope's motorcade and reduced to reading the gospels. Impressed by Matthew's violence (10:34), he began *Il vangelo*. Pro Civitate Christiana provided funding.
8. Pasolini said *Il vangelo* superimposes a brusque, literal (Rossellinian) treatment of Matthew on traditional Christian iconography, juxtaposing the natural and supernatural like some of the films of Rossellini, Dreyer, and Mizoguchi (Stack 1969: 9). Critics often note Pasolini's camera's reverential style (see Walsh 2019: 32–4).
9. Compared to Hollywood epics, "neorealism" is an understandable description, but is less accurate in the history of Italian cinema. Pasolini rejected neorealism for the "cinema of poetry" (see Pasolini 1988: 167–88). Naomi Greene argues that Pasolini evokes neorealism to subvert it with his religious sensibility, that he rejects the "natural" for a violent consecration/deconsecration of things, and that his camera confronts reality head on rather than waiting for it to reveal itself (1990: 21–52). Significantly, Pasolini saw reality as already ideological and always constructed (Viano 1993: 53–72).
10. Unless otherwise noted, parenthetical scripture references are all to Matthew.
11. Irazoqui resembles Byzantine Christs or those in Georges Rouault's work (see, e.g., the 1922 etching *Forever Scourged*; the 1937 *Head of Christ*). Irazoqui was a nineteen-year-old Spanish economics student when Pasolini chose him to play Jesus. Irazoqui, an agnostic, was in Italy to solicit support against Franco. He became a literature professor and a chess referee. Pasolini dubbed over Irazoqui's voice with that of Enrico Maria Salerno. Ironically, Rossellini used Irazoqui's voice for his Jesus in *Il messia* (1975). Italian audiences would recognize Salerno's

voice (Viano 1993: 138), and Salerno later dubbed the Italian for Clint Eastwood in Sergio Leone's *Dollars* trilogy.

12 Matthew 6:25-34 has as background music Bach's "Erbarme dich, mein Gott" from *St Matthew Passion*. This plea for mercy recurs twice before the end of part one: when the authorities complain about Sabbath eating and when the rich young man cannot follow Jesus.

13 While scholars often marvel at the atheist Pasolini's deployment of miracles, Zygmunt Barański notes that he includes only six of Matthew's (1985: 88–90). Later, Pasolini expressed regret about the miracles' sentimentality (Stack 1969: 87–91).

14 Pasolini started to cut this section, but left it in for his Catholic friends (Tatum 2013: 115).

15 For a list of scenes in which Jesus smiles, see Baugh (1997: 103).

16 In the passion, Caiaphas, wearing a black hat, becomes a distinct character. Pasolini does not differentiate types of religious leaders. The religious leaders' bizarre hats "quote" the headgear of Christian religious leaders in a specific panel, "Heraclius' Return of the Cross to Jerusalem," in Piero della Francesca's mid-fifteenth-century *Legend of the True Cross* fresco cycle in the Church of San Francesco in Arezzo, Italy (Fuller 2004: 55–73; 2006). Piero is also important in Pasolini's depiction of the pregnant Mary. See his *Madonna del Parto* (1460).

   In striking contrast to Matthew's Jesus, Pasolini's Jesus is never in a synagogue. Does this mitigate the potential anti-Semitism in a film that makes the (Jewish) religious leaders more culpable for Jesus's death than any other film up to its time?

17 "Kole Nidre," "all vows," is part of the evening Yom Kippur service and asks for the forgiveness of vows to God as part of the search for forgiveness.

18 Carol Hebron asserts this appearance Christ figures Judas (2016b: 134). Cf. Judas's flight to his suicide here to the similar depictions in *Jesus Christ Superstar* (1973) and *The Passion of the Christ* (2004).

19 Ironically, Pasolini's political film indicts Jesus on the priests' charge of blasphemy (Tatum 2013: 118–19). Is there a connection here with Pasolini's own recent condemnation for blasphemy because of *La ricotta*? See Stack (1969: 63). All filmmakers link themselves with their Jesuses, but Pasolini's Jesus is particularly autobiographical. His mother plays Mary. Jesus meets Pasolini's lover, Ninetto Davoli, playing with a child (18:1-4; Vargo 2003: 49–50). Most importantly, Pasolini sees himself, like his Jesus, as a Gramscian intellectual (or poet) in a world ripe for revolution, but ultimately forsaken by his people (see, e.g., Sicilano 1982: 251–66; Schwartz 1992: 445; Baugh 1997: 100–1; Walsh 2003: 107–9).

20 Pasolini minimizes the mockery at the cross.

21 One shot strongly resembles, in reverse, Mantegna's *Lamentation of Christ* (1480).

22 Antonio Gramsci was an Italian Marxist philosopher famous for his notion that the elite controlled others through ideological means (cultural hegemony), rather than through violence. Gramsci called for working class intellectuals to construct alternative ideologies/art. See Stack 1969: 8, 22–5; Greene 1990: 27–35, 54–60; Page 2021: 131.

23 Pasolini chose Matthew because it was the only gospel with a "national-popular epic" (Gramscian) quality. "Mark's seemed too crude, John's too mystical, and Luke's sentimental and bourgeois" (in Greene 1990: 72). In his script for a Paul film, Luke, the author of Acts, becomes the wealthy, oppressive institutional church's representative and an agent of Satan. See Walsh (2019: 23, 30–1).

24 Reinhold Zwick notes that Pasolini's script included all of Matthew and that he shot over four hours of film. By Zwick's estimation, the film uses eighty-six of Matthew's one hundred fifty pericopes (2013: 109). Barański claims that 60 percent of Matthew is absent, that Pasolini

amplifies those sections he keeps, and that he subverts Matthew's narrative sequence from 4:21 to 21:1. Pasolini offers silences and focuses on faces/location in contrast to Matthew's logocentrism. Further, Pasolini's camera moves away from a pietistic focus on Jesus in the passion, and instead films others watching Jesus (1985: 82, 88, 99). See also Viano (1993: 331–3), Testa (1994), Aichele (2002), Walsh (2003: 95–120), and Tatum (2013: 112–17).

Pasolini also adds non-Matthean material from Isaiah and John. Pasolini claimed to prefer John to Matthew, but not for filming (Stack 1969: 95).

25 For an argument that *Il vangelo* is populist but not Gramscian or Marxist, see Nowell-Smith (1977).
26 Zwick compares *Il vangelo* with Italian neorealism, Dreyer, and Bresson (as well as Méliès's cinematic magic) (2013: 111–12). See Page (2021: 131–2, 135–6), and the sources cited therein, for Pasolini's place in Italian cinema. Page argues that *Il vangelo* now functions as aesthetic icon for Italian (religious) cinema. Art cinema differs, of course, from Italian peplum and the spaghetti Westerns. Amusingly, Pasolini played the revolutionary priest Don Juan in *Requiescant* (1967), who teaches the protagonist—the adopted son of a pacifist preacher—the Bible's (violent) revolutionary significance.
27 For a discussion of Christ figuring and redemptive motifs in Pasolini's mythological quartet, see Zwick (2014).
28 While biblical critics might see a Christ figure in the visitor, Pasolini apparently imagined a fertility god or an Old Testament deity (Schwartz 1992: 519–22). The narrator cites Jer. 20:7 during the film.
29 Barth Schwartz wonders if Pasolini would have completed a Trilogy of Death, repudiating his Trilogy of Life, if he had lived—and if it would have included Pasolini's long-planned Paul film (1992: 689). See n6 above.
30 The critique of institutional religion—and intellectuals—is even more pronounced in Pasolini's Paul script. See n6.

8

The Greatest Story Ever Told

George Stevens, director, George Stevens Productions/United Artists, 1965

PLOT SUMMARY: FRAMING JESUS IN THE WESTERN LANDSCAPE[1]

Instead of opening historically, this massively expensive epic's camera[2] looks up at an Orthodox church's oculus (with passion week scenes) and then slowly pans down as a narrator recites Jn 1:1-5. Reaching a Greek inscription, the film's Jesus translates: "I am he." The narrator resumes with Jn 1:2 as the camera finds the apse image of a priestly Christ, which resembles the film's adult Jesus (Max von Sydow).[3] A dissolve to a starry sky accompanies "the life was the light of men," and a star becomes an oil lamp's flickering flame in a cattle stall—thus, "the light shineth in darkness." The camera focuses on a baby's hand, the narrator announces the film's title, and the baby's hand dissolves into a solar disk. Jesus (and this film) is light breaking into a dark world, which "comprehended it not."[4]

This lengthy prologue is the first of three frames for Jesus. It indicates Jesus's story (and the film) belongs to the church. The film's conclusion returns to this same church. In between, the film meditates ritualistically on Jesus's ideas.[5] Typically, one scene slowly dissolves to the next. Voices linger across scenes or begin early, creating voiceover effects.[6] At the double climax (Lazarus's resurrection and Jesus's passion), triumphant religious music overwhelms speech and ambient sound.

The second frame is (Herodian) politics. The prologue segues to fortress Jerusalem as the wise men approach. On his throne, black-clad Herod (Claude Rains), with his son Antipas (José Ferrer) and other advisors, receives them. The wise men report a star-destined child (remember the prologue's star/flame), so Herod's advisors search the scriptures and "pious" Herod quotes Mic. 5:2. The guards, whom Herod sends after the wise men, line the horizon, looking down on the nativity like a Western's "Indians" or cavalry.

An inner voice tells Joseph to flee. The scholarly Herod receives his guards' Bethlehem report and then orders the slaughter of the innocents (Jer. 31:5) as a "more fitting" prophecy than Mic. 5:2.[7] His spear-wielding cavalry rides down upon the village, leaving children dead in the streets (the violence is offscreen). Herod, however, collapses after hearing the "good" news. The empty manger and the open door through which the family escaped mean Micah 5:2 is still in play.

Thus, the second frame is actually politics versus prophecy (cf. Humphries-Brooks 2006: 47–8), and this film utilizes more Hebrew Bible texts than any previous Jesus film.[8]

In Egypt, Joseph reads Isa. 9:6 from a scroll as the holy family rests beside a palm-lined lake. Accordingly, the elite do not dominate this film as they do *King of Kings* (1961).[9]

When Herod's son, Antipas, fails to maintain order, Roman soldiers arrive, while the people languish sick and defeated, and the holy family returns down a road lined with crosses (with voiceovers from Pss. 61; 103; 22). A dramatic medium shot, in a film filled with (extreme) long shots, shows baby Jesus staring at the crosses. Even though Antipas tells the Romans that the messiah is someone who will never come, someone watches from the shadows.

The third frame is the majestic, mythic Western landscape of John Ford Westerns.[10] Like Pasolini, Stevens toured Israel, but rejected it in favor of southern Utah (e.g., Moab is Bethlehem; the Sermon is in what is now Canyonlands National Park), Nevada (Pyramid Lake is the Sea of Galilee), and California (Death Valley National Park is Jesus's wilderness). This landscape, playing a role like that of *King of Kings*' political times, dwarfs the human characters (Tatum 2013: 94–5).

Like Western heroes, the Baptist and Jesus belong to and navigate the landscape. John (Charlton Heston)[11] is literally a voice(over) crying from the wilderness, calling the people to repent (Hos. 6:6). As the camera pulls up from the temple's sacrificial altar and dissolves to a line of people trudging into the wilderness, the voice predicts the Lord's wilderness highway (Isa. 40:2-5). The camera pans down the Jordan valley to people awaiting baptism, and the voice offers selections from the gospels' Baptists' teachings as well as Mal. 3:1; 5:2. After a medium shot of John baptizing, the film presents John and then Jesus in closeup. Having quoted Mic. 5:2, John baptizes Jesus and claims Jesus is the one awaited (cf. Lk. 7:19). The sleeping world is ready to awake. After embracing John, Jesus walks into the wilderness in an extreme long shot.

John shouts (Ps. 24:7) as the scene dissolves to Jesus climbing arduously, as John's voice echoes (Isa. 40:9-10). At night, Jesus finds a high cave. There, the chuckling Dark Hermit (Donald Pleasance),[12] Stevens's invented demonic figure, tempts Jesus: "And it [life] can be easy, friend. If a man knows the way to power and glory in this world." The voice comes from within the dark cave, as Jesus stands backlit by a huge, full moon in the cave's mouth. The Hermit tempts the fasting Jesus with food and then with world rule, angelic protection, and miraculous bread as they sit on the precipice's edge.[13]

At dawn, John's voice describes the messiah's restorative acts (Isa. 29:17; Ps. 9:18) climaxing with "arise, shine, for thy light is come, and the glory of the Lord is risen upon thee" (Isa. 60:1). Climbing even higher, the sunlit Jesus stands silhouetted in an extreme long shot before the Western sky and landscape, so distant that his words also seem a voiceover: "All the tribes of the earth shall see the Son of Man coming in the clouds of heaven, power, and great glory."[14]

The landscape speaks. It is prophecy (cf. Babington and Evans 1993: 141–2). Jesus learns spiritual lessons in this wilderness, and wisdom emerges from his psychological/spiritual struggle. The script describes the Dark Hermit as Jesus's consciousness (Forshey 1992: 97) and the dark cave is almost too Jungian (cf. Skywalker's cave in *The Empire Strikes Back* 1980). The prophecies ringing through the landscape could also be part of Jesus's consciousness (the cultural super ego?), so Jesus's wilderness struggle is his (Jungian) maturation.[15] Jesus becomes the Son of the West (Stern, Jefford, and DeBona 1999: 159).

When Jesus returns, the Baptist identifies him as the shepherd (not God's lamb), and Judas (David McCallum), Peter (Gary Raymond), Andrew, and John follow. Settling under a bridge with desert flowers and buttes as background, Jesus introduces his semi-ascetic trust God message: to labor for everlasting bread, not perishable fruit (Jn 6:27, 33, 50); to trust in God's provision (Lk. 12:22-26; 28b-31); to know the kingdom within (Lk. 17:21); to place no value in things (cf. Mt. 6:19); to be light to those in darkness, not a judge (Mt. 5:40, 16; 7:1-2); and, again, to trust God's provision (Mt. 6:28-29).[16]

The film's twofold pattern for Jesus's ministry is thus set. First, brief—often dark interior—scenes illustrate the political elites' deadly worries about troublesome prophets. Pilate (Telly Savalas) is the true power, and Antipas and Caiaphas (Martin Landau) must support Roman order while they pursue their own goals.[17] Their Jerusalem is a massive walled fortress dominating the surrounding countryside and people,[18] which Jesus describes succinctly with Lk. 13:34-35 as his ministry begins. Second, longer—usually sunny exterior—scenes depict Jesus's itinerancy among the people (see Stern, Jefford, and DeBona 1999: 158). While some healings occur, teaching dominates. Other key teaching scenes take place in Lazarus's courtyard, in Capernaum, in the Sermon, and at the Jordan.

In Bethany, Lazarus (Michael Tolan) invites his "good friend" Jesus into his home. As they relax in a garden, Jesus teaches about the greatest commandment (Mk 12:28b-34, pars). Agreeing this is more important than burnt offerings (cf. Hos. 6:6), Lazarus wants to go with Jesus; however, Jesus knows Lazarus's wealth is too great a burden. Their dialogue evokes the camel's needle (Mk 10:17-25) as Jesus elaborates that one cannot serve God and money (Mt. 6:21, 24) and tells of a widow who gave two pennies (Lk. 21:1-4). Lazarus wonders who could do such a thing; nonetheless, Jesus promises not to forget Lazarus.

Jesus's ministry centers around Capernaum. As he enters, Jesus "declares" his Father in his heart (cf. Jn 14:9) and the Father's love to the tax collector Matthew (Roddy McDowall). Matthew follows Jesus into the synagogue where Jesus counters a message of judgment (cf. the Baptist's message) with one of salvation, faith, and Hos. 6:6. In illustration, Jesus "heals" the lame man Uriah (Sal Mineo) by encouraging him to try walking. Leaving alone, Jesus pauses prayerfully to touch the mezuzah.

After the Baptist's violent arrest,[19] Jesus teaches at the Galilean lakeshore and in the wilderness (Mt. 11:28-30; Jn 6:35). As Jesus becomes more popular, Caiaphas sends Sorak (an invented character, Victor Buono) to spy on him. Nicodemus (Joseph Schildkraut)[20] and Joseph of Arimathea accompany Sorak. During a long shot of sheep on the hills, Jesus declares himself the Good Shepherd (voiceover, Jn 10:14, 16). Meanwhile, the Baptist tells Antipas that Jesus, the shepherd, gathers souls. Later, Jesus sits on a mountain with children, looking down on Capernaum (Mk 10:14-15).[21]

Jesus returns to Capernaum in public triumph. The Dark Hermit and Caiaphas's spies watch as Jesus offers stones to those innocent enough to stone the woman taken in adultery (Magdalene [Joanna Dunham]) before forgiving her sins.[22] The sick jostle him for cures, and he tells them their faith cures them. Political revolt begins in Galilee and Judea.

Antipas executes the Baptist,[23] but John's voice (repent) lingers on.[24] Antipas then sends his palace guard to arrest Jesus (a third Herodian attack on Mic. 5:2). The guard leaves Antipas's fortress and enters the wilderness in a dramatic long shot from above as Jesus speaks (voiceover) of the blessed persecuted. A dissolve moves to Jesus, in an extreme long shot, perched precipitously above a canyon landscape. His Sermon calls his followers to be the light of the world before reciting the Lord's Prayer with them (Mt. 5:10-11, 3-9, 13a, 14a, 16; 6:9-10). In a bucolic scene, Jesus asks his disciples, including Magdalene and Uriah, who he is. For Judas, Jesus is the greatest teacher, but Peter, the church's rock, knows Jesus's messianic identity (Mt. 16:16-19). Pharisees warn Jesus about Antipas, so Jesus goes to Nazareth (citing Lk. 13:31-33). Antipas's guard arrives at the desolate Sermon site, hopelessly late.

Rejected at Nazareth and struck by a stone (Mk 6:4; Lk. 4:18-19), Jesus walks away to visit his mother (Dorothy McGuire). Their visit is cut short when the sickly Lazarus warns his good friend that soldiers are coming for him. Alone, Jesus stops and heals blind Aram (Ed Wynn) at Nazareth's well. At the Jordan, after learning that Lazarus is dying, one melancholic disciple asks, "Are men like circles in the water? Do they just float away, and are lost? It was right there where John the Baptist stood." The scene ends with them all reciting the Lord's Prayer.

They arrive in Bethany for the funeral (Martha caustically notes). In a closeup, Jesus declares he is the resurrection (Jn 11:25-26) and leaves everyone (including most of the film's important characters) below as he ascends, in a (very) long shot, up a steep hill to Lazarus's tomb. Once there, the audience sees Jesus framed against the Western blue sky (cf. the Dark Hermit's cave scene). In his most dramatic scene, a contorted Jesus prays for Lazarus's resurrection (reportedly von Sydow improvised the prayer from Exod. 15:11; Isa. 43:13; Job 5:18; Ezek. 37:9) (see Figure 8.1). As the tomb opens, the audience sees Jesus from the inside.[25] After shots of awed, fearful people in the crowd, swelling music overrides any ambient sound (except for thunder). Then Jesus and Lazarus stand outside the tomb at such a distance they cannot be identified. The Hallelujah Chorus rises, but people ask what happened (particularly Judas), as three witnesses (Bar Amand [Van Heflin], Uriah, and Aram) run to fortress Jerusalem shouting to its four heralds (perhaps

Figure 8.1 Jesus prays outside Lazarus's tomb in *The Greatest Story Ever Told*, directed by George Stevens, George Stevens Productions/United Artists, 1965. All rights reserved.

symbolizing the four Gospels) that the Messiah has come, and testifying (respectively) to Jesus's miracles (raised the dead, healed the lame, and the blind). The soaring music nearly overwhelms, and ends part one.

After the intermission and Jesus's anointing (by Magdalene for his burial; Jn 12:1-8), Jesus, dressed in new white robes,[26] leaves Lazarus's home for the Jerusalem triumph. Ambient sound, hosannas, and hallelujahs (with the music rising again) attend the scene, which is seen from above, from afar (with Jesus almost indistinguishable in the crowd), and (framed) from within the city gate. The frenzied crowds worry the authorities, but Caiaphas's guard cannot arrest Jesus. Jesus violently cleanses the temple (citing Hos. 6:6 [Mt. 9:13] again). Before the altar, Jesus speaks for scripture (Mt. 5:17)[27] but against the watching black-clad religious leaders (Mt. 23:3, 5, 7-10).[28]

That night, beside the altar fire, torch-wielding Jesus teaches that he has come to bring salvation and light (Jn 12:46-47). He bids the people walk in the light (12:35-36) and to become sons of the light. He assures them that faith, hope, and love abide (citing 1 Cor. 13:13!) and that he is with those gathered in his name (Mt. 18:20).[29] As he leaves with his disciples, the people recite Ps. 23. Ominous sounds of marching precede the Romans, whom Pilate has sent to arrest Jesus. They slaughter the people even though Bar Amand briefly delays the inevitable by turning the other cheek.[30]

Judas departs the upper room, standing in the shadows outside as Jesus enters and shuts the door. Judas almost collides with the Dark Hermit lurking in the shadowed streets as he hurries to Sorak and Caiaphas (cf. the portrayal in *From the Manger to the Cross* 1912). He proposes to give his "good friend" Jesus to them, the purest man he knows, whom he loves.[31] The confused priests agree to do their best to see that no harm comes to Jesus.

Returning to the upper room, Judas sits alone at the table's end as Jesus (with light forming a nimbus in a recess behind him) announces the hour has come (Jn 12:23). As Jesus offers bread and wine, the camera returns repeatedly to Judas, who does not partake. Jesus sends Judas away (Jn 13:27) and speaks to the others about martyrdom's power (Jn 12:23-24).

Stevens cuts repeatedly between Judas's receipt of the money and Jesus's agonizing Gethsemane, and finally to Judas's arrival with the temple guard. Saving Judas from Peter's sword, Jesus asks the guard why they come in the dark when "all my life, I have walked in the light and spoken in the light" (reinforcing the film's light-dark dichotomy).

A dissolve leads to Jesus's Sanhedrin trial, where Caiaphas charges him with sedition, sorcery, blasphemy, and "so many" crimes. Blind Aram, however, refuses to confirm any charges (cf. Jn 9:24-34). Outside, the Dark Hermit prompts Peter's denial. Nicodemus arrives and protests the illegitimate proceedings: "Are we Romans now that we disregard decency?"[32] Nonetheless, Caiaphas extracts Jesus's blasphemous "I am," sealing his fate and reducing Nicodemus (in a closeup) to silence.

Another dissolve leads to the Roman trial where Jesus responds to Pilate's polytheism with the Shema; to his agnosticism by saying Pilate has not looked for God; and to his politics by saying his kingdom is not of this world. After a lengthy sidebar with Claudia, Pilate sends the innocent Jesus to Herod Antipas.

A drunken Antipas mocks Jesus with a robe, saying "now you are the king you were born to be" (citing Mic. 5:2). As Jesus is taken back to Pilate, a medium shot shows the Dark Hermit, who surprisingly speaks Jn 3:16 in voiceover,[33] before Jesus comes face to face with Peter's denial.

In the Ecce Homo scene, Pilate sits in an open-air courtyard with Jesus standing forlornly before him. Despite people speaking for Jesus, the Dark Hermit cries loudly for Jesus's crucifixion and claims to have no king but Caesar (in counterpoint to Jesus's second claim to an otherworldly kingdom). After Pilate washes his hands, his voiceover of the creed's "under Pontius Pilate crucified ... " accompanies a closeup of his face.

After another dissolve, Jesus is on the Via Dolorosa. He staggers under a dark cross with no ambient sound or crowd noise. Music overwhelms the scene. The first diegetic sound occurs when Jesus falls the first time and the cross hits stone. Jesus tells women not to weep (Lk. 23:28-31). Stevens cuts to a long shot of Judas throwing his money in the temple and then back to Jesus falling again. A Black man (Sidney Poitier) shoulders Jesus's cross, and they both move forward. Through an open gate, one sees a cross raised on distant Golgotha.[34] A cut shows Judas ascending the temple altar's steps in a long shot. An even longer shot, from inside the city gate, shows Jesus's cross ascending Golgotha with Jesus following. After one hears the hammering of nails, another cut shows Judas falling into the altar fire. In another long shot, through the city gate, one sees Jesus's cross raised.

Most of the crucifixion scene is long shots of the three crosses on the hill or medium shots (e.g., Nicodemus, Joseph of Arimathea, Simon, and Aram) and closeups of Jesus's anguished followers (e.g., Mary and Magdalene). Jesus utters all seven traditional words from the cross. Closeups of Jesus occur during the "I thirst" and "Into thy hands" sayings. After the last saying, Jesus's eyes go blank, and a thunderstorm begins. Jesus's head falls onto his chest in a long shot, and the centurion (John Wayne) confesses the Son of God (the darkness makes it difficult to identify Wayne). A final shot shows the (guilty) city in the distance.

After the burial, Pilate posts a tomb guard at Caiaphas's request (because "Jesus tread the path of prophecy"). In a dissolve, one sees disciples throwing rocks into the Jordan, recalling the disciples' discussion of death. Then, the film shifts abruptly to sunrise, trumpets (four heralds on the distant city walls), the Hallelujah Chorus, and the open tomb. Knowing Jesus will rise, Magdalene leads Peter and John to the empty tomb. After Caiaphas says it will be forgotten in a week, a dissolve leads to a gigantic "sky" Jesus commissioning the disciples and repeating his semi-ascetic trust God message (Jn 13:34; Mt. 6:33-34; 28:20b). A final dissolve returns to the prologue's church art.

MEMORABLE CHARACTERS

1 While Stevens embellishes Jesus "Jewishly" (with scriptures and rituals), Jesus is "the light [that] shineth in the darkness." The church's Christ, he is not chary with Johannine "I ams" (and is repeatedly accused of blasphemy). His final rise into the Hallelujah Chorus and church art hardly surprises.

2. The Western landscape is as important a character as Jesus.[35] It represents the divine and prophecy. Jesus is a son of this (American) West as is the Baptist, who is the wilderness's voice.

3. The Dark Hermit is the demonic opposition, agitating for evil at crucial moments. He is the voice for the easy life (versus Jesus's message of semi-ascetic trust in God). He appears in the woman taken in adultery scene (calling Jesus Son of David), in the street's shadows as Judas leaves the Last Supper, in Caiaphas's courtyard (asking Peter if he is with Jesus), in the streets when Antipas sends Jesus back to Pilate, and in the mob (where he cries for Jesus's crucifixion and declares Caesar his only king). Black-clad Sorak, also invented, is the Dark Hermit's human counterpart, appearing frequently "against" Jesus (e.g., before the Capernaum spy mission, at Judas's betrayal arrangement, and at the Jewish trial).

4. Fortress Jerusalem (vis-à-vis the Western landscape) is Jesus's (and the people's) worldly opponent. The Herodians represent the "war on prophecy" (Mic. 5:2). Pilate is Roman order incarnate. At the Jewish trial, black-clad Caiaphas represents judicial corruption vis-à-vis the noble, gray-clad Nicodemus.

5. Despite limited screen time/dialogue, Magdalene may be Jesus's true follower (cf. Jn 20:29).[36] After her redemption (from adultery), she is among the disciples and is the first to believe (without seeing) and to bear witness to the resurrection.

6. By contrast, Judas and Lazarus represent the difficulties in following Jesus's semi-ascetic message. Jesus is simply "too good" for Judas's mere humanity (see n31) and his teaching too much for Lazarus. A composite of John's Lazarus, the interested scribe (Mk 12:28b-34), and the anonymous rich man (Mk 10:17-25), he is Jesus's friend but not his disciple. Is he left outside the circle of followers or does his resurrection augur hope even for Judas and for wealthy Americans (see Cultural Location)? Jesus's followers do gather at his house before the resurrection appearances.

MEMORABLE VISUALS

1. The priestly, iconic Christ of the church at the beginning and end.
2. The sunlit blue sky, unbounded West (Jesus) versus fortress Jerusalem and the elite's dark interiors.
3. Sermon overlooking Western canyons.
4. The Baptist forcibly "baptizing" Antipas's soldiers as they arrest him.
5. Children playing "army" as Jesus walks into Nazareth.[37]
6. Jesus praying at and seen from within Lazarus's tomb.
7. Sermon by torchlight in the temple court.
8. Golgotha viewed through the city gate; Jesus surrounded by Romans.

KEY AUTHORITY/SCRIPTURE

1 The Western landscape and the church vie to be the film's ultimate authority.

2 The Hebrew scriptures ("Jesus tread the path of prophecy") and the prophetic voice(over) crying in the wilderness are other important authorities. Micah 5:2 (in particular, initiating the prophecy versus politics theme) occurs several times (from Herod, the Baptist, and Antipas). Hosea 6:6 substantiates Jesus's personalized, ethical view of religion. It occurs four times (in the Baptist's voiceover "above" temple sacrifices, in Jesus's response in the Capernaum synagogue, and in Jesus's comments as he cleanses the temple [Lazarus also alludes to it in his first conversation with Jesus]).

3 The Gospel of John provides the film's structure (with the church frame, the significance of Lazarus's resurrection, and Jesus's frequent references to his hour [Jn 12:24]). The light versus darkness ideology is even more important (and Johannine; see Walsh 2018c). Stevens also uses many of the Johannine "I am" sayings.

4 Jesus's semi-ascetic teaching is not particularly Johannine, however, nor is his emphasis upon the kingdom within (Lk. 17:21).

CULTURAL LOCATION/GENRE: WESTERN (EPIC UNDONE)

Epics are metanarratives reflecting or aiming at a unifying cultural identity. Stevens's epic Jesus is too late for US cultural unity and not awe-inspiring or socially prescriptive enough to promote unity. The Civil Rights Movement and growing opposition to US involvement in Vietnam indicated a world of fragmented personal narratives (see Forshey 1992: 103–4; Stern, Jefford, and DeBona 1999: 149–54; Tatum 2013: 104–8).

Aware of this context, Stevens adapted the epic Jesus in two distinctive ways. First, rather than a social contract, his film stresses the privatized, subjective, expressively individualistic religious faith beginning to dominate the 1960s US religious landscape (see Walsh 2003:10–13, 167 n20, 177–80). Accordingly, Jesus twice tells Pilate his kingdom is not of this world. From the beginning, Jesus speaks of the kingdom within or of the Father within. Jesus's issue is personal faith, and Jesus repeatedly tells people, like Uriah, that their faith (not he) heals them.

The stress on subjective individualism has deep currents in American thought, extending back at least to Ralph Waldo Emerson, and Stevens's Jesus is a self-reliant, divinity-within Emersonian (or follower of Thoreau), rather than a European existentialist (Walsh 2003: 152–7). Although political leaders are threatened by Jesus's activities, Jesus has nothing to say to politics or economics. Such concerns, as Jesus says to Lazarus, distract one from (the) God (within). Stevens's Jesus is a counter cultural sage wandering the wildlands away from the city (the modern world), which kills such prophets (Lk. 13:34-35) (see Babington and Evans 1993: 142–6; Stern, Jefford, and DeBona 1999: 155–9).

This Jesus is not epic then because he is not at home in the 1960s United States.[38] He belongs to the church, to myth, to children's stories, or to the West—that most romantic of American spaces—and transplanting Jesus to this West is Stevens's second modification of the Jesus epic.³⁹ The classic West(ern), or the frontier, is where the true American is born and belongs. The West is to the United States as the wilderness is to biblical Israel. It creates a "sacred discontent" with (modern) civilization (see Schneidau 1976; Moss 2004: 181). Accordingly, discussions of the Western often turn on polarities between it and the city (see Stern, Jefford, and DeBona 1999: 157; Walsh 2003: 156–62), and Stevens's Jesus Western juxtaposes the wilderness/itinerant Jesus with the rulers of fortress/civilization. Stevens's Jesus is the self-reliant Western hero, untroubled by his conflict with corrupt society. But, he is from another time/place.

Lazarus says it all, for the West and epic come undone in him.⁴⁰ He lives at ease, just outside the city walls in his comfortable "country" estate. Like so many 1960s people, he is a seeker; he is discontent with a materialistic life, but he cannot follow Jesus. Who could do such a thing? He speaks to the disconnect between US materialism and Jesus's semi-ascetic trust in God. Lazarus stands between Jesus and the Dark Hermit as well as between the wilderness/frontier and the city. The US audience knows Lazarus. He is their door/frame into the Jesus epic, but they are not at home there.⁴¹

DIRECTOR

Stevens's early camera work was with 1920s Laurel and Hardy slapstick comedies, and perhaps that early work contributes to his Jesus film's aura of the natural world's goodness. By the 1930s Stevens was directing features like *Swing Time* (1936) and *Gunga Din* (1939). During the Second World War, he filmed the Allied armies' entry into Dachau. In the 1950s, he directed the critically acclaimed *A Place in the Sun* (1951), *Shane* (1953), *Giant* (1956), and *The Diary of Anne Frank* (1959). Nominated for the Best Director Oscar for each, he won for *A Place in the Sun* and *Giant*.

Shane has obvious connections to *Greatest Story*. The film opens with a lone frontiersman (Shane) riding out of the mountains into the settled valley below. Meanwhile, a young boy, Joey, playfully hunts deer until he sees the stranger arrive. (Joey's POV renders *Shane* yet another children's story.) On the farm, Joey's father, Joe Starrett (Van Hefflin), offers Shane (Alan Ladd) a job, and Joey's mother, Marian (Jean Arthur), provides him with food (and some longing looks).ABandoning his gun, Shane settles down to a new life.

Unfortunately, trouble has already been brewing in the valley, because Rufus Ryker, a cattle rancher, has been trying to oust farmers. After various hostilities and hired gunslingers' arrival, Starrett decides to confront the rancher. Shane, knowing the hired guns outman Starrett, knocks him out and goes to town in his place. There, in a saloon, where he has previously been humiliated, Shane defeats the outlaws and the head rancher, as Joey watches. He leaves, telling Joey "a man has to be what he is."⁴²

The parallels with *Greatest Story* (and the Gospel of John) are obvious. Both protagonists are strangers from beyond. Both associate themselves with a small, endangered community that they educate and save (Shane educates Joey in self-reliant maturity). Both stories are told from the "saved" community's perspective, which alone knows the protagonist's identity. Finally, in an echo of *Shane* that Stevens's aficionados could not miss, Starrett/Bar Amand (Van Heflin) runs through a cemetery to the walls of Jerusalem to announce

Lazarus's resurrection, like Shane's departure, riding through the gravestones on Cemetery Hill into the setting sun.[43]

Insofar as the protagonist of *Greatest Story* dies (founding a sectarian group), while the protagonist of *Shane* delivers his community, Shane is more messianic than Stevens's Jesus.[44]

MGM HOME ENTERTAINMENT, 199 MINUTES, 2001
DVD Extras (two disks)

Two-page descriptive insert of the film's production
Disk 2
"He Walks in Beauty" Documentary (41 minutes):[45] The title alludes to Navajo mythology's Changing Woman, no doubt because the film was shot near the Navajo Reservation with some Navajos as extras.

1. George Stevens as director, 0:00
2. Max von Sydow on "Jesus," 9:16
3. Camera shot philosophy, 12:56
4. Influence of Stevens's "Dachau experience," 25:53
5. Production cost and time, 31:00
6. The role of great art, 37:18
7. Credits, 40:20

Theatrical Trailer (3:29 minutes)
Still gallery

1. Original production art
2. George Stevens during pre-production
3. Production camp and the Glen Canyon location
4. Behind the scenes of the John the Baptist sequence

Costume Sketches
Deleted Scene (alternate version of the Via Dolorosa sequence, 2:09 minutes)
"Filmmaker" Documentary (about 26 minutes): The documentary has four parts, but no chapters, and no way to move randomly from one part to another. The first three parts are each about eight minutes. The fourth part is three-and-a-half minutes. The timer resets to zero with each part.

1. Lighting, composition; touring Israel, the geography of the American Southwest's religious significance.
2. Costumes, planning Salome's dance and the Baptist's death.
    Carl Sandburg's Jesus as the "ideal man," the "universal man."

3 Filming Lazarus's resurrection.
4 Jesus's anointing and film editing.

Disk 1
    Languages
    French (dubbed)
    Subtitles: French, Spanish

DVD Chapters

(The Dark Hermit's appearances are in italics)

1 Main Title
2 In the Beginning, 4:48
3 The Three Kings, 7:20
4 Jesus, Mary, and Joseph, 11:31
5 Escape from Bethlehem, 17:40
    Baby Jesus looks at crosses, 23:20
    Jesus in the shadows, 25:30
6 John the Baptist, 26:15
    Sacrifice of lambs in the temple, 26:22
7 Jesus's Temptation, 31:52
    Dark Hermit's first appearance, 31:59
8 Gathering His Flock, 39:30
    Teaching under the bridge, 41:17
    Work starts in Galilee, 46:53
9 "Love Thy Neighbor [Lazarus]," 51:55
10 "Bring the Baptist to me," 56:15
11 [Matthew] The Tax Collector, 57:55
12 "Do Unto Others," 1.01:34
    Jesus demands mercy in Capernaum synagogue (Mt. 9:13; Hos. 6:6)
    (A shadow of a cross appears on Jesus's chest)
13 John before Herod, 1.08:03
    John "baptizes" Herod's soldiers
14 The Flock Grows, 1.11:47
    Simon (the Zealot) tells Jesus of John's arrest
    "All ye who labor" (Mt. 11:28-30), 1.12:30
        "Bread of life" (Jn 6:35), 1.13:05

116 | Jesus, the Gospels, and Cinematic Imagination

    Nicodemus: "I've always been fond of children's stories," 1.14:07
    "Good shepherd" (Jn 10:14, 16), 1.14:25
  Receiving the kingdom like a child (Mk 10:13-15)

15 "Cast the First Stone," 1.19:37
  Magdalene
  The Dark Hermit: "Hail, Son of David," 1.20:49

16 "I'm Cured," 1.23:32
  Woman touches Jesus's clothing, 1.24:13
  Salome's dance, John's death, 1.25:31
    "He's the one prophesied, born in Bethlehem"
  "Arrest the Nazarene," 1.31:17

17 "Blessed are the Meek," 1.31:25
  Sermon on the Mount (including Magdalene)
  "Who do men say that I am?" (including Magdalene), 1.34:10
  Pharisees warn Jesus of murderous Herod (Lk. 13:31-33), 1.35:43

18 A Prophet in His Home, 1.36:54
  Blind Aram at a pool (Jn 9:6-8)
    Children playing army
  "Spirit … upon me" (Lk. 4:18), 1.38:30
  "You shall not tempt the Lord your God" (Mt. 4:7; Lk. 4:12), 1.40:15
  Jesus and his mother, 1.41:29
    Lazarus warns Jesus about possible arrest (Jn 11:1-3)

19 Restoring Sight, 1.43:30
  "Lazarus is sick, dying" (Jn 11:1-3), 1.45:20

20 The Lord's Prayer, 1.46:05

21 Lazarus Comes Forth, 1.47:47

Intermission, 1.59:48

22 Jesus in Jerusalem, 2.03:00
  Cleansing the temple, 2.10:32
  "I desire mercy" (Mt. 9:13; Hos. 6:6), 2.11:24
  Herod Antipas, the priests, and Pilate, 2.13:24
    "He's telling people to love their enemies" (Mt. 5:43; Lk. 6:27), 2.14:29
  At night in the temple courts, 2.14:49
    "A light into the world" (Jn 12:46-47)
    Bar Amand turns the other cheek to Roman soldiers, 2.18:00

24 Judas's Betrayal, 2.18:54
    The Dark Hermit in the shadows, 2.20:25
25 The Last Supper, 2.24:24
    "If a grain of wheat dies" (Jn 12:24)
26 "Your Will Be Done," 2.34:00
    "All my life, I've walked in the light, and spoken in the light" (Jn 12:35-36)
27 Jesus's Trial, 2.39:05
    Before the Sanhedrin
        The Dark Hermit, 2.41:59
        Nicodemus interrupts (Jn 7:49-52), 2.42:57
28 Pilate's Sentence, 2.45:30
    Pilate sends to Herod, 2.48:32
        "From you Bethlehem, shall he come forth"
    The Dark Hermit, "For God so loved the world" (Jn 3:16), 2.51:31
    Second time before Pilate, 2.52:52
    The Dark Hermit, "Crucify him!" 2.53:25, 2.54:09, 2.55:49
        Simon of Cyrene is in the crowd, 3.00:50
        The Dark Hermit, "No king but Caesar" (Jn 19:15), 2.56:41
        Pilate washes his hands, 2.57:24
29 Carrying the Cross, 2.57.39
    Veronica, 2.58:53
    Judas throws down the thirty pieces, 3.00:10
    Simon of Cyrene, 3.00:50
30 Calvary, 3.02:26
    Judas throws himself into the altar, 3.04:30
31 "It is Finished," 3.06:46
    "Into thy hands" (Lk. 23:46), 3.08:38
    "Truly this man was the Son of God" (Mk 15:39), 3.09:25
    Temple veil torn, 3.09:40
    Laid in the tomb, 3.10:28
    Caiaphas: "Jesus tread the path of prophecy," 3.10:38
32 "He is Risen," 3.11:09
    Disciples throw stones in the Jordan River
    The prophecy (Lk. 24:6-8), 3.13:00
    Lazarus, 3.13:21
    "Teach all nations … love one another" (Mt. 28:18; Jn 13:34), 3.15:07

NOTES

1. Stevens cut his four-hour-plus film to 225 minutes for the premiere and edited it again to 199 minutes. A general release version of 141 minutes also appeared. For different "takes" on seeing the premiere and edited version, see Egan (2018) and Kunkel (2018). The MGM DVD is the 199-minute version.
2. 20th Century Fox budgeted 10 million, the largest to that time for one of their films, but they withdrew after Stevens spent over 2 million before shooting began. United Artists took over, and the film finally cost approximately 20 million, making it the most expensive Jesus film ever. Twenty million is approximately 164 million 2020 dollars. Note the disjoint between the film's cost and Jesus's semi-ascetic message.
3. Jesus was von Sydow's first US film role. He had an outstanding reputation for work in Ingmar Bergman films: the Crusader who plays chess with Death in *The Seventh Seal* (1957); a traveling magician claiming supernatural powers in *The Magician* (1958); and characters troubled by God's silence in two of the films in Bergman's *Silence of God* trilogy (*Through a Glass Darkly* 1961 and *Winter Light* 1963). Later he was Father Merrin in *The Exorcist* (1973). Von Sydow's aristocratic, "European" demeanor contributes to his aura as a stranger from afar. See Walsh (2018c: 181 n13).
4. On cinematic Johannine prologues, see Walsh (2018c). The prologue is the story; the following, "an extended denouement" (Stern, Jefford, and DeBona 1999: 130).
5. Stevens said he wanted to emphasize Jesus's "ideas" (Moss 2004: 271, 277). The film credits Fulton Oursler's popular novel of the same name. Oursler was a reporter, novelist, and editor at *Reader's Digest*. He became a Roman Catholic in 1943 after becoming convinced of Christian ethics' importance versus communism. He adapted a radio series (beginning in 1947) into the novel (Oursler 1950: viii–x). 20th Century Fox acquired the film rights soon thereafter. Like Stevens, Oursler emphasizes Jesus's ideas (calling Jesus's ministry a lecture tour, 1950: 98; see also 98–101, 253–6, 290–9) and understands Jesus's religion in ethical, not ritual, terms (1950: 78–9, 87–9). The film and novel also place Capernaum at the center of Jesus's ministry (1950: 106), understand Judas's motivation similarly (1950: 229–33), and depict the Jewish trial almost identically (1950: 248–61).
6. Donald Richie says Stevens's slow dissolves suggest "subjective, prophetic, elegiac, or magical" connections (1970: 44–5). Marilyn Ann Moss says Stevens's use of the dissolve (in *Shane*) "couple[s] two shots together to show their difference *and* simultaneity" (2004: 196; emphasis in source).
7. Herod says to Antipas, "The child of imagination is the child I fear."
8. For a partial list, see Stern, Jefford, and DeBona 1999: 344–7.
9. Ray treats the elite as a unified group while Stevens typically depicts them independently.
10. Bruce Babington and Peter Evans describe the film as an "American Pastoral" and say the call of the wild(erness) pervades it (1993: 139). The film is extremely "wide." It was shot in Ultra Panavision 70 and originally projected using the single projector Cinerama system onto a huge, deeply curved screen (Moss 2004: 281–2, 285).
11. The 1950s biblical epic actor, Heston, won an Oscar for Best Actor for *Ben-Hur* (1959). He also played the lead role in *Planet of the Apes* (1968), also filmed at Lake Powell. In that film, Roddy McDowall (*Greatest Story*'s "Matthew") was Heston's ape counterpart, "Cornelius."
12. Pleasance specialized in insane and evil characters (*Austin Powers* parodied him as Dr. Evil), but is best known for playing the psychiatrist Samuel Loomis in *Halloween* films.

13 Do the temptations begin and end with "bread" to augur Jesus's semi-ascetic trust God message?
14 This "quotation" liberalizes passages like Mt. 24:20 and Rev. 1:7, which speak instead of people mourning when they see the heavenly Son of Man (or his sign).
15 The protagonist of *Jesus* (1999) also comes of age in his wilderness trial.
16 The melancholic film and its Jesus lack joy and humor. In a 1969 interview, Stevens contended, "All the great wilderness is sad. The great open plains under the mountains are sad, the wind blows sadly. When you hear it, it's the melancholy" (Moss 2004: 194–5). Nevertheless, when Jesus calls them men of little faith, the disciples laugh, and Jesus plays the straight man for Peter's comical worries about his stolen coat.
17 As in *King of Kings*, reports to these officials allude to gospel incidents not depicted otherwise.
18 Even *Il vangelo* (1964) does not achieve a single image as evocative of the city's oppression of the people.
19 Antipas's men's arrival on the horizon above the Baptist echoes the composition of the slaughter of the innocents. Cf. also the cavalry that goes after Jesus.
20 Schildkraut played Judas in *The King of Kings* (1927). He died while shooting this film, so his role was adjusted. Was Jn 3 lost in process or never shot?
21 Stevens often interlocks scenes by matching visuals with words. In this sequence, John and Jesus's words about shepherds correspond with adjacent scenes where disembodied shepherds' voices discuss Jesus while sheep are visible in the wilderness. Similarly, Sorak dismisses reports about Jesus as ridiculous tales for children, while Nicodemus and Joseph extol the value of such stories. A few scenes later, Jesus sits with the children (of the kingdom).
22 Her red apparel stands out like the girl's red coat in *Schindler's List* (1993) or the red gradually appearing in *Pleasantville* (1998).
23 One hears the executioner's sword fall before Salome finishes her dance. Antipas orders Jesus's arrest immediately. *King of Kings*' dance scene is more lascivious.
24 *King of Kings* and *Greatest Story* both expand the Baptist's character. Ray focuses on the Baptist's career/fate as Jesus's ominous forerunner. For Stevens, the Baptist incarnates the "voice in (of?) the wilderness."
25 This scene is as important to this film as the Sermon is to *King of Kings*. It is the longest and may be the most definitive treatment in Jesus films. Its shot of Jesus from within the tomb inspired directors like Zeffirelli, Scorsese, Young, and Hayes and Sokolov (see Staley 2021: 45–7; Staley also points out that Stevens fails to demonstrate Lazarus's sisters' faith). Curiously, John Ford closes *The Searchers* (1956), which many saw as indebted to Stevens's *Shane*, with a similar shot, photographing from within a dark house Ethan Edwards (John Wayne) standing in the doorway.
26 Jesus wears white throughout the film. Villains are often in black (Sorak) or red (Romans).
27 The speech takes place at such a distance and with so many cuts that it is almost a voiceover.
28 Antipas and Pilate bond laughing at Jesus's teaching about loving your enemies.
29 Whether recognizing the irony or not, Stevens repeats Jesus's voiceover of Mt. 18:20 with shots of the dead bodies in the courtyard.
30 Contrast *King of Kings*' focus on the slaughter, rather than Jesus's temple teaching.
31 At their first meeting, Lazarus's sister Mary fears for Jesus because he is too good. Does Jesus's goodness make Judas feel unworthy enough to betray (see Walsh 2010: 86–8)? In Oursler's novel, Judas betrays to escape Jesus's spell (1950: 230–2).
32 The emphasis upon a divided Sanhedrin, like the inventions of the Dark Hermit and Sorak, mitigates anti-Semitism (if not supersessionism).

33 Given the prophecy versus politics theme, it is tempting to see this curious scene and Judas's confused betrayal as indications of prophecy's victory. Does it also account for the Dark Hermit's Jn 3:16 voiceover?

34 See the opening discussion of Stevens's three frames for Jesus. Stevens frequently depicts Jesus in doors/gates (or entering/leaving spaces), but the framing is most obvious in the crucifixion sequence. See Richie (1970: 48–50).

35 Moss says Stevens considered "the ever-present expansiveness of the landscape" to be "one of the film's [*Shane*] characters" (2004: 196).

36 While Mary appears in many scenes (in Nazareth, at Lazarus's tomb, on the Via Dolorosa, at the cross, and in Lazarus's house on Easter morning), she is hardly as important as she is in *King of Kings*. She speaks only in the nativity. Peter's comic coat, the acknowledgment that he is the church's rock, his denial, and his mourning at the chair where Jesus was anointed still do not make him a dominant character.

37 When asked about the use of guns in *Shane* (and Joey's fascination with them), Stevens often said he "was disturbed to see groups of children in Germany playing with guns, emulating American cowboys, the mythic heroes who reminded them of the America soldiers who had defeated Hitler" (Moss 2004: 179).

38 Tom Aitkin says the film's artificiality proclaims it "has nothing whatsoever to do with everyday life as you, the audience, know and understand it" (in Baugh 1997: 29).

39 For a discussion of the film as an attempt to "materialize" a sacred other (Jesus, the West, etc.), see Walsh 2003: 153–6. Leandro Castellani says the film is an "incurable ill of Americanisms" (in Baugh 1997: 247 n99).

40 The time of the classic, cinematic Western was already past. Its comfortable dichotomies had come undone. See John Ford's late Westerns (e.g., *The Searchers*), Stevens's own *Giant* 1956 (if one considers that a Western), or the popular Spaghetti Westerns.

41 Was semi-asceticism still an ideal? John F. Kennedy's nomination speech (July 15, 1960) and his inaugural address (January 20, 1961) spoke of the hard work and sacrifice required of all Americans who should ask "what you can do for your country."

42 Donald Richie claims that Stevens's oeuvre struggles with the Romantic problem, life in a hostile world. Characters achieve maturity (like Shane and Jesus) by "owning" their outsider status (1970: 7–12, 52–73). Richie also contends that the distinction between using violence (Shane) and suffering it (Jesus) is less important than acting decisively and maturely (1970: 60–70).

43 Moss says, "After the war Stevens especially understood that death is part of living. His look back on America's—and his own—childhood in the West has become a beautiful elegy [in *Shane*]" (2004: 200).

44 Or perhaps an apocalyptic Christ compared to Stevens's more gnostic figure. See Walsh (2003: 159–65).

45 A seventy-five minute "Making of" video can be found on YouTube, which begins with this forty-minute piece, then adds another video just past the forty-seven-minute mark (https://www.youtube.com/watch?v=vkzWkyCA6ws&list=PL6WkSHx0QUfXGKOu89ZIJPpA9QEWt9fYJ&index=6&t=0s).

9

Godspell

David Greene, director, Columbia, 1973

PLOT SUMMARY: SINGING AND CLOWNING THE GOSPEL

The end of the studio monopoly and the Hays Code, as well as the increasing influence of foreign film on Hollywood, meant more experimental Jesus films were possible.[1] These were small budget films, anticipating smaller audiences than the big budget epics, whose era was temporarily over. In 1973, three Jesus films featuring musical numbers appeared, each aiming at a different market: *Godspell* for a mainline church audience (March 21); *Gospel Road* for an evangelical Protestant audience (March 31);[2] and *Jesus Christ Superstar*, with the biggest budget, for a broader audience (August 15).

Godspell was playwright John-Michael Tebelak's attempt to liberate Jesus from his staid church entombment.[3] Like *Il vangelo* (1964), *Godspell* is set in modernity, although in New York City, not southern Italy.

The film opens with a shot of a crudely drawn sun on a graffiti-tagged corrugated fence (cf. graffiti's importance in *Son of Man* 2006). Amidst wind noise, a voiceover begins as the camera pulls back, revealing the sun to be a flower, and then pans right to view, from under the Brooklyn Bridge, the Manhattan skyline across the East River. The (unfinished) Twin Towers dominate the skyline. During this shot, a voiceover from God (King, most in potency, maker of all things) announces, "I have made all of nothing for man's sustentation and of this pleasant garden that I have mostly goodly planted. I will make him gardener for his own re-creation."[4] The voice presages the film's story of new creation, although "garden" is misleading.[5]

Traffic noise replaces the wind, and the camera focuses on a man walking into Manhattan, pulling a red circus cart across the Brooklyn Bridge. The film's title moves into view from the distance: *Godspell: A Musical Based on the Gospel According to St. Matthew*. The man hums "Prepare Ye the Way of the Lord" (Mt. 3:3).[6] A rainbow and dove floating above clouds decorate his cart. He wears a ringmaster's coat with a silver fish across its shoulders and two clasping silver hands on its belt. A shofar is visible on top of the cart.

A jet roars overhead as the Twin Towers come into view.[7] Suddenly, the camera picks out eight people, slightly calmer than their peers, in Manhattan's bustling streets. These people catch glimpses of the ringmaster and hear the shofar.[8] Leaving the everyday, they follow his call, singing "Prepare Ye the Way of the Lord," the first of the songs structuring the film (see DVD Chapters).[9]

The ringmaster leads the singing, dancing, smiling group into Central Park to the angel-topped Bethesda Fountain, named for the Jerusalem "pool" (Jn 5:2) where healing awaited the first person to step into the water after an angel "troubled the water" (Jn 5:4).[10] The camera returns repeatedly to the eight-foot-tall, bronze, female "Angel of the Waters." As the troupe frolics in the pool (being healed?), the ringmaster espies a blond, afro-haired figure, clad only in shorts. The ringmaster is the Baptist calling for a change of mind/life (3:11).[11] Suddenly, the afro-coifed fellow, a resplendent red heart on his forehead, is in the pool ready to "get washed up" (3:13-15). The scene frames this figure, whose words identify him as Jesus (Victor Garber),[12] with John in a medium shot beneath the onlooking angel. Jesus rises from the waters in a Superman t-shirt and clown pants and shoes singing "God Save the People." Now dressed as clowns (see Cox 1969: 167–90), the troupe follows Jesus and John through Central Park into the city's eerily empty streets—dancing and singing.

The film has magic, but no miracles;[13] yet, the characters' changed actions, the song and dance, and the city's emptiness indicate the troupe has entered a sacred, alternative place—a place of play, recreation, rebirth—a place of clowns and trickster figures.[14] The film's title plays on an Old English word, "gōdspel" (gōd = good, spel = tidings) from which the modern English "gospel" derives. But "spel" also has magical connotations, and the characters have come under God's spell or into divine ecstasy (Baugh 1997: 43, 47; Walsh 2003: 73–84; Pippin 2013).[15]

Their gambols bring them to a fenced junkyard on Wards Island (near Hell Gate Bridge). They play, turning trash into new toys. Jesus paints his followers' faces, and the troupe performs his teachings in a comic vaudevillian style, mixing performances and dialects (see Baugh 1997: 42–3). Jesus hosts a variety show.

Jesus's teaching, augmented by parables, comes from a revised Sermon on the Mount. Along with the songs, the Sermon frames the film's first act (see Table 9.1). Like *Il vangelo*, *Godspell* selects and rearranges Matthew's Sermon, but delivers it piecemeal (unlike *Il vangelo*). The teaching continues as the troupe leaves the junkyard, singing "Day by Day," and frolics through an empty city (locations in Table 9.1). They, and Jesus's teachings, are itinerant.[16]

While *Il vangelo*'s Jesus angrily monologues, *Godspell*'s Jesus is happy, with his troupe. While *Godspell*'s Jesus starts (e.g., the Prodigal Son) or caps most of the teaching (e.g., the Beatitudes), the community performs the teaching (see Walsh 2003: 81–5). This communal enactment, along with its music, makes *Godspell* distinctive. The film also includes more parables than any Jesus film up to its time: the Pharisee and the Tax Collector, the Unmerciful Servant, the Sheep and the Goats, the Good Samaritan, Lazarus and the Rich Man, and the Prodigal Son.[17] The troupe enacts the parables as skits (in different styles: e.g., call-and-response sermon and finger puppets).

The communal Sermon advocates righteousness, humility (e.g., 5:17-20; 6:22-24; 6:2-4), forgiveness, and love (e.g., 5:25-26; 5:38-39; 7:3-5; 5:44; 7:12), while enjoining trust in God's provision (5:1-12; 6:28-30; 7:9-11). *Godspell*'s Sermon moves from responsibility to blessing by postponing the Beatitudes and by pairing the Sermon with songs similarly moving from responsibility/mission ("Day by Day," "Turn Back") to blessing ("Bless the Lord," "All for the Best," "All Good Gifts"). The Sermon's basic message is the importance of (religious) community, which the inclusion of Lukan materials underlines.

Table 9.1 *Godspell*'s "Matthean" sermon, scripture, and song.

Sermon	Other scripture	Song	Location	Time
5:17-20	Lk. 18:9-14		Junkyard	15:34; 18:00
5:25-26	18:23-35		Junkyard	19:33; 19:58
		Day by Day	Junkyard On the Road	
5:38-39	25:31-46		Military Memorial Monument	25:55; 26:50
6:22-24		Turn Back	Andrew Carnegie Mansion	29:21
	Lk. 10:30-35		Parking Lot	35:11
6:2-4	Lk. 16:19-31		Grant Memorial	37:45; 38:53
		Bless the Lord	Guggenheim Bandshell	
5:1-12			Guggenheim Bandshell	44:32
		All for the Best	Lincoln Center Times Square Twin Towers	
7:3-5		All for the Best	Twin Towers	48:54
5:44	13:3-8, 9-23		Lincoln Center	51:55
		All Good Gifts	Umpire Rock	
6:28-30			Central Park	56:24
	Lk. 15:11-31		Cherry Lane Theatre	58:44
7:9-12			Pier	1.04:59
5:13-16		Light of the World	Tugboat Statue of Liberty	1.05:40

To see the narrative flow, read right from the Sermon column and then return to the left.

The Prodigal Son's dramatic enactment in the Cherry Lane Theatre, where the play *Godspell*, with Stephen Schwartz's score, was first performed Off-Broadway (May 17, 1971), climaxes the first act. The troupe performs the parable as a commentary on clips from early silent comedies.[18] As in those comedies, everyone (important) is saved. The father sees to it that the two brothers embrace. Similarly, after the Sheep and the Goats' enactment, Jesus returns to collect the Goats as well, and Jesus draws a smiley heart on a window while the troupe sings "Turn Back, O Man." Comedy and happiness overcome all—in the first act.[19]

The troupe makes its way to a decaying pier where they embark on a tugboat, singing "Light of the World" (5:13-16). This paean to US nationalism frequently displays the boat's American flag and a troupe member mimics the Statue of Liberty pose (in the background). Lines about the city of God, however, recall the film's story of human recreation. Significantly, any dichotomy between Sermon and song has vanished. The Sermon is song.[20]

Back on the pier, the second act opens with Jesus declaring that this is the beginning (recalling either Jn 12:23 or the film's prologue and Gen. 1:1). A robot, representing the scribes and Pharisees, emerges from a warehouse to challenge Jesus (21:23-27; 22:16-21, 36-40).[21] In his most aggressive, violent scene, Jesus harangues the robot in "Alas for You" (based primarily on 23:13, 33-34, 16, 36).[22] During the song, Jesus tears the (emperor's new) clothes from the robot, leaving it broken on the ground, and then walks away lamenting Jerusalem's fate (23:37-39, in a medium shot facing the camera).

The troupe sings "By My Side" to comfort the sad, lonely Jesus.[23] The Baptist (now "Judas"), however, reminds the audience of Judas's betrayal (26:14-16).[24] The troupe then dances through the city one last time, singing "Beautiful City," about building a city of man (not a city of angels) out of brokenness and despair. The song echoes the prologue, and the troupe returns through Central Park, passing by the redemptive "Angel of the Waters" on their way to the junkyard.

In the evening, Jesus and Judas lay down a red door as a table, and Jesus cleans the troupe's painted faces (cf. Jn 13:1-12). Announcing the betrayal, Jesus sends Judas away "quickly" (merging 26:21-22, 25 with Jn 13:27). Sitting before a painted sunrise on the wall behind him, Jesus pronounces Jewish blessings and eucharistic words over the bread and wine. Offscreen, a group sings "On the Willows" (based on Ps. 137).[25] The lament foreshadows the question awaiting them in Jesus's absence: "How shall we sing the Lord's song in a foreign land?"

Having said his goodbyes, Jesus prays alone. Greene merges Jesus's garden struggle to accept the cup with the Matthean temptations (4:1-11).[26] Banishing Satan, Jesus determines to worship God alone (4:10).[27] Police cars arrive, their headlights illumining the junkyard, and a reluctant Judas returns. When he starts to run away, Jesus encourages him. Judas kneels before Jesus (recalling the baptismal scene) and they embrace. Calling him friend, Jesus kisses him on each cheek.

Returning to his ringmaster role, blowing a whistle, and humming, Baptist/Judas ties Jesus to the junkyard's chain-link fence with bright red ribbons (see Figure 9.1).[28] The troupe hurls itself onto the fence where Jesus hangs, and they begin the "Finale," with Jesus addressing God ("Oh God, I'm bleeding," "dying," and "dead") and the troupe responding ("Oh God, you're bleeding … ").[29] Jesus's head slumps and the (police) lights go out.[30]

With a dissolve, morning arrives. The disciples awake and start singing the "Finale" again, but now it is "Long Live God" (mixed with "Save the People," "Beautiful City," and "Prepare Ye") as they take Jesus's body down and carry it cruciform into the empty city, still singing. Gradually, the funeral march becomes upbeat as those not carrying Jesus begin to clap and dance. Fittingly, the song becomes "Day by Day" (cf. Lk. 9:23). They turn a corner and vanish. The New York City streets are suddenly busy again. The troupe lost, the song goes on, despite crowd noise.

Figure 9.1 The red ribbon, chain-link fence crucifixion in *Godspell*, directed by David Greene, Columbia, 1973. All rights reserved.

MEMORABLE CHARACTERS

1 Jesus is a clown (Tebelak and Schwartz 2012: iv); he belongs to Harvey Cox's *Feast of Fools* (1969)—to the hope that festivity, fantasy, and play may recreate the world. The faded Superman t-shirt distinguishes this Clark Kent-Jesus from more powerful cinematic Christs.

2 The clown troupe is as important as Jesus.[31] They perform his teachings, share in his suffering and death, and continue his song in the modern city.

3 The Baptist/Judas is Jesus's call/destiny, the ringmaster of Jesus's inescapable fate. He stands with the "Angel of the Waters" and has red ribbons at hand. Nonetheless, he is in the troupe that carries the dead Jesus back into the city.

MEMORABLE VISUALS

1 Jesus clad in faded Superman t-shirt and clown pants.
2 Baptisms in Bethesda Fountain, Central Park.
3 The Prodigal Son "film."
4 Red-ribbon crucifixion on a chain-link fence (see Figure 9.1).
5 The troupe carrying the cruciform Jesus into the city.

KEY AUTHORITY/SCRIPTURE

1 The chief authority is the alternative, sacred reality of fantasy, play, and clowning (cf. the function of *Il vangelo*'s southern Italy and peasants, or *Greatest Story*'s West

[1965]), and the music evoking both tradition (the Episcopal hymnal and scripture) and popular folk-rock style.

2 The scriptural authority is an adapted Matthew focusing on the Baptist, Sermon selections, and a drastically condensed passion (conflict stories, Supper, garden/betrayal, and death)—and ultimately turned into song. In this regard, "Light of the World" (5:13-16) is the film's most important text (followed closely by "Day by Day").[32]

3 Notably, this Matthew is also quite Lukan, given its inclusion of Lukan parables, like the Prodigal Son, which the film renders even more inclusive than Luke's version.

CULTURAL LOCATION/GENRE: MUSICAL COMEDY, VAUDEVILLE, PANTOMIME

Godspell's vaudevillian roots and clowns distinguish it from *Jesus Christ Superstar* and *Gospel Road*. As a musical comedy, songs and laughter are more important to *Godspell* than dialogue or character/plot. Realism is also not required. *Godspell* is less spectacular than *Jesus Christ Superstar*; it has no big, show-stopping numbers. It is naïve, simple, and playful—as befits vaudeville (and the community theater where it has thrived).

The costumes, hair, and music also indicate connections with the countercultural 1960s and with its youth (and Jesus) movements. Nonetheless, the creators stress *Godspell*'s connections with clowns, rather than hippies (Tebelak and Schwartz 2012: iv). The film has an important precursor in *Parable*,[33] a short film produced by the Council of Churches of New York City for the 1964–5 World's Fair.[34] Before *Parable*'s opening titles, a narrator says that Jesus taught in parables and a modern parable might imagine a circus (world) in which one person dared to be different. The rest of the film is mime; it has no narration. A black screen gives way to morning at the circus (the set is the Circus World Museum in Baraboo, Wisconsin). Magnus the Great (Gordon Oarsheim) prepares for the day, and a circus parade proceeds down the road.

At the rear of the parade, almost unnoticed, a clown rides on a donkey (Clarence Mitchell) in white face and white clothing. He walks around the circus grounds taking on the burdens of the elephant caretaker, a man in a dunking booth, and a magician's female assistant. His actions entice them to follow him, but angers others (e.g., the barker, the magician). The clown and his followers ultimately enter the big tent where the puppeteer Magnus has hoisted clowns to the rafters, manipulating their strings abusively. After wiping the audience's feet (all children), the clown frees the puppets from their strings and dons one of their harnesses. Those he has angered beat him, and Magnus hoists him aloft for more abuse. The clown dies with a loud scream (startling in a pantomime). Magnus is left sitting dejectedly on his throne.

The next morning, the clown's followers comically help each other prepare for the day. Magnus also prepares, but this time he dons white face paint. The parade begins again. Time passes; the clown is missing; then a figure in white (presumably Magnus) rides a donkey down the road.

If it is, indeed, Magnus, then *Parable* is even more optimistic and inclusive than *Godspell*. Notably, however, neither film—despite their comedy—imagines the complete displacement of the System (circus or city). The clowns simply represent difference.

DIRECTOR

John-Michael Tebelak wrote *Godspell* as part of his master's thesis in drama at Carnegie-Mellon University in Pittsburgh, Pennsylvania. He wanted to liberate Jesus's message from the church's stifling confines (see Barker 1975). He worked with theater students at Carnegie-Mellon who improvised scenes for biblical verses and first performed the play on campus in 1970.[35]

A Carnegie Mellon alumnus (Charles Haid) brought the play to producers who sponsored a run at the Off-Off-Broadway La MaMa Experimental Theatre Club. The producers then hired Stephen Schwartz, also a Carnegie Mellon alumnus, to redo the music and lyrics.[36] Subsequently, the play opened Off-Broadway at the Cherry Lane Theatre on May 17, 1971. After various roadshow productions, the play opened on Broadway in 1976 (and again in 2011).

David Greene directed the play's film version, but he is best known for television productions (he was a co-director of *Roots* [1977] and won Emmy awards for the TV features *The People Next Door* [1969] and *Friendly Fire* [1979]).[37]

PROBLEMATIC ISSUE: VISUALIZING THE SACRED

Building upon Paul Schrader's famous *Transcendental Style in Film*, Vivian Sobchack describes three ways, out of many, in which cinema visualizes the transcendent: (1) figural literalism mimetically represents the sacred other that, it asserts, transcends the material world; (2) transcendence in immanence lets the sacred emerge in and from the material world; (3) figural gap imagines a sacred other wholly beyond human ken, which is therefore inexpressible materially, except for the awareness of a rift in the material world (2008).

The first is the style of Jesus film generally—particularly those films which present Jesus as a divine figure visiting a world where he does not (wholly) belong. In the scenes in which the Baptist and Jesus flicker into sight, *Godspell* partakes in this "way," as does its creation of a play space in an eerily empty city. Realistic film photography and film's tendency to hallow itself, however, are avenues to Sobchack's second "way." Celebrities are also immanent sacreds. *Il vangelo*'s lingering closeups on peasant faces are a Jesus film example of the second "way." *Godspell* reaches that "way" when the song lingers after the troupe vanishes into the city. The third "way" typically appears in art (or "difficult") film. Schrader cites the works of Ozu, Bresson, and Dreyer as examples. Such films (and their sacreds) are hard to consume and assimilate. They confront and deny identification and sentimentality (Schrader 2018: 177–85). Most Jesus films, by contrast, work to identify Jesus (however transcendent) with their audiences (to comfort and even deify them).

COLUMBIA, 103 MINUTES, 2000
DVD Extras

English, Spanish, Portuguese, Chinese, Korean, and Thai subtitles. Widescreen on side A.
Musical Numbers: Highlights
   (These filmed songs function like music videos.)

1 Prepare Ye (The Way of the Lord)
2 Save the People
3 Day by Day
4 Turn Back, O Man

Talent Files (text only)
   David Greene (director)
   Victor Garber
   Katie Hanley
   David Haskell

Bonus trailers
   Bye Bye Birdie
   Oliver!

DVD CHAPTERS

(All scripture references are to Matthew unless otherwise indicated)
(Non-Matthean material is in italics)

1 Start
2 Prologue, 1:15
3 "Prepare Ye the Way of the Lord," 7:34
      "I baptize you with water" (3:3, 11, 13-15), 10:00
4 "Save the People," 10:37
      Parable of the Pharisee and the tax collector (Lk. 18:9-14), 18:00
5 "Day by Day," 22:30
6 "Turn Back O Man," 30:36
      Parable of the Good Samaritan (Lk. 10:30-35), 35:11
      Parable of the Rich Man and Lazarus (Lk. 16:19-31), 38:53
7 "Bless the Lord," 41:40
8 "All for the Best," 46:05
      The song ends on top the unfinished Twin Towers, 49:50
      "All your wrongs will be redressed," 50:20

9 "All Good Gifts," 55:03

    Parable of the Prodigal Son (Lk. 15:11-32), 58:44

10 "Light of the World" (5:13-16), 1.05:40

    "By whose authority?" (21:23-27; 22:16-21, 36-40; 23:2, 5-9), 1.08:00

    ("This is the beginning")

11 "Alas for You" (23:13-15, 33-34, 36), 1.10:38

    "Jerusalem, Jerusalem" (23:37-39), 1.12:16

12 "By My Side," 1.13:53

    Judas Iscariot (26:14-16), 1.16:58

13 "Beautiful City," 1.17:51

    Bethesda Fountain and junkyard

    The Last Supper (26:20-29), 1.21:08

14 "On the Willows" *[Ps. 137]*, 1.25:02

    "Stay here" (26:36-41, 34, 42), 1.27:14

    Temptation (4:3-11), 1.29:09

    Betrayal (26:47-56), 1.30:12

    Crucifixion (27.33-55), 1.32:30

15 Finale, 1.32:49

    Death, 1.35:00

    Easter morning (28:1-10), 1.35:52

    City alive, 1.38:40

16 End Credits, 1.38:54

NOTES

1 For example, atheist Luis Buñuel's *Nazarín* (1959) traces a simple priest's degradation. This Christlike figure's naïve piety, not unfaithfulness or corruption, contributes to his ruin. Jesus's teaching is irrelevant to modernity, but the film indicts the world's maliciousness as well. In Buñuel's *La Voie lactée* (The Milky Way 1969), two impious pilgrims travel the Camino de Santiago and also journey through a cynical recap of Christian history and Roman Catholic dogma/heresy. They meet Jesus and Mary in historical guise—and sometimes recognize them. Buñuel's Jesus is unorthodox; the film ends with Jesus's unsuccessful "healing" of two blind men. In Peter Medak's *The Ruling Class* (1972), a schizophrenic English lord thinks he is Jesus Christ until electroshock "resurrects" him as Jack the Ripper (amusingly, people prefer Jack!). *Godspell*'s piety obviously distinguishes it from these films.

2 In *Gospel Road*, a black-clad, Bible-wielding Johnny Cash sings and narrates a pilgrimage through modern Israel and the evangelistic (gospel) road of salvation. The film's director, Robert Elfstrom, plays a blond, smiling, mute Jesus. Ruth Carter Cash, one of the few "historical" characters to speak/sing, plays Magdalene and dramatizes her exorcism/salvation (Lk. 8:2) in the film's most important scene. Incongruously, the crucifixion appears against

various modern urban backdrops. In the last shot, Jesus, seen from behind, strikes a Rio de Janeiro *Christ the Redeemer* pose. Billy Graham used the film evangelistically. See Cochran (2021).

3   Tebelak says the play's idea began when he attended a glum, chilly Easter Vigil that seemed to pile stones on Jesus's tomb. See Barker (1975).
4   The actor playing Jesus delivers this voiceover, if it appears, in play versions. See Laird (2014: 23, 353 n35). It is not in Tebelak and Schwartz (2012). The film's narrator sounds like Jesus/Victor Garber, but the credits do not confirm it. The film credits simply list the actors, and no one is addressed by name in the film. The play's script designates characters by the original actor's names, except for Jesus and the Baptist/Judas. In the play's original prologue and musical number, "Tower of Babble," the eight cast members argue philosophically, creating a chaos to which the play's Baptist and Jesus respond. The film's noisy city streets provide a similar chaos.
5   Barnes Tatum claims that God is the film's theological center (2013: 135).
6   Parenthetical scripture references are to Matthew unless otherwise noted.
7   After September 11, 2001, the jet engine's juxtaposition with the Twin Towers seems eerily prescient.
8   David Haskell plays the ringmaster/Baptist/Judas. He appeared in the original play as did Robin Lamont, Gilmer McCormick, Joanne Jonas, and Jeffrey Mylett. *Godspell* was Haskell's most memorable acting role.
9   Many are from the Episcopal hymnal: "Save the People," "Day by Day," "Turn Back, O Man," "Bless the Lord," "All Good Gifts," and "We Beseech Thee" (not in the film) (Tebelak and Schwartz 2012: vii). While there are solos, the songs typically become communal ("Alas for You" is a notable exception). Guitar, bass, keyboard, and percussion accompany the songs.
10 Prior, the AIDS victim protagonist of Tony Kushner's 1993 award-winning play *Angels in America* (and 2003 film), sits at the fountain in that play's conclusion.
11 *Godspell*'s Baptist is non-judgmental. The play's Baptist is more challenging as its script includes Mt. 3:7-8, 10-11 (Tebelak and Schwartz 2012: 7-8).
12 Garber appeared as Jesus in the 1972 Toronto production of *Godspell*. Gilda Radner and Martin Short were also in that cast. Garber has had a lengthy stage, film, and TV career. Canadian, of Russian Jewish descent, and homosexual, he differs somewhat from the Hollywood Jesus norm, as does his afro, shaven face, and clownish garb.
13 A "miracle" occurs when a blonde woman plants a little sumac in a pot. While she is distracted, the Baptist replaces the shrub with a larger tree. Having seen Jesus water the shrub, she thinks "it's a miracle." The sequence parodies film's cut-away "editing" miracles. The ringmaster and Jesus's sudden appearances employ similar (primitive) editing techniques. In many ways—especially in its vaudevillian style—the film recalls early silents.
14 Beginning and ending in a modern city contrast dramatically with the church opening and conclusion in *Greatest Story*. Of course, *Godspell* does leave the city for its God spell.
15 See Nietzsche's notion of philosophy as dance ([1887] 1974), van Gennep's notion of ritual transition ([1909] 2019), Huizinga's discussion of play (1949), Turner's discussion of liminality (1967: 93-111), or Bakhtin's notion of carnival (1984). Most critics note the influence of Harvey Cox's notions of festival and clowning on *Godspell* (Tebelak and Schwartz 2012: iv). Cox saw his *Feast of Fools* (1969) as a supplement to his *The Secular City* (1965).
16 Jesus's teaching means differently according to its context. Like *Il vangelo*, *Godspell* removes the teaching's canonical certainty. See Walsh (2003: 69-73).

17 Parables did appear as silent shorts. See, for example, *L'enfant prodigue* (Zecca) 1901, 1907, 1909.
18 The scene indicates *Godspell*'s vaudevillian and silent film connections. Early films were often shown in vaudeville halls and as part of variety shows. Further, the commentary on silents here recalls the sermonic lectures accompanying early Jesus lantern slides and films.
19 Unlike Jesus epics, the film does not cut away to scenes featuring elite opposition, but it suggests conflict when Jesus slaps the Baptist to illustrate his "turn the other cheek" teaching. (The Baptist almost returns the favor before reconsidering it.) The disciples also quarrel briefly until Jesus tells them to love their enemies. More importantly, in one ominous moment, Jesus has difficulty completing the beatitude the Baptist begins about persecution (5:11).
20 The play has an intermission, with the characters mingling with the audience, here.
21 Why a robot? Early play productions used tin foil to represent wealthy clothing. See Tebelak and Schwartz (2012: 61). The robot might reflect the System that 1960s countercultural movements rejected, or the modern industrial society rejected by American Romanticism. See Chapter 8 and Walsh (2003: 73-7). Reading *Godspell* in connection with the 2011 Occupy movements, Tina Pippin (2013) argues that the film is less negative about "the city" than Walsh claims.
22 This harangue is the film's most Pasolini moment—although one can hardly imagine *Il vangelo*'s Jesus bursting into song.
23 The question about where Jesus is going has a Johannine aura (cf. Jn 14). Other Johannine elements include the idea that the troupe was first the Baptist's disciples (Jn 1:35-37), the face-washing (cf. Jn 13:1-12), Jesus's command for Judas to do it quickly (twice) (Jn 13:27), and the arrival of the arrest party with lights (Jn 18:3).
24 That one actor plays both the ringmaster Baptist and Judas connects the baptism and passion, emphasizing Jesus's prophetic destiny. See Walsh (2010: 61-3).
25 Judas begins this song in the play's Broadway revival. See Tebelak and Schwartz (2012: 78).
26 Other filmmakers also present Jesus's temptation near the story's end. See, for example, *The King of Kings* (1927) and *The Last Temptation of Christ* (1988). Like *Godspell*, *Jesus Christ Superstar* (1973), *Jesus* (1999), and *The Passion of the Christ* (2004) place the crucial test in the garden.
27 These words are deployed less effectively than in *King of Kings* (1961).
28 *Son of Man* "crucifies" its Jesus with red ribbons too. See Staley (2013b: 98-102).
29 The troupe's words are ambiguous. Is their "Oh God" an expletive like "Oh shit," or do they address Jesus as God?
30 Perhaps, Jesus's junkyard death echoes his death outside the city in the gospels. As he dies alone in the garden, his death is almost inexplicable. The story (or fate) determines it. See n24.
31 Some see *Godspell* as the story of a Christian community and of Christ figure(s), rather than as a Jesus story. Any Jesus relocation raises such interpretative possibilities.
32 Most of Matthew—even more than in *Il vangelo*—is missing: for example, the infancy; fulfillment citations; miracles; synagogues and temple; Peter's confession and installation as the church's rock; transfiguration; Mt. 10; 18; 24-25 (except for the Sheep and Goats parable); triumph and temple act; trials; mockery and abuse; burial; and resurrection appearances.
33 Tebelak said that the short influenced *Godspell* (Lindvall and Quicke 2011: 15).
34 Rolf Forsberg directed *Parable*. He later directed the dramatic sequences for *The Late Great Planet Earth* (1978) (narrated by Orson Welles).

35 Tebelak was only twenty-two. He directed *Godspell* revivals and other plays before his death in 1985. The film credits him as co-writer and creative consultant. He was the dramaturge for the Cathedral Church of St John the Divine in New York, and some say he considered going to seminary.
36 Schwartz is famous for theatrical (e.g., *Wicked* 2003) and cinematic (e.g., *The Prince of Egypt* 1998) music and lyrics. He has won three Grammy Awards (one for *Godspell*) and three Academy Awards (one for *The Prince of Egypt*).
37 He directed Victor Garber again in the title role in *Liberace: Behind the Music* (1988), a Canadian TV-production.

10

Jesus Christ Superstar

Norman Jewison, director, Universal, 1973

PLOT SUMMARY: ROCKING THE GOSPEL

While *Godspell* reflects the worlds of vaudeville and local theater, *Jesus Christ Superstar* is a Broadway spectacle. Beginning as a single song (1969), it became Andrew Lloyd Webber (composer) and Tim Rice's (lyricist) twenty-eight song, two LP album (1970),[1] a touring rock opera concert (1971), and a Broadway production (October 12, 1971).[2]

Faithful to its rock opera roots, everything is sung.[3] There is silence (e.g., during the final credits) and ambient noise (e.g., the nailing to the cross), but no spoken dialogue. The songs' independence—as well as the abrupt editing and camera—makes the film more episodic than the gospels (Goodacre 1999: 8–9). The obvious difference between the film and staged versions is the film's location in Israel's Negev desert. That landscape, like *Greatest Story*'s (1965) iconic West, becomes its own character, emphasizing the film's aura of alienation and anguish.[4]

The film opens in silence. The camera pans the Negev bringing into view the ruins of Nabataean Avdat with modern scaffolding. Dust rises in the distance, and a bus, lettered in Hebrew and Arabic, comes into view. The instrumental "Overture" begins. A wood cross and other theatrical paraphernalia are atop the bus. It stops; energetic young people pile out, unload, and don 1970s era costumes. They have come to perform *Jesus Christ Superstar*.[5] The film barely develops the notion of a play performance (contrast *Jésus de Montréal* 1989), but 1970s modernity still intrudes (Reinhartz 2013a: 118).

The troupe sings and dances ritualistically, as a Black actor, dressed in red, walks out into the desert. Black-clad actors, with Pasoliniesque hats (the religious leaders), and (Roman) soldiers in purple tank tops and chrome helmets stand watching. Within the ritual circle, a blonde character salutes the sun (with "Jesus Christ Superstar" instrumental background). Women slip a white biblical-epic-looking robe over his naked back. An abrupt cut moves to a closeup of this Jesus (Ted Neeley).[6] Meanwhile, the black-clad, vulture-like leaders climb into Avdat's scaffolding. The film's title appears.

After a fade to black, an extreme longshot depicts a barely discernible figure perched on a ridge that should signify Jesus and his wilderness preparation. Instead, it is Judas's "tempting" (Carl Anderson).[7] The camera approaches him from multiple perspectives in a rapid series of cuts and zooms as he sings the first song, "Heaven on Their Minds."[8] Emphasizing Judas's alienation, Jewison cuts between this angry, stalking character and Jesus calmly teaching his followers.[9] Judas rues the group's descent into mythology. Now

Jesus believes everything they say of him, and Judas fears the Romans will destroy them all. In its greatest innovation (beyond its music), the film continues to present Jesus largely from Judas's (and Magdalene's) POV.[10]

Underneath marching soldiers, Jesus's group rests in a cave.[11] Through an oculus, a shaft of light falls on Jesus as the apostles sing "What's the Buzz?" They wonder when they will "ride" to Jerusalem, but Jesus warns them not to worry about the future (cf. Mt. 6:34). Meanwhile, in the first (erotic) anointing scene, Magdalene (Yvonne Elliman)[12] washes Jesus's face and feet (cf. Lk. 7:36-50). When Judas complains about Jesus associating with women of her kind/profession ("Strange Thing Mystifying"), Jesus tells him, if innocent, to cast the first stone (equating Magdalene with the woman taken in adultery). Then, Jesus berates his disciples for not caring whether he comes or goes.

A cut leads to Annas (Kurt Yaghjian) and Caiaphas (Bob Bingham) in flickering lamplight, deciding Jesus's fate[13] ("Then We Are Decided").[14] In the cave, Magdalene anoints Jesus a second time, as she and a female chorus support him with "Everything's Alright" (echoing Mt. 6:34?) (see Figure 10.1). Judas complains on behalf of the poor (Jn 12:3-8), so Magdalene and the women comfort him as well. After farewell words (cf. John's farewell discourse), Jesus and Judas clasp hands. But Judas turns away from Magdalene's continuing "comfort" of Jesus.

A dissolve leads to circling vultures, followed by the vulturous leaders mounting their scaffolding. Beneath them, a small group walks toward the ruins, hosannaing "Jesus Christ Superstar." The leaders decide "This [dangerous] Jesus Must Die" (cf. Jn 11:49-50).[15] Jesus rejects Caiaphas's demand to silence the crowd (see Lk. 19:39-49) and teaches the people that they can "win" the kingdom. They, however, have other concerns and want "JC" to do something for them—even die. The last sobers Jesus (in freeze-frame closeup), but the scene ends happily with him holding a child.[16]

After a cut, "Simon Zealotes" and others materialize out of the desert, dancing into columned ruins (with slow motion and freeze-frame accentuating their athleticism). They want Jesus to take power (over the Romans). Soldiers and Judas watch while the dancers prostrate themselves around Jesus, but Jesus attacks, saying none of them understand power and glory. As Magdalene comforts him, Jesus mourns "Poor Jerusalem," and muses that dying is the way to conquer death.

A dissolve leads to "Pilate's Dream" of a haunted-looking Galilean refusing to answer questions and leaving Pilate to take the blame.[17] Another dissolve segues to the cleansing of "The Temple," a modern bazaar selling everything, including sex and weapons. Jesus smashes it all.[18] Suddenly, he walks alone through the wilderness ruing his ministry's long, weary road. Black-clad figures rise from the cliffsides, demanding healing (cf. *Il vangelo*'s [1964] tower of the sick) and overwhelming Jesus. The music speeds frenetically as he begs to be left alone.

A fade to black leads to Magdalene comforting Jesus in her tent. It is another "anointing" scene, reprising "Everything's Alright" and introducing her signature song, "I Don't Know How to Love Him." Like Judas, Magdalene knows Jesus is "just" a man and regrets becoming a frightened lover after so many previous men.[19] Jewison ends the scene by superimposing their two faces.

In an eerie silence, tanks crest the wilderness horizon and roar to life, descending on Judas. Running helter-skelter to the scaffold-poised leaders, he betrays Jesus, but pleads not to be "Damned for all Time." Annas and Caiaphas offer him "Blood Money" to tell them where they can arrest Jesus (Gethsemane, Thursday night). Suddenly, Judas is in the desert again. Fighter jets shriek low overhead.

An intermission occurs here in stage presentations. The episodic film's first act has moved from adoration ("Orchestra") to murderous plots ("Blood Money"), and from Judas's demythologizing ("Heaven on Their Minds") to the "sad solution" ("Damned for all Time"). Judas has dominated. The second act's opening scene, however, echoes the early "What's the Buzz?" scene.

A shepherd leads his sheep, and the apostles, walk into a garden for a Da Vinci-style picnic ("Last Supper").[20] Again, Jesus berates them, turning institutional words about wine and blood into an accusation about the disciples' callousness and claiming it mad to think he will be remembered.

Jesus and Judas scream names-become-epithets at one another: "You Judas!" "Christ!" Knowing his destiny as betrayer, Judas wonders if his disobedience would ruin Jesus's ambition. He leaves only when Jesus, himself ambivalent (he follows Judas with a cloak and caresses him), chases him away. As Judas runs, he scatters the flock of sheep.

In one of the film's best scenes (equaling Judas's opening temptation), Jesus climbs a mountain (cf. *Greatest Story*'s temptation scene) as the camera looks down on him (a divine POV; Humphries-Brooks 2006: 63–6). Jesus is sad and tired ("Gethsemane"). Gradually, abandoning "why" (which God is not "hot on"), Jesus agrees to die. Jewison presents this destiny in a montage of twenty-three shots of crucifixion art in twenty-six seconds (Forshey 1992: 109).[21] Jesus agrees to drink God's "cup of poison," for the nonce, but warns God that he may change his mind.

The camera dissolves to Judas, Jesus's doppelgänger, approaching Jesus from behind and kissing him. After "The Arrest," Jewison shows, from on high, soldiers taking Jesus down a lonely road to Caiaphas (they pass another shepherd and his flock). Mimicking reporters, people badger Jesus with questions. Jesus responds to Caiaphas's blasphemy question evasively (cf. Mt. 27:11), but Caiaphas sends him to Pilate anyway. At a lonely desert well, Peter[22] denies Jesus ("Peter's Denial").[23]

In his cliff fortress, Pilate mocks Jesus as "someone Christ, King of the Jews" and marvels at his silence ("Pilate and Christ") before sending him to Herod Antipas as the mocking crowd reprises the triumph's "Hosanna." On his pleasure island, Herod mocks Jesus in a vaudevillian-style performance for failing to walk across his swimming pool.

As soldiers march Jesus back to Pilate, a dissolve moves to Magdalene and Peter singing "Could We Start Again Please?" (with Jesus shimmering in and out of the scene). Seeing the beaten Jesus in a dungeon cave, Judas returns the blood money, lamenting he will be dragged through the slime and the mud ("Judas's Death"). Alone, on his knees, he echoes Magdalene's theme song as he too does not know how to love this man. Judas then runs, under a darkening sky, into the wilderness. Finding a barren tree on a hill, he hangs himself with his moneybag-rope belt, berating God for murdering him. The chorus sings "So long, Judas," as he hangs silhouetted (in a long shot).[24]

The camera pulls back to the ruins of a Roman amphitheater (in Beit She'an National Park) for the "Trial Before Pilate." Pilate tries to avoid executing this sad, little man, who may have a kingdom "somewhere," by having Jesus flogged (counted in slow motion). Women pull an anguished Magdalene away. After the scourging, Pilate holds Jesus pietà-like as Jesus tells him that things are fixed, unchangeable. Threatened further by the crowd, Pilate washes Jesus's blood from his hands, telling the "innocent puppet" to die if he desires.

In a surprising Ecce Homo-like scene, Jesus is transfigured into clean white garments. Judas, also in transfigured white, descends from a black sky on a lighted cross for "Jesus Christ Superstar." With female backup dancers and chorus, an angry Judas still asks who Jesus is and if Jesus believes what they say about him.[25]

Little revelation occurs despite the heavenly spectacle. The climactic scene simply renews the questions of Judas's opening song. It makes no confession. The passing of time (story) has only deepened the elegiac mood (cf. Goodacre 1999: 12).

Jewison cuts repeatedly between this spectacle and Jesus on the Via Dolorosa (in silence). The song ends as Jesus is audibly nailed to his cross. Canned mockery accompanies the cross's raising. Magdalene suffers more noticeably than Jesus.[26] After a shot from the top of the cross toward the mocking soldiers (cf. the camera placement in *King of Kings* 1961), "Crucifixion" begins. Jesus asks God to forgive them (in a medium shot), asks why God has forgotten him, and entrusts his spirit to the father's hands (both in closeup, although somewhat obscured by the sun behind Jesus). Jesus's head slumps forward. The music stops.

New instrumental music begins ("John 19:41") as everyone walks away and boards the bus—in street clothing. Yvonne Elliman and Carl Anderson are the last to board. Ted Neeley is not seen boarding (nor did he visibly deboard the bus earlier). The sun sets behind the empty cross. In the shadows below, a barely visible shepherd crosses the hill with his sheep.[27] The camera pulls back. The screen fades to black and the credits roll in silence.

MEMORABLE CHARACTERS

1 Judas's opening and climactic solos establish him and his accusatory questions as the film's POV (cf. Jesus's angry questions in the garden).[28] Tim Rice famously said that the opera grew from Bob Dylan's question: "Whether Judas Iscariot had God on his side" (in his 1964 song, "With God on Our Side"; Miller 2016). Judas is the 1960s antihero suspicious of celebrity and the Establishment; nonetheless, Judas eventually bows to Jesus/God/destiny's demands, so the traditional story continues.

2 The film's primary spokespersons (Judas and Magdalene) know Jesus is "just a man." Appropriate to his humanity, Jesus's hair moves (a Jesus film rarity). "Christ" never appears with its traditional theological connotations. It is epithet and surname. In Gethsemane, Jesus finds his own accusatory questions. Like Judas, he receives no answer unless it is the montage of crucifixion art. Like Judas, he acquiesces to destiny or to the story.[29]

3 Magdalene replaces Mary as Jesus's comforter, repeatedly caressing and anointing him. The film fleshes out the ménage à trois suggestion in DeMille's *The King of Kings* (1927), forming the most erotic relationships in Jesus film before *Last Temptation*

(1988; see n19; Baugh 1997: 250 nn38–9).³⁰ Jaime Clark-Soles claims Magdalene "has become a mulatto whore who is a site of contest between two alpha males" (2013: 144; see Figure 10.1). The film does go out of its way to slur Magdalene, equating her with the woman taken in adultery.

MEMORABLE VISUALS

1 Judas alone, in the distance, in the Negev.
2 Magdalene "comforting" Jesus (see Figure 10.1).
3 Jesus and Judas's Last Supper argument.
4 Jesus's Gethsemane accusations and the crucifixion art montage.
5 Judas's repentance (1.24:54) and eventual suicide (see n24).
6 Judas's descent from heaven for his transfiguration with Jesus.

KEY AUTHORITY/SCRIPTURE

1 Rock-and-roll music and a youthful anti-Establishment/tradition dominate, so traditional certainties and answers become accusatory questions (see Problematic Issue). Not even Jesus has visionary certainty.
2 Magdalene's repeated "anointing" of Jesus provides a significant undercurrent, enabling a perplexed Jesus to carry on. Sometimes a biblical incident can dominate a film, like Jesus's temptation in *Last Temptation*, but no other film gives as much attention to the anointing (cf., however, *From the Manger to the Cross*'s [1912] two anointings).
3 The film paraphrases scripture. Jesus's story or cultural memory is important, not specific gospel texts. Accordingly, the irreducible, mysterious nub of the gospel/story for this film is Jesus and Judas's shared, tragic destiny (see Walsh 2010: 23–50).

Figure 10.1 Magdalene comforts Jesus as Judas looks on in *Jesus Christ Superstar*, directed by Norman Jewison, Universal, 1973. All rights reserved.

CULTURAL LOCATION/GENRE: ROCK OPERA/PASSION PLAY

Produced four years after the Stonewall riots, *Jesus Christ Superstar* was the first Jesus movie to hire openly gay men for lead roles (e.g., Pilate).[31] Opening during the Senate Watergate hearings, the movie (and its rock opera precursor)[32] reflects the anti-Establishment youth movement of 1960s America,[33] but the successful album, play, and movie actually indicate consumer capitalism's annexation of the 1960s counterculture.[34] Accordingly, Jesus Christ becomes another troubled, money-making celebrity (rather than the Messiah, the Son of God).[35]

Traditionally, passion plays offer a set of moral lessons for the faithful by absolutizing villains' negative characteristics and glorifying heroes. Not surprisingly, Judas and the Jews fare quite badly, and some even claim anti-Semitism inherent to the passion play's structure. To combat this tendency, filmmakers build or create characters (like *The King of Kings*' Caiaphas), minimize/eliminate material (like the blood curse; the Jewish trial in *King of Kings* 1961), or ennoble Judas (as here). Filmmakers relocating Jesus to modernity, however, often emphasize offensive gospel passages to attack modern villains. For example, *Il vangelo*'s "Jewish" religious leaders are the modern bourgeoisie. Similarly, Jewison's modern religious opponents are the Establishment, not Jews.[36]

Further, Jewison undoes some of the traditional anti-Semitism by concentrating on Judas's POV and on the protagonists as "fated"; nonetheless, his Judas's death returns to a traditional perspective. Further, raising Judas from the dead to sing "Jesus Christ Superstar" hardly challenges consumerism or celebrity culture.

DIRECTOR

Canadian Norman Jewison was a respected, successful director by the time he co-wrote and directed *Jesus Christ Superstar*.[37] During his career, he directed twelve actors to Oscar nominations, three of whom won. Five of his films were nominated for Best Picture. *In the Heat of the Night* (1967) won. He was nominated three times for Best Director.

Prior to *Jesus Christ Superstar*, Jewison worked on *Fiddler on the Roof* (1971), which relied on stories by Sholem Aleichem and had been a Broadway musical (1964). Tevye (Topol), the father of five girls, struggles to maintain his Jewish tradition in the face of modern opposition. The similarities to *Jesus Christ Superstar* are obvious—Tevye even repeatedly talks to God—but *Fiddler* is a gentler, romantic comedy in which Tevye and his wife struggle to accept their daughters' willful decisions to marry for love.[38] The religious persecution causing the family to emigrate to the United States is a darker element, but more context than story, which details the quest to live a happy (traditional) life like a "fiddler on the roof."

Jewison's *Agnes of God* (1985) modernizes the virgin birth more completely and more cynically than *Jesus Christ Superstar* does the passion. In a nunnery outside Montreal, the novice Agnes (Meg Tilly) gives birth to a child, subsequently found dead in her wastebasket. A court-appointed psychiatrist, Martha Livingston (Jane Fonda), investigates Agnes's sanity (Martha has a sister Mary who died as a nun, and she is barren due to an abortion). After a long struggle with the Mother Superior (Anne Bancroft), Martha hypnotizes Agnes and learns the novice believes she has been divinely impregnated.

A flashback with heavenly light and doves supports this claim, but Martha suspects rape and murder. The court ultimately rules Agnes not guilty by reason of insanity and remands her to the nuns and regular psychiatric treatments. Perhaps, Jewison's Judas, given the option, might have chosen a similar treatment for Jesus.

Jewison is now most famous for his "social ills" films.[39] Given the concerns about *Jesus Christ Superstar*'s racism (see n8), his racial injustice trilogy is worth mentioning: *In the Heat of the Night* (1967), *A Soldier's Story* (1984), and *The Hurricane* (1999).[40] In the first, racist Chief Gillespie (Rod Steiger) arrests Virgil Tibbs (Sidney Poitier) for the murder of a wealthy local as Tibbs boards a train to leave town. The Southern policeman learns to his embarrassment that Tibbs is a homicide detective from Philadelphia. Tibbs's chief delegates him to assist with the case, which he ultimately solves despite racist opposition. In the two most memorable scenes, (1) Tibbs advises a racist cop, "They call me *Mister* Tibbs," and (2) after a wealthy racist slaps Tibbs, Tibbs returns the affront. Along the way, Tibbs twice escapes a racist mob (with Gillespie's help). Ultimately, Gillespie and Tibbs grow to respect one another and work together.[41]

In *A Soldier's Story*, Captain Richard Davenport (Howard E. Rollins, Jr.), a Black military lawyer, is sent to investigate the shooting death of Black sergeant Vernon Waters at a segregated military base in Louisiana in 1944, against the wishes of the base's commanding officer Colonel Nivens. Davenport learns that Waters's company has been assigned menial tasks (or baseball), rather than active duty, and that Waters was himself a tyrannical racist responsible for the death of various Black soldiers (a lynching and a hanging suicide). While most suspect the KKK responsible for the murder, Davenport finally extracts Pfc. Peterson's (Denzel Washington) confession that he killed Waters in revenge because Waters forced his friend to commit suicide. In the larger context, the company leaves for the European theater.

The Hurricane tells the story of Rubin "The Hurricane" Carter's (Denzel Washington) wrongful 1966 conviction and imprisonment for a triple murder, and his nearly twenty-year quest for justice. Carter claimed racism was the foundation of his conviction. A child living in Toronto reads Carter's autobiography and convinces his foster family to work on Carter's case. Ultimately, a Federal Court judge (played by Rod Steiger) overturns the verdict as based on racism.[42]

In all three films, (democratic) law overcomes racism. Most see the "law" in Jesus films, including Jewison's, differently.

Problematic Issue: Celebrity

Godspell removes the Jesus story from the church to "resurrect" it religiously. *Jesus Christ Superstar* relocates the Jesus story similarly, only to reveal Christian discourse's uncertainty outside worship.[43] Christian confessions become (Jobian) questions or very tentative grabs for meaning. Jesus and Judas rail at each other with the epithets (or passion play roles): "Judas"; "Christ." Pilate succinctly captures the ambiguities when he refers to Jesus as "someone Christ, King of the Jews."

In fact, "King of the Jews," "messiah," and "Christ" are not important terms. They need updating. In the rock opera/Broadway context, "Superstar" or "celebrity" carries more meaning—however fleetingly—and translates "messiah/Christ" for (that) modernity.[44] One should not pass by this translation too quickly. What does messiah/Christ mean (even in Christian discourse) if superstar/celebrity translates it?

The film's title—and movement from the demythologizing "Heaven on Their Minds" to the climactic, transfiguring, mythologizing "Superstar"—announces that its concern is the making and fate (mythologizing) of celebrity (not messiahs).[45] Judas's opening song says it all. Jesus comes undone as he becomes "superstar." Everyone is simply acting. Pilate has the blame, Judas is "damned for all time," and Jesus is an "innocent puppet" because those are their (temporary) roles (see Chapter 16). Everything is "fixed."

If that is all, then the film is simply a story about the dangers of celebrity and the gospels are simply stories about the dangers of messiahs. Perhaps, however, there is more. Hauntingly, the actor playing Jesus does not board the troupe's bus after the play is done. Like Daniel in *Jésus de Montréal*, has he identified too closely with his role—and is that role Jesus—or celebrity?[46]

SUPERSTARS: THE MAKING AND REUNION OF THE FILM

Tedhead Records and Frunkrock Pictures, 2015
The Reunion, 1:56
1. The Israel Experience, 5:00
    Norman Jewison (in 1972), talking about the Israeli filming sites
    Ted Neeley "Jesus of Nazareth," 6:25
    Yvonne Elliman "Mary Magdalene," 8:10
    Kurt Yaghjian "Annas," 9:27
    Norman Jewison, on charges of anti-Semitism, 9:55
    Barry Dennen "Pilate," 10:44
    Larry Marshall "Simon Zealotes," 12:16
    Bob Bingham "Caiaphas," 13:29
    Joshua Mostel "Herod," 15:46
2. Directed by Norman Jewison, 18:35
    "It would make a hell of a movie," 19:28
    Cast members talk about Jewison as director, 19:31
    The difference between the Broadway production and the film, 21:43
    Picking Ted Neeley for the role of Jesus, 24:11
    Picking Yvonne Elliman for the role of Mary Magdalene, 26:24
    How Jewison dealt with other actors on the set, 27:42
    Neeley on the film's impact, 31:32

3. This Jesusmania, 32:44
      The reunion tour
      Ted Neeley on playing "Jesus" today, 39:57
      "Jesus, will you bless my child?" 41:05
      Barry Dennen on playing Pilate today, 42:03
      Jewison, "It has something to say," 44:16
   4. Carl Anderson: Heaven on Our Minds, 44:58
      Jewison on picking Anderson for the role of Judas
      "I couldn't refuse him the role because of his color"
      Carl Anderson on the role of "Judas," 45:35
      Died in 2004

New York City Reunion April 27, 2015 (50 minutes)
Welcome, 1:16
Norman Jewison, 8:17
"Let's talk about the making of the film," 14:40
Different actors talk about their memories on set
Jewison talks about the choreographer and "Simon Zealotes," 26:32
"Herod," 28:17
"Mary Magdalene," 37:10
Jewison on "Jesus" at the film's end and the accidental shepherd, 40:57

UNIVERSAL DVD, SPECIAL EDITION, 107 MINUTES, 2004

DVD Extras

Languages
   Spoken: English, French, captioned for the hearing impaired (English)
   Subtitles: English, Spanish, French
Bonus Materials
   An exclusive interview with master lyricist Tim Rice
      Genesis, 0:00
      The Music Men, 0:55
      The Album, 2:49
      Rock Opera, 4:41
      Controversy, 6:26
      Cast, 8:26
         Comments about racial issues
      The Film, 10:54
      Legacy, 12:38
   Feature Commentary with director Norman Jewison and actor Ted Neeley
   Photo Gallery

DVD Chapters

1. Heaven on Their Minds, 0:20
    Title, 5:30
    Judas on a mountain alone, 5:48
2. What's the Buzz? 10:56
    Magdalene washes Jesus's feet (Lk. 7:36-50; 10:38-42)
3. Strange Thing Mystifying, 13:17
    Plots against Jesus (Mk 3:6, 14:1-2), 15:54
4. Everything's Alright, 18:10
    Magdalene anoints Jesus (Jn 12:1-7)
    Caiaphas and the Council (Jn 11:48-53), 22:21
    Triumphal entry (Jn 12:12-19), 23:57
5. Hosanna, 26:03
6. Simon Zealotes, 29:40
    Lament over Jerusalem (Mt. 23:37-39; Lk. 13:34-35), 34:42
7. Pilate's Dream, 35:37
8. The Temple, 37:21
9. My Temple Should Be, 39:14
    Needy overcome Jesus, 40:39
    Jesus and Magdalene, 43:14
10. I Don't Know How to Love Him, 44:09
11. Damned for All Time, 49:24
12. The Last Supper, 53:33
    Judas's response to Jesus's "prophecy," 56:55
    Jesus goes to Judas, 58:28
13. Gethsemane, 1.00:50
    Crucifixion art, 1.04:22
    "Cup of poison," 1.05:51
14. The Arrest, Part 1, 1.07:03
15. The Arrest, Part 2, 1.08:57
    Trial before Caiaphas, 1.10:12
16. Peter's Denial, 1.11:14
    Magdalene reproaches and comforts Peter, 1.12:17

17 Pilate and Christ, 1.13:54
18 King Herod's Song, 1.16:10
19 Could We Start Again Please? 1.19:29
20 Judas's Death, 1.23:14
    How to love, 1.25:00
21 Trial before Pilate, 1.28:00
    Magdalene's grief during Jesus's scourging, 1.32:03
22 Superstar, 1.35:01
    Judas's song-and-dance descent to Jesus, 1.35:35
    Via Dolorosa, 1.38:04
23 The Crucifixion, 1.39:07
    Magdalene lamenting, 1.39:49; 1.41:06
    Death, 1.41:50
    Yvonne Elliman, 1.43:10
    Carl Anderson, 1.43:14

NOTES

1   Ian Gillan, Deep Purple vocalist, sang the part of Jesus on the album. Murray Head was Judas (and sang that part on the original song), Yvonne Elliman was Magdalene, Barry Dennen was Pilate, and Michael d'Abo was Antipas. Lloyd Webber and Rice collaborated on several musicals, including *Joseph and the Amazing Technicolor Dreamcoat* (cantata 1968; Broadway 1982) and *Evita* (album 1976; Broadway 1979). Both are among a small group to have won an Oscar, an Emmy, a Grammy, and a Tony.

2   It was the first time in forty years that an actor played Jesus on Broadway (Bial 2015: 61). Tom O'Horgan, who also directed *Hair* (Broadway 1968), directed it at the Mark Hellinger Theatre. Jeff Fenholt was Jesus, Ben Vereen was Judas. Elliman and Dennen continued their album roles. Bob Bingham was Caiaphas. Carl Anderson understudied Vereen and took the role while Vereen was ill. Ted Neeley understudied Jeff Fenholt. In the film, Neeley and Anderson played Jesus and Judas, with Elliman, Dennen, and Bingham continuing their Broadway roles.

    Of many revivals, Gale Edwards's 1996 London production (Broadway 2000) is noteworthy. It featured Glenn Carter as Jesus, Tony Vincent as Judas, and Renée Castle as Magdalene. A recording, directed by Edwards and Nick Morris, appeared on PBS's Great Performance series in April 2001 (and in the UK in 2000). Glenn Carter played Jesus, Jérôme Pradon was Judas, and Renée Castle was Magdalene. NBC aired a live concert version (John Legend as Jesus, Brandon Victor Dixon as Judas, and Sara Bareilles as Magdalene) on Easter Sunday 2018 and again on Easter Sunday 2020.

3   The DVD Chapter titles indicate most of the songs. For a complete list, see *Imdb.com (Jesus Christ Superstar: Soundtracks)*. For the lyrics, see *LyricWiki: Jesus Christ Superstar* 1973. Some film songs were expanded (notably "Trial Before Pilate") and some lines were altered to avoid

offending religious audiences (e.g., in the same song, Jesus is not ignorant about his kingdom). See *Imdb.com (Jesus Christ Superstar: Trivia)*. "Then We Are Decided" was written for the film. "Could We Start Again Please?" was written for Broadway and appears in the film.

5   Jewison says the image came from watching a Jordanian bus drive up and offload tourists while he was exploring filming sites in Israel (The List: Norman Jewison, Part 2 of 3, 16:46 (YouTube https://www.youtube.com/watch?v=bJ13Q23N_kI). Neeley says the bus was his and he used it for music gigs (DVD commentary). Stephenson Humphries-Brooks thinks it alludes to Ken Kesey's 1964 psychedelic bus trip to the NYC World Fair (2006: 66–7). The Beatles *Magical Mystery Tour* (1967) also draws on Kesey's psychedelic bus trip. Intriguingly, the first three digits of the bus's license plate are "666."

6   Jewison found Neeley in Los Angeles, playing the lead in the Who's rock opera, *Tommy*. Neeley had played Claude in the 1968 Los Angeles staging of *Hair*, which led to an audition for Judas for the Broadway *Jesus Christ Superstar*. Neeley reprised "Jesus" repeatedly (into his seventies), most famously in a five-year tour, with his longtime friend Carl Anderson, beginning in 1992.

7   The red clothing could mark Judas as a Satanic tempter. See Walsh (2010: 76) and Clark-Soles (2013: 142). Like the epics, the film cuts from Jesus's group to the elite, but Jewison prefers to cut to the alienated Judas.

8   In addition to reprises of "Judas," Anderson had a prolific singing career. Some African American Baptist ministers complained to Universal about the racism of casting a Black man as Judas (Forshey 1992: 113). See Director and n24. In NBC's "live" 2018 performance, Black actors play both Jesus and Judas.

9   In contrast to *Godspell*, Jesus's teaching appears only in this mimed scene and in a few lines of song lyrics.

10 The wilderness solo is a soliloquy in which Judas reveals his inner thoughts to the audience. Jewison frequently uses closeups (to end scenes and) for such "revelations."

11 The scene recalls *Greatest Story*'s "under the bridge" teaching. The striking cave is the Bell Cave in Beit Guvrin National Park.

12 Elliman had three top-ten Adult Contemporary songs in the 1970s and toured with Eric Clapton. Edward Blum and Paul Harvey note that Elliman's Hawaiian, Japanese, and Chinese ancestry hint of an interracial relationship with Jesus that the Supreme Court had legitimized only six years earlier in *Loving v. Virginia 1967* (2012: 233).

13 They consider him a threat to "law and order," a phrase conservatives used to agitate against the Civil Rights movement.

14 John's Annas, Caiaphas's father-in-law (18:3), becomes Caiaphas's youthful "second."

15 While the film has no miracles, Annas calls Jesus "miracle wonder man" and mentions "a trick or two with lepers." See also "King Herod's Song."

16 The use of this Jesus film trope is striking here given children's absence from the troupe.

17 In Mt. 27:19, Pilate's wife (traditionally named Claudia) has the troubling dream. A woman (Claudia?) brings Pilate his laurel crown here and reappears in both of Pilate's subsequent scenes.

18 Reportedly, nothing was left unbroken after the second take. See *Imdb.com (Jesus Christ Superstar: Trivia)*.

19 Cf. *The King of Kings*' Magdalene who thought she could "handle" Jesus as she did other men. This Magdalene does not, however, clearly "convert." She is "in love."

20 Jewison had an olive grove watered for four months to create this grassy area (Hebron 2016b: 154).

21 Because of this montage, the film has two crucifixions, not counting Judas's hanging.
22 Paul Thomas (birth name Philip Charles Toubus) went on to act in over 500 adult films and direct nearly 300 more. He was inducted into the X-Rated Critics Organization Hall of Fame in 1986.
23 Jewison dubbed his own voice for the old man challenging Peter.
24 Cf. the suicidal flights into the wilderness in *Il vangelo* and *The Passion of the Christ* (2004). In a personal conversation on September 13, 2016, Ted Neeley told Jeffrey Staley that Jewison was quite familiar with *Il vangelo*.

   The scene looks like a lynching. Citing Wood (1989: 135–45), Humphries-Brooks claims the lynched man is always innocent in American film (2006: 65). While far less sanguine, James Cone also reads the cross in the context of lynching (2012: 180) and with artists (2012: 93–119) to find in it an emblem of God's suffering with "the crucified of history" (2012: 121–50; cf. *Intolerance* 1916). See also *Color of the Cross* (2006), where a Black Jesus is crucified as the result of racism.
25 Amusingly, Judas also wants to know Jesus's opinion about Buddha and Muhammad. The question reflects growing interest in the United States with "other" religions.
26 Magdalene's replacement of the Virgin Mary is most obvious here.
27 Cf. the shepherd walking on the mountain during *King of Kings*' Sermon. According to DVD commentary, the shepherd accidentally appeared as the camera was rolling. Jewison liked the symbolism (and sunset) and kept the shot. On subsequent viewings, this "accident" makes the other shepherds and sheep in the film quite noticeable. Lloyd Baugh claims, however, these other shepherds mean the last shepherd is not the resurrected Christ (1997: 51).
28 Anderson turns his questions into accusations, becoming a Job-Judas. See Paffenroth (2001: 85–99) and Walsh (2010: 76–84). In Gethsemane, Jesus also becomes a Jobian figure.
29 Barnes Tatum says Jesus's (ignorant) devotion heightens his faithfulness/obedience (2013: 134). One should not forget, however, that Jesus and Judas both know their future reputations.
30 See Chapter 5 for a discussion of the pre-DeMille history of this romantic triangle.
31 Biblical epics have depicted villains, like Nero and Antipas, effetely since the silent era.
32 See nn1–2 above. Some saw *Jesus Christ Superstar* as a more sophisticated version of *The Who's Tommy* (album 1969; tour 1969–70) (Stern, Jefford, and DeBona 1999: 188). Robert Stigwood managed the musicals *Hair* (1968) and *Jesus Christ Superstar* (1971), and (co-)produced the films *Jesus Christ Superstar*, *Tommy* (1975), *Saturday Night Fever* (1977), and *Grease* (1978).
33 Gerald Forshey says the film's target audience was the non-revolutionary left (1992: 105–6, 112; cf. Stern, Jefford, and DeBona 1999: 184–90).
34 Lloyd Webber has often been criticized for such commercialization.
35 Humphries-Brooks (2006: 55–6). He argues that this Jesus film is the first to depict Jesus in terms of Hollywood heroism and thus the foundation for Scorsese and Gibson's films (2006: 67). For a broader discussion of Jesus's move from church to American icon, see Prothero (2003).
36 This interpretation makes Judas a villainous "sell out." Many critics attacked the film for anti-Semitism. A TV talk show even hosted a debate on the point (Forshey 1992: 112–16).
37 He worked with CBC-TV from its inception in 1952, directing musicals and variety shows, before moving to NBC in 1958 for similar work.
38 Jewison's earliest films were comedies, but *Moonstruck* (1987) is his most famous romantic comedy.

39 His first "serious" film was *The Cincinnati Kid* (1965), which dealt with the problem of (gambling) addiction.
40 Traveling across the American South after his service in the Second World War, Jewison was appalled by segregation. He left the United States for England in the late 1960s because of social justice concerns.
41 For a critique of such films for merely pacifying audience concerns about racism through the formation of a single mixed-race friendship, see Runions (2003: 43–63). *A Soldier's Story* may be more thought-provoking.
42 The first and last films in this trilogy have protagonists with Christ-figure qualities. See, for example, Heetebrij (2020) and Barsotti and Johnston (2004: 176–7).
43 *Life of Brian* (1979) and *Jésus de Montréal* similarly call attention to interpretation.
44 Celebrity is a brand-name commodity. See Chapter 12.
45 See n35. *Life of Brian* is more concerned with the making and fate of messiahs.
46 Ironically, Neeley spent the rest of his professional life playing "Jesus."

11

Il messia (The Messiah)

Roberto Rossellini, Orizzonte 2000, 1975

PLOT SUMMARY: THE PHILOSOPHER KING

Il messia was Roberto Rossellini's penultimate film. Streaming versions are readily available, but none in English (see Cultural Location).[1] Nevertheless, it is so innovative among Jesus films that it demands inclusion here.[2]

Rossellini's first innovation is his starting point. An Italian intertitle provides a date, the eleventh century BCE.[3] Returning to the Promised Land, the Hebrews face Philistine oppression (a soldier kills one boy), so the tribal elders request a king from Samuel. Per his style, Rossellini films the discussion in a long shot with the camera panning the group and zooming backward and forward. The techniques avoid a fixed POV and create what Rossellini described as a neutral or objective (POV) aesthetic (Brunette 1996: 343).[4] The techniques produce a sense of everyday, communal reality—a second Rossellini innovation in a tradition trending toward spectacle and the unique.[5]

Samuel summarily rejects the elders' request because "there is no king in Israel …. the king of Israel is the Eternal."[6] After Samuel takes their request to God, he reports God will give them the king they deserve (cf. 1 Sam. 8). Arrogant Saul and murderous Herod bookend Israel's resulting history of war and tears. The prophets, however, give the humble the hope of a "just king," the messiah to come. Rossellini's third Jesus film innovation then is to set Jesus in a populist framing of Israel's long discussion of the king.[7]

In 1 CE (an Italian intertitle), evil Herod has spies keep track of wise men's search for the messiah (eventually citing Mic. 5:2). The wise men say they have followed this king's star, although no star appears onscreen, and neither virginal conception nor angels are mentioned.[8] The wise men bring their gifts to an ordinary-looking family, barely visible in the darkness. A man (angel?) warns Joseph, and the family flees to Egypt. The nativity is over in seconds, and babies' cries and a few running people depict the slaughter of the innocents. As Peter Brunette observes, Rossellini reduces iconic events like the nativity, Via Dolorosa, and crucifixion to signs or notations (1996: 345).

Underlining his evil-king theme, Rossellini deploys Josephus's report that Herod ordered important men's deaths to coincide with his to ensure mourning at his death (*Antiq.* 17.6.174-75). The resulting violence is more graphic than the innocents' slaughter.

In 12 CE (another Italian intertitle), Rome is in control, but white-clad Jewish pilgrims come to Jerusalem for festivals and await the messiah's just, "flaming sword" destruction of tyrants.[9] In an encampment outside Jerusalem's walls (cf. *Greatest Story*'s [1965] fortress Jerusalem), Mary, still as young as at Jesus's birth,[10] prepares Jesus for his coming of age as a man of the law, wrapping him in a tallit.[11]

As Joseph takes him into the temple, Jesus asks about the red-clad soldiers. Joseph replies that Jews must follow Roman orders but that only God is their master. As the lamb they purchased is sacrificed, Rossellini offers a rare closeup—of the boy's face—foreshadowing Jesus's similar fate.

Near a pen of lambs awaiting slaughter, children sing the playful *Chad Gadya*, sung at the end of the Passover Seder.[12] The song lists accumulating calamities, beginning with a goat eaten by a cat and ending with the angel of death's arrival. Some think the song details Israel's history of foreign oppression (cf. the prologue's theme). When Jesus goes missing, Mary and Joseph find him listening to a priest talking about the Passover lamb (continuing the lamb motif).

After another Italian time intertitle (28 CE), a dog howls,[13] and pilgrims walk to the "Jordan" to see the Baptist, preaching of a coming messiah (Isa. 11:1, 4). Jesus, with some of his future disciples, is already at the Jordan (cf. Jn 1:35-42). The Baptist harangues the rich and powerful (Lk. 3:7-14). Some repent, and Jesus (Pier Maria Rossi)[14] strips to his loincloth and kneels for baptism—without heavenly voice or descending dove. Andrew declares Jesus the lamb of God (cf. Jn 1:29, 36). Some of John's disciples, and then Peter, Philip, and Nathaniel, become Jesus's disciples (Jn 1:37-51). The scene ends with a closeup of Jesus.[15]

In the temple,[16] an unnamed disciple (John) jostles a man who drops and breaks a jar. After a shocked pause, Jesus takes a bystander's coiled rope and flails about, overturning tables and releasing doves (quoting Mk 11:17). Another cut leads to Jesus's conversation with the Samaritan woman, and his open acknowledgment that he is the messiah (Jn 4:26). In a night scene, the Baptist's disciples describe Jesus's success, and the Baptist reminds them he is not the messiah (Jn 3:28-30). The Baptist's public attack on incestuous Herodias, which nearly instigates a street riot, leads to his arrest. Antipas visits John's cell for a conversation (cf. *King of Kings* 1961), which reiterates the film's themes: Antipas claims the king above reproach and John claims only God is king.[17]

Susanna (not yet named) interrupts Mary's prayers (Ps. 92) to tell her Jesus has returned to Nazareth as a prophet (an ominous appellation given the Baptist's arrest). At the synagogue, Jesus declares "the year of the Lord," inciting the villagers to chase him out of town (Lk. 4:16-28, without attempting to kill him). In a fourth innovation, Rossellini's Mary follows her son, assisting him thereafter with his village gospel work, sometimes taking the lead in teaching.[18]

After the miraculous catch/call of disciples,[19] they complain about corrupt tax collectors. Jesus, however, counsels them not to judge (Lk. 6:37-38; Mt. 7:21, 24-27). Beginning his village gospel mission, he shapes a winnowing fork while teaching (see Figure 11.1). The emphasis on village teaching rather than miracles or controversy is Rossellini's fifth Jesus film innovation.[20] The religious leaders complain about Jesus's company when he eats in a tax collector's house. The Baptist's disciples arrive with his questions. A disciple replies boisterously with miracle reports, but Jesus quiets him, focusing instead on the gospel for the poor (cf. Lk. 7:22-23).

As they eat grain in a field, Jesus instructs his disciples about the Baptist's preparatory role (Lk. 7:24-34). He responds to leaders' complaints about Sabbath violations by elevating the people's judgment above the priests'. To defend their authority, the leaders plot Jesus's end. Later, as a smiling Jesus holds and talks with children, a foregrounded Judas (unnamed) defends his master's democratic law to their dinner host and counters the leaders' charge of blasphemy with Ps. 82:6. When a disreputable woman races in and falls at Jesus's feet, women hurry the children away from her, and the Pharisee condemns Jesus for consorting with such, but Jesus defends her greater love (see Lk. 7:36-50).[21] Meanwhile, as Antipas feasts, the chained Baptist speaks to Antipas as an equal.

In a sequence that nicely visualizes Rossellini's village gospel, Mary, Susanna (still unnamed), and Susanna's children make bread. Others work at everyday tasks; Jesus makes a plow and teaches (the parable of the weeds [Mt. 13:24-30], an expanded version of the parable about leaven [13:33], and the parable of the net [13:47-50]) as the village men fish (cf. Figure 11.1). When one of Susanna's sons asks Mary where the kingdom is, she tells him it is here on earth (cf. Lk. 17:21): "When all have remembered to be good ... then there will be the kingdom of heaven," a place of peace and plenty. "It is enough that all really love one another." Echoing scriptures describing the true king's just, peaceful realm (see n7), Mary's "sermon" answers the prologue's tragedy of kings.

An abrupt cut leads to a young Salome's brief dance and horrible request. "Lapdogs" urge Antipas to kill the Baptist, who refuses to kneel before Antipas, so Antipas's men behead him on the spot. The scene recalls Saul's first kingly act—the slaughter of an ox. A cut segues to the sleeping village. Mary leads others, including Jesus, in a Kaddish. When he walks away, the group tells the village about the Baptist's death so everyone can decide what to do. Accordingly, Susanna (still unnamed) and her family leave in the dark as Jesus names his disciples.

In the dark, Jesus delivers (selections from) his Sermon (Mt. 5:17, 20-24; 18:15, 22; 5:33-34, 37, 27-28, 31-32, 38-40, 42; 7:12; 5:43-44, 46). As birds signal the dawn, Jesus asks the sleeping disciples if they too will leave. They cannot because he alone has the words of life (Jn 6:67-69). Walking away, Jesus invites them to take his cross and his yoke (Mk 8:34; Mt. 11:29-30). He steps up on a small mound to deliver the Beatitudes (Mt. 5:3-12; omitting "in spirit" from the beatitude on the poor). He then breaks bread, which the disciples distribute. Instead of a miracle, one sees the small "multitude" eating.

Jesus repairs a fishing boat while he explains the disciples' mission (Mt. 10:16; 9:37-38; Lk. 9:3; Mt. 6:26, 28-29). They then proclaim the kingdom for the poor to working villagers (illustrated with Lk. 16:19-31; Mk 10:17-22), while Jesus himself tells a group he is the good shepherd (Jn 10:11-16b).

Back at the village, women wash clothes as Jesus and disciples return. A scribe asks Jesus how he might have eternal life and Jesus responds with the parable of the Good Samaritan (Lk. 10:25-37).

The group sets out again quickly (another Italian time intertitle, 32 CE). As they cross a bridge, a very somber Jesus warns them he has brought fire and division, and that discipleship is hard (Lk. 12:49, 51-53; 14:31-33; Mt. 7:13-14). The pilgrims arrive in Jerusalem for the Festival of Booths, where Mary and Susanna (still unnamed) are in the listening crowd. When priests pour water upon the altar, Jesus offers himself as living water (Jn 7:37-38). The leaders challenge his authority and purity, so Jesus curses them on behalf of the oppressed people (selections from Mt. 23). The temple guard cannot arrest Jesus, however, because of the people. The leaders argue (cf. Jn 7:45-52), as they search to entrap this false teacher. They try unsuccessfully to use the woman taken in adultery[22] and the healed blind man (Jn 9:13-30) to this end.

A final Italian time intertitle (33 CE) opens the film's last section. At the village, everyday tasks busy the group. A tired Jesus, for once not working, tells them about servant-greatness and answers their questions about prayer. On the road again, Jesus teaches them the Lord's Prayer, which they recite. Meanwhile, the religious leaders, who have heard rumors about Lazarus's resurrection and worry about a man who teaches people to make their own decisions, consider their options. Caiaphas decides Jesus must die for the nation (Jn 11:50).

When the disciples entreat him not to go to Jerusalem, Jesus calmly predicts the Son of Man's passion.[23] Without a change of scene, Jesus orchestrates his happy triumph. Cries lauding the "liberator of the oppressed" and "the one who will bring us peace and justice" mix with traditional Hosannas (recall the citation of Isa. 61:1-2 in the Nazareth synagogue).[24] Leaders protest, but Judas declares, "the stones will cry out his glory." A young man/servant (an unidentified Mark) runs to Susanna's home (finally identified)[25] to tell Mary that "he has come."

Fearing the people will try to enthrone Jesus and provoke a bloody Roman response, the religious leaders send two men to suborn Judas, flattering him with his knowledge of the law.[26] Judas pays for the disciples' food for Seder, but continues on his own way.[27] At the meal, Mark (now named) is present, but no women are. After the foot washing, Jesus identifies the betrayer privately to John and tells Judas to do it "quickly." After the institution words, Jesus calls for love for one another and warns the world will oppose them (selections from Jn 14-17; and Lk. 22:35-38).[28]

Outside, the group chants a Passover song, the *Dayenu* ("It Would Have Been Enough"), and moves to the garden. In a brief scene, Jesus accepts his cup and God's will. Judas (leading police without torches) betrays Jesus with a bow (no kiss). In the following melee, Mark flees nearly naked (Mk 14:51-52) to report to Magdalene and Mary, who presciently knows details of Jesus's passion (cf. *The Passion of the Christ*'s [2004] Mary).

Before the Sanhedrin Jesus is calm as he is slapped, spit upon, and charged with blasphemy for saying, "You have said it," when Caiaphas asks if he is the Son of God (harmonizing the various gospel accounts). Peter's denial is noticeably absent. John reports to Mary while the priests take Jesus to Pilate.

The priests accuse Jesus of inciting revolt, forbidding tax payments, and claiming to be king (cf. Lk. 23:2). Dismissing everyone, Pilate tells (king) Jesus that his own people have betrayed him (cf. the intimate scene between Antipas and the Baptist). Jesus admits to a kingdom not of this world and to bearing witness to the truth (Jn 18:36-37). Sending Jesus to be scourged, Pilate declares Jesus's innocence, so the priests bring a crowd to accuse Jesus. As Mary, Magdalene, John, and Mark watch from the background, Pilate descends to deal with the small mob. Soldiers bring Jesus in royal robe and crown of thorns so that he stands on stairs slightly above Pilate and the crowd (Ecce Homo).[29] In a final (sixth) dramatic move away from the Jesus film tradition, Rossellini shows neither scourging nor mockery (and will not show the Via Dolorosa or much of the crucifixion).[30] Thereby, Rossellini shifts from (the powerful's) spectacle to the people's experience (and the village gospel). After releasing Barabbas, Pilate washes his hands, a priest utters the infamous Mt. 27:25, and another claims that Caesar alone is king (cf. the prologue's theme).

Everyone disperses except for the holy witnesses. Mark brings news that Jesus is to be crucified, so they all run to Calvary. Instead of Jesus's Via Dolorosa, however, Rossellini films Mary's. She falls twice on the way as children sing the *Chad Gayda* offscreen and then onscreen, recalling Jesus's childhood Passover trip to Jerusalem.

The camera pans past these children to Roman soldiers on the city walls and then, as if by happenstance, to Jesus and the other two crucified victims. Jesus dies, like Stracci (in *La ricotta* 1963), practically unnoticed. A few soldiers loll beneath the crosses as the holy group arrives. The women lament (in a passing zoom shot), and Rossellini zooms in to Jesus's head dropping in death and then back to a closeup of Mary's face. The traditional last words are not spoken. The cross, like other icons, has become mere sign (Brunette 1996: 345).

An abrupt cut leads to the icon that remains—the ever-youthful Mary in a room, holding her dead son in a pietà pose. She anoints and caresses her son tenderly while Magdalene and Susanna watch and John says, "Father, forgive them." Mary asks Magdalene for the burial cloths. When the burial party approaches the tomb, Magdalene collapses sobbing, but Mary walks stoically away as priests seal the tomb.

On Easter morning, as Mary and some disciples approach the tomb, soldiers run past them. A sobbing Magdalene says, "It's empty!" Mary runs ahead and peers into the tomb. From within the tomb, a camera presents a closeup of her face as she smiles and kneels in an orant pose.[31] The final shot is skyward to blue sky and passing clouds.

MEMORABLE CHARACTERS

1 Jesus is Rossellini's "philosopher king," establishing, like the Hebrew Bible's ideal king, a (village) kingdom community of justice, peace, and love (see Figure 11.1). The focus on teaching and community-building gives the film a "slow," philosophical quality, almost as if it were "the words of an oratorio, declaimed by actors seated on stools on an empty stage" (Baugh 1997: 86). Despite the abundant lamb imagery, neither Jesus nor Rossellini gives much attention to his death.

2 Mary is perpetually young. Perhaps, her youth relies on the Italian tradition of Michelangelo's *Pietà*, which itself may depend upon Dante's notion that the Virgin Mary was the "daughter of her son" (*Paradiso*, canto 33; cited in Brunette 1996: 347). She works with Jesus in his village gospel efforts, and the film focuses on her passion, not her son's. She is the film's "heart" (Brunette 1996: 347) and the ideal disciple (cf. Baugh 1997: 88).

3 The (false) kings—Saul, Herod, Antipas—are the primary villains, seconded by the urban elite religious leaders. Pilate is impossibly innocent,[32] given the castigation of kings. Judas usually listens attentively near Jesus, but his betrayal is signified (like other Christian icons/signs), not explored.

4 Minor characters—like Susanna, John, and Mark—are as important as the tradition's leading characters because of Rossellini's village gospel and neutral style. He seldom introduces anyone by name, if at all, until after they have made several screen appearances. Susanna is important as Mary's village friend and perhaps as one of the movement's benefactors (cf. Lk. 8:3).

MEMORABLE VISUALS

1 The striking antiquity of the eleventh century BCE prologue.
2 The boy Jesus, in tallit, staring at the sacrificial lamb's preparation.
3 Mary following her son out of Nazareth into his mission.
4 Judas defending his master in a wealthy man's home and during the triumph.
5 The zoom of the working village as both Jesus and Mary teach (with Mary teaching Susanna's little boy) (cf. Figure 11.1).
6 Mary falling on her Via Dolorosa.
7 *Pietà*, with Mary putting the dead Jesus's hand to her cheek.
8 Mary's resurrection face.[33]

Figure 11.1 While working on a winnowing fork, Jesus teaches his village gospel in *Il messia*, directed by Roberto Rossellini, Orizzonte 2000, 1975. All rights reserved.

KEY AUTHORITY/SCRIPTURE

1 Rossellini's aesthetic, which creates the sense that one sees (village) reality, naturalizes his populist gospel.[34]

2 Mary's explanation of the possible kingdom is the film's populist answer to the problem of corrupt, oppressive kings and is the village gospel's most concise statement: a call to create the kingdom through goodness and love. This emphasis and the focus on the poor, outcast, and disreputable lead some to compare the film with Luke (as does the film's "historical" approach).

3 The film's structure for Jesus's ministry, however, relies heavily on John (but Lazarus's resurrection is absent, except as rumor).

CULTURAL LOCATION/GENRE: ITALIAN CINEMA AND AMERICAN CATHOLICISM

Il messia belongs first to Italian cinema's long history and thus rejects the Cinecittà peplum aesthetic as much as that of the Hollywood epic (see Page 2021: 132–3). *Il messia* also belongs to the Italian (European) tradition of public artists/intellectuals who critique society from a (sometimes ill-defined) left-wing position. *Il vangelo* is the most famous Jesus film example. Arguably the crucial (iconic) moment in Italian biblical film, *Il vangelo* is influential on all subsequent Italian Jesus films (Page 2021: 131–2, 135–6).[35]

Both films reject the Jesus epics' aesthetic, differing from them at almost every point (see Chapter 7). Rossellini may be even more dismissive than Pasolini, as Pasolini retains the miraculous and, therefore, many iconic moments. Both films speak for the people versus corrupt power, although Rossellini focuses on "kings" while Pasolini increasingly concentrated on consumer capitalism's hegemony. Both privilege the people and their villages. Rossellini does so through his neutral aesthetic, the long shot and long take (see n4). Pasolini privileges the people with location shots, black-and-white photography, and closeups. Those closeups, as well as Pasolini's abrupt cuts, handheld camera, and POV shots sharply distinguish him from Rossellini. *Il vangelo*'s eclectic, interpretative background music also separates it from *Il messia*, which relies primarily on ambient noise and diegetic music.

Further, while (a form of Gramscian) Marxism animates *Il vangelo*, *Il messia* is more vaguely populist and humanist. Pasolini's hope lay in the people's revolution, while Rossellini believed, at least in his historical period, in their educational improvement. Consequently, their Jesuses are drastically different. Pasolini's Jesus is a firebrand revolutionary hardly ever deigning to dialogue. Rossellini's Jesus is a philosophical sage always looking for conversation. The difference might be as simple as that between a Markan Jesus (Pasolini) and a Lukan/Matthean one (Rossellini). Finally, the people are more important in *Il messia* than in *Il vangelo*. Rossellini's teaching Jesus lives and works among the people. Pasolini's alienated Jesus strides angrily ahead.

Il messia is not well-known in the Americas due to its complicated distribution history.[36] Fr Patrick Peyton, a Notre Dame-trained Catholic priest, secured the film's initial funding. He founded the *Family Rosary Crusade* and the popular *Family Theater* radio and television program in 1947, which gave him access to Catholic Hollywood stars and important Catholic leaders (Johnson 2008: 357–8).[37] In the hagiographic account, he was devoted to the Virgin Mary because of a (miraculous) cure from tuberculosis when he was thirty, and appealed to the Blessed Virgin for help in creating a film Christ.[38] Less than two days later, he was in Rossellini's home (Brunette 1996: 341–2; Gallagher 2012: 5:37). Some say that Rossellini and Fr Peyton signed the film contract in front of Michelangelo's *Pietà* (Brunette 1996: 342).[39]

Ultimately, the De Rance Corporation of Milwaukee, Wisconsin, associated with Father Peyton, held the US distribution rights for *Il messia*. When Eric Sherman tried to screen *Il messia* at the 1978 Filmex festival in Los Angeles, the De Rance Corporation obtained a restraining order. Presumably, because of the narrow devotional piety of (or akin to) Fr Peyton, the De Rance Corporation agreed to the film's exhibition only in a severely edited version that would "cut thirty minutes of the film, rearrange the scenes, and add a voice-of-God narration" (Brunette 1996: 342–3; cf. Gribble 2011: 280–1). Rossellini always resisted such changes. Accordingly, *Il messia* was never released to US theaters.

DIRECTOR

After making propaganda films for Italy's fascist regime,[40] Rossellini, with the help of Federico Fellini, created one of neorealism's early exemplars, the internationally acclaimed *Roma città aperta* (Rome, Open City 1945), not long after Rome's liberation.[41] Neorealistic films create a documentary (or realist) feel by employing episodic narrative structures about the people's everyday lives, coupled with location shooting, available light, and non-professional actors (see Chapter 7). Rossellini, however, admitted his film's "look" had as much to do with limited resources and a Rome devastated by war, as any aesthetic choice.

Roma città aperta is also rather "dramatic"—more so than the later *Il messia*—for neorealism (contrast, e.g., Vittorio De Sica's *Ladri di biciclette* [Bicycle Thieves 1948]). Connections with *Il messia* are readily evident, however, in the concentration on the people's struggles to live amid corruption and oppression. As in *Il messia*, some people conspire with the (German) overlords and some resist them—but in the name of human dignity, rather than faith—as the Germans stamp out the resistance.

The priest Don Pietro (Aldo Fabrizi) supports the resistance to help those in need and to practice charity humbly. He stands somewhere between Pasolini and Rossellini's Jesuses. Major Bergmann, the German occupation leader, demands that the priest betray the rebels' identities, but Don Pietro replies, "I believe that anyone fighting for justice and liberty walks in the ways of the Lord, and the ways of the Lord are infinite" (cf. Mary's potential kingdom description).[42] In the film's climax, the Germans force Don Pietro to watch the lengthy, brutal torture and murder of the resistance leader. With tears streaming down his beatific face, Don Pietro extols Manfredi's sacrifice, declaring, "It is finished" (Jn 19:30). The next morning, the Italian firing squad deliberately misses Don Pietro, but a German officer shoots him in the head. Before dying, Don Pietro manages to say, "God forgive them" (Lk. 23:34). Interestingly, this film focuses more on these Christlike martyrs' sufferings than *Il messia* does on Jesus's passion. As in *Il messia*, however, there is no resurrection. The boys the priest taught do support him—by whistling a resistance song.

In the United States, Rossellini is known for *Il miracolo* (1948) because Catholic organizations protested it as a blasphemous (modernized) nativity parody (see n8). The New York Board of Regents censored the film and that decision was appealed to the US Supreme Court. In a landmark 1952 case, the Supreme Court argued that films should "enjoy the same First Amendment rights of freedom of expression applied to other media" and that "sacrilege could no longer serve as a basis for censorship" (Brunette 1996: 97).

Rossellini's most sincerely religious film,[43] apart from his two biblical forays, is *Francesco, giullare di Dio* (*Francis, God's Jester* 1950, but usually called *The Flowers of St. Francis* in English).[44] The film, based on two medieval works about St Francis and acted primarily by Franciscan monks, is a series of parabolic episodes illustrating St Francis's teaching (about humility, joy, and the kingdom's "children") and presenting it, as *Il messia* does Jesus's teaching, as something beneficial to modernity. Unlike *Il messia*, the film is quite whimsical, containing several slapstick scenes (cf. *Parable* 1964; *Godspell* 1973). An epigraph from 1 Cor. 1:27 nicely captures its style and St Francis's teaching.

Rossellini ended his career (except for *Il messia* and a documentary completed postmortem [*Beauborg, centre d'art et de culture Georges Pompidou* 1977]) with a didactic, ten-film, made-for-television Grand Historical Project—begun in 1964. It included *Atti degli apostol* (The Acts of the Apostles 1969)[45] and *Agnostino d'Ippona* (Augustine of Hippo 1972), although the only critically acclaimed film was *La prise de pouvoir par Louis XIV* (The Rise of Louis XIV 1966). Rossellini forsook cinema and turned to television, which he believed could spread culture to larger audiences. Rossellini's goal was to improve humans by helping them become more rational (Bondanella 1993: 125–6; Brunette 1996: 253). He believed he could do that by expunging the "mystical and spiritual" in favor of "reconstruct[ed] history" (Brunette 1996: 253). The films focus on a "great man" who represents a change in human consciousness (Brunette 1996: 254). While not technically in this ten-part project, *Il messia* has the same aura, aesthetic, and ambition.

IL MESSIA

Streaming on YouTube (Croatian subtitles)[46]
(Italian intertitle chronology from the Santa Fe Communications distributed VHS version are in italics)

1 Prologue, 0:00
2 Hebrew people return to their promised land, 1:58

The eleventh century BCE, 2:33

    Canaanite attack, 4:05

    Samuel: "[N]o king for our people," 7:52

Saul chosen king, 11:45

    Summary of Israel's monarchies, 12:27

    The prophets' messianic hope, 13:26

3 *Year 1 CE*, 13:32

Wise men seek the messiah, 14:22

The wise men visit the newborn king, 15:51

Slaughter of innocents, 17:32

Herod's deathbed, 17:51

People rejoice at Herod's (supposed) death, 18:38

4 *Year 12 CE*, 21:10

Jewish pilgrims await the coming messiah

First view of Jesus and his parents, 21:26

> Mary recites the tradition of the tallit, 22:31

In the temple, 24:18

> Slaughter of the lamb, 26:03

Children sing *Chad Gadya*, 26:15

The lost child, 27:21

Jesus listens to priests discuss the Passover lamb's blood, 29:12

5 *Year 28 CE*, 29:35

Pilgrims go to the Jordan, 30:10

> (Quote of Isa. 11:1, 4)

> Jesus's baptism, 32:37

First disciples called, 33:39

> "You are Simon, son of John," 34:05

> Philip and Nathaniel, 34:13

Cleansing the temple (Jn 2:13-25), 35:31

Samaritan woman (in blue and red) at the well, 36:02

John the Baptist's disciples, 38:00

John the Baptist's arrest, 38:54

> Antipas: "I am your king. I have no sins," 42:06

Nazareth rejection (Lk. 4:16-27), 42:38

> Susanna: "They say he looks like a prophet!" 43:11

> Expelled from the synagogue, 45:22

> Mary follows Jesus (into their joint ministry), 46:20

Fisherman's call/catch, 46:47

> Judas (unnamed; first appearance) beside Jesus, 47:32

> Judas mimics Jesus's actions, 48:00

> Judas and Jesus look at each other, smiling, 48:48

Tax collectors (Matthew), 48:54
Jesus making a winnowing fork, 51:06
    "Not everyone who cries out, 'Lord, Lord,'" 51:11
    The house built on a rock, 51:27
        Pharisees condemn Jesus's "preaching to the rabble," 51:58
    Tax collector Matthew's call
        (unnamed, but visible at 48:58; 51:11), 52:30
        In the tax collector's house, 52:52
Baptist's disciples' questions, 53:57
    A disciple reports miracles, 54:40
Plucking grain on the Sabbath, 55:08
    "What did you go out to see in the desert?" 55:33
    "Shame! Working on the Sabbath!" 56:42
Plots against Jesus, 57:23
    In the Pharisee's house, 58:55
        Judas converses with the host, 59:00
        "I've heard it said that he insinuates he is the Son of God," 59:33
        Judas answers with Ps. 82:6, 59:41
Anointing woman, 59:57
Conversation between Antipas and the Baptist on "true freedom," 1.00:53
Parable of the weeds, 1.03:32
    Jesus teaching and making a plow, 1.04:16
        Judas takes notes as Jesus teaches (see below, 1.44:43)
Parable of the yeast, 1.05:17
    Mary tells Susanna's little boy that the kingdom will come when everyone is good and loves, 1.05:36
Parable of the net, 1.07:23
Salome's dance and the Baptist's death, 1.08:02
    The Baptist's disciples report John's death, 1.10:32
        Call of the disciples, 1.11:51
        Susanna, leaving, hugs Mary: "Forgive us. The children," 1.12:05
Sermon on the Mount, 1.12:08
    "Seventy times seven" (Mt. 18:21-22), 1.13:09
    "You have the words of eternal life" (Jn 6:67-68), 1.16:12
    A follower "must take up his cross each day" (Lk. 9:23), 1.16:25

Beatitudes, 1.16:43
Feeding the 5,000, 1.18:24
Sending out of the Twelve, 1.19:13
> Jesus repairs a boat while Judas leans on it, 1.19:21
> Disciples' teaching mission, 1.20:27
>> Parable of Rich Man and Lazarus, 1.20:33
>> The rich young ruler, 1.21:33
> Parable of the Good Shepherd, 1.23:10
Disciples return, 1.23:46
> Mary and other women wash clothes, 1.23:43
Parable of Good Samaritan, 1.24:30

6 *Year 32 CE* (1.26:02)

Jesus and disciples walk across a bridge (toward Jerusalem)
> Jesus warns them of their cause's hardships (Lk. 9:23a, 12:49, 51-53; 14:31-33; Mt. 7:13-14)

Jerusalem's Festival of Booths, 1.28:07
> "If anyone is thirsty," 1.29:44
> "Woe to you Pharisees," 1.30:49
> Mary, Susanna, and John are there, 1.31:21; 1.31:30
> Failed arrest, 1.31:47
> Woman caught in adultery, 1.32.50
> Blind man healed, 1.34:51

7 *Year 33 CE* (1.36:37)

Village work and teaching
> Who will be greatest in the Kingdom? 1.37:12
> Lord's Prayer, 1.37:27

Plots against Jesus, 1.38:20
> "He can't be thinking of coming to the Holy City for Passover!" 1.39:05

Prophecy of death, 1.39:42
> Triumphal Entry, 1.40:32
> A Sadducee to Judas: "Silence these people!" 1.43:34
> Mark tells the others that Jesus is going to the temple, 1.43:51

Sanhedrin, 1.44:18
> Two men suborn Judas, 1.44:43

Passover meal prepared, 1.45:26

Foot washing, 1.46:51

    "I am the way the truth and the life," 1.51:30

    "The man who has a purse must carry it; buy a sword," 1.53:37

    "Here are two swords" (table knives), 1.53:52

Garden prayer, 1.53:52

Betrayal and arrest, 1.55:40

    "Who is it you want?" 1.56:14

    Mark runs away, leaving his tunic behind, 1.56:30

Before the Sanhedrin, 1.57:08

    Jesus slapped, 1.57:27

    False witnesses, 1.57:36

    "Blasphemy!" (Caiaphas rips shirt), 1.58:53

    Spit upon, 1.59:05

    Mary, Magdalene, and Mark meet John for news, 1.59:09

At Antonia Fortress, 1.59:49

    Mary, Magdalene, John, and Mark enter the courtyard, 2.04:07

    Priests return with a "crowd" of accusers, 2.05:17

    Jesus returns in a royal robe and crown of thorns, 2.05:52

        "Behold the man," 2.06:09

        Barabbas, 2.06:51

        John, Mark, Mary, and Magdalene watching, 2.07:17

            Pilate washes his hands, 2.07:21

    "His blood be on us and on our children," 2.07:38

    Mary: "They don't know what they do," 2.08:34

    Mark reports Jesus's crucifixion

Mary's Via Dolorosa, 2.08:56

    Mary falls twice

    Children seen singing the *Chad Gadya* in two different circles, 2.09:9

    Roman soldiers march to Calvary high above the singing children

First view of the three crucified victims, 2.09:35

    Magdalene cries; Mary stands stoically, 2.10:03

    No words, the wind blows; Magdalene sobs, 2.10:21

Death, 2.10:47

Pietà, 2.10:56

    At the doorway, John says, "Father, forgive them," 2.12:03

"Magdalene, the cloths," 2.12:20

Six disciples help carry the body to the tomb, 2:12:37

Sealing the tomb, 2.13:45

Magdalene falls, weeping, 2.14:31

Mary and the disciples Easter morning, 2.15:55

Soldiers run past them; Magdalene says, "It's empty!" 2.16:06

Mary runs, 2.16:08

Mary looks in, 2.16:33

Mary kneels praying, 2.16:40

View of clouds; music, 2.16:48

Credits, 2.17:00

NOTES

1 To date, the film's only authorized English production is an out-of-print, subtitled VHS (Santa Fe Communications, Milwaukee, WI, 1999). Ironically, the original script was supposedly in English (Gallagher 2012: 6:05). A character does say "Thank you" in English at 1.24:12. At this writing, three streaming versions are available on YouTube: one with Croatian subtitles, one dubbed in Spanish (Castilian vocabulary, but Latin American pronunciation), and one that can be enabled with rather archaic English subtitles. The Spanish version and a Korean-subtitled edition are also available on DVD. The Croatian subtitled version differs slightly from the other Italian version. For example, many scenes shot with a blue ("night") filter appear in broad daylight in the Croatian subtitled version.

The YouTube Italian version (https://www.youtube.com/watch?v=-O2AR7rWCck) has English subtitles that can be activated. These somewhat archaic English subtitles sometimes quote the Douay-Rheims Bible (translated from the Latin Vulgate in 1582). The film's English subtitles are taken from the artsubs.wz.cz website. The origin of these artsubs.wz.cz subtitles is unclear.

In a worst-case scenario, the Spanish-dubbed version available online (https://www.youtube.com/watch?v=1J_gll4hkIU) has poor, auto-generated English subtitles that can be enabled by clicking on the settings icon. From there, click on subtitles/cc auto-generated; then scroll down to and click on English.

2 Most biblical film scholars have not discussed the hard-to-acquire film in depth, but see Baugh (1997: 84–93) and Page (2016b; 2021).

3 Hebrew Bible tableaux in passion plays are similar, but the tableaux work allegorically, not historically. See Shepherd (2013: chaps. 1–2). The time intertitles do not appear in the streaming versions. Rossellini treats the biblical/Jewish tradition more seriously than previous Jesus filmmakers (Brunette 1996: 344). But, see *Greatest Story*'s attention to prophecy and the subsequent *Jesus of Nazareth* (1977).

4 Rossellini invented a remote-controlled Pan Cinor zoom lens that he mounted on a dolly to roam locations at will, zooming in and out on characters (see Bondanella 1993: 128–9; Gallagher 2012: 4:57; Page 2016b: 628). The zoom facilitates Rossellini's beloved lengthy

takes (aka plan-séquence), which allowed him to achieve (what he called) a neutral, objective aesthetic (avoiding a fixed, privileged POV). See the Capernaum teaching scenes, where one long take is nearly two minutes, and another is a minute and sixteen seconds.

5 Brunette says Rossellini has a "penchant for understatement" (1996: 345). Although speaking about Rossellini's *Atti degli apostoli* (Acts of the Apostles 1969), Matt Page claims Rossellini minimizes what Hollywood epics exaggerated: no romantic subplots enliven the action; characters report supernatural/miraculous events; and leading figures' persecution is underplayed (2016b: 630–1).

6 Cf. the Zealots motto: "No king but God." See Josephus *Antiq.* 18.1.6.

7 Many Hebrew Bible texts discuss whether Israel should have a king, and if so, what the nature of such a king (messiah) might be. See, for example, 1–2 Samuel, the royal psalms, and messianic prophecies. Luke is also Rossellini's precursor, as its opening echoes 1 Samuel extensively. However, Luke (and Acts) subsequently concentrates, like the Former Prophets and unlike Rossellini, on a succession of (rejected) prophets.

Among Jesus films, *King of Kings* also focuses on the king/messiah's nature, but its exploration is more spiritual and less political than Rossellini's. Other films—like *Jesus Christ Superstar* (1973), *Life of Brian* (1979), and *Jésus de Montréal* (1989)—focus instead on the making of messiahs.

Dennis Grunes (2007) compares *Il messia* to Rossellini's *Socrate* (1971). Plato's *The Republic* features Socrates's dialogue with various people on the just state (to be led by a philosopher king). While *Socrate* relies more on *The Apology* and *Crito*, Rossellini's Socrates does say, "It [politics] should be not the art of domination, but the art of showing us what justice is." That quote nicely describes *Il messia*'s main concern, if not that of Rossellini's entire historical period. Brunette says *Socrate* foregrounds the philosopher's "Christlike" elements, as both he and Jesus engage "in the same quest for truth." Rossellini's Socrates even discusses "what it means to be a 'good shepherd'" (1996: 300).

8 Rossellini minimizes the miraculous/supernatural throughout. Virgin birth is more important in *Il miracolo*, the second part of his 1948 anthology film *L'Amore*. A wanderer gets a goatherd girl drunk and leaves. When she wakes, she concludes he was a miracle (St Joseph).

9 Pilgrimage is a major motif, reflecting Rossellini's own philosophical quest for truth (see Page 2016b). Jesus and Mary his mother wear white, although Jesus occasionally wears a black cloak on his travels and Mary dons a black shawl at Jesus's death. The white clothing recalls Muslims on a hajj. Many of the extras have Muslim names as the film was shot in Tunisia in forty-two days in summer 1975 (Gallagher 2012: 6.00). *Jesus of Nazareth*, *Life of Brian*, and *Last Temptation* (1988) were subsequently shot in North Africa.

10 Sixteen-year-old Mita Ungaro played Mary. Most of Rossellini's actors are nonprofessionals or unknowns.

11 Mary's friend, Susanna (unnamed until the passion), does the same for her son (behind and to Mary's left).

12 The song was well known in 1970s Italy. Popular folk singer, Angelo Branduardi, sang a version, *Alla fiera dell'est*, on his similarly named 1976 album.

13 Ambient noise is quite noticeable. It contributes to Rossellini's neutral aesthetic. The next time marker is 32 CE, sixty-five minutes later, when Jesus enters Jerusalem for the penultimate time. The time markers create a four-year ministry. The sixty-five minutes allow Rossellini to explore Jesus's village teaching slowly.

14 Jesus was his most important role. Rossellini dubbed the film, using Enrique Irazoqui's voice for Jesus (see Gallagher 2012: 6:04). Irazoqui played Jesus in *Il vangelo* but Pasolini dubbed over his voice. See Chapter 7.
15 Rossellini films at a distance, so medium shots seem closeups. See, for example, the shot of Mary's head and shoulders as the Nazareth rejection scene begins. Closeups are most common in the Last Supper scene.
16 This placement follows the Johannine, rather than Synoptic, order.
17 Jesus's later conversation with Pilate about kingdom and truth echoes this scene.
18 Cf. the Marys in *King of Kings* and *Son of Man* (2006).
19 All one sees is a boat full of fish. Like *King of Kings*, Rossellini refers to miracles through reports.
20 Although the aura differs, *Godspell* is precursor.
21 Judas sits at Jesus's feet, after the Pharisee indicts Jesus, in a visualization that deliberately rejects Jn 12:3-8.
22 DeMille's Caiaphas uses the adulterous woman to trap Jesus in *The King of Kings* (1927). The adulteress is the not yet named Magdalene.
23 This prediction comes much later than similar gospel predictions.
24 The dubbed Spanish version has some call Jesus "the king of the poor."
25 The home is significantly wealthier than the earlier village homes. Does this evoke Lk. 8:1-3? Magdalene (not named) is also in the home, and the Last Supper takes place there.
26 Cf. the Saul/Paul in Rossellini's *Atti degli apostol* (Brunette 1996: 292–3, 312) and *Jesus of Nazareth*'s scholarly Judas.
27 While Judas is the group's treasurer, the film makes no reference to a betrayal price and never shows Judas's arrangements with the priests.
28 Rossellini's use of the zoom is quite noticeable here, as are the closeups of Jesus.
29 Jesus visually usurps Pilate's position as judge (see Page 2016b: 632). Contrast this demeanor with that of Ray's bowed-head victim in *King of Kings*.
30 As Rossellini treats the passion's iconic moments elliptically (or in "a few incisive glances"; Luigi Bini, cited in Baugh 1997: 90), Jesus film's typical sadomasochism is absent.
31 The shot resembles *Greatest Story*'s shot of Jesus from within Lazarus's tomb.
32 This portrayal may stem from Christian tradition (and anti-Semitism), or simply reflect Rossellini's love of Rome and its (Roman) heritage.
33 The most memorable visuals may be the minimalization or omission of iconic Christian moments.
34 Pasolini, who understood reality as ideologically created, would be appalled (see Chapter 7), but Rossellini argued his didactic films were free from ideological bias (Brunette 1996: 256–7, 261–2).
35 See Baugh's comparison of the Sardinian *Su Re* (2012) with *Il vangelo* (2018; 2021). Unfortunately, *Su Re* is not available with English subtitles.
36 Like *Il vangelo*, *Il messia* was a joint Italian-French production. It premiered at the Italian Montecatini Film Festival on October 25, 1975. Its French premiere was February 18, 1976. A rare public showing (with English subtitles) occurred in the United States at New York City's Museum of Modern Art on November 17, 2006 (see MOMA n.d.).
37 *Pray: The Story of Patrick Peyton* is forthcoming from *Family Theater Productions* n.d.
38 Richard Gribble finds no evidence of the special plea to Mary and offers evidence that Peyton met Rossellini on a trip to Athens in 1973 (2011: 275–6).

39 Does Mary's importance come from Rossellini's cultural Catholicism or from Peyton's Marian piety?
40 Brunette divides Rossellini's long career into: (1) before *Roma città aperta*; (2) the war trilogy and after; (3) the Bergman era; (4) India and the commercial period; and (5) the Grand Historical project (1996). For a discussion of Rossellini's oeuvre as a move from humanism to an Augustinian understanding of human sin and spiritual search (in *Il miracolo* 1948 and *Stromboli, terra di Dio* 1950), through his famous rejection of cinema ("cinema is dead"), and then back to humanism again in his final, educational TV project, see Page (2016b).
41 Rossellini's war/neorealist trilogy includes this film, *Paisà* (Paisan 1946), perhaps a better example of neorealism, and *Germania anno zero* (Germany, Year Zero 1948).
42 Don Pietro models Christlike mercy when he agrees to officiate the ashamed, pregnant Pina's (Anna Magnani) wedding to Francesco. When Pina is shot down in the street (in the film's most famous scene) running after a German truck taking Francesco away, Don Pietro holds her pietà-like.
43 See also *Giovanna d'Arco al rogo* (Joan of Arc at the Stake 1954). Based on the oratorio of the same name by Paul Claudel and Arthur Honegger, the film is Joan's stake-fantasy, wherein a priest shows her life's nobility and influence.
44 The film is on the same 1995 Vatican list of best films in the religious category that included *Il vangelo*. Pasolini said it was one of the most beautiful in Italian cinema (Gallagher 1998: 355).
45 For information on *Atti degli apostol*, see Page (2016b: 629–30) and Walsh (2016e: 502–3; 2018a; 2019).
46 The hours/minutes/seconds listed refer to the most easily accessible, Spanish-dubbed, YouTube version (online: https://www.youtube.com/watch?v=1J_gll4hkIU). English quotations, however, are from the Santa Fe Communications VHS tape. See n1 above. The time of scenes in the VHS differs because it adds thirty-two seconds of Santa Fe Communications VHS credits at the beginning.

12

Jesus of Nazareth

Franco Zeffirelli, director, ITC Films/RAI, 1977

PLOT SUMMARY: IF NOT YOUR JESUS, WHOSE?

This television miniseries[1] about Jesus (out) of Nazareth explores his messianic identity in three movements. The first movement—from Rabbi Yehuda's opening synagogue sermon to Jesus's opening synagogue sermon—leaves village, messianic Judaism behind when the Nazareth villagers expel blasphemer Jesus. The second movement pursues Jesus's Galilean kingdom enterprise and Peter's "creation" as the apostolic church's rock, beginning with a Capernaum ministry in which Jesus gradually entices "stupid" Peter to follow, and ending with two contrasting scenes: the messianic revelation to Peter and Peter's reluctance to accept Jesus's death. The third movement (much of it taking place in the temple) centers on Jesus's death and resurrection, the foundation of the apostolic church's "born again" message. It moves from Lazarus's resurrection to Jesus's, highlighting various Johannine "I ams." At the Roman trial, Pilate asks, "Whose Jesus is this?" He is Jesus "of Nazareth," then rejected as blasphemer/false prophet in Nazareth, Capernaum, and Jerusalem, and judged "not ours" by Jewish leaders before Pilate, before becoming the church's resurrected Lord. Ultimately, "Jesus" also belongs to commercial television's consumer capitalism (see Problematic Issue).

The film opens on a long shot of Nazareth. In the film's most memorable innovation, Franco Zeffirelli zooms in to focus on that Jewish village's life and religion, despite excursions elsewhere[2] (for an hour and forty-eight minutes).[3]

The trip to Bethlehem is for the census and birth (with repeated citations of Mal. 5:2; cf. *Greatest Story* 1965). Zeffirelli highlights Mary's labor contractions (Olivia Hussey).[4] The shepherds (Luke) and kings (Matthew) visit the holy family at separate times. The kings meet just before finding the holy family and they never visit Herod (Peter Ustinov). Melchior identifies Jesus as the king of Israel taking away the sin of the world.

The wise men warn the family, so the flight to Egypt avoids Herod's slaughter of the innocents. Rapid camera movements, screams, shadows, and bodies in the street display the slaughter indirectly. Just before the holy family returns to Nazareth, Rabbi Yehuda (Cyril Cusack) tells Nazareth that God will send a deliverer. The holy family looks down on Nazareth (cf. the film's opening shot) with the baby Jesus blessing the village from Joseph's arms (cf. the Infant of Prague).[5]

The first trip to Jerusalem is for Jesus's presentation in the temple (circumcision; cf. Lk. 2:21-39).[6] The second trip is at Passover when Jesus is twelve (cf. Lk. 2:42-50).[7] Ominously, Jesus carries a lamb into the temple,[8] but he also introduces the film's subjective, spiritual message by instructing the leaders that "prayer from the heart" is more important than sacrifice or temple.

Nazareth's village Judaism is always these excursions' backdrop.[9] It is Jesus's "whence."[10] It also ensconces Jesus in television domesticity as Zeffirelli starts with Joseph (Yorgo Voyagis) and Mary's betrothal and wedding difficulties.[11] After Mary's Lukan-annunciation response to moonlight (an unseen, unheard angel), she tells an incredulous Joseph of her pregnancy. A nightmare of her stoning (resembling the woman taken in adultery story) and an angel (the film's only supernatural voice), however, convince him to marry Mary.

Instead of utilizing apocryphal gospel stories about Jesus's childhood (e.g., from *The Infancy Gospel of Thomas*), Zeffirelli invents new episodes.[12] In one, Joseph teaches carpentry to children (including a blond-haired, blue-eyed Jesus),[13] which he glosses theologically: a ladder may lead to heaven (Gen. 28:11-12). An inquisitive Jesus climbs the (Jacob's) ladder into hazy light, if not heaven (cf. Jn 1:51).

In the next scene, the eerily blue-eyed Jesus reads Torah at his bar mitzvah. Roman soldiers interrupt the celebration, rudely conscripting food and causing Zealots to wonder "how long?" When a villager claims God has abandoned them, Zeffirelli zooms, in answer, into Jesus's watchful blue eyes and dissolves to Jesus's childhood Passover lamb.

These visuals depict different understandings of messiah. Further, Herod refers earlier to messiahs as bad dreams "disguised as a solution to every problem" and promises there will be none while he lives. Rabbi Yehuda, however, defines "messiah" definitively when he claims, in the film's opening, that the king messiah will stand on the temple's roof and proclaim deliverance (also citing Isa. 60:1; cf. Jesus's Nazareth sermon). For Zeffirelli, (village) Judaism is messianic (cf. *Il messia*'s [1975] more communal village).

Years later, aged Yehuda sits alone in the synagogue, still reading messianic prophecies (e.g., Isa. 40:2; Mal. 3:1).[14] After a closeup of the scroll, the film dissolves to the Baptist (Michael York) haranguing incestuous Antipas (Christopher Plummer) outside his palace. At the Jordan, John speaks of the coming kingdom/Lord and repentance as he baptizes en masse. (He also quotes Isa. 40:3-4, continuing Yehuda's synagogue reading.)

At Nazareth, a young Mary sits with the dying Joseph who entrusts his shop to younger men in the room's shadows[15] and his spirit to God's hands (Ps. 31:5; Lk. 23:46). The rabbi and Mary recite the Shema. Suddenly, Jesus appears at the Jordan (cf. Jesus's move to his "work" after Joseph's death in *Jesus* 1999). Crosscut closeups show John and the adult Jesus (Robert Powell)[16] for the first time. Jesus's first words speak of fulfilling righteousness (Mt. 3:15). As John baptizes him, a dove flies overhead, and John claims to hear the Eternal say, "This is my beloved son." John then tells two disciples to follow "the lamb of God who takes unto himself the sins of the world." Immediately, Antipas's cavalry (cf. the innocents' slaughter) arrives to arrest John.

Jesus returns to Nazareth.[17] Mary enters the synagogue as Jesus claims to fulfill Isa. 61:1-2. A villager objects because this is a messianic prophecy and Jesus angrily says that the kingdom comes unexpectedly (Lk. 17:20b).[18] Only Mary believes. The villagers try to stone the blasphemer (Andrew disarms one man), but Andrew and Philip follow Jesus. Jesus "touches" them in welcome—the first of his many intimate physical connections.[19]

Jesus's Capernaum synagogue teaching opens the film's second movement, the Galilean ministry. Jesus focuses on a law written on hearts (Jer. 31:31-34), the end of captivity to sin, and the God coming to them (cf. Isa. 40:1-5).[20] His first miracle is a dramatic exorcism,[21] whose staging may reflect *The Exorcist*'s (1973) recent popularity. Backlit by natural light, with hand raised in blessing, Jesus commands, "Satan! Leave him!" Audibly expelling breath (?), the boy is healed. Zeffirelli's camera lingers on the drama; he does not cut away and back.[22]

At the Sea of Galilee, Jesus interacts with fishermen, the contemplative John (John Duttine) and the angry Peter (James Farentino), who wants a holy man that can feed starving children. The great catch follows, visualized in a long shot with hazy light reflecting on water, and then the nets spilling on the shore (is it a miracle?). Matthew, the tax collector, watches closely.

As a crowd threatens to overwhelm anxious Peter's house, Jesus compares the kingdom to a hidden treasure, a valuable pearl, and a net, and says the kingdom is at hand (quoting Lk. 12:54-56). The paralytic is let through the roof and healed (onscreen), but critics accuse Jesus of blasphemy for forgiving the man's sins.

That night, despite his disciples' objections, Jesus eats in Matthew's house. Eventually, a drunken, angry Peter (shot in profile as he often is in the film) stands with the other disciples at the door as Jesus recounts the Prodigal Son.[23] In the film's best scene, Zeffirelli reconciles everyone with crosscuts displaying Jesus, Peter (in profile), and Matthew's changing faces. After Peter cries, "I am just a stupid man," Jesus ushers them into an embrace (see Figure 12.1).

Embarking on Galilean travels,[24] Jesus teaches about the kingdom's divisiveness (in a rare cinematic use of Mt. 10:34; Lk. 12:51-53) and demands (losing home/life). Jairus interrupts, asking for help with his daughter. Jairus's servant Thomas doubts Jesus can help, so Jesus encourages Thomas to believe without seeing (cf. Peter's final speech), raises the girl, and makes Thomas a disciple.

Salome's erotic dance forces a reluctant Antipas to have the Baptist beheaded (offscreen). Onscreen, John's disciples bury him, and Zealots, led by Amos, plan revenge. Judas (not identified; Ian McShane)[25] tells them he will become Jesus's disciple (apparently as a Zealot spy).

Crowds, including Judas, Simon the Zealot, and Joseph of Arimathea (James Mason), listen as Jesus tells them to abandon anxiety and seek the kingdom (cf. Mt. 6:25-34). The rich, young ruler turns away sadly when Jesus tells him to sell his possessions (from Mk 10:17-25; Mt. 6:24). That night, Judas offers his scholarly services to an exhausted Jesus who allows Judas to stay—even though saying, "The tree is known by its fruit" (Mt. 12:33).[26]

The infirm rush to Jesus. After he raises a wavering hand, everyone takes fish from a seemingly bottomless basket. In closeup, an awed Magdalene (Anne Bancroft),[27] previously identified as a prostitute, weeps over her bread.[28] Judas (along with Simon the Zealot) now believes that people must change first, but the Zealot Amos wants to force the Sadducees to acclaim Jesus king.

In his house, Simon the Pharisee wants to know if Jesus accepts "our laws."[29] Joseph of Arimathea knows the law's heart is the Shema, but not who his neighbor is. Jesus does not answer with the Good Samaritan. Instead, the disreputable Magdalene interrupts to weep at his feet. Forgiving her (Lk. 7:36-50), Jesus clasps her face with both hands and entrusts her with his burial ointment (cf. Mk 14:8; Mt. 26:12).[30]

Jesus sends his disciples by twos with mission instructions, ending with "freely give" (Mt. 10: 8-11, 14-16, 19-20). After Zealots botch an assassination attempt, Antipas orders the captured killed (cf. Herod's slaughter of the innocents). Judas comforts the mourning Simon with hopes that they will bring in the kingdom by dealing with the Sanhedrin.

When the excited disciples return, Jesus queries them about people's views about his identity (adding "in Galilee" to Mk 8:27), leading to Peter's confession that Jesus is Messiah, Son of God. Divine revelation has redeemed Peter's "stupidity," so Jesus names him the church's rock (although he has been "Simon Peter" from the beginning) and gives him the kingdom's keys (Mt. 16:23-33). Jesus admonishes secrecy until the time to go to Jerusalem. An ecstatic Judas thinks the leaders will "recognize" Jesus, but a weeping Jesus rebukes Judas (not Peter) and prophesies the Son of Man's death and resurrection. As the music crescendos and the camera pulls back, Jesus stands—with welcoming, outstretched, palm-open hands—in firelight, smoke, and then darkness.[31]

After a fade to black, the next scene opens with a view of the sky (heavens) seen through tree branches. In voiceover, Jesus begins the Beatitudes—a closeup locating Jesus at Mt. 5:8 and Jesus appearing in (glowing) cruciform for Mt. 5:11-12. The abbreviated Sermon ends with Jesus's solo recitation of the Lord's Prayer. The placement and camera present the Sermon as a soliloquy revealing Jesus's inner resolve. In subsequent closeups, Jesus speaks more and more directly to the audience/camera (see nn31–32).

That night, Peter wakes from troubled sleep to implore Jesus not to go to Jerusalem/death. An anguished Jesus (in a rare profile shot) rejects Peter/Satan (Mt. 16:22-23).

The film's third movement begins as celebrating pilgrims trek to Jerusalem for Passover, passing crucifixion scaffolding. As some discuss Jesus's words about death and resurrection, a man reports Lazarus's deadly illness. Jesus stops at Bethany where Martha, who already believes in the life-giving Christ, greets him (cf. Jn 11:21-22, 27). In a long shot, Jesus approaches Lazarus's tomb alone. Then, in a shot from within the tomb, Jesus prays, addressing either audience or God (11:25-26).[32] No one else could possibly hear. In a second shot from the tomb (cf. *Greatest Story*'s cinematography), Jesus calls forth Lazarus.[33] Lazarus emerges in an extreme long shot. After a closeup of Jesus speaking Jn 11:25b, the scene ends.

In Jerusalem, people carry lambs into the temple while worshipers chant prayers and the Shema. Judas meets privately with Zerah (a character invented by Burgess, played by Ian Holm).[34] After mocking Judas's peace-through-messiah/Jesus plan, Zerah promises Judas that Jesus will prove himself before the Sanhedrin.

Passing the crucifixion scaffolding, Jesus enters Jerusalem in triumph. Judas is deliriously happy. As Roman soldiers and Zerah watch, Jesus cleanses the temple with a large wooden staff.[35] Jesus ignores Zerah's conversational attempts and declares he will raise this destroyed temple in three days (Jn 2:19; cf. Mt. 26:21). A disappointed Judas, still not understanding Jesus's "heart" message, chastises Jesus for not dialoguing with the open-minded, powerful Zerah.

Jesus teaches in the temple as he did earlier in Galilean synagogues (cf. Lk. 19:47). He invites the humble and sinful to come to him and the kingdom (Lk. 10:23-24, 21; Mk 10:43-45; Mt. 20:26-28; 11:28; 25:34-40—sheep only) as Nicodemus (Laurence Olivier) watches. In a complex sequence, Jesus rejects Barabbas's (Stacey Keach) pleas to lead a Zealot revolt (Mt. 26:52), in favor of loving one's enemies (Mt. 5:44). After the "authority" trap, Jesus, holding a child, tells children's stories (Mt. 21:28-32) and expounds his love-teaching (from Mt. 5:39-46; 7:12 [in negative form]; Lk. 6:37: Mt. 5:48; 7:7-12). He forgives the woman taken in adultery (Claudia Cardinale)[36] and heals a Roman centurion's (Ernest Borgnine) servant (cf. Mt. 8:5-13).[37] The latter turns Barabbas completely against Jesus, "friend of the Romans."

Encountering a man born blind (Jn 9; quoting 9:5), who simply wants alms, Jesus daubs his eyes with mud as others hold the man down. When the man washes his eyes, he sees light on water (cf. the miraculous catch) and then sees clearly (cf. Mk 8:22-26). The leaders' dismissal of this miracle leads to Jesus's Mt. 23 diatribe, which ends with his claim to a special connection with God (Jn 10:30), sparking cries of blasphemer (as in the Nazareth and Capernaum synagogues). In the tumult, Barabbas kills a Roman soldier and steals a standard. Arrested, he calls loudly for the false prophet Jesus's stoning. Judas's peace-through-messiah/Jesus plan seems lost.

In the late afternoon, Nicodemus warns Jesus of Sanhedrin opposition, and Jesus tells Nicodemus he must be "born again." The scene ends with Jn 3:16-17. Jesus's temple teaching is over.

In an invented scene (ameliorating anti-Semitism), the Sanhedrin discusses Jesus, with Joseph of Arimathea and Nicodemus speaking on his behalf (cf. *Greatest Story*'s divided Sanhedrin). Nicodemus wonders whether Jesus might be the messiah, but Caiaphas (Anthony Quinn) contends the false prophet must die to preserve the people (Deut. 13:1-5; Jn 11:50). Like Judas, Joseph and Nicodemus want Jesus to meet the Sanhedrin, which Zerah facilitates by duping Judas into identifying Jesus's location.

At the Last Supper, Jesus predicts Peter's denial and Judas's betrayal, identifying the traitor to John alone. Judas leaves smiling, thinking he does Jesus's bidding, but he disappears into dark streets (cf. *From the Manger to the Cross* [1912] and *Greatest Story*'s similar staging). In one of the film's most supersessionist moments, institution words replace the bread and wine's Passover significance with new eucharistic meaning (Zeffirelli 1984: 101). Staring unblinkingly into the camera, Jesus says he is the way, the truth, and the life (Jn 14:6). In the garden, a smiling Judas kisses Jesus to identify him. The other disciples abuse him, but Judas does not realize he has betrayed Jesus until Zerah gives him money and tells him the "meeting" is a blasphemy trial.

Despite Joseph and Nicodemus's opposition, Caiaphas attains Jesus's conviction for blasphemy when Jesus claims to be the Son of God.[38] Reciting the Shema, Caiaphas sends Jesus to Pilate. En route, Jesus sees Peter before the denials, after which Peter runs crying through the dark streets. The film segues from Peter to Judas running, to complete their parallel stories. In a dissolve to the morning, Judas is shown hanging from a tree, with a closeup of the money spilled at his feet.

In the streets, people cry for Barabbas's release, as Pilate (Rod Steiger) arrives for Passover. When the harried Pilate agrees to speak to the priests' Jesus, they claim he is not theirs, causing Pilate to wonder to whom Jesus belongs (the film's central question). Jesus admits he is a king (not of this world) and a witness to the truth. When Pilate asks about truth, Zeffirelli zooms, in answer, into a closeup of the silent Jesus. Pilate orders the dreamer flogged (the violence captured in shots of Jesus's hands and face, horses' fear, and the floggers' exertion) while he and Zerah (replacing Caiaphas) watch and discuss Jesus's fate. The beaten, mocked Jesus—backlit by natural light—returns to Pilate in the Ecce Homo scene. Finding no escape (there is no meeting with Antipas), Pilate submits to the people's choice. Most of the crowd screams for Barabbas, with one man beating Magdalene into silence, and Pilate sentences the treasonous Jesus to crucifixion.

In contrast to the trials' slow pace, the Via Dolorosa proceeds rapidly. With crosscuts to Zerah pacing the temple (often shot from above), Jesus carries his crossbar. People mock and Veronica wipes his face, but Jesus does not fall and no Simon carries the cross.[39] Nicodemus watches from a distance. As in *The Passion of the Christ* (2004), the camera focuses on the nails driven into Jesus's hands. Soldiers then haul Jesus roughly onto the scaffolding seen previously.[40]

Romans push the mocking crowd away (cf. Jesus silents), and the pace slows so that Jesus can speak the sayings from the cross (omitting only "I thirst"). The centurion (Borgnine) allows Jesus's mother and Martha to approach the cross, and then Magdalene, after Mary identifies her as "family." Finally, Nicodemus, taking on a narrator/voiceover role like that of Rabbi Yehuda in the film's first movement, recites Isa. 53:3a, 7, 4-5, concluding with a whispered "Born again." The centurion removes his helmet, but makes no confession (nor is there a spear thrust). Zeffirelli zooms out from the dead Jesus to a gentle rain and to Peter praying, "My God, my Lord. Please help me."

Taking Jesus's body from the scaffolding, soldiers drop it in the mud. Wailing, Mary grasps him pietà-like, and Magdalene kisses his feet (recalling the earlier Lk. 7 scene). Zerah arranges for a Roman guard at the tomb. On Easter morning, the women come to the tomb, with Magdalene carrying the ointment Jesus gave her. Gardeners (conflating Jn 20:12 and 20:15) ask them why they look for the living among the dead, and the women find the tomb empty.

Magdalene reports Jesus's resurrection and appearance to the timid disciples (Jn 20:15-17). Thomas does not believe, and Magdalene storms off.[41] As the others argue, Peter (in profile again) says he believes because Jesus said so. Peter declares them all "Judases"—and forgiven ("succeeding" Jesus by looking directly into the camera). Meanwhile, Zerah enters the tomb (only he and the soldiers do) and concludes: "Now it begins." Finally, Jesus appears to the hiding disciples and commissions them to teach the nations and, speaking directly to the camera, tells them to fear not: "I am with you everyday until the end of time." The last camera shot is of the empty graveclothes.

MEMORABLE CHARACTERS

1. Jesus is more "of Nazareth" than any previous cinematic Jesus. He is also an iconic, unblinking, divine figure,[42] made intimately available to the audience in one centered closeup after another. His blatant Johannine confessions leave him repeatedly open to blasphemy charges.

2. Zeffirelli develops the apostles more than any other Jesus filmmaker, creating vignettes out of their traditional epithets: for example, doubting Thomas; Simon the Zealot; Matthew/Levi the tax collector; and (John) the beloved disciple. Mary the eternally young virgin and Magdalene the reformed prostitute are similarly traditional. The formation of the "church's" rock is so crucial that the film is practically a Peter film. Significantly, Peter is the first to believe "without seeing."[43]

3. Pilate is the most important elite figure opposing Jesus. Ameliorating the tradition's anti-Semitism, Pilate orders Jesus's crucifixion without foisting responsibility onto the Jews.

4. Zerah, Burgess's invention (cf. Sorak and the Dark Hermit in *Greatest Story*), sidelines Caiaphas who, nevertheless, still makes the most succinct "false prophet" statement. The Machiavellian Zerah is the Sanhedrin's face vis-à-vis Jesus/Judas and Pilate.

5. Judas is Zerah's dupe, not that of an oracle or of Satan. Zeffirelli redeems Judas somewhat through an editorial segue from Peter the denier to Judas the betrayer,[44] and by having the upper room's Peter describe all present as forgiven Judases. Nonetheless, the intellectual Judas still does not "belong" in a film about the "heart."

6. Like John's gospel (12:42; 19:38), the film creates Jews sympathetic to Jesus (ameliorating anti-Semitism): Yehuda; Joseph; Joseph of Arimathea; and Nicodemus.

MEMORABLE VISUALS

1. Rabbi Yehuda and Jesus reading Torah in the synagogue.
2. Mary's labor pains.
3. The child Jesus climbing Jacob's (?) ladder.
4. Crosscut closeups of Jesus, Peter, and Matthew during the Prodigal Son parable (see Figure 12.1).
5. Closeups of the iconic, non-blinking, divine Christ.[45]
6. Magdalene washing Jesus's feet with tears in the Lk. 7:36-50 scene and at the deposition.
7. The segue from remorseful Peter to anguished Judas after the Sanhedrin trial.
8. Backlit (transfigured?), scourged, and mocked Ecce Homo looking skyward.
9. Nicodemus reciting Isa. 53 and "born again" at the cross.

Figure 12.1 Jesus reconciles fiery Peter and tax collector Matthew in *Jesus of Nazareth,* directed by Franco Zeffirelli, ITC Films/RAI, 1977. All rights reserved.

KEY AUTHORITY/SCRIPTURE

1 The zoom into a closeup or extreme closeup creating the illusion one has knowledge of a character's thoughts or that the unblinking Son of God speaks directly to the audience.

2 Rabbi Yehuda and Nicodemus's voiceovers authorize the sense that apostolic Christianity "fulfills" messianic Judaism. Those who think Jesus a blasphemer/false prophet are on the wrong side of (supersessionist) history.[46] Notably, this narrative structure resembles Luke-Acts.

3 Nicodemus's quotation of Isa. 53:3a, 7, 4-5 as he watches the crucifixion, which he glosses evangelically with "Born again."

4 Johannine "I ams" (and the closeups of the unblinking Powell) express the film's Christology.

CULTURAL LOCATION/GENRE: RELIGIOUS DRAMA, TELEVISION MINISERIES

Jesus of Nazareth was an international production appearing almost simultaneously on televisions in the UK, Italy, and United States (see n1). In Italy the film continued a long tradition of Jesus-adjacent stories. It also marked the beginning of a series of

Italian made-for-television productions. Compared to *Il vangelo* (1964) and *Il messia*, it represented a conservative turn (Page 2021: 133–4).[47] While sharing village settings and populism with those movies, *Jesus of Nazareth* validates the institution (the apostolic church and consumer capitalism).[48] Accordingly, many of *Jesus of Nazareth*'s actors and actresses are celebrities.

The film's camera techniques serve this ideology. Pasolini's closeups reveal the material hardships of the people's lives (and male beauty); Zeffirelli's reveal the depths of personalities or a Jesus intimate with every viewer. In the United States, Zeffirelli's constructions of the person and religion resonated well with the burgeoning evangelical movement[49] epitomized by the election and inauguration of the first "born again" US president, Jimmy Carter.[50] Again, while Rossellini's zoom builds community, Zeffirelli's zoom exposes individual's "depths." Zeffirelli's focus on individual personality helps explain, if it does not require, the stable of celebrities. As befits television, *Jesus of Nazareth*, unlike *Il vangelo* and *Il messia*, belongs to consumer culture (see Problematic Issue).

Jesus of Nazareth appeared initially on NBC television without commercial breaks (see n1). It was "prestige TV," an example of the emerging miniseries, which grew out of older serializations of (classic) novels.[51] (The US miniseries tended to rely on popular, not classic, novels.) Filmmakers marketed miniseries as surpassing popular television series in plot and character development—touting their nature as "one-time events" and their spectacle of celebrities. The first US example was *QB VII* (1974), but *Roots* (1977), premiering a few months before *Jesus of Nazareth*, was the first blockbuster. *Jesus of Nazareth* was a financial and critical success and quickly replaced *The King of Kings* (1927) as the most seen Jesus film due to its repeated television broadcasts.[52] Like *The Passion of the Christ* more recently, *Jesus of Nazareth* created the "canonical" Jesus for a whole generation (Humphries-Brooks 2006: 81).

The television medium, of course, differs significantly from film (in ways beyond the miniseries' length). Before digital and pay television, two key differences were commercial interruptions (see Problematic Issue) and visual quality. Analog televisions of the 1970s were small screens with lower resolutions and less color definition than film. Consequently, television typically opted for medium shots and closeups, rather than the epic's longshots. Interaction between characters replaces conflict with nature and vast historical movements (Stern, Jefford, and DeBona 1999: 198–9, 213). Domesticity replaces nature/history. Accordingly, *Jesus of Nazareth*'s first movement situates Jesus in a happy family and then sends him off on a mission (typically a war or a career). Nazareth becomes ancient Galilee's Mayberry.[53] As intimacy replaces wide-open spaces, *Jesus of Nazareth*'s camera zooms in repeatedly to closeups of good-looking celebrities, and its Jesus intimately, but non-erotically, embraces everyone.[54]

Television of the 1970s represented "family values" and the status quo. Everything is in good taste. Sex, and to a lesser extent violence, is suggested rather than represented. Nothing can disturb the political-social status quo.[55] After all, television has replaced the nickelodeon and cinema as the working classes' nightly entertainment. At most, viewers might be asked to buy something (see Problematic Issue)—even religion, now seen as a commodity.

DIRECTOR

Zeffirelli began his career as an opera scene designer and his films are known for excessive or baroque productions (see Baugh 1997: 77–9; Kandell 2019). Scenery is more important than character (cf. *La vie et passion de notre seigneur Jésus Christ* 1907), as in his elaborate recreation of Nazareth.[56] His productions look good—if they sometimes lack substance (Lane 2019).

Critics often disparaged his work, but most of his productions were immensely popular. The Metropolitan Opera staged his version of *Falstaff* (1964) for over forty years, and his film *Romeo and Juliet* (1968) grossed 50 million dollars on a budget of 1.5 million (Kandell 2019). The latter made Shakespeare appealing to younger audiences through its youthful leads (with an unknown, fifteen-year-old Oliva Hussey as Juliet [and as Mary in *Jesus of Nazareth*]). Zeffirelli's oeuvre often seems to be deliberately popularizing difficult material (cf. his *Hamlet* 1990 and *Jesus of Nazareth*).[57]

A "miraculous" escape from a car crash influenced Zeffirelli's religious films, *Jesus of Nazareth* and *Brother Sun, Sister Moon* (1973).[58] Usually disparaged in comparison with Rossellini's *Francesco, giullare di Dio* (1950), *Brother Sun* is a *Romeo and Juliet* version of the St Francis story, designed to appeal to young audiences, starring two impossibly beautiful "flower children" (Graham Faulkner and Judi Bowker) romping through the woods in sentimental, pastel scenes.

At home, sick from war, wealthy Francesco has troubling nightmares about his past and "visions" of God's demands, but returns to his profligate life. Gradually, nature's beauties and "treasure in heaven" transform him (his subsequent teaching depends upon Jesus's Sermon). After his father humiliates him publicly (to "save" him from his madness), naked Francesco leaves Assisi for a wandering, ascetic life. With some of his friends—and the beautiful Clare, who works with lepers—he rebuilds a ruined church. Facing hostility from the Assisi wealthy, Francis walks to Rome for Pope Innocent III's advice (Alec Guinness). When angry authorities expel Francis for rejecting the church's wealth in favor of Jesus's "poor," the pope supports the "innocent" Francis, kissing his feet. Despite its sentimentality, the film does emphasize the critical disjoint between Jesus's teaching and the institutional church (cf. *Il vangelo*), something never hinted at in *Jesus of Nazareth*.

PROBLEMATIC ISSUE: JESUS COMMODIFIED

In 1965, George Stevens sued Paramount and NBC to prevent the airing of his *A Place in the Sun* (1951) with commercial interruptions. He lost, but he and others continued the battle, arguing, "A motion picture should be respected as being more than a tool for selling soap, toothpaste, deodorant, used cars, beer and the whole gamut of products advertised on television" (in Cronin 2005). Some once felt similarly about the Jesus story.

While *Jesus of Nazareth* was initially shown without commercial interruption, Zeffirelli had already cut his film for future advertising spots, as indicated by the repeated fades to black. Commercial television's constant interruptions mean that a television "story" never stands alone. The audience's attention is constantly diverted—constantly serving two masters, the most important of which is the commercial. Early cinema's grand pageants and epics become (Hallmark) postcards (Humphries-Brooks 2006: 77; cf. Baugh 1997: 75, 79).[59] Jesus must compete for attention, for his market share. Jesus is a commodity and, in "the cultural logic of late capitalism," no overarching myth or institution controls the commodity's meaning.[60] Perhaps, in a capitalist society, there is little point in contesting its logic. After all, many now describe religion's recent forms in capitalist terms (consider, e.g., religious marketing and branding).

In this context, Zeffirelli's Jesus, like that of *Jesus Christ Superstar*, is simply another malleable celebrity (see Chapter 10). As in *Greatest Story*, the surrounding celebrities overwhelm Jesus (the relatively unknown Robert Powell). Further, recognizable actors' other roles follow them into the film. Meaning is not restricted to the church or the gospel; it is always intertextual.[61] Thus, the Jesus in *King of Kings* (1961) is inevitably a teenage heartthrob, a surfer Jesus. The centurion in *Greatest Story* steps out of the American West, bringing the cavalry to Calvary.

Thus, in *Jesus of Nazareth*, Nero orders the baby Jesus's death (Peter Ustinov in *Quo Vadis* 1951). Juliet gives birth to Jesus (Olivia Hussey in *Romeo and Juliet* 1968). When the kings visit the holy family, the Dark Hermit (Donald Pleasence in *Greatest Story*), Darth Vader (James Earl Jones in *Star Wars: Episode IV* 1977), and drug lord Frog One (Fernando Rey in *The French Connection* 1971) do homage to the child. Captain Von Trapp has the Baptist executed (Christopher Plummer in *The Sound of Music* 1965).[62] Mrs. Robinson anoints Jesus's feet (Anne Bancroft in *The Graduate* 1967). Humbert Humbert (James Mason in *Lolita* 1962) and Hamlet (Laurence Olivier in *Hamlet* 1948) try vainly to defend Jesus, but Bilbo Baggins orchestrates his execution (Ian Holm in *The Lord of the Rings: The Fellowship of the Ring* 2001). Bill Gillespie sentences him to death (Rod Steiger in *In the Heat of the Night* 1967). Finally, lovable, butcher Marty (Ernest Borgnine in *Marty* 1955) oversees the crucifixion.

Is it any wonder that directors often seek little known actors to play Jesus?

ARTISAN HOME ENTERTAINMENT, 382 MINUTES, 2000
DVD Extras (First DVD)

Trailer (0:37)
Cast and Crew (filmography updated through 1999)
Historical Information (20 pages, the named source is Henri Daniel-Rops, *Daily Life in Palestine at the Time of Christ* 1962).

DVD Chapters

First DVD

1 *Jesus of Nazareth*

2 [Opening Synagogue] Sermon, 2:20
      "[W]hen the messiah comes … " 2:27
3 The Marriage Contract, 4:54
4 Betrothal to Each Other, 7:13
5 [Non-spectacular] Message from God, 9:06
6 King Herod, 13:06
7 Blessed Mary, 15:37
      "My soul doth magnify," 18:08
8 A Special Child, 18:40
9 Joseph's Dilemma, 21:50
10 Nightmares, 25:51
      Joseph's nightmare, 26:11
      Angel voice tells Joseph to marry, 26:47
11 Wedding Day, 27:18
12 Discussion of a Census, 30:35
13 Fulfilling the Prophecy (Mal. 5:2), 33:06
14 Traveling to Bethlehem, 36:05
      Laboring Mary, 36:23; 37:05; 37:44; 38:22
      Crosscuts to each of the three kings, 36:38; 37:19; 37:56
15 Three Kings, 38:34
16 No Room in the Inn, 42:54
17 A Child Is Born, 46:37
      Shepherds see the star, 46:37
      Birth pangs, 47:04
18 The Shepherds Come, 49:40
19 News of the Birth, 52:15
      (Angry) Herod starts to quote Mal. 5:2; 52:56
20 A Seal in Flesh, 54:11
      Simeon, 55:56
21 Gifts from the Wise Men, 57:54
      Wise men send the family to Egypt, 1.02:05
22 Slaughter of the Innocents, 1.04:19
23 A Home in Nazareth, 1.07:27
      Child Jesus blesses Nazareth, 1.09:42

24 Gifts from God, 1.10:28
   Jesus climbs ladder, 1.11:18
25 Roman Soldiers, 1.12:52
   Bar mitzvah, 1.13:00
26 Pilgrimage to Jerusalem, 1.17:44
   A lamb on Jesus's shoulders, 1.19:06
   Jesus: "The prayer from the heart is more important" 1.20:14
27 An Unholy Marriage, 1.21:15
   Rabbi Yehuda reading a collage of messianic scriptures in synagogue.
   The Baptist, 1.22:38
28 John the Baptist, 1.26:33
29 Not the Messiah, 1.29:37
   Salome listens—Herodias demands that Antipas arrest John, 1.31:19
   Sanhedrin to the Baptist: "Who are you?" 1.32:43
30 Returning to God, 1.34:57
   Joseph: "Into thy hand," 1.36:40
   Mary recites the Shema
31 The Messiah, 1.37:57
   Jesus returns to Nazareth, 1.42:05
   John arrested, 1.42:29
32 The Scriptures Are Fulfilled, 1.43:00
   Kingdom not foreseen, 1.45:54
33 The First Followers, 1.47:18
   "Stone the blasphemer," 1.47:31
   Andrew and Philip are Jesus's first disciples, 1.48:15
34 Driving out Satan, 1.49:47
35 Fishermen, 1.54:57
   Great catch of fish, 1.56:46
   It's a miracle. It's not a miracle, 2.00:56
36 Reading the Signs, 2.01:20
   Kingdom of heaven is like a treasure, a pearl, a net, 2.03:05
37 [Matthew] The Tax Collector, 2.05:15
   Paralytic (Mk 2:1-12), 2.06:56
38 The Home of a Sinner [Matthew], 2.09:56

39 A Story of [Prodigal] Brothers, 2.14:03

    Peter: "I am just a stupid man," 2.20:15

40 Unfairly Imprisoned, 2.21:16

    Baptist: "Before kingdoms change, men must change"

41 A Difficult Decision, 2.27:43

    Peter leaves his fishing boat

42 Healing the Child, 2.30.00

    "I've come not to bring peace, but a sword ... " (Mt. 10:34)

43 Doubting Thomas [Jairus's Servant], 2.35:03

44 Start of a New Life, 2.37:22

    Matthew to Peter: "We'll never be the same"

45 The Princess's [Salome] Dance, 2.39:42

46 The Head of the Baptist, 2.47:07

47 [His Disciples] Burying John, 2.49:01

    Judas (to Zealots): "Let him fulfill his mission"

48 [Prostitute] Mary Magdalene, 2.53:41

49 Entering the Kingdom of Heaven, 2.57:53

    Rich young ruler, 3.02:14

50 The Scholar Judas, 3.03:53

    Multi-lingual, scholar Judas: "Do you need a man like me?"

Second DVD

51 Endless Fish and Bread, 0:00

    "He's a prophet sent from God!" 5:45

52 Plans of Revolt, 5:56

    Zealots plan to force Sadducees to declare Jesus king

53 A Tainted Woman [Magdalene] (Lk. 7:36-50), 10:15

    Joseph of Arimathea: "It is the law that has enabled us to survive as a people"

    "Who is my neighbor?" 12:58

54 Blessed among Women, 16:23

    Sending out the Twelve (Mt. 10:5, 8-16, 19-20)

    Mary tells John, "Anyone who obeys our Father in heaven is brother ... " (Lk. 11:17-28; Mk 3:31-35), 18:35

55 [Zealot] Assassination Attempt [on Antipas], 19:24

    Judas and Simon the Zealot talk about Zealot deaths, 22:12

56 Peter Has Spoken the Truth, 23:12

    Time to go to Jerusalem, which delights Judas, but Jesus reprimands him

57 [The Beatitudes and] The Lord's Prayer, 28:23

58 The Holy City, 31:51

    At night, Peter tries to stop Jesus going to Jerusalem/death (Mt. 16:22-23)

59 Raising Lazarus from the Dead, 37:23

60 "Proclaim Jesus King in Judea," 43:46

    Lambs brought to the temple

    Judas (to Zerah): "Let Jesus prove himself before the Sanhedrin"

61 Palm Sunday, 48:27

    Cleansing the temple, 51:15

62 Services at the Temple, 55:46

63 Religious Zealots, 59:27

    (Forgiving) Jesus meets (vengeful) Barabbas, 1.01:00

64 Out of the Mouth of Babes, 1.04:22

    "By what authority?' 1.05:08

65 "Seek and Ye Shall Find," 1.07:50

66 Adulteress, 1.10:18

67 [Jesus] Friend to the Romans, 1.13:29

    Healing of Centurion's slave (Mt. 8:5-13) angers Barabbas

68 The Blind Man Can See [Jn 9], 1.16:40

69 The High Priests, 1.21:48

    "I and my father are one" (Jn 10:30), 1.26:45

    Judas is heartbroken when Barabbas is arrested, 1.28:26

70 Warning, 1.28:33

    Nicodemus (Jn 3), 1.29:34

71 The Temple Elders [argue about Jesus], 1.31:52

72 Judas's Decision [to work with Zerah], 1.41:49

    Judas: " … he says the heart is more important"

73 Passover, 1.45:15

74 The First Communion, 1.50:45

75 The Betrayal, 1.56:53

    Judas and Zerah arrive, 1.58:40

76 An Invaluable Help, 2.01:37

    Zerah: "No meeting; there's a trial"

    Thirty pieces of silver, 2.02:49

77 The Son of God [before the Sanhedrin], 2.04:10
78 [Peter's] Three Denials, 2.10:11
    Judas hangs himself, 2.12:28
79 Pontius Pilate, 2.12:56
    Jesus appears, 2.15:19
    Pilate washes his hands, 2.15:32
80 Trial, 2.17:45
81 [Scourging and] Mockery of a King, 2.23:31
    "Behold the Man," 2.25:27
    Prisoner's release, 2.28:23
82 The People Shall Decide, 2.29:33
    Pilate sentences treasonous Jesus to be crucified, 2.34:20
83 The Crucifixion, 2.35:19
    Via Dolorosa, 2.35:51
    Veronica, 2.38:25
    Crucified, 2.39:15
84 Two Thieves, 2.40:43
85 A Mother's Sorrow, 2.42:56
    Magdalene, "one of the family"
    John, the Beloved Disciple comes, 2.44:50
    Nicodemus quotes Isa. 53:3a, 7, 4-5; born again, 2.47:38
    "Father, into thy hands," 2.49:42
86 End of Suffering, 2.50:45
    Peter weeping, 2.51:11
    Deposition, 2.51:49
87 An Empty Tomb, 2.53:45
    Women visit tomb, 2.56:04
88 [Magdalene reports] He Has Risen, 2.58:49
89 A Question among Disciples, 3.04:21
    Peter believes without seeing
90 Appearing to the Disciples, 3.07:30
    In the empty tomb, Zerah: "Now it begins"
91 Closing credits, 3.10:49

NOTES

1. The film was a joint UK (Lew Grade)-Italian project. ITV (UK) aired the film on April 3, 1977. Italy's RAI 1 broadcast the film in five episodes from March 27 through April 25. In the United States, NBC aired the miniseries in two three-hour installments on Palm Sunday (April 3) and Easter Sunday 1977 (April 10). In 1979, NBC showed an expanded version in four two-hour installments. Various networks have since repeatedly aired the film. The Artisan DVD (and YouTube version) is the 1977 version. Abridged versions are available on YouTube and elsewhere.
2. After the annunciation, Mary visits pregnant Elizabeth. In a rare cinematic moment, Zeffirelli includes the Baptist's birth and circumcision. Elizabeth first names Mary's (unborn) son the messiah.
3. Cf. recent films about Jesus's childhood (e.g., *The Nativity Story* 2006; *The Young Messiah* 2016).
4. While this is the first Jesus film to show the child's birth on screen, Mary's labors evoke sexual orgasm or spiritual ecstasy more than childbearing pain (cf. Mary at the 47:54 mark with Bernini's *Ecstasy of Saint Teresa*).
5. The baby's "Christian blessing" gesture is only one of many instances where Jesus already belongs to Christianity. See, for example, Joseph of Arimathea asking if Jesus will accept their laws and the sign of the fish drawn in the dirt in the woman taken in adultery scene.
6. Jesus's circumcision is rare cinematically (see *The Savior* 2014; Chattaway 2021: 24).
7. On journeys, Mary always rides a donkey.
8. The Baptist declares Jesus the lamb of God (1.41:45). Sheep are repeatedly in the mise-en-scène (see, e.g., 52:00; 58:49; 1.11:18; 1.19:06; DVD 2, 43:46; as they are in *Jesus Christ Superstar*; *Last Temptation* 1988) although no one stresses that Jesus is the sacrificial lamb until Nicodemus quotes Isa. 53 at the cross.
9. Zeffirelli used Jews from an ancient community on the Isle of Djerba as extras (Tatum 2013: 144). On anachronisms, see Maccoby (1977) and McGeough (2021: 117, 122).
10. Paul VI's 1965 *Nostra Aetate* inspired Zeffirelli to focus on Jesus's Judaism (Tatum 2013: 143) as it touted Christians and Jews' common spiritual patrimony and denied that "the Jews" were responsible for Jesus's death. The Last Supper scene (see Reinhartz 2007: 50–1) and the film's overall structure (see Walsh 2003: 37–8), however, are supersessionist.
11. Zeffirelli, born out of wedlock, often spoke of his search for a "father" and the bastard-epithet's painfulness. The film gives more attention to Joseph than any other Jesus film (except for infancy films; see n3). Later in life, Zeffirelli, as an ultraconservative Italian senator, strenuously opposed abortion.
12. Anna is Mary's mother according to the *Protoevangelium of James*.
13. Zeffirelli had blond hair and blue eyes.
14. The effect resembles those of epic voiceover and the silents' intertitles.
15. Are these Joseph's sons? See Chattaway 2021: 22.
16. Powell had a long television career. Italian and British critics lauded his "Jesus," but he said, "I hope Jesus Christ will be the last in my line of sensitive young men for quite a while."
17. Zeffirelli claims he omitted the temptation because he could not film this mystery (1984: 151).
18. Despite its internalized construction of religion, the film does not quote Luke 17:21.
19. The television medium almost demands crosscuts from one closeup to another (in dialogue scenes), but Zeffirelli increases the intimacy by having Jesus touch almost everyone—with notable exceptions like the rich young ruler and Judas (Page 2019).

20 The message of Jesus and the Baptist (and Rabbi Yehuda) is more similar here than in most other films.
21 An exorcism is Jesus's first miracle in Mark (1:21-27); however, Zeffirelli visualizes something more like Mt. 17:14-19.
22 According to Bruce Babington and Peter Evans, Zeffirelli gives "a bravura treatment" to miracles (1993: 104). The matter may reflect Zeffirelli's love of opera. Stephenson Humphries-Brooks says that Zeffirelli's camera is always the unblinking "eye of faith" (2006: 78; cf. Staley 2021: 47–8). The original screenwriter, Anthony Burgess, had something less hagiographic in mind (1977). In *Man of Nazareth* (1979), based on his screenplay, Burgess has a skeptical Greek merchant relate what he saw after the crucifixion. For a comparison of novel and film, see Holderness (2015: 67–86). Suso Cecchi D'Amico, a prolific screenwriter who worked with most of the post-war Italian directors, revised Burgess's script.
23 As in *Godspell* (1973), the parable redeems two men.
24 Like the epics, Zeffirelli cuts away to the elite (Herod or Antipas), but he spends more time developing "minor" characters (e.g., the wise men; John's disciples and the Zealots; Joseph of Arimathea; Nicodemus; Zerah), who often come to Jesus.
25 The English actor is best known for roles in *Lovejoy* (1986–94), *Deadwood* (2004–6, 2019), and *American Gods* (2017–21).
26 The first Artisan DVD ends here, but the Galilean ministry is not over. The scene ends with an intimate closeup of their faces, nicely foreshadowing the betrayal kiss (cf. various intimate scenes in *The Last Temptation*).
27 Bancroft won the Best Actress Oscar as Anne Sullivan, the tutor to Helen Keller, in *Miracle Worker* (1962) and was nominated four other times.
28 Jane Schaberg says that this scene completes Magdalene's conversion (1996: 39).
29 Zeffirelli claims he thought of his Jesus as a Pharisee (1984: 45).
30 Schaberg doubts that the fiery Magdalene/Bancroft would kneel at Jesus's feet (1996: 39).
31 Most filmmakers, including Zeffirelli, omit the transfiguration (see, however, *La vie et passion de notre seigneur Jésus Christ* and *The Jesus Film* 1979), but Zeffirelli does "transfigure" Jesus: for example, in this scene, backlit at the first miracle, and backlit in the Ecce Homo scene. The frequent iconic closeups, centering Jesus's face in the screen, function similarly. This scene ended the first segment of the initial, two-part showing on NBC in 1977.
32 Barnes Tatum argues that Zeffirelli's film harmonizes the gospels more adroitly than any other by placing most of Jesus's Johannine divine speech after Peter's confession (2013: 150, 156). The camera work, however, has already deified Jesus and critics have called him blasphemer since his Nazareth sermon.
33 On the scene's photography and this rare privileging of believing Martha, see Staley (2021: 47).
34 Burgess said that he created Zerah to facilitate interaction between the Sanhedrin and Jesus, and imagined Judas's story as a tale of lost innocence (1977; for Zeffirelli's interpretation, see 1984: 186–98).
35 The Baptist brandished a similar staff when he challenged the Sanhedrin's representatives. Burgess says that he wanted a manly, tigrine Christ (1977).
36 Jesus draws a fish (an early Christian symbol) in the sand.
37 This scene highlights Jesus's temple teaching as the Prodigal Son scene did the Galilean teaching. It also seems to replace the (missing) controversy about paying imperial taxes.
38 Jesus speaks so slowly that it seems "halting." His response to Caiaphas is the slowest moment in a "seemingly interminable epic" (Reinhartz 2007: 102).

39 Jesus's painful gasps recall Mary's gasps in labor. Both may symbolize the spiritual ecstasy of being "born again." See n4.
40 Even though Jesus dies on this scaffolding, Zeffirelli offers several traditionally—and visually impossible—iconic shots of the cross.
41 Schaberg says the resistant, feminist viewer leaves with Magdalene and that her message vanishes beneath Peter's belief (1996: 41–2). Contrast *Mary Magdalene*'s (2018) end.
42 Zeffirelli said of Powell's screen test: "Something was happening that made us think of a miracle … Even more impressive was a kind of light 'not his' … " (1984: 96). "Powell's eyes … became two intense beacons of light … " (1984: 79). The makeup team applied dark blue eyeliner to his upper eyelid and white to the lower to intensify this effect.
43 Peter's transformation resembles that of the Peter of Luke-Acts. The cinematic transformation is more miraculous because the Lukan transformation takes place after resurrection appearances.
44 The sequence makes them seem (of) one character. See Walsh (2010: 36 n35).
45 Jesus blinks at least twice in the film, during his lengthy Sanhedrin testimony.
46 For a more positive reading of these outcasts, see Walsh (2005: 165–72).
47 Lloyd Baugh calls the film the "polar opposite" of *Il vangelo* (1997: 262 n15).
48 Populism is most evident in the "personality" closeups and in Joseph of Arimathea's Sanhedrin paean about "the people." The film also celebrates Nazareth (small town) over Jerusalem (big city) and the heart over (misguided) intellectuals (see Humphries-Brooks 2006: 76).
49 Bob Jones III urged a film boycott (without seeing it), which led General Motors to abandon the project. Proctor and Gamble took over the film's sponsorship (Forshey 1992: 170).
50 One of the effects of the 1960s countercultural movements, of the US defeat in Vietnam, and of the Watergate scandal was a retreat to personal enhancement. Religion became a matter of individual (evangelical) conversion. See Henderson (1977), Forshey (1992: 166), Stern, Jefford, and DeBona (1999: 218–29), and Walsh (2003: 12–13). In cinema, the move was from "issues" cinema to escapist fantasies like *Star Wars: Episode IV* (1977) or *Rambo* (1982). For a comparison of *Jesus of Nazareth* and *Star Wars*, reliant on Joseph Campbell's hero-within-mythology and discovering an Obi-Wan Jesus, see Stern, Jefford, and DeBona 1999: 218–27).
51 In the United States, Powell's aristocratic British accent might also have lent the film prestige (although such accents typically belong to the biblical epics' imperial villains).
52 *The Jesus Film*, used extensively in evangelistic missions, and *The Passion of the Christ* may now have surpassed *Jesus of Nazareth*'s audience.
53 Mayberry is the fictitious small town of *The Andy Griffith Show*, one of television's most popular shows from 1960 to 1968.
54 In this context, Baugh notes lepers' absence (1997: 77).
55 This rhetorical choice reflects the film's international status. In the United States, however, the film makes two subtle political moves. First, it mainstreams Roman Catholicism, refreshing the waning Protestant establishment (Humphries-Brooks 2006: 78–80). Protestant evangelicals and Roman Catholics would unite again in praise of *The Passion of the Christ*. Zeffirelli's film is quite Marian, and Peter plays a greater role than in any previous Jesus film. Second, while it does not compare with Moses's Statue of Liberty pose, which ends *The Ten Commandments* (1956), Zeffirelli's wise men—traditionally representing Asia (Melchior), Europe (Caspar), and Africa (Belshazzar)—are red, white, and blue, joined together under one bright star. It must be happenstance that Caspar is rational, Melchior religious, and Belshazzar least knowledgeable. Note, however, that Assisi's colors are also red and blue.

56 Zeffirelli first began working in film with Luchino Visconti, who became his lover and is known for *Ossessione* (Obsession 1943), based on James M. Cain's *The Postman Always Rings Twice*, and *Senso* (1954), an attempt to break away from neorealism. Zeffirelli credited Visconti with teaching him "how to bring together a world of culture" embodying "an idea" (in Kandell 2019).
57 Andrew Rissik says Zeffirelli does "for the Bible what the *Reader's Digest* does for novels, and it's the very inoffensiveness of the thing that ultimately makes it so offensive" (in Baugh 1997: 75).
58 He also became *metteur en scène* (scene setter) for many Vatican events (Lane 2019).
59 *La ricotta* (1963) is precursor.
60 This language alludes to "postmodernism's" unending semiosis (so Jameson 1991). Many consider television, in contrast to cinema, an inherently postmodern medium. Of course, the "church" loses control of Jesus's meaning whenever Jesus appears in art, popular culture, etc. See the discussions in Chapters 7 and 10.
61 Intertexuality is not about the sources an author uses to create a text. It is about everything (including texts) a reader uses to read a text. See Kristeva (1980).
62 Plummer narrates *The Gospel of John* (2003).

13

Monty Python's Life of Brian

Terry Jones, director, Handmade Films, 1979

PLOT SUMMARY: "HE'S NOT THE MESSIAH. HE'S A VERY NAUGHTY BOY!"

Like a Jesus epic, *Life of Brian* opens with an infancy. Astrologers, following a star, worship a Capricorn baby named Brian in a dark cowshed. As they leave, they see the illuminated Hallmark manger with haloed family. Realizing their mistake, they return, roughly retrieve their messianic gifts, and take them to the epic messiah. The film, however, stays with the ordinary Brian, Jesus's hapless doppelgänger. Amusingly, people confess Brian a "lucky bastard" (a chosen one?) on three separate occasions (in prison, after his fall from UFO heavens, and on his Via Dolorosa).

In the ensuing (Terry Gilliam) animated title sequence, buildings and monuments fall, as does an angel, flying too close to the sun. Subsequently, Brian also falls (from a tower, from the UFO, from a balcony, into the hermit's pit) or is thrown down (repeatedly before Pilate). He is never, however, raised or glorified. Even his cross is profane. A James Bond-like title song ("Brian," sung by teenager Sonia Jones) accompanies the animation and understates Brian's banal growth to adulthood.[1]

The film reopens on a historically realistic, first-century scene, but with incongruous titles: "Saturday Afternoon," "About Teatime."[2] Crowds stream into the wilderness to hear Jesus (Kenneth Colley)[3] deliver Beatitudes (Mt. 5:1-12). As in Jesus adjacents, Jesus is far away—so his faint words are misheard (peacemakers become cheesemakers; the meek become Greeks) and misinterpreted (cheesemakers become anyone involved in dairy products).[4] Epic reverence has become a querulous brawl at the back of the crowd. Members of the (unidentified) People's Front of Judea (PFJ) have better seats, so they understand the peacemaker-Jesus blessed those with status quo investments.

Jesus will not return, although an unhappy leper testifies to a cure. Yet, Jesus does not truly vanish; his story sets the stage for Brian (Graham Chapman), who replaces Jesus as (disputed) messiah and crucified one—with amusing and perhaps parabolic results.

Brian and his mother Mandy (Terry Jones) leave Jesus's pacifist Sermon for a stoning, which Mandy attends by donning a fake beard. The intended victim (like Jesus epics' woman caught in adultery) goes free, but only because the crowd switches its ire to the religious official (John Cleese) who inadvertently utters the divine name while explaining the accused's blasphemy.

Even though Brian and Mandy pass by crosses with skeletons (cf. *Greatest Story* 1965), a humorous, slightly askew view continues. Brian meets a disgruntled ex-leper (Michael

Palin), who complains he cannot collect alms because the "bloody do-gooder" Jesus healed him. At home, a Roman soldier awaits the prostitute Mandy. The scene continues the film's skewed Jesus model when Mandy (not a heavenly voice) tells Brian he is a centurion's "bastard" (not the beloved son). Still, the "revelation" inaugurates Brian's public career—an effort to prove his Jewish (not his messianic) identity.[5]

Working the Children's Matinee in an almost empty Jerusalem Coliseum,[6] Brian sells refreshments to the bumbling PFJ who never actually revolt because they talk endlessly[7] and split into ever-smaller groups (one consists of one individual). As if emphasizing their "mere talk," the PFJ sends Brian to paint anti-Roman graffiti. A Roman centurion (John Cleese) catches Brian, pedantically corrects his Latin, and forces him to write the corrected slogan 100 times.

The next, less educationally minded Roman detachment tries to apprehend Brian, who runs for his life, thus beginning an extended, comic chase sequence whose series of near escapes (cf. *Intolerance* 1916) ends incongruously with Brian's crucifixion.[8] Brian meets Judith Iscariot (Sue Jones-Davies) who takes him to the PFJ's secret headquarters. As the PFJ plots Pilate's wife's kidnapping, a wag points out that empire has benefits, which the revolutionaries hilariously list: aqueducts, sanitation, roads, wine, and peace. Judith and Brian's sudden arrival scares the PFJ into hiding, but they recover to attach Brian to their kidnapping squad.

In the palace, the kidnappers encounter and squabble with another rebel group, leaving only Brian alive. Having bemusedly watched the revolutionaries kill themselves, Romans arrest Brian. Jailed, he meets a law-and-order (or masochistic), Roman-loving prisoner (Ben/Michael Palin). Having been chained to the wall for five years, he thinks Brian is a "lucky bastard," who is thus likely to "get away with crucifixion" for his first offense. He also claims crucifixion is the best thing the Romans ever did for Jews (mocking the earlier "benefits" scene).[9]

Pilate's (Michael Palin) lisping speech reduces the Roman guard to uncontrollable laughter, allowing Brian to escape. Pursued to a tower, Brian falls, but a passing UFO miraculously saves him—a parody of Jesus's "exaltations" (see Walsh 2013b: 191).[10] But, like Icarus (in the animated title sequence), Brian falls back to earth when the UFO is shot down.

When the "lucky bastard" walks away unscathed, the Roman chase begins again. Brian runs through the marketplace where a Blood and Thunder Prophet (Terry Gilliam), a False Prophet, and a Boring Prophet (Michael Palin) harangue a crowd. Brian buys a beard and a gourd from Harry the Haggler (Eric Idle). Going to PFJ headquarters, he interrupts the reading of a martyrs' roster, which includes his name (an upper room resurrection appearance?). The Romans come three times to this secret headquarters, twice searching the impossibly small room with an impossibly large number of soldiers while Brian hides on a rickety balcony.

When Brian's balcony collapses, Brian falls atop the Boring Prophet. To fit in, Brian preaches (appropriating Jesus's words without attribution; cf. Mt. 7:1; 6:28; 25:14-30).[11] But Brian is no Jesus. His audience criticizes and questions (cf. *Last Temptation*'s [1988] teaching scene). Still, when Brian retreats, the crowd pursues the "messiah" of their choosing because they take his reluctance as a sign that he is the (secret) messiah.

The fleeing Brian loses a sandal, and his followers quarrel over whether the (dropped) gourd or the sandal is his chief symbol. Trying to disappear into the wilderness, Brian jumps into a pit onto a hermit (Simon the Holy Man/Terry Jones), causing Simon to break an eighteen-year vow of silence. The noise alerts Brian's followers who demand food and other miracles. (When Brian suggests they eat from a nearby juniper, they see a miracle.) A blind man, thanking Brian for his restored sight, falls into the pit, and the crowd acclaims Brian for restoring Simon's speech when he complains about his broken vow (cf. the "tree" miracle in *Godspell* 1973). Brian's continuing denials lead to further ecstasies, as the crowd believes only the true messiah would so demur.[12] When Simon objects to these irrationalities, Brian's followers harass the heretic. The entire scene parodies messianic sectarian developments (like the apostolic church?) and the development of legendary sayings/miracles (like the Christian gospels?).

The next morning, at Mandy's house, Brian awakes alongside the naked Judith. Sauntering naked to the window[13] and throwing open the shutters, Brian finds his followers awaiting their messiah's revelations.[14] Mandy dismisses the crowd, saying, "There's a mess [here], all right, but no messiah …. He's not the messiah. He's a very naughty boy!" She reconsiders when they hail her as the blessed mother/virgin. Rejecting "following," Brian exhorts his followers to think for themselves, but his message is lost as they, except for one dissenting voice, chant in unison, "We're all individuals. We are all different" (see Figure 13.1).[15]

When the crowd floods Mandy's house, Reg (John Cleese), the leader of the PFJ, starts managing his new savior's campaign, lining up lepers and women taken in sin for Brian to heal. When Brian sneaks outside, an ecstatic Judith hails him as the revolution's leader causing a passing centurion (John Cleese) to arrest Brian.

Figure 13.1 Brian prompts his "followers" to think for themselves in *Monty Python's Life of Brian*, directed by Terry Jones, Handmade Films, 1979. All rights reserved.

Pilate callously adds Brian to the day's 139 crucifixions.[16] The ever-plotting, never-acting PFJ only discusses liberating Brian. The bureaucratic Nisus Wettus (Michael Palin) lines up the crucifixion party in good "Roman" (or British) order. Brian's claim to be a Roman and request for a lawyer go unheeded.

Jones cuts repeatedly between the "crucifixion party" and a laughing crowd's demands for the release of various criminals simply to hear Pilate and Biggus Dickus's (Graham Chapman) lisping mispronunciations of their names. Ben harangues the "lucky bastards" on the Via Dolorosa from his cell, a saint helps a man bear his cross only to be added to the crucifixion party in his place, and vendors sell candle crosses. Finally, in Pilate's courtyard, Judith gains "Bwian's" (belated) release.

Brian tries to convince the soldier crucifying him that he does not have to follow orders (cf. his balcony message), but the Roman, predictably, likes orders. Mr. Cheeky (Eric Idle) encourages Brian with the hope of rescue. The crucifixion sequence, however, repeatedly douses these hopes. Reg and the PFJ arrive, but only to celebrate Brian's martyrdom, singing "For He's a Jolly Good Fellow." The centurion arrives with Brian's reprieve, but everyone claims, "I'm Brian" (cf. the end of *Spartacus* 1960), and the wrong man goes free (Mr. Cheeky, not Barabbas). The Judean People's Front's suicide commandoes chase off the soldiers, but commit suicide rather than saving the crucified. Like the PFJ, Judith thanks Brian for his noble death, and Mandy chastises him for leaving her. Instead of saving Brian, others determine his death's (non-)meaning.

Finally, Mr. Frisbee III (Eric Idle) tries to cheer Brian with life's absurdity by leading the crucified in the film's song-and-dance finale, "Always Look on the Bright Side of Life (Death)" (written by Eric Idle).[17] As the camera pulls back from the hill of crosses, Mr. Frisbee advertises the record for sale in the foyer (parodying Jesus musicals).[18]

MEMORABLE CHARACTERS

1 Brian is a "naughty boy." His portrayal against the Jesus backdrop proliferates messiahs, traditions, and crosses, profaning Jesus and undoing Christian (messianic) semiotics. He is not Christ or antichrist, but "unchrist" (see Cultural Location; Problematic Issue; Aichele 2007).

2 Mandy and Judith function similarly. They mean and amuse, respectively, only against the backdrop of the Virgin Mary and Magdalene/Judas.

3 The PFJ and Romans are also comic, bungling versions of their gospel counterparts. Only Pilate and Jesus appear with their "gospel" names/identities. Jesus is the iconic, epic Christ. The Jewish leaders are glaringly absent, except for the stoning victim.

MEMORABLE VISUALS

1 The astrologers pushing Mandy aside to recover their gifts.
2 The crowd's misunderstandings of the Sermon.
3 The ex-leper's complaints about lost revenue.
4 The miracle of the hermit.

5 The crowd repeating Brian's teaching in unison: "We're all individuals" (see Figure 13.1).
6 The song-and-dance crucifixion finale.

KEY AUTHORITY/SCRIPTURE

1 The iconic, epic Jesus is the film's basic authority. The story/humor fails without his story (see Dyke 2002).
2 The key scripture might be Mk 13:5-6, 21-22. The plurality of messiahs makes identities disputable. While comedy relishes identity mistakes (and other errors), sectarian identities demand certainty.

CULTURAL LOCATION/GENRE: ANTI-ESTABLISHMENT COMEDY, PARODY, AND PARABLE

Like *Godspell*, *Life of Brian* creates vaudevillian (and television variety show) sketch comedy (see Chapter 9). Both films rely on other stories for any narrative sense. The Pythons always push toward the next laugh, regardless of the direction.[19] In one breath, the troupe praises empire or individualism and, in the next, mocks them. Nothing is stable. Everything is grist for the anarchic mill. All that matters is the next laugh, for only the laugh is sacred.[20]

Identity is temporary, at best. Comedy relies on mistaken identity and cross-dressing;[21] consequently, the Pythons play various roles. Chapman is Brian and Biggus Dickus. Cleese is PFJ leader Reg, the centurion who arrests Brian, and Arthur, who knows Brian is messiah because he has "seen a few." Eric Idle is Stan/Loretta, Mr. Cheeky, and Mr. Frisbee. Terry Jones is Mandy, Simon the Hermit, and the Saintly Passerby. Michael Palin is the ex-leper, prisoner Ben, Pilate, and Nisus Wettus. All of them play "both sides," denying heroes and villains' finality.

As a collage of sketches, the film moves rapidly from genre to genre—from epic, to animated comedy, to epic again, to science fiction, to musical, and so on. Reality is not stable—it has no meaning—or has multiple meanings depending upon the perspective (sketch or genre or identity) momentarily adopted. Such comedy denies the finality of things (cf. Crossan 1975).

Where *Godspell*'s comedy hopes for restoration, *Life of Brian*'s is happily cynical.[22] What matters is the critique of established institutions and myths (the commonsense) that define "ordinary" life—the critique of (institutional, imperial) Romans or British who "can't take a bloody joke."[23] That the Pythons see genuine change as unlikely leads to the final song.

Nothing survives the laugh. Traditional parody imitates an exemplar's style to mock it, writing in the heroic style, for example, about non-heroic subjects. Similarly, *Life of Brian* adopts epic historical realism, but places the ordinary Brian at its center. It treats the Jesus epic as *Blazing Saddles* (1974) does the Western. Some recent critics, however, see parody as the intertextual attempt to innovate in the face of dominant genres, texts, and institutions (Genette 1997: 17). In this sense, *Life of Brian* creates new meaning, but not one completely separable from its gospel, epic, and other intertexts.

In the latter sense, parody is not far from parable, whose etymology suggests "[a story] thrown alongside." And the Pythons certainly throw Brian alongside Jesus, who jostles Jesus aside, reducing him to a bit player (cf. the bit-player Jesus in *Hail, Caesar!* 2016). Some understand parables in contrast to myth, which supports the establishment or the cultural dominant (e.g., Crossan 1975; on this sense of myth, see Barthes 1972). If an antimyth contests—perhaps even seeks to replace—the reigning myth (as an antichrist opposes Christ), a parable seeks to bring myth's (political and semiotic) workings into view (like the unchrist [Brian] vis-à-vis Jesus Christ).

If *Life of Brian* is parabolic, one might imagine it beginning, "There was a young Jewish bastard …." Such a parable might clear a space for reflection amid taken-for-granted Christian discourse that names (the nobody) Jesus of Nazareth messiah and declares one Roman crucifixion, among many, the world's prophesied salvation. Such parable profanes the sacred/myth, as comedy laughingly insists on the non-finality of stories/institutions (Crossan 1975; Walsh 2013b: 189–91).[24] The film's last song is thus crucial. Intriguingly, the film's meaning, if there is one, is at the cross(es)—as in Western Christianity—although no one in this Jesus adjacent converts to Christianity (see Problematic Issue).

DIRECTOR

The Pythons achieved fame with the sketch comedy *Monty Python's Flying Circus* (BBC 1969–74; first seen in Canada in 1970 and in the United States in 1974). They also made films, the most famous of which are *Monty Python and the Holy Grail* (1975) and *Life of Brian*. Both are often included on all-time best film comedy lists.[25]

The former, more sketch-like film, treats Arthurian legends as *Life of Brian* does Jesus stories. Miming the riding of horses, King Arthur (Graham Chapman) and Patsy, his squire (Terry Gilliam), look for knights for Arthur's Round Table. In one scene, Arthur defeats the Black Knight (John Cleese), by cutting off appendage after appendage as the knight makes light of his injuries (cf. *Life of Brian* characters dismissing crucifixion). The knights acquired are hardly legendary heroes, and they never find the grail. They move from one sketch to another, including a barrage of catapulted animals (and manure), the murder of an effeminate prince at his (forced) wedding, the terrifying, deadly Rabbit of Caerbannog, an animated cave monster (cf. *Life of Brian*'s UFO scene), and the Bridge of Death's trials. The story ends with the arrest of Lancelot (John Cleese), Arthur, and Bedevere (Terry Jones) for the murder of a modern historian who happens into the story. The camera is broken in the melee—resulting in an even more subversive ending than *Life of Brian*'s.

The Meaning of Life (1983) is a series of sketches loosely arranged around the question of life's meaning and the conceit of an abstract "life" from birth to death. In its finale, one of the troupe, in drag, opens an envelope, reads its statement about life's meaning, and notes that its message of self-preservation, peace, and harmony is rather trite (cf. Brian's bland balcony

Sermon). This mockery allows the troupe and its fans temporary flight from the dominant culture's values/stories.

That only *Life of Brian*'s Mr. Cheeky escapes crucifixion (and not for the first time) is no coincidence. Neither, of course, is the final song's lyrics declaring life absurd and "a piece of shit," and advising a grin in the knowledge that "the last laugh is on you." For the troupe, the only good is sitting lightly (comically) in life.

PROBLEMATIC ISSUE: (MAKING) MESSIAHS: "I'VE SEEN A FEW"

Life of Brian is a Jesus adjacent movie. The epic Jesus is there, and Brian's story intersects with that holier narrative. *Life of Brian* does not, however, have the proper Jesus adjacent tone. No one converts or even acts reverently. There is no "lust for glory," no hagiography. Everything is every day, and everyone is painfully ordinary. Brian is not enough of a Christ figure for the Jesus adjacent mechanics to work smoothly.[26]

When people try to make him a messiah—to heed his teaching (or symbols) and laud his miracles—everything goes comically awry (even for wise men); the messianic significations come undone. His followers succeed only in bringing him—against his own wishes—to the empire's attention, which crucifies him with dispatch—despite administrative bungling. Everyone left standing then assigns whatever meaning they like to Brian (cross/death).

The epic Jesus—and that of Jesus cinema typically—is, of course, wholly "Christ." Brian is more "Jesus" than "Christ." At least, Brian is a Jewish (or British) nobody—a Brian ~~Jesus~~ of Nazareth (or Liverpool).[27] As noted earlier, Brian is unchrist (not antichrist). Placing him within Christian or messianic discourse causes far greater confusion than when *Jesus Christ Superstar* (1973) replaces messiah with celebrity. Christian discourse's certainty vanishes when everyone has "seen a few [messiahs]" (cf. the anxiety in Mk 13:5-6, 21-22).

In the gospels (and Christian discourse), God or destiny "makes" the messiah. In *Jesus Christ Superstar*, story (or Christian discourse or spectacle) makes the messiah—despite Judas and Magdalene's resistance, and everyone else's horror. Horror cinema typically dismisses "messiah" as suicidal or murderous delusion—as "nut job," an increasingly popular signification in mass media (see Walsh 2021a). Brian is no more horror-messiah, however, than he is Christ figure. Instead, *Life of Brian* explores more thoroughly than *Jesus Christ Superstar* (and in a comic mode) fans' role in making messiahs. Brian then is not only unchrist; he is also the human need to follow (to create messiahs).

CRITERION DVD, 94 MINUTES, 1999
DVD Extras

The title sheet insert includes a two-page history of the film's production, and the DVD title menu adds six additional features. These include two commentaries, a documentary, deleted scenes, theatrical trailers, and British radio ads.

Commentary One—Terry Gilliam, Eric Idle, and Terry Jones

1 The Virgin Mandy
2 Angst and Animation
3 The Dogsbody of the Group
4 A Pile of Poo
5 A Great Leading Man
6 Keith Moon
7 Day for Night
8 The Effluents of Jerusalem
9 Comedy Rules
10 Exploding Cigars
11 The Art of the Deal
12 *Jesus Christ—Lust for Glory*
13 Hermit in a Hole[28]
14 Nether Regions
15 Cockadoodle-do
16 Mr. Cheeky
17 Tunisian Comic
18 Troglodytes
19 "I'm Brian"
20 The Wrong Crosses

Commentary Two—John Cleese and Michael Palin

1 Human Nature
2 Terry's Bits
3 Slips of the Tongue
4 Baby Oil
5 A Decent Chap
6 Judith Iscariot
7 Schoolboys
8 The Metronome
9 Pig Latin
10 "A Load of Old Rubbish"
11 Python Philosophy
12 Lost Laugh

"The piece of gourd that passeth all understanding."
13 Hermits
14 "How Shall We Fuck Off?"[29]
15 Doing God a Favor
Malcolm Muggeridge's critique
16 A Terrible Nice Bloke
17 A Rabble of Rubble
18 An Instrument of Torture
19 Strange New Revolutionaries
20 The World is Full of Loonies

Deleted Scenes
    Sheep, 4:36
    Pilate's Wife, 1:59
    Otto, 4:26
    "The Sign That Is the Sign," 1:15
    Souvenir Shop, 0:42
Theatrical Trailer, 2:45
British Radio Ads
    Michael Palin
    Eric Idle
    Terry Gilliam
    John Cleese

The Pythons' Documentary

1 Prologue: Graham Chapman Rests, 0:00
2 The Phenomenon, 3:34
3 Hail, the Pythons, 5:15
4 Python·esque\pi-the-'nesk\, 17:44
5 Insomniacs, Intellectuals and Burglars, 20:21
6 Nth-Rate Philosophers with Attitude, 24:47
7 Judea AD 33, 32:00
8 Tunisian Tummy, 25:52
9 Transplants, Teeth and Tax Evasion, 37:12
10 Python on Python, 40:29
11 Fellow Travelers, 46:59

12 Epilogue: An Orgy with Cherryade, 49:15

DVD Chapters

1 Logos/Three Wise Men, 0.00
        Star appears, 0:30
2 Opening titles animation, 4:20
3 Judea AD 33, 6:54
        Sermon on the Mount, 7:00
        Stoning, 10:40
4 "Alms for an ex-leper," 14:17
5 "You're one of them," 16:21
        "Your father was a Roman centurion," 17:17
6 The People's Front of Judea, 18:12
7 "Romans go home," 23:52
8 Raid on Pilate's palace, 31:02
9 Pilate, 38:19
10 Crash landing, 42:36
        UFO rescue, 43:13
        Various prophets, 44:52
11 Haggling, 46:16
12 The shoe and the gourd, 52:27
        Brian speaks Jesus's words, 52:50
        (Messianic) Kingdom secrets, 55:15
13 Give us a sign, 57:46[30]
        Healing the "dumb," 58:26
        Miraculous food in the desert, 1.00:10
14 Hail Messiah, 1.00:22
        Healing the blind, 1.01:00
15 "A very naughty boy," 1.02:56
        "You are all individuals," 1.07:08
            George Harrison's cameo appearance, 1.09:00
        Arrest, 1.09:56
16 "One cross each," 1.11:33

17 Pilate's Passover address, 1.14:15

    "I shall weleaseBwian!" 1.21:30

    Via Dolorosa, 1.21:34

18 The Jewish section, 1.22:32

    The People's Front of Judea

    A forest of crosses, 1.23:04

    "Penitent thief," 1.24:51

19 The Rescue Committee, 1.25:11

    The JPF Suicide squad, 1.28:08

    Judith, 1.28:33

    Brian's mother, 1.29:00

20 Always look on the bright side of life, 1.29:28

NOTES

1. Cf. John Barry (Prendergast)'s Bond themes (the first written in 1962). These song lyrics, those for "Always Look on the Bright Side of Life," and the film script are available at http://www.montypython.net/scripts/briansng.php#.
2. Shot on location in Tunisia, the film used some of *Jesus of Nazareth*'s locations and sets. For a comparison to biblical/Jesus films, see Telford (2015).
3. Colley is best known as the villainous Admiral Piett in *Star Wars: Episode V* (1980) and *Episode VI* (1983).
4. This physical distance represents the gap between Jesus and his audience/followers/church.
5. Brian "owns" a litany of slanders used against Jews: "I'm a Kike! A Yid! A Hebe! A Hook-nose! I'm Kosher, Mum! I'm a Red Sea Pedestrian, and proud of it!" See Reinhartz 2015. Brian's mission is personal, not the "no king but God" Zealot mission.
6. Three film incidents allude to *The Sign of the Cross* (1932): (1) spectators snacking during gladiator fights; (2) a prisoner hanging from dungeon walls; and (3) a mute/deaf prison guard.
7. Stan's demand to be called Loretta and insistence on his right to bear children hijacks the meeting.
8. The gospels (and Acts) are also a series of improbable comic escapes ending incongruously at the cross (or house arrest).
9. The finale's bloodless crucifixions minimize this brutality, but Helen Bond claims the finale is "gallows humor" resisting empire (2015).
10. The UFO or sci-fi "transcendence" is appropriate for a *Star Wars*' generation in which many have lost a sense of traditional, supernatural transcendence. See Walsh (2013b: 191). Davies claims the "fairly tacky" fantasy replaces the gospels' "ultimate reality" (1998: 412–13).
11. The film's greatest Jesus-subversion lies here in the crowd's rejection of Brian's "Jesus" teaching and his collapse into nonsense. See Crossley (2015: 71–2, 81).
12. In an era of "fake news," one's laughter may turn to tears in the face of such overwhelming cognitive dissonance or confirmation bias.

13 Reportedly, the troupe reshot this scene because it was too obvious that Brian was not Jewish. A rubber band saved the day.
14 The staging resembles speeches from St Peter's Square balcony.
15 Modern film constructs and relies upon the (modern) myth of individualism. *Life of Brian* both supports and mocks this myth.
16 The numbers profane Christianity's unique cross (cf. *Spartacus*, *King of Kings* 1961 and *Greatest Story*). Like *La ricotta* (1963), *Life of Brian* also profanes the cross by focusing on a nobody's cross.
17 Some compare the song's perspective to existentialism (see, e.g., essays in Hardcastle and Reisch 2006). Barnes Tatum points to similarities with Ecclesiastes (2013: 165).
18 The song was released as a Double A side single with the title song "Brian."
19 On their television show, the Pythons relied on Gilliam's animation to connect their skits. They avoided structure in their sketches, trying not to end with the big gag. Sometimes, players would simply walk away as if confused, or someone/something (like the UFO) would interrupt.
20 Many considered the film blasphemous. See Hewison (1981), Tatum (2013: 168–72), and Tollerton (2015). In a now famous 1979 BBC program, hosted by Tim Rice, John Cleeves and Michael Palin discussed the film with Malcolm Muggeridge and Bishop Mervyn Stockwood who savagely attacked and simultaneously dismissed it. See https://www.youtube.com/watch?v=1ni559bHXDg. By contrast, Richard Burridge argues *Life of Brian* provides an ecclesial opportunity (2015).
21 Python humor also exhibits a school-boyish fascination with sex, human waste, and buffoonish authority (e.g., lisping Pilate and the Latin instructor-centurion).
22 Some (e.g., Frye 1982) consider Christianity and its gospels comic because of their "happy endings" (resurrection). Others claim Christianity has less in common with comedy because they define comedy in terms of episodic classical comedy whose themes included sexual license, crude behavior, and disrespect for authority. Historically, the "church" resisted such comedy, sometimes even calling it blasphemous. See Aichele (2018) and n21. The first camp might be describing *Godspell* and the second *Life of Brian*. On the rarity of comic biblical cinema, see Shepherd (2015) and Aichele (2018).
23 UK audiences may be more likely than US viewers to see the humor's political nature. See Stern, Jefford, and DeBona (1999: 259–62).
24 When re-released in theaters on its twenty-fifth anniversary, *Life of Brian* comically resisted *The Passion of the Christ*'s (2004) heavy-handed interpretation of the Christ's substitutionary, sacrificial death—with an unchrist's cross and with the multiple meanings others attached to Brian's death.
25 Eric Idle reprised *The Holy Grail* as the musical *Spamalot* (Broadway 2005; West End 2006). He, with John Du Prez, also revised *Life of Brian* as the oratorio, *Not the Messiah: He's a Very Naughty Boy* (2007 premiere at the Toronto Luminato festival).
26 If parabolic, the "Brian Christ" may unsettle as effectively as "Good Samaritan." The troupe's humorous, working title was *Jesus Christ: Lust for Glory* (see, e.g., Morgan 1999: 224–5). Ironically, that title nicely summarizes Christian discourse's spiritualizing (glorifying) of the Jewish Jesus. In rejecting that title, the troupe may feign reverence, but they simultaneously undo Christian discourse (see Problematic Issue). Accordingly, the troupe considered a scene in which the crucified Jesus angrily complains about the cross's shoddy workmanship, but decided Jesus did not "fit" their comic style, which centers around ordinary bunglers—hence, the more banal Brian.

27 On Brian and historical Jesus research, see Davies (1998: 400–6), Crossley (2011), and Taylor (2015). Philip Davies claims, "Brian both *is* Jesus and is clearly *not* Jesus" (1998: 406). Leaving aside the Sermon's iconic Christ, the Pythons present "a Jesus [Brian] in human drag" (1998: 409). James Crossley compares Brian to some "subversive" historians' Jesuses: a non-messianic, illegitimate, Jewish revolutionary. Cf. the passion play Jesus in *Jésus de Montréal* (1989). Davies also uses the film to critique historical Jesus scholarship's creation of messianic traditions (via the historical Jesus; 2015). Crossley laments that the Pythons did not really "go for Jesus," thereby challenging scholars' "too comfortable" Jesuses (2015: 81).

28 The Criterion DVD title menu and title sheet insert list nineteen chapters. In commentary one, the missing DVD chapter stop is #13. This list adds that stop and titles it "Hermit in a Hole." Subsequent chapters in this list are one number greater than the title menu and title sheet.

29 See n28. The missing chapter stop in Commentary 2 is #14, titled here "How shall we fuck off?" All subsequent chapters are one number greater than the title menu and title sheet.

30 See n28. The missing chapter stop in the DVD chapter list is #13, titled here "Give us a sign." All subsequent chapters are one number greater than the title menu and title sheet.

14

The Jesus Film

John Krish and Peter Sykes, directors, The Genesis Project/Warner Bros., 1979
John Heyman, producer

PLOT SUMMARY: THE ~~ROMANS~~ LUKAN ROAD TO SALVATION[1]

The film's marketing and paratext[2] claim the film presents Luke (Today's English Version; now known as the Good News Bible) literally or objectively.[3] The film adapts Luke's preface accordingly. The camera pans the Galilean countryside as the narrator recites 1:3-4, omitting the reference to other Jesus stories in 1:1 and substituting "absolute truth" to describe the film rather than the GNB's "full truth" or the KJV's "certainty."[4] The narrator also asserts the film's historical truth by combining 1:5 and 2:1 (the on-location in Galilee visuals reinforce this claim).

This preface appears eight minutes into the film. Pre-2001 versions open with a shot from outer space,[5] as the camera descends to earth with a scrolling intertitle of Jn 3:16-17 à la *Star Wars: Episode IV* (1977).[6] This older prologue succinctly expresses the film's evangelistic ideology. Since 2001, the opening camera still descends to earth, but a new introduction places the film/Jesus in a *Heilsgeschichte*, which moves from creation/fall to substitutionary sacrifice and the messiah prophesied to suffer for humans.[7] The narrator concludes by asking if Jesus is this messiah (cf. *Jesus of Nazareth*'s [1977] fundamental query). This introduction renders the film/Luke the Lukan road to salvation.

The filmmakers necessarily added sound and visuals. While music is sometimes intrusively obvious (e.g., before the ascension), ambient sound simply adds depth. Offscreen or fringe characters ask non-Lukan questions or make non-Lukan comments furthering the evangelical adaptation of Luke. Non-Lukan children laugh and play and plead to see Jesus, and then express their delight when they do. The narrator also makes heavy-handed evangelical comments (see Table 14.2). While some visual translations rely entirely on a narrator's recitation (e.g., the *New Media Luke* 1979), this film deploys speaking characters. These voices, except for Brian Deacon's Jesus, have been dubbed by other (British) actors.[8] Generally, speaking characters quote Luke, with Jesus deviating from Luke only once (when he greets a small child in Nazareth).

Shot on location in Israel with Israeli actors and Palestinian extras (cf. *Gospel Road* 1973), the film has a "realistic" look (cf. the epics and *Jesus of Nazareth*). Like *Jesus of Nazareth*, the film also has a television-like quality. Like other visual translations (and later television miniseries; e.g., *The Bible* 2013), the film intensifies the supernatural with blinding-light angels (in the annunciation and at the tomb) and violence (e.g., Jesus's non-Lukan beating before Antipas and non-Lukan scourging before Pilate). Like *Jesus of Nazareth*, the film handles miracles with bravura (not cutting away editorially). Its visualization of the miraculous catch and feeding of the multitude particularly resemble those of *Jesus of Nazareth*. Numerous other scenes are also indebted to the Jesus film tradition (see Table 14.2). For example, Mary carrying a water jar before the annunciation visually imitates *From the Manger to the Cross* (1912).[9]

The film's camerawork and editing are unobtrusive, deliberately fostering the illusion of objectivity, like the classic Hollywood style. Accordingly, the effects that occur are quite noticeable: for example, the flashback of the raising of the Nain widow's son; the young girl's "imagination" of the Good Samaritan; the panning of the disciples at the Last Supper; Pilate throwing his judgment scroll in slow motion; the God's eye POV shots on the Via Dolorosa and at the cross; and the zoom into an extreme closeup of Jesus for his dying words (23:46).

The Jesus Film eschews fictional subplots to adhere to Luke, so it is episodic, even stilted, like *Il vangelo* (1964) or early silents. The film achieves a tapestry effect—and some plot/characterization—by photographing the same characters in several scenes (e.g., Peter, Judas, Magdalene, and Joseph of Arimathea) and by adding non-Lukan material to "fill out" characters like Peter and Magdalene. The film further changes Luke by including textually suspect passages, adding material from other gospels, and creating material (see Table 14.2). It also omits significant Lukan material (see Table 14.1) and rearranges what is left (see DVD Chapters). The resulting "Luke" fits well the film's evangelical ideology.

Table 14.1 Omissions from Luke.

Luke	Omitted incidents
1:5b-25	Baptist's birth predicted
1:49-80	Part of Mary's hymn and the Baptist's birth
2:36-38	Prophetess Anna
3:23b-38	Genealogy
4:32-37	Synagogue exorcism (Capernaum)
4:38-41	Capernaum healings
4:42-44	Synagogue preaching tour
5:12-16	Man with skin disease healed
5:17-26	Paralyzed man healed
5:33-39	Fasting controversy
6:1-11	Sabbath controversy
8:43-48	Cloak-touching woman healed
9:1-6	Twelve's mission
9:7-9	Antipas's confusion
9:49-55	Other exorcists and ungrateful Samaritan village

10:1-22	Mission of the 70 (72)
10:38-42	Mary and Martha
11:14-26	Beelzebul controversy
11:29-32	Demand for a miracle
11:37-12:3	Attack on Pharisees, scribes, and hypocrites
12:3-12	Fear God
12:13-21	Rich fool parable
12:35-48	Watchful, unfaithful, and faithful servants
12:49-13:5	Miscellaneous teachings
13:6-9	Unfruitful fig tree parable
13:20-21	Yeast parable
13:22-30	Narrow door
13:31-35	Lament over Jerusalem
14:1-6	Sabbath healing of sick man
14:7-24	Wedding seat and wedding feast parables
14:25-35	Discipleship's cost
15:1-10	Lost sheep and coin parables
15:11-32	Prodigal son parable
16:1-15	Shrewd manager parable and other teaching
16:18-31	Rich man and Lazarus
17:7-10	Servant's duty
17:11-19	Grateful Samaritan leper
17:26-37	Time of Noah and Lot
18:1-8	Widow and judge parable
19:11-27	Gold coins parable
20:27-47	Controversy about marriage in resurrection and messiah
21:5-38	Destruction of Jerusalem prediction
22:9-13	Passover directions
24:13-32	Emmaus road

This table is not exhaustive. It focuses on pericopes, not verses.

Table 14.2 Additions to Luke.

Luke	Item	Source
2:20	Shepherds are first evangelists	Narrator
2:4-50	Whose child is this?	Character
2:46	The Baptist talks to Jesus	Character
4:1-12	Reverberating-voice snake-devil	Gen. 3?

4:16-30	Only messiah can fulfill such prophecy*	Character
4:16-30	Jesus identifies self as messiah; these Jews reject	Narrator
4:31	People longed for a messiah, versus tyranny	Narrator
8:40-41	Capernaum synagogue teaching	Isa. 55:6-7, 12
5:27	Luke's Levi is called Matthew	Mt. 9:9; 10:3
7:36	Is he the messiah?	Simon
7:36-50	Woman is Magdalene	Tradition
9:13-14	Boy provides the "starter" loaves and fish	Jn 6:9
9:23	Woman plays stringed instrument by fire	
11:1-4	"Father in heaven" Lord's Prayer	Mt. 6:9-13
13:18-20	Laughing, "I have no idea what he's talking about"	Woman
10:29	Romans are not our neighbors	People
18:43	Crowds want to know the way to salvation	Narrator
19:26	Jesus knew he was to be killed for human's sins	Narrator
19:37	Palm branches in triumph	Jn 12:13
19:45-46	Tables overturned, animals released	Mk 11:14; Jn 2:15
19:46	Pilate tells priests to control Jesus	
22:17	Jewish blessings over bread and wine	Tradition
22:19b-20	Blood poured out for you	Disputed text
22:30	There is no traitor!	Peter
22:39	Betrayal for thirty pieces of silver	Mt. 26:15
22:39	Jesus knows death for sins of others approaches	Narrator
22:43-44	Angels and sweating blood	Disputed text
22:62	Peter's prayer of repentance	Sinner's Prayer
23:1	Vicious Pilate crucified thousands	Narrator
23:11	Antipas's men beat Jesus	
23:11	Boy picks up Jesus's lost robe	*The Robe*
23:18	Priests suggest choice between Barabbas and Jesus	
23:22	Scourged before Pilate	
23:27	Old woman gives Jesus water	*Ben-Hur*
23:33	Nails driven (through wrists)	*Jesus of Nazareth*
23:33	Crowd cheers the cross raising	
23:34	Crucified … fulfillment of prophecies	Narrator
23:38	Inscription in three languages	Jn 19:20
23:34	Mockingly, no ordinary mystic's garment	Soldier
23:53	Spices sprinkled on corpse	Jn 19:39-40
24:51	Great Commission	Mt. 28:18-20

* This addition completely reverses 4:22.

The film abbreviates the infancy, abandoning Luke's two-birth-infancy structure by omitting material about the Baptist's birth. It highlights the supernatural with angels of light and by twice mentioning the virgin that Luke mentions once. The shepherds are the first evangelicals, spreading the gospel (cf. 2:20).

Older versions introduced Jesus's "public life" with titles proclaiming the film's "documentary" status. The first section (from Lk. 3-7) depicts Jesus's baptism, temptation, and Nazareth rejection as well as his "conversion" of apostles in Capernaum. The adult Jesus first appears, photographed from behind and approaching John, in concert with 3:16. As the music swells (3:17), Jesus appears in crosscut closeups with the Baptist. He kneels and baptizes himself, looking smilingly heavenward, the narrator supplying the heavenly voice. In the wilderness, a talking snake, with a reverberating voice, tempts Jesus. In his first film words, Jesus quotes scripture to the snake (4:4, 8, 12).

In Nazareth, a smiling Jesus greets a child and preaches in the synagogue. As in *Jesus of Nazareth*, a man objects that only the messiah can fulfill Isa. 61, but the narrator claims Jesus is the messiah and adds that the people longed for a liberating messiah.

In Capernaum, Jesus "converts" Peter and Matthew. The filmmakers bring the Pharisee and tax-collector parable (18:10-14) forward to explain their conversions (the 1916 *Intolerance* uses the same parable to introduce its Jesus fragments). Peter (evangelically) confesses his sin (5:8), and Matthew follows Jesus mutely, simply at his word. Unsurprisingly, Jesus's miracles respond to or call forth obedience and faith (e.g., 5:1-11; 8:40-42, 49-56).

Abruptly, Jesus calls his apostles and delivers an abbreviated Sermon, walking among the people and riffing off what he sees (cf. *King of Kings* 1961). He illustrates his introductory parable by addressing 6:32-33 to a prostitute and 6:38-41 to people who judge him for dealing with such a woman. Jesus ends his Sermon by blessing those who obey God's word (11:28). Simon the Pharisee wonders if Jesus is the messiah and asks him to dinner where, of course, the prostitute finds forgiveness while the Pharisee does not. The narrator identifies this woman as Magdalene, who, with other women, supports Jesus throughout the film.

People flock to Jesus. But a narrative comment about Antipas's imprisonment of the Baptist introduces opposition and the second section of Jesus's Galilean ministry (selections from Lk. 8-9; 11-13).

Jesus responds to the Baptist's questions by reiterating his messianic claims (7:22-23). He teaches a crowd the parable of the seeds, with happy children on people's shoulders (cf. Zacchaeus), but explains it only to his disciples later. When his family visits, Jesus describes his true family (again) as those who obey God's word (8:18-21). More miracles follow (8:22-39; 9:10-17), with children added everywhere. Thus, a young boy provides the "starter" loaves and fish (cf. Jn 6:9).

Peter confesses Jesus as messiah, and Jesus predicts the Son of Man's death (9:22, omitting any reference to the religious leaders), even though he has faced little opposition. His death is a theological (salvific), not political, matter. A woman sings and plays a stringed instrument as Jesus talks about discipleship (9:61-62, 23-27; see Cultural Location). The transfiguration, rare in film, follows (but, see *La vie et passion de notre seigneur Jésus Christ* 1907). Moses and Elijah (in soft focus) stand beside Jesus, who appears in blindingly white clothing, which he will wear into the passion. Moses and Elijah speak (turning 9:31 into dialogue) in reverberating voices (like the snake's), but the narrator supplies the heavenly words (9:35).

Jesus continues working miracles (9:37-43; 13:10-13) and teaching about (seeking) the kingdom (selections from 11-12). Objections grow to Jesus's associations, to which Jesus responds with 5:30-32, and his healing on the Sabbath, which provokes Jesus to anger for the first time (13:14-17).

While it is not clearly demarcated, Jesus sets out for Jerusalem (taken largely from Lk. 17-19; 10). When rich men, keeping their wealth, want to know when the kingdom will come, Jesus replies with 17:20-21. As they pass four crosses, two with crucified men (visualizing 9:23, 51; see Figure 14.1),[10] Jesus prophesies the Son of Man's suffering again (17:22, 24-25). During a rest, Jesus relates the Good Samaritan parable (10:30-37), visualized through a little girl's imagination.[11] She answers Jesus's questions, so he, laughing, picks her up and declares that such are of the kingdom (18:16-17; 9:47-48).

Jesus heals a blind man with a non-Lukan touch (18:35-43), and the narrator comments that the crowds press Jesus "to show them the way to salvation." A happy Jesus brings salvation (himself?) to Zacchaeus's house (19:9)—another converted tax collector (recalling the film's thematic parable). Less happily, Jesus prophesies the Son of Man's death (at the hands of Gentiles) a third time (18:31).

As the Jerusalem story begins, the narrator comments that resolute Jesus (9:51) knew he was to be killed for humanity's sins (non-Lukan language). A muted triumph follows, so that the leaders' objections seem petty. Jesus weeps because Jerusalem did not recognize "her visitation," and cleanses the temple, overturning tables and releasing animals (not in Luke, but see Mk 11:14; Jn 2:15).

The tumult attracts Pilate's attention, who tells Caiaphas, in an invented scene, that he is responsible if Jesus threatens the peace (cf. *Greatest Story* 1965). Conflict grows during Jesus's temple teaching (the film omitted most of the Galilean controversies), but Jesus attacks only the "hypocritical section" of the religious leaders.

At the Last Supper, the filmmakers include textually suspect passages about Jesus's sacrificial death (22:19b-20).[12] The focus, as in Luke, is on Peter's upcoming denial and Satan's testing. Judas's betrayal arrangements occur after the supper when Satan "enters" him (22:3). This rearrangement illustrates Jesus's remarks about Satan's desires/temptations (22:31-38) and Peter's (invented) claim that "there is no traitor." As is common in film, Judas vanishes into dark streets (cf. *From the Manger to the Cross*; *Greatest Story*; *Jesus of Nazareth*; and *The Gospel of John* 2003).

As Jesus prays on the Mount of Olives, the narrator comments (in non-Lukan language) that Jesus knew the hour of his death was approaching—a death "for" humanity's "sins." The filmmakers include the textually suspect strengthening angel (in blinding light) and the "great drops of blood" (22:43-44). Jesus's clothing is no longer transfigured white. The passion soils him.

The temple guard beats Jesus, and Peter denies Jesus (in crosscuts, although Luke treats the events separately). After Jesus looks at Peter, Peter weeps (22:62) and prays (a non-Lukan "Sinner's Prayer") for forgiveness. The Council condemns Jesus, and after more beatings, sends him to Pilate.

In an invention, the narrator describes vicious Pilate, who had sent thousands to "a slow death by nailing them to wooden crosses."[13] Nonetheless, Pilate tries to avoid judging Jesus, sending the Galilean to Antipas, who orders Jesus beaten (not in Luke). As he is taken back to Pilate, Jesus loses Antipas's mocking robe. A small boy grabs it and runs away (cf. *The Robe* 1953).

Again, Pilate tries to dismiss Jesus, saying he will whip and release him. The priests ask for the choice between Barabbas and Jesus (not in Luke), and the crowds clamor for Barabbas's release and for Jesus's crucifixion.[14] Whipped onscreen (not in Luke), soldiers throw Jesus at the priests' feet. Then, from a balcony, Pilate throws the scroll with Jesus's death sentence down at Jesus's feet (it falls in slow motion toward the camera).

Soldiers push back the clamoring crowd as Jesus carries his crossbar down the Via Dolorosa (cf. *Jesus of Nazareth*). When Jesus falls, the soldiers conscript Simon to carry the bar. When Jesus falls a third time, an old woman gives him water (cf. *Ben-Hur* 1959). At the cross, the filmmakers show the nails driven, as does *Jesus of Nazareth*, but these nails pierce Jesus's wrists (cf. Jn 20:25-27). The violence far surpasses the previous film tradition (and Luke). When the cross is raised, the crowd cheers. Jesus speaks all the Lukan words from the cross (23:34, 43, 46) while people mock and his disciples watch (23:49?). After the prayer for forgiveness, the narrator adds that Jesus "was crucified ... in fulfillment of the prophecies." Holding Jesus's tunic, the centurion mockingly observes that this is "no ordinary mystic's garment" (not in Luke), and a soldier nails the placard above Jesus's head. After Jesus promises the good thief paradise, the narrator describes the torn temple curtain and the (supernatural) darkness. Then, the camera draws in for an extreme closeup of Jesus's commitment of his spirit to the Father, followed by a God's eye POV shot from atop the cross (cf. *King of Kings*; *Jesus Christ Superstar* 1973).

Joseph of Arimathea, who looked plaintively at Jesus on the Via Dolorosa, leads five women and a man carrying Jesus's body into an ornate tomb. The camera remains in the tomb as it is closed. At sunrise, "Sunday" morning, the women find the body gone. Suddenly, a blinding light and two angels appear in the tomb to remind them of what Jesus said (24:5-7). The disciples do not believe their report, but Peter runs to the tomb, collapsing into the grave clothes. As two men report the Emmaus Road appearance, Jesus, in transfigured white, stands among the apostles and commissions them as they kneel (24:36-49). They walk outside the city, and Jesus commissions them again (Mt. 28:18-20). As he speaks, the camera rises from the earth (cf. the opening camera work). The screen fades to clouds/white.

An epilogue, with shots of scrolls and fragments of film scenes, rehearses messianic prophecies to present Jesus as the messiah dying for people's sins. This fulfilment proves God's word "flawless." Finally, the narrator invites any who wish to join him in a "Sinner's Prayer."[15]

MEMORABLE CHARACTERS

1 Jesus is the messiah who dies for humanity's sins. While evasive before Caiaphas (22:70)—and never claiming divinity (10:21-22 is absent)—Jesus is often in blindingly white (transfigured) clothing (cf. *The King of Kings*' [1927] glowing Jesus). He laughs and smiles more than any previous cinematic Jesus (but see *Jesus* 1999).

2. Peter, the only other developed character, is the converted, repentant sinner—a model for all who would come to Jesus.
3. In the service of the same evangelical ideology, Magdalene is church tradition's converted prostitute. She accompanies Jesus in his work (8:1-3) and is present for the resurrection appearance and commissioning.
4. Horribly, Judas is simply "possessed" (22:3).

MEMORABLE VISUALS

1. The film's opening shot from the heavens.
2. Dove resting on Jesus's shoulder.[16]
3. Jesus perpetually smiling.
4. Blinding light transfiguration and Jesus's subsequently bright white clothing.
5. Jesus, Peter, and Judas passing four crosses—two empty—on the way to Jerusalem (see Figure 14.1).

Figure 14.1 Jesus, Peter, and others walk past four crosses in *The Jesus Film*, directed by John Krish and Peter Sykes, The Genesis Project/Warner Bros., 1979. All rights reserved.

6   Jesus with Zacchaeus.
7   Nails driven into Jesus's wrists at the cross.

KEY AUTHORITY/SCRIPTURE

1   The key authority is the evangelical paratext (introduction and epilogue), rendering Luke the evangelical "Lukan road to salvation." In earlier versions, Alexander Scourby's recognizable voice also added authority.
2   The key Lukan text is the Pharisee and the tax-collector parable (18:10-14), as it "models" evangelical salvation.
3   Ironically, Luke itself is less authoritative than is this evangelical or Johannine reading of it.
4   Jesus films, particularly *Jesus of Nazareth*, are an unmistakable visual authority.

CULTURAL LOCATION/GENRE: THE EVANGELISTIC JOURNEY OF FAITH/VISUAL TRANSLATIONS

The film's cultural context is American Protestant evangelicalism.[17] The filmmakers produced the film as an evangelistic tool, and it is still used to that end today (see n3). Film marketing claims it has been translated into more languages and has been seen by more people than any other Jesus film.[18]

In addition to the various adaptations of Luke already mentioned, two further items are worth noting. First, in its oldest versions (although not the present ones) the film's narrator was Alexander Scourby. To an older evangelical generation, his recognizable voice[19] lent the film evangelical authority.

Second, the film packages Jesus's teaching on discipleship (following Peter's confession) as if it were a nighttime campfire vigil for evangelical teenagers, including a singer playing a stringed instrument ("guitar"; cf. the nighttime confession scene in *Jesus of Nazareth*). Peter's confession reflects the testimonies, conversions, and rededications common to such youth retreats. If one pushes the analogy, the transfiguration is akin to the camp's closing worship service, and Peter's wish to build housing is akin to evangelical teenagers' reluctance to leave the camp "high" for ordinary life. Peter's post-denial prayer for forgiveness might also resonate with such teenagers' "backsliding" experiences.[20]

The film is the best-known example of a "visual translation." Given its massive adaptations of Luke, it is more like *Il vangelo* (not always considered a part of this genre) than other visual translations. This film foregrounds (and replicates) Lk. 18:9-14, as *Il vangelo* did Mt. 10:34, to trumpet its ideology. Accordingly, the film is more evangelistic tract than documentary.

The Jesus Film is a shorter version of a lengthier, more "literal" visualization of Luke (KJV) known as *The New Media Bible: The Gospel According to St. Luke* and *Word-for-Word, The Bible on Video: Gospel of Luke* (1979; the US video box title). In *New Media Luke*, Luke (Richard Kiley) appears at the film's beginning and end reading his gospel from a scroll to people on a hill. He narrates the entire film; although, on occasion, characters speak historically appropriate languages in the background.[21] The film was released only on reel (for church viewing) and VHS.

Subsequent visual translations have more in common with *New Media Luke* than with *Il vangelo* or *The Jesus Film* (see Walsh 2021b). They more faithfully follow the gospel text they translate. Unlike *New Media Luke*, however, they deploy speaking characters, even though they all have overbearing, ubiquitous narrators. Examples include *The Visual Bible: Matthew* (1993) and *The Visual Bible: The Gospel of John*. The recent *Lumo Project Gospels* (2014–16) are a different matter, as they feature narrators reading the entire gospel. One can hear ambient noise and characters speaking a faux-Aramaic in the background. The project uses the same actors for all four gospels (but different narrators) and sometimes the same visuals (even though the visuals necessarily match one gospel better than another). The project is also notable for its deployment of a non-European-looking Jesus (Selva Rasalingam) (see Taylor 2017).

DIRECTOR/PRODUCER

The motivating force behind *The Jesus Film* was film agent, producer, and financier John Heyman.[22] He formed the for-profit company, the Genesis Project, in 1974 with Chaim Topol (Tevye in *Fiddler on the Roof*) and Michael Manuel (former general manager of the Metropolitan Opera touring company) to create films promoting biblical literacy in a television era. The original plan was to create ten short biblical films (each fifteen to twenty minutes long), "without interpretation," then to market them, with supporting educational materials tailored for different religious groups (Blau 1976). Pricing its product too dearly, the project was unsuccessful. Having completed work on a Genesis film and hard at work on a Luke film, Heyman agreed to produce a shorter Luke film for Campus Crusade in return for financial assistance for his larger project.[23]

John Krish and Peter Sykes directed *The Jesus Film*. Krish was one of his time's finest British documentary filmmakers, but his *Guardian* obituary does not include *The Jesus Film* in his significant work (Brownlow 2016). The Australian Sykes worked primarily in UK television and Hammer horror films. Curiously, both Krish and Sykes directed episodes of the British television show, *The Avengers*. Heyman, however, had more influence on *The Jesus Film* than did these directors.

PROBLEMATIC ISSUE: THE GOSPEL TRUTH

The film's parataxis claims the film presents Luke unmediated. Heyman insisted that the film have no credits because it translated Luke "without interpretation" (cf. Blau 1976). Of course, scholars know all translations are interpretations, and any comparison with Luke will reveal the film's massive adaptations. The film's claims to objectivity are thus more rhetorical than descriptive, appealing to an evangelical target audience with views of scripture's infallibility (if not inerrancy) and inscribing the film with similar authority. The film's Jesus captures the film's rhetorical goal: "Happy are those who have no doubts about me" (7:23).

Such rhetoric creates a "gospel effect,"[24] a sense that films present Jesus or the gospel directly, nude, without mediation (or that they should).[25] In reality, films create the gospel effect when they are successfully marketed to the appropriate audience (e.g., visual translations) or vague enough or broad enough that more disparate audiences can resonate with the films' reprises of the gospel/Christian message (e.g., epics). To do so, films tread quite closely to Jesus's popular cultural memory (harmonizing the gospels). Further, they employ specific stylistic choices to create the gospel-effect rhetoric: for example, using iconic Christian imagery; creating (the illusion of) historical realism; utilizing authoritative voiceovers; and deploying Johannine rhetoric/ideology (see Chapter 4). *The Jesus Film* makes use of all these devices to bypass troublesome interpretation(s).[26]

THE STORY OF JESUS FOR CHILDREN

Streaming at *The Jesus Film* Project
https://www.jesusfilm.org/watch/the-story-of-jesus-for-children.html/english.html
(Excerpts from *The Jesus Film*, cobbled together with a detective-like story where children try to find out who Jesus is.)

The Jesus Film, 2-Disc Limited Collector's Edition DVD, 120 minutes, 2003
(Remastered with a new prologue)
Streaming on *The Jesus Film* Project website
Excluding the new Old Testament prologue, the titles[27] and numbers below reflect the paper "Event Index" included with the *2-Disc Limited Collector's Edition* DVD.

Old Testament prologue, 0:00
    Journey across the solar system (Ps. 19), 0:23
    Creation (Gen. 2:7), 1:03
    Temptation and Fall (Gen. 3:1), 1:44
    A coming one who would be the ultimate sacrifice (the Messiah), 5:11
    Who was the Messiah? 7:12
        The story of Jesus based on eyewitness accounts, 7:34
        An actor plays "Jesus," 7:45

1. Prologue-Annunciation (1:3a-4), 8:00
    A Nazareth virgin (1:26), 8:25
2. Mary visits Elizabeth (1:39), 9:12
3. Jesus's birth (2:1), 9:53
4. Shepherds and Angels (2:8-20), 10:48
5. Simeon's prophecy (2:21), 11:31
6. Jesus with teachers in the temple (2:41), 12:35
    Film Title, 13:44
7. Jesus's baptism (3:1), 14:14

8   Wilderness temptation (3:23a), 17:54
9   Jesus of Nazareth (4:16), 20:29
10 Jesus at Capernaum (4:31; 5:1), 23:11
11 Pharisee and tax collector (18:9-14), 24:18
12 Miraculous catch (5:1-11), 25:12
13 Teaching in a synagogue (9:56), 27:05
14 Jesus raises Jairus's daughter (8:40), 27:33
15 Jesus calls Matthew (5:27), 29:40
16 Jesus chooses the apostles (6:12), 30:53
17 Sermon on the Mount [sic] (6:17), 33:05
18 Simon the Pharisee (7:36), 37:35
18 Jesus teaches (8:1), 40:28
19 John the Baptist in prison (7:18), 41:03
    (begins with 3:19-20; then moves to the Nain widow's son, 7:11-17), 41:18
20 Parables (8:4), 42:52
21 Lamp illustration (8:16), 45:14
22 Jesus's true family (8:19), 45:45
23 Jesus stills the storm (8:22), 46:02
24 Jesus heals the demoniac (8:26), 47:54
25 Jesus feeds 5,000 (9:12), 50:03
26 Who do the crowds say I am? (9:18), 52:33
27 Death and resurrection foretold (9:21-22), 53:28
28 Discipleship's cost (9:61-62, 23-27), 53:50
    "What will it profit a man?" (camera focuses on Judas)
29 Transfiguration (9:28), 55:40
30 Jesus heals the demoniac boy (9:37), 57:20
31 Lord's Prayer (11:1), 59:30
32 Teachings on prayer (11:9), 1.00:20
33 Worry and faith (12:22), 1.01:12
34 Kingdom of God teaching (17:1), 1.02:39
    Mustard seed (13:18-20), 1.03:28
    Sinners, not the righteous (5:30-32), 1.03:45
    Sell possessions (12:32-34), 1.04:08
35 Sabbath healing of woman (13:10), 1.04:39
36 Rich young ruler (18:18), 1.06:00

37 God's kingdom within (17:20), 1.07:15
   Jesus, Peter, and Judas pass four crosses, 1.07:36
38 Great commandment (10:24), 1.08:14
39 Good Samaritan (10:29), 1.08:49
   Suffer the little children (18:16-17; 9:47-48), 1.10:00
40 Jesus heals the blind man (18:35) 1.10:54
41 Zacchaeus (19:1), 1.12:12
   Third prophecy of death (18:31-33), 1.14:27
42 Triumph (19:35), 1.15:01
43 Jesus weeps over Jerusalem (19:41), 1.16:28
44 Jesus cleanses the temple (19:45), 1.17:07
45 Political and religious leaders oppose Jesus (20:20), 1.18:45
46 Widow's mite (21:1), 1.19:36
47 Jesus's authority challenged (20:1), 1.20:02
48 Vineyard parable (20:9), 1.21:00
49 Render unto Caesar (20:20), 1.22:37
50 Last Supper (22:1), 1.23:27
51 Greatest in the kingdom (22:26), 1.26:20
52 Plot to kill Jesus (22:2), 1.28:37
   Satan enters Judas (22:3), 1.28:44
53 Gethsemane [sic] (22:39), 1.28:54
54 Arrest (22:47), 1.31:07
55 Peter's denial (22:54), 1.33:17
56 Trial (22:63), 1.36:00
   Sanhedrin, 1.36:26
   Pilate, 1.38:18
   Antipas, 1.39:28
   Pilate, 1.41:02
   Barabbas's release (not shown), 1.41:44
57 Crucifixion (23:26), 1.35:27
   Via Dolorosa (23:26a), 1.43:34
   Simon of Cyrene (23:26b), 1.44:16
   Jerusalem women (23:28), 1.45:30
   Nailed to cross (23:33), 1.47:00
   Mocking (23:35), 1.49:13

Drawing lots (23:34), 1.50:05

"King of the Jews" (23:38), 1.50:44

Sour wine (23:36), 1.51:07

Penitent thief (23:39), 1.52:11

Darkness (23:44), 1.53:05

Temple veil torn (23:46), 1.53:34

58 Death (23:46), 1.54:18

Centurion's witness (23:47), 1.54:23

59 Burial (23:50), 1.54:40

60 Resurrection (24:1), 1.56:34

61 Emmaus Road (24:13), 1.59:15

62 Appearance to Disciples (24:33), 1.59:38

63 Ascension (24:50), 2.01:02

Reprise of major themes, 2.02:14

Sinner's prayer, 2.05:45

NOTES

1. "The Romans road to salvation" is a popular evangelistic tract. Cf. Bill Bright's 1952 "The Four Spiritual Laws."
2. Gérard Genette's "paratext" refers to a text's packaging, frame, or threshold, which influences reading/interpretation often without being noticed (1997).
3. Warner Brothers, who released *Monty Python's Life of Brian* in August, premiered *The Jesus Film* in theaters on October 19, 1979, in the southern and western United States (and to more theaters in the north and east in the spring). Campus Crusade began worldwide distribution, dubbing into various languages that spring (Tatum 2013: 185). A slightly shorter VHS version was available in 1979 (omitting the woman healed by touching Jesus's cloak and using a shorter version of the Nain widow's son's raising; see *Imdb.Trivia*). See Cultural Location, as well as Turner (2008: 181–7), Page (2010), and Eshleman (2016).

    The Jesus Film Project website (https://www.jesusfilm.org/) offers free film downloads and information on available languages and audience numbers. The project has repeatedly repackaged the film (e.g., *The Story of Jesus for Children* 2000). A re-mastered, high-definition DVD was completed in 2014, celebrating the film's thirty-fifth anniversary, and using the TEV 2nd ed. (1992). The website lists a 2015 release date for an "enhanced Blu-Ray edition" and the DVD has a 2016 date on it.
4. The phrasing asserts scripture's infallibility (if not inerrancy). All scripture references, unless noted, are to Luke.
5. While a rocket first captured a photo of the earth from space in 1946, NASA's lunar missions made dramatic photographs available, including the famous Blue Marble taken by the crew of Apollo 17 (December 7, 1972).

6   This opening is available at https://www.youtube.com/watch?v=HodqXGFhDXE. This version's intertitles do acknowledge other Jesus accounts (cf. 1:1).
7   This Hebrew Bible interpretation is more blatantly supersessionist than that in *Jesus of Nazareth*.
8   Despite his olive complexion, the British Deacon "stands out" amidst the Israeli and Palestinian cast—with theological (transcendence) and imperialist consequences.
9   The home, like that in some annunciation paintings and Tissot's Bible, is improbably wealthy. Its plastered walls are painted in two colors, and it has latticed alcoves and nine-foot ceilings. At least four other film scenes rely on Olcott/Tissot: (1) twelve-year-old Jesus sandwiched between his parents as they leave the temple; (2) the dove perched on Jesus's left shoulder at his baptism; (3) the naked, curly-headed Gerasene demoniac; and (4) the yellow-robed and yellow turbaned Zacchaeus, lying across a tree branch in Jericho.
10 Are the empty crosses for Jesus and Peter (or for those who follow Jesus daily)?
11 Jesus's parable answers the "who is my neighbor" question, but ignores shouts from the crowd that deny Caesar and soldiers (who watch) that status (cf. Barabbas's response to Jesus's healing of the centurion's servant in *Jesus of Nazareth*).
12 Western Christianity almost universally holds that Jesus's death is salvific. Of the gospels, however, Luke gives least emphasis to Jesus's salvific death.
13 This potentially anti-Semitic eschewing description, as well as Pilate's warning to Caiaphas about Jesus, is inconsistent with Pilate's subsequent "innocent" portrayal as he twice declares Jesus innocent (see Reinhartz 2007: 242). Luke's Pilate says this three times (23:4, 14-16, 22).
14 Some shout, "Set him free," and some shout, "He is the messiah."
15 In the pre-2001 version(s), the narrator succinctly assured people that Jesus wished to enter everyone's heart, and Jesus recited Jn 11:25-26 in voiceover.
16 The dove-on-the-shoulder shot (enticed by seeds) took over two hours. As a result, Deacon contracted pneumonia, so Heyman and Eshleman took turns replacing Deacon on the cross during filming (Eshleman 2016: 50).
17 Evangelicals constitute the single largest group of US Christians. Evangelicals focus on personal conversion, biblical authority, the substitutionary atonement, and missions.
18 Mark Noll offers three different possible interpretations of the film's broader connection to US culture and empire: (1) the film's missionary use is American imperialism; (2) the film's missionary use enables local agency; and (3) the film's message offers personal hope and guidance to the needy (2009: 71-2).
19 He was known for his audio recordings of the KJV (beginning in 1953) and for his audio-recordings (of approximately 500 books) for the blind.
20 "Backsliding" accounts for evangelical failures without dismissing the evangelical doctrine of "eternal security," which claims that Christians cannot "lose" their salvation—if their conversions were sincere.
21 The film is available at https://www.youtube.com/watch?v=JTb4UIbnOHE.
22 For a concise summary of his career, see his *Variety* obituary (Dagan 2017). His son David Heyman is a producer of the Harry Potter films.
23 With Bright's help, Heyman received three million dollars in funding from Bunker and Carol Hunt. See Noll (2009: 87).
24 This phrasing echoes Roland Barthes's "reality effects," or texts' non-story-essential, descriptive elements suggesting the texts represent reality, but which represent rhetoric (1986: 141-8).

25 Roland Barthes (1972) describes the work of myth as presenting historical choices as if "true" or "natural." George Aichele (2001) describes a similar semiotics in gospel interpretation as the "canon mechanism."
26 See Table 14.2 for some of the film's use of non-Lukan gospel material. Notably, Heyman also had Lazarus's resurrection filmed.
27 Some of the "Event" titles are shortened. The DVD has twenty-seven unnamed chapters.

15

The Last Temptation of Christ

Martin Scorsese, director, Universal, 1988

PLOT SUMMARY: THE QUEST FOR GOD

As Barnes Tatum observes, *The Last Temptation of Christ* has three parts: (1) the three main characters' introduction, reprising the triangles of *The King of Kings* (1927) and *Jesus Christ Superstar* (1973),[1] and ending with Judas and Jesus agreeing to a joint mission; (2) an eccentric presentation of familiar gospel/cinematic incidents; and (3) Jesus's death-throes "last temptation" fantasy (2013: 193–5). The last ensured the film's notoriety,[2] but it is only part of the film's greatest innovation—Jesus films' first subjective, introspective, human Jesus (Willem Dafoe).[3] *Last Temptation* brings the audience into Jesus's own troubled experience, following the lead, as an opening intertitle says, of Nikos Kazantzakis's novel ([1955] 1988).

The film opens with screeching birds,[4] and the camera pans aggressively through trees as if searching for prey.[5] Suddenly, the camera looks down on a sleeping/dreaming man.[6] His voiceover begins: "Then the pain starts. Claws slip under the skin and tear their way up." He wakes, and the scene shifts to a rude house filled with carpenter's implements. The interior voiceover (IV hereafter) continues: the carpenter Jesus says the pain and voices returned even though he fasted and whipped himself.[7] He lifts a beam onto a stand and with outstretched arms "tries it for size." Startled, he asks who is following him (IV).

As if in answer, Judas (unidentified; Harvey Keitel)[8] bursts in, challenging, "Are you ready?"[9] This Zealot sneers at the coward making Roman crosses and asks him how he will ever pay for his sins. When Jesus says, "with my life," Judas turns back from the open door to cradle Jesus's face[10]—but beats him mercilessly when Jesus says he plans to finish the cross.

Strapping on an iron-studded belt, Jesus carries the crossbar to a crucifixion site.[11] People throw rocks at him and a prostitute (the unidentified Magdalene; Barbara Hershey)[12] spits in his face.[13] The Zealot awaiting crucifixion calls the people to messianic revolt as a bored officer reads the charges. Jesus assists those driving nails into the victim's feet (whose whispered name is Lazarus),[14] and blood splatters Jesus's face.[15]

This opening shockingly inverts, yet still foreshadows Jesus's destiny (see Walsh 2010: 56–9). While cross forebodings are a Jesus film trope (e.g., *From the Manger to the Cross* 1912; *The King of Kings*), no other film foreshadows so early—and none makes Jesus a crucifier. Jesus is not ready for his destiny.[16] He learns God's plan in fits and starts.

That night Jesus writhes on a dirt floor as his mother comforts him. The pain makes him want (IV) God to stop loving him. He shapes crosses to make God hate him. In the morning, Jesus's mother prepares food for his wilderness quest and asks if it is God or Satan who torments him (cf. Mk 3:22-30).

As Jesus walks alongside a lake, he hears footsteps. A bird screams and Jesus collapses in agony, repeatedly whispering "Magdalene" (IV). In bustling Magdala, he enters a house with black-and-white copulating snakes painted on its door.[17] Across the courtyard, he sees Magdalene having sex with one customer after another.

After Magdalene finishes her long, sweaty day, Jesus approaches haltingly, begging her forgiveness. Later, after her aborted stoning, he will stoop to wipe blood from her feet with his robe (inverting Lk. 7:36-50).[18] Unforgiving Magdalene, however, hates Jesus and the God who has consumed him.[19] She wants him to save her body, but Jesus rejects her a final time.

In a desert monastery, a man welcomes Jesus but tells him the Master he has come to see has died. When Jesus sees the corpse the next morning, he recognizes it as the man who welcomed him. The moment ensnares the audience in Jesus's dreams/visions (cf. Walsh 2010: 110–11), making those visions the cinematic "real."[20]

A young monk envies Jesus's visions, but Jesus knows only fear. He worries it is Lucifer telling him that he is God. That night, two snakes appear in Jesus's hut and, speaking in Magdalene's voice, forgive him. As Jesus leaves the hut, the lurking Judas grabs him, pressing a knife to his throat. Surprisingly unafraid,[21] Jesus so stupefies Judas that he (temporarily) forgoes his Zealot-orders to kill the cross-maker and agrees to help Jesus. Although he becomes Jesus's first disciple,[22] Judas swears to kill Jesus if he strays from the revolutionary path.

The film's second part—a skewed version of gospel episodes—is equally frenetic.[23] Jesus's mission of love/pity begins with Magdalene's aborted stoning during which both she and Jesus are struck by several stones. Jesus begins his halting, confused teaching immediately afterwards. Some dismiss the Nazarene (Jn 1:46); others dismiss his teaching (about a sower spreading love) as an impractical children's story.[24] Jesus walks manically within the small group (the camera jerkily following), explaining God's love as if in private conversations.[25] He ends the Beatitudes and woes forlornly when people race off to kill the rich—not heeding his love message.[26]

Nevertheless, Jesus's followers grow (in dissolves as they walk along a lake). One night, Judas and Jesus talk intimately (their heads captured in one medium shot, instead of in shot/countershot).[27] When Judas objects to Jesus's "turn the other cheek" conduct, Jesus explains that spiritual freedom is more important than political freedom/change—reiterating the opening intertitle's dualism. Thinking that he should have killed Jesus, Judas demands that Jesus visit the Baptist for messianic assessment. The scene closes with a closeup of the fearful Jesus sleeping on Judas's bosom (see Figure 15.1)—dreaming of an apple tree growing instantly from a seed (Eden; Mk 4:28?).

At the Jordan, orgiastic, writhing dancers surround John.[28] The Baptist is unsure about baptizing Jesus (the moment is soundless, except for running water). That night, while Judas looks on from above, the Baptist tells Jesus that the rotten tree requires an axe, and sends him into the desert[29] to meet God (or Satan).[30] A snake with Magdalene's voice, a lion with Judas's voice, and an archangel/Satan/pillar of fire (telling Jesus he is God) tempt him.

When an apple tree appears again, Jesus eats the fruit (which turns his mouth bloody), then cuts down the tree with a magically appearing axe. The vision(s) climaxes with the Baptist telling Jesus "he's the one."

Returning to civilization, Jesus stays with Mary and Martha, who restore him. Later, he finds his squabbling disciples beside a fire. Judas has barely held them together. Backlit, Jesus removes his heart and offers it, inviting them to leave home and fight the devil—in the temple if need be.[31] When Jesus foreswears love for the Baptist's axe, a delighted Judas (not Peter) confesses, "Adonai."[32]

In a surreal, slow-motion scene (with music gradually overtaking ambient sound), Jesus wrestles with the possessed who crawl from pits (cf. Jesus overwhelmed by the sick in *Jesus Christ Superstar*). After healing a blind man with a poultice and spittle, Jesus goes, with Magdalene, to Nathaniel's cousin's Cana wedding. When someone objects to her "impurity," Jesus rejects the law as against his heart. Offscreen, the water becomes wine, and Jesus tells Nathaniel to make sure he has enough. Meanwhile, Jesus dances joyfully in the film's happiest scene.

Nazareth's villagers reject Jesus, however, throwing stones at the possessed/lunatic/magician after he claims, in the street outside the synagogue (not inside), that he fulfills fiery judgment prophecies (not the Lord's acceptable year). Gathering an army of crippled, blind, and poor, he rejects his own mother.[33] Jesus's "ministry" climaxes with Lazarus's resurrection. Seen from within the tomb in slow motion, Jesus gestures violently, striving to draw out Lazarus (cf. von Sydow's contortions in *Greatest Story* 1965; Staley 2021: 48). With ambient sound muted, Lazarus's hand thrusts out. Jesus gingerly grasps it, and Lazarus/death pulls him into the tomb. Both Jesus and Lazarus re-emerge to faint music and ambient noise. No one makes any Johannine confessions (although Jesus says, as Lazarus embraces him, "Adonai. God, help me").[34]

Entering Jerusalem and a temple flowing with blood, Jesus violently disrupts its business. After Roman coins float through the air in slow motion, the high priest picks up an idolatrous coin and confronts the presumptuous Jesus. Jesus counters that he ends the old law and begins a new one (pace Mt. 5:17-20). He is God (cf. Jn 10:30), and the "saint of blasphemy." He has brought a sword (a rare cinematic occurrence of Mt. 10:34) and will destroy the temple in three days, for "God's an immortal spirit who belongs to everybody .... God is not an Israelite!" Jesus's disciples pull him away from the ensuing melee (cf. Lk. 4:16-30). The Zealot leader Saul (Paul) demands to know why Judas has not killed this magician and then kills the corpse-like Lazarus himself, so that Jesus's miracles will not diminish the chances of revolution.[35]

In another intimate conversation with Judas, Jesus changes his message a second time.[36] Jesus describes what the audience sees—a vision in which he read portions of Isa. 53:4-7 with Isaiah (played by Scorsese)—from a blank scroll. Jesus explains that he is the (messianic) lamb (cf. Jn 1:29, 36) and that the cross is the shadow that has followed him.

Wearing a headcloth (see n16), Jesus enters Jerusalem a second time, accompanied by a small triumphal cohort (with upbeat music and with Judas crying out, "King of the Jews!"), and heads toward a Roman imperial statue. He disturbs temple business again, trying to spark a revolt. In a moment of eerie silence, Jesus prays (IV) for God to let him die here. Jesus tells the crowd he has come to set fire to the world (cf. Mt. 3:10-11). Soldiers gather ominously; Peter rallies the crowd; and everything quiets as Jesus (IV) pleads with God for the axe, not the cross. Stigmata overwhelm Jesus, and Judas spirits him away as soldiers attack and women wail.

Alone, Jesus asks Judas for forgiveness. Despite Judas's caresses and protests (cf. the duo's first scene), Jesus says he dies to reconcile God and man, and asks Judas to keep his (wilderness) promise to kill him for straying from—or failing at—the revolutionary path. When Judas argues that God should kill Jesus if it is necessary, Jesus says God will do it—through Judas. Jesus has the easier job, to be crucified; Judas is the stronger one with the harder task.[37] Jesus (not Judas) completes his betrayal, by telling Judas to bring the temple guards to Gethsemane.

The streets flow with sacrificial lambs' blood; Mary serves the Last Supper, which other women, including Magdalene, attend. During the institution, the shared wine transubstantiates in Peter's mouth and hands.[38] Seeing this as his cue, Judas departs and Scorsese cuts abruptly to Gethsemane—with camera shots through tree branches (cf. the film's opening). Shot from a God POV, Jesus prays for forgiveness and asks to be spared the cup/cross. After all, God miraculously delivered others. Suddenly, John's angelic double (John still sleeps on the ground nearby) offers Jesus God's cup/answer. Judas arrives with the guard, kissing Jesus fully on the mouth and embracing him.[39] Looking at Judas, Jesus finally answers Judas's first (film) question: "I'm ready."

Cavalierly currying his horse, Pilate (David Bowie) passes judgment on Jesus, who is more dangerous than the Zealots because he wishes to change the way people think. Jesus's paraphrase of Dan. 2:31-46 solidifies Pilate's decision. After all, Golgotha already has 3,000 skulls: "I do wish you people would go out and count them some time. Maybe you would learn a lesson." The Jewish trial and manipulative religious leaders are notably absent.

In a short, brutal sequence, soldiers beat the nude Jesus, scourge him (including a God POV shot), and crown him with thorns. The camera pulls away to show Jesus's bleeding, nude back before an iconic closeup of Jesus's face against a black background (not quite the *vera icon*). With the crowd's jeers reduced to whispers, Scorsese presents the Ecce Homo and Peter's denials.[40] Abruptly, from another God POV, Jesus staggers down the Via Dolorosa, banging the cross beam against walls (cf. Jesus's earlier cross-bearing for another). Then, in a medium Bosch-like shot, Jesus struggles under the cross (all ambient sound gone, but with musical background)—surrounded by faces, but without the hopeful faces of Bosch's good thief, Veronica, and Simon.[41] The muted sound, a technique Scorsese has used throughout to enhance the audience's sense of sharing Jesus's experience, suggests the perspective of one beaten to a stupor.

Jesus ascends Golgotha, a hillside strewn with bones and skulls, followed by black-garbed women. Jesus sees a cross ready for him, in camera shots echoing the preparation of Lazarus's cross. Jesus wonders (IV) where his mother and Magdalene are. He steps toward his mother to apologize for being a bad son before a soldier pulls him back. Soldiers lay Jesus on the cross and drive nails through his wrists, as Jesus begs God to stay with him (IV). He and his mother scream in pain. As the cross is raised, Scorsese films the now nude Jesus from behind, offering glimpses of the crowd from Jesus's POV.[42] The camera moves to a closeup of Jesus as he whispers "Father, forgive them." Mockery and an approaching storm nearly drown out his words.

When Jesus screams in desolation (Mk 15:34), ambient sound disappears again. After a lengthy silence, Jesus looks down upon a young girl/guardian angel.[43] She claims the merciful God who saved Isaac is his father too (cf. Jesus's garden plea) and that Jesus need die only in a dream. She levitates, removing Jesus's thorny crown and nails.[44] As they walk away, she tells him he is not the messiah. She leads him into a garden—a striking contrast to the film's typical desert settings—for his marriage to Magdalene. Magdalene cleanses his wounds (in a pietà pose); they make love as the angel watches; and Magdalene becomes pregnant. One day she hears something unusual and is bathed in light. She smiles. A bird, like those of Jesus's torments, screams harshly. Jesus returns to find her dead. When he picks up the (always handy) axe, the guardian angel asks if he plans to kill God. Relenting, Jesus digs his wife's grave. Then, the guardian angel encourages him: "There's only one woman in the world." So Jesus has children with Mary and Martha.[45]

Years later, Jesus hears an evangelical-sounding Saul/Paul preaching about salvation through Jesus's death-resurrection. Jesus angrily brands Saul/Paul a liar. Saul/Paul follows Jesus, telling him if he must crucify and resurrect Jesus to save the world, he will. People prefer Saul/Paul's story to Jesus's truth.[46]

Finally, an elderly Jesus lies dying as Jerusalem burns (70 CE), attended by the angel, Mary, and Martha. Peter and others enter the house;[47] angry, bloody, and battle-weary, Judas arrives last, from the battle. He complains Jesus betrayed them when he left his divinely assigned cross.[48] As Jesus's stigmata return, Judas exposes the guardian angel as Satan (she becomes the wilderness pillar of fire)[49] and berates Jesus for hiding as a mere man.

The repentant Jesus crawls toward the cross. Kneeling in an orant pose, Jesus asks God to forgive his prodigal son. He accepts his destiny. Suddenly, Jesus is back on the cross.[50] Ambient noise returns as Jesus looks at the camera through blood and sweat. He smiles, declaring "it accomplished" (twice; Jn 19:30), and dies. Keening, strobe lights,[51] and clanging (church?) bells overwrite Golgotha.

MEMORABLE CHARACTERS

1 Scorsese's is the first introspective, subjective Jesus in Jesus films. He is a tortured, alienated visionary bordering on the neurotic[52]—a typical Scorsese character—but one who eventually discovers God's plan. His "moral [voluntary] choice" of the cross (Tatum 2013: 202) makes him an exemplar for others (cf. Kazantzakis [1955] 1988: 2–4; Deacy 2001: 85–9).

2 The Zealot Judas is Jesus's "bosom buddy" (cf. Jn 13:23), his first and most beloved disciple, and his deadly destiny (see Walsh 2010: 49–84). Jesus betrays Judas, rather than vice versa. As Judas calls Jesus back to his messianic destiny, there is no redemption without Judas.

3 The prostitute Magdalene represents the hero's temptation to domesticity. In the film's androcentric world, she represents the flesh that the spiritual hero must overcome/ reject (Babington and Evans 1993: 165–6).[53]

Figure 15.1 Jesus asleep on Judas's chest in *The Last Temptation of Christ,* directed by Martin Scorsese, Universal, 1988. All rights reserved.

MEMORABLE VISUALS

1 Jesus seen from above, writhing on the ground in the throes of a painful possession (three times in part one).
2 Jesus making crosses and helping crucify a Zealot.
3 Flowing, spurting blood; butchered lambs; Jesus's beating heart and stigmata.
4 Jesus asleep on Judas's chest (see Figure 15.1).
5 Jesus's fantasy of an "ordinary" family life.
6 Jesus's smiling, messianic death on the cross.

KEY AUTHORITY/SCRIPTURE

1 As an opening intertitle indicates, Kazantzakis's novel, with its notion of the human struggle between the spirit and the flesh, provides the film's worldview and key authority (but see Problematic Issue).
2 Jesus's interior monologues (IV), dreams, and visions are the primary avenue to the spirit. They gradually become the only (cinematic) reality. Accordingly, the audience's experience is comparable to Jesus's gradual discovery of God's plan.
3 While Scorsese endlessly revises, Jesus films are also authoritative.[54] Scorsese thought *Il messia* (1975) a major influence on the film's dirty, gritty, "village feel" (Keyser 1992: 170), but the shaky, frenetic camera and rugged editing, as well as Jesus's frenetic pace and violence (e.g., the axe; cf. Mt. 3:10-12; 10:34), suggest *Il vangelo*'s influence (1964; Babington and Evans 1993: 150; Baugh 1997: 254 n49). *Barabbas* (1962) is worth

mentioning as the cross's shadow torments that film's alienated, protagonist (see Walsh 2003: 33–4, 174; 2008a).

4 Jesus finally decides that Isa. 53 defines his messianic destiny. The gospels do not employ this text to interpret Jesus's death, but film often does (e.g., *Jesus of Nazareth* 1977; *The Passion of the Christ* 2004).[55]

5 While the film's title suggests the gospels' temptation narratives might be key, and Scorsese does dramatize the scene, Scorsese extends the temptation throughout as the (human) struggle between the spirit and the flesh.[56] Jesus is so uncertain about God's plan and even about voices/angels' identity that the gospel pericope about the identity of the spirit(s) possessing Jesus may be a more important gospel authority (e.g., Mk 3:21-35).

CULTURAL LOCATION/GENRE: NON-EPIC BIOPIC

Political and religious conservatism surged in the 1980s United States. By the end of the decade, however, the Moral Majority's heyday was over, and televangelists had suffered several public relations crises. Evangelicals, however, still publicly attacked their longstanding "secular humanist" enemy (e.g., intellectuals, artists, and Democrats), promoting "culture wars" (Forshey 1992: 172–4). Scorsese's *Last Temptation*, despite its many conservative Christian features, was an appealing target.

Last Temptation failed to cohere with audience expectations. Jesus epics ended with *Greatest Story*, but the most successful Jesus film thereafter, *Jesus of Nazareth*, had simply reformatted the epic (and religious orthodoxy) for television. Despite his miniscule budget and cast, Scorsese's film looked like it had similar epic pretensions; however, almost every scene deliberately inverted that tradition. *Il messia*'s village Christianity and *Il vangelo*'s populist, rebellious leaders—as well as Pasolini's frenetic camera and jagged editing—are far more influential. *Last Temptation* bespeaks auteur film, foreign film, a rough aesthetic, and an obtrusive camera/editing as well as contemporary, "exotic" music (see Babington and Evans 1993: 150–1, 158; Stern, Jefford, and DeBona 1999: 285–6; Humphries-Brooks 2006: 84).

Despite the attention to mise-en-scène, which audiences would accept as historically realistic (see McGeough 2021), the focus on Jesus's interior, human development lets history slip into psychological character exploration or biopic.[57] In one sense, that move coheres with cinematic trends, a culture of self-expression, and a rejection of religious institutions in favor of spirituality (or interior, privatized religion).[58] The era's popular American cinema/religion tended to find triumphant deities within, not external arduous struggles between God/Satan, spirit/flesh, or good/evil (Walsh 2003: 176, 181; see Problematic Issue).

Last Temptation also eschewed the facile moral dichotomies of Reagan's revitalization of Cold War rhetoric and of nostalgic, triumphant cinema like *First Blood* (1982), *Rambo: First Blood Part II* (1985), *Red Dawn* (1984), and *Rocky IV* (1985) for something more like the struggles of *The Godfather* (1972) (Stern, Jefford, and DeBona 1999: 288–90). In this context, *Last Temptation*'s greatest (cultural) offense might simply be its distance from the triumphant, self-confident Jesus popular in the United States (cf. Walsh 2003: 173–85; Humphries-Brooks 2006: 98–9).

DIRECTOR

Early reviewers saw *Last Temptation* as a buddy film (e.g., Corliss 1988: 44) largely because of Judas's significance and because of Scorsese's earlier *Mean Streets* (1973). *Last Temptation* seems that earlier film's "apotheosis." Charlie (Harvey Keitel) plays a mid-level Italian mobster racked by Catholic guilt. As the opening voiceover (spoken by Scorsese) remarks, one atones for one's sins on the streets and in the home—not in church. The words fit Scorsese's Jesus equally well. Charlie tries to find salvation by balancing his place in the mob, his friendship with Johnny Boy (Robert DeNiro), and his love for Johnny Boy's cousin, Teresa (Amy Robinson). As in *The Last Temptation of Christ*, the buddy relationship is more important than the hero's relationship with the girl.

Charlie's "salvation" strategy becomes untenable when Charlie's boss outlaws his relationships with Teresa and Johnny Boy and when the romantic, suicidal Johnny Boy refuses to pay his gambling debts. As in *Last Temptation*, Charlie, like Judas, tries sacrificially to save his impractical, suicidal friend. (The film is replete with religious imagery, including Charlie's damaged hand and Charlie kneeling in blood and water.) The friend's demise effectively marks both films' ends, and the buddy's world (Keitel in both movies) comes undone.

In terms of Scorsese's larger oeuvre, however, the buddy seems less important than Scorsese's trademark, alienated heroes vacillating between different values. Jesus is another Charlie, Travis Bickle (*Taxi Driver* 1976), or Jake La Motta (*Raging Bull* 1980). The audience sees the world through these protagonists' tortured perspectives, which "push" them toward their (tragic or messianic) destinies (Forshey 1992: 179). As Les Keyser observes, Scorsese's protagonists are on arduous, sacrificial quests: "Scorsese's Jesus and his cross join a long line of Scorsese heroes—Alice Hyatt and her songs, Jake La Motta and his boxing gloves, Jimmy Doyle and his horn, Fast Eddie and his pool cue—all torn between a larger mission and a yearning for normal life, torn between their inspiration and their common sense, just as Scorsese himself felt torn between his camera and his domestic life" (1992: 180–1).

These films are "visions taken from the point of view of the cross" (Stern, Jefford, and DeBona 1999: 291). Scorsese grew up in a Catholicism (educated early by the Sisters of Mercy) that saw humans as bearing the guilt of original sin (understood sexually) and salvation as possible only down a long road of sacrifice. Scorsese drew pictures of the crucifixion and storyboards for a Jesus movie when he was just ten years old (Kelly 1991: 161). Later, he wrote a passion script set in 1960s Manhattan entitled *Jerusalem, Jerusalem!* (Baugh 1997: 52–3, 57–8; Burnette-Bletsch 2021: 200–1).

Scorsese's fascination with Jesus's passion is not restricted to his ostensibly religious films.[59] Pauline Kael famously observed of *Raging Bull* that Scorsese turned the boxer's life into a "ritual of suffering" in which Jake seemed to be crying out, "Crucify me, crucify me," from the ring—all in Scorsese's own effort to become "the saint of cinema" (1980).

"Mad superman" Howard Hughes (Abrams 2009: 89) in *The Aviator* also fits this image (see Staley 2016).

The more recent *Silence* (2016), reprising Shūsaku Endō's 1966 novel, indicates Scorsese's continuing cinematic efforts at redemption. Fr Rodrigues (Andrew Garfield), who provides numerous IVs (like Jesus), goes to seventeenth-century Japan with another Jesuit monk in search of his mentor, the heroic Fr Cristóvão Ferriera (Liam Neeson), rumored to have apostatized in the face of Japanese persecution. The film, another vision from the cross, reports Rodrigues's kenotic salvation (Burnette-Bletsch 2021: 204–9). Rodrigues begins his quest, thinking of himself as a heroic Christ figure. But after his betrayal by the non-heroic Kichijiro (a Judas figure; Yōsuke Kubozuka), Rodrigues eventually apostatizes, trampling a *fumie* (an image of Christ). *Silence* suggests this apostasy is the moment where proud Rodrigues becomes humbly (kenotically) Christlike.[60] After this point, Rodrigues loses control of the narrative (he no longer narrates; see Burnette-Bletsch 2021: 204–9) and ceases to practice Christianity. During his cremation, however, the audience sees a crucifix in his hand (a detail not in the novel). In Scorsese's rendering, in his apostasy, Rodrigues became one with those to whom he came to minister, the hidden Christians. In this end, Rodrigues may be more Christlike than *Last Temptation*'s Jesus.[61]

PROBLEMATIC ISSUE: GNOSTICISMS

As non-substantial, flickering light, film's medium is prone to gnosticism (see Roszak 2005; Wilson 2006). Moreover, with its always-transfigured protagonists, Jesus cinema moves inexorably toward such theologies. At least, high Christologies are so much the Jesus cinema norm that "Christ" overwrites "Jesus," and theologians lament the tradition's inadequate notion of the incarnation (see, e.g., Baugh 1997). Finally, the move in US Jesus cinema (since, at least, *Greatest Story*) toward privatized, subjective understandings of religion reflects a similar theological drift, but also, and perhaps more importantly, a larger cultural slide toward gnostic anthropologies (conceiving the individualistic human as triumphant and true; see Cultural Location).[62]

Aware of this context, Paul Schrader, *Last Temptation*'s original scriptwriter, called the film "Arian" (Schrader 1990: 139). He saw this not as heresy, but as an "incarnational" intervention in a gnostic or docetic Jesus film tradition (see, Stern, Jefford, and DeBona 1999: 285–95; Deacy 2001: 104–37; Holderness 2015: 37–66). That is, if there is too much divinity in the tradition, one might add some humanity.[63] Notably, Scorsese himself said repeatedly he wanted to create a Jesus with whom one could identify (in Corliss 1988: 36; see also the discussion of *Silence* in Director).

CRITERION DVD, 163 MINUTES, 2000
DVD Extras

The title sheet insert includes a four-page summary of conservative Catholic and Protestant fundamentalist pre-release reactions to the film. Special DVD features include

Commentary; Scorsese's visual research; Costume designs; Production and publicity stills; On location in Morocco; and Peter Gabriel.

Commentary

Recorded in 1997 for the *Criterion Collection*. Martin Scorsese, Willem Dafoe, Paul Schrader, and Jay Cocks. The commentary chapters match the DVD Chapters below although they have different names.

1 Scorsese introduction
2 "God as a headache"
3 An ancient controversy
4 Plagued by God
5 Barbara Hershey
6 Fully human, fully divine
7 The language of Christian times
8 Telling stories
9 Casting Jesus
10 A wild revivalist meeting
11 A sense of humor
12 The natural and the supernatural
13 The Jesus curse
14 "We left Hollywood behind"
15 Jesus's power
16 An existentialist book
17 "Judas plays everyman"
18 Peter Gabriel
19 A Roger Corman technique
20 A blood cult
21 An unplayable scene
22 David Bowie
23 Time limits
24 Camera positions
25 The last temptation
26 Controversy
27 The great democratic equalizer
28 Death Muppet

29 Humiliation

30 "Why do you want me to do it?"

Scorsese's visual, bibliographic research

1 *The Biblical Archeology Review*

2 *National Geographic*

3 Paintings

4 Books and films

Costume designs
Production and publicity stills
On location in Morocco
    From the original VHS Video master (16 minutes)
        Tomb of Lazarus, 0:00
        Baptism of Jesus, 0:55
        Wedding at Cana, 7:55
        End of Crucifixion, 9:57
Peter Gabriel (interview conducted August 29, 1996)
    Introduction
    Video interview (12 minutes)
    Photo gallery

DVD Chapters

1 Logos, 0:00

2 The Feeling Begins, 0:29

3 Condemned to Die, 7:03

4 Magdalene, 12:25

      Jesus's mother asks if it is God or the devil, 12:31

5 Jesus: "I need you to forgive me," 17:28

6 The Master, 23:00

7 Purified, 28:17

      Judas, the first disciple, 30:13

      Magdalene's stoning, 33:46

8 The Sermon on the Mount, 37:27

9 The Foundation, 42:07

      "We'll go see John the Baptist," 46:45

10 John the Baptist, 48:12
    Baptist sends Jesus to the desert, 53:09
11 "Speak to me in human words," 53:46
12 Return from the Desert, 1.01:40
    Mary and Martha (of Bethany) take Jesus in
    Jesus's sacred heart, 1.07:59
    "I believed in love, now I believe in this [the axe]," 1.08:58
13 Casting out Devils and Working Cures (Lk. 13:32), 1.09:13
    Wedding at Cana, 1.11:30
14 Rejected at Nazareth, 1.14:56
    "He's insane, he has a demon," 1.17:13
15 Lazarus, 1.19:20
16 The Saint of Blasphemy, 1.23:33
    "When I say 'I,' rabbi, I'm saying God" (Jn 10:30), 1.27:06
    "I came to bring a sword" (Mt. 10:34; Lk. 12:51), 1.27:24
17 The Shadow of the Cross, 1.29:05
    Saul kills Lazarus
    "I am the lamb" (Jn 1:29, 36), 1.31:36
    Shadow of the cross, 1.33:13
18 "King of the Jews," 1.33:53
    Triumphal entry, 1.35:50
    Cleansing the temple again, 1.37:12
19 Waiting for the Sign, 1.37:45
    Stigmata, 1.39:24
    "God gave me the easier job," 1.42:40
20 Passover/Last Supper, 1.43:41
    Peter's stigmata, 1.47:36
21 "Do I have to die?" 1.48:16
    "John" hands Jesus a cup, 1.51:36
    Judas's "betrayal," 1.52:37
22 Pontius Pilate, 1.53:49
23 Golgotha, 1.58:18
    Via Dolorosa, 1.59:15
    Golgotha, 2.00:54

24 "Why have you forsaken me?" 2.05:00

    Guardian angel, 2.07:08

25 The World of God, 2.09:39

    "Who's getting married?" 2.10:35

26 "There's only one woman in the world," 2.17:56

    Mary and Martha, 2.18:19

27 Paul, 2.21:57

28 Moving On, 2.28:25

    Jerusalem burns, Judas returns, 2.32:27

    Satan revealed, 2.35:40

29 "It is accomplished," 2.36:55

    Death, 2.39:26

30 Credits, 2.39:28

NOTES

1. On this triangle, see Chapter 5.
2. *Last Temptation* was the most controversial Jesus film ever (see, e.g., Kelly 1991: 161–80; Forshey 1992: 171–7; Flowers and Middleton 2005). Some conservatives objected to the sex, but, for theologians, the issue is the film's scandalously human Jesus. See Problematic Issue.
3. Dafoe played the "good" sergeant in the moral allegory *Platoon* (1986), for which he earned the first of four Academy Award nominations. He has played psychopaths and villains (e.g., *To Live and Die in L.A.* 1985) more often than heroes. His Jesus is more "intense" than any other cinematic Jesus (except for Enrique Irazoqui in *Il vangelo*).
4. Kazantzakis describes the spirit as a "carnivorous bird" ([1955] 1988: 2).
5. The film has no "church" music. Peter Gabriel, who wrote the music, touts "world" music, and Scorsese asked him for music with a Middle Eastern "feel" (Kelly 1991: 232–5; Papanikolaou 2005; see n38). Scorsese's request and the film's Morocco/Arab/Islamic "setting" all bespeak Orientalism. See Chapter 3; McGeough (2021).
6. Is the entire film Jesus's dream? Lloyd Baugh says the entire film is an extended interior monologue in which Jesus struggles to come to terms with himself (1997: 70). Jesus film cameras typically look up at Jesus (or glimpse him from afar or treat his face as an icon). There are earlier exceptions (e.g., the camera atop the cross in *King of Kings* 1961 and *Jesus Christ Superstar*), but films after Scorsese increasingly use the downward POV (e.g., *Jesus* 1999; *The Passion of the Christ*).
7. Kazantzakis's Jesus often refers to his invisible companion ([1955] 1988: 130, 159, 362–3, 387, 423, 442, 479)—eventually equated with the fantasy's archangel. The novel also frequently refers to the cross's shadow following Jesus.
8. Keitel has acted in many Scorsese films (most recently *The Irishman* 2019), as well as several Paul Schrader and Quentin Tarantino films. Despite later diversification, he was frequently a thug or mobster in his early career.

9   Some reviewers criticized the actors' "New York" accents (particularly Keitel's), but it ties the film closely to Scorsese's early work, particularly *Mean Streets*. See Director.
10 Visually footnoting the tradition's lamb trope and foreshadowing Jesus's ultimate destiny, sheep pass behind Judas as he asks this question. The film features more "slaughtered lambs" than any previous Jesus film: see, for example, the wedding at Cana; the sheep heads carried before Jesus's group entering Jerusalem; and the Passover lambs. Sheep are visually important in *Jesus Christ Superstar, Il messia,* and *Jesus of Nazareth*.
11 The crowds are small. When Paramount withdrew because of religious opposition, Scorsese convinced Universal to take over on the non-epic budget of 6.5 million dollars. The average Hollywood budget in 1988 was 18 million (Stern, Jefford, and DeBona 1999: 286).
12 Hershey starred in Scorsese's first feature, *Boxcar Bertha* (1972, which also featured a crucifixion), and she gave him a copy of Kazantzakis's novel then. In the late 1980s, she was one of Hollywood's finest actresses, receiving a Golden Globe nomination for best supporting actress for her Magdalene.
13 Jesus's mother and Magdalene interact with Jesus during this first Via Dolorosa. They do not appear during Jesus's final Via Dolorosa, but are at Golgotha.
14 The novel simply calls him "the Zealot."
15 On the film's blood, appearing dramatically against the film's typically brown palette, see Keyser (1992: 182–4) and Baugh (1997: 57–62; n28).
16 The script and novel ([1955] 1988: 52, 66) connect Jesus more closely with the crucified victim, as Jesus takes the victim's bloody "headcloth." The script is available online: https://sfy.ru/?script=last_temptation_of_christ_1988.
17 A cruciform lizard is painted above the door. Does the cross already "top" sex/domesticity?
18 Jesus asks for forgiveness from Magdalene, Judas, his mother, and God (repeatedly). Returning to the cross, he refers to himself as God's "prodigal son."
19 In Kazantzakis, the clawing torments begin at Jesus and Magdalene's unsuccessful betrothal. Consequently, Magdalene turns to prostitution ([1955] 1988: 26, 89–97).
20 Graham Holderness argues that Kazantzakis's poetry has a dreamlike, deceptive aura while Scorsese's camera gives the dreams/visions a "real" quality (2015: 60). For a recent depiction of Jesus's surreal visionary life, see *Last Days in the Desert* (2015) and Pippin (2018).
21 Kazantzakis's Jesus sees death as a way to God ([1955] 1988: 399).
22 In the script, Jesus sees God's face in Judas's.
23 The handheld, too-close camera and rough editing, along with Dafoe's manic acting, contribute to this sense.
24 Only villains dismiss children in Jesus films. Kazantzakis's Jesus teaches in parables because he is illiterate. His parables, like those in *Godspell* (1973), redeem everyone. Even Lucifer may eventually be redeemed ([1955] 1988: 183, 202, 217, 224).
25 The camera and staging parody those of *King of Kings* and *The Jesus Film*'s (1979) Sermons.
26 Scorsese grants Jesus's teaching neither gospel nor epic authority. Jesus changes his message twice (Walsh 2003: 72). Scorsese cites this scene as exemplary of the film's humor (in Kelly 1991: 241–2).
27 Other than *Il vangelo*, this was the most homoerotic Jesus film until *A Primeira Tentação Cristo* (The First Temptation of Christ 2019). Schrader's first script was more blatantly so (Kelly 1991: 236). On biblical film's heteronormativity, see Graybill (2018).
28 Jesus reflects on having seen John before (IV), perhaps in a dream. Is he associating the Baptist with the monastery's dead master?

29 The brown, dusty desert and villages—the film was shot on location in Morocco—are part of the non-epic aura and are as evocative as *From the Manger to the Cross*'s Holy Land locations, *Il vangelo*'s southern Italy, or *Greatest Story*'s American West.
30 The script's Jesus remarks that the Baptist's tongue (who kissed him aggressively) felt like a burning coal (Isa. 6:7).
31 This scene is one of the few without antecedent in the novel.
32 Judas calls Peter a rock, teasing him for his slowness.
33 A woman tells the rejected Mary that she saw armies of angels behind Jesus.
34 The major ministry incidents come from (reordered) John.
35 The script supplies this explanation; the film is not clear about why Saul executed Lazarus. In the novel, Barabbas kills Lazarus ([1955] 1988: 413–14).
36 A vexed Judas reviews Jesus's shifting messages: love, axe, death.
37 Judas is co-redeemer. Here, Jesus seems more forerunner (Baptist) than messiah.
38 Incongruously, the Islamic confession of faith is sung during the institution (see Kelly 1991: 233; Baugh 1997: 59–60). Baugh criticizes the transubstantiation and "sacred heart" scenes as overly "literal" (1997: 58).
39 Scorsese includes a slow-motion healing of the servant's ear.
40 Peter runs through the streets and into another running man (whom the script names Philip). Cf. the cut from Peter to Judas in *Jesus of Nazareth*.
41 *Christ Carrying the Cross*, 1500–35, in the Museum of Fine Arts, Ghent. See https://en.wikipedia.org/wiki/Christ_Carrying_the_Cross_(Bosch,_Ghent). Most now attribute this painting to a Bosch follower.
42 The depiction reprises Antonello da Messina's 1475 *Crucifixion* (Royal Museum of Fine Arts, Antwerp). For the image, see https://en.wikipedia.org/wiki/Crucifixion_(Antonello_da_Messina).
43 The script's angel is an old man; Kazantzakis's is a Black boy ([1955] 1988: 451).
44 This guardian angel (fantasy) is the only supernatural event at the crucifixion.
45 Kazantzakis's Jesus lives as "Lazarus" with these two ([1955] 1988: 458–66).
46 Stephenson Humphries-Brooks says that Paul's portrayal rejects evangelical Christianity as a way forward for the United States (2006: 95). *Last Temptation*'s John also thinks what people believe is more important than the truth. Cf. also "The Grand Inquisitor" (Forshey 1992: 179) and Fr Leclerc in *Jésus of Montréal* (1989). Kazantzakis uses this scene to motivate Jesus to return to the cross ([1955] 1988: 473–80). Kazantzakis does, however, impugn Matthew for misunderstanding prophecy and for making up stories that Jesus neither likes nor remembers (see, e.g., [1955] 1988: 341–3, 348–9, 389–92, 407, 415).
47 Behind them, seen through the door and black tree limbs, is a bright red (fiery, bloody) world. Cf. film posters and some (e.g., Criterion Collection) DVD covers. The opening and Gethsemane scenes also portray Jesus through (similar) tree limbs.
48 At Keitel's request, Scorsese lay on the pallet in Dafoe's place for Judas's harangue (Kelly 1991: 230).
49 Satan reminds Jesus he promised, in the wilderness, to meet him again.
50 In both script and novel ([1955] 1988: 443, 495–6), Jesus's final fantasy interrupts the cry of desolation. Baugh opines that despair, not domesticity, should be the final temptation (1997: 260 n175).
51 Many think the lights suggest resurrection, but film damage caused the effect. Scorsese liked the effect and left it, saying that people should decide what it means. Notably, keening continues into the credits (cf. Baugh 1997: 69).

52 Jerold Abrams claims that Scorsese (and Michel Foucault) thinks Christ is most like us in madness (2009: 83).
53 Humphries-Brooks says Magdalene—"temptation"—never converts (2006: 87–9).
54 Scorsese "studiously reshoots standard [Jesus film] scenes" "to undo their effect" (Humphries-Brooks 2006: 84).
55 One might see the film as a struggle over which biblical text will define its Jesus: Isa. 53 (Jesus and Isaiah) or Gen. 22 (the guardian angel)?
56 Contrast the way other films, for example, *The King of Kings*, transfigure Jesus throughout.
57 On Jesus films as biopics, see Reinhartz (2007). On biblical film's shift from epic to biopic, see Moore (2018: 42–5).
58 The film promotes such "spirituality" with its "realization" of Jesus's interior struggle, as well as its rejection of domesticity and Torah, in favor of the heart and a God who belongs to the world (Walsh 2010: 111).
59 Nor is the matter always Christian (crucifixion) imagery. See *Kundun* (1997) and Jeffrey Staley's (2016) discussion of mother goddesses in *The Aviator* (2004).
60 In a later conversation with Kichijiro (and then Jesus/God), Rodrigues seems to think in these terms.
61 Alternatively, he may be a bodhisattva turning away from nirvana "to save" others. In this case, the crucifix may simply be "an analogy" for those who need Christian references to understand the film.
62 Given this cultural gnosticism, cinematic heroes/heroines are often visually transfigured—without need of Christian discourse and without, thereby, being Christ figures. In one classic example, *The Aviator*'s (2004) Howard Hughes (Leonardo DiCaprio) sits naked, in a screening room director's chair as the projector's light casts a saintly penumbra around his head (Staley 2016: 239–40).
63 Baugh argues that the film's flawed anthropology, not its Christology, is the theological problem (1997: 71).

16

Jésus de Montréal

Denys Arcand, director, 1989

PLOT SUMMARY: BECOMING THE SON OF MAN

Jésus de Montréal has three distinct parts. In part one, actor Daniel Coulombe (Lothaire Bluteau) researches, writes, and rehearses a modernized passion play as he prepares to play Jesus.[1] In part two, Daniel and his small troupe enact this play on the grounds of the St Joseph's Oratory shrine to rave media reviews and to rector Fr Leclerc's consternation.[2] Part three depicts Daniel's growing transformation into a "Christ" or "son of man," and his own passion.[3] The film deals with the difficulties of reconstructing Jesus, reprises the earliest Jesus film type (filmed passion plays), and becomes a Christ-figure film (see Problematic Issue).[4]

The film opens on a play. An actor playing Smerdyakov, the illegitimate son in *The Brothers Karamazov*, blames his murder of his father on his half-brother Ivan's "death of God … everything is permitted" philosophy. Smerdyakov hangs himself, pronouncing woes on suicides who damn themselves, and cursing the God who beckons them. The play foreshadows the tragedy (death) to follow and limns the film's "death of God" world.[5]

The media lavish praise on Pascal (Cédric Noël), the actor playing Smerdyakov. A woman opines that she wants Pascal's head for her *Homme sauvage* cologne campaign (see Figure 16.1). Reinforcing Baptist allusions, Pascal (and the camera) diverts the critics' praise to Daniel (unidentified), who has just arrived, by saying, "There's a good actor" (cf. Mk 1:7). Daniel tells Pascal his next part is "Jesus" and that he needs "inspiration."

The film's title, *Jésus de Montréal*, follows. Although a first-time viewer may not realize it, Daniel is already more "*Jésus de Montréal*" than Daniel.[6] The city becomes a film character with its skyline serving repeatedly as background and with so many of its recognizable places in the mise-en-scène (see n2; cf. Nazareth's function in *Jesus of Nazareth* 1977).

A choir featuring two women rehearses Pergolesi's *Stabat Mater* in a church loft. When Daniel enters the sanctuary, he looks up at the choir director,[7] missing Fr Leclerc (Gilles Pelletier) standing behind him.[8] Fr Leclerc has hired Daniel to modernize a passion play Leclerc wrote thirty-five years ago and has staged every summer at the shrine. With Leclerc, Daniel watches a videotape and takes notes. The play begins at the shrine's statue of Jesus condemned to death, the First Station of the Cross.[9]

Daniel collects his troupe (disciples), beginning with the maternal Constance (Johanne-Marie Tremblay)—whom Daniel finds working at a soup kitchen, a crucifix displayed prominently on the wall behind her. The two of them recruit Martin (Rémy Girard)[10] in an amusing scene where he voices different characters in a porno.[11] The three pick up

Constance's daughter, who is immediately enthralled with Daniel (cf. film's Jesus among the children trope).[12]

Daniel researches "Jesus," talking to a furtive Deep Throat-like professor in a parking garage about new Jesus information[13] and reading impressive library tomes. A dour librarian reassures Daniel, saying Jesus will find him.[14] Daniel also returns to the shrine to muse upon the First Station. When he gets home, he interrupts a tryst between Constance (now the woman taken in adultery) and Fr Leclerc. Leclerc laments his aborted theater career,[15] but rejects Constance's offers of "a place with her" because he cannot face poverty.[16] Surprisingly, Arcand treats this failed priest (a cinematic trope) almost empathetically.[17]

Daniel and his disciples invite René (Robert Lepage)[18] into the troupe. René subsists by narrating documentaries—Daniel and friends interrupt his dubbing of one about the universe's vast, inhuman quality. Reluctant to join them (like "doubting Thomas," he wants to see the evidence/script), René directs them to another prospect.

Arcand cuts to this young woman, a scantily clad Mireille (Magdalene; Catherine Wilkening) walking on water in a Milan Kundera-inflected[19] commercial for Esprit #7 (Holy Spirit?) cologne.[20] Her lover/director Jerzy values her only for her sexual appeal, so she joins Daniel's troupe. René appears at Constance's flat and joins after Daniel agrees to allow him to recite Hamlet's soliloquy in the play. They celebrate a friendly first supper of pizza and wine—despite René's reminder of the superstition that doing tragedy is dangerous.[21]

The troupe rehearses the new play (acting out the kingdom?) in front of the First Station statue. Their play refers to Jesus as the prophet Yeshua ben Panthera, questions the gospels' reliability, and highlights modernity's "distance" from Jesus.[22]

Part two of the film is the new passion play's first performance, which begins with (and at) the First Station of the Cross.[23] Soldiers (Constance and Mireille) bring the bound Jesus before a philosophical Pilate (René). He dismisses Jesus's impractical teaching (Jn 18:36, 38; 15:13), but sentences Jesus to death at Caiaphas's (Martin) urging (Jn 11:50), after describing crucifixion's horrors and musing about an afterlife's possibilities.

A jaded security guard escorts the audience to the Second Station, an archaeological dig (rather than Jesus bearing his cross). Archaeologists Constance and Mireille relate "facts" about the Jewish Jesus who thought the world's end near, whose facial features are unknown,[24] and whom some considered a Roman soldier's illegitimate son (see Mk 6:3). Leading the way to the next station, they talk about the era's belief in magic/miracles. Martin and René portray other magicians (e.g., Simon the Magician),[25] and Daniel/Jesus walks on water (Mt. 14:22-31), heals a blind woman, and raises Jairus's daughter (Mk 5:35-43). A devout Haitian maid intrudes upon the play, begging her Lord's forgiveness, before the exasperated security guard removes her.[26] Jesus teaches trust in God, nonviolence, and forgiveness (Sermon selections), as he passes out bread to the audience (the miracle of the loaves) and eats with his disciples.

Suddenly, Jesus demands to know what people say of him. When Peter (Martin) names him the Christ, Jesus responds strangely, "Never say I am the Christ. I am the son of man" (selecting freely from Mk 8:29-31; see Walsh 2018d: 305-8). Leaving his disciples (Jn 13:36), Jesus is arrested, despite the Haitian maid's warnings.[27]

The security guard leads the audience to the next station, where Jesus is whipped. Mireille and Constance comment on crucifixion's banality and its use to enforce public morality (with thousands pilloried as signposts on major roads).[28] Jesus carries his cross beam (the traditional Second Station), refuses narcotic wine, is stripped nude (Tenth Station), and is nailed to the cross (Eleventh Station) in a pose like that seen in Daniel's library research (and in *Last Temptation* 1988). As often in Jesus films, the audience sees the nails driven. The women describe crucifixion's horrors (death by exposure, exhaustion, and suffocation). Jesus says he is thirsty, and mumbles "Forsaken," without reference to God (cf. Mk 15:34). Constance says Romans left crucified bodies to rot, and with only the film's audience present, an actor thrusts a spear into Jesus's side. Blood spews.

Having left Jesus alone on the cross, the security guard takes the audience underground for resurrection ruminations (not the Fourteenth Station's entombment). Constance says years have passed, and René recites Hamlet's ("perchance to dream") soliloquy. Suddenly, Magdalene (Mireille) runs up announcing the resurrection to a skeptical Peter (Martin).[29] A cloaked stranger (René) appears to two disciples on the road to Emmaus (Martin and Constance).

Mireille and Constance minimize these reports' trustworthiness but point out that the resurrection hope made life bearable for those lost in a bewildering universe (cf. Fr Leclerc's later claims about the hopeless' need of the church). Finally, the troupe summarizes its gospel: "You must find your own path to salvation. No one can help you. Look to yourself with humility and courage .... Love one another. Seek salvation within yourselves" (cf. Lk. 17:21). The lights go out, applause begins, and Daniel/Jesus descends—with light streaming down behind him—to rejoin the troupe.

The critics who touted Pascal in the film's prologue now mob the troupe, praising them with similar words. A famous actor flirts with Constance; a jealous Pascal leaves without speaking to Daniel; and, amusingly, two Raëlians (including Daniel's dour librarian) discuss alien "contact" with Martin and René. Daniel, however, descends into the tunnel (hell) to speak with the apoplectic Leclerc who angrily dismisses the play (saying the Bible "can be made to say anything").[30] His priestly superiors will decide the play's fate.

This enactment is the play's most complete version. Subsequent performances are fragmentary and farcical, in contrast to this first "miraculous" performance (Testa 1995: 105). More importantly, the reenactments take second place to Daniel's increasingly important story (Baugh 1997: 119).[31] Notably, when Daniel returns to the happy troupe, they call him "Jesus."

A media blitz celebrates Daniel's miraculous "triumph" in the "Passion on the Mountain."[32] At Constance's apartment, Mireille washes (anoints) Daniel and asks him to attend a commercial audition. Even the shrine's *Stabat Mater* singers are there. The woman agent, who wanted Pascal's head, and Jerzy, Mireille's former lover/director, are in charge and deliberately abase Mireille. An enraged Daniel trashes the set (the temple) and chases the "money men" away.

At the play's next performance, Jesus/Daniel does more Sermon teaching, adding woes/curses drawn from Mt. 23, as well as lessons about humility in a faceoff with the religious officials. Police detectives interrupt Jesus/Daniel's lonely cross reverie (the play's audience already awaits the resurrection), arresting him for assault and property destruction. Consequently, Jesus/Daniel is a no-show at the resurrection.

Daniel appears before a judge (played by Arcand). When Daniel refuses counsel (Richard Cardinal) and pleads guilty, the judge orders a psychological evaluation. After Daniel's release, pending sentencing, the lawyer invites him to lunch atop a Montreal skyscraper, offering him acting roles, wealth, "this city," and charity spokesperson roles. Daniel is not tempted.

Meanwhile, Fr Leclerc rehearses the old play with the recalcitrant troupe, saying no one knows when Daniel will return (Mk 13:34-37?). Daniel appears, however, and watches the troupe from behind Leclerc as Constance "hams up" "Behold the Son of God." The others join the humorous mockery, acting the passion in different modes: comédie Française; New York method acting; New York street slang (cf. *Last Temptation*); and kabuki.[33] Daniel completes the last mode, miming ritual suicide (another ominous foreshadowing).[34]

When Leclarc stalks angrily away, Daniel follows him into the sanctuary where Leclerc berates him for ruining their lives and for failing to recognize that the church provides what the despairing need.[35] Daniel feels the institution has worn the once radical Leclerc "down." By contrast, the fearless Daniel thinks there is "more to life than quietly waiting for death."

Overlooking the city, the troupe has a last supper of pizza and wine. Mireille exhorts them to one last performance by testifying that the troupe/play has "saved" her (from selling her body). They get into costume, and Daniel pushes them past the security guard, insisting the guard has no authority.

As Daniel hangs on the cross (for the third time), an enhanced security detail stops the performance. The head security guard, standing in cruciform before the crucified Jesus/Daniel, remonstrates with the unhappy audience: "Look, he dies on the cross and is resurrected. No big deal. Talk about slow!" The ensuing brawl knocks over Jesus's cross.[36] Mireille tries unsuccessfully to rouse "Daniel" (who has "become Jesus").[37]

An ambulance crew takes the unconscious Daniel, along with the women, to St Mark's (no such hospital exists in Montreal). Hopelessly overwhelmed, the hospital cannot help, but Daniel revives and the trio leaves. They descend into a subway (hell) on an escalator (shot from below). Daniel monologues, juxtaposing humanity's quest for happiness with life's harshness and mystery. He notes his father forsook him (as the crucified Jesus?) before segueing—with Pascal's head in the *Homme sauvage* cologne advertisement displayed behind him—into a demythologized apocalyptic rant (Mk 13:2, 14-18, 21-22, 24-25 [paraphrased as "shaken heavens"], 32-33). Daniel collapses as a blue subway train[38] arrives. Constance runs for help, leaving Mireille holding him in a pietà (see Figure 16.1).

The same ambulance crew rushes Daniel to the Jewish General Hospital (which does exist). The staff attends to Daniel immediately, but it is too late. Daniel is brain dead. A doctor, dressed in a white coat (cf. Mk 16:5) and speaking English, asks Constance and Mireille in a dark waiting room, in eucharistic language, to "give us his body." Daniel's type-O blood is a "Godsend."

As Daniel lies cruciform, doctors harvest his organs. Arcand intercuts the organs' delivery[39] with Daniel's cremation and the lawyer's offer to help the troupe create the "Daniel Coulombe Theatre." Rejecting this project, Mireille, Daniel's beloved disciple, walks alone on the shrine's hill. Music begins as the two women from St Joseph's loft choir (and the beer commercial) sing the *Stabat Mater* in the subway, busking under Pascal's billboard poster head.[40] Art's commodification is blatant.[41]

As the music continues, the camera pans away and ascends through what appears to be rock and concrete. The credits scroll and ascend. As the camera moves past stained glass, upbeat electric guitar music begins. After a black screen, a traditionally shaped, empty cross appears—Montreal's flickering lights behind it.[42] In some DVD versions, after a final black screen, the DVD returns to its menu, which displays the First Station of the Cross statue.

MEMORABLE CHARACTERS

1 Daniel produces a modernized passion play in which he plays Jesus (Daniel's miraculous aesthetic ministry) and then becomes a modern Jesus or son of man in the film's final third (Daniel's passion; see Walsh 2018d).

2 "Jesus" is different representations: the First Station of the Cross's statue, the passé passion play's role, an academic reconstruction, evangelical and artistic creations, an object of pious devotion (Raëlian, Haitian, and sacred heart), and, most importantly, the figures created by Daniel's art and life (see Baugh 1997: 115–18; Walsh 2003: 31–3).

3 Father Leclerc is the chief antagonist. He is a Judas betraying art and himself, choosing an easy life over integrity (cf. *Greatest Story*'s [1965] tempting Dark Hermit). Like the ringmaster in *Godspell* (1973), Pascal is both Baptist (losing his head to commercialism) and Judas (forsaking artistic integrity).

4 The troupe alludes to various gospel characters. Constance is both mother and the woman taken in adultery. Mireille is Magdalene. Martin is Peter, and René represents doubting Thomas. The women are the stronger characters, providing the gospel message and (play) commentary and Daniel's support system (cf. Lk. 8:1-3). Mireille is Daniel's beloved disciple.

MEMORABLE VISUALS

1 Repeated panoramas of Montreal's skyline.
2 The First Station of the Cross statue.
3 The security guard standing cruciform before Daniel/Jesus on the cross.
4 Daniel/Jesus falling from and crushed by the cross.
5 Daniel's subway rant and pietà before Pascal's "head" (see Figure 16.1).
6 Daniel cruciform; his organs harvested.

Figure 16.1 Mireille holds Daniel in a pietà beneath Pascal's "head" in *Jésus de Montréal*, directed by Denys Arcand, 1989. All rights reserved.

KEY AUTHORITY/SCRIPTURE

1 The play's Sermon and the troupe's tomb/resurrection gospel reflect an optimistic faith in the individual's capacity for integrity and ability to love/respect others.

2 The cinematic world assumes modern reason's reliability (scientific and historical discoveries).

3 The prologue's play, Daniel's apocalyptic subway rant, and Mireille and Daniel's commitment to their play resemble Albert Camus's call to creation in an absurd world (see Walsh 2003: 55–7, 61–2; 2018d: 302–4, 310–11). Perhaps, the key authority then is hope in the authentic artist and in art's salvific qualities (Arcand, cited in Loiselle 1995: 157).

4 While the film draws eclectically on the canonical gospels, Arcand claimed Mark inspired his film (in Testa 1995: 110 n13; see also Walsh 2018d: 296). Arcand's "Mark" reflects a world of even more radical exile or God-forsakenness than that in canonical Mark. Crucified, Daniel/Jesus can manage only "forsaken" (cf. Mk 15:34).[43] Daniel's audience does not have comfort like that of Mk 13:20. The apocalyptic rant's only religious/theological references are warnings about false christs/prophets (Mk 13:21–22). Further, Daniel/Jesus rejects Peter's Christ-confession so that Mk 8:29-31(and 3:28) become important (see Problematic Issue).

CULTURAL LOCATION/GENRE: PASSION PLAY

In the 1960s, Québec went through a Quiet Revolution that effectively shifted it from a traditional Roman Catholic society to a modern "secular" state. The period saw an improved economy and standard of living as well as a rise in (French Canadian) nationalism and in lifestyle choices. Joie de vivre replaced Roman Catholic spirituality (Stern, Jefford, and Debona 1999: 318–19).

Soon, however, French Canadian cultural critics like Arcand began to lament society's commercialization and hedonism (Baugh 1997: 113–14). As US media products dominated, French artists and intellectuals critiqued "Hollywood" and strove for more local products.[44] Accordingly, *Jésus de Montréal* rejects religion (Jesus) and bodies' (Mireille) commodification and exalts (non-commercial) art. In a world without transcendence (or metanarrative), the artistic play with "surfaces" may be the only hope (cf. Walsh 2003: 61–2). Juxtaposition (Daniel and Jesus), parody, pastiche, intertextuality, frame breaks (between play and primary reality), and irony are everything. According to Adele Reinhartz, these tensions in *Jésus de Montréal*—for example, between the radical, revolutionary (passion play) Jesus and the conventional Christ figure (Daniel)—mirror "the tension in post-1970 Québécois society between the Catholicism that shaped its past identity and the radical secularity that shapes its present self-understanding." She argues further that the film deploys Christ ironically (a failed Christ) and offers an uplifting secular message, pointing to "both the hope and the fear that Québec's secular future may bring" (2021: 251–3; cf. Beavis 2013).

Not surprisingly, then, Arcand abandons the Hollywood spectacle and star system for a return to Jesus film's earliest style: filmed passion plays. Arcand's recent precursors include *The Lawton Story* (1949; cf. *Jesus Town USA* 2014), *Celui qui doit mourir* (He Who Must Die 1957), *La ricotta* (1963), and *Jesus Christ Superstar* (1973). Reinhartz refers to such films as "the passion in present tense," and sees them as a subset of films placing the Jesus story alongside a modern story (e.g., *Intolerance* 1916) (2013: 116–25). Among such films, *Jésus de Montréal* stands between extremes that show none of the passion play (e.g., *Celui qui doit mourir*) and those that show little of the modern "frame" narrative (*Jesus Christ Superstar*).

Jesus epics and "histories" tend to present their audiences with a comfortable message, obscuring interpretative problematics and differences between the Jesus story and the present. By contrast, films that present Jesus relocations—whether parables, metaphors, allegories, or Pasolini's "analogy"—foreground the audience's "need" to interpret. *Jésus de Montréal* is such a parable, both by presenting the passion in present tense and through the fecundity of its conflicting Jesus representations (see Problematic Issue; Walsh 2018d: 308–11).

DIRECTOR

Denys Arcand is the best-known French-Canadian director. In addition to Genie Awards for best film, director, and writer for *Le Déclin de l'empire américain* (The Decline of the American Empire 1986) and *Jésus de Montréal*, the first film won the International Critics Prize at Cannes and the second a Jury Prize. Both films were also nominated for Academy Awards for Best Foreign Language Film. Arcand won that award in 2004 for *Les invasions barbares* (The Barbarian Invasions 2003).

Educated as a historian, Arcand's first films were social activist documentaries. The most famous is *On est au coton* (We Work in Cotton 1970), which dealt with textile workers' exploitation. The film caused such uproar that the National Film Board refused to distribute it for several years. It also made Arcand famous as a social critic and a filmmaker of despair (Harkness 1989: 235).

In a "second career," Arcand began to make French features. *Le Déclin de l'empire américain* was his first major success—and the top-grossing French-Canadian film up to its time.[45] In that film, eight middle-age people, who work in a university history department or are affiliated with those who do, leave town for a weekend retreat. The men and women spend the day separately, engaging in multiple conversations about sex, in which words (representations) clearly replace experience. A taped interview with the historian Dominque (Dominique Michel) about her new book, *Variations on the Idea of Happiness*, begins and ends the film, and creates irony through juxtaposition with the conversations, as Dominque contends societies decline to the extent that notions of personal happiness permeate them (cf. the Quiet Revolution's effects). During the day it becomes clear that Rémy (Rémy Girard) has had affairs with all the group's women.[46] After the group hears Dominque's interview, Rémy's wife Louise debunks Dominque's theories, which leads Dominque to reveal her affair with Rémy—with destructive consequences (see Loiselle and McIlroy 1995b: 4). The next morning, as the film ends, matters remain unresolved.

Arcand brought back most of this film's cast for the sequel *Les Invasions barbares*. Philandering Rémy, now divorced from Louise, is dying from cancer. His son Sébastian (Stéphane Rousseau), who has a successful business career in London, who despises his father for his adulteries, and whom his father belittles for his lack of culture, returns home to care for Rémy. Sébastian struggles to find proper health care for his father and finally buys heroin from a drug addict, Diane's daughter Nathalie (Marie-Josée Croze), to ease his father's pain.

Rémy's friends take him to the country to console him (cf. the "set" in *Le Déclin*). Their conversations reveal their passé (Quiet Revolution) views. They wonder if the 9/11 attacks mark the onset of modern barbarian invasions. Rémy dies peacefully with his friends after his "guardian angel" Nathalie gives him another heroin injection.[47]

Despite the film's subject (death) and title, *Les Invasions barbares* is more hopeful than Arcand's documentaries and *Le Déclin*'s cultural wasteland. Like *Jésus de Montréal*, it finds some hope in a world of despair and (the) death (of God) in a small community. *Jésus de Montréal* may be more hopeful still, in its modest glimmer of personal integrity and art.[48]

PROBLEMATIC ISSUE: JESUSES

The secularization of society (e.g., Canada's Quiet Revolution) means the church no longer controls society's institutions. Outside that institutional control, "messiah" and "Jesus" mean differently as other ideologies come into play. Moving beyond *Jesus Christ Superstar* and *Life of Brian*, *Jésus de Montréal* creates a bewildering number of "Jesuses" (see Memorable Characters).[49] In a society of "mechanical reproduction" (Walter Benjamin's famous phrase [1968]), "Jesus" no longer even bears art's authenticity. "Jesus" is endlessly producible and plastic—like everything else in a society of representation or simulation. Not surprisingly, then, *Jésus de Montréal*'s church loses control of its Jesus/passion play. Even the return to the "original" play fails in a flurry of different theatrical representations.

The film is thus deeply concerned with acting roles—as are most filmed passion plays. While Daniel is more Christlike than is the Jesus role he plays, *Jésus de Montréal* does not Christ figure him as previous filmed passions would have done; nor does Daniel (reverently) imitate Christ as a Jesus-adjacent or Christ figure should. The revelation of what truly is transpiring takes place, as in the gospels and film tradition, at the disciples' confession. Notably, like Mark's Jesus (Mk 8:29-31), Daniel's Jesus is not satisfied with "Christ." He is the "son of man" (see Walsh 2018d: 305–8). "Son of man's" implicit plurality here (cf. the "humans" of Mk 3:28) is as important as the film's plurality of Jesuses. It is after all Camus's world (see Key Authority).

ARROW DVD, 120 MINUTES, 2006[50]

DVD Extras

English subtitles
Interview with Denys Arcand (November 28, 2005)
    About *Jesus of Montreal*, 2:30–13:00; 26:15

DVD Chapters

1 Leclerc's Project, 0:00
    Smerdyakov's suicide
    Title, 3:15
    Pergolesi's *Stabat Mater*, 3:41

2 Looking for Constance, 6:49
    "Peter," 7:53
    "Crucifixions," 11:37
    "Woman caught in adultery," 14:00

3 Casting, 17:19
    "Thomas," 20:45
    "Magdalene," 21:00

4 First Rehearsal, 25:35
    "Little children," 25:37

5 The Passion Play, 28:25
    First Station, 28:40
    Archaeological dig, 32:55

        Miracles and teaching, 35:55

            "Speak to me, sweet Jesus," 37:45

            Sermon (excerpts from Mt. 5-6), 38:27

            "I am the son of man," 40:41

            Arrest, 41:09

        The Passion, 41:18

            Scourging, 41:28

            Crucifixion's history, 41:33

            Via Dolorosa, 42:41

            Crucifixion, 43:14

            Death, 45:35

        Entombment, Last Station of the Cross, 45:54

            Hamlet's soliloquy, 46:48

            Resurrection appearances, 48:41

6   The Critics, 51:42

        Raëlians, 54:08

        Fr. Leclerc's reaction, 55:39

7   All Right! 57:22

        "Anointing woman," 1.00:09

8   Mireille's Audition, 1.01:09

        "Temple cleansing," 1.06:14

9   Trial, 1.07:40

        Play's second performance, 1.07:46

            Woes against the Pharisees and scribes, 1.07:59

        Daniel's arrest on the cross, 1.09:15

        Daniel's absence, 1.10:58

        "Trial before Pilate," 1.11:11

            Psychological evaluation, 1.12:56

        "Temptations," 1.15:18

10 Considerable Modifications, 1.19:13

        Return to original script, 1.19:55

11 Cancelled, 1.27:30

        "Last Supper," 1.27:40

        Play's third performance, 1.31:00

        Falling cross, 1.32:54

St. Mark's Hospital, 1.33:52

"Forsaken by my father," 1.37:24

"Apocalyptic discourse" (Mk 13:2, 14-33), 1.37:38

"Death of the Baptist" (Mk 6:27-28), 1.38:12

"Pietà," 1.40:45

Jewish General Hospital, 1.40:58

12 Daniel's End, 1.41.06

"Give us his body," 1.43:55

New heart, 1.47:18

The theater in his name, 1.47:30

"Magdalene" leaves, 1.48:08

New eyes, 1.48:14

Pergolesi's *Stabat Mater*, 1.49:24

Credits, 1.50:50

Empty cross, 1.53:10

NOTES

1 Bluteau won the 1990 Genie Award for best leading performance for *Jésus de Montréal*. His next role was the seventeenth-century French Jesuit priest, Paul LaForgue, in *Black Robe* (1991), another Genie Award winning film. Ironically, given his "Daniel's" commitment to local theater, most of Bluteau's roles have been outside Canada.

2 Saint Joseph's Oratory of Mount Royal dominates Montréal's skyline, but the shrine refused permission to film on site. The "garden" locations are near the École Polytechnique de Montréal. The church interiors are from the Church of St Michael and St Anthony. The Brock Tunnel was the location for the last Station of the Cross. See http://www.urbexplayground.com/urbex/brock-tunnel-relic-past.

3 Bart Testa reads part two as Daniel's miraculous ministry and part three as his passion, a descent into the suffering "city," previously obscured by the consumer society's façade (1995: 101–8).

4 Lloyd Baugh depicts *Jésus de Montréal* as a "transition" from Jesus to Christ-figure films (1997: 113–29). Testa sees the film as an *imitatio Christi* (1995: 105–6).

5 The film is French Canadian and was made after the Quiet Revolution (1960s) that ended the Roman Catholic domination of Montréal/Québec. See Cultural Location. For some of the film's intertexts, most of which deal with the "death of God," see Walsh (2018d: 303–4).

6 The characters have mentioned "Jesus" three times. "Daniel" does not occur until the media praise the actor who played Jesus in the "Passion on the Mountain." Fr Leclerc does call Daniel "Mr. Coulombe" in the post-title scene. Coulombe means "dove" or "dove-keeper," and extends the opening's "Baptist" allusions.

7 Here, Daniel looks up to the camera while the *Stabat Mater* looks up to her son on the cross. The music is the *Stabat Mater*'s next to last movement, in which the believer calls on the Virgin Mary (and the victorious cross) for protection (see Reinhartz 2007: 38).

8   The tempter's traditional location.
9   This statue/station becomes a film leitmotif. It portends Daniel's fate.
10 A respected actor, Girard has received more Genie nominations than anyone else, winning the award for supporting actor for this film.
11 A similar scene occurs in *The Favour, the Watch, and the Very Big Fish* (1991), when Louis Aubinar (Bob Hoskins), a holy card photographer, dubs a porno for a sick friend and impresses Sybil (Natasha Richardson). Fortuitously, Louis unwittingly employs Sybil's previous boyfriend (The Pianist/Jeff Goldblum), a recently released criminal, to pose as Jesus for his holy cards. Thereafter, matters become a farcical, comic twist on *Jésus de Montréal* as supposed miracles and other events lead the Pianist to "believe" his role and to drown when he tries to walk across a swimming pool.
12 Daniel is itinerant or homeless.
13 The professor fears he will lose his post if he tells the truth about Jesus. He envies Daniel's artistic freedom. "Deep Throat" was the code name of Bob Woodward's secret source in *All The President's Men* (1976).
14 It is a passion prediction, as Jesus's fate does "find" Daniel. The librarian is a Raëlian.
15 Ironically, Leclerc admires tragedy: *Richard III* and *Lorenzaccio*.
16 At the scene's end, Constance collapses over Daniel's legs as if a repentant woman at Jesus's feet (a trope depending on Jesus films, rather than the gospels; but see Lk. 7:38).
17 For Arcand, integrity is rare and difficult.
18 LePage is an internationally respected Canadian playwright.
19 Amusingly, the Czech/French novelist's most famous work is *The Incredible Lightness of Being*, a Nietzsche-inspired look at human life's insignificance, reduced by the commercial's creators to lightness—to walking on water.
20 Her attire is reminiscent of that of Jesus crucified or deposed.
21 Amusingly, Daniel cannot uncork the bottle (contrast the miracle at the wedding at Cana).
22 Arcand, a historian, privileges non-gospel material in Daniel's radical reconstruction of Jesus. For critique, see Reinhartz (2007: 27, 29, 31–40).
23 Jesus's statue is now blindfolded. The Stations of the Cross are fourteen artistic renderings of Jesus's suffering. See Chapter 20. The film's passion play follows these stations loosely, explicitly referencing only five.
24 The women point out Jesus's different, early artistic depictions, including the youthful, beardless Hermes and the bearded Greek Orthodox priest.
25 They also mention the rumor of Jesus's childhood in Egypt.
26 The Haitian maid's intrusion blatantly foreshadows the film's major theme: the confusion between Daniel's "historical" Jesus and Daniel as "Christ" or "son of man."
27 The frustrated guard tries to explain the separate realities of the play and its audience (thus calling attention to a "wall" Arcand repeatedly violates).
28 Actors often provide voiceover narration while others act. The effect is like that of silent intertitles or epic voiceovers—as well as the commentary sometimes supporting silents.
29 The music is "Pritouritze Planinata," performed by Stefka Sabotinova, of the award-winning folk musical group, Le Mystère Des Voix Bulgares. The piece is also heard when Daniel/Jesus walks on water. For the film soundtrack, see https://www.discogs.com/Yves-Laferri%C3%A8re-J%C3%A9sus-Of-Montr%C3%A9al-Original-Music-by-Yves-Laferri%C3%A8re/release/11455358.
30 Acrand has made similar comments about the Bible (see Barker 1990: 4).

31 Baugh says Arcand undercuts the play's Jesus in favor of the Christlike Daniel through transgressions of narrative boundaries, through turning everything into a media event, and through various comic elements (1997: 120–1).
32 Arcand intercuts critics saying contradictory things about Daniel, to humorous effect. Is he commenting on gospel vagaries?
33 Ironically, a Japanese produced kabuki adaptation of *Jesus Christ Superstar* appeared in 2009 (see Lies 2009).
34 Cf. the humorous "suicide squad" at Brian's cross in *Life of Brian* (1979).
35 In the play's last station (the tomb), Constance speaks similarly of resurrection belief among the bitter and desperate.
36 No providence (or prophecy) directs these events. René does have a superstitious premonition about tragedy (repeated after the ambulance leaves) and the film includes tragic foreshadowing (e.g., the First Station of the Cross's statue's repeated appearance). Arcand says he knew Daniel had to die because modernity cannot accept such uncompromising figures, but he wanted to undermine the tragedy, so he "chose a rather grotesque death for the actor, having him fall under his cross, as if the performance itself killed the performer" (in Loiselle 1995: 157). Peter Wilkins wonders why "no critic suggests that Arcand might be viewing the original Jesus as an actor of sorts growing into a role" (1995: 129). See the comparison between Jesus as Son of Man and Daniel as Jesus in Walsh (2018d). Arcand himself notes the line between an actor and his/her role is often fragile and permeable. See Barker (1990: 4), Schechter (1985: 123–6), and Walsh (2018d: 305–8).
37 Daniel's death is his life's end, but not its culmination. His life is an act of absurd creation in response to the prologue's suicidal, death of God play. Daniel's "creation" is also a response to Leclerc and Pascal's betrayals. See the previous note; Walsh (2003: 56–7).
38 "The blue train" is a common metaphor for loss in American jazz, blues, and folk music traditions. See the songs by John Coltrane (1958), Johnny Cash (1962), and Linda Ronstadt (1988).
39 The woman receiving Daniel's eyes joyously exclaims, "the light." A sacred heart picture looms in the background. By contrast, Leclerc shuts his window on a view of rainy Golgotha.
40 They sing the *Stabat Mater*'s last movement, where the worshiper confesses hope in her soul's heavenly safety as her body decays. See Baugh (1997: 129) and Reinhartz (2007: 38).
41 Barnes Tatum says it is a move from organ to boom box (2013: 218). Could it also bespeak Jesus's liberation from a rich, corrupt church?
42 For a reading of this sequence as affirming the resurrection, see Baugh (1997: 127–9). More see the organ harvesting as a "modern resurrection." Consider also the music discussed in n40. Nonetheless, any affirmation sits incongruously beside (Leclerc and) the tomb station's reflections on the miserable's need for the resurrection.
43 Outside of the film's pre-title sequence and the troupe's farcical rendering of Fr Leclerc's play, the word "God" only occurs as an expletive.
44 In 1999, Stern, Jefford, and DeBona estimated that as much as 97 percent of cinema in Canada was from Hollywood (1999: 328). They argue that Arcand, working after the Quiet Revolution, is trying to tell a Jesus story in a world with no coherent way to represent God (1999: 322–6).
45 *Jésus de Montréal* followed this success. It is, therefore, a reflection on Arcand's own struggles with "commercial" art's temptation.

46 John Harkness contends that Arcand's films are about betrayal. Rémy's infidelities in *Le Déclin* are examples, but Harkness also observes that the revelation of infidelity near the film's end betrays the comic film's previous atmosphere (1989: 235, 238). Note also Arcand's tendency to juxtaposition, pastiche, and irony.

47 Arcand continued tracking these aging characters in *L'Âge des ténèbres* (Days of Darkness or The Age of Ignorance 2007). The comedy follows an aging, depressed bureaucrat who retreats into sexual fantasies. Despite its title, *La chute de l'empire américain* (The Fall of the American Empire 2018) is not a sequel.

48 Reinhartz finds *Jésus de Montréal* the most hopeful of the French-Canadian Christ-figure films she reviews (2021: 251–3).

49 Matters are more confusing in the recent TV series *Preacher* (2016–19). In the present, God has rejected Jesus because of his affair with Magdalene, and God himself has gone missing because of a conflict in heaven. The Grail has cloned multiple Jesuses, hoping to find the one that will usher in their apocalyptic empire. Unfortunately, the clones are idiots. Meanwhile, Preacher Jessie Custer searches for God and assesses his own messianic powers. Jesse—the messiah who opposes God—and his misfit band ultimately stop the apocalypse and save the world. The original Jesus, part of the supporting cast, rejects his apocalyptic destiny and God dies in heaven. In the end, matters are "simply" human (cf. *Jésus de Montréal*'s mortal son of man).

50 Koch Lorber released a DVD in 1989, but the Arrow DVD is the only widescreen version.

17

Jesus

Roger Young, director, Lux Vide, 1999

PLOT SUMMARY: HUMAN, FOR LOVE

Jesus has three parts: (1) an opening family drama (Walsh 2003: 7, 28–9); (2) the young man's subsequent Johannine career; and (3) the passion.¹ The first part is the most innovative, reflecting the production company's desire to create "family television" (cf. *Jesus of Nazareth* 1977; see Cultural Location). Jesus is a dreamy adolescent who is close to his father, despite sullen moments. Joseph's death sparks Jesus's coming of age, and he leaves home as his father had hoped he would (a biopic motif; see Reinhartz 2007: 18). Thereafter, Jesus's Johannine career stretches from the wedding at Cana to Lazarus's resurrection. Scriptural language, however, is rare (see Page 2006b; Tatum 2013: 226, 228–30). The passion is more traditional, but it pits the lamb of God against the Zealots, not the religious leaders (cf. Zealot troublemakers in *King of Kings* 1961; *Jesus of Nazareth*). The Romans play everyone as a farce for their amusement.

Like *Last Temptation* (1988), *Jesus* starts with a subjective point of view. Jesus dreams of violent events "in [his] name" (including the Crusades, Joan of Arc's burning, and a dying soldier's screams [for Jesus] in a First World War battle). Mimicking Scorsese's innovative POV, Roger Young's camera looks down on the prone Jesus (Jeremy Sisto)² as he wakes. This Jesus, however, has his father Joseph (Armin Mueller-Stahl) as companion. Joseph also pushes Jesus to his "mission."

Turning from this father–son scenario, *Jesus* introduces other significant characters—Mary (Jacqueline Bisset) at a well; Magdalene (Debra Messing) working as a prostitute;³ and, at more length, Pilate's arrival in Jerusalem (Gary Oldham).⁴ Like the Jesus epics, *Jesus* has several scenes focusing on the elite (opposition). The invented Livio (G. W. Bailey) comments on Jewish customs and serves as a Dark Hermit-like troublemaker. Livio welcomes Pilate, introduces him to Antipas, and helps facilitate, for his own amusement, a conflict between Pilate and Caiaphas (Christian Kohlund). When Caiaphas and other priests heroically offer "their necks," rather than allow Roman insignia to profane the temple (cf. *King of Kings*' priests who resist Pompey), Pilate withdraws. Later, however, Pilate will triumph, duping Caiaphas in Jesus's passion.

As the family drama continues, Joseph and Jesus make repairs at their "blood relatives'" home (Lazarus, Martha, and Mary [Stefania Rocca]).⁵ Jesus has a tender, adolescent romance with Mary of Bethany (contrast *Last Temptation*'s more adult relationships and *The King of Kings*' [1927] implied love triangle). When Joseph and Jesus return to Nazareth, they find their home ransacked and their goat taken for Roman taxes.⁶ Joseph bitterly laments, wondering when the people's suffering will end. Jesus stomps away petulantly, thinking his father⁷ is telling him to end their suffering. Mary follows Jesus, mending family fences. When they return, they find Joseph dying. Joseph's last words are that he loved Jesus "as his own." After Joseph's funeral, in the family tomb, Jesus tearfully begs God to raise/return his father/companion, instead of leaving him alone in his new work.⁸

When he fails at carpentry, his mother reminds him of his special past (a flashback shows Joseph's disbelief as Mary reports the annunciation)⁹ and tells him it is time to find his answers. His father (which one?) asks it.

Leaving for self-discovery, Jesus breaks his romantic ties with Mary. His old life is over, and he is not who she thinks he is. In contrast to Willem Dafoe's emotional wreckage in *Last Temptation*, Jeremy Sisto understates his devastating loss of Mary of Bethany (love), Joseph (fatherly mentor), and home (Mary).

At the Jordan, the Baptist (David O'Hara) screams for (political) justice. At a campfire, the cousins reminisce about their childhood trip to Jerusalem.¹⁰ A long flashback shows lambs taken to slaughter,¹¹ people chanting Hebrew scriptures, and the young Jesus teaching authorities about the prince of peace. John's most haunting memory, however, is of the crucifixions lining the road.¹² Instead of responding to this memory, Jesus asks John if he will baptize him (creating a link between baptism and cross). John agrees—if Jesus confesses his sins and dedicates his life to God.

At his baptism, an unearthly light engulfs Jesus. There is thunder;¹³ Jesus stands, bathed in more radiant light, and everyone kneels while the Baptist whispers, "the lamb of God." Jesus then wanders into the wilderness for his "testing" (not "temptation"; cf. *King of Kings*, which privileges and repeatedly returns to Lk. 4:12).

Satan appears as a woman in a modern, flowing red garment to tell Jesus he must become "like them," giving up divinity (cf. the kenosis in Phil. 2:5-11). As Jesus agrees, the earth shakes, and the camera looks down upon the screaming Jesus in a God's eye POV (cf. *The Passion of the Christ*'s [2004] shot of the defeated Satan at the cross). Satan welcomes Jesus to (human) life, disappears, and returns instantly as a man in a modern dark suit (Jeroen Krabbé). Employing various special effects, he tempts Jesus to use his divine power to solve humanity's problems and become the world's leader (be #1). Jesus retorts that he will create the kingdom through God's word and by being the poorest, the lamb of God. Laughing, Satan departs saying the test has only begun (cf. Lk. 4:13). Surprisingly, Jesus collapses laughing as well. Despite these Synoptic Gospel trappings, Jesus's Johannine ministry has begun—he has become "human" (Jn 1:14).

Laughter and joy mark Jesus's mission (he is the happiest Jesus in Jesus films). Like the troupe in *Godspell* (1973), he never walks when he can dance—frolic with children, roughhouse, or water-fight (see Figure 17.1). His disciples are less playful.

A dusty Jesus (Gen. 2:7?) returns to Nazareth. Andrew and John, who saw his baptism, are waiting for "the one." Jesus laughs when Andrew is not sure if Jesus is the messiah and when his mother mentions his followers. Mary insists, however, on Jesus's divine destiny by recalling (with flashbacks) his miraculous childhood (cf. *Infancy Gospel of Thomas* 2:1-3) and the magi's adoration.

At his cousin's wedding in Cana, Jesus drinks and dances (cf. *Last Temptation*'s dancing Jesus). Appalled at this "non-kingdom" profligacy, Andrew believes only when Jesus turns the water into wine—at his mother's insistence (contrast Jn 2:4-5).[14] Miracles induce faith here more than in any other Jesus film (except for *The Jesus Film* 1979).[15] Peter and James follow only after the miraculous catch;[16] and Thomas, after publicly berating Jesus as a charlatan, follows only after Jesus heals a lame boy. Later, the stilling of the storm and the walking on the water lead a disciple to confess, "the Son of God."

The calls of Judas and Matthew differ. Happening upon a Zealot attack on Roman tax collectors, Jesus tries to stop the carnage.[17] Barabbas slits a soldier's throat anyway and slaps blood onto both of Jesus's cheeks (cf. Mt. 5:39).[18] Jesus tells Barabbas he will be free only when he learns to love (Jesus's two basic themes), but Barabbas chooses the sword (cf. Judas's choice in *King of Kings*). A cowardly Judas emerges from the shadows to confront Jesus for weeping over (the non-human) Romans, and to reject Jesus's offer of friendship (cf. *Jesus of Nazareth*'s Barabbas's rejection of "the friend of the Romans"). Judas follows, however, when Jesus claims to be "the way" to freedom (Jn 14:6; cf. *Last Temptation*'s dichotomy between political and spiritual freedom).[19]

One of the attacked tax-collectors was Levi, whom Jesus renames Matthew. Despite Peter's objections (cf. *Jesus of Nazareth*'s similar scene), Jesus and the disciples relish a meal in Matthew's house as Jesus teaches Peter to love his enemies.

After the Baptist's beheading, Caiaphas sends his (invented) assistant Jared with the woman taken in adultery to expose "Joseph of Nazareth" (Jared corrects the name to "Jesus") as a fraud (cf. *The King of Kings*' similar trap). Their arrival interrupts Jesus's only film parable (Mt. 13:44). After doodling a fish in the dirt (cf. *Jesus of Nazareth*), Jesus refuses to condemn the woman. Magdalene watches, amazed that Jesus treats the adulteress as if she were "worth something." Jesus invites Magdalene to follow him to freedom, exactly as he has invited men (cf. *Mary Magdalene* 2018).

Suddenly, in mid-ministry, Jesus cleanses the temple, with Peter and Judas's assistance, denouncing the priests for caring more for Caesar than God.[20] Troublemaking Livio tries to trap Jesus on Roman taxes and, in the next scene (which opened the televised miniseries' second evening), reprises the incident as a satirical skit for Pilate's amusement.

Laughingly asking his disciples if they think he has anything to say, Jesus delivers a brief Sermon beside the Sea of Galilee. People laugh with Jesus as he blesses the poor and persecuted. He enjoins people to mercy and reliance on God, rejects purity regulations (cf. Mk 7), and (with a closeup of his pained mother) claims that those who do God's will, not she who birthed him, are blessed. That evening, Mary begins mentoring Magdalene after she comforts Mary over Jesus's rudeness.[21]

Jesus selects twelve disciples (kissing only Judas) as if picking sides for a game. He sends them away across the lake after a "holy huddle." A disciple's acclamation of Jesus as Son of God while he walks on the water functions like the Synoptic Gospels' confession and transfiguration scenes.[22]

On the way to Jerusalem for Passover, a Canaanite woman begs for help for her daughter (cf. Mt. 15:21-28). In a scene found only here (or in visual translations of Matthew) in Jesus films, this woman helps Jesus realize his message is also for Gentiles—

to Judas's (nationalistic) consternation. When he angrily demands Judas give the poor the (ominous) thirty pieces he has collected, Jesus further alienates Judas. Treating Magdalene more tenderly, Jesus tells her that speaking for him, not gender, makes one a disciple.

Word that Lazarus is dying interrupts the happy group's next-day travels. The mourning Mary of Bethany knows who Jesus is now (she did not when he left for the wilderness) and thus believes him when he says, "I am the resurrection." Jesus raises Lazarus[23] that they might believe, and Thomas embraces "the evidence." This triumphant scene contrasts vividly with Jesus's failure to raise Joseph.

The film's passion section opens as a divided Sanhedrin (cf. *Greatest Story* 1965 and *Jesus of Nazareth*) discusses the Lazarus miracle. Finally, Caiaphas asserts they must stop this false messiah with his rumored miracles before he starts a revolt Rome will crush (cf. Jn 11:50).[24] Meanwhile, Judas promises the Zealots Jesus will lead a revolt. Instead of arresting Jesus, Pilate plans to manipulate Caiaphas.

When Judas advises Jesus it is time to revolt, Jesus announces that his death will free people from sin, not from Rome. Aghast, Judas calls Jesus a traitor. He proves himself the film's villain by threatening Jesus that he "may have no choice" but to lead a violent revolution—a stance diametrically opposed to Jesus's freedom-of-choice message (see Walsh 2010: 141). Jesus dismisses Peter as "Satan" when he also opposes Jesus's plan (cf. Mk 8:33). Alone with his mother, Jesus says he dies to prove God's love (cf. Phil. 2:5-11; Jn 3:16; 15:13).

When the Zealots "cleanse the temple," the Romans quash the revolt (as in *King of Kings* and *Jesus of Nazareth*). Rejecting (the invented) Mordecai's support for Jesus in the Sanhedrin, Caiaphas falls into Pilate's trap by agreeing to bring Jesus to him for elimination.

The Last Supper is cinematically traditional. Judas arranges Jesus's betrayal with (the invented) Seth. Judas betrays (for thirty pieces) because Jesus is "not the man I thought he was" (contrast Mary of Bethany's new knowledge). In the garden, Jesus faces Satan's last test (cf. *Passion of the Christ*'s garden struggle).[25] Satan tells Jesus he dies in vain; humans cannot love, and they will kill in Jesus's name (visuals reprise Jesus's opening nightmare). As in the wilderness, Satan urges Jesus to make earth a paradise by fiat. Faithful to his free-will message, however, Jesus responds that he dies to show God loves enough to give freedom of choice (cf. Jn 3:16), so that people can make the divine image shine again (cf. *Godspell*'s opening voiceover).[26]

After Judas and Peter betray Jesus,[27] and a brief Sanhedrin trial, Caiaphas brings Jesus to Pilate. Pilate and Livio treat the trials, the people's choice, and the Ecce Homo as an amusing game. Pilate even tries to engage Caiaphas in the fun. Livio facilitates Pilate's desired outcome, urging the crowd to call for Barabbas's release.[28] In an aside to this smirking "devil," Pilate calls his hand washing the final blow (against Caiaphas?). Pilate does, however, condemn Jesus to crucifixion (as in *Jesus of Nazareth*; *The Jesus Film*), as Caiaphas closes his eyes (in sadness or weariness?).[29]

Mary, John, and Magdalene watch Jesus carry his crossbeam while Peter and Judas quarrel about whose betrayal was worse. At Golgotha, the soldiers nail Jesus (through his wrists) to the crossbeam as the holy trio agonizes. Everything happens swiftly.[30] As the soldiers hoist the crossbeam, Jesus asks God to forgive, but sarcastic, cynical Livio tells the "Messiah" they know "exactly" what they are doing. Jesus asks why God has forsaken him, but still commends his spirit to God.³¹ After he dies, an earthquake destroys the aqueduct behind him, and water floods around the cross.³²

Mary holds Jesus in a pietà as a gentle rain falls. Sarah Brightman sings "Pie Jesu" as background music.³³ After mourners carry Jesus to the tomb, his mother gently wipes his face. On Easter morning, Magdalene finds the empty tomb and reports the body's theft to the disciples. Peter, John, and Magdalene run to the tomb, where John believes "before seeing" and convinces Peter (cf. Jn 20:1-9). Lingering, Magdalene sees the risen Jesus. Thomas does not believe her report, until Jesus appears in the upper room (Jn 20:28). Jesus blesses those who believe without seeing (Jn 20:29) and commissions the disciples. As he walks to the window, he is transfigured into light, and disappears. Jesus's mother, clearly in charge, stands and calls Magdalene and then the others into a final "holy huddle."

In the international release, a modernly clad Jesus appears in a modern city laughingly embracing a swarm of children.³⁴ In the DVD version, LeAnn Rimes sings "I Need You," as the credits roll.³⁵

MEMORABLE CHARACTERS

1. Jesus is an ordinary guy (Reinhartz 2007: 106), except for the special effects (Walsh 2003: 29, 32). No other cinematic Jesus laughs and plays as much. Unlike *Last Temptation*'s human Jesus, this Jesus becomes (inhumanly) certain about his identity in the wilderness. Ironically, the certainty comes as Jesus "empties" himself of divinity (cf. Phil. 2:5-11) to demonstrate God's love to humans. He is not, however, very Jewish. He does not preach in synagogues, "break" the Sabbath, or debate the Pharisees.

2. In this family drama, Joseph and Mary are supportive, nurturing parents. "Father's" referent is often ambiguous, not clearly distinguishing between Joseph or Jesus's heavenly father. While Jesus begins his ministry (coming of age) only after Joseph's death, he never leaves Mary, his spiritual mentor, behind (cf. *King of Kings* and *Il messia*'s [1975] Marys). She is the leader of the post-resurrection community (cf. *Il messia* and *Son of Man*'s Marys).

3. While Magdalene is tradition's forgiven prostitute, she is also one of, if not chief among, Jesus's disciples (cf. *Mary Magdalene*).

4. Satan and Judas are Jesus's opponents, tempting him with power and dismissing the film's virtues of freedom and love. Judas also represents the Zealot folly. Like Judas in *Jesus of Nazareth*, Caiaphas is more dupe than villain. Still, he is the most noble Caiaphas in Jesus films to this point.

5. Pilate and Livio represent callous Rome, mildly amused at the colonials beneath them. Livio reprises earlier cinematic inventions like Sorak, the Dark Hermit, and Zerah (and noble Lucius in a different way).

Figure 17.1 Jesus roughhousing with his disciples in *Jesus*, directed by Roger Young, Lux Vide, 1999. All rights reserved.

MEMORABLE VISUALS

1 Montage of violence in Jesus's name in opening and in Gethsemane.
2 Special-effects baptism and wilderness (and, to a lesser extent, walking on water).
3 The laughing Jesus dancing and playing (roughhousing with the disciples [see Figure 17.1]).
4 Jesus learning from the Canaanite woman.
5 The fight between Judas and Peter while Jesus is on the Via Dolorosa.
6 Mary mentoring Magdalene and leading the disciples into a "holy huddle" after Jesus's departure.
7 The resurrected Jesus embraced by a swarm of children in a modern city.

KEY AUTHORITY/SCRIPTURE

1 The modern values of individualism (free choice) and love are the film's chief authorities.

2   The Jesus film tradition is another authority. Almost every scene alludes to a cinematic precursor. *Jesus* is a family-friendly, G-rated version of *Last Temptation*. *Jesus of Nazareth* is another major influence/authority.

3   Among the gospels, *Jesus* relies most upon John, but at a distance. Despite Johannine Easter emphases, *Jesus*'s miracles evoke a non-Johannine faith. Nevertheless, the ministry does move from Cana to Lazarus, and Jesus dies to demonstrate God's love (Jn 3:16).

4   The most important scriptural authority is Phil. 2:5-11, whose kenotic Christology the film employs (in the wilderness) to bridge the gap between its very human Jesus and his divine identity.

CULTURAL LOCATION/GENRE: FAMILY DRAMA, TELEVISION BIBLE

Italian entrepreneurs established the Lux Vide S.p.A production company in 1992 to create family-oriented television films for an international audience (Tatum 2013: 223). They have worked with RAI, Mediaset, Sky, and TNT. Their website touts *The Bible Collection* (1994–2002), sold in 144 countries, as a typical product. The collection is available in the United States from TNT in a seventeen-set DVD.[36] *Jesus* is part of that collection, but was first shown in the United States on CBS.[37] Except for *Genesis: The Creation and the Flood* (1994), the collections' films are comparable to *Jesus*, featuring political intrigue and romance in a historical setting—like Jesus epics generally (Chattaway 2001).[38] Roger Young and Raffaele Mertes, *Jesus*'s cinematographer, directed several of the films (five and six, respectively).

Other projects have aspired to film the Bible, including the failures of Dino De Laurentis (completing only *The Bible: In the Beginning ...* 1966) and John Heyman's New Media Bible (completing only *Genesis* and *Luke* [both in 1979]; see Chapter 14). Further, certain film trilogies' biblical spans are loosely comparable to that of *The Bible Collection*: Cecil B. DeMille's *The Ten Commandments* (1923), *The King of Kings*, and *The Sign of the Cross* (1932), and Sir Lew Grade's *Moses the Lawgiver* (1974), *Jesus of Nazareth*, and *A.D.* (1985).

More comparable now is Roma Downey and Mark Burnett's *The Bible*, broadcast weekly on the History Channel in March 2013, footage from which ultimately became the (unremarkable) feature *Son of God* (2014).[39] Five hours of the ten-hour miniseries covered HB/OT material (Genesis material through Abraham; the Exodus; the conquest of Jericho; Samson; Saul; David; Solomon; Exile [Daniel]; and Return). Four hours covered gospel material, while the last hour moved from resurrection appearances and Pentecost through Paul and martyrdoms to Revelation. The miniseries' popular success led to a sequel, *A.D.: The Bible Continues*, which aired on NBC in April–June 2015. It covered material in Acts 1–12.

Jesus (and its surrounding collection) is an international project, appealing broadly to a "family values audience," but not necessarily a religious one. By contrast, *The Bible* appeals to US evangelical Protestants. It has more violence and more special effects than *The Bible Collection*, gesturing (sometimes garishly) at the supernatural. By contrast, *Jesus* opens with a painful acknowledgment of the violence done in "the name of Jesus."[40] More than *The Bible*,[41] it belongs among other 1990s television comedies and dramas. Young's Jesus could easily walk onto the set of *Seinfeld* (1989–98) or *Friends* (1994–2004).[42] The film deals gently with family crises about sullen, but loving children; parents looking for work; children struggling to come of age and to find their own "life"; young adults wrestling with romance and love; and pushy, recently widowed, empty-nester mothers.

DIRECTOR

Roger Young was a successful director and producer of commercials in Chicago, even forming his own company before beginning a Los Angeles commute to work in various television capacities. He won an Emmy for outstanding direction in 1980 (for *Lou Grant*) and directed several pilots, including *Magnum, P.I.* (1980). Roger Young found his career niche, however, in directing television miniseries.

Young is one of the most prolific Bible film directors of all time. In addition to *Jesus*, he also directed *Joseph* (1995), *Moses* (1996), *Solomon* (1997), and *St. Paul* (2000) in *The Bible Collection*. All were shot in Morocco,[43] and TNT aired the first two initially in the United States. While *Joseph* won an Emmy for best miniseries, Peter Chattaway claims the series "comes of age" with Young's *Moses*. Compared to other Moses film directors, Young downplays violence and special effects. Further, Young's Moses (Ben Kingsley) stands out among cinematic Moses for his emotion, humor, and humanity (see Chattaway 1996).

Young's Jesus is quite similar. Despite his divinity, he is a model of/for authentic modern individuation (Walsh 2003: 29). Young treats Paul similarly in *St. Paul* (Walsh 2016e: 504), providing him with an understandable, modern psychological dilemma. Where Young's Jesus moves from one dead father to another heavenly father, Young's Paul must choose between two living father figures, representing different kinds of Judaism: Gamaliel's tolerant Pharisaism, and the invented Reuben's violent ethnocentrism. Despite his long friendship with Reuben and his temporary flirtation with Reuben's persecution of Christians, Paul gradually moves toward a "spiritual" path like that of Young's Jesus, characterized again as a message of love and freedom of choice. *St. Paul* demonstrates the message's victory through Paul's repeated escapes from Reuben's murderous traps (often helped by Reuben's wife Dinah, formerly Paul's love interest), Reuben's death, and Paul's arrival in Rome.

After *The Bible Collection*, Young directed more historical-period television (e.g., *Imperium: Augustus* 2003) and biblical fare (*Barabbas* 2012; *The Red Tent* 2014). The latter, based on Anita Diamant's 1997 novel, is the best known. Lifetime, which aired the miniseries on December 7–8, 2014, used it to return to original programming. The film's protagonist is Jacob's only daughter Dinah (Rebecca Ferguson). The film provides the biblical character (Gen. 34) with a backstory in the red tent, where women spend their time of menstruation and share a tradition/religion hidden from the tribe's men; with a love story involving (not a rape by) Shechem; and with an afterlife of Egyptian exile partially paralleling that of her more famous brother Joseph. Even more non-biblical than *Jesus*, it, like that precursor, creates a larger, formative place in the "biblical" story for women.

TRIMARK DVD, 174 MINUTES, 2000
DVD Extras

Music Video
    LeAnn Rimes, "I Need You" (from the *Jesus* soundtrack)

Soundtrack Presentation (7:30 minutes long)
    LeAnn Rimes
    98 Degrees
    Steven Curtis Chapman
    Yolanda Adams
    Lonestar
    DC Talk
    Jaci Velasquez
    Edwin McCain
    Hootie and the Blowfish
    Avalon
    Sarah Brightman
    Patrick Williams

Letter from the Pope
    November 25, 1999
Subtitles: English, French, Spanish

DVD Chapters

1. Main Credits
       Jesus's nightmare, 0:12
2. Mary, 3:04
       Livio, 3.07
       Magdalene, 6:34
3. Corruption, 7.26
4. Carpenter, 11:24
5. Suffering, 16:25
       Joseph dies, 19:22
6. Angel, 20:04
       Jesus visits Mary and Martha, 25:21
7. John the Baptist, 25.24
8. Jerusalem, 31:22
       Flashback to crosses, 37:02

9 The Lamb, 37:20

      Baptism, 37:46

      "To be like them," 38:52

10 Morning star, 41:10

11 Messiah, 46:40

      Mary relates the bird miracle, 49:00

      Mary recalls kings' gifts, 51:04

12 Water into Wine, 52:35

      Mary: "It's time!"

13 Sinner, 56:38

      Great catch of fish/call, 58:25

14 The Word, 1.02:20

      Doubting Thomas sees Jesus heal lame man, 1.03:16

15 Zealots, 1.07:38

      Barabbas slaps Jesus on both cheeks, 1.10:38

      Jesus (to Judas): "I am the way" (Jn 14:6), 1.12:25

      Jesus instructs Peter to love his enemy, Matthew, 1.13:44

16 Forgiveness [in Matthew's house], 1.13:58

      Livio sees Salome's dance (Mk 6:17-28), 1.15:38

17 Celebration, 1.19:53

      Magdalene watches woman caught in adultery scene, 1.21:00

18 [Cleansing the] House of Prayer, 1.25:40

      Livio asks about Roman taxes

19 Deliverer, 1.27:35

      Livio's skit for Pilate

20 Ownership [of the world], 1.30:50

      Jesus's Sermon: "What can they buy with all that money?"

          "Blessed the womb," 1.34:33

21 Apostles, 1.34:56

      The twelve, 1.36:12

22 Faith, 1.40:09

      Walking on water (Mt. 14:28-36)

      Livio reports feeding of the five thousand to Antipas, 1.43:56

      Canaanite woman's daughter, 1.44:45

23 Friend, 1.46:38

    Mary brings Magdalene to Jesus

    Jesus demands Judas give the thirty pieces to poor, 1.48:48

24 Resurrection [of Lazarus], 1.51:24

25 Peacekeeper, 1.55:20

    Caiaphas: What to do with Jesus?

    Triumph, 1.57:55

    Barabbas's men ask Judas when Jesus will lead revolt

26 God's will, 1.59:09

    Livio tells Pilate to arrest Jesus

    Judas wants Jesus to lead revolt, 2.00:27

    Jesus calls Peter "Satan," 2.02:26

    Jesus tells his mother privately: "I must die to prove God's love," 2.03:15

27 Sacrifice, 2.03:47

    Romans put down Zealot revolt in temple

    Caiaphas blames Jesus (Jn 11:50), 2.04:26

    Amused, Pilate and Livio dupe Caiaphas

28 Last Supper, 2.07:57

    Judas's betrayal, 2.12:01

29 Judas, 2.13:19

    Peter's betrayals prophesied

    Satan tests Jesus again, 2.16:11

30 Betrayal, 2.17:58

    Satan shows Jesus the future killing in his name again

    Judas's betrayal, 2.20:16; 2.21:13

    To Caiaphas, 2.22:00

        Peter's betrayals

31 Believe, 2.24:40

    Caiaphas brings Jesus to Pilate (Jn 18:28-38), 2.25:38

32 Kings, 2.29:30

    Livio and Antipas

    Back to Pilate, 2.32:52

        Livio leads the cries for Barabbas

33 Sentenced, 2.35:55

    Pilate and Livio: "Hail the king of the Jews," 2.36:30

    Barabbas mocks Jesus, 2.36:49

    Pilate washes hands, 2.37:11

    Via Dolorosa, 2.37:50

34 Crucifixion, 2.39:51

    Earthquake; aqueduct breaks, 2.43:25

    Deposition, 2.43:48

    Burial, 2.44:17

    Magdalene to tomb, 2.45:18

35 Ascension, 2.45:21

    Peter and John to tomb

    "Woman, why are you weeping?" 2.47:22

    Thomas, 2.49:08

    Great Commission, 2.51:35

    Ascension, 2.52:13

NOTES

1. The international versions are longer than the US versions. Imdb.com lists the most important material missing from US versions: (1) Joseph rejects the pregnant Mary (in a longer scene); (2) Lazarus throws Jesus out after Jesus rejects Mary; (3) Joan of Arc's execution appears during Jesus's Gethsemane test; (4) a longer treatment of Jesus's crucifixion; (5) Judas's hanging; and (6) Jesus's modern, post-resurrection appearance (shot on Malta) with children. For more detail, see Pagano (n.d.). The film was shot in Morocco.
2. Sisto was twenty-five when he played Jesus. While recognizable from previous film roles in *Grand Canyon* (1991), *Clueless* (1995), and *Suicide Kings* (1997), he is better known for long-running television roles in *Six Feet Under* (2001–5), *Law & Order* (2008–11), and *Suburgatory* (2011–14).
3. Messing had just begun her role as Grace in NBC's *Will & Grace* (1998–2006, 2017–20).
4. Oldham is the film's most accomplished actor. He won the Academy Award for Best Actor for his performance as Churchill in *Darkest Hour* (2017). His villains are particularly highly regarded (e.g., in *True Romance* 1997; *Léon: The Professional* 1994; and *The Fifth Element* 1997).
5. Jesus is an only child.
6. The movie does not portray the family as poor "enough" to alienate its modern audience. Mary almost always wears the elite's red- and blue-dyed clothes (as in later Christian art), and the family house has a second story. Jesus sleeps in his own room, on a bed with sheets and a pillow.
7. "Father's" referent is particularly ambiguous in this sequence.
8. The scene foreshadows and merges elements of Lazarus's resurrection, Jesus's Gethsemane trial, and the cry of dereliction.

9   No one mentions the virginal conception—only angelic visits.
10 Arriving in Jerusalem, Joseph says they are not in Nazareth anymore, which Adele Reinhartz compares to the famous line in *The Wizard of Oz* (1939) (2007: 7).
11 Jesus is the lamb of God, but the film makes less of lamb imagery than *Jesus Christ Superstar* (1973), *Jesus of Nazareth*, and *Last Temptation*.
12 Mary tries to shield Jesus from this sight. Cf. Mary's actions in *Son of Man* (2006) at the slaughter of the innocents and the infant Jesus looking at the crucified in *Greatest Story*.
13 Is this thunder the voice from heaven? The international version includes the heavenly voice (Pagano n.d.).
14 Andrew is more important than in any other Jesus film.
15 The film does not explain the contradiction between Jesus's wilderness renunciation of miraculous powers and his ministry's faith-inducing miracles. While the latter contradicts the Johannine notion of faith, John believes in the resurrection "without seeing" and the resurrected Jesus quotes Jn 20:29.
16 Jesus renames Simon "Peter" at their first meeting.
17 Notably, oppressive Roman taxation (and Joseph's death) "called" Jesus to his ministry. See also Livio's later trap.
18 *Last Temptation* also presents this teaching as an incident, reported by Judas.
19 Perhaps he follows because Jesus mysteriously knows his name.
20 Jesus does not touch the sacrificial animals.
21 Mary does not judge (Magdalene) because she has been judged. In the international version, Joseph initially rejects Mary's "annunciation story." Later, Jesus's acceptance of the former prostitute causes his mother to tell him that his father "would be so proud." When Jesus asks, "Which one?" Mary laughingly answers, "Both" (1.47:44).
22 Livio reports the multitude's feeding to Antipas. Livio repeatedly taunts Antipas suggesting Jesus is the Baptist revived. Earlier, he helped catalyze the Baptist's execution.
23 As is now cinematic tradition, the camera frames Jesus at the tomb's entrance from within. See Staley (2021).
24 When he first arrived in Jerusalem, Pilate called the temple the heart of Jewish resistance to Rome.
25 Barnes Tatum calls this scene the film's theological center (2013: 231), but it is so only when paired with the wilderness temptation and Jesus's interactions with Judas about true freedom.
26 That Jesus dies to show God's love is a major atonement theory (touted famously by Abelard), but cinema prefers to show Jesus's death as a sacrifice for sins or as a conflict with Satan.
27 Jesus predicts Peter's "betrayal" (not denial), thus pairing Judas and Peter. Both *Il vangelo* (1964) and *Jesus of Nazareth* also pair the characters' flight and grief. See Telford (2005).
28 In a rare moment in Jesus films, Barabbas also mocks Jesus.
29 The former would make this character film's most sympathetic Caiaphas (see Reinhartz 2007: 220).
30 About ten minutes elapse between sentencing and entombment, so the crucifixion is less than 6 percent of the film.
31 The film does not include Simon of Cyrene, the penitential thief, spear thrust, or centurion's "confession."
32 This scene may recall Jn 19:34 or the (rain) water and blood flowing from the cross and healing Ben-Hur's leprous family (1959).

33 The song, continuing through the burial, comes from Andrew Lloyd Webber's "Requiem." As Webber merges the traditional "Pie Jesu" with the "Agnus Dei," Jesus is again the lamb of God, who takes away the sins of the world.
34 This end is available on YouTube. See https://www.youtube.com/watch?v=sO0yX7Y-xtU.
35 The music merges religious and romantic love as popular music often does. Nonetheless, the lyrics recall film themes/scenes: Rimes finds both freedom and love in him (the film Jesus's basic teaching); she needs him "like water" (cf. the torrent at the cross); and, most religiously, she needs him "like mercy from heaven's gate." The DVD advertises a soundtrack of adult contemporary music, *Jesus: Music from and Inspired by the Epic Mini-Series*, including this song, which was released before the miniseries aired in the United States and was designed to promote and capitalize upon the miniseries. For critique, see Ruhlmann (2000). Cf. the mockery of such crass commercialism in *Life of Brian*'s (1979) final voiceover.
36 The collection also includes *Abraham* (1993), *Genesis: The Creation and the Flood* (1994), *Jacob* (1994), *Joseph* (1995), *Moses* (1995), *Samson and Delilah* (1996), *David* (1997), *Solomon* (1997), *Jeremiah* (1998), *Esther* (1999), *The Apocalypse* (2000), *Joseph of Nazareth* (2000), *Mary Magdalene* (2000), *St. Paul* (2000), *Judas* (2001), and *Thomas* (2001).
37 TNT envisioned a "fantasy," with Jesus flying through the air and Gabriel "emceeing," while performing magic, but Lux wanted a more "historical" production (Dempsey 1998). Accordingly, the film was shown on CBS in the United States on May 14–15, 2000. It aired in Italy on December 5–6, 1999. In Italy, it was the year's highest-rated program, reaching an audience comparable to those of soccer world championships (Schneider 1999).
38 Matt Page compares *Jesus* and *Jeremiah* specifically (2016a).
39 *The Bible* promotes Jesus's divinity overtly and subtly. The actor playing Jesus (Diogo Morgado) appears as "messenger/God" in some HB/OT scenes, and Robert Powell (*Jesus of Nazareth*'s divine "Jesus") narrates *The Bible*'s UK version. For a comparison of the miniseries and *Son of God*, see Chattaway (2014).
40 Contrast *Jesus of Nazareth*'s affirmation of apostolic, institutional Christianity. In *Jesus*, religion is more personal and radically individual. Further, *Jesus of Nazareth*'s emphasis on inward spirituality becomes freedom of choice in *Jesus*. Religion is also now something that "feels good." One can almost imagine this Jesus saying that life can be "easy" (cf. the temptation of *Greatest Story*'s Dark Hermit).
41 As with *Jesus of Nazareth*, (rapid) fades to black often suggest commercial locations (see Chapter 12). The CBS broadcast sandwiched commercials about noodles in a cup, cosmetics, Gas-X, IAMS cat food, US West ("I've got the power!"), and Kentucky Fried Chicken between Jesus's baptism and his wilderness test. Without irony, the film ended with a commercial advertising a phone number where viewers could place orders for VHS tapes of the movie for $29.98. See also n35.
42 Young directed Sisto again in episodes of *L.A. Law*.
43 Part of *St. Paul* was shot in Malta.

18

The Miracle Maker

Derek W. Hayes and Stanislav Sokolov, directors, BBC, 2000

PLOT SUMMARY: A LITTLE CHILD SHALL LEAD THEM

This stop motion puppetry film is set in a realistically constructed first-century Palestine, like those of the epics,[1] but it presents its story from a child's POV (Tamar) and for children.[2] The opening camera draws in on a walled city, "Sepphoris, Upper Galilee; Year 90 of the Roman occupation,"[3] near Nazareth where day-laborer Jesus might find work (tektōn in Mk 6:3; see Chattaway 2007).

Jairus and his pre-adolescent daughter Tamar enter crowded Sepphoris.[4] A Roman soldier rudely shoulders Jairus aside, but family friend Cleopas (of Lk. 24:18) greets them warmly. He points out new synagogue construction, on which Jesus (unidentified) works. Jairus is seeking help for chronically ill Tamar. While her father consults a doctor, Tamar watches Jesus (still unidentified) stop a cruel overseer from whipping "Mad Mary" (Magdalene).[5] Sadly, the doctor has only palliatives for the failing Tamar. Both the family and Jesus (still unidentified) leave the city.[6]

Jesus returns to his mother's home in Nazareth and tells her he has quit his job because he "has other work,"[7] prompting her memory of her twelve-year-old in the temple "about" his "father's business" (Lk. 2:43-50).[8] The film deploys her memory in hand-drawn (cel) animation, this film's device for flashbacks, embedded stories, and characters' interior views.[9] Jesus spends the night, and as he sleeps, Mary remembers the nativity (in cel animation).

Abruptly, the film segues to a river where the Baptist speaks of a coming powerful one (Lk. 3:16). Jesus arrives, and John identifies him as the lamb of God who takes away the sin of the world (Jn 1:29). Jesus baptizes himself (all the baptisms shown are self-baptisms) and then rises into an ethereal spotlight. A heavenly voice addresses Jesus as beloved son (three times), and a bird's shape is briefly visible in the intensifying light.

In the wilderness ("for battle," according to John), a shadowy, animated man/bird follows Jesus. When Jesus collapses, cel animation presents a special-effects temptation sequence (following Luke's order). The sequence ends, as in *King of Kings* (1961), with Jesus refusing to test God (Lk. 4:12). Notably, Satan has a Roman haircut and wears Roman-style clothing, while Jesus has a more Semitic appearance.[10]

After another abrupt cut, Jesus meets his friend Lazarus at a spring and goes home with him (cf. *Greatest Story* 1965, *Last Temptation* 1988, and *Jesus* 1999). There, Jesus talks with Mary about his new work, building God's kingdom (Mt. 6:10), while Martha complains

(Lk. 10:38-42). The next day, on a grassy hill, Jesus teaches a small group—including Cleopas, Tamar, and her mother Rachel—to trust God (Mt. 7:7, 11), to act on his word (Mt. 7:24-27; cel animation illustrates the "parable" for children seated around Jesus), and to come "unto him" if they hunger and thirst (cf. Jn 6:35, 37).

Religious leaders scowl in the background, and ill Tamar, who refuses to leave, collapses in the sun. Zealots watch from a nearby cave as Judas argues Jesus's unusual powers could empower a successful revolt (cf. the Judases in *King of Kings*, *Jesus of Nazareth*, and *Jesus 1999*). An animated sequence illustrates Judas's violent desires before he leaves to follow Jesus.

In Capernaum, Roman soldiers mill about ominously; Matthew fails to collect taxes from Mad Mary (her frightful delusions appear in cel animation) and from Simon, who has had "no catch." Jesus walks imperially onto Simon's boat at quitting time, ordering Simon to push out again. After teaching about the mustard-seed kingdom (Lk. 13:18-19), Jesus sends Simon farther out to catch fish that "hide from the sunlight." After the miraculous catch, Jesus forgives Simon (cf. the repentant Peter in *The Jesus Film* 1979) and promises to make him a fisher of men.

From a balcony, Tamar watches crowds overrunning Simon's house. Jesus tells people to avoid judging others (illustrated by slapstick cel animation) before people let a paralytic through the roof. Jesus's (healing) forgiveness of the paralytic angers (invented) Asher ben Azarah, a Jerusalem priest preparing a report on Jesus for the authorities (cf. *Greatest Story*'s Sorak). The healed man, however, dances in the streets while Jairus's family looks on forlornly.

That rainy night, Mad Mary roams the streets. The film shifts to cel animation, illustrating Magdalene's tormented, demonic world (Lk. 8:2). Jesus releases her from her fragmented selves (cf. Magdalene's exorcism in *The King of Kings* 1927).

At a well, Jesus plays with children and haltingly calls his disciples, starting with Simon, whom he names the Rock (Peter). The most dramatic choices are those of Thomas, who realizes slowly that Jesus is talking to him, and the tax-collector Matthew.

Rachel finally demands that Jairus take Tamar to Jesus. Meanwhile, wealthy Simon (the film never uses the word "Pharisee") agrees to invite Jesus to his house for "review." The wealthy critique Jesus's disreputable associations, but he explains he has come to call sinners. As if in illustration, Magdalene (as the sinful woman of Lk. 7:36-50) arrives to anoint Jesus's feet with her tears. When Jesus forgives her, Asher and the religious leaders, except for Jairus (and Cleopas), declare Jesus a demoniac and those "with Jesus" God's enemies (cf. Mk 3:22-30).

At home, Jairus's daughter is near death, so he rushes to Jesus. Jesus agrees to help, but the hemorrhaging woman delays him, and Tamar dies before his arrival. Jesus tells Jairus to believe and his daughter will be well (Lk. 8:50; cf. cinema's portrayal of Lazarus's resurrections). Jesus walks into Tamar's room, and she "wakes" into the light (cf. the blind girl's healing in *The King of Kings*).[11] Now Tamar dances in the streets.

The joy is short-lived, however, as word arrives that Antipas has killed the Baptist. Foreshadowing Gethsemane, Jesus weeps alone on "the cold stone." Meanwhile, Asher and an elderly accomplice goad Antipas into action against this kingdom-destroying

Jesus, because Antipas (with Roman haircut) fears Rome's reprisals. As if in concert, Jesus tells Peter the time has come, and Judas, drawing his sword, thinks victory over Rome has finally arrived.[12]

Everyone, including Jairus's family, sets off for Passover in Jerusalem. There, Pilate discusses crowd control with the centurion/tribune Quintilus, who has recently put down a Galilean revolt. Pilate arrested its leader Barabbas, Judas's friend, and crucified 117 Jews.[13] Pilate plans to execute Barabbas on Passover, the Jewish day celebrating freedom. Meanwhile, the disciples argue about their kingdom status, but Jesus, holding a toddler, defines the kingdom's greatest as "humble children." Tamar looks on admiringly. In response to questions about neighbors, Jesus tells the Good Samaritan parable (cel animation).[14]

Early the next morning, word arrives of Lazarus's deadly illness. When Tamar wonders why Jesus does not hurry to help his friend, Jesus ominously replies that their grief has a purpose—God's glory. The disbelieving Asher reports the "dark deception" of Lazarus's resurrection (in cel animation) to urge Caiaphas to deal with the mob's miraculous messiah.

The triumphal entry, including Jairus's family and Cleopas, follows immediately. Judas has a vision (cel animated) of victory over the oppressive city. Caiaphas calms frightened priests, saying they will aim Caesar's anger at one man to save the people (Jn 11:47-51). As Jesus enters the temple, a cel-animated flashback recalls his pre-adolescent temple experience. After he cleanses the temple, Jesus responds to a question about paying Roman taxes. His answer mollifies Quintilus, but disillusions Judas who struggles with the horror of a crucified, defeated messiah (cel animated). Jesus finally predicts the Son of Man's death (cel animation), and the animation segues back to puppetry, with Jesus still talking about the Son of Man giving his life (Mk 10:45). Judas runs away in angst, sees his imprisoned friend Barabbas, and has a horrifying cel-animated vision of crucifixion, his betrayal of Jesus, and his subsequent luxury. Thereafter, Judas betrays Jesus to Asher.

Jesus celebrates a Da Vinci-style Last Supper, as Jairus's family, Cleopas, Magdalene, and others sit nearby at smaller tables. Tamar notices Jesus's distinctive manner of holding the bread high aloft to bless it. After the eucharistic language,[15] Jesus tells Judas several times, as if forcing betrayal, to do what he must do. When Judas leaves, Jesus again says it is time. Outside, Cleopas and Jairus want explanations, but Jesus demurs, saying he will come to them soon. He tells Tamar (not Peter) she cannot go with him, but that she will be with him in his father's house (from Jn 13:36-14:2).

In the cel-animated garden sequence, Jesus sees "the cup" aloft before him and asks repeatedly for another way. Satan parts the trees, like the Red Sea, for Jesus's escape, but Jesus accepts his father's will. The film returns to puppetry, and Judas betrays Jesus with a kiss (Jesus cites Lk. 22:48).[16] A brawl breaks out and Peter slices a guard's ear, but Jesus shouts "No!" White light stops everything. When visuals return, Jesus heals the guard, tells Peter violence is not the way, and tells the guards this is their (dark) time.

Peter's denials and Jesus's trial before the Sanhedrin are intercut (as in John). Joseph of Arimathea objects to illegalities,[17] but Caiaphas silences him. Jesus refuses to respond because they do not believe, but finally says they will see the Son of Man enthroned. Accusing Jesus of blasphemy, the Sanhedrin sends him to Pilate. Jesus locks eyes with Peter en route, after Peter's last denial (Lk. 22:61).

The priests accuse Jesus of "stirring up the people," of refusing to pay taxes to Caesar (only in Lk. 23:2), and of claiming to be king of the Jews. Finding no cause against Jesus, Pilate sends the Galilean rebel to Antipas (only in Luke). After mockery, Antipas returns "the king of the Jews" to Pilate. Seeing Jesus in transit, Judas futilely laments his betrayal of an innocent man to callous Asher.[18] Spotlit, Judas lies crumpled in the dark streets.

When Pilate declares Jesus innocent, Asher provokes a small crowd to cry out (meekly) for Jesus's crucifixion and then to ask for Barabbas's release. After Caiaphas threatens Pilate "with Caesar," Pilate washes his hands (Mt. 27:24) and tells the centurion to "deal with their king according to Roman law" (cf. the Roman condemnations in *Jesus of Nazareth*; *The Jesus Film*; *Jesus* 1999).[19]

As Jesus carries the crossbar on the Via Dolorosa (with few watching), Jairus's family awakes and rushes inside the city. Jesus falls on the Via Dolorosa, and Tamar, not Veronica or Ben-Hur, reaches out to comfort him (see Figure 18.1). The procession quickly ascends a hill. A hammer rises and falls, but the nailing is not onscreen. As a storm approaches, Jesus's cross is raised amidst two others. The priests and Satanic inner voices tempt Jesus to prove his messianic identity by leaving the cross. Instead, Jesus entrusts his spirit to God (Lk. 23:46) and declares it finished (Jn 19:30). The temple veil rips, and the centurion declares Jesus, hanging on the cross in the dark, the Son of God (not "innocent" as in Lk. 23:47).

Jairus's family deposes Jesus in a spotlit scene and forms part of the burial party. Magdalene laments—and echoing her Mad Mary past—runs wailing from the tomb to the empty cross.

Later, she joyously discovers the empty tomb and meets the resurrected Jesus, but Peter, calling her mad (Mary), does not believe. When he visits the tomb (Lk. 24:34?), he sees Jesus and believes. Thomas does not believe Peter's claim or the Emmaus road report (cel animation).[20] In the cel animation, Tamar recognizes Jesus because of the distinctive way he holds the bread aloft. Thomas believes only when Jesus appears to him (Jn 20:28-29).

The film closes with Jesus commissioning his apostles (combining Mt. 28:19-20 and Acts 1:8a) and ascending (fading into light). Tamar has the last word as she comforts a frightened child with Jesus's words to her in the garden (Jn 14:1-2). Looking directly at the camera, she says the kingdom has come and he is with us forever. The camera pans to a blue sky and the credits begin, accompanied by Anne Dudley's "Pie Jesu."

MEMORABLE CHARACTERS

1 The filmmakers amplify Jairus's unnamed daughter in Lk. 8:40-56 by inventing scenes and by imputing gospel characters' words (e.g., Peter in Jn 13:36) and other film characters' actions to her (like Ben-Hur on the Via Dolorosa). *The King of Kings*' Mark is the only comparably important child in Jesus films. Strictly speaking, Tamar does not provide the film's POV, but she serves as Jesus's chief witness (cf. Greydanus 2021: 81–2), speaking the film's Jesus message directly to the camera/audience in the finale.

2 Jesus is a craftsman and teacher (cf. *Il messia* 1975). The film contains an unusual amount of Jesus's teaching for a children's film—although primarily in brief snatches

and in several parables' effective cel animation. Surprisingly, the film does not concentrate on Jesus's miracles except for its three resurrections: Tamar's, the story's foundational miracle; Lazarus's, remarkably downplayed (see Staley 2021: 49); and Jesus's (only *Risen* 2016 gives it as much attention). The film has a lofty Christology, but still presents Jesus humanly, as capable of humor (cf. *Jesus* 1999), grief, and temptation—particularly in cel animation "inside views" during his wilderness and garden struggles (cf. Jesus's depiction in *Last Temptation*).

3 Cel-animated inside views also humanize Magdalene and Judas. Unfortunately, the film equates "Mad Mary" (Lk. 8:2) with the woman of Lk. 7:36-50. After the anointing, she is often in Jesus's company and is the resurrection's first witness.

4 Cel-animated inside views show Judas's Zealot desires. Despite his crumpled, pathetic repentance in the dark streets, he, like the rest of the story, remains quite conventional.[21]

5 While the film creates sympathetic "Jewish characters" (see n10), the typical elite villains are all callously, politically motivated. As in many other films (e.g., *Greatest Story*, *Jesus of Nazareth*, and *Jesus* 1999), the chief villain, Asher ben Azarah, is an invented character catalyzing Jesus's rejection and crucifixion.

MEMORABLE VISUALS

1 The cel-animated inside views of Jesus's trials, Magdalene's horrible, demonic world, and Judas's path to betrayal.

2 The enlivening of Jesus's teachings through cel animation (e.g., the two foundations, the log in the eye, and the Good Samaritan).

Figure 18.1 Tamar reaches out, Ben-Hur style, to comfort Jesus in *The Miracle Maker*, directed by Derek W. Hayes and Stanislav Sokolov, BBC, 2000. All rights reserved.

3 Jesus's work on the Sepphoris synagogue.
4 Jesus lamenting John's death.
5 The many scenes in which Jesus is with children, but particularly those where he is with Tamar.
6 Tamar's Ben-Hur scene in which she "just" touches Jesus's hand on the Via Dolorosa (see Figure 18.1).

KEY AUTHORITY/SCRIPTURE

1 The cel animation of characters' subjectivity gives the film an authoritative aura like that provided by silent intertitles and epic voiceovers. The inside views take the audience places humans cannot ordinarily go.
2 Murray Watts, the screenwriter, says Lk. 8:40-56 was the script's starting point (although Mk 5:21-43 also provides details). Richard Burridge, film advisor, claims more broadly that Luke is the film's primary source (see Reinhartz 2007: 270 n17). Matt Page finds only three film scenes prior to the resurrection without Lukan parallels (Mt. 7:24-27; Jn 11:1-46; Jn 11:47-48). Further, Page identifies seven film episodes found only in Luke (in their order of appearance: 2:16-17, 42-50; 10:38-42, 25-37; 24:33-35, 13-32, 48-53) (Page 2006c).
3 The film also relies on non-Lukan gospel material, particularly John (e.g., lamb of God; Lazarus's resurrection; resurrection appearances; and Tamar's "many houses" finale).
4 Appropriately, the children's film emphasizes accepting the kingdom like a child (Mk 10:15) in deliberate contrast to Judas, Jesus's disciples, and the elite's power politics. Tamar's ubiquity and "final word" underline the investment in children's authority.

CULTURAL LOCATION/GENRE: CHILDREN'S ANIMATED (BIBLE) STORY

The Miracle Maker was released in 1999 as a Welsh language video and later aired on S4C television. Televised English versions later appeared in the UK and in the United States (on ABC on April 23, 2000). S4C's remit is the airing of Welsh-language television. It commissions work from BBC Cymru Wales (and others) and has a reputation for airing children's animation, including the highly touted, award-winning *Shakespeare: The Animated Tales* (twelve thirty-minute episodes [1992-4]). It was a joint Welsh-Russian production and utilized a mixture of animation techniques including stop motion puppetry, hand-drawn cels, and digitally manipulated paintings. The series has been widely used to introduce children to Shakespeare.

S4C followed this successful venture with a similar treatment of nine thirty-minute Hebrew Bible tales in the 1996 *Testament: The Bible in Animation*. Created by Naomi Jones and developed by Derek W. Hayes, the series included episodes on Creation and the Flood, Abraham, Joseph, Moses, Ruth, David and Saul, Elijah, Daniel, and Jonah. Its success led

S4C to the feature-length *The Miracle Maker*, also a Russian-Welsh production. The film uses a variety of animated styles and utilizes many of the series' people in its production and cast.

The Miracle Maker is the first, well-known, feature-length Jesus animation.[22] Biblical animation, however, is now mushrooming, so more animated Jesuses may soon appear.[23] Animation's low-budget possibilities and family-friendly appeal make it attractive. Most of the biblical offerings so far have tended, like *The Miracle Maker*, toward conservative theology (Heard 2016: 275–81).[24]

The Miracle Maker is distinctive in biblical animation for its characters' "Semitic" appearance.[25] Following a trend going back to S4C's *Shakespeare: The Animated Tales*, *The Miracle Maker* deliberately avoids Disney animation's big-eyed sentimentality. Given the use of Russian puppeteers, the puppets tend to an orthodox or iconic mien. According to Murray Watts, this iconic choice was intentional because one must see "through" a material representation to find "the essence of the human being" (in DVD Extra, "Making of" Documentary).

FILMMAKERS

Successful playwright Murray Watts scripted both S4C's animated *Beowulf* (1998) and this film. He is best known for *The Miracle Maker*, its novelization (2000), and the *Lion Bible for Children* (1991), which has been translated into several languages and has sold over a million copies. Watts also wrote the script for *KJB—The Book That Changed the World* (2011).

Stanislav Sokolov directed the Russian stop motion puppetry. Before *The Miracle Maker*, he was known primarily for film shorts. He directed two of the *Shakespeare: The Animated Tales*, "The Tempest" (1992) and "The Winter's Tale" (1994), both of which were stop motion puppetry.

Derek W. Hayes was the director in Wales. A British animator since 1973, Hayes formed Animation City in 1979 with Phil Austin. He has produced commercials (Lego, Carlsberg), music videos (Madonna, Rod Stewart, Elton John), television titles (*Jeeves and Wooster* 1990–3), and graphics. He directed the award-winning television short *Prince Cinders* (1993). Before directing *The Miracle Maker*, he developed *Testament: The Bible in Animation*, and directed two of its episodes: "Elijah" and "Ruth" (both in 1996). He also directed *Y Mabinogi* (Otherworld 2003), a collection of medieval Welsh legends, for S4C. Based on a graphic novel, the film was for older children and adults.

FAMILY HOME ENTERTAINMENT DVD, 87 MINUTES, 2000[26]

DVD Extras

"Making of" Documentary (29:09)
    "A fifth gospel, from a child's eye-view," 3:45
    Orthodox iconography and Jesus's image, 7:34

Making the puppets, 11:01
Historical accuracy, 11:53
Animation for flashbacks, parables, inner thoughts, 15:04
Bringing the puppets to Russia, 17:33

Trailer
Cast and Crew
Production Notes
Audio Features: English, Spanish

DVD Chapters

1 The Miracle Maker

2 Building a New Synagogue, 1:30
    Jesus works on a Sepphoris synagogue, 2:30
    Mad Mary, 2:53, 3:45

3 His Father's Work, 4:49
    Jesus walks home, 5:19
    Flashback to twelve-year-old Jesus in the temple, 6:14
    Flashback to nativity, 7:36

4 John the Baptist, 8:18

5 Tests, 10:45

6 Build a Strong Foundation, 13:06
    Jesus teaches in Lazarus's home (Mt. 6:10), 14:39
    Jesus teaches on a grassy hill (Mt. 7:7), 14:47
    Zealot Judas watches from a cave, 17:25

7 An Abundant Catch, 18:34
    Roman taxation, 18:53
    "Push the boat out," 20:15

8 Healing the Sick, 23:40
    Asher, the authorities' spy, 24:28
    The paralytic at Simon's house, 24:38
    A log in your own eye (Mt. 7:3; Lk. 6:41), 25:14

9 Expelling the Demons from Mary, 28:04
    The twelve, 29:38

10 Invitation to a Feast, 32:37
    Anointing (Lk. 7:36-50)
    "In league with the devil," 34:31

11 [Tamar] Raised from the dead, 34:40
12 King Herod's Wrath [caused by Asher's report], 39:55
    Jesus weeps over John's death.
    "The hour has come [for Jerusalem]" (Jn 12:27), 41:45
13 The Good Samaritan, 43:04
14 Lazarus Is Risen [in Asher's report], 48:01
15 A Den of Thieves, 51:31
16 Judas's Torment, 57:15
    Mk 10:45, 57:18
17 The Last Supper, 58:17
18 "Your will be done" [Jesus's internal struggles], 1.01:19
19 Betrayed with a Kiss, 1.04:06
    Sanhedrin trial, 1.06:10
20 Denied Three Times, 1.07:42
21 The King of the Jews, 1.08:46
22 A Passover Tradition, 1.10:58
    Pilate's second declaration of innocence, 1.11:22
23 The Crucifixion, 1.12:57
    Via Dolorosa
    "Come down now" (temptation), 1.15:05
24 "I've seen the Lord" [Magdalene], 1.16:36
    Burial, 1.17:14
    Easter morning, 1.17:52
25 Jesus Appears on the Road [to Emmaus], 1.20:08
    Jesus appears to Peter
    Cleopas and Jairus, 1.21:10
26 Doubting Thomas, 1.24:18
    Mt. 28:19-20 and Acts 1:8, 1.25:33
    Tamar: "In my Father's house … " (Jn 14:2), 1.26:13
27 "The Kingdom of God has come," 1.26:20
28 End credits, 1.26:57

NOTES

1 Christopher Heard says animation's "core contribution to film" is to make "the unbelievable believable" (2016: 267). Cf. the discussion of Méliès in Chapter 2.

2. Adele Reinhartz describes the film as a children-accessible, parent-acceptable version of *Jesus of Nazareth* (1977) (2013a: 61).
3. Excavation of this site began in 1983.
4. Tamar is Jairus's unnamed daughter (Mt. 9:18-26; Mk 5:21-43; Lk. 8:40-56). Luke says she is "about twelve" (Lk. 8:42), although she appears younger here.
5. Cf. Jesus giving Ben-Hur water denied by a cruel Roman (1959).
6. While the elites are here, as in the Jesus epics, this film cuts more frequently to Jairus's family scenes.
7. Ralph Fiennes voices Jesus. A renowned Shakespearian actor, Fiennes is better known for his cinematic villains: for example, Amon Göth in *Schindler's List* (1993), Rameses in *The Prince of Egypt* (1998), and Lord Voldemort in the 2005–11 *Harry Potter* series. The elite and Jesus speak an educated "British," while the people, particularly Peter, tend to Scottish dialect (see Greydanus n.d.). American William Hurt "stands out" as Jairus.
8. Before Icon Pictures' involvement, the film's working title was *In My Father's House* (Chattaway 2007).
9. The animation makes Jesus's teaching come "alive" (cf. Jesus's teachings' different revitalizations in *Godspell* 1973 and *Il messia*). It is the cel animation of interior views, however, that is the film's truly distinctive, memorable technique.
10. In 2007, Reinhartz said this was the only Semitic-looking Jesus on screen (2007: 48). One can now add "Islamic" film Jesuses (see Bakker 2013; Zwick 2021), as well as the *Lumo Gospels*' Jesus (Selva Rasalingam; Taylor 2017). Apart from the Romans (and Satan), the film's entire cast looks Semitic (Malone 2012: 145).
11. While this gospel resurrection is cinematically common, it is more important here than elsewhere (but, see *La vie du Christ* 1906; *La vie et passion de notre seigneur Jésus Christ* 1907).
12. The sequence contrasts Antipas, Caesar, Jesus, and Judas's different constructions of power.
13. The film repeatedly implies Galilee is rebellious.
14. Even the children know that the prevailing cultural code reviles Samaritans.
15. Not only does the film include words that are textually suspect in Luke (22:19b-20), it also adds "for the forgiveness of sins," which appears only in Mt. 26:28.
16. As in *Last Temptation* and *Jesus* (1999), Jesus faces his most difficult trial at the end.
17. Cf. *Greatest Story* and *Jesus of Nazareth*'s divided Sanhedrins.
18. Jesus's innocence is a distinctive Lukan emphasis (see 23:4, 14-15, 22, 47).
19. The film does not have a scourging (only threatened in Lk. 23:17, 22), nor a (developed) Ecce Homo scene, Barabbas's release, blood curse, nor Simon of Cyrene.
20. Jairus is the ruler seeking help for his daughter and the unnamed disciple of Lk. 24:23-35. Like Judas, he has trouble understanding the messiah's death as a common criminal.
21. See Reinhartz (2007: 18) and Greydanus (n.d.; 2021: 80).
22. The Korean *Yesu* (1998), edited together from the television series, *Jesus: A Kingdom without Frontiers* (1996), makes this qualification necessary. See Malone (2012: 144–5). Although not animated, *The Story of Jesus for Children* (2000) edits selections from *The Jesus Film* into a sixty-one-minute "children's POV" story.
23. On biblical animation, see Heard (2016). Other than *The Prince of Egypt*, the exemplars are family friendly, children's direct-to-video or television fare: for example, CBN's *Superbook* (fifty-two time-traveling episodes, 1982–3; new series, 2009–13); Hanna-Barbera's *The Greatest Adventure: Stories from the Bible* (direct-to-video release of thirteen biblical episodes [three devoted to Jesus] featuring time-traveling children archeologists, 1986–92); Nest

Family Entertainment's two direct-to-video series, created by Richard Rich—the twenty-four-episode *Animated Stories from the New Testament* (1987–91, 1995–7, 1999–2004) and the twelve-episode *Animated Stories from the Old Testament* (aka Animated Stories from the Bible, 1992–5); and the biblically themed, direct-to-video *VeggieTales* (1993–2015; including some television airings and feature-length films). In comparison to *The Miracle Maker*, Hanna-Barbera's "Miracles of Jesus" (1989), presenting miracles primarily from the healed's POV, is notable, as is *Animated Stories from the Bible: Friends and Heroes* (a thirty-nine-episode TBN/BBC program, 2007–9), which pairs a CGI-story about children, with biblical stories in cel animation helping the children navigate their CGI-lives (Heard 2016: 272, 275). For pedagogical critique, see Heard (2000; 2016), Rohrer-Walsh (2002), and Scholz (2012).

24 *The Prince of Egypt*, arguably the most famous biblical animation (apart from *VeggieTales*), is rather "liberal" in this context. See Rohrer-Walsh (2018).

25 On biblical animation's typically "Caucasian" characters, see Heard (2016: 273; cf. 2000), Scholz (2012), and n10.

26 Lionsgate released a special edition DVD in 2007. It includes an audio commentary with co-director Derek Hayes, which is not on the 2000 DVD (Chattaway 2007).

19

The Gospel of John

Philip Saville, director, Visual Bible, 2003

PLOT SUMMARY: DIGITALIZING THE WORD

The Gospel of John is the "most literal" visual translation considered here (see Chapters 7 and 14). Following the American Bible Society's commission, the filmmakers adhere strictly to the Gospel of John's words (TEV/GNT). Images (and background music) are another matter (see Brant 2008),[1] and the camera (including mise-en-scène and editing) creates the film's distinctive "plot" and "characterization."

John's prologue alludes to Gen. 1, but the film opens with an ordinary beach sunrise as Christopher Plummer,[2] the film's narrator, recites John's prologue.[3] The sunrise anticipates the "rise" of the incarnate light (Jesus is repeatedly associated with sunlight; e.g., 1:9, 29),[4] but the cosmic setting of Genesis/John is gone.[5] The film's end replays this sunrise, and Jo-Ann Brant argues both scenes are the same day. If so, the film begins at its end, with Jesus watching Galilean fisherman (Jn 21)[6] and with Jesus as the (divine) camera (2008: 157)—hardly the gospel's perspective.[7]

The sun is fully risen as Plummer recites 1:4b-5a, but the screen fades to black with 1:5b. Before Plummer continues, visuals depict a busy campsite, then John baptizing (1:6-8).[8] At 1:9, Jesus's shadow appears, then sunlight through tree branches, and then Jesus's feet. The audience shares Jesus's POV of people (1:10-13), then Jesus's shadow appears after 1:13, before the camera pans up to the first full shot of Jesus (Henry Ian Cusick)[9] walking (1:14a), before moving into a closeup (1:14).

The Baptist, the first speaking character, appears again at 1:15 along with the Beloved Disciple (unidentified but wearing a distinctive beige skull cap) and Andrew. Jesus appears in a long shot (1:16). As he walks toward the camera in soft focus, a closeup shows his profile more distinctly on the frame's left (1:17). The profile remains during 1:18. Once the camera, Jesus has now been digitalized, photographed, rather than incarnated (see Walsh 2021b: 107).

The camera and Plummer's narration dominate. Plummer speaks more often than anyone else (and has top billing), delivering comments that might belong to characters (e.g., 3:16-21, 31-36).[10] He takes over for God (12:28), angels (20:13), and even Jesus (e.g., [part of] 1:47; 11:4).

At the Jordan, the Baptist argues with Jerusalem priests and Levites (including "the Young Levite"). As the Baptist identifies the approaching lamb of God, Jesus is backlit by sunlight (after 1:29). The first flashback, a technique the film employs to enliven Johannine material, shows Jesus rising (twice; once in closeup) from the Jordan's waters as John reports the baptism (1:32-33).[11] In closeup, John confesses Jesus is the Son of God (1:34).[12] The Beloved Disciple, who appears on screen more than anyone except Jesus,[13] and Andrew follow the lamb of God (1:36), and Jesus finally speaks: "What are you looking for?" (1:38).

Andrew fetches his brother Simon, fishing on the (opening) seacoast, even though Simon is a fisherman only in the Synoptic Gospels (but see Jn 21). Simon, renamed Peter, and Philip, the next disciple, "know" Jesus before he speaks, but Jesus knows Nathaniel first having already "seen" Nathaniel's visionary experience. Nathaniel's experience (not described in John) appears as a flashback (connecting Jesus with sunlight again). John's language suggests the audience shares Jesus's POV (but see n3) and Nathaniel does appear in an "awed face" confession/closeup (1:49; see n12).

The film interprets the signs and discourses of Jn 2-12 with mise-en-scène, through camera movement, and by creating characters.[14] The film invents characters by giving an actor speech that John attributes to groups (e.g., the Leading Pharisee often speaks for John's authorities) and by extending a character's screen time beyond John's explicit mentions (e.g., the Beloved Disciple, Nicodemus, and Magdalene). The latter also creates some narrative continuity (e.g., Nicodemus first appears in the temple cleansing, rather than in dialogue with Jesus).

Both the wedding feast and the temple cleansing have elaborate mise-en-scènes. Empty cups, Jesus's violent use of the whip, and coins falling in slow motion enliven the scenes. The wedding guests are shocked, the priests are horrified, and Jesus is happy among the people and angry with the leaders. Interestingly, the film eschews miracles at 2:23-25. Instead, Jesus, alone in an empty room, closes shutters against the people's cries.[15]

Philip Saville shifts locations/backgrounds during Jesus's conversation with Nicodemus. Plummer speaks Jn 3:16, not Jesus (increasing "direct audience address"; but see n10). Visuals show Jesus and his disciples, from above and afar, leaving Jerusalem (during the harsh 3:19). Despite 3:22, visuals show John baptizing, not Jesus (harmonizing with 4:2?). After the Baptist says Jesus must increase (3:30), a montage shows Jesus's followers gradually increasing (3:31-4:2; cf. the similar montage in *Last Temptation* 1988).

The Samaritan woman's amusement (4:11-12, 15) and bemusement (4:19-20, 26) animate the next dialogue, as does the camera that follows her while she accosts people in the street. When the Samaritans return to Jesus (the crops being ripe),[16] Jesus, in keeping with Jesus films (but not John), holds a child as he teaches. After 4:38, Jesus lovingly "touches" the Samaritans he walks among, as the narrator (not Samaritans) calls Jesus the savior of the world (4:42).

The (Roman) government official seeking healing for his son arrives on a galloping horse (4:46-53). Saville (and editor Michel Arcand) employs the first black-and-white flashback to visualize the official's memory of Jesus's announcement, not the miracle (John does not narrate the miracle either). That the official and his "servants" are Roman soldiers harmonizes John with Mt. 8:5 and Lk. 7:2. This depiction also means Samaritans, Galileans (but see 4:44), and Romans respond positively to savior-of-the-world Jesus before his conflict with Jewish authorities begins (Jn 5).[17]

At the pool of Bethzatha, the lame man's joints audibly pop as he stretches his malformed legs, and the camera focuses on his bandaged feet as he gingerly walks. The Young Levite chastises the man for breaking the Sabbath, but the Leading Pharisee, in a distinctive black turban and curly black ringlets, becomes Jesus's main opponent (5:15). Jesus addresses most of 5:19-47 to him, following him around the courtyard before tapping him pointedly with a scroll (5:46). Black-and-white flashbacks illustrate the witnesses Jesus marshals: John (versus the authorities; 5:33), the healed lame man (5:36), and a scroll ripped from a leader (5:39).

Near the Sea of Galilee, Jesus gently touches people in a crowd. As in the Synoptic Gospels (but not John), the disciples distribute the multiplied loaves and fishes. That evening, Jesus walks to his disciples' boat on a stormy sea. The next day, Magdalene (dressed in exotic, prostitute red)[18] is in the crowd (although John mentions her first at 19:25). Face-to-face with her, Jesus speaks 6:27-28. Moved, she leans toward him so intimately that she seems about to kiss him. She stays with Jesus, despite people's grumbling, as Jesus, monologuing, moves inside a synagogue (6:42)—a provocative, if not offensive, setting for his "eucharistic" language (6:51-57). Standing by the scrolls, Jesus claims to be the bread from heaven (6:58). Magdalene and Peter remain loyal, but others doubt (including Jesus's brothers, 7:1-5).[19] In the background previously, Judas becomes the focal point during the betrayer's condemnation (6:64, 71).

Back in the temple, the Leading Pharisee directs the temple's Head Guard, wearing a spiked metal helmet, to arrest Jesus, but nods off the guard when this proves impossible (7:30). That night, the Head Guard tries to arrest Jesus in a home, but steps back in awe when Jesus opens the door (7:33-34). The next day, the guard watches with the Leading Pharisee and the Young Levite as Jesus talks about living water, and as Nicodemus defends Jesus (7:51). When the trap of the woman taken in adultery (not Magdalene)[20] set by the Leading Pharisee and the Head Guard fails, the guard throws her angrily to the ground.

Standing before a lit menorah, Jesus announces he is the light of the world (8:12). Facing off with the Leading Pharisee, Jesus declares he will die in his sins if he does not believe Jesus is "I am who I am" (8:24). A fade to black leads to Jesus teaching about freedom to masons working on the temple. Judas, the Beloved Disciple, and Magdalene are in the background. An angry Jesus utters the infamous 8:44. While the crowd is amused at first, masons move forward with stones after 8:58. The disciples courageously intervene, and Jesus disappears (8:59).

When Jesus heals the blind man with spittle on the Sabbath, the Leading Pharisee interrogates the man. The narrator mentions Jesus's followers' synagogue expulsion (9:22, 34), and Jesus walks among sheep before the blind man gratefully kneels before him (9:38). Sheep are everywhere as Jesus touches people and talks about the good shepherd. As often in Jesus films (but not John), Jesus seems to be teaching a young girl (10:14). In the temple, people rise to stone Jesus (10:30), and he disappears again (10:39).

Jesus weeps (one tear at 11:33) with Lazarus's sisters. People stagger back from the opened tomb's stench. Notably, the film does not frame Jesus from within the tomb (as is the cinematic trope). The camera moves toward the dark tomb with Jesus's command (11:34). Lazarus emerges as a shadow on the wall, the camera focusing on awed faces.

Then Caiaphas announces his deadly plan (11:49-50). As Plummer talks about the priests' murderous decision, Jesus and his disciples walk along a ridge at twilight (cf. *The Seventh Seal*'s [1957] danse macabre; Page 2006a).

At the anointing, Judas grins greedily while talking about money. During the triumph, the authorities look down from above. The Leading Pharisee speaks 12:19. Jesus wears a purple shawl, for the hour has come. He crumples to the ground (12:27) before Plummer speaks for "heaven" (12:28). Jesus walks alone while Plummer recites Isaiah's judgmental words and the camera looks down upon the "blind" leaders. While the Head Guard is visibly upset, Nicodemus smiles at Jesus's words about eternal life (12:50).

The filmmakers utilize all their visual strategies during the supper's interminable monologue (13-17).[21] Background characters have important actions. Magdalene, a gray cloak covering her red clothing, enters with Jesus. A temple guard watches from the dark street. Judas eats hungrily beside Jesus, who talks with the Beloved Disciple. Jesus stands and strips for the footwashing as shocked Magdalene watches. Jesus laughs at Peter's "full bath" request. The camera focuses on Judas before and after Jesus's comment about all but one being clean (13:10b). Finally identified (13:23, 25), the Beloved Disciple asks who the betrayer is. Following Jesus films (not John), Judas meets the Head Guard in the dark streets. Magdalene rushes to Jesus's side when he speaks of leaving (13:33) and watches as Jesus comforts Peter after predicting his denial.

On the roof (14:15), Magdalene and the Beloved Disciple are nearest Jesus who places his hand on the disciple's leg. When he talks about this world's ruler (14:30-31), non-Johannine visuals show Judas and the Head Guard with a priest. Jesus and his entourage, including Magdalene, move by torchlight through a vineyard (15:1). Sitting by a fire, Jesus tosses a dead branch into it (15:6). Walking alongside the Beloved Disciple, Jesus talks about love.

As the group passes through a tunnel, black-and-white flashbacks to the ministry begin. Jesus, still in a purple shawl, says he chose them (15:16) as the Beloved Disciple, Andrew, and Philip's "calls" replay.[22] When Jesus talks about the world's hatred (15:18), the attempted stoning of Jesus replays. Flashbacks show Jesus feeding the multitude, teaching in the temple, the Leading Pharisee calling off the Head Guard (15:22), the blind man's healing (15:24), the Leading Pharisee's interrogation of the blind man (15:25), and another attempted stoning (16:10). Suddenly, a color flashforward shows judging Pilate (16:11). As the group continues underground, more non-Johannine visuals crosscut to Judas approaching with torch-carrying guards (16:24, 28).

Black-and-white flashbacks accompany Jesus's prayer about glory (17:1): walking on water; Lazarus's resurrected shadow; the lame man's feet; the lame man carrying his pallet; Andrew calling Peter; Nathaniel's visionary awe; and Cana's red wine (in color; 17:4-9). Everyone, including Magdalene, kneels for Jesus's anointing touch. A black-and-white flashback shows Jesus's shadow entering the world (17:18) before various nationalities come to Jesus (some not previously seen, 17:20-22). A closeup displays Jesus's final glory (17:24-25) before everyone crosses the Kidron, with a disciple assisting Magdalene.

When Jesus says, "I am he," those who have come to arrest him step back, but do not fall (contra 18:6). Judas watches, horrified, as Jesus demands his followers' release. The Beloved Disciple and Magdalene watch Jesus bound. At the high priest's house, the Beloved

Disciple (the "other disciple" of 18:15) enters the house while Peter remains outside (for his denials). The Head Guard slaps Jesus (18:22).

In the morning, Pilate receives the authorities outside, but interrogates Jesus inside. A closeup frames the duo together for 18:36-38. When Pilate finds no reason for condemnation, the Leading Pharisee and the Young Levite lead shouts for Barabbas's release (18:40). The scourging appears as shadows on a wall (cf. *The King of Kings* 1927); the crown is only carried; but Pilate presents the bloody Ecce Homo. The Leading Pharisee and the Young Levite lead calls for Jesus's crucifixion.

The Via Dolorosa and the crucifixion, as in John, are incredibly brief. Neither the nailing nor the cross's raising appears on screen (19:17-18). Instead, the film focuses on Pilate's placard and the Beloved Disciple, Mother Mary, and Magdalene's arrival. The Johannine last words pass quickly. The most violent moment is the breaking of the other victims' legs. Joseph of Arimathea and Nicodemus take the body to the tomb.

In the resurrection appearance to Magdalene, Jesus hides behind a small palm when speaking. Stepping forward, he pulls off his headscarf to be recognized (so visuals rather than his voice "reveal" him; contra 20:16). Magdalene, however, walks stunned through the streets. Her report to the disciples is not depicted. The words to Thomas about believing without seeing seem incongruous in a visual translation (20:29).

In an appendix (Jn 21), Jesus appears on the prologue's beach. After Jesus evokes Peter's triple confession, a flashforward shows Roman soldiers chaining Peter (21:18). The film ends with a closeup of the Beloved Disciple, which freezes and morphs into a digitalized black-and-white photograph, identifying the film's "textual" source (21:24-25; see Figure 19.1). A coda including Jn 3:16 calls the audience to faith.

MEMORABLE CHARACTERS

1 The narrator is more important than John's. He is not the Beloved Disciple (and thus not the gospel's author).[23]

2 Understating his Johannine glory, the film still presents Jesus as "I Am That I Am," the light come into the world (cf. *The King of Kings*), and the savior of the world (see the diverse people acclaiming Jesus before Jn 5 and the visuals of various ethnicities accompanying 17:20-22). The film's Jesus smiles more often than John's angry words imply (see 2:4; 7:6-8; 8:39-59).

3 The Beloved Disciple is the Baptist's other disciple (1:35-40) as well as the disciple accessing the high priest's house (18:15). Onscreen almost as much as Jesus, the film's final image freezes and digitalizes his face/witness.

4 Magdalene is Jesus's other premier disciple. She is intimately near him after the miraculous feeding and during his last evening. The camera focuses on her when Jesus uses the metaphor of childbirth (16:21-22), and she gasps on the Via Dolorosa when Jesus falls.

5 The Leading Pharisee is Jesus's chief opponent (seconded by the Young Levite and Head Guard).

Figure 19.1 Digitalizing the apostolic witness (book) in *The Gospel of John,* directed by Philip Saville, Visual Bible, 2003. All rights reserved.

MEMORABLE VISUALS

1 Daybreak at the sea in Jn 1:1; 21:4.
2 Jesus's first appearance as shadow, then with rays of sunlight.
3 Jesus facing off against the Leading Pharisee.
4 Jesus's intimacy with people, but particularly with Magdalene and the Beloved Disciple.
5 The flashbacks during the farewell discourse.
6 The final digitalizing of the Beloved Disciple's face (see Figure 19.1).

KEY AUTHORITY/SCRIPTURE

1 The camera is the film's chief authority and so dominates that it renders Jesus's words in 20:29 almost nonsensical. It often tells a different story than John's words (see n3), and it harmonizes the film with the other gospels and with Jesus films (see n11).
2 The almost ubiquitous narrator is the film's second authority. His effect far surpasses that of silents' intertitles and other cinematic narrators like that in *King of Kings* (1961). His omniscient voice creates a powerful "word of God" (or gospel) effect (see Walsh 2021b).
3 The Beloved Disciple is the chief witness. Following Jesus (1:14) almost immediately into the film's visuals (1:15; cf. 1:37), he is also the film's "last man standing" in the digitalized finale (21:24; see Figure 19.1).

4 The TEV/GNT John is the film's "script." That some film versions begin and end with Jn 3:16 is appropriate to this translation and the Visual Bible series' tendencies (see Cultural Location).

CULTURAL LOCATION/GENRE: VISUAL TRANSLATION

Visual translations follow the tradition of recorded Bibles by notables like Alexander Scourby and, more recently, James Earl Jones. In a broadband culture, the shift to visualizations is understandable, if not inevitable. Like recordings, visual translations' true home is a format easily accessible for church or private devotional use (DVD or streaming). At present, visual translations belong to evangelical Protestant agendas (see Chapter 14). Nonetheless, *The Gospel of John* premiered at the Toronto Film Festival and had a brief theatrical run (Tatum 2013: 249–52).[24]

The film's lack of financial success—partly attributable to *The Passion of the Christ*'s phenomenal success (2004)—contributed to Visual Bible International's bankruptcy and the Visual Bible Project's end. In addition to *The Gospel of John*, the project completed films on *Matthew* (1993) and *Acts* (1994).[25] Bruce Marchiano played Jesus in the two earlier films. Visual Bible marketed them as visualizations of the New International Version. Neither film, however, follows its text as closely as *The Gospel of John* does. They create elaborate backstories for their authors, both of whom appear in their films as both characters and narrators.

Thus, *Matthew* begins with Matthew (Richard Kiley) introducing himself as a former Roman tax-collector transformed by Jesus's invitation to "follow me," and saying that he writes to show through scriptures that Jesus is the long-awaited Messiah.[26] After a pause, he continues (curiously), "the following is a word for word account of the Gospel according to Matthew." The movie cuts between Matthew teaching the gospel to a young boy (sometimes through call and response)—or reciting so two scribes can transcribe it—and characters acting out the Matthean text, either narrated by Matthew or spoken by characters.

After Mt. 28:20, the film fades to black and then shows first Jesus's feet and then a full shot of Jesus from behind as he turns smiling and gesturing at the viewer to follow. The scene recalls the adult Jesus's first appearance in the movie at his baptism (first his feet, then his reflection in the water, and then his smiling face), and replicates Matthew's own "follow me" experience. Jesus does not speak. There is no need. The film has spoken (cf. Walsh 2021b: 107).

The similarities with Jesus's gradual visualization in *The Gospel of John*'s prologue, as well as the fact that both introductions preview the films' conclusions, are striking. *The Gospel of John*, however, appeals to apostolic authority in a more restrained way. Its evangelistic agenda is also less evident, although some versions do conclude with an evangelistic invitation to faith (cf. *The Jesus Film* 1979).

This evangelistic agenda makes the TEV/GNT's choice as the film's "script" unsurprising.[27] The American Bible Society created the TEV/GNT for children and people learning (or with limited) English. *Good News for Modern Man: The New Testament in Today's English Version* (TEV) appeared in paperback in 1966. The Protestant Bible appeared in 1976 and an inclusive language revision in 1992. Because it was viewed as a paraphrase, the American Bible Society renamed the TEV the GNT in 2001 to eschew that reputation. The TEV/GNT does, however, clearly follow Eugene Nida's "dynamic equivalence" translation theory, which aims to translate "ideas," rather than "words," or at readability, rather than fidelity to its source.

Like the NIV, the TEV/GNT has a conservative theological agenda. One point where this is evident is the high Christological rendering of "I am he" (8:24, 28, 13:19) as "I AM WHO I AM" (cf. Exod. 3:14). Presumably, it is the modern desire to avoid anti-Semitism that leads to the rendering of John's "the Jews" as "Jewish authorities."

DIRECTOR

Philip Saville had a long, successful television career (beginning in 1955). He won two Bafta awards for directing the miniseries *Boys from the Blackstuff* (1982) and *The Life and Loves of a She-Devil* (1986). He was particularly well known for the innovative direction of filmed plays (directing over forty episodes of *Armchair Theater* [1956–74]). As *The Gospel of John* is essentially a filmed play (text; see Greydanus 2003), Saville seems particularly suited for the project. His work for *Armchair Theater* often involved filming live plays. His trademark was his innovative use of camera with rapid movement, angles, framing, and mirrors (Wake n.d.; Hadoke 2017). That expertise certainly helps alleviate the tedium of the film's devotion to the TEV/GNT.

VISUAL BIBLE INTERNATIONAL, 180 MINUTES, 2003
DVD Extras

Setup
    Spoken Language: English
    Subtitles
        Spanish
        French
    Special Features: Enhanced Viewing
        An interactive icon that can be turned on or off, giving access to pertinent historical and geographical information
Two-hour version of the film (The following features are on the two-hour DVD only)
Historical Background (*Note: the forward arrow within sections is not active*)
    Jesus, Son of God (in order of appearance), 7:20 minutes
        Peter Richardson, Bruce Waltke, Charles Hedrick, Alan Segal, Stephen Breck Reid, Patricia Dutcher-Walls
    The World of Jesus (interviews with Academic Advisory Committee), 7:48 minutes
        In order of appearance: Patricia Dutcher-Walls, Peter Richardson, Alan Segal

Glossary of Terms
Bibliography and Filmography
Production Design: The Making of *The Gospel of John*
   Director: Philip Saville, 7:45 minutes
   Screenwriter: John Goldsmith, 11:48 minutes
      The summing up of the Farewell Discourse, 4:22
      The Leading Pharisee, 6:32
      Anti-Semitism vs. anti-clericalism, 6:50
      Like a silent movie, 8:40
      John, the beloved disciple, 9:12
   Director of Photography: Miroslaw Baszak, 6:45 minutes
   Production Designer: Don Taylor, 10:19 minutes
      Filmed in Spain's Sierra Nevada
   Costume Designer: Debra Hanson, 10:08 minutes
   Musical Score: Jeff Danna, 10:21 minutes
   Hair and Make Up Design: Trefor Proud, 5:35 minutes
   Cast and Filmmakers Featurette
About the Cast (Only Henry Ian Cusick [Jesus] and Christopher Plummer [narrator] have video segments related to their characters)
   Jesus, 5:40 minutes
   Narrator, 6:05 minutes
About the Filmmakers
Academic Advisory Committee
Interactive Map of the Holy Land: The Miracles of Jesus
Trailer
Production Credits for DVD and Special Features

DVD Chapters

1 Prologue and the Word of Life (1:1-28)
      Beloved Disciple appears (1:15), 3:48
      Young Levite appears (1:19), 4:34
2 Lamb of God, the First Disciples (1:29-50), 6:04
3 The Cana Wedding; Jesus Goes to the Temple (2:1-22), 12:51
4 Jesus and Nicodemus, Jesus and John (2:23-4:2), 19:37
5 Jesus and the Samaritan Woman (4:3-44), 25:35
6 Healing the Official's Son, Healing the Lame Man (4:45-5:14), 31:35
      Leading Pharisee appears, 37:48
7 Authority of the Son, Witness to Jesus (5:15-6:1), 37:55
8 Feeding the Five Thousand, Walking on Water (6:2-24), 43:05
      Magdalene appears, 49:25

9   Bread of Life, Words of Eternal Life (6:25-70), 49:52
10 Festival of Shelters, The Attempted Arrest (7:1-44), 57:57
      Head Temple Guard appears (7:27), 1.01:05
11 The Adulterous Woman, the Light of the World (7:45-8:30), 1.04:10
12 Truth Will Set You Free, Jesus and Abraham (8:31-59), 1.11:23
13 Jesus Heals a Man Born Blind (9:1-12), 1.16:06
14 Pharisees Question the Blind Man (9:13-34), 1.19:38
15 Spiritual Blindness; Jesus the Good Shepherd (9:35-10:21), 1.23:01
16 Jesus Is Rejected (10:22-40), 1.27:01
17 Jesus Is the Resurrection and the Life (11:1-27), 1.30:31
18 Lazarus Brought to Life (11:28-45), 1.34:17
19 The Plot against Jesus (11:46-57), 1.38:50
20 Jesus Anointed at Bethany (12:1-11), 1.40:51
21 The Triumphal Entry into Jerusalem (12:12-50), 1.43:15
22 Jesus Washes His Disciples' Feet (13:1-20), 1.51:12
23 Jesus Predicts His Betrayal and Denial, the Way to the Father (13:21-14:14), 1.56:00
24 The Promise of the Holy Spirit, the Real Vine (14:15-15:6), 2.02:23
25 Love One Another (15:7-16:11), 2.05:58
26 Victory over the World (16:12-17:9), 2.10:54
27 Jesus Prays for His Disciples (17:10-26), 2.15:55
28 The Arrest of Jesus, Peter's Denial (18:1-27), 2.18:58
29 Jesus before Pilate (18:28-19:12), 2.24:31
30 Jesus Is Crucified (19:13-37), 2.31:25
31 The Burial, the Empty Tomb (19:38-20:18), 2.39:41
32 Jesus Appears to His Disciples (20:19-30), 2.43:57
33 Jesus and Peter, Conclusion (21:1-25), 2.47:33
34 Credits, 2.54:02

NOTES

1 Marketing touted the film's historical realism and expert advisors, including Adele Reinhartz. It was filmed in Spain (location shots) and in the Toronto Film Studios. Its largely British (Shakespearian actors) cast and educated British accents, however, hardly stray from the tradition's Eurocentrism (Greydanus 2003; Tatum 2013: 249–50).
2 The Canadian Plummer is one of few to have received an Academy, Tony, and Emmy award. He played Antipas in *Jesus of Nazareth* (1977), but is better known for roles like Georg von Trapp in *The Sound of Music* (1965).

3   The disjoint between words and visuals often creates a sense of two different stories. For example, the closeup of Nathaniel's awed face seems to indicate that the subsequent flashback is his memory, but John 1:48 says Jesus "saw" this event. Brant argues the persistency of such disjoints culminates in different ideologies: the visuals being more open to the world than the hostile text (2008: 150, 157–8). She claims the visuals overwhelm the words. Reinhartz agrees, although she refers to anti-Semitic visuals overriding the opening titles' caveats (2007: 276 n19).
4   Cf. John's tendency to verbal puns (e.g., again/above in Jn 3).
5   *Son of God* (2014), a feature film constructed out of *The Bible* materials (2013), opens with the aged John's voiceover (selecting from John's prologue) as visuals present *Heilsgeschichte* moments. Christology overwhelms as the actor playing Jesus (Diogo Morgado) appears in or provides the voice for various *Heilsgeschichte* theophanies (see Burnette-Bletsch 2016c: 301–2).
6   The resulting structure (from Galilee to Galilee) resembles Mark more than John.
7   Cf. the descending/ascending Jesus POV camera beginning/ending *The Jesus Film*. Brant attributes "the camera is Jesus" to scriptwriter John Goldsmith's comments (in DVD Extras).
8   The film often pauses between Johannine passages, so that many visuals appear between Johannine verses (as a gloss). Further, the camera often leads, as the words try "to catch up" (Brant 2008: 153).
9   The Scottish-Peruvian Cusick's other famous role is that of Desmond Hume on *Lost* (2005–10).
10 Translators punctuate the Jn 3 monologues differently to indicate who speaks the words (narrator or character). The film follows the TEV/GNB, which places closing quotes after 3:13. A note, in the TEV/GNT, says the "quotation" may continue through 3:21.
11 Perhaps, the flashback suggests that John only reports the baptism. It also harmonizes John with the Synoptic Gospels. Other harmonizations include visualizing Simon Peter's call by the sea in 1:40, suggesting Mk 1:16 as much as Jn 1:41; the Roman official's (centurion) request for help for his son, as in Mt. 8:5 and Lk. 7:2, but not Jn 4:46-53; the disciples' distribution of the loaves and fishes (as in the Synoptics); Jesus the carpenter, following Mk 6:3 when visualizing Jn 7:1-5; cuts to Judas and the religious authorities during Jesus's last night following the Synoptics, not John (Judas is absent from John from 13:30 until 18:2); and the sponge on a long stick (Mk 15:36), not a hyssop (Jn 19:29). Perhaps, the film tradition (not the Synoptics) determines some of these.
12 The film makes a trope of closeups of "confessional faces."
13 As in John, the Beloved Disciple is not named until 13:23 and never equated with John, Zebedee's son. Goldsmith identifies him as John in DVD Extras.
14 According to Barnes Tatum, the film's structure follows the TEV/GNT's introductory outline of John: 1:1-18; 1:19-51; 2:1-12:50; 13:1-19:42; 20:1-31; 21:1-25 (2013: 241–5).
15 Visual translations and television miniseries are notorious for adding violence and (supernatural) miracles to the gospel accounts. Neither is true here.
16 While shots of surrounding fields punctuate the scene, Jesus gestures at the arriving people as he says these words.
17 If this suggests anti-Semitism, the film generally strives to avoid such calumny. For example, John infamously describes Jesus's opponents simply as the "Jews." Without any support from Greek texts, the TEV/GNT often translates this phrase as "the Jewish authorities" and the film follows along. The film also opens with titles eschewing anti-Semitism by asserting

that crucifixion was a Roman method of execution, not approved by Jewish law, that Jesus and his earliest followers were Jewish, and that the gospel came into being during a time of antagonism between those followers and the Jewish religious establishment.

18 In DVD Extras, Debra Hanson, the film's costume designer, confirms that Magdalene's clothing is that of a prostitute. Saville agrees, but also calls her Jesus's first female disciple.
19 With 7:1-5, Jesus works on a piece of wood in a village—even loading a donkey—recalling the always working village Jesus in *Il messia* (1975).
20 This scene appears in John in modern translations, but not in the oldest Greek manuscripts. It appears in some manuscripts of the Gospel of Luke.
21 Tatum claims that the sequence has some of the finest technical filmmaking in Jesus films (2013: 243).
22 The time manipulations are non-Johannine, but Goldsmith, in DVD Extras, justifies them by arguing that the farewell discourse summarizes Jesus's ministry.
23 In addition to the offscreen/onscreen distinction, the narrator's voice differs noticeably from that of the Beloved Disciple (cf. 1:38; 19:35).
24 More recently, the first Lumo Gospel had a "premiere" on Netflix in December of 2014. The Lumo Project is the first to complete films of all four gospels. The other films went directly to DVD or streaming packages (see Taylor 2017; Walsh 2021b: 108; as well as the project's homepage: https://www.lumoproject.com/).
25 Reportedly, a Gospel of Mark film was in the works before the project's demise.
26 *The New Media Luke* also begins (and ends) with Luke (Richard Kiley) reading his gospel to others. *The Visual Bible: Acts* (1994) begins with an even more elaborate introduction of Luke (Dean Jones) on a storm-tossed ship, as doctor, author of Luke and Acts, and friend of Paul. Like *The Visual Bible: Matthew*, it cuts between Luke telling and actors enacting the story.
27 The NIV has a similar ideology. The move from the NIV to the TEV/GNT had more to do with financial issues than with a shift in the project's theology/ideology.

20

The Passion of the Christ

Mel Gibson, director, Icon, 2004

PLOT SUMMARY: THE SORROWFUL MYSTERIES

This film falls into three roughly equal parts: (1) Jesus's arrest and trial before Caiaphas (thirty-eight minutes); (2) trial before Pilate, including beatings (thirty-two minutes); and (3) road to the cross and crucifixion (forty-four minutes). The Stations of the Cross structure the film more than they do *Jésus de Montréal*'s (1989) passion play.[1] Only two (#8, #14) do not appear (see Table 20.1),[2] but the First Station occurs over an hour into the film. The earlier material reflects other Catholic devotional practices,[3] including the sorrowful mysteries of the Rosary and the more recent fourteen-station "Scriptural Way of the Cross."[4] All the sorrowful mysteries (three before the First Station) and the "Scriptural Way" (six before the First Station) appear in the film.

Much of the film relies on Anne Catherine Emmerich's imaginative passion visions (Tatum 2013: 258). Thomas Boomershine says every non-gospel "touch" in the film comes from Emmerich. Further, as Gibson uses no New Testament material not also appearing in Emmerich, William Campbell claims Gibson and co-writer Benedict Fitzgerald "could have scripted the screenplay without ever reading the Gospels" (quoted in Boomershine 2005: 3).[5]

Table 20.1 Catholic passion devotion.

Stations of the Cross	Scriptural way of the cross	Rosary's sorrowful mysteries
	In the garden (1)	Agony in the garden (1)
	Betrayed by Judas and arrested (2)	
	Condemned by the Sanhedrin (3)	
	Denied by Peter (4)	
	Judged by Pilate (5)	
	Scourged, crowned with thorns (6)	Scourging at the pillar (2)
		Crowning with thorns (3)

Condemned to die (1)		
Takes up his cross (2)	Takes up his cross (7)	Carrying the cross (4)
Falls the first time (3)		
Meets his Mother (4)		
Simon of Cyrene (5)	Simon of Cyrene (8)	
Veronica (6)		
Falls the second time (7)		
Meets Jerusalem women (8)	Meets Jerusalem women (9)	
Falls the third time (9)		
Stripped (10)		
Nailed to the cross (11)	Crucified (10)	Crucified (5a)
	Promise to repentant thief (11)	
	Mary and John united (12)	
Dies (12)	Dies (13)	Dies (5b)
Taken from cross (13)		
Laid in tomb (14)	Laid in tomb (14)	

Except for the Icon Production company image (and its lightning), the film opens without credits. An epigraph, taken from Isa. 53:5, appears, providing the interpretative perspective ("for us")—and justification for the film's graphic violence. One of cinema's most detailed Garden of Gethsemane scenes ensues (but cf. *Jesus* 1999). With haunting background music, dark clouds menace a full (Passover) moon. The camera pans down into the dark garden, circling sinisterly around the praying Jesus. A predatory bird screams as Jesus (Jim Caviezel)[6] calls out "Adonai" (twice). The film's dialogue is Aramaic (with some Hebrew) and Latin. The first English subtitle appears when Jesus chastises his inner circle for failing to watch and pray.[7] Peter and John, framed together, are perplexed.

The film segues from Peter looking up at the moon to Caiaphas looking at the same moon before offering Judas the thirty pieces (Judas stands across from a line of priests and temple police). Another priest pitches the money bag to Judas (in slow motion, as in *Jesus Christ Superstar* 1973), who fumbles it and then grovels for the coins. The film segues back to the inner circle watching Jesus, who is also kneeling—in anguished prayer—creating a striking visual contrast to Judas. Although kneeling, Jesus's body arches painfully, framed in a shaft of moonlight as if already hanging (cf. the arched body in Matthias Grünwald's Isenheim Altarpiece *Crucifixion*).[8]

Jesus prays for his Father's protection (selected Psalms), but an androgynous Satan (Rosalinda Celentano) appears in the background to tell Jesus the task is too much. Refusing to look at Satan, Jesus prays. The camera cuts back and forth, but never frames the two faces together. This is no dialogue. After Jesus accepts Abba's will, clouds cover the moon and Jesus collapses.

The POV captures the sprawled Jesus from above.[9] As moonlight returns, the tip of a serpent's tail becomes visible in Satan's nostril, then the camera pans down Satan's body to the serpent emerging from his robes. Another God's-eye POV shows the snake crawling toward the prone Jesus. Satan smiles as the snake crawls onto Jesus's hands.[10] Jesus gathers his strength and rises—for the first of many times—as if he, like a Western/action hero, has suffered enough to justify his violent revenge. Looking at Satan for the first time, Jesus dramatically stomps the snake's head (rendering Gen. 3:15 messianic). When Jesus looks back at Satan again, the torch-bearing arrest party arrives.

In less than ten minutes, Gibson has established Jesus's vicarious suffering, visually aligned Judas, Caiaphas, and the temple guard with Satan,[11] and anticipated the suffering hero's ultimate triumph. Little characterization follows—except for flashbacks displaying Jesus's ministry.[12] The visuals ending the crucifixion (in the film's last five minutes) simply reprise this scene. Between, one sees the most brutal, horrifying passion yet filmed (see Problematic Issue).

After the temple guard forces Judas to identify Jesus, a melee ensues. Judas and John flee, with John losing his cloak (cf. Mk 14:51-52), and Peter struggling against several guards. After Jesus heals Malchus's ear (Jesus's only film miracle), the guards bind and beat Jesus. An abrupt cut introduces a waking, frightened Mary, who has sensed her son's sufferings. Except in flashbacks, Mary's face hereafter will be stricken, held rigidly in pain. She is the passion's chief witness and co-redeemer, suffering with her son. Appropriating Passover Haggadah language, she asks, "Why is this night different from every other night?"[13] Replying apropos, Magdalene comforts her: "Because once we were slaves and we are slaves no longer." Then, John bursts in with news of Jesus's arrest.

The guards throw Jesus from a bridge, where he hangs suspended by chains before the distraught Judas. When the guards jerk Jesus upward, animalistic snarls begin and a demon/beast hurtles, screaming in the darkness, from behind Judas.

In the high priest's courtyard, Judas watches among people bribed to be there.[14] The holy trio (Mary, Magdalene, and John) arrives. Mary embraces Peter, and Magdalene asks Roman soldiers (including Cassius) for help before a guard dismisses "crazy" Mary (cf. Mad Mary in *The Miracle Maker* 2000). Nonetheless, the soldiers alert Abenader, Pilate's assistant/centurion, of "troubles."[15] Jesus sees a carpenter working and flashes back to a happy time with his mother, building a table.[16] In the present, Mary meets Jesus's glance and affirms: "It has begun, Adonai. So be it."

Annas and Caiaphas interrogate Jesus; liars testify; and people abuse Jesus[17] while Judas, gnawing at his hand, watches. Leaders shunt aside Joseph of Arimathea and Nicodemus's objections.[18] After Jesus's "I am" (closeup) and the blasphemy verdict, the trial degenerates into a vicious (sometimes slow-motion) beating.[19]

After his last denial, Peter catches Jesus's baleful eye (a flashback shows Peter's memory of Jesus's prediction of his denial). Fleeing, Peter falls at Mary's feet, confessing his betrayal. He does not appear again except in flashbacks.

Caiaphas dismisses Judas's repentance.[20] Little children, morphing demonically into "little satans," curse Judas, as a handheld camera captures his whirling "descent into hell." In the first of many ground-level shots, an empathetic Mary puts her ear to the pavement, showing she knows where her suffering son hangs below (see Figure 20.1). As the sun rises, demonic children, with Satan, chase Judas along a hill's crest. Lips chewed to tatters, Judas holds his head and screams—his world undone; everything eerily quiet, the children gone. The film's first section ends as (Beelzebub's) flies buzz around a donkey's rotting carcass. Judas takes its rope and hangs himself (cf. Judas's flight and hanging in *Il vangelo* 1964 and *Jesus Christ Superstar*).

The film's second part continues slowly toward the First Station of the Cross. The Antonia fortress doors are opened, and the camera follows the priests who march the shuffling, chained Jesus into the courtyard. Pilate stands on a balcony with Abenader, looking disbelievingly at the savagely beaten wretch below. Caiaphas and Annas claim a dangerous sect hails Jesus as king.

Pilate receives Jesus inside, sending away his guard (except for Abenader), and offers Jesus drink.[21] In the interrogation's climax, the camera frames Pilate and Jesus's faces intimately together (cf. Jn 18:33-38).[22] Above the courtyard, Pilate declares he finds "no cause" against Jesus and sends the Galilean to Antipas (Claudia approves). The priests accompany Jesus to a foppish, dissolute Antipas (cf. *Jesus Christ Superstar* and *Jesus of Nazareth*'s [1977] similar characterizations).[23] When Antipas dismisses "crazy" Jesus, the priests return him to Pilate. In the interim, Pilate tells Claudia that he must prevent a revolt (by Jesus or Caiaphas's followers) to avoid Caesar's bloody retaliation.[24]

Sitting and drinking in judgment above the courtyard, Pilate repeats that he finds "no cause" for Jesus's death. Abenader's soldiers control the ensuing brawl. Fearing an imminent revolt, Pilate offers a choice between the buffoonish Barabbas and messiah Jesus, and Caiaphas leads the cries for Barabbas's release and Jesus's crucifixion. Looking disbelievingly at Claudia, Pilate instead orders Abenader to have Jesus scourged severely (before being released).

"Severely" understates the film's most brutish moments.[25] Seen from above (like Gethsemane and Golgotha) and chained to a post, a determined Jesus (twice) whispers, "My heart is ready, Father." The priests watch as loutish soldiers laugh mockingly, hurling various (untranslated) insults. Two soldiers beat Jesus with rods as the officer in charge counts the blows. The extreme violence makes some soldiers look away. Satan enters, walking in slow motion behind Annas and Caiaphas.

The scourging over, Jesus kneels at the post—his hands spasming. When Jesus sees Mary arrive, he rises (echoing Gethsemane), so the officer orders an additional flogging, now with cats o' nine tails. The flesh flays from Jesus's body and his blood splatters the mocking soldiers' faces. Distraught, Mary turns away, asking, "My son, when, where, how will you choose to be delivered of this?" Sound fades, except for Magdalene's weeping. Sympathetic Claudia offers the women white towels.

Jesus, a bloody mass, is seen splayed on the ground from above (cf. Gethsemane). Now the officer orders Jesus flipped so the soldiers whip his front. The audience shares Jesus's POV of these soldiers and of Satan behind them, walking (in slow motion) with a grotesque baby in arms. Jesus flashes back from a soldier's bloody foot to washing John's feet (and to speaking about the world's hatred and the Father's helper; Jn 15:18, 26). Abenader returns and stops the scourging, obviously disgusted by the brutality. After another POV from above Jesus's bloody body, the soldiers drag him away (the audience shares Jesus's upside-down POV). Miraculously, Jesus's loincloth remains intact and unsoiled.

The camera lingers lovingly on the torture instruments in the deserted court. The holy trio returns, and Mary wipes up Jesus's (eucharistic) blood. Inside, soldiers press a crown of thorns onto Jesus, mock him as "king of the worms" with a red robe, and continue beating him. Outside (with only background music), Magdalene wipes up Jesus's blood with her headscarf. On the ground, she flashes back to Jesus's deliverance of her (she is the woman taken in adultery).

Incredulous at the beating's savagery, Pilate tenderly helps Jesus face the crowd for the Ecce Homo (the words are spoken in Latin). Caiaphas, threatening Pilate with Caesar's disapproval, leads the cries for crucifixion. When fighting breaks out again, Pilate demands water brought and Jesus flashes back to the last supper's handwashing. Pilate declares his innocence and tells the priests to look to it, as Caiaphas smiles evilly.[26]

As the film's third part begins, Abenader, on horseback, leads the crucifixion party out the fortress gates (seen from outside). The two thieves take up their crossbeams, and Jesus kneels, caressing his cross: "I am your servant, Father ... " The impenitent Gesmas mocks Jesus as a fool. Whipping Jesus, a soldier demands that "his highness" move. Still smiling, Caiaphas follows on a donkey (contrast the triumphal entry). While Roman soldiers beat and whip Jesus along the Via Dolorosa, a Bosch-like crowd mocks Jesus and throws stones. A closeup of Jesus's bloody eyes leads into a triumphal entry flashback.

Mary and Satan watch each other, and John rushes Mary and Magdalene through back alleys so that Mary can meet her son. Beaten and pushed, Jesus falls in slow motion atop his cross. He rises and falls again; his cross falls heavily upon him (in slow motion) as Mary watches from an alley.[27] She gathers strength from a flashback memory of helping her child rise after a fall and rushes through the crowd to her son. In the film's tenderest moment, Jesus shares her memory before declaring, "See, Mother, I make all things new" (Rev. 21:5).[28] He rises, and awed Cassius stares at Mary.

Black-clad women wail, Pilate watches from afar, and Jesus falls again. Abenader stops the beatings as Jesus cannot continue. The soldiers and women press Simon into service. He reluctantly agrees after asserting loudly, "I'm an innocent man, forced to carry the cross of a condemned man."[29] Here, and hereafter, the camera frames Simon and Jesus's faces intimately.

When Jesus falls again, Veronica walks unmolested to him with a cup of water. He wipes his bloody face with her headscarf, but a soldier knocks away the water (cf. the famous scenes in *Ben-Hur* 1959). To end the abuse, Simon threatens to stop carrying Jesus's cross.[30] The procession continues, leaving Veronica behind. With effort, viewers can see the "true icon" on her scarf (contrast *La vie du Christ*'s [1906] dramatic "revelation").

Abenader gallops through the city gates, and Golgotha appears for the first time through the gates (cf. *Greatest Story*'s [1965] similarly framed shots). Outside, Jesus falls again (in slow motion). The audience shares his reeling POV (from above), and then his view of Simon from the ground. Helping Jesus rise again, Simon says, "We're almost there." As they look up at Golgotha, Jesus flashes back to his call to love your enemies (Mt. 5:43-46).

The black-clad priests look down on Jesus as he crests Golgotha (cf. *Jesus Christ Superstar*'s vulture-priests). Jesus flashes back to his words about laying down his life for his sheep (and taking it up again; Jn 10:11, 18). Seen from below, Jesus falls again. Casting off the cross, Simon falls face to face with Jesus. A soldier pulls Simon brusquely away telling him he is "free to go."[31] As he stumbles away weeping, the holy trio arrives.

Soldiers tell his "highness" to rise, which he does only after locking eyes with Mary (as he did mid-scourging). Stripped to his loincloth, Jesus flashes back to the last supper's cloth-wrapped bread. He crawls to the cross, and John flashes back to Jesus's words about "greater love" (Jn 15:13). Seen from above, Jesus crawls onto the cross, his hands trembling, the camera cutting repeatedly to Mary (and slightly less often to Magdalene, John, Abenader, and Caiaphas).

As a nail is pressed into his left palm (by Gibson) and then driven, Jesus flashes back to more last supper words (13:33-34; 14:1, 6). The soldiers dislocate Jesus's shoulder to force his right hand to the nail hole. Seen from above, Jesus asks his Father to forgive them during the blood dripping, second nailing. Another nail is driven (in slow motion) through his feet, blood spraying. Mary claws at the ground in anguish. The cross is turned over (in slow motion) so that Jesus hangs horizontally, looking down at the ground as the soldiers bend the nails into place. They flip the cross again so that it falls roughly (cf. the scourging). Caiaphas and other priests watch the placard nailed.

A "eucharistic" flashback, continuing to merge crucifixion and its ritual recreation in the mass, shows the bread/body "given up for you." A closeup of John watching both unites the moments.[32] As Jesus lifts the bread, the film segues to the cross's raising, shot briefly from above. Mary rises with her son, dropping handfuls of dirt; the cross falls into place and Magdalene covers her head (a new scarf—or is she covered by the blood?). Blood drips down the cross, and the story flashes back to the eucharistic blood of the covenant. Again, closeups of John connect both moments before returning to a lingering shot of the bloody cross.

Gesmas, the soldiers, and Caiaphas (strutting forward) taunt Jesus. Again, Jesus asks God to forgive them, and Dismas tells Caiaphas that Jesus speaks specifically to him. Jesus promises Dismas paradise, but a crow pecks out Gesmas's eye.

After a long shot of Golgotha, a storm arrives; blood drips from the cross; soldiers gamble; and the sky darkens (cf. Gethsemane's clouding moon). The soldiers are scared; the crowd and the priests leave; and Mary comes forward (passing Cassius) to kiss her son's bloody feet. Cassius passes Jesus a sponge on a spear. Despite Mary's wish to die with Jesus, Jesus commends Mary and John to each other.

Gesmas mocks Jesus's forsakenness and Jesus looks up, weeping, to ask why. Declaring it accomplished, his head falls forward. He lifts his head one last time (seen in closeup from above in one of the film's most popular images) to entrust his spirit to God, and then gasps in death.

As background music continues softly, a distant God's-eye POV looks down on Golgotha, photographed in a blue palette.[33] A CGI raindrop/teardrop falls to earth. When it strikes the ground (seen at ground level), storm sounds return; Pilate's fortress shakes; the temple is split in two (cf. *The King of Kings*' [1927] earthquake); and soldiers mill about wildly. The soldiers break the thieves' legs, but a tremor prevents them from breaking Jesus's. Abenader throws Cassius a spear and he pierces Jesus's side. Blood and water shower down (cf. the healing water flowing from *Ben-Hur*'s cross), and Cassius kneels in it (in apparent) conversion. Abenader removes his helmet, but makes no confession. In the ruined temple, weeping Caiaphas grabs his head in anguish (cf. the similar gestures by Judas before his suicide and by Caiaphas in *The King of Kings*' ruined temple), and the soldiers flee. Finally, Satan, seen from above in a red-tinted Golgotha, looks upward. The camera recedes, as he screams in pain and anguish (cf. Judas and Caiaphas's anguish).

A dissolve returns to Golgotha, where four Roman soldiers (including Abenader and Cassius), Joseph of Arimathea, and the holy trio depose Jesus. Mary holds her son in a pietà. Closeups linger on the bloody "arms of Christ," before another closeup of the Stabat Mater's bloody face. The camera pulls back as Mary stares unblinkingly into space. The sad scene (contrast *La ricotta*'s [1963] deposition mockery) fades slowly to black.

Seen from within, the tomb's stone rolls away. In a play of light and shadows, the grave clothes sag as if abandoned. Then Jesus, transfigured, rises (yet again) to martial music. The gigantic CGI-nail holes in his hands are visible for all Thomases.

MEMORABLE CHARACTERS

1 Jesus is the bloody, battered meat of Isa. 53, Catholic passion devotion, and evangelical Protestant atonement. Despite intimations of divinity (e.g., ascribing Rev. 21:5 to him), he is the suffering action hero that Mel Gibson portrayed throughout his film career.

2 Mary is the most important character other than Jesus. She is mediator, co-sufferer, and co-redeemer. She channels Jesus's suffering for the viewer. She comforts Jesus, but does not instruct him (contrast the Marys in *King of Kings* 1961, *Il messia* 1975, and *Son of Man* 2006). Magdalene, the converted adulteress, and John form the rest of the holy trio, and are the other important passion witnesses (as, to a lesser extent, is Veronica).

3 Simon of Cyrene is Gibson's "manly man," who helps Jesus bear his cross, and is thus a Christ figure and imitator of Christ (see Linafelt 2004). An ideal Protestant evangelical, he is set free at the cross.

4 The Romans are the most complex characters. Pilate and Abenader are law-and-order men aghast at Jesus's sadistic treatment. They may be the film's most human characters. The common soldiers are brutal beasts. Cassius and Claudia convert to Jesus.[34]

5 Satan is Jesus's chief opponent and Jesus films' most monstrous (androgynous), reptilian Satan (cf. Revelation's dragon). His/her most obvious cinematic precursors are *Greatest Story*'s Dark Hermit and *Jesus*'s (1999) Satan. Gibson also "Satanizes" Judas (in his demonic punishment) and Caiaphas, whose most important forerunner is *The King of Kings*' Caiaphas.

Figure 20.1 Mary, as co-sufferer, listens for her child's groans in *The Passion of the Christ*, directed by Mel Gibson, Icon, 2004. All rights reserved.

MEMORABLE VISUALS

1 Jesus rising to crush the snake's head (Satan) in the garden, echoed when Jesus rises from the scourging, repeatedly on the Via Dolorosa, before the nailing, and, of course, in the tomb (with martial music).
2 The androgynous Satan.
3 Mary's empathy (her ear pressed to the pavement [see Figure 20.1]) and co-suffering with her son. Her face, almost in rigor, is the passion's primary witness (particularly as the camera pulls back during the pietà).
4 Upside down POV shots from Jesus, looking up from the ground.
5 Jesus and Simon framed intimately throughout their Via Dolorosa struggles.
6 The CGI teardrop falling from heaven, ushering in God's judgments on the Romans, Caiaphas, and Satan (cf. also Judas's demonic persecution and the scavenging bird attacking Gesmas).

KEY AUTHORITY/SCRIPTURE

1 Catholic passion devotion and Emmerich's imaginative passion visions are the film's chief authority. As Mary is the chief witness, she is also a part of this authority. The choice of Latin, rather than Greek, as one of the film's "original" languages increases the Catholic aura. Both the ancient languages and the subtitles force the viewer to fixate—meditatively—on the film.
2 Gibson also relies heavily on other Jesus films. *The King of Kings* may be the most important precursor (with its villainous Caiaphas and its cross-earthquake), other than *Braveheart* (see Director).

3 A messianic Isa. 53 epigraph explains that the suffering is "for us."
4 While the film borrows from all the gospels, the film's Roman trial and triumphant passion are noticeably Johannine (for the supersessionist, sacrificial death, see Heb. 9:11-14, 26-28; 10:12).

CULTURAL LOCATION/GENRE: 9/11 EPIC/HORROR

According to conventional wisdom, the biblical epic died in the 1960s with Ray's *King of Kings* and Stevens's *Greatest Story*. While the Hollywood epic moved to other "historical" moments, to outer space and to fantasy, no one believed that biblical epics could be profitable. *The Passion of the Christ*'s surprising success, however, returned that possibility. The most famous biblical epics since have been *Noah* (2014) and *Exodus: Gods and Kings* (2014), but neither was as successful as *The Passion of the Christ* and neither was a Jesus film. Jesus did return to the big screen (e.g., *The Nativity Story* 2006, *Son of God* 2014, and *The Young Messiah* 2016), but no epic Jesus has succeeded *The Passion of the Christ*. Thus, Gibson's legacy now seems less the biblical epic's return and more pre-release, religious marketing's miraculous possibilities and Hollywood's increasing openness to smaller market, conservatively oriented religious films (or television "events," like *The Bible* [2013] from which *Son of God* arose).

The Passion of the Christ had incredible success as a religious event appealing to evangelical Protestants and to Catholics practicing (or remembering) passion devotions.[35] In the United States, and perhaps in the "West" more broadly, the film also became part of post-9/11 rhetoric and debate.[36]

Stephenson Humphries-Brooks tracks Jesus's portrayal as an American hero in the penultimate chapter of his *Hollywood's Making of the American Christ*. He discusses the rise of reluctant action heroes, or American Christs, from some sadistic beating (or even death) to enact a justified, violent revenge (2006: 101–16): for example, Ben-Hur, Spartacus, Shane, Eastwood's Stranger, Eastwood's Preacher, Neo, Martin Riggs, and William Wallace.[37] While Hollywood eschews Revelation's similar figure, Gibson's Jesus is close kin to these heroes (2006: 117–32), as his (repeated) rise from sadistic tortures indicates.

The film's post-9/11 situation is clearer in the film's sympathetic treatment of imperialist Romans (Americans) and in its anti-Semitism. While the ("Eastern") soldiers are brutes, the Roman leaders (Pilate and Abenader) strive to maintain imperial order against foreign, Semitic revolutionaries (terrorists). Further, Jesus and the Jews who move forward with him are not "too Jewish."[38] They look modern, European, American. Those left behind are "Other," medieval stereotypes, and "Eastern"[39] peoples standing in for contemporary Semites (cf. Said ([1978] 1994). The empire is Christian or, at least, redeemable, and, not surprisingly, imperial teardrops fall in righteous vengeance upon the Orientalized Other after the empire's (9/11) wounding.[40]

Finally, the frequent (film noir) blue-wash, the use of unsettling minor keys in the musical background, Gethsemane's entire mise-en-scène, the monstrous, androgynous

Satan, Judas's demonic possession/punishment, the relentless focus on bodily violence and fluids (blood), the Bosch-like faces, and the affects of fear and disgust all identify the film as horror (see Problematic Issue).[41]

DIRECTOR

While often appearing in comedies, Mel Gibson's basic persona, as actor and director, is the suffering action hero, the "American Christ," described by Humphries-Brooks (see Burnett 2002; and, more broadly, Copier 2008). Consequently, Gibson's Jesus most resembles his William Wallace in *Braveheart* (1995).

The chief structural difference is the elaborate backstory that Gibson develops for Wallace, which justifies the reluctant hero's violence. In short, Wallace responds to the evil Edward Longshanks and his henchmen's murderous, oppressive history, whose victims include Scottish nobles, William's father and brother, and William's "secret" wife (Murron). Her death "calls" Wallace to his mission—Scotland's freedom.

The film's passions are so similar that Gibson's *Braveheart* seems a dress rehearsal for his *Passion*. Even though a self-styled "Judas" (Robert the Bruce) betrays Wallace and both protagonists reject "tyranny,"[42] the closest parallels are in the films' temptation and torture scenes (cf. Walsh 2008b). Wallace, too, has a "dark [Gethsemane] night of the soul." His lover (the princess) visits his cell on the eve of his public execution to bring him drugs to dull his senses during the torture to come. He takes the drugs, but spits them out when she leaves, throwing himself to the ground to pray for the strength to die well. Wallace faces the light streaming through an open cell window—echoed in Jesus's moonlit kneeling.

Both films use interminable tortures at their "climax" to display their heroes' integrity. Wallace is repeatedly stretched cruciform, but the film's slow-motion concentration on the manly endurance of physical pain is a closer connection. Both cut repeatedly from this violence to the followers' horrified, awed faces and to those guilty for the travesties. *Braveheart* even includes slow-motion shots of Murron (not Satan) walking slowly through the crowd.[43]

Gradually, both transform their spectacles of imperial power into their heroes' triumphs. Like Jesus, Wallace rises manfully from the ground during his terrible tortures. As Wallace screams his last, triumphant words ("Freedom!" instead of the "Mercy" that would have brought death's release), the film cuts to shots of his admiring followers and the dying, clearly defeated Longshanks. One of the last shots looks up to the cruciform Wallace and to his dying hand dropping Murron's scarf (cf. *The Passion*'s heavenly teardrop), and beyond that to a brilliant blue sky. Thereafter, the betrayer (Robert the Bruce) fights for Scottish freedom (Wallace's cause). Martial music, like that in *The Passion*'s tomb, and Wallace's voiceover accompany the Bruce's attack on the English. Jesus's triumph is lonelier.[44]

PROBLEMATIC ISSUE: VIOLENCE

While many critics denounced the film's anti-Semitism, it received an "R" rating because of its unprecedented (Jesus film) violence. Roger Ebert speculated that a similar film with any other protagonists would have been rated NC-17 (2004). Other reviewers saw the violence as merely one of many features bespeaking horror (see Cultural Location), even calling the film torture porn or splatter horror (see Walsh 2005c).

Those who defended the film's violence typically focused on the horror as (justifiable) passion mysticism (e.g., Irwin 2004; cf. Goodacre 2004).[45] They have a point. As film scholar Isabel Pinedo observes, a "stunning combination of bloody spectacle and excess-driven narrative" is characteristic of both horror and the passion (devotion; quoted in Pieto 2011: 54–5). Apart from the admittedly intensified gore,[46] Gibson employs traditional Jesus film techniques for hallowing the passion: (1) staging it as recognizable Christian art/pageant; (2) littering it with talismans (the blood, the Eucharist, and the "arms of Christ"); (3) presenting it as a cinematic spectacle, with various special effects (Satan's CGI child, the teardrop, and the earthquake); (4) presenting it as the cinematic climax of Jesus's (action hero) life; and (5) cutting from it to closeups of the followers' awed faces.

Still—and even if the crosscutting of crucifixion and Eucharist transubstantiates the film—the violence seems gratuitous (see n45), except in a film aiming at horror affects (which include disgust; see Carrol 1990; Brinkema 2014). Further, it is not just the barbaric scourging (and ubiquitous abuse); it is also that characters must look away.[47] Even (Christ figure) Simon runs from the crucifixion (perhaps, back to the child he left on the road). Those who cannot escape look on with faces from Bosch or cinematic horror—held in rigor, disgust, and post-traumatic stress.[48]

That troubles. And if Gibson has faithfully, masterfully, brutally visualized Western Christianity's crucified imagination, as his defenders say, then perhaps it is not just the film that is horrific. It is that tradition and/or its "world" (including its God and humans; see Cultural Location; Walsh 2005c: 11–14).

20TH CENTURY FOX HOME ENTERTAINMENT DVD, 126 MINUTES, 2007

DVD Extras

Disk One
Passion Recut
   (This "recut" version does not differ from the 2004 release)
Commentaries
   Filmmakers' Commentary by Director/Producer/Co-Screenwriter Mel Gibson, Cinematographer Caleb Deschanel, and Editor John Wright (on/off)
   Production Commentary by Producer Stephen McEveety, Visual Effects Supervisor/Second Unit Director Ted Rae, and Special Make-up and Visual Effects Designer Keith Venderlaan (on/off)
   Theological Commentary by Director/Producer/Co-Screenwriter Mel Gibson, Language Consultant and Aramaic/Latin Translator Father William Fulco, and Theologians Gerry Matatics and Father John Bartunek (on/off)

Music Commentary by Composer John Debney (selected scenes) (on/off)
Footnotes
    "With footnotes selected, interesting facts and trivia will appear throughout your viewing experience of the film" (on/off)

Disk Two
Filmmaking
    By His Wounds, We Are Healed: Making *The Passion of the Christ* (1.40:20)

1. Introduction
2. Script Evolution
3. Language Barriers
    Fr. William Fulco SJ, on the biblical languages
4. Finding Jerusalem
5. Artistic Inspiration
6. The Right Role
    "Mary the mother"
    "Pilate"
    "Mary Magdalene"
    "Judas"
    "Jesus"
7. Evil Personified
8. Tailoring a Perfect Fit
9. The Director
10. Grace in Photography
11. Make-up and Visual Effects
12. The Earthquake
13. The Crucifixion
14. Jim Suffering
15. Breaking the Tension
16. Wrapping Production
17. The Cutting Room
18. The Score
19. Designing the Sound Effects
20. Guerilla [sic] Marketing
21. Spiritual Journey

Below the Line Panel Discussion (13:50)
    Deleted Scenes
        Pilate (2:09)
        Don't Cry (2:25)
The Legacy
    Through the Ages
        (Art and Iconography)
    Paths of a Journey
        (The Via Dolorosa in Jerusalem)
    On Language
        (Fr. William Fulco, SJ)
    Crucifixion: Punishment in the Ancient World
    Anno Domini
        (The afterlives of some of Jesus's disciples and others associated with early Christian legends)
Galleries (a series of still images [drawings])
    Production Art
        Costume and Set Design
        Technical Drawings
        Storyboards
            Garden of Olives
            The Flogging
            Crucifixion FX
            Raising the Cross
    Historical Texts (Mt. 26-28; Mk 14-16; Lk. 22-24; Jn 13-21)
    Art Images (categorized by the fourteen Stations of the Cross)
    Characters and Their Actors
    Unit Photography
    Trailers and TV Spots
    DVD Credits

DVD Chapters

Widescreen. English and Spanish subtitles. English (audio) commentary for the visually impaired, English (additional text) for the hearing impaired.

1 The Beginning, 0:00
        Isa. 53:5, 0:21
            Thirty pieces, 3:23
        Satan appears, 5:53
        Jesus stomps the serpent, 9:10
        Arrest, 11:15

        Mary and Magdalene, 14:09

        Judas under the bridge, 15:35

    Caiaphas, 23:13

        Peter confesses to Mary, 31:10

        Judas repents, 31:43

            Child bites Judas (cf. *The King of Kings*), 33:30

        Mary's ear to the ground, 34:54

        Judas's death, 35:38

    Jesus before Pilate, 38:29

        Pilate's first refusal to condemn, 43:25

    Antipas, 44:10

    Pilate and Claudia again, 46:20

        Pilate (second refusal to condemn), 51:40

            Scourging, 52:05

            Mary looks at Jesus; he rises, 55:01

            Second whipping, 56:12

                Claudia brings cloth to Mary, 59:57

            Satan's child, 1.01:26

        A crown of thorns, 1.05:02

        Mary and Magdalene collect Jesus's blood, 1.05:47

2   Station I (see Table 20.1), 1.08:12

        "Ecce Homo," 1.08:52

        Pilate washes his hands, 1.11:00

        Pilate's third refusal to condemn Jesus, 1.11:59

3   Station II, 1.12:33

4   Station III, 1.15:24

5   Station IV, 1.16:38

        Mary comforts Jesus, 1.17:45

6   Station V, 1.20:47

        Simon of Cyrene, 1.21:28

7   Stations VI & VII, 1.23:18

        Veronica, 1.26:59, 1.27:10

8   Station VIII, 1.27:27 (see n2)

9   Station IX, 1.28:13

        Simon: "We're nearly there," 1.29:00

"Free to go," 1.32:09

10 Station X, 1.34:33

11 Station XI, 1.34:52

    Nailed to the cross, 1.36:36

    Raising the cross, 1.41:02

12 Station XII, 1.43:11

    Two thieves, 1.43:29

    Darkness, 1.46:33

    Casting lots, 1.47:03

    Mary kisses Jesus feet, 1.49:00

    Death, 1.52:22

        Heavenly tear, 1.52:36

        Earthquake, 1.52:49

        Pilate, 1.53:04

        The temple and Caiaphas, 1.53:26

        Spear thrust, 1.54:17

        Satan, 1.55:18

13 Station XIII, 1.55:44

14 Station XIV, 1.57:22[49]

15 Credits, 1.58:50

NOTES

1. The well-known list became widespread in the eighteenth century. The stations grew out of pilgrimages and Franciscan devotions. See Marini n.d.
2. Black-clad women are ubiquitous on the Via Dolorosa, and Jesus meets these women (Eighth Station) in a deleted scene (see DVD Extras).
3. The Eucharist is intercut with the cross. Peter Malone calls this crosscutting the film's greatest strength (2012: 164).
4. As Stations three, four, six, seven, and nine have little gospel precedent, Pope John Paul II inaugurated "The Scriptural Way" in 1991 as a "biblical" alternative.
5. Emmerich was a nineteenth-century nun who claimed Mary mediated passion visions to her. Clemens Brentano, a German Romantic poet, claimed Emmerich reported her visions to him, which he recorded as *The Dolorous Passion of Our Lord Jesus Christ* (1833). These visions are more violent and anti-Semitic than Gibson's film. See Webb (2004b), Boomershine (2005), Eberhart (2005), Tatum (2013: 259–63), and Holderness (2015: 115–7). Film details from Emmerich include the Gethsemane moon, the garden Satan, bribed people in the priests' courtyard, proto-Christian Claudia and "innocent" Pilate, Judas's demonic punishment, Mary's empathetic knowledge of Jesus's sufferings, "Satanic" Caiaphas, the scourging's details, Claudia's towels, Mary and Jesus's Via Dolorosa intimacy, and the Via Dolorosa's multiple falls.

6   Caviezel's first major role was in *The Thin Red Line* (1998). Devoutly Catholic, playing "Jesus" was the opportunity of a lifetime. In 2018, he played Luke in *Paul, Apostle of Christ*.
7   Gibson reluctantly added subtitles late in production.
8   On the film and Christian art, see Morgan (2004) and Apostolos-Cappadona (2004).
9   Cf. the introductory POV looking down on the prone Jesus in *Last Temptation* (1988). That uncertain Jesus, however, differs dramatically from this film's unwavering Jesus. The Jesus in *Jesus* (1999), also seen prone early, stands between these two extremes.
10 Cf. Jesus's restless hands to those in Grünwald's *Crucifixion*.
11 Critics justifiably accused the film of anti-Semitism. For a humorous mockery, see *South Park*'s "The Passion of the Jew" (broadcast March 31, 2004). On the film's anti-Semitism, see the Ad Hoc Scholars Report (2003) and Blizek (2004). Alluding to the skull-capped "little satans," Adele Reinhartz says no other Jesus film so graphically portrays Jn 8:44 (2007: 195; 2013a: 71–2). She also notes the Jewish authorities' (dressed in black and depicted in red settings) visual association with Satan and Gibson's inclusion of all the gospels' anti-Semitic materials (2007: 195, 216–17, 248). She finds the film comparable to *Der Galiläer* (1921), the Jesus tradition's most anti-Semitic film. Barnes Tatum, however, thinks a few film elements minimize anti-Semitism: cries of dissent at the blasphemy charge; the designation of Simon as "Jew"; Dismas telling Caiaphas that Jesus prays for him; and Joseph of Arimathea's deposition assistance (2013: 260, 263–4). Paula Fredriksen (2004) sees the film as an educational opportunity for combatting anti-Semitism.
12 The flashbacks (1) personalize Jesus and those who watch his suffering and (2) assist passion meditation. Cf. Webb (2004a) and Holderness (2015: 122).
13 She "appropriates" because the film's rhetoric applies this language to Jesus's suffering.
14 People in the crowd seem as if they arrived from a Bosch painting. Cf. the faces on the Via Dolorosa in *Last Temptation*.
15 Claudia first appears here, whimpering in her sleep. She is as prominent only in *A.D.: The Bible Continues* (2015).
16 Except for grotesqueries (e.g., the Bosch-people, Antipas, and Barabbas), the scene is the film's only comic relief. Jesus playfully splashes his mother with water (cf. the rough housing in *Jesus* 1999). The flashbacks are characters' "memories"—primarily Jesus's, but also those of Mary, Peter, Magdalene, and John. The audience shares Jesus's POV in (some of) these sequences, and in other moments (e.g., when the world turns topsy-turvy during the scourging, Via Dolorosa, and nailing).
17 One accuser says Jesus claimed to be the bread from heaven (Jn 6:35-56).
18 Caiaphas silences this dissent so efficiently that the scene is hardly the "divided Sanhedrin" of *Greatest Story*, *Jesus of Nazareth*, and *Jesus* (1999).
19 The film uses slow motion more than other Jesus films, forcing meditation on Jesus's suffering. Along with the slow motion, flashbacks, and CGI effects, a gothic (horror) aura and film noir palette are the film's distinctive visual techniques.
20 The scenes parallel Peter and Judas (cf. similar treatments in *Il vangelo*, *Jesus of Nazareth*, and *Jesus* 1999; see Telford 2005).
21 Increasing the intimacy, Pilate speaks Aramaic to Jesus who answers in Latin.
22 This intimacy contrasts with the refusal to frame Satan and Jesus's faces together in the garden. The Sanhedrin trial is mixed on this point, bringing Caiaphas near Jesus for the blasphemy question, and several priests, including Annas, close to Jesus for blows or spitting. That tumult contrasts with Pilate's calm, judicial conversation.

23 The scene is textbook Orientalism. A leopard (a nod to Magdalene's exotic boudoir in *The King of Kings*) is even present.
24 "Positive" portrayals of Pilate or Caiaphas (or the religious authorities) depend upon characterizing them as struggling to maintain a fragile order amidst competing forces and under threats from greater authorities. If one character gets positive treatment (here Pilate), the other is usually vilified (here Caiaphas).
25 Less than a verse in each of the gospels (and only threatened in Luke), the scourging takes up almost eight film minutes.
26 Given recent films' emphasis on Pilate's judicial condemnation of Jesus, the return to early films' association of the Jews with the crucifixion is tellingly anti-Semitic. The blood curse is not subtitled, but Caiaphas says it in Aramaic.
27 Jesus falls repeatedly on the film's Via Dolorosa (but only three times in the stations; see Table 20.1).
28 Identity in Revelation is notoriously fluid, but God seems to be the speaker in Rev. 21:5.
29 The words invert the epigraph's substitutionary atonement language. Does Simon fear that what happened to the saintly cross-bearer in *Life of Brian* (1979) might also happen to him?
30 One soldier mockingly tells the Jew (Simon, the exemplar of Christian discipleship) to continue. In an interesting shot, Simon and Cassius (the good Roman soldier) lift the cross together.
31 Cf. Lucius's dismissal of Barabbas in *King of Kings*. The sequence makes Simon the film's most important character other than Jesus and Mary. He models (manly) Christian discipleship. Cf. John Bunyan's Pilgrim in *A Pilgrim's Progress*.
32 John is an interesting witness as the Gospel of John is the only gospel lacking the institutional words.
33 This shot "supersizes" *King of Kings* and *Jesus Christ Superstar*'s POV shots from the top of the cross.
34 Claudia in the BBC/HBO *The Passion* (2008) differs. She holds her nose at the city's stench as she and Pilate, with the aid of brutal soldiers, enter Jerusalem (cf. Claudia in *King of Kings*). A Galilean nobody/prophet enters the city on its opposite side while Caiaphas, also differing from Gibson's demonic figure, spends time happily with his daughter and pregnant wife. Caiaphas is caught between the prophet and Pilate's competing images of kingdom. The four-part series, clearly aiming to challenge Gibson's rendering, aired on the BBC March 16–23, 2008. HBO has not aired it in the United States and no DVD is available in region 1. For more information, see http://www.bbc.co.uk/thepassion/archive.shtml.
35 For a discussion of the places and groups where and with whom the film was popular, see Malone (2012: 167–70) and Tatum (2013: 267–73).
36 Gibson is Australian and shot the film in Italy at Matera (where Pasolini shot part of *Il vangelo*) and Cinecittà, but Gibson is also thoroughly Hollywood. For a discussion of biblical film scholars' complicity in the post-9/11 debate, see Vander Stichele and Penner (2006). Neoliberalism, not just neoconservatism, participates in empire.
37 See also Jewett (1984), Jewett and Lawrence (1977), and Walsh (2003: 173–85). On Gibson's Jesus as an action hero, see Walsh (2005c; 2008b).
38 Here, Jesus "so white" is a reflex of a larger Orientalizing discourse.
39 For a discussion of historical Jesus studies' similar characterizations, see Arnal (2005) and Crossley (2008; 2012).

40 Humphries-Brooks draws out the allegory: true Christians must convert the secular state (Rome) to Christian values to save the United States from the "Jew" within (everyone who is not a heteronormative, conservative Christian) and so become strong enough to resist Semitic terrorists (2006: 131).
41 See Walsh (2008b), McGeough (2018), and Seesengood (2018).
42 Jesus rejects Satan's tyranny and Pilate's authority over him (Jn 18:36; 19:11).
43 In an earlier scene, Wallace confronts Murron (who wears a hooded robe) in a dark wood (cf. *Passion of the Christ*'s Gethsemane).
44 Rumors persist, however, of a *Passion 2*.
45 More cinematically, one might ask whether the violence is strong (stopping one's thoughts parabolically) or weak (that of guilt-free entertainment or mythic certainty). See McKinney (1993) and Walsh (2017b) (and the citations therein).
46 Roman crucifixion glorified empire by displaying the shamed, abused victim's dying/dead body. The gospels' audaciously different stories glorify God by minimizing the details (thus, Gibson's most important move away from the gospels is his focus on the details of suffering), telling a Jewish—rather than Roman—story (which now seems anti-Semitic), and stressing the passion's providential direction and outcome (often utilizing irony).
47 Alternatively, because Jesus's groin is always covered, the audience in encouraged to look at the bodily (male) violence.
48 Of course, the horrible "sights" "mean" only because of the Isaiah epigraph and other interpretative allusions (e.g., to the Eucharist and Stations of the Cross). Cinematic epigraphs (and caveats), however, are notoriously ineffective compared to their films' visual experiences. Further, death "means" only in the living's eulogies. See the amusing play with this point in *Life of Brian*'s crucifixion scene.
49 The DVD Scene Selection insert lists DVD chap. 14 as "Jesus Rises from The Dead," which is not a Station of the Cross, in contrast to DVD chaps. 2–13. The Fourteenth Station is Jesus's burial. Cf., however, the "resurrection message" in the Fourteenth Station in Daniel's passion play in *Jésus de Montréal*.

21

Son of Man

Mark Dornford-May, director, Spier Films, 2006

PLOT SUMMARY: THIS IS MY WORLD

After a cosmic prologue, Dornford-May's film covers Jesus's entire life—from annunciation to death—in three (approx.) twenty-five-minute parts: (1) the annunciation through the call of Jesus's disciples; (2) Jesus's public activity, emphasizing four sermons; and (3) Jesus's passion. The film concludes with a ten-minute dénouement including Jesus's exaltation. A BBC-like Channel 7 TV news report appears near the beginning of each section; a fourth precedes the women's protest of Jesus's disappearance (cf. Zwick 2013: 110–11; Tatum 2013: 276–87).

After an extreme closeup of a locust,[1] the prologue merges Satan's fall (Rev. 12:7-9?)[2] with Matthew's temptation narrative (4:1-11). Satan and Jesus (Andile Kosi) sit on a sand dune. Satan has a topknot, a snake tattoo on his cheek, an earring, wears black over a red t-shirt, and carries a distinctive goat-hoofed cane. He haunts the film, like the "Satans" in *Greatest Story* (1965) and *The Passion of the Christ* (2004).

White clay covers Jesus's face, and he wears a white robe, indicating participation in a Xhosa circumcision ritual (which appears later).[3] When Satan offers Jesus the world, Jesus pushes him down a sand dune. With the camera on the fallen Satan, Jesus finally speaks: "Get thee behind me, Satan" (Mt. 16:23); "This is my world!" The screen erupts in flames, and Satan counters: "No, this is my world!" The cosmic conflict has begun.

The flames become a burning building and the first TV news report—about "continuing violence in the Kingdom of Judea, Afrika"—appears. The Jesus story has been relocated to modern Africa, *Son of Man*'s most distinctive feature—along with its Black African cast (see Cultural Location).[4] A "Democratic Coalition" has invaded Herode's [sic] territory to "bring peace."[5] An unidentified young woman dodges Herode's militia (wearing distinctive yellow t-shirts) by hiding among slaughtered children in a classroom.[6] Satan, with his distinctive cane, passes through the room.

A child angel in a white loincloth and with white feathers on his chest announces that the woman (Pauline Malefane) will give birth to Jesus. After a beautiful *Magnificat*,[7] a modern infancy includes shepherds (children herding goats), wise men, and the slaughter of the innocents. The infancy includes ominous locust stridulations and child angels who protect Jesus (from Satan) and play with him.[8] They also sing "Sun Will Rise in Spring" (the theme song's first occurrence).[9]

Following angelic instructions, the holy family flees, but finds Herode's militia on the road, slaughtering children (the locust and Satan appear again).[10] At first, Mary covers

Jesus's eyes (he seems about five), but then forces him to gaze upon the horror. *Son of Man*'s plot and characterization hang on this moment. Mary harangues the angel about this injustice "to children" before stalking away. The angel tries to remove Jesus, but he refuses this protection, repeating the prologue's words: "This is my world!" Jesus then follows his mother, under whose tutelage he will stand with the oppressed (see Rohrer-Walsh and Walsh 2013: 167–9).

A dissolve segues to Jesus bathing in the sea with other young men his age. This "baptism" is a Xhosa coming-of-age circumcision ritual (see Giere 2013: 25–7). A flashback to the prologue indicates Jesus's adulthood is a struggle with Satan for "this world." The scene closes with Jesus wiping his face, creating a "true image" in clay on a cloth.

Jesus sets out for work (in Khayelitsha), calling his twelve disciples—three of whom are women (Simone, Phillippa, and Thaddea). Gun-runner Judas, who sells to gangsters identified as the elders Caiaphas and Annas, receives special attention.

The film's second section opens with the second television news report, which announces Herode's death and the Democratic Coalition army's installation of an interim government. Governor Pilate (identified in the credits) promises his forces will withdraw after establishing a secure peace. Meanwhile, Jesus's first sermon calls for nonviolent struggle against poverty, overcrowding, lack of education, epidemics, and thuggery. No one has the right to kill; every life is important. While there are faint gospel echoes (cf. Mt. 5:38-42), the words sound more like those of Steve Biko.[11] When he complies with Jesus's demand that his followers relinquish their weapons, Judas flashes back to executing prisoners as a child soldier.

A man, wearing a red-plaid shirt and carrying a goat-hooved cane, represents the black-clad Satan (who also continues to appear). He oversees an adulteress's necklacing (named Magdalene in the credits).[12] After Jesus and coalition soldiers stop this lynching, the woman sells her jewelry and buys perfumed oil. Finding Jesus at a wedding, she anoints his feet (cf. Lk. 7:36-50). Judas angrily objects to this waste (Jn 12:4-5) and sneaks away that evening to conspire with the elders, as Satan and Jesus watch.

Judas videotapes Jesus's second sermon, which renounces obsession with moral trivialities in favor of a struggle with "real (social) sin." Denying that all authority is divinely instituted (contra Rom. 13:1-7), Jesus offers peace—without destroying beliefs or traditions (cf. Mt. 5:17-20)—and warns hatred will destroy their future if they do not forgive. Meanwhile, two women bring a lame boy over tin roofs as Jesus says those with imperial histories prefer to forget them while blaming Africa's problems on tribalism and corruption. These empires lie, Jesus says, punctuating a litany of imperial injustices with the refrain, "Evil did not fall." "Evil will fall," Jesus says, when his followers denounce the lie that people "just disappear."[13] Then, the lame boy is handed through the roof for Jesus's healing (cf. Mk 2:1-12).[14]

As Jesus and the disciples ride in a "bakkie" (pickup), he tells them, in his third sermon, that they must be above suspicion and must believe in human goodness. At a funeral, Judas videotapes (the unidentified) Lazarus's resurrection. A rainbow appears over Khayelitsha as Peter paints a graffito of this miracle. Jesus also exorcises a girl, seen in videotape and graffito. The elders dismiss Judas's report of these matters as "mumbo jumbo for children"[15] and demand Judas secure proof of Jesus's political ambitions.

Accordingly, Judas videotapes Jesus's (fourth) sermon (on an outhouse) as soldiers keep watch.[16] Claiming that collective dialogue will pierce deaf ears, Jesus calls for solidarity in the quest for human dignity. Peter beats a drum and the people chant (apartheid-era protest tactics). As soldiers approach and a loudspeaker demands the illegal assembly's dispersal, Peter picks up chunks of concrete and advances toward the soldiers. Jesus stops him (cf. Jn 18:10-11), but in an abrupt cut, Judas delivers the "got him" videotape. Another graffito depicts the outhouse sermon.

The third television report, with images of the military suppressing riots, announces the imposition of martial law. Mothers protest outside the governor's palace by placing their small children in the street (cf. the earlier slaughter of the innocents). Jesus sits with these children in solidarity (contrast the Jesus film children-trope's typical sentimentality). Mary packs a bag (ominously containing a picture of Jesus) and travels to him.[17] Jesus processes through Khayelitsha in triumph (in a cart). The Synoptic Gospel controversies become a meeting in which the elders (with the demonic red-shirted man in the background) warn Jesus not to imperil the peace. Demanding a voice for the people, Jesus walks away.

The film's third part opens when the elders (and the demonic man) take Jesus's videotaped outhouse sermon to Pilate. Finding no actionable evidence therein (but mere "tales for children"), Pilate, like so many film Pilates before him, leaves Jesus to the elders: "It will have nothing to do with me, if he disappears." As he says these words, he spills a glass of water on his hands (cf. Mt. 27:24).

A last supper follows, and as the group drinks ceremoniously from a pail, a flashforward shows Jesus's cross while flashbacks (in red) recall slaughtered innocents. After another flashforward to his cross (in red; see Figure 21.1), Jesus predicts his betrayal and denial. In the "garden" (a construction site), Satan and Jesus's guardian angel wait. Despite Jesus's pleas for this to pass, the arresting party arrives with flashlights, led by the demonic man. Satan watches. Judas videotapes his betraying kiss, seen in slow motion (as evidence for his fee?).[18] The arresting party (seen from above) hustles Jesus to the elders. Pilate is not involved. In an industrial shack, the elders beat Jesus as Judas (in his final film appearance) vomits outside. After an Ecce Homo-shot of Jesus's beaten face, Jesus asks how long it will take (to kill him), using words attributed to Steve Biko during his "disappearance."[19] The beatings continue (seen from outside) before henchmen throw Jesus's limp body into a car. Satan watches smilingly as ominous lightning crackles—and Peter denies Jesus in the "garden" (with a cock crowing).

The action cuts between Satan walking the earth (in his final film appearance) and Jesus's "disappearance." As Jesus's body is dumped in an unmarked grave, the elders' TV interview focuses on the need to work closely with coalition forces. The demonic man takes Jesus's boots (becoming more like Satan who wears similar boots), and another man shoots the corpse repeatedly. "Hundred" (Centurion), not yet identified, looks back at the grave.

Learning that Jesus was taken, Mary and other women disrupt the final news report—an interview with Pilate—with photographs of the disappeared (Jesus). The community sings and dances in a night protest, burning the governor's effigy while holding photos of Jesus. Mary wails in grief when Hundred tells her about Jesus's burial site. The screen fades into flames (cf. the prologue's end). Satan and Jesus still contest the world.

At the grave, Mary exhumes Jesus's body and holds it pietà-fashion in a bakkie (without musical background). The child angels wait as Mary and others tie Jesus to a cross with red ribbons (cf. *Godspell*'s [1973] crucifixion; see Staley 2013b), displaying the battered, "disappeared" body on a hill above Khayelitsha (see Figure 21.1). Crowds stream up the hill (cf. Jn 12:32). Mary begins the film's dirge/protest, "The Land is Covered in Darkness," and Peter begins the *toyi-toyi* resistance dance (see Runions 2013). A helicopter flies overhead as armed soldiers arrive. They demand the crowd disperse and fire over the protesters' heads. Mary rises from the ground, looks at the soldiers and then Jesus, and strides toward the soldiers to begin the *toyi-toyi* again.

In the denouement, the crucifixion appears as a graffito. Then Jesus's shadow, accompanied by angel shadows, appears over the empty grave. The thematic "Sun Will Rise in the Spring" begins in the background[20] as Jesus marches with a host of child angels up a sandy hill (cf. the prologue) to his red-ribboned cross. He turns in slow-motion triumph, and the camera freezes on an image of him with upraised fist. The film segues to a title, Gen. 1:26 (cf. *Godspell*'s prologue). The credits follow, with thirty-five shots of Khayelitsha's children and everyday life (without any signs of empire or Satan), and a reprise of the film's music (except for the protest songs; see Nkadimeng and Baugh 2013: 46–7). The film's final shot, as the credits end, is a rainbow over Khayelitsha.

MEMORABLE CHARACTERS

1 Like the Marys in *King of Kings* (1961) and *Il messia* (1975), this Mary mentors her son. Like that in *Jesus* (1999), she leads the post-passion community. Jesus is more son of Mary than Son of God (Rohrer-Walsh and Walsh 2013: 169). In effect, the film is *The Gospel of Mary* (see Nadar 2013: 64–7) or *Mary and the Mothers* (Rohrer Walsh and Walsh 2013).

2 The Steve Biko-Jesus resists poverty, disease, ignorance, political corruption, global capitalism, and empire. He is more interested in political reform than *Il vangelo*'s (1964) Jesus. The slaughter of the innocents psychologically "founds" his social justice concerns.

3 Satan is Jesus's chief opponent. Symbolized by a locust and marked by his goat-hooved cane, he is the lord of "this [violent, oppressive] world," of which Pilate, Caiaphas, Annas, and the demonic man, also carrying a goat-hooved cane, are the human face.

4 Childhood violence shapes Judas's identity. He is the most eager, determined traitor in Jesus films, repeatedly searching for "damning" evidence. By contrast, Peter's graffiti makes him Jesus's personal portrait artist.

MEMORABLE VISUALS

1 Locust (extreme closeup).
2 Child angels.

Figure 21.1 Jesus crucified in protest above Khayelitsha in *Son of Man*, directed by Mark Dornford-May, Spier Films, 2006. All rights reserved.

3 Slaughtered children at the annunciation; the slaughter of the innocents; women protesting in the streets with their children; and women attacking the governor's news conference.

4 Jesus's white-faced, adult circumcision (baptism).

5 Mary's face framed with electric fan halo in the "stable," and Mary meeting Magdalene under a billboard, advertising, "The first. The original."

6 The bakkie pietà.

7 The post-mortem, crucified display of the "disappeared" on the hill above Khayelitsha, including the *toyi-toyi* (see Figure 21.1).

KEY AUTHORITY/SCRIPTURE

1 Satan's fall and continued conflict with Jesus over this world echo Rev. 12:1-9 (and Mt. 4:8) and indicate how authoritative the Chester Mysteries are.

2 Those who resisted apartheid or other oppressive states and "disappeared" like Steve Biko are also key authorities. The film thus rejects Rom. 13:1-7.

3 Jesus's exaltation on the cross is quite Johannine (see, particularly, Jn 12:32).

4 Reflecting on the absence of the words "Son of Man" in the film, Barnes Tatum posits the film's title suggests "what it means to become a human being and to act humanely in the face of 'The Powers that Be'" (2013: 289). In Dan. 7, a heavenly human kingdom (of the Son of Man) does replace those of the beasts, and the film's citation of Gen. 1:26, joined with the epilogue's (hallowing) visuals of Khayelitsha's daily life, may suggest something similar (cf. Rohrer-Walsh and Walsh 2013: 175–6).[21]

CULTURAL LOCATION/GENRE: POSTCOLONIALISM, JESUS RELOCATIONS

Mark Dornford-May's film made its debut at the Sundance Film Festival in February 2006, where it was nominated for the Grand Jury Prize in the "World Cinema—Dramatic" category. Although it did not win the award, audiences loved the film, and it drew positive reviews at subsequent festivals.[22] Because the film did not secure a distributor, most people did not see it until its 2009 DVD release. In January 2010, an international symposium on biblical films and violence at the Akademie Franz Hitze Haus in Münster, Germany, previewed the film for a small group of biblical scholars. Later that year, more saw it under the auspices of the Film and Bible Consultation at the Annual Meeting of the Society of Biblical Literature in Atlanta, Georgia.

Arguably the most important, complex Jesus film since *Jésus de Montréal* (1989), the film's political concerns invite comparison with *Il vangelo* (see Zwick 2013: 115–17; Baugh 2021). The film is closest, however, to *Godspell* and to other films relocating Jesus to modern cities (Staley 2013b; cf. Bakker 2021). While their red-ribboned crucifixions visually connect *Godspell* and *Son of Man,* the latter is a postcolonial rendering of *Godspell*, placing the Jesus story in the contested world of adult politics, rather than reveling in a face-painting play date that leaves (US) empire uncontested (see Staley 2013b: 102–8).

Son of Man certainly invites a postcolonial reading, and the Biko-Jesus's sermons are far more specific than those of *Il vangelo* or *Jésus de Montréal*'s Jesuses. Scholars have argued that the film advocates for postcolonial agency (Punt 2013) and have compared the Jesus/film's message not only to Steve Biko's but also to the efforts of South Africa's Truth and Reconciliation Commission (Giere 2013: 29–30), African women's *imbokodo* movements (Nadar 2013), and Desmond Tutu's *ubuntu* (reconciliation) theology (Middleton and Plate 2013: 137). For Gerald West and the African students with whom he reads the film, however, important questions remain unanswered: for example, "is nonviolence enough, or do we not need substantive macro-economic structural change? Is caring for our child enough or is that not a clear image of Africa's future?" (2013: 20).

For Erin Runions, the film's cultural merit is its incitement to everyday resistance to empire—in the climactic *toyi-toyi* and the epilogue's images of everyday life in Khayelitsha. She argues the film "takes a story line (the Gospel), and art form (film), and a politics (democracy), all of which the United States claims is its own, and resistantly transforms them using African (specifically Xhosa) culture" (2013: 179). *Son of Man* offers a (Black) non-European Jesus that biblical film scholars have treated seriously (see Problematic Issue).

DIRECTOR

Mark Dornford-May had directed just one film, *U-Carmen eKhayelitsha* (2005), prior to *Son of Man*. Both films reset their precursors in Xhosa and in Khayelitsha, are dominated by traditional African music, and have protagonists murdered in the films' climaxes.

Pauline Malefane, Dornford-May's wife, plays the leading role in both films. Further, both films grow out of touring theatrical productions by Dimpho di Kopane (Combined Talents), a South African theater cooperative founded by Dornford-May in 2000.

Son of Man is the film version of Dimpho di Kopane's *The Mysteries—Yiimimangaliso*, which opened in London in 2001 and in the United States in 2004. *The Mysteries* modernize the Chester Mystery plays, themselves community theater, with which Mark Dornford-May has had significant experience.[23] The play is more similar to the mysteries' structure than the film is (e.g., including more Old Testament material; for a concise summary of the play, see Hoile 2003). As in the film, Andile Kosi played Jesus (and God) in London. When the play was reprised in London in 2009, Pauline Malefane played Jesus/God (and another woman played Satan). The reprise also toned down the 2001 play's politics (at least, a white Cain no longer killed a Black Abel, although the police still wielded sjamboks [Billington 2009]).

PROBLEMATIC ISSUE: GLOBAL JESUSES OR FINDING NON-EURO-AMERICAN JESUSES

Because of the historical power of Euro-American empires, as well as the cultural imperialism of Euro-American Christian missions, the cinematic Jesus has too often been the uncritical "face" of such imperialism.

Global cinematic Jesuses, however, are increasingly important. *Karunamayudu* (Ocean of Mercy 1978) sets the Jesus story firmly in Indian bhakti devotion (see Friesen 2008; 2010; Middleton and Plate 2013: 139–41). The Iranian *Al-Masih* (The Messiah 2007) presents the Jesus story so that it coheres with the Quranic Jesus (see Bakker 2013; Middleton and Plate 2013: 141–4; cf. *Histoire de Judas* [Story of Judas 2015] on which see Zwick 2021). Set so completely in these new cultural contexts and worldviews, these films thoroughly remythologize the Jesus story (creating new myths; not anti-myths or parables).[24]

The Italian *Seduto alla sua destra* (Black Jesus 1968) is much closer to *Son of Man*. It transforms the story of Patrice Lumumba (the film's Maurice Lalubi) into an African Jesus. After one of Lalubi's men betrays him, he is imprisoned with two white felons (one a thief) and then tortured (with nails hammered into his hands) before being put to death with the thief. Channeling Lumumba, Lalubi (Woody Strode) confronts the European imperialists at one point saying, "We're not your monkeys any longer." After Lalubi is "disappeared," a young African boy, like one of *Son of Man*'s child angels, stands in the road, impervious to the assassins' weapons, blocking their escape (see Baugh 2013: 120–6).

The Color of the Cross's (2006) depiction of the last two days of its Black Jesus's life targets racism directly. Because he is Black, the Sanhedrin refuses to credit messianic claims about Jesus (Jean-Claude La Marre, also the film's scriptwriter and director). The Romans also treat Black Jews as more troublesome than white Jews. While not well received critically, Darren Middleton and Brent Plate find the film culturally significant (in the United States) for its representation of the divine in the image of Black believers and for its (racially) crucified (lynched) Jesus (2013: 137–9).[25]

As James Cone observes, "It is one thing to think about the cross as a theological concept or as a magical talisman of salvation and quite another to connect Calvary with the lynching tree in the American experience" (2012: 180). Although he does not discuss *The Color of the Cross* or *Son of Man*, Cone and these films reject the cross as salvific talisman in favor of the cross as an emblem of God's suffering with "the crucified of history" (2012: 120–51; see also Walsh 2017b; cf. *Intolerance* 1916).[26] Barnes Tatum speaks similarly of *Son of Man*'s cross. For Tatum, *Son of Man* turns what was once a brutal instrument of empire (Roman law and order) into a protest against such empires (2013: 290).[27]

LORBER DIGITAL, 91 MINUTES, 2009
DVD Chapters

(The TV News Reports are in italics)

1 His Name Shall Be Jesus, 0:00
    Locust (extreme closeup), 0:56
    Satan tempts Jesus, 1:03
    TV News 1: "Reporting from the Kingdom of Judea, Afrika," 2:39
    Annunciation, 5:11

2 Birth, 8:18
    No room in the inn, 9:37
    Child goat herders, 10:09

3 Register with the Authorities, 16:04
    Magi, 16:37
    Angel warns Joseph, 17:40
    Slaughter of innocents, 19:57
    Baptism, 22:08

4 You Are a Man Now, 23:21
    "Veronica's veil," 24:34
    The Twelve, 24:39
    TV News 2: Pilate's interim government, 28:21
    Jesus's First Sermon, 29:12
    Woman caught in adultery, 32:13
    Anointing Jesus's feet (Lk. 7:36-50; Jn 2:1-11; 12:1-8), 34:51
    Judas takes recording to elders, 38:15

5 Finding Peace, 39:45
    Jesus's Second Sermon

Paralytic healed, 40:13

Jesus's Third Sermon, 42:20

Lazarus's resurrection, 43:38

Peter's first graffito, 45:43

Exorcism, 45:58

Second graffito, 47:29

Jesus's Fourth Sermon, 47:35

Judas's video evidence, 50:30

Third graffito, 50:39

TV-News 3: Governor announces martial law, 50:54

Jesus sits with children, 52:59

Triumphal entry, 53:38

6 Taken Away, 55:27

Pilate "washes" his hands, 57:00

Last Supper, 57:32

"Garden," 1.00:13

Beating seen from afar (with Ecce Homo), 1.03:19

Peter's denials, 1.05:40

7 Shot and buried, 1.07:48

8 Searching, 1.09:17

TV-News 4: Women interrupt governor's press conference

Women at the gravesite, 1.11:05

Bakkie pietà, 1.12:07

Red-ribbon cross, 1.12:45

Above the city (Jn 12:32), 1.13:26

Toyi-toyi, 1.16:20

Cross graffito, 1.19:50

"The Sun in spring will rise," 1.20:10

Title: Gen. 1:26, 1.22:00

End Credits, 1.22:21

NOTES

1 Hugh Pyper (2018) has an intriguing postcolonial/translation-oriented reading of the opening credits and prologue. Thabang Nkadimeng and Lloyd Baugh connect the recurring locust and helicopter sounds with Satan (2013: 44).

2   This prologue reflects the medieval Chester Mystery Plays' influence. See Zwick (2013: 111-13) and Director.
3   The image may trouble viewers familiar with Frantz Fanon's 1952 *Black Skin, White Masks* (Pyper 2018: 216).
4   The film's low-budget camera and editing are not remarkable. Its narrative is more episodic than the gospels and relies heavily on them, as does *Il vangelo*, for its meaning (Baugh 2021: 144). The film also mixes "styles": it moves from magical realism and mystery plays through TV newsreel footage to musical theater and a sacred (or sentimental) celebration of ordinary life in Khayelitsha—the poor, violent township near Cape Town where much of the film was shot.
5   The report's language and Pilate's later speeches recall presidential language justifying various US invasions of the Middle East. See Runions (2013: 179-81).
6   The scene turns Luke's annunciation—often rendered pastorally, even sentimentally in art—into a text of terror.
7   Pauline Malefane's professional singing is the high point, but most of the music is the "people's" (see Baugh 2021: 145). Other than in the Jesus musicals, music is as important only in *Il vangelo*. For a translation of the lyrics, see Nkadimeng and Baugh (2013).
8   Sometimes, only Jesus sees the angels (cf. the garden scene).
9   On the film's theatrical nature, see Zwick (2013: 111-13), Holderness (2015: 140-2), and Bakker (2021: 157-9, 162).
10 Gerald West (2013) argues the gospel overwhelms the modern African situation. He claims these children would be conscripted, not slaughtered. Similarly, the Magdalene's necklacing would be for apartheid collaboration, not adultery.
11 The film contains no parables and nothing like the Johannine Christological teaching (although the actor who plays Jesus also plays God in the theatrical production; see Director). Jesus sounds like the "gospel Jesus" only in incidental words spoken to a prostitute, during healings, or in language associated with the passion (e.g., "do quickly," "you will deny," "let this cup"). His themes (psychological liberation from oppression, human dignity, and solidarity) and language (particularly in the outhouse sermon) are reminiscent of Steve Biko's writings (1978). See Mokoena (2017).
12 On necklacing, see n10; Tutu 2007: 19. In the Chester Mysteries, the two key "incidents" in Jesus's ministry are the woman taken in adultery and Lazarus's resurrection (Zwick 2013: 112).
13 The saying functions like a gospel passion prediction. On the "disappearance" of those who oppose police states, see Giere (2013: 27-30).
14 This is Jesus's first miracle in *The King of Kings*, *King of Kings*, and *Greatest Story* (see Staley 2018: 85-8). Jesus's miracles are collages. The child lowered through the roof echoes Mk 2:6, but the mother's cry, "My child is dying," recalls Jairus's words (Mk 5:23). In Lazarus's raising, the carrying of the casket is more reminiscent of the raising of the widow's son (Lk. 7:12).
15 Dismissing children marks one as a villain in Jesus films.
16 Cf. *Il vangelo*'s presentation of Mt. 23. A helicopter flies overhead, a semiotic substitute for the (Satanic) locust that merges Satan and imperial "peace-keepers" (see n1).
17 In a context where families posted their disappeareds' pictures, the photo may be a passion prediction. See nn 13, 19.
18 On the film itself as betrayal (a handing over), see Aichele (2013).
19 On the similarity between Jesus's end and Biko's "disappearance," see, for example, West (2013: 17-18).

20 The dirge (or protest song), "The Land is Covered in Darkness," and "The Sun Will Rise in Spring over the Mountain," which responds to the dirge, are the film's most important music. The second and thematic song appears in different modalities ten times (e.g., at the announcement to the shepherds, when Mary turns Jesus's face to the slaughter of the innocents, at Lazarus's resurrection, when women with children protest in the streets, and when Jesus and the angels ascend crucifixion hill; see Nkadimeng and Baugh 2013: 40–4).
21 This epilogue resembles the divine voiceover opening *Godspell* (which accompanies visuals of graffiti and New York City) about "gardener" humans recreating themselves.
22 It won the Founders Prize at Michael Moore's Traverse City Film Festival (2006); Best Feature at the Pan African Film Festival in Los Angeles (2006); Seattle Weekly Award for Best Film at Sundance (2006); and Best Director, Best Cinematography, and the Special Jury Prize for Original Creative Vision at the River Run International Film Festival in Winston-Salem (2007).
23 Mark Dornford-May has said, "The plays of the Chester Mystery Cycle form some of my earliest memories. As an eight-year-old angel in front of the north side of Chester Cathedral, I remember being really and truly in awe of God because his face was painted gold and he spoke in a language (Latin) that was at once thrilling and mysterious. My father directed at least seven productions of the Chester Mystery Cycle plays, all of which I appeared in, although much as he loved me, even he never cast me as an angel again!" (Amer 2013).
24 Using Julie Sanders's terminology, the films "appropriate," rather than "adapt," the Jesus story (2006: 1–41). For Sanders however, appropriations tend to be critical and surreptitious. These films are neither. In Theodore Ziolkowski's language, they are fictional transfigurations (1972). None of these observations imply an "original" or an "essence." They speak only of changes in a tradition. See this volume's introduction.
25 While *Color of the Cross* comes from "within the empire," biblical film scholars have made it clear that not all Euro-American Jesus films reflect Hollywood/US history and ideology. See, for example, on silent film (Shepherd 2013; 2016b); on Dreyer's films (Vander Stichele 2016); on German Jesus films (Zwick 2016; 2018); on Cinecittà (Page 2021); on the Sardinian *Su Re* (Baugh 2018; 2021); and on Canadian "Christs" (Reinhartz 2021).
26 Any film noticing (the pain of) other crucifixion victims also has the potential for such "solidarity." Pasolini's crucified Stracci (*La ricotta* 1963) is particularly noteworthy here as is *Il vangelo*'s focus on a thief's pain (not Jesus's) as he is nailed to his cross.
27 For a different reading, objecting to the film's hallowing of death, see Walsh (2013a: 200–4).

22

Mary Magdalene

Garth Davis, Universal, 2018

PLOT SUMMARY: A WOMAN'S POINT OF VIEW

Told from Magdalene's POV, the film has three segments: (1) Mary of Magdala's life before she meets Jesus (about seventeen minutes); (2) Mary's experience with Jesus's ministry (about forty-nine minutes); and (3) Mary's experience with Jesus during a Jerusalem Passover (about forty-four minutes).

The film opens with sounds of breathing, a black screen, and a woman sinking into water (seen first from below and then above).[1] A female voiceover reports a conversation, transforming Jesus's parable about a man (e.g., Lk. 13:19) to one about a woman: "What will it be like—the Kingdom?" (Visuals show the woman sinking deeper.)[2] "And he said, it is like a seed, a single grain of mustard seed, which a woman took and sowed in her garden. And it grew and it grew. And the birds of the air made nests in its branches."

In an abrupt perspective change, the Sea of Galilee (presumably) appears in an establishing shot with the film's title.[3] More titles set the historical stage as the camera zooms down: Judaea 33 CE (cf. *Il messia*'s [1975] titular dates).[4] Rome's puppet Antipas rules, but sedition grows and the people long for the prophesied messiah/kingdom of God (cf. *King of Kings*' [1961] opening voiceover). The camera settles on two women. When a man calls frantically, Mary (Rooney Mara)[5] rushes to help her sister-in-law Leah through a difficult childbirth, lying beside her and repeatedly saying, "Look at me." She could be Emmanuel.

In a Sabbath synagogue service, the man with whom Mary's family has arranged her marriage, Ephraim (a slightly older widower with children), stares at Mary. She averts her eyes. In an abrupt cut, women fish (working strenuously as men hasten to hear "that man" speak).[6] Later, Mary finds a new betrothal dress waiting for her. At that evening's meal, Mary listens to her brother Joseph's discussion of "that man's" teaching (about a new, just world), exorcisms, and the Baptist. Mary still cannot hold Ephraim's gaze and runs wildly to the synagogue (see Fletcher 2021: 57–9) and then to the sea before the village rabbi can alert her family. At home, her brother Daniel accuses her of shaming their family and insists there will be a marriage this time.

That night, Daniel wakes her (seen from above) to take her to the sea where he and male villagers forcibly "baptize" her, exorcising the "unnatural thing" inside her. The next morning, Joseph wakes his father, who is holding Mary (seen from above again), and asks permission to fetch the healer.

When he arrives (see Cultural Location), she denies she is possessed, claiming ruefully she has only unhappiness and shame inside. The healer Jesus (Joaquin Phoenix)[7] finally appears on screen when she confesses she longs to know God[8] and admits she sometimes senses God in the stillness. Smiling, Jesus says, "There are no demons here" (contrast Mary's exorcisms in *The King of Kings* 1927; *The Miracle Maker* 1999; and *Magdalena: Released from Shame* 2007).

Later, Mary leaves her nets to hear Jesus talk about the kingdom and being born anew like children. Eventually, he chastises his rancorous listeners: "Wake up, Magdala [village or Mary?]. Open your eyes. Look at the [suffering] people."[9] Alluding to Mary's desires, he asks whether there is something in the silence. Unidentified, Peter (Chiwetel Ejiofor)[10] baptizes while Jesus heals a blind woman using spittle.[11] When the sick overwhelm Jesus (cf. similar scenes in *Jesus Christ Superstar* 1973 and *Last Temptation*), Mary comforts him before Peter angrily pushes her away.

The next morning Mary leaves her family to join Jesus's band and do, as an unidentified Judas (Tahar Rahim)[12] says, "just as they [the male disciples] do" (cf. the offer to Magdalene in *Jesus* 1999). She walks into the lake, and Jesus baptizes her, submersing her three times: "I baptize you with water to cleanse you. I baptize you with light and with fire. I baptize you to be born anew, awake, and ready for the day to come." An angry Peter tells Judas that Magdalene will divide the community.

Mary trails the group, and as Jesus starts up a hill alone, Judas befriends Mary, telling her Jesus is "talking to the angels." Judas then confides that he lost his wife and daughter to drought and Roman taxes. Now he awaits Jesus's kingdom when the dead will rise. Despite Judas's pleas for patience, the disciples discuss strategies for a Passover revolt in Jerusalem. When Mary speaks instead of the prophet's prince of peace, Peter brusquely silences her.

In an intimate moment, Mary tells Jesus that she and her brothers, as children, tried to see how long they could hold their breath underwater—feeling almost bodiless. When she asks if that is what it feels like to be one with God, an amazed Jesus says no one has ever asked how it feels. She smiles, and he looks away. Growing bolder, she, like the Syrophoenician woman (Mk 7:24-30), advises Jesus to include others (women, not Gentiles) in his ministry.

In Cana (identified by intertitle), Jesus goes where women wash clothes (there is no wedding) and asks Mary publicly what he should teach. She advises him to teach the women as he would men. In a scene mixing elements of the Samaritan woman and the woman taken in adultery, Jesus tells the women that they must obey God before men and that they must forgive oppression. A woman responds with the unforgiveable story of a husband who raped and drowned his wife after finding her with another man. Jesus still insists forgiveness is the only way to enter the kingdom because hate consumes a person. Mary baptizes the women, using Jesus's baptismal words.

In an abrupt cut, Mary awakes and rouses the others to follow Jesus. Now, Mary walks behind Jesus at the column's head (not at the rear), until they find Lazarus (whose family does not know Jesus) prepared for burial. Stroking Lazarus's chest, Jesus lies beside him, just as Mary lay beside Leah.[13] With sounds of heavy breathing (cf. the prologue), Lazarus's chest begins to rise, and he stares at the weeping Jesus. Peter (not Martha) confesses Jesus as Son of God and claims people will shout it from the rooftops (cf. *Greatest Story*'s [1965] messianic proclamation to Jerusalem).

The traumatized Jesus, however, enters a cave where he sobbingly reveals that his path goes into darkness/Jerusalem (a passion prediction). Promising to walk the same path, Mary comforts him, "I'm here now. Be here with me" (cf. *Jesus Christ Superstar*'s "Everything's Alright" scene or *The Passion of the Christ*'s [2004] Mary comforting Jesus on the Via Dolorosa). Jesus collapses into her embrace (cf. Jesus in Judas's embrace in *Last Temptation*).

The next day, the crowds line the streets holding candles, lauding Jesus. He responds by quoting the Baptist's prayer about the humble's kingdom. Sending Mary, as his hands, to bless them, he continues with the Lord's Prayer. Led by women, the crowd acclaims him messiah. Finally, Jesus instructs Peter, who thinks the revolt is beginning, to send everyone to preach and to heal, and to take Mary with him.

As they go through Samaria (identified by intertitle), Peter leads, telling a skeptical Mary about the coming glorious revolt. They come upon a burned, crucified corpse and then a corpse-filled village (cf. *Son of Man*'s [2006] annunciation scene). Although Peter is anxious, Mary nurses a dying woman: "Look at me. You're seen and heard in every act of care. You answer to God with every act of love" (cf. Mary's treatment of Leah). As Peter tends to the woman's dying child, a Roman cavalry man arrives. But Mary stands firmly in the road until he turns away.[14] When she and Peter leave, she leads.

After they meet Jesus's mother on the way to Jerusalem (another intertitle), Mother Mary tells Magdalene about Jesus's childhood terrors (his friends claimed him possessed) and of her sense that he was "never completely her own." Mother Mary tells Magdalene she must prepare herself to lose him.[15]

As they approach Jerusalem (identified by intertitle), they pass crosses (in the background). The disciples think the kingdom is coming (cf. *Last Temptation*'s disciples' expectation as they approach Jerusalem), but people pay little attention. In the temple, a montage shows some money changing hands, but also images of blood and animal sacrifice as well as what appear to be fragments of Jesus's own bloody crucifixion.[16] Jesus's demand for repentance is delivered to an insignificant priest at the bustling crowd's edge.

When Jesus begins to destroy things, the priests hustle him away. Like the *Last Temptation*'s Judas, Peter rescues the traumatized Jesus as Roman soldiers arrive. Mary and Judas hide in tunnels, and Judas wonders why Jesus did not seize the kingdom-moment.

In a home, Mary listens to Judas beg Jesus to bring the kingdom so the blessed dead (his family) will rise. Collapsing, Jesus fails to comfort Judas. After Mary washes Jesus's feet, he anoints her eyes as the Baptist anointed him: "Open your eyes to the light. It has begun. Don't stop it now" (cf. Jesus's call of "Magdala"). The prophetic succession is clear: Baptist; Jesus; Mary (see Figure 22.1).

At the brief Seder (reciting parts of Ps. 136),[17] Mary sits at Jesus's right hand. In the garden, Jesus prays at a great tree (not a cold stone), sad that he must go to God. Philip suggests removing Jesus forcibly to safety, but Mary insists that Jesus does what God asks. Later, Mary wakes (shot from above as birds squawk) to find Judas kissing Jesus.[18] The trio stands frozen for a moment before the chaos in which a Roman soldier knocks Mary unconscious (cf. Judas's fate in *Histoire de Judas* 2015).

When Mary wakes, Judas is bathing her wound and telling her Jesus will have to act to save himself, and "the righteous will rise again." Mary races through the city to find the bloody Jesus already carrying his cross beam. Dazed, she collapses sobbing. Abruptly, Jesus hangs on the cross—his mother watching.

Still lying on the Via Dolorosa (seen from above; cf. *Il messia*'s focus on Mother Mary's Via Dolorosa), Mary envisions the prologue's woman sinking in water, but now that woman hangs cruciform. As a barely conscious Jesus hangs on the cross, the camera adopts his POV. A shadow walks forward, merging with the cross's shadow (cf. the cross shadows in *From the Manger to the Cross* 1912 and *King of Kings*). Mary emerges from the shadows to hold Jesus's gaze, helping him through the pain (as she did Leah and the Samaritan woman; cf. *Il messia*'s climactic interaction between Mother Mary and the crucified Jesus).[19] Jesus dies without speaking.[20] His death is not sacrificial, atoning, or heroic.

Mary and Judas watch Jesus's mother cradle his body and kiss his wounds. Judas tells Mary ominously that he is going "to his family," but she remains alone at the tomb. In the morning, the camera zooms in slowly on Judas hanging in a doorway. Mary hears someone calling her name and finds Jesus (seen from afar) outside the tomb.

Mary tells Peter that she saw Jesus alive. The disciples do not believe—they want something more apocalyptic—but she argues, scoffing: "Did he ever say this to you? … [The kingdom is] here within us. All we have to do is to let go of our anguish and resentment and we become like children, just as he said …. It grows with us with every act of love and care, with our forgiveness." Skeptically, Peter asks, "Why would he come to you alone?" John almost believes, but Peter insists on the patriarchal kingdom/church: "Every *man* in this room is his rock, his church, upon which he will build his glorious new world."[21] Mary rejects this as Peter's message, not Jesus's, and refuses to be silenced.[22]

Alone on a hillside with her, Jesus says, "You do not lose heart, even now. Didn't you ask what will it be like? The kingdom?" Looking at each other, they laugh. Then Mary walks through city streets as women watch and follow (including Mother Mary and Cana's [unforgiving] woman; cf. *Son of Man*'s final shots of everyday Khayelitsha). The opening female voiceover about the mustard seed recurs along with the underwater visuals, but now many women float in the water. In the final shot, Mary strides toward the camera (without quite holding its gaze).

Closing titles assert that the gospels say Mary was present at Jesus's death and burial, and was the resurrected Jesus's first witness; that Pope Gregory named her a prostitute in 591; and that in 2016 the Vatican identified her as Apostle of the Apostles, their equal—the resurrected Jesus's first messenger.

MEMORABLE CHARACTERS

1 Mary Magdalene is Jesus's chief apostle, witness, and support (cf. Mother Mary in *Il messia* or *Son of Man*, or Judas in *Last Temptation*). Even Lk. 8:2 becomes mere

patriarchal calumny as the film strenuously rehabilitates Mary's reputation (see Greydanus 2021: 85; Fletcher 2021).[23] Like *Last Temptation*'s Jesus, Mary is a spiritual seeker.

2 Jesus senses God's presence and talks with angels. He is a calm version of *Last Temptation*'s Jesus. He learns from Mary. He speaks of creating supportive community, of becoming like children, and of performing the kingdom—as Mary says more clearly than he after the resurrection proclamation (see *Godspell* 1973 and *Il messia*'s performed kingdoms). Like *Il messia*'s Jesus, he is not the center of attention.

3 Welcoming Mary as fellow disciple, Judas is Jesus films' most engaging, sympathetic Judas (cf., however, the protagonist of *Histoire de Judas*). After the loss of his family, he betrays Jesus to force the kingdom's miraculous arrival and their apocalyptic return. Peter and the other disciples take over some film Judases' Zealot desires.

4 Jesus's other traditional opponents never appear (cf. the absence of white imperialists in *Son of Man*). The primary villain is patriarchy, particularly in Mary's oppressive family and Peter, who tries to oust her from the post-Jesus, patriarchal church.

MEMORABLE VISUALS

1 Mary (one supposes) diving underwater in the prologue and the epilogue (with other women) as well as in a flashback on the Via Dolorosa.
2 Mary baptizing women at Cana.
3 Mary and Jesus lying with and gazing empathetically at those in pain or dead.
4 Mary and Jesus's longing looks.
5 Jesus anointing Mary's eyes as his successor (see Figure 22.1).
6 Mary "helping" Jesus die on the cross by supporting him with her gaze.

Figure 22.1 Jesus anoints Mary's eyes in *Mary Magdalene,* directed by Garth Davis, Universal Pictures, 2018. All rights reserved.

KEY AUTHORITY/SCRIPTURE

1 Jesus films are visually authoritative: the lingering looks at awed, expressive faces, particularly Mary's (cf. *La passion de Jeanne d'Arc*'s [1928] shots of Joan; see Page 2018; and *Il vangelo*'s [1964] shots of the people); the Southern Italy locations, particularly Matera cum Jerusalem (cf. *Il vangelo* and *The Passion of the Christ*);[24] the focus on village life and female leadership (cf. *Il messia*; *Son of Man*; and *La vie du Christ*'s [1906] ubiquitous women); the shots from above of spiritual seekers (cf. *Last Temptation*); and intimacies between Mary and Jesus (cf. *Jesus Christ Superstar*).

2 Mary Magdalene's female presence, voice, and POV. She mentors Jesus and succeeds him (cf. *Il messia* and *Son of Man*'s mothers). Her final face-off with Peter and his patriarchal church is more like the *Gospel of Mary*'s end than those of the canonical gospels (see Hasted 2018).[25]

3 The parable of the mustard seed (Lk. 13:19) and the born anew notion (becoming like children; Jn 3:3-5) are the scriptural source of Jesus and Mary's message. Materials reminiscent of Jesus's Sermon (e.g., forgiveness and love) seem more (psychological) self-help than religious wisdom (Greydanus 2021: 86).

CULTURAL LOCATION/GENRE: WOMAN'S POV; JESUS ADJACENT[26]

Women play active roles alongside men in *Il messia* and *Son of Man*. At the very beginning of Jesus cinema, Alice Guy focused so much on the women around Jesus (Lk. 8:2-3)—eschewing a Jesus-centric focus—that her *La vie du Christ* is virtually a Jesus adjacent film. In striking contrast to Guy's film, however, *Mary Magdalene* does little with (the many women of) Lk. 8:2-3—before its epilogue. Nevertheless, *Mary Magdalene* surpasses its precursors in privileging a woman's POV more consistently.[27]

Michele Fletcher (2021) has demonstrated both the importance of Mary's POV[28] and Mary's maturation as she learns to hold the male gaze. That transformation, however, depends at least as much on seeing Mary, as it does on what Mary sees. In fact, as with the awed faces so often dominating Jesus adjacents (e.g., Demetrius in *The Robe* 1953), Mary's expressive face and eyes are more often on camera (as object of Jesus, Judas, or Peter's gaze) than they are (imagined to be) the camera. The result is a somewhat problematic feminist lens (cf. the discussion in Chapter 1).

The frequent use of Scorsese-like, God's-eye POV shots of a recumbent Mary (e.g., when Daniel wakes Mary for her exorcism; when Joseph wakes Mary and her father; when she lies with Jesus en route to Jerusalem; and when she wakes in the garden, on the Via Dolorosa, and at the tomb)[29] may be the best example of this other ideology. It is evident in Mary and Jesus's first meeting, which follows upon the God's-eye shot of Mary recumbent with her father.[30]

Mary feigns sleep, lying on the floor, as her father tells a man offscreen that he does not know his daughter anymore. During the next minute and twenty-two seconds, the camera alternates between medium closeups and closeups of Mary lying on the floor. She and the man to whom her father spoke discuss her demons. Finally, sandalled feet come into view as this man approaches her from behind. When he asks what she longs for, she replies, "To know God." The camera cuts to Jesus's first (film) appearance, lingering on him like a third conversation partner for fourteen seconds (medium long shot, to medium shot). Mary finally turns to look at Jesus after he says, "And yet you've felt God's presence." The camera slowly pans right, toward Jesus, and Mary replies, "Sometimes, in the stillness, I think I feel it." Jesus responds, "It's always been there. All it needs is your faith." Mary looks up at Jesus, who smiles and says, "There are no demons here." Jesus's POV of Mary returns as he says, "Rest in the light."

Despite the film's feminist concern for Mary's POV and experience, this camerawork reflects a decidedly "orthodox Christian" predisposition about Jesus's identity, and a paternalistic[31] leading of the viewer to "confess" Jesus as "God," before Mary herself is capable of such a confession. Later, after Lazarus's resurrection, Peter confesses Jesus as Son of God, but Mary never does. It does not matter. The camera has already made this confession in the duo's first encounter, drowning out, at least for the moment, Mary's more (questioning) feminist perspective.

DIRECTOR/FILMMAKERS

While women have been significantly involved in the Jesus film tradition, this film's heavy reliance on women filmmakers recalls women's importance in early silents (e.g., Alice Guy; Gene Gauntier). The critically acclaimed Helen Edmundson and Philippa Goslett wrote the script, which deliberately tries to counter Mary's traditional "bad reputation" (see Hasted 2018; Fletcher 2021: 56). In collaboration with Jóhann Jóhannsson, Hildur Guðnadóttir, who won an Academy Award for Best Original Score for *Joker*, composed the music.

Director Garth Davis's previous, feature-length film was the Academy Award-nominated *Lion* (2016). Greig Fraser was the cinematographer and Alexandre de Franceschi the film editor for that film and this. Rooney Mara also performed in *Lion*.

Like *Mary Magdalene*, *Lion*'s story centers on a person who feels he does not "belong" in his family. Saroo, the Indian protagonist, has been adopted by an Australian family. And as in *Mary Magdalene*, his feelings of being different send him on a quest to find his authentic self. Unlike Magdalene, however, Saroo is searching for his lost family. As a boy, he and his older brother Guddu stole coal to help their poor family survive. One day, having lost touch with his brother, Saroo jumped a train, thinking Guddu was on board, and fell asleep. When he awoke, he was in Calcutta, where he did not understand the local language. After misadventures, he was institutionalized and adopted. Later, as a young adult, Indian food sparks a memory of home. He uses Google Earth (improbably) to find his village and his mother. Perhaps, as improbably, Magdalene finds the supportive, egalitarian Jesus (family) amid a patriarchal culture (i.e., her family and then Peter).

WATER PRODUCTIONS LIMITED AND SPIRIT FILM, 120 MINUTES, 2019

DVD Extras

Cast and Crew Interviews (40:47 minutes)
    Rooney Mara (Magdalene), 0:00
    Chiwetel Ejiofor (Peter), 3:03
    Garth Davis (Director), 6:31
    Philippa Goslett (Writer), 14:51
    Iain Canning (Producer), 17:46
    Tahar Rahim (Judas), 21:25
    Liz Watts (Producer), 25:05
    Ariane Labed (Rachel, Magdalene's sister-in-law), 31:44
    Fiona Crombie (Production Designer), 34:46
    Denis Menochet (Daniel, Magdalene's older brother), 38:32
Featurettes (theatrical trailers with selected excerpts from the "Cast and Crew Interviews," above)
    Director Featurette, 1:54
    Cast Featurette, 2:26
    Story Featurette, 2:01
    Behind-the-Scenes Footage, 14:04
    Theatrical Trailer, 2:23

DVD Chapters

(Numbered only. Chapter titles supplied)

1 Prologue (breathing), 0:04
    Title, 2:30
    Judea, 33 CE (intertitle), 2:43
    Sabbath service, 7:22
    Mary and women fish, 9:45
2 Mary's Refusal, 10:51
    Marriage offer, 12:23
    Daniel: "Mary, get up," 16:54
    Jesus appears, 22:06
3 Mary Follows Jesus, 23:47
    Jesus's "first" sermon, 24:18
4 Disciple Mary, 31:13
    Into the water for baptism, 35:12

5 Wary Mary, 37:27
    Judas befriends Mary, 38:36
    Mary and Jesus together, 42:17
    Cana (intertitle), 45:40

6 Mary's Leads Women, 50:12
    Lazarus, 52:00
    "The Baptist's prayer," 59:23
    "Lord's Prayer," 1.00:19
    Mission of the Twelve, 1.01:30

7 Samaria 1.02:12

8 Road to Jerusalem, 1.09:52
    Mother Mary arrives, 1.10:13, 1.10:20
    Passover, 1.14:10
        Triumphal entry, 1.15:27

9 Jerusalem, 1.16:27
    In the temple, 1.16:42
        Crucifixion montage, 1.18:57
        Judas with Mary: "It was the perfect time," 1.23:09
    Mary, Jesus, and Judas, 1.25:00
    Mary washes Jesus's feet, 1.27:11
    Last Supper, 1.29:26

10 The Last Supper, 1.29:27
    Judas's kiss, 1.34:58
    Judas wakes Mary, 1.35:36
    Via dolorosa, 1.36:29
    At the cross, 1.38:31
        Underwater, 1.39:22
    Shadow approaches cross's shadow, 1.40:14
    Jesus dies, 1.41:24
    Judas and Mary, 1.42:05
    To the tomb, 1.43:12
    Judas hangs from a doorway, 1.44:22
    Easter, 1.45:02

11 Behind Closed Doors, 1.45:36
    Mary walks out, 1.50:57

Mary sees Jesus again, 1.51:02

12 Like a Seed, 1.52:01

Mary walking (voiceover replays prologue)

Women underwater, 1.52:29

Credits, 1.53:37

NOTES

1. In private correspondence, Michelle Fletcher reports that the underwater scenes were choreographed and shot by freediver Julie Gautier. See https://juliegautier.com/.
2. Cf. Mary's kingdom conversation with Susanna's child in *Il messia*'s village.
3. The film often uses long shots from above, of the landscape and Jesus's group traversing the landscape, and shots of people lying on the ground, asleep or in distress.
4. The opening camera work seems deliberately obtrusive, calling attention to the prologue. The film also repeatedly echoes the prologue's underwater scene: for example, in Mary's exorcism, her baptism, her discussion with Jesus about "feeling" God, her baptism of other women, her Via Dolorosa vision, and in the epilogue.
5. A popular actress, Mara's notable performances include *The Girl with the Dragon Tattoo* (2011), for which she was nominated for the Academy Award for Best Actress, and *Carol* (2015), for which she was nominated for Best Supporting Actress.
6. The visuals contrast women's confinement with men's freedom.
7. Phoenix began his career as a child actor (with his brother River) and won the Academy Award for Best Actor for *Joker* (2019). Other notable film roles include *Gladiator* (2000, as Commodus), *Walk the Line* (2005, as Johnny Cash), *The Master* (2012, the alcoholic veteran enthralled by an L. Ron Hubbard-like figure), and *Her* (2013). He has been cast as Napoleon Bonaparte in the upcoming *Kitbag*.
8. The conversation about "longing" recalls film Magdalenes amorously attracted to Jesus (e.g., in *Jesus Christ Superstar*; *Last Temptation*), but this Mary seeks God—not a man.
9. Jesus's manner presents him as a "seeker," rather than a divine authority. His message—create supportive community with the suffering—is like that of *Il vangelo*, *Il messia*, and *Son of Man*'s Jesuses.
10. One of Ejiofor's best-known roles is Solomon Northup in *12 Years a Slave* (2013) for which he was nominated for the Academy Award for Best Actor.
11. The blind healed in the gospels are all men.
12. The French Rahim, of Algerian descent, was the lead in the 2009 French *Un prophète*, about the rise of a criminal through Corsican and Muslim gangs.
13. The shot from within Lazarus's tomb is so traditional (see Staley 2021) that the camera depicts Jesus arriving on scene from within a dark, tomb-like space.
14. Fletcher sees this moment as Mary's peripetia. Here and hereafter, she has learned to "hold the [male] gaze" (2021: 59).
15. This mother is far more "realistic" than the tradition's holy norm. Private conversations between the two Marys are common in Jesus films (see, e.g., *King of Kings*; *Jesus* 1999).
16. While cross foreshadowings are traditional (see, e.g., *From the Manger to the Cross*'s cross shadow falling across the young Jesus or *Greatest Story*'s baby Jesus looking at a forest of crosses), this flashforward is most like that of the red-ribboned crucifixion at *Son of Man*'s

last supper. The POV is ambiguous (the film does not use techniques that typically "flag" an entry into a mental state), but the montage seems to be Jesus's mental perspective or, perhaps, a "vision" shared with Mary, as she watches him so intently.

The film rarely adopts Jesus's POV. Other examples include Jesus's initial meeting with Mary, their discussion of his ministry's purpose, Mary's comforting him after Lazarus's resurrection, her washing his feet, and her appearance before him at the cross.

17 There are no words of institution.
18 This film moment most resembles *The King of Kings*' ménage à trois opening.
19 The film's cinematographer (Greig Fraser) was proudest of this shot (Goldman 2019: 29, 30).
20 None of Jesus's words from the cross appear (they are also absent, e.g., from *Il messia*; *Barabbas* 1962; and *Histoire de Judas*). Jesus's trials and torture are also absent as Mary is unconscious when they would have happened.
21 On the film's construction of male gender, see Emmett (2020).
22 Fletcher reads this scene as fulfilling Jane Schaberg's hopes for a cinematic Jesus story from a woman's POV (see Schaberg 1996). Schaberg bemoans Magdalene's silencing in *Jesus of Nazareth* (1977), while Fletcher highlights this Magdalene's refusal to be silenced (2021: 55, 60–1). Fletcher does worry, however, about casting decisions which create a scenario in which a white woman reproves a Black man (2021: 61; see also Warren and Edwards 2018). Against such whitewashing, Davis claims the story of Malala Yousafzai (2014 Nobel Peace Prize winner) reminded him of Magdalene (in DVD Extras), and costume designer Jacqueline Durran employed women from a Jordanian refugee camp to embroider the actors' and actresses' clothing (Minthe 2018).
23 On Magdalene in film, see Reinhartz (2007: 125–49), O'Brien (2016), Hornik (2019), and Fletcher (2021: 62–3 nn4–5).
24 Davis used CGI to superimpose an archeologically accurate second temple onto Matera.
25 Given the message of light/new birth and a faint Johannine structure (Cana through Samaritan woman to Lazarus's resurrection and foot washing [each differing from their Johannine counterparts]), one might argue that the film's Mary is the "beloved disciple," and even the Johannine tradition's source.
26 The film's opening sequences flirt with romance genre clichés (a headstrong woman rejects a suitor and then serendipitously falls under a mysterious stranger's spell), as do Mary and Jesus's longing looks.
27 *La vie du Christ*'s climactic moment—Veronica's display of the "true image" to the audience and the Via Dolorosa women—does, however, privilege women's POV. Nevertheless, Guy's film does not reject patriarchy's public-male/private-female dichotomy as completely as *Mary Magdalene* does (if only for Mary). Even though her women are often in public, Guy simply repositions the divide by rigidly arranging its women and Jesus together in opposition to the hostile, male political world. Curiously, both films have women triumph over (mounted) Rome. Magdalene faces down a Roman cavalry man in a decimated Samaritan village. In *La vie du Christ*, a mounted Roman soldier forces the pregnant Mary away from shelter and a second mounted Roman leads Jesus's Via Dolorosa procession. In the climax, however, Roman soldiers flee in fright while women (and female angels) worship at the empty tomb. Cf. *Mary Magdalene*'s triumphant women epilogue.
28 Mara, director (Garth Davis), and cinematographer (Greig Fraser) all emphasize the importance of Mary's POV in establishing the film's female/Mary affect (see DVD Extras, "Cast and Crew Interviews").

29 Note how often these are "awakenings," visually embodying the theme of Mary's search for God.
30 Following Schaberg's reading of *Jesus of Nazareth*, Fletcher demonstrates that *Mary Magdalene* rewrites the patriarchal Jesus film tradition. This scene may challenge Jesus's meeting with Magdalene in her house of prostitution in *Last Temptation*. That Jesus, however, must wait his turn to be alone with Magdalene.
31 At this point, perhaps Mary is simply shifting from one loving father to another.

A Gospels Harmony of Select Jesus Films

Twenty-two films are listed alphabetically by director in the parallels below. If there are two directors, only the first director is named. DVD chapters are in parentheses; hour/minutes/seconds follow. Since Saville's film follows the exact order of John's gospel, its scenes are easily accessible and only referenced when other films visually portray the Johannine scene. If a director has combined multiple gospel stories, the film scene is referenced more than once.

This gospel parallels list is not intended to be exhaustive. For example, not every visual reference to Magdalene is listed. However, the listed parallels are those most useful for comparative canonical gospel studies (see also the topic index).

The hour/minute/second markers listed below are not uniform across all platforms, internet streaming sites, or computers. However, if one starts with this "Harmony" to see if films have the desired episode, one can then go to the chapters ("DVD Chapters") on those films to see what scenes are near the desired episode, then go to the streaming versions and fast-forward with "educated guessing" to find them.

Arcand, *Jésus de Montréal* (Arrow Special Edition), 1989
Davis, *Mary Magdalene*, 2018
DeMille, *The King of Kings*, 1927
Dornford-May, *Son of Man*, 2006
Gibson, *The Passion of the Christ*, 2004
Greene, *Godspell*, 1973
Griffith, *Intolerance: Love's Struggle throughout the Ages*, 1916
Guy, *La vie du Christ*, 1906
Hayes, *The Miracle Maker: The Story of Jesus*, 2000
Jewison, *Jesus Christ Superstar*, 1973
Jones, *Monty Python's Life of Brian*, 1979
Krish, *The Jesus Film*, 1979
    (remastered, 2014; streaming at Jesus Film Project)
Olcott, *From the Manger to the Cross*, 1912
Pasolini, *Il vangelo secondo Matteo*, 1964 (no DVD chapter divisions)
Ray, *King of Kings*, 1961
Rossellini, *Il messia*, 1975 (streaming on YouTube only)
Saville, *The Gospel of John*, 2003
Scorsese, *The Last Temptation of Christ*, 1988
Stevens, *The Greatest Story Ever Told*, 1965
Young, *Jesus*, 1999

Zecca, *La vie et passion de notre seigneur Jésus Christ*, 1907
Zeffirelli, *Jesus of Nazareth*, 1977

Preface Mt. 1:1-17; Mk 1:1; Lk. 1:1-4; Jn 1:1-18
    Jn 1:1-18
        Saville (1) 0:50
        Stevens (2) 4:48
    Lk. 1:1-4
        Arcand (4) 27:56
        Krish 8:00
    Other
        Arcand (1) 0:03
        Davis (1) 0:04
        DeMille (1) 0:27; (2) 1:15
        Dornford-May (1) 0:56
        Gibson (1) 0:21
        Greene (1) 0:15; (2) 1:16
        Griffith (1) 0:10; (3) 8:38
        Jewison (1) 0:20
        Krish 0:00
        Olcott (1) 0:22
        Pasolini 2:57
        Ray (3) 6:14
        Rossellini, 0:00 (1 Sam. 8) 9:28
        Saville (1) 0:00 (Jn 3:16); (1) 0:04
        Scorsese (2) 0:49
            (This chapter can only be accessed when starting the film from the beginning, after choosing an audio version)

John the Baptist
    Birth and Early Life: Lk. 1:57-80
        Zeffirelli (8) 19:45
    Preaching: Mt. 3:1-12; 14:4-5; Mk 1:2-8; 6:18-19; Lk. 3:1-18; Jn 1:19-28
        Arcand (1) 2:42
        Greene (3) 7:32
        Hayes (4) 8:18
        Krish 14:38
        Pasolini 22:47
        Ray (8) 26:55; (13) 44:32, 46:38
        Rossellini 31:05, 32:00, 38:54
        Scorsese (10) 48:12, 51:41
        Stevens (6) 26:29; (7) 36:43, 38:34
        Young (7) 28:02; (13) 56:38
        Zeffirelli (27) 1.22:38; (29) 1.32:43; (69) 1.26:22

Baptizing: Jn 3:23-36 (see Jesus's baptism)
    Arcand (5) 46:10; (6) 53:38, 51
    Rossellini 38:00
    Saville (4) 23:24
    Zeffirelli (31) 1.42:10

Arrest: Mt. 4:12-16; Mk 1:14; Lk. 3:19-20
    Ray (14) 48:33
    Rossellini 40:00
    Stevens (13) 1.08:04
    Zeffirelli (29) 1.31:19; (31) 1.42:29

In Prison: Mt. 14:3; Mk 6:17-20; Lk. 3:2
    Krish 41:03
    Pasolini 32:03
    Rossellini 40:16
    Stevens (14) 1.15:17
    Young (14) 1.06:55
    Zeffirelli (33) 1.48:44; (40) 2.21:16

Messengers from John: Mt. 11:2-19; Lk. 7:18-35
    Krish 41:03
    Pasolini 55:47
    Ray (18) 1.02:12; (21) 1.10:38; (25) 1.19:50
    Rossellini 53:57, 55:33
    Stevens (14) 1.11:47
    Zeffirelli (32) 1.49:57

Salome's Dance/John's Death: Mt. 14:6-12; Mk 6:21-29; Lk. 3:19
    Arcand (1) 1:57; (11) 1.38:12 (death only)
    Davis (3) 11:46
    Hayes (12) 39:57 (death only)
    Pasolini 1.07:55
    Ray (22) 1.12:30; (25) 1.21:19
    Rossellini 1.08:02, 1.10:38
    Scorsese 1.03:54 (death only)
    Stevens (16) 1.25:31
    Young (16) 1.15:38
    Zeffirelli (29) 1.30:05; (40) 2.25:08; (45) 2.39:42

Burial
    Rossellini 1.10:58
    Zeffirelli (47) 2.49:01

Jesus's question about John's baptism: Mt. 21:23-27; Mk 11:27-33; Lk. 20:1-8
    (See "Controversy," "By whose authority?")

Jesus's Birth and Early Life
Joseph and Mary's betrothal and marriage: Mt. 1:18; Lk. 1:26-27

  Zeffirelli (3) 5:10; (4) 7:13; (8) 18:54; (11) 27:18
Announcement (Mary): Lk. 1:26-38
  Dornford-May (1) 5:11
  Krish 8:25
  Olcott (1) 1:01
  Young (6) 23:02
  Zecca (1) 0:20
  Zeffirelli (5) 9:06
Announcement (Joseph): Mt. 1:18-25
  Olcott (1) 3:00
  Pasolini 3:04
  Young (6) 23:58
  Zeffirelli (9) 21:50
Mary Visits Elizabeth: Lk. 1:39-56
  Krish 9:12
  Stevens (4) 11:34
  Zeffirelli (7) 15:37; (8) 18:40
Bethlehem Journey: Lk. 2:1-6
  Dornford-May (2) 8:21
  Guy 0:39
  Krish 9:53
  Olcott (1) 4:30
  Ray (5) 12:57
  Zecca (1) 1:29
  Zeffirelli (12) 20:35; (14) 36:23, 37:05, 37:44, 38:24; (16) 42:54
Birth: Lk. 2:7
  Arcand (3) 23:13; (5) 34:05; (6) 55:53
  Dornford-May (2) 9:37
  Jones (5) 16:39; (9) 39:41; (15) 1.07:59
  Krish 9:53
  Ray (5) 13:44, 14:40
  Stevens (2) 5:54
  Zecca (2) 4:47 (miraculous appearance)
  Zeffirelli (17) 47:04
Shepherds' Announcement and Visit: Lk. 2:8-20
  Dornford-May (2) 10:09
  Guy 2:18
  Hayes (3) 7:36
  Krish 10:48
  Ray (5) 14:52
  Stevens (3) 10:51
  Zecca (2) 2:39, 4:05
  Zeffirelli (17) 46:37; (18) 49:57

Wise Men's Journey and Visit: Mt. 2:1-12
    Dornford-May (2) 14:05
    Guy 2:51
    Hayes (3) 7:43
    Jones (1) 0:30
    Olcott (1) 7:36
    Pasolini 6:40
    Ray (5) 14:25
    Rossellini 13:32
    Stevens (2) 6:37; (3) 10:17; (4) 11:59
    Young (11) 51:04
    Zecca (2) 4:05, 4:41
    Zeffirelli (14) 36:38, 37:19, 37:56; (15) 38:34; (19) 52:27

Circumcision and Temple Presentation: Lk. 2:21-40
    Dornford-May (3) 22:08
    Krish 11:31
    Zeffirelli (20) 54:11

Flight into Egypt and return: Mt. 2:13-15, 19-22
    Arcand (5) 35:45
    Dornford-May (2) 17.40
    Olcott (1) 13:17
    Pasolini 14:55; 21:21
    Ray (6) 17:24, 18:39
    Rossellini 17:26
    Stevens (4) 13:45; (5) 17:40; (5) 22:31
    Young (11) 48:50
    Zecca (2) 7:30
    Zeffirelli (21) 1.02:05; (22) 1.06:54; (23) 1.08:29

Slaughter of Innocents: Mt. 2:16-18
    Dornford-May (3) 19:57
    Pasolini 17:20
    Ray (6) 16:50, 18:09
    Rossellini 17:32
    Stevens (4) 15:10
    Zecca (2) 6:52
    Zeffirelli (21) 1.03:12

Herod's Death: Mt. 2:19
    Dornford-May (4) 28:21
    Pasolini 20:20
    Ray (6) 18:38
    Rossellini 17:51
    Stevens (4) 16:56; (5) 18:28
    Zeffirelli (23) 1.07:27

Nazareth Childhood: Mt. 2:23; Lk. 2:51-52
    Davis (8) 1.12:30
    Gibson (5) 1.17:45
    Olcott (2) 15:29
    Ray (7) 20:51
    Scorsese (5) 22:20 (Magdalene)
    Stevens (5) 22:31
    Zeffirelli (23) 1.09:35

Miracles
    Baby Jesus miraculously appears in the manger
        Zecca (2) 4:47
    Baby Jesus sleeps through the Slaughter of Innocents
        Zecca (2) 7:37
    Sleeping baby Jesus protected by singing angels
        Guy 4:19
    Holy family hidden from Herod's soldiers
        Zecca (2) 9:47
    Holy family given water from a rock on journey to Egypt (cf. 1 Cor. 10:4)
        Zecca (2) 10:25
    Life to a dead bird (cf. *Infancy Gospel of Thomas* 2:1)
        Young (11) 49:00

Jesus at Twelve in the Temple: Lk. 2:41-50
    Hayes (3) 6:14; (15) 53:53
    Krish 12:35
    Olcott (2) 16:44
    Rossellini 21:10
    Young (7) 21:14
    Zecca (3) 13:55
    Zeffirelli (26) 1.17:44

Carpentry work: Mt. 13:55; Mk 6:3
    Arcand (5) 34:38
    DeMille (9) 35:21, 35:50; 36:18; 41:35
    Gibson (1) 19:55
    Hayes (2) 2:30; (3) 5:19
    Jewison (1) 8:02
    Olcott (2) 21:25
    Ray (34) 1.51:56
    Rossellini 51:06; 1.04:17; 1.19:20
    Saville (10) 57:43
    Scorsese (2) 3.55
    Young (1) 0:55; (2) 4:28; (4) 11:47, 15:28; (6) 22:22
    Zecca (2) 12:03
    Zeffirelli (24) 1.10:29

Joseph's Death
> Young (4) 19:22
> Zeffirelli (30) 1.34:57

Baptism: Mt. 3:13-17; Mk 1:9-11; Lk. 3:21-22; Jn 1:29-34
- Davis (9) 1.27:11
- Dornford-May (4) 28:21
- Greene (3) 10:20
- Hayes (4) 8:43, 9:24
- Krish 14:14
- Olcott (3) 21:35
- Pasolini 26:25
- Rossellini 32:27
- Ray (10) 33:30
- Scorsese (10) 50:42
- Stevens (6) 28:42
- Young (7) 29:32; (9) 37:47
- Zecca (3) 14:41
- Zeffirelli (31) 1.39:12

Temptations: Mt. 4:1-11; Mk 1:12-13; Lk. 4:1-13
- Arcand (9) 1.15:18
- DeMille (15) 1.08:48
- Dornford-May (1) 1:03; (4) 23:22
- Gibson (1) 5:53
- Greene (14) 1.29:09
- Hayes (5) 10:45; (18) 1.03:24; (23) 1.15:05
- Jones (10) 43:13 (Mt. 4:5-6; Lk. 4:9-11)
- Krish 17:54
- Pasolini 28:35
- Ray (11) 36:55; (27) 1.32:28
- Scorsese (11) (53:06); (24) 2.07:08
- Stevens (6) 31:00; (18) 1.40:14
- Young (9) 38:52; (29) 2.16:11
- Zeffirelli (31) 1.42:05 (allusion)

Disciples' Call (alphabetical order)
- Andrew (not John's disciple): Jn 1:35-40
  - Davis (3) 23:52
- Galilean Fishermen: Mt. 4:18-22; Mk 1:16-20
  - Dornford-May (4) 24:39
  - Olcott (3) 23:23
  - Pasolini 33:55
  - Ray (11) 42:05
  - Rossellini 46:47
  - Saville (2) 8:57

    Scorsese (9) 42:08
    Stevens (8) 40:36 (Andrew, Peter, and John)
    Zeffirelli (35) 1.54:57
James (little): Mt. 10:3; Mk 3:18; Lk. 6:15
    Stevens (8) 47:30 (Matthew Levi's brother)
    Zeffirelli (38) 2.13:56 (Matthew Levi's brother)
John's disciples: Jn 1:35-42
    Greene (3) 8:37
    Hayes (4) 9:12 (Peter)
    Pasolini 23:41 (Andrew, John)
    Ray (10) 35:14; (11) 41:26 (John, Andrew)
    Rossellini 33:39 (Andrew and Simon)
    Saville (2) 7:59 (Beloved Disciple [John], Andrew)
    Stevens (8) 39:00 (Judas), 40:36 (Andrew, Peter, and John);
        (14) 1.11:47 (Simon the Zealot)
    Young (7) 28:16 (John and Andrew); (11) 46:40
    Zeffirelli (28) 1.28:47; (31) 1.41:33; (33) 1.47:34, 1.48:15 (Andrew, Philip)
Judas: Mt. 10:4; Mk 3:19; Lk. 6:16 (see also "Judas," p. 342)
    Hayes (6) 18:22
    Ray (19) 1.04:12
    Saville (9) 57:18
    Scorsese (7) 30:13 (the first disciple); (12) 1.08:58
    Stevens (8) 40:29 (the first disciple)
    Young (15) 1.12:12, 1.13:05
    Zeffirelli (50) 3.03:53
Magdalene (not the "Woman caught in adultery" or "Anointing woman,"
    see "Controversy")
    Davis (4) 35:58
    Saville (8) 49:25, 51:39, 54:50, 55:34, 56:46; (23) 1.59:10; (26) 2.12:19; (30) 2.33:27
        with disciples at Peter's confession: Matt 16:13-23; Mk 8:27-33; Lk. 9:18-22;
        Jn 6:68-71
    Stevens (17) 1.34:01; 1.34:51 (she sits up when she hears Peter's words)
    Young (17) 1.24:52 (see [2] 6:34; [16] 1.19:33); (21) 1.34:56; (23) 1.46:57, 1.49:58
    Zeffirelli (48) 2.53:41
Matthew: Levi, the Tax Collector Mt. 9:9-13; Mk 2:13-17; Lk. 5:27-32
    DeMille (9) 40:41
    Hayes (7) 19:09; (9) 30:50
    Krish 29:40
    Rossellini (unnamed) 52:30 (first appearance, 51:11)
    Stevens (11) 58:38
    Young (15) 1.07:48, 1.12:35
    Zeffirelli (36) 2.02:21; (37) 2.05:15; (41) 2.28:42
Nathaniel (see "Philip")

Others
    Arcand (2) 7:08
    Ray (19) 1.04:01
    Saville (2) 10:18
    Stevens (14) 1.12:55 (Thaddeus), 1.18:28 (James)
Peter: Lk. 5:1-11; Jn 1:41-42
    Arcand (2) 7:53
    Davis (7) 1.08:12
    Hayes (7) 19:44
    Krish 25:12
    Ray (11) 42:05
    Saville (2) 9:32
    Stevens (8) 40:47
    Young (13) 58:25
    Zeffirelli (35) 1.56:46; (38) 2.09:56; (39) 2.14:02, 2.20:05; (41) 2.28:49;
        (44) 2.37:22
Philip and Nathaniel Jn 1:45-50
    Rossellini 34:13
Simon the Zealot: Mt. 10:4; Mk 3:18; Lk. 6:15
    Jewison (6) 29:40
    Stevens (14) 1.11:47
    Zeffirelli (52) 8:34
Sons of Zebedee: (James and John)
    Scorsese (8) 41:12 (see "John's disciples")
Thomas: Mt. 10:3; Mk 3:18; Lk. 6:15; Jn 11:16; 14:5; 20:24-29
    Arcand (3) 20:45; (3) 24:42
    Stevens (14) 1:12:55; (17) 1.34:37
    Young (14) 1.06:35
    Zeffirelli (42) 2.32:31; (43) 2.35:43

Twelve Chosen: Mt. 10:1-4; Mk 3:13-19; Lk. 6:12-16; Jn 6:66-71
  Greene (4) 15:33
  Hayes (9) 29:38
  Krish 30:53
  Pasolini 36:00
  Ray (30) 1.39:16
  Rossellini 1.09:48
  Saville (9) 56:15
  Stevens (17) 1.31:35 (seated closest to Jesus)
  Young (21) 1.36:12

Twelve Sent: Mt. 10:1-11; Mk 6:7-13, 30; Lk. 9:1-6, 10
  Davis (6) 1.01:30
  Ray (30) 1.41:13

Rossellini 1.19:13, 1.23:46 (return)
Zeffirelli (54) 16:34; (56) 23:20 (return)

Peter's Confession/First Prophecy of Death: Mt. 16:13-23; Mk 8:27-33; Lk. 9:18-22; Jn 6:68-71

Arcand (5) 40:17, 40:28; (12) 1.47:30
Davis (12) 1.49:16
Dornford-May (5) 42:02; 49:27 (Peter, "the Rock" picks up concrete, and Jesus tells him to put it down)
Jones (14) 1.01:20
Krish 53:28
Pasolini 1.14:50
Rossellini 1.15:56; 1.39:42 (Lk. 18:31-34)
Saville (9) 56:55
Scorsese (12) 1.06:20; (17) 1.31:00
Stevens (17) 1.33:56, 1.34:48 (Magdalene is in the scene)
Young (26) 2.00:32, (Judas) 2.02:03
Zeffirelli (56) 23:35; (58) 33:06

Miracles
General
Arcand (5) 35:55
Jewison (9) 40:39
Olcott (3) 25:23; (4) 34:34; (5) 48:24
Scorsese (13) 1.09:26 (exorcisms)
Stevens (16) 1.26:05
Reports
Davis (2) 11:27
Ray (20) 1.08:05
Rossellini, 54:40
Stevens(16) 1.26:52; (17) 1.33:12
Young (22) 1.43:56
Not New Testament
Blind Girl
DeMille (5) 15:20 (quoting Mk 3:2)
Childhood miracles (see "Jesus's Birth and Early Life")
Exorcism of violent man
Ray (19) 1.04:36
On Via Dolorosa
DeMille (23) 2.02:22, 2.04:25
In alphabetical order
Bent woman: Lk. 13:10-17
Krish 1.04:39 (Sabbath)
Blind from Birth: Jn 9:1-41
Jones (14) 1.01:00

Rossellini 1.34:51
Saville (13) 1.16:06
Stevens (18) 1.36:54, 1.39:02; (19) 1.43:55; (21) 1.55:11; 1.59:28; (27) 2.39:37; (31) 3.09:20
Zeffirelli (68) 1.18:00; (69) 1.22:06

Blind Bartimaeus: Mt. 20:29-34; Mk 10:46-52; Lk. 18:35-43
Krish 1.10:54
Olcott (4) 42:16

Blind man and spittle: Mk 8:22-26
Arcand (5) 36:48
Davis (3) 28:52
Scorsese (13) 1.10:30

Blind men: Mt. 9:27-31
Olcott (3) 28:42
Ray (15) 53:51

Boy possessed by a spirit: Mt. 17:14-21; Mk 9:14-29; Lk. 9:37-43
DeMille (8) 30:32
Dornford-May (5) 45:58
Krish 57:20
Zeffirelli (34) 1.52:00 (see "Capernaum Synagogue" under "Teaching")

Canaanite woman's daughter: Mt. 15:21-29; Mk 7:24-29
Young (22) 1.44:45

Catch of fish: Lk. 5:1-11
Hayes (7) 21:53
Krish 25:12
Rossellini 46:47
Young (13) 58:25
Zecca (3) 21:01
Zeffirelli (35) 1.57:56

Centurion's servant/son healed: Mt. 8:5-13; Lk. 7:1-10; Jn 4:46-54
Saville (6) 31:35
Zeffirelli (67) 1.13:40; (85) 2.48:59

Coin in fish's mouth: Mt. 17:27
DeMille (9) 35:53, 41:10

Ear of slave (see "Betrayal and Arrest")

Feeding 5,000: Mt. 14:13-21; Mk 6:30-44; Lk. 9:10-17; Jn 6:1-15
Arcand (5) 38:20
Jones (13) 1.00:10
Krish 50:03
Pasolini 52:07
Rossellini 1.18:24
Saville (8) 43:05
Zeffirelli (51) 2:27

Fig tree cursed: Mt. 21:18-22; Mk 11:12-14, 20-24
> Greene (5) 24:02 (see "Teaching," "Parables," "Mustard Seed")
> Pasolini 1.26:14; 1.42:50

Gerasene demoniac: Mt. 8:28-34; Mk 5:1-20; Lk. 8:26-39
> Krish 47:54

Hemorrhaging woman: Mt. 9:20-22; Mk 5:25-34; Lk. 8:42-48
> Hayes (11) 37:02
> Olcott (3) 28:39
>> (Male leper kisses hem of Jesus's robe.)
> Stevens (16) 1.24.12

Jairus's daughter: Mt. 9:18-26; Mk 5:21-43; Lk. 8:40-56
> Arcand (5) 37:25
> Guy 6:38
> Hayes (11) 34:40
> Krish 27:33
> Ray (20) 1.07:52
> Zecca (3) 18:58
> Zeffirelli (42) 2.31:47

Lame man: Jn 5:1-18
> Pasolini 50:02 (on Sabbath; see "Withered hand")
> Saville (6) 34:14

Lazarus raised: Jn 11:1-46
> Davis (5) 52:00 (see "Widow's son raised")
> DeMille (11) 45:37
> Dornford-May (5) 43:36, 45:43
> Hayes (5) 13:06; (14) 48:09
> Olcott (4) 37:57
> Rossellini 1.38:20; 1.39:01 (report only)
> Saville (17) 1.30:31
> Scorsese (12) 1.01:40; (15) 1.19:22; (17) 1.29:05 (killed by the future Apostle Paul); (26) 2.18:19 (Jesus marries sisters Mary and Martha)
> Stevens (8) 49:22, 50:30; (9) 51:55; (18) 1.42:03; (20) 1.45:19; (21) 1.47:47; (22) 2.03:42; (32) 3.13:21
> Young (4) 11:24; (6) 25:21; (23) 1.48:56; (24) 1.51:24
> Zecca (3) 22:16
> Zeffirelli (59) 38:10

Leper cleansed: Mt. 8:1-4; Mk 1:40-45; Lk. 5:12-16
> Jones (4) 14:38
> Olcott (3) 28:24
> Pasolini 38:44

Magdalene's demons cast out: Lk. 8:2
> Davis (2) 16:54, 20:16
> DeMille (3) 1:52; (6) 21:30, 22:15

Hayes (2) 2:53, 3:45; (7) 18:52; (9) 28:07
    Krish 40:28
Mute man cured: Mt. 9:32-33; Mk 7:31-37
    Jones (13) 58:26
Paralytic healed: Mt. 9:1-8; Mk 2:1-12; Lk. 5:17-26
    DeMille (4) 10:26
    Dornford-May (5) 40:13
    Hayes (8) 24:41
    Olcott (3) 29:08
    Ray (15) 52:03
    Stevens (11) 1.00:55 (Sabbath); (17) 1.34:22; (21) 1.49:31, 1.55:20, 1.59:22
    Young (14) 1.03:16
    Zeffirelli (36) 2.01:20; (37) 2.06:54
Paralyzed man by pool (see "Lame man")
Raising of Lazarus (see "Lazarus raised")
Stilling the Storm: Mt. 8:23-27; Mk 4:35-41; Lk. 8:22-25
    Krish 46:02
    Ray (20) 1.07:52
Syrophoenician woman's daughter (see "Canaanite woman")
Transfiguration: Mt. 17:1-8; Mk 9:2-8; Lk. 9:28-36
    Krish 55:40
    Zecca (3) 23:38
Walking on water: Mt. 14:22-33; Mk 6:45-52; Jn 6:16-21
    Arcand (5) 35:55
    Olcott (4) 34:21
    Pasolini 54:20
    Saville (8) 47:21
    Young (22) 1.40:09
    Zecca (3) 20:23, 21:03
Water into wine: Jn 2:1-11
    Davis (5) 48:28 (in Cana with women; no wedding)
    Griffith (11) 1.01:56
    Olcott (3) 26:25
    Saville (3) 12:51
    Scorcese (13) 1.11:30
    Young (11) 52:05
    Zecca (3) 15:26
Widow's son raised: Lk. 7:1-10
    Davis (6) 52:00
    Dornford-May (5) 43:36
    Krish 41:18
    Olcott (3) 31:31
Withered hand (Sabbath): Mt. 12:9-10; Mk 3:1-3; Lk. 6:6-8

Pasolini 50:02 (see "Lame man" and "Controversy" "Sabbath [no miracle]")

Teaching (alphabetical order)

    Apocalyptic discourse: Mt. 24:1-51; Mk 13:1-37; Lk. 21:5-36
        Arcand (11) 1.37:38, 1.37:38
        Jones (10) 44:52; (12) 52:39
        Pasolini 1.41:50
        Scorsese (22) 1.55:35
        Zeffirelli (69) 1.26:00

    Capernaum Synagogue: Mk 1:21-28; Lk. 4:31-37; Jn 6:25-59
        Saville (9) 52:40
        Stevens (11) 1.00:55
        Zeffirelli (34) 1.50:25

    Conditions of discipleship (after Peter's confession): Mt. 16:24-28; Mk 8:34-9:1; Lk. 9:23-27
        Gibson (1) 25:54
        Greene (12) 1.13:53 (see [5] 22:30)
        Hayes (15) 56:37
        Jones (15) 1.06:38
        Krish 53:50
        Pasolini 1.16:50
        Ray (16) 56:33
        Rossellini 1.16:25, 1.26:56
        Stevens (9) 53:24
        Young (26) 2.01:14

    Greatest commandment: Mt. 22:34-40; Mk 12:28-31; Lk. 10:25-29, 37
        Greene (10) 1.09:34
        Hayes (13) 45:51
        Krish 1.08:14
        Pasolini 1.34:54
        Ray (27) 1.27:57
        Rossellini 1.24:30
        Stevens (9) 51:55
        Zeffirelli (53) 12:24

    Lord's Prayer: Mt. 6:9-15; Lk. 11:2-4
        Davis (6) 1.00:19
        DeMille (16) 1.12:55
        Hayes (6) 14:39
        Krish 59:30
        Ray (28) 1.35:05
        Rossellini 1.37:49
        Stevens (17) 1.32:56; (20) 1.46:45
        Zeffirelli (57) 30:40

Mary at Jesus's feet: Lk. 10:38-42
    Davis (9) 1.27:11 (see "Controversy," "Anointing Woman")
    Greene (5) 22:30
    Hayes (6) 13:36
    Jewison (2) 12:21 (Magdalene; see "Controversy," "Anointing Woman")
    Olcott (4) 35:15
    Scorsese (12) 1.03:40
    Zecca (3) 16:49 (Magdalene)
Mission discourse: Mt. 10:5-42; Lk. 10:1-24
    (see "Controversy," "Division in households")
    Dornford-May (4) 29:12
    Griffith (11) 1.02:35
    Pasolini 36:00
    Rossellini 1.19:13, 1.26:56
    Zeffirelli (42) 2.30:00, 2.31:16; (54) 16:34; (62) 56:25
Nicodemus: Jn 3:1-21 (see Sanhedrin meeting Jn 7:50-52; Jn 19:39-42)
    Davis (3) 24:51, 27:52, 28:19; (4) 36:26; (6) 50:06 (born anew)
    Saville (4) 19:37
    Zeffirelli (70) 1.29:34
Parables (alphabetical order)
    Good Samaritan: Lk. 10:29-37
        Greene (6) 35:11
        Hayes 45:51
        Krish 1.08:49
        Ray (27) 1.28:24
        Rossellini 1.24:30
    Good Shepherd: Jn 10:1-18
        Gibson (9) 1.31:05
        Ray (27) 1.28:24
        Rossellini 1.23:10
        Saville (15) 1.24:18
    Lamp: Mk 4:21-25; Lk. 8:16-18
        Krish 45:14
    Lost sheep: Mt. 18:10-14; Lk. 15:1-17
        Pasolini 1.18:45
        Ray (19) 1.05:35
    Mustard Seed: Mt. 13:31-32; Mk 4:30-32; Lk. 13:18-19
        Davis (1) 1:45; (12) 1.52:01
        Greene (5) 24:02
        Hayes (7) 20:53
        Krish 1.03:28
    Net: Mt. 13:47-50
        Rossellini 1.07:23

Pharisee and Tax collector: Lk. 18:9-14 (cf. Mt. 6:6-5)
    DeMille (see "Controversy," "Woman caught in adultery")
    Greene (4) 18:00
    Griffith (3) 10:04
    Krish 24:18
Prodigal Son: Lk. 15:11-32
    Greene (9) 58:44
    Scorsese (29) 2.37:18
    Zeffirelli (39) 2.14:54
Rich man and Lazarus: Lk. 16:19-31
    Greene (6) 38:53
    Rossellini 1.20:33
Sheep and goats: Mt. 25:31-46
    Greene (5) 26:50
    Zeffirelli (62) 58:06
Sower: Mt. 13:1-23; Mk 4:1-20; Lk. 8:4-15
    Greene (8) 52:48
    Jones (12) 55:15 (secrets)
    Krish 42:52
    Olcott (4) 33:45
    Pasolini 2.09:57
    Scorsese (7) 37:33
    Stevens (18) 1.40:33
Talents: Mt. 25:14-30; Lk. 19:12-27
    Jones (12) 54.00
Treasure, pearl, net: Mt. 13:44-50
    Young (17) 1.22:03
    Zeffirelli (36) 2.03:09
Two sons: Mt. 21:28-32
    Arcand (5) 40:00
    Pasolini 1.29:55
    Zeffirelli (64) 1.05:52, 1.07:13
Unmerciful Servant: Mt. 18:23-35
    Greene (4) 19:58
Wedding banquet: Mt. 22:1-14; Lk. 14:16-24
    Pasolini 1.32:15
Weeds: Mt. 13:24-30, 36-43
    Ray (16) 56:41
    Rossellini 1.03:32
Wicked tenants: Mt. 21:33-41; Mk 12:1-12; Lk. 20:9-19
    Krish 1.21:00
    Pasolini 1.30:44

Repent, kingdom of God is near: Matt 4:12-17; Mk 1:14-15; Lk. 4:14-15
    Pasolini 33:37
    Zeffirelli (32) 1.45:59; (36) 2.04:25; (36) 2.05:05; (52) 6:10
Rich young man: Mt. 19:16-30; Mk 10:17-31; Lk. 18:18-30
    Krish 1.06:00
    Pasolini 1.05:20
    Rossellini 1.21:33
    Scorsese (12) 1.08:44
    Stevens (9) 51:55
    Zeffirelli (42) 2.30:45, 2.31:26; (49) 3.02:05
Samaritan woman: Jn 4:1-42
    Davis (6) 1.02:07 (Lk. 10:51-55; passing through)
    Guy 5:48
    Hayes (11) 29:28
    Rossellini 36:02
    Saville (5) 25:35
    Stevens (18) 1.37:02 (perhaps)
    Zecca (3) 17:56
Sermon on the Mount/Plain: Mt. 5:1-7:28; Lk. 6:12-49; 11:9-13; 12:22-34
    Arcand (5) 37:20, 38:27, 40:11; (9) 1.07:46
    Davis (6) 59:23
    DeMille (6) 21:53 (Mt. 7:7)
    Dornford-May (5) 47:35; see (5) 42:02
    Gibson (9) 1.29:36
    Greene (4) 15:35, 19:34; (5) 25:55, 29:21; (6) 37:45; (7) 44:32; (8) 48:54; 51:55; (9) 56:24, 1.04:59
    Hayes (6) 14:47
    Jones (3) 7:00; (12) 52:50
    Krish 33:05; 59:30; 61:44; 1.01:12
    Pasolini 41:35
    Ray (26) 1.21:51; (27) 1.25:09
    Rossellini 51:06, 1.12:08, 1.19:13
    Scorsese (8) 39:45; (9) 44:24
    Stevens (8) 41:34; (17) 1.31:25
    Young (15) 1.10:00; (20) 1.31.44
    Zeffirelli (42) 2.3:35; (49) 2:58:48; (50) 3.06:23; (53) 11:54; (57) 28:23; (63) 1.01:51; (65) 1.07:50
Woes against Pharisees and scribes: Mt. 23:1-39; Lk. 11:37-52
    Arcand (9) 1.07:59, 1.08:48
    Greene (10) 1.10:02
    Pasolini 1.35:26
    Rossellini 1.30:49

Stevens (23) 2.12:45
Zeffirelli (69) 1.25:12
Woes against unrepentant cities: Mt. 11:20-24; Lk. 10:13-15
Pasolini 58:52

Controversy (alphabetical order)

Anointing woman: Lk. 7:36-50
Arcand (7) 1.00:09 ("Magdalene")
Davis (9) 1.27:11 (see "Teaching," "Mary at Jesus's feet," and "Bethany Anointing")
Dornford-May (4) 34:51
Guy 8:13 (Magdalene)
Hayes (9) 32:26 (Magdalene)
Jewison (2) 12:21; (9) 43:14; (19) 1.19:44 (Magdalene; see "Teaching," "Mary at Jesus's feet," and "Bethany Anointing")
Krish 37:35 (Magdalene)
Olcott (3) 32:30
Rossellini 59:57
Stevens (22) 2.03:42 (Magdalene)
Zecca (3) 16:49 (Magdalene)
Zeffirelli (48) 2.53:43; (51) 5:19; (53) 13:00 (Magdalene)

By whose authority? (John's baptism): Mt. 21:23-27; Mk 11:27-33; Lk. 20:1-8
Arcand (5) 40:45
Greene (10) 1.08:00
Krish 1.20:02
Zeffirelli (64) 1.05:08

Coin in Temple treasury (see "Widow's mite")

Division in households: Mt. 10:34-36; Lk. 12:51-53
(see "Teaching," "Mission Discourse")
Pasolini 38:32
Rossellini 1.27:00
Scorsese (16) 1.27:24
Zeffirelli (42) 2.30:00

Little children: Mt. 18:1-5; 19:13-15; Mk 9:33-37; 10:13-16; Lk. 9:46-48; 18:15-17
Arcand (4) 25:37
DeMille (10) 42:46
Dornford-May (5) 51:52
Griffith (16) 1.36:58
Hayes (13) 44:46
Krish 1.19:36
Pasolini 1.07:13, 1.17:24
Rossellini 1.37:12
Stevens (14) 1.18:07

Prince of demons: Mt. 12:22-24; Mk 3:19-22; Lk. 11:14-16
    Gibson (1) 25:21
    Hayes (10) 34:31
    Scorsese (4) 12:31 (14) 1.17:13
Rejection in Nazareth: Mt. 13:54-58; Mk 6:1-6; Lk. 4:16-30; Jn 4:43-45
    Krish 20:29
    Pasolini 1.02:34
    Saville (5) 31:10
    Scorsese (14) 1.14:56
    Stevens (18) 1.36:54
    Rossellini 42:38
    Zeffirelli (32) 1.43:00
Rejection of family: Mt. 12:46-50; Mk 3:31-35; Lk. 8:19-25
    Davis (4) 31:13, 34:06; (5) 47:20
    Jones (15) 1.04:00
    Krish 45:45
    Pasolini 1.00:52, 1.01:29, 1.02:45, 1.02:55, 1.03:22
    Scorsese (14) 1.18:10
    Young (20) 1.34:33
    Zeffirelli (54) 18:35
Render unto Caesar: Mt. 22:15-22; Mk 12:13-17; Lk. 20:20-26
    DeMille (9) 35:53
    Dornford-May (5) 39:45
    Greene (10) 1.08:50
    Hayes (15) 55:07
    Jones (7) 28:24
    Krish 1.22:37
    Pasolini 1.32:50
    Young (18) 1.26:24 (see [5] 16:25; [15] 1.07:59); (19) 1.27:35
Sabbath (no miracle): Mt. 12:1-8, 11-12; Mk 2:23-28; 3:4; Lk. 6:1-5; 14:5
    Pasolini 48:00
    Rossellini 55:08, 56:42
    Scorsese (7) 33:46 (see "Woman caught in adultery")
    Zeffirelli (53) 10:54
Tax collectors and sinners: Mt. 9:10-13; 11:19; Mk 2:15-17; Lk. 5:29-32; 7:34
    Arcand (3) 24:33
    Griffith (13) 1.13:28
    Hayes (10) 32:55
    Jones (7) 28:24
    Krish 1.03:45
    Ray (27) 1.29:37
    Young (16) 1.13:58 (see [5] 16:25; [15] 1.07:59)
    Zeffirelli (38) 2.09:56, 2.12:04; (48) 2.57:06; (53) 10:22

Temple taxes: Mt. 17:24-26
    DeMille (9) 35:53
Temple teaching: Jn 7:1-52; 8:20-59; 10:30-33
    Jones (3) 10:40 (stoning for blasphemy)
    Olcott (4) 36:56
    Rossellini 1.29:44
    Saville (11) 1.09:39
    Stevens (23) 2.14:54
    Zeffirelli (69) 1.26:45
Widow's mite: Mk 12:41-43; Lk. 21:1-4
    Krish 1.19:36
    Stevens (9) 54:22
Woman Caught in Adultery: Jn 7:53-8:11
    Arcand (2) 14:00
    DeMille (12) 52:06; (13) 55:45
    Dornford-May (4) 32:13
    Gibson (1) 1.06:11 (Magdalene)
    Griffith (13) 1.13:28
    Jones (14) 1.02:50
    Ray (16) 57:03 (Magdalene)
    Rossellini 1.32:50 (Magdalene)
    Saville (11) 1.05:17; (25) 2.08:22
    Scorsese (7) 33:46 (Magdalene; see [3] 9:06; [4] 14:59)
    Stevens (15) 1.19:38 (Magdalene)
    Young (17) 1.21:00 (Magdalene watches)
    Zeffirelli (66) 1.10:18
Zacchaeus: Lk. 19:1-10
    Krish 1.12:12

Jerusalem Journey: Matt 20:20-28; Mk 10:32-45; Lk. 9:51-53; 22:24-27
    Davis (8) 1.09:56
    DeMille (10) 42:46
    Dornford-May (5) 52:12
    Hayes (12) 41:45; (15) 57:18
    Krish 1.06:00
    Ray (34) 1.52:04, 1.53:00
    Rossellini 1.37:27
    Scorsese (18) 1.33:53
    Stevens (18) 1.42:16
    Young (23) 1.48:48
    Zeffirelli (58) 33:04, 35:19
Jerusalem Lament: Mt. 23:37-39; Lk. 13:34-35
    Greene (11) 1.12:16
    Jewison (6) 34:42

Krish 1.16:28
Pasolini 1.40:50
Stevens (8) 50:02
Zeffirelli (69) 1.26:35

Bethany Anointing: Mt. 26:6-13; Mk 14:3-9; Jn 12:1-11
Davis (9) 1.27:11 (see "Controversy," "Anointing Woman")
Jewison (4) 18:10 (Magdalene) for Judas's response, see (1) 6:35; (9) 43:14; (19) 1.19:44 (see "Controversy," "Anointing woman")
Olcott (4) 42:55
Pasolini 1.43:00
Saville (20) 1.40:51
Stevens (22) 2.03:42 (Magdalene)
Zeffirelli (53) 15:50 (Magdalene; see "Controversy," "Anointing woman")

Triumphal Entry: Mt. 21:1-9; Mk 11:1-10; Lk. 19:28-40; Jn 12:12-19
Davis (8) 1.15:27
DeMille (15) 1.06:12; (16) 1.12:02; 1.12:27
Dornford-May (5) 53:38
Gibson (3) 1.14:10
Guy 9:17
Hayes (15) 51:31
Jewison (4) 23:24, 23:57; (5) 26:07
Krish 1.15:01
Olcott (5) 45:18
Pasolini 1.20:50
Ray (35) 1.53:28
Rossellini 1.40:32
Saville (21) 1.43:15
Scorsese (18) 1.35:50
Stevens (15) 1.20:28 (Capernaum); (22) 2.07:50
Young (25) 1.57:55
Zecca (3) 24:33
Zeffirelli (61) 48:35

Temple Cleansing: Mt. 21:12-16; Mk 11:15-19; Lk. 19:45-48; Jn 2:12-22
Arcand (8) 1.06:14
Davis (9) 1.16:42
DeMille (14) 1.01:10
Hayes (15) 53:36
Jewison (8) 37:21
Krish 1.17:07
Olcott (5) 46:27
Pasolini 1.24:19
Rossellini 35:21
Saville (3) 16:26

Scorsese (16) 1.24:42; (18) 1.37:12
Stevens (23) 2.10:32
Young (18) 1.25:40; (19) 1.28:28
Zecca (3) 25:16
Zeffirelli (61) 51:16; (64) 1.04:39

Plots against Jesus: Mt. 12:14; 26:1-5; Mk 3:6; 14:1-2; Lk. 6:11; 13:31-33; 20:20; 22:1-2
Arcand (6) 55:39
DeMille (12) 52:06
Dornford-May (5) 54:21
Griffith (7) 26:47
Hayes (8) 23:41; (12) 40:49; (15) 57:06
Jewison (3) 15:54
Krish 1.18:45
Olcott (5) 47:24
Pasolini 51:50; 1.42:00
Ray (29) 1.38:46
Rossellini 57:23; 1.44:18
Stevens (14) 1.13:22; (16) 1.31:17; (17) 1.35:54; (22) 2.10:12, 2.12:41, 2.13:18
Young (17) 1.21:30; (22) 1.43:56; (26) 1.59:12
Zeffirelli (60) 46:10; (61) 55:18; (68) 1.17:18

Sanhedrin Meeting: Jn 7:50-52; 11:46-53
Arcand (5) 28:44; (10) 1.22:50
Hayes (15) 52:56
Jewison (4) 22:21, 23:58
Rossellini 1.31:48, 1.38:20
Saville (11) 1.04:42; (19) 1.38:50
Young (25) 1.55:24; (27) 2.04:26
Zeffirelli (71) 1.31:52

Judas: Mt. 10:4; Mk 3:19; Lk. 6:16
Prior to meeting Jesus
    Davis (5) 38:36
    Hayes (6) 17:25
    Ray (8) 23:33; (9) 28:56; (16) 54:58
    Young (15) 1.07:57, 1.11:43
    Zeffirelli (47) 2.50:17; (49) 2.58:20
Becomes disciple (see "Disciples' Call")
Questions and concerns
    Jewison (1) 6:05
    Scorsese (3) 4.21; (12) 1.06:20
    Young (22) 1.46:08; (23) 1.47:45; (26) 2.00:27
    Zeffirelli (52) 6:32; (55) 22:12; (56) 27:10; (63) 1.02:27; (69) 1.28:26
Betrayal plans: Mt. 26:14-16; Mk 14:10-11; Lk. 22:3-6; Jn 6:70-71
    DeMille (16) 1.13:42

    Dornford-May (4) 38:15; (5) 46:35, 50:12
    Gibson (1) 3:23
    Greene (12) 1.16:58
    Hayes (16) 57:16
    Jewison (10) 48:14
    Krish 1.28:44
    Olcott (5) 49:34
    Pasolini 1.45:45
    Ray (37) 2.01:02; (38) 2.08:42
    Rossellini 1.44:43
    Saville (9) 57:18; (23) 1.56:00; (24) 2.04:35
    Scorsese (9) 43:41; (19) 1.40:36; (28) 2.34:04
    Stevens (24) 2.18:53; (25) 2.33:06, 2.33:45; (26) 2.35:56
    Young (26) 2.02:36; (28) 2.12:01
    Zeffirelli (60) 46:10; (72) 1.41:49; (73) 1.50:04
  Betrayal (see "Betrayal and arrest")
  Repentance: Mt. 27:3-5
    Davis (10) 1.42:05
    DeMille (22) 1.59:30, 2.00:30
    Dornford-May (6) 1.04:07
    Gibson (1) 31:43
    Hayes (22) 1.11:00
    Jewison (20) 1.23:20
    Pasolini 2.00:36
    Ray (44) 2.27:01
    Stevens (29) 3.00:11
    Young (33) 2.39:40
  Death: Mt. 27:3-10; Acts 1:15-20
    Davis (10) 1.44:22
    DeMille (22) 2.00.34, 2.01:10; (24) 2.09:18; (25) 2.17:37, 2.20:07
    Gibson (1) 35:38
    Jewison (20) 1.27:12
    Olcott (7) 58:59
    Pasolini 2.01:50
    Ray (49) 2.41:35
    Stevens (30) 3.03:06, 3.04:05, 3.04:30
    Zeffirelli (78) 2.12:28
  Resurrection
    Jewison (22) 1.35:40
Washing Disciples' Feet: Jn 13:1-17
  Gibson (1) 1.02:10
  Greene (13) 1.21:24
  Olcott (6) 51:28

Rossellini 1.46:51
Saville (22) 1.51:12

Last Supper: Mt. 26:20-35; Mk 14:17-31; Lk. 22:14-38; Jn 13:18-16:33
Arcand (11) 1.27:40
Davis (9) 1.29:26
DeMille (17) 1.15:28
Dornford-May (6) 57:32
Gibson (1) 30:01; (2) 1.11:11; (9) 1.34:09; (11) 1.35:10, 1.36:40, 1:37:27, 1.40:54, 1.42:39, 1.38:11
Greene (13) 1.21:08
Guy 10:06
Hayes (17) 58:17
Jewison (12) 53:33
Jones (12) 55:35 (gourd and sandal)
Krish 1.23:27
Olcott (6) 52:29
Pasolini 1.46:20
Ray (38) 2.02:49
Rossellini 1.45:26, 1.48:10
Saville (22) 1.51:37
Scorsese (20) 1.44:50
Stevens (24) 2.18:53; (25) 2.24:24
Young (28) 2.07:59
Zecca (4) 26:19
Zeffirelli (73) 1.45:15

Garden Prayer: Mt. 26:36-44; Mk 14:32-40; Lk. 22:39-46; Jn 17:1-26
Davis (10) 1.31:40
DeMille (18) 1.25:50
Dornford-May (6) 1.00:13
Gibson (1) 0:56, 4:39
Greene (14) 1.27:14
Guy 11:32
Hayes (18) 1.01:19
Jewison (12) 1.00:17
Krish 1.28:54
Olcott (7) 56:01
Pasolini 1.49:50
Ray (39) 2.09:25
Rossellini 1.53:52
Saville (26) 2.14:30
Scorsese (21) 1.52:39
Stevens (26) 2.33:30
Young (29) 2.13:19

Zecca (4) 27:22
Zeffirelli (74) 1.55:45; (75) 1.56:53
Betrayal and Arrest: Mt. 26:45-56; Mk 14:41-52; Lk. 22:47-53; Jn 18:1-12
Arcand (5) 41:09; (9) 1.09:15; (11) 1.30:55
Davis (10) 1.34:53
DeMille (18) 1.26:55, 1.30:54
Dornford-May (6) 1:02:13
Gibson (1) 10:31, 11:15
Greene (14) 1.30:12
Guy 13:01
Hayes (19) 1.04:08
Jewison (13) 1.06:30
Jones (15) 1.09:56
Krish 1.31:07
Olcott (7) 57:55
Pasolini 1.53:38
Ray (40) 2.13:00
Rossellini 1.55:40 (Mark runs away nearly naked)
Saville (26) 2.13:04, 2:13:45; (27) 2.18:48
Scorsese (21) 1.52:37
Stevens (26) 2.38:05
Young (29) 2.15:26; (30) 2.20:16, 2.21:33
Zecca (4) 27:02, 28:27
Zeffirelli (75) 1.58:39
Jesus and High Priest/Sanhedrin; Peter's Denials: Mt. 26:57-27:2; Mk 14:53-15:1; Lk. 22:54-23:1; Jn 18:13-38
DeMille (19) 1.35:12
Dornford-May (6) 1.05:40
Gibson (1) 16:33; 23:13
Guy 14:01, 16:03
Hayes (19) 1.06:10
Jewison (15) 1.10:12
Jones (3) 10:40 (stoning for blasphemy)
Krish 1.33:17, 1.36:00
Pasolini 1.56:25, 1.59:50
Ray (40) 2.14:04
Rossellini 1.57:08
Saville (28) 2.21:36
Scorsese (23) 1.58:48 (denials only)
Stevens (27) 2.39:04
Young (30) 2.22:00
Zecca (4) 29:13
Zeffirelli (77) 2.04:37

Pilate Trial: Mt. 27:11-31; Mk 15:2-20; Lk. 23:2-6, 13-25; Jn 18:28-19:16
  Questions
    Arcand (5) 28:44; (9) 1.11:11, 1.14:42
    DeMille (20) 1.40:00
    Dornford-May (6) 56:13
    Gibson (1) 38:03, 38:29, 48:19; (2) 1.08:21; (12) 1.53:04
    Guy 17:37
    Hayes (21) 1.08:51; (22) 1.11:22
    Jewison (17) 1.14:03; (21) 1.28:10
    Jones (15) 1.10:08; (see [9] 38:20)
    Krish 1.38:18, 1.41:02
    Olcott (7) 1.00:01
    Pasolini 2.02:33
    Ray (41) 2.26:37
    Rossellini 1.59:49
    Saville (29) 2.24:31
    Scorsese (22) 1.53:49
    Stevens (28) 2.45:30, 2.52:52
    Young (31) 2.25:38; (32) 2.32:51
    Zecca (4) 30:30
    Zeffirelli (79) 2.14:14; (80) 2.17:49; (81) 2.25:27
  Scourging/thorn crown: Mt. 27:26-31; Mk 15:15-20; Lk. 22:16, 22; Jn 19:1-3
    Arcand (5) 41:28
    DeMille (20) 1.45:49; (21) 1.47:38
    Dornford-May (6) 1.03:19
    Gibson (1) 52:05, 56:12 (scourging), 1.05:02 (crown of thorns)
    Guy 20:12
    Hayes (21) 1.10:41
    Jewison (21) 1.31:20
    Krish 1.42:09
    Olcott (7) 1.02:10
    Pasolini 2.04:15
    Ray (44) 2.25:41
    Rossellini 2.05:52
    Saville (2) 2:27:54
    Scorsese (22) 1.57:36
    Stevens (28) 2.53:53 (stated, not carried out)
    Young (32) 2.35:14, 2.35:56
    Zecca (4) 31:35
    Zeffirelli (81) 2.23:31
  Pilate's wife's dream ("Claudia"): Mt. 27:19
    DeMille (20) 1.45:12
    Gibson (1) 22:20, 38:03, 43:02, 46:20, 51:36, 59:57; (2) 1.08:49, 1.09:26, 1.10:28, 1.12:15

　　　　Guy 19:33 (Pilate's wife begs him not to harm Jesus)
　　　　Jewison (7) 35:37 (Pilate's dream)
　　　　Ray (44) 2.25:57
　　　　Stevens (22) 2.09:50; (25) 2.32:33
　　Barabbas released: Mt. 27:15-21, 26; Mk 15:6-15; Lk. 23:18-25
　　　　Arcand (8) 1.12:47
　　　　DeMille (20) 1.47:10; (22) 1.54:11
　　　　Gibson (1) 49:19
　　　　Guy 18:24, 18:40
　　　　Hayes (22) 1.12:12 (stated, not shown)
　　　　Jones (17) 1.14:29, 1.20:45; (19) 1.26:51
　　　　Krish 1.41:44
　　　　Pasolini 2:03:27
　　　　Ray (45) 2.28:27
　　　　Rossellini 2.06:51
　　　　Saville (29) 2.27:18 (stated, not shown)
　　　　Stevens (28) 2.54:25
　　　　Young (32) 2.33:54; (33) 2.36:16, 2.36:31
　　　　Zeffirelli (79) 2.12:56; (81) 2.28:23; (82) 2:31:10
　　Pilate washes hands: Mt. 27:24-25
　　　　DeMille (22) 1.58:52
　　　　Dornford-May (6) 56:13
　　　　Gibson (2) 1.11:00, 1.11:46
　　　　Guy 18:47
　　　　Hayes (22) 1.12:38
　　　　Jewison (21) 1.34:40
　　　　Olcott (7) 1.03:35
　　　　Pasolini 2.03:33 (Pilate holds helmet near well; does not wash)
　　　　Rossellini 2.07:21
　　　　Stevens (28) 2.57:24
　　　　Young (33) 2.37:11
　　　　Zecca (4) 33:20
　　　　Zeffirelli (79) 2.15:32
Antipas: Lk. 22:7-12
　　Arcand (9) 1.12:56
　　Gibson (1) 44:10
　　Hayes (21) 1.10:09
　　Jewison (18) 1.16:14
　　Krish 1.39:28
　　Olcott (7) 1.01:12
　　Ray (43) 2.22:30
　　Stevens (28) 2.48:36
　　Young (32) 2.29:30

Via Dolorosa: Mt. 27:31-32; Mk 15:20-22; Lk. 23:26-32; Jn 19:16-17
    On the way
        Arcand (5) 42:41
        Davis (10) 1.36:29
        DeMille (23) 2.01:26
        Gibson (2) 1.12:34
        Griffith (24) 2.34:13; (27) 2.56:37
        Guy 21:24
        Hayes (23) 1.12:59
        Jewison (22) 1.38:04
        Jones (17) 1.19:32, 1.21:34; (18) 1.22:41, 1.23:02
        Krish 1.43:34
        Olcott (7) 1.04:45
        Pasolini 2.05:00
        Ray (46) 2.32:05
        Saville (30) 2.33:19
        Scorsese (23) 1.59:15
        Stevens (29) 2.57.39
        Young (33) 2.37:50
        Zecca (4) 33:32
        Zeffirelli (83) 2.35:51
    Veronica (Bernice, in *The Acts of Pilate*)
        Dornford-May (4) 24:34
        Gibson (5) 1.20:05; (7) 1.23:44, 1.26:59, 1.27:10, 1.27:21
        Guy 23:34
        Ray (46) 2.24:25
        Stevens (29) 2.58:53
        Zecca (5) 34:15
        Zeffirelli (83) 2.38:24
    Simon of Cyrene: Mt. 27:32; Mk 15:21; Lk. 23:26
        DeMille (23) 2.05:05
        Gibson (6) 1.21:28; (7) 1.25:30; (9) 1.29:00, 1.30:16, 1.30:54, 1.32:09
        Guy 21:18, 27:57
        Jones (17) 1.20:25; (18) 1.23:58
        Krish 1.44:16
        Olcott (7) 1.05:51
        Pasolini 2.05:23
        Ray (46) 2.34:13
        Stevens (28) 2.55:55; (29) 3.00:45; (31) 3.07:20
Crucifixion: Mt. 27:31-32; Mk 15:20-22; Lk. 23:26-32; Jn 19:18-22
        Crucifixions—not Jesus
        Arcand (2) 11:37; (5) 41:33, 43:04, 43:48; (11) 1.31:00
        Davis (8) 1.14:25

Jones (4) 14:31; (11) 50:25; (15) 1.10:20; (16) 1.13:20; (17) 1.16:54;
(18) 1.22:48, 1.23:04
Krish 1.07:36
Pasolini 2.07:05
Ray (4) 12:14; (48) 2.39:38
Scorsese (3) 7:46; (18) 1.34:43; (22) 1.57:02
Stevens (5) 22:54
Young (8) 37:02

Nailed to cross: Mt. 27:35-38; Mk 15:25-27; Lk. 23:32-34; Jn 19:18-22
Arcand (5) 43:14
Davis (10) 1.38:31
DeMille (24) 2.09:29
Gibson (11) 1.36:36
Greene (15) 1.32:30
Guy 28:16
Hayes (23) 1.14:16
Jewison (22) 1.39:08
Jones (18) 1.24:23 (Brian)
Krish 1.47:00
Olcott (7) 1.06:57
Pasolini 2.08:30
Ray (47) 2.37:05
Saville (30) 2.34:00
Scorsese (23) 2.02:48
Stevens (30) 3.04:16
Young (34) 2.40:34
Zecca (5) 36:43
Zeffirelli (83) 2.39:15

Three crosses: Mt. 27:38; Mk 15:27; Lk. 23:33
Davis (10) 1.39:02, 1.39:56, 1.40:25 (no speaking)
Rossellini 2.09:35 (no speaking)

Chief priests and others mock: Mt. 27:39-44; Mk 15:29-32; Lk. 23:35-38
Arcand (11) 1.31:09
DeMille (24) 2.10:40
Gibson (12) 1.44:00
Guy 28:34
Hayes (23) 1.14:57
Jewison (23) 1.40:07
Jones (19) 1.25:21 (see "Centurion's witness")
Krish 1.49:13
Scorsese (23) 2.04:34; (24) 2.06:41
Stevens (30) 3.05:44
Young (34) 2.41:22

    Zecca (5) 38:21
    Zeffirelli (83) 2.40:04; (85) 2.46:20
Dividing garments: Mt. 27:35; Mk 15:24; Lk. 23:34; Jn 19:23-27
    Gibson (12) 1.47:03
    Krish 1.50:05
    Olcott (7) 1.07:22
    Rossellini 2.08:34 (Mary's words); 2.12:03 (John's words)
    Saville (30) 2.35:40
    Young (34) 2.42:27
    Zecca (5) 38:31
Penitent thief: Lk. 23:29-44
    DeMille (24) 2.12:19-2.15:18
    Gibson (12) 1.43:29, 1.44:52, 1.45:10, 1.50:39, 1:53:44
    Jones (18) 1.24:51
    Krish 1.52:11
    Olcott (7) 1.07:48
    Ray (47) 2.37:52
    Stevens (30) 3.05:55
    Zeffirelli (84) 2.41:19
Darkness: Mt. 27:45, 51-53; Mk 15:33; Lk. 23:44
    Arcand (11) 1.40:34
    DeMille (25) 2.15:17
    Dornford-May (6) 1.05:40, 1.14:21
    Gibson (12) 1.46:30
    Griffith (29) 3.11:21
    Hayes (23) 1.14:10, 1.15:24
    Krish 1.53:05
    Olcott (7) 1.09:07
    Pasolini 2.11:23
    Ray (48) 2.40:51
    Scorsese (24) 2.05:24
    Stevens (31) 3.09.02 (thunderstorm)
    Young (34) 2.42:16
    Zecca (5) 38:53
    Zeffirelli (86) 3.50:49
Wine with myrrh: Mt. 27:34; Mk 15:23
    Arcand (5) 43:00
    DeMille (24) 2.08:55
    Pasolini 2.06:21
Sour wine on a stick: Mt. 27:49; Mk 15:38; Lk. 23:36; Jn 19:28-29
    Arcand (5) 44:29
    Gibson (12) 1.49:10
    Krish 1.51:07

        Olcott (7) 1.08:11
        Pasolini 2.10:30
        Saville (30) 2.37:09
        Stevens (31) 3.07:54
Death: Mt. 27:50, 55-56; Mk 15:37, 40-41; Lk. 23:46, 48-49; Jn 19:30
        Arcand (5) 44:51; (9) 1.09:15; (12) 1.42:31
        Davis (10) 1.41:25
        DeMille (25) 2.17:00
        Dornford-May (6) 1.06:22
        Gibson (12) 1.52:22
        Greene (15) 1.35:00
        Griffith (29) 3.11:21
        Hayes (23) 1.16:04
        Jewison (23) 1.41:58
        Krish 1.54:18
        Olcott (7) 1.09:41
        Pasolini 2.10:52
        Ray (48) 2.40:44
        Rossellini 2.10:47
        Saville (30) 2.37:54
        Scorsese (29) 2.39:26
        Stevens (31) 3.09:07
        Young (34) 2.43:08
        Zecca (5) 38:51
        Zeffirelli (85) 2:50:25
Spear thrust/breaking legs: Jn 19:31-37
        Arcand (5) 45:30
        DeMille (25) 2.20:26
        Gibson (12) 1.54:17
        Guy 29:10
        Saville (30) 2.38:02
        Zecca (5) 39:02
Centurion's witness: Mt. 27:54; Mk 15:39; Lk. 23:47
        DeMille (25) 2.20:35
        Dornford-May (6) 1.10:08
        Gibson (12) 1.52:47, 1.53:07; (13) 1.54:50
        Hayes (23) 1.16:26
        Jones (19) 1.25:21
        Krish 1.54:23
        Ray (49) 2.41:16
        Stevens (31) 3.09:26
        Zecca (5) 39:09
        Zeffirelli (85) 2.48:59 (see "Miracles," "Centurion's servant/son healed")

Veil of Temple torn: Mt. 27:51; Mk 15:38; Lk. 23:45
    DeMille (25) 2.20:53
    Gibson (12) 1.53:26, 1.53:36, 1.54:57
    Hayes (23) 1.16:04
    Krish 1.53:34
    Stevens (31) 3.09:40
Earthquake: Mt. 27:51-52; 28:2
    DeMille (25) 2.19:06
    Gibson (12) 1.52:49
    Olcott (7) 1.09:24
    Pasolini 2.10:53
    Young (34) 2.43:25
    Zecca (5) 38:53
Deposition: Mt. 27:57-59; Mk 15:42-46; Lk. 23:50-53; Jn 19:38-40
    Arcand (11) 1.40:16
    Davis (10) 1.41:33
    Dornford-May (6) 1.12:07
    Gibson (13) 1.55:44
    Greene (15) 1.35:30
    Guy 30:03
    Hayes (24) 1.16:38
    Krish 1.54:40
    Pasolini 2.11:57
    Ray (49) 2.41:52
    Rossellini 2.10:56
    Saville (31) 2.39:41
    Young (34) 2.43:48
    Zecca (5) 39:14
    Zeffirelli (86) 2.51:49

Burial: Mt. 27:60-61; Mk 15:46-47; Lk. 23:53-56; Jn 19:41-42
  Arcand (12) 1:46:09
  Davis (10) 1.43:12
  Dornford-May (6) 1.06:22, 1.11:05
  Guy 31:03
  Hayes (24) 1.17:14
  Krish 1.55:01
  Pasolini 2.13:42
  Ray (49) 2.43:14
  Rossellini 2.13:45
  Saville (31) 2.40:27
  Stevens (31) 3.10:29, 3.11:09
  Young (34) 2.44:17
  Zecca (5) 40:32

Resurrection Appearances

Roman guards: Mt. 27:62-66; 28:4, 11-15
    DeMille (26) 2.23:32
    Guy 32:29
    Pasolini 2.14:37
    Stevens (31) 3.10:37; (32) 3.12:44
    Zecca (6) 41:31
    Zeffirelli (87) 2.53:46; (88) 2.58:49; (90) 3.07:30

Descent into Hell: 1 Pet. 3:19
    Arcand (5) 46:26; (11) 1.36:38

Easter (no resurrection)
    Arcand (5) 46:26; (9) 1.10:58
    Greene (15) 1.35:52
    Jewison (23) 1.43:40
    Jones (20) 1.29:33

Easter morning: Mt. 28:1-10; Mk 16:1-8; Lk. 24:1-12; Jn 20:1-18
    Arcand (5) 48:41; (11) 1.36:11; (12) 1.47:12, 1.47:30, 1.48:14, 1.53:50
    Davis (10) 1.45:02
    DeMille (26) 2.22:42
    Dornford-May (6) 1.12:45
    Gibson (14) 1.57:22
    Guy 32:14
    Hayes (24) 1.17:52
    Krish 1.56:34
    Pasolini 2.14:59
    Ray (50) 2.44:31
    Rossellini 2.15:35
    Saville (31) 2.40:46
    Stevens (32) 3.12:07, 3.13:33
    Young (35) 2.45:22
    Zecca (6) 41:13
    Zeffirelli (87) 2.56:04

Emmaus: Lk. 24:13-32
    Arcand (5) 49:15
    Hayes (25) 1.21:06
    Krish 1.59:17

Closed doors: Lk. 24:33-49; Jn 20:19-29
    Davis (11) 1.45:35
    DeMille (26) 2.29:22
    Hayes (24) 1.20:43; (25) 1.24:19
    Krish 1.59:40
    Saville (32) 2.44:09
    Stevens (32) 3.12:36

　　　　Young (35) 2.48:37
　　　　Zeffirelli (43) 2.35:42; (88) 2.59:05; (90) 3.08:41
　　Great catch: Jn 21:1-23
　　　　Ray (51) 2.46:33
　　　　Saville (33) 2.47:33
　　Great Commission: Mt. 28:16-20
　　　　Arcand (12) 1.46:43, 1.47:30
　　　　Davis (12) 1.51:02
　　　　Hayes (26) 1.25:30
　　　　Krish 2.01:33
　　　　Pasolini 2.16:04
　　　　Stevens (32) 3.15:07
　　　　Young (35) 2.51:36
　　　　Zeffirelli (90) 3.09:32
　　Ascension: Lk. 24:50-52; Acts 1:6-11
　　　　DeMille (26) 2.36:25
　　　　Dornford-May (6) 1.20:10
　　　　Guy 32:25
　　　　Hayes (27) 1.26:09
　　　　Jewison (22) 1.35:23
　　　　Krish 2.01:02
　　　　Stevens (32) 3.14:56
　　　　Young (35) 2.52:13
　　　　Zecca (6) 42:06
　　Apostle Paul preaches Jesus's death and resurrection: Acts 9:1-22; 1 Cor. 15:3-9
　　　　Scorsese (27) 2.22:15

REFERENCES

Abel, Richard (1994), *The Ciné Goes to Town: French Cinema 1896–1914*, Berkeley: University of California Press.

Abel, Richard (1999), *The Red Rooster Scare: Making Cinema American, 1900–1910*, Berkeley: University of California Press.

Abrams, Jerold J. (2009), "The Cinema of Madness: Friedrich Nietzsche and the Films of Martin Scorsese," in Mark T. Conard (ed.), 75–91, *The Philosophy of Martin Scorsese*, Lexington: University of Kentucky Press.

Ad Hoc Scholars Report (2003), "Reviewing the Script of the Passion." Available online: https://www.bc.edu/content/dam/files/research_sites/cjl/texts/cjrelations/resources/reviews/Passion_adhoc_report_2May.pdf (accessed October 25, 2020).

Aichele, George (1985), *The Limits of Story*, Chico: Scholars.

Aichele, George (2001), *The Control of Biblical Meaning: Canon as Semiotic Mechanism*, Harrisburg: Trinity.

Aichele, George (2002), "Translation as De-Canonization: Matthew's Gospel According to Pasolini," *Crosscurrents*, 51: 524–34.

Aichele, George (2007), "Unchrist," *Postscripts: The Journal of Sacred Texts and Contemporary Worlds*, 3.2–3: 186–200.

Aichele, George (2013), "Film as Betrayal: Some Thoughts on *Son of Man*," in Walsh, Staley, and Reinhartz 2013: 206–16.

Aichele, George (2018), "Comedic Films and the Bible," in Walsh 2018e: 73–8.

Aichele, George and Richard Walsh, eds. (2002), *Screening Scripture: Intertextual Connections between Scripture and Film*, Harrisburg: Trinity.

Altman, Rick (1999), *Film/Genre*, London: British Film Institute.

Amer, Matthew (2013), "Exclusive: Mark Dornford-May on Why the Chester Mystery Plays Are So Important to Him," *London Theatre*, August 20. Available online: https://officiallondontheatre.com/news/exclusive-mark-dornford-may-on-why-the-chester-mystery-plays-are-so-important-to-him-107332/ (accessed November 1, 2020).

Andrew, Geoff (1991), *The Films of Nicholas Ray: The Poet of Nightfall*, London: Charles Letts.

Anonymous (2015), "'Head of Christ,' Has Influenced Culture's Image of Jesus for 75 Years," *Covenant Companion*, October 29. Available online: https://covenantcompanion.com/2015/10/29/head-of-christ-has-influenced-cultures-image-of-jesus-for-75-years/ (accessed May 13, 2020).

Apostolos-Cappadona, Diane (2004), "On Seeing *The Passion*: Is There a Painting in This Film? Or, Is This Film a Painting?" in Plate 2004: 97–108.

Arnal, William (2005), *The Symbolic Jesus: Historical Scholarship, Judaism and the Construction of Identity*, London: Equinox.
Babington, Bruce and Peter Williams Evans (1993), *Biblical Epics: Sacred Narrative in the Hollywood Cinema*, Manchester: Manchester University Press.
Bakhtin, Mikhail (1984), *Rabelais and His World*, trans. Hélène Iswolsky, Bloomington: Indiana University Press.
Bakker, Freek L. (2009), *The Challenge of the Silver Screen: An Analysis of the Cinematic Portraits of Jesus, Rama, Buddha, and Muhammad*, Leiden: Brill.
Bakker, Freek L. (2013), "Islamic Views of Jesus and Mary: Two Iranian Films," in Marek Lis (ed.), *Cinematic Transformations of the Gospel*, 55–74, Opole: University of Opole Press.
Bakker, Freek L. (2021), "Jesus in a Modern Contemporary Context," in Walsh 2021c: 153–64.
Barański, Zygmunt G. (1985), "The Texts of *Il Vangelo Secondo Matteo*," *The Italianist*, 5: 77–106.
Barker, Adam (1990), "Actors, Magicians & the Little Apocalypse," *Monthly Film Bulletin*, 57.672: 4.
Barker, Thomas A. (1975), "All Good Gifts," *Dramatics Magazine*, January. Available online: https://dramatics.org/all-good-gifts/ (accessed June 11, 2020).
Barsotti, Catherin M. and Robert K. Johnston (2004), *Finding God in the Movies: 33 Films of Reel Faith*, Grand Rapids: Baker.
Barthes, Roland (1972), *Mythologies*, trans. Annette Levers, New York: Hill and Wang.
Barthes, Roland (1986), *The Rustle of Language*, trans. Richard Howard, New York: Hill and Wang.
Baugh, Lloyd (1997), *Imaging the Divine: Jesus and Christ-Figures in Film, Communication, Culture and Theology*, Kansas City: Sheed & Ward.
Baugh, Lloyd (2013), "The African Face of Jesus in Film," in Walsh, Staley, and Reinhartz 2013: 120–32.
Baugh, Lloyd (2018), "A Revolutionary Passion Film: Giovanni Columbu's *Su Re* (The King)," in Walsh 2018e: 346–57.
Baugh, Lloyd (2021), "Three Revolutionary Gospel Films: By the People, with the People, and for the People," in Walsh 2021c: 141–51.
Beavis, Mary Ann (2013), "*Jesus of Montreal* (1989)," in Reinhartz 2013b: 145–50.
Benjamin, Walter (1968), "The Work of Art in the Age of Mechanical Reproduction," in *Illuminations*, trans. Harry Zohn, New York: Shocken.
Bial, Henry (2015), *Playing God: The Bible on the Broadway Stage*, Ann Arbor: University of Michigan Press.
Biko, Steve (1978), *I Write What I Like*, London: Bowerdean.
Billington, Michael (2009), "The Mysteries—Yiimimangaliso," *The Guardian*, September 16. Available online: https://www.theguardian.com/culture/2009/sep/16/the-mysteries-review (accessed November 7, 2020).
Blau, Eleanor (1976), "A Movie Translation of Entire Bible Begun to Transmit Faith to Today's Nonreaders," *The New York Times*, January 26. Available online: https://www.nytimes.com/1976/01/26/archives/new-jersey-pages-a-movie-translation-of-entire-bible-begun-to.html (accessed July 13, 2020).
Blizek, William L. (2004), "Special Issue: *Passion of the Christ*," *Journal of Religion & Film*, 8.1. Available online: https://digitalcommons.unomaha.edu/jrf/vol8/iss1/ (accessed October 25, 2020).
Blum, Edward J. and Paul Harvey (2012), *The Color of Christ: The Son of God and the Saga of Race in America*, Chapel Hill: The University of North Carolina Press.

Boillat, Alain and Valentine Robert (2016), "*La Vie et Passion de Notre Seigneur Jésus-Christ* (Pathé-Frères, 1902–05): Tableau Variation in the Early Cinema," in Shepherd 2016b: 24–59.

Bond, Helen K. (2015), "'You'll Probably Get Away with Crucifixion': Laughing at the Cross in *Brian* and the Ancient World," in Taylor 2015: 113–26.

Bondanella, Peter (1993), *The Films of Roberto Rossellini*, Cambridge/New York: Cambridge University Press.

Boomershine, Thomas E. (2005), "Mel, Go to Seminary, Please: A Biblical Storyteller's Reflections on 'The Passion of the Christ,'" *Journal of Theology*, 109. Available online: http://gotell.org/wp-content/uploads/MelGoToSeminaryPlease.pdf (accessed October 25, 2020).

Bordwell, David (2017), "Anybody but Griffith," *David Bordwell's Website on Cinema*, February 27. Available online: http://www.davidbordwell.net/blog/2017/02/27/anybody-but-griffith/ (accessed February 23, 2020).

Brant, Jo-Ann A. (2008), "Camera as Character in Philip Saville's *The Gospel of John*," in Shepherd 2008: 149–64.

Brinkema, Eugenie (2014), *The Forms of the Affects*, Durham/London: Duke University Press.

Brownlow, Kevin (2016), "John Krish Obituary," *The Guardian*, May 23. Available online: https://www.theguardian.com/film/2016/may/23/john-krish-obituary (accessed July 23, 2020).

Brunette, Peter (1996), *Roberto Rossellini*, Berkeley: University of California Press.

Burgess, Anthony (1977), "The Gospel According to Anthony Burgess," *The New York Times*, April 3. Available online: https://www.nytimes.com/1977/04/03/archives/the-gospel-according-to-anthony-burgess-the-gospel-according-to.html (accessed July 6, 2020).

Burgess, Anthony (1979), *Man of Nazareth*, New York: McGraw-Hill.

Burnett, Fred (2002), "The Characterization of Martin Riggs in *Lethal Weapon 1*," in Aichele and Walsh 2002: 251–78.

Burnette-Bletsch, Rhonda (2016b), "General Introduction: The Bible and Its Cinematic Reception," in Burnette-Bletsch 2016a: 1–14.

Burnette-Bletsch, Rhonda (2016c), "God at the Movies," in Burnette-Bletsch 2016a: 299–326.

Burnette-Bletsch, Rhonda (2021), "Scorsese's Jesus: Christology in *The Last Temptation of Christ* and *Silence*," in Walsh 2021c: 199–211.

Burnette-Bletsch, Rhonda, ed. (2016a), *The Bible in Motion: A Handbook of the Bible and Its Reception in Film*, Berlin/Boston: De Gruyter.

Burridge, Richard A. (2015), "The Church of England's Life of Python—Or 'What the Bishop Saw,'" in Taylor 2015: 19–41.

Carrol, Noël (1990), *The Philosophy of Horror: Or, Paradoxes of the Heart*, New York: Routledge.

Chattaway, Peter T. (1996), "Review: *Moses* (dir. Roger Young, 1995)," *FilmChat*, December 1. Available online: https://www.patheos.com/blogs/filmchat/1996/12/review-moses-dir-roger-young-1995.html (accessed August 29, 2020).

Chattaway, Peter T. (2001), "Review: *The Bible Collection* (dir. Various 1994–1999)," *FilmChat*, April 29. Available online: https://www.patheos.com/blogs/filmchat/2001/04/review-the-bible-collection-dir-various-1994-1999.html (accessed August 28, 2020).

Chattaway, Peter T. (2007), "*The Miracle Maker: Special Edition*," *FilmChat*, March 16. Available online: https://www.patheos.com/blogs/filmchat/2007/03/the-miracle-maker-special-edition.html (accessed September 25, 2020).

Chattaway, Peter T. (2014), "*The Bible* and *Son of God*: Just How Different Are They?" *FilmChat*, July 27. Available online: https://www.patheos.com/blogs/filmchat/2014/07/the-bible-and-son-of-god-just-how-different-are-they.html (accessed August 29, 2020).

Chattaway, Peter T. (2021), "Obscure Gospel Elements in Jesus Films," in Walsh 2021c: 19–30.
Clark-Soles, Jaime (2013), "*Jesus Christ Superstar*," in Reinhartz 2013b: 140–5.
Cochran, James M. (2021), "'Walk[ing] upon That Gospel Highway': Experiencing Physical Pilgrimages, Places, and People in *The Gospel Road: A Story of Jesus*," in Walsh 2021c: 189–98.
Cone, James H. (2012), *The Cross and the Lynching Tree*, Maryknoll, NY: Orbis.
Copier, Laura (2008), *Preposterous Revelations: Visions of Apocalypse and Martyrdom in Hollywood Cinema 1980–2000*, Enkhuizen: Raamwerken.
Copier, Laura and Caroline Vander Stichele, eds. (2016), *Close Encounters between Bible and Film: An Interdisciplinary Engagement*, Atlanta: SBL.
Corley, Kathleen E. and Robert L. Webb, eds. (2004), *Jesus and Mel Gibson's Passion of the Christ: The Film, the Gospels and the Claims of History*, New York: Continuum.
Corliss, Richard (1988), "Body and Blood: An Interview with Martin Scorsese," *Film Comment*, 24 (October): 36–42.
Cosandey, Roland, André Gaudreault, and Tom Gunning, eds. (1992), *Une invention du diable? Cinéma des premiers temps et religion/An Invention of the Devil? Religion and Early Cinema*, Lausanne and Quebec City: Payot Lausanne/Presses de l'Université Laval.
Cox, Harvey (1965), *The Secular City: Secularization and Urbanization in Theological Perspective*, New York: Macmillan.
Cox, Harvey (1969), *The Feast of Fools: A Theological Essay on Festivity and Fantasy*, New York: Harper & Row.
Critical Dave (2013), "War of the Remake: *Jesus Christ Superstar*(s) (1973, 2000, 2012)," *Critical Dave*, November 6. Available online: https://daveandhiscriticisms.wordpress.com/2013/11/06/war-of-the-remake-jesus-christ-superstars-1973-2000-2012/ (accessed June 15, 2020).
Cronin, Paul (2005), "George Stevens: A Filmmakers Journey: About George Stevens," *PBS: America Masters*, July 13. Available online: http://www.pbs.org/wnet/americanmasters/george-stevens-about-george-stevens/710/ (accessed July 4, 2020).
Crook, Zeba (2011), "Jesus Novels: Solving Problems with Fiction," in Delbert Burkett (ed.), *The Blackwell Companion to Jesus*, 501–18, Chichester: Blackwell.
Crossan, John Dominic (1975), *The Dark Interval, toward a Theology of Story*, Niles, IL: Argus.
Crossley, James G. (2008), *Jesus in an Age of Terror*, London: Equinox.
Crossley, James G. (2011), "Life of Brian or Life of Jesus? Uses of Critical Biblical Scholarship and Non-Orthodox Views of Jesus in Monty Python's *Life of Brian*," *Relegere: Studies in Religion and Reception*, 1: 93–114. Available online: https://relegere.org/relegere/article/view/10 (accessed July 20, 2020).
Crossley, James G. (2012), *Jesus in an Age of Neoliberalism*, Sheffield: Equinox.
Crossley, James G. (2015), "The Meaning of Monty Python's Jesus," in Taylor 2015: 69–81.
Custen, George F. (1992), *Bio/Pics: How Hollywood Constructed Public History*, New Brunswick: Rutgers University Press.
Dagan, Carmel (2017), "John Heyman, Distinguished Financier and Producer, Dies at 84," *Variety*, June 9. Available online: https://variety.com/2017/film/news/john-heyman-dead-dies-producer-1202460783/ (accessed July 13, 2020).
Davies, Philip R. (1998), "*Life of Brian* Research," in J. Cheryl Exum and Stephen D. Moore (eds.), *Biblical Studies/Cultural Studies: The Third Sheffield Colloquium*, 400–14, London: Continuum.

Davies, Philip R. (2015), "The Gospel of Brian," Taylor 2015: 83–9.
Deacy, Christopher (2001), *Screen Christologies: Redemption and the Medium of Film*, Cardiff: University of Wales Press.
Deacy, Christopher (2006), "Reflections on the Uncritical Appropriation of Cinematic Christ-Figures: Holy Other or Wholly Inadequate?" *Journal of Religion and Popular Culture*, 13 (Summer). Available online: https://www.utpjournals.press/doi/abs/10.3138/jrpc.13.1.001 (accessed January 19, 2020).
Deleuze, Gilles (1997), *Cinema 1: The Movement Image*, trans. Hugh Tomlinson and Barbara Habberjam, Minneapolis: University of Minnesota Press.
DeMille, Cecil B. (1959), *The Autobiography of Cecil B. DeMille*, ed. Donald Hayne, Englewood Cliffs: Prentice-Hall.
Dempsey, John (1998), "'Jesus' Won't Bless TNT," *Variety*, July 20. Available online: https://variety.com/1998/tv/news/jesus-won-t-bless-tnt-1117478602/ (accessed August 28, 2020).
Detweiler, Robert (1964), "Christ and the Christ Figure in American Fiction," *The Christian Scholar*, 47.2: 111–24.
Dolkart, Judith F., ed. (2009), *James Tissot the Life of Christ: The Complete Set of 350 Watercolors*, London/New York: Merrell.
Doré, Gustav ([1859] 2014), *The Dore Gallery of Bible Illustrations, Project Guttenberg*. Available online: https://www.gutenberg.org/files/8710/8710-h/8710-h.htm (accessed March 4, 2020).
Drew, W. M. (1986), *D.W. Griffith's Intolerance: Its Genesis and Its Vision*, Jefferson, NC: McFarland.
Dyke, Carl (2002), "Learning from *The Life of Brian*: Saviors for Seminars," in Aichele and Walsh 2002: 229–50.
Eberhart, Christian A. (2005), "The 'Passion' of Gibson: Evaluating a Recent Interpretation of Christ's Suffering and Death in Light of the New Testament," *Consensus*, 30.1: 37–74. Available online: https://scholars.wlu.ca/cgi/viewcontent.cgi?article=1202&context=consensus (accessed October 25, 2020).
Ebert, Roger (2004), "*The Passion of the Christ*," *Roger.Ebert.com*, February 24. Available online: https://www.rogerebert.com/reviews/the-passion-of-the-christ-2004 (accessed January 5, 2021).
Egan, Joseph (2018), "*The Greatest Story Ever Told*," December 7. Available online: http://www.josephmartinegan.com/2018/12/07/the-greatest-story-ever-told-p1/ (accessed May 21, 2020).
Eisenstein, Sergei (1949), "Dickens, Griffith, and the Film Today," in Sergei Eisenstein (ed.), *Film Form: Essays in Film Theory*, trans. Jay Leyda, 195–255, New York: Harcourt, Brace & World.
Emmett, Grace (2020), "'You Weakened Him': Jesus's Masculinity in *Mary Magdalene*," *Religion and Gender*, 10: 97–117.
Eshleman, Paul (2016), *I Just Saw Jesus*, 3rd ed., Abbotsford, WI: Aneko.
Family Theater Productions (n.d.), "*Pray: The Story of Patrick Peyton*." Available online: https://www.praythefilm.com/ (accessed June 25, 2020).
Fillon, Mike (2020), "The Real Face of Jesus," *Popular Mechanics*, April 10. Available online: https://www.popularmechanics.com/science/health/a234/1282186/ (accessed May 13, 2020).
Fletcher, Michelle (2021), "Seeing Differently with *Mary Magdalene*," in Walsh 2021c: 55–65.
Flowers, Elizabeth H. and Darren J. N. Middleton (2005), "Satan and the Curious: Texas Evangelicals Read *The Last Temptation of Christ*," in Middleton 2005: 147–55.
Forshey, Gerald (1992), *American Religious and Biblical Spectaculars*, Westport: Praeger.

Foster, Charles (2000), *Stardust and Shadows: Canadians in Early Hollywood*, Toronto: Dundurn.
Foster, Diana (2014), "The History of Silent Movies and Subtitles," *Video Caption Corporation*. Available online: https://www.vicaps.com/blog/history-of-silent-movies-and-subtitles/ (accessed February 28, 2020).
Foster, Gwendolyn (2013), "Alice Guy's *La Vie du Christ*: A Feminist Vision of the Christ Tale," *Film.int*, September 3. Available online: http://filmint.nu/?p=9219 (accessed February 23, 2020).
Fredriksen, Paula (2004), "Controversial 'Passion' Presents Priceless Opportunity for Education," *Christian Science Monitor*, February 2. Available online: https://www.csmonitor.com/2004/0202/p09s02-cogn.html (accessed October 15, 2020).
Friedrich, James L. (n.d.), "*Day of Triumph*," *Gospel Film Archives*. Available online: https://www.gospelfilmsarchive.com/dot.html (accessed May 7, 2020).
Friesen, Dwight H. (2008), "*Karunamayudu*: Seeing Christ Anew in Indian Cinema," in Shepherd 2008: 165–88.
Friesen, Dwight H. (2010), "An Analysis of the Production, Content, Distribution and Reception of *Karunamayudu* (1978), an Indian Jesus Film," PhD diss., University of Edinburgh.
Friesen, Dwight H. (2016), "*La Vie et Passion de Notre Seigneur Jésus-Christ* (Pathé-Frères, 1907): The Preservation and Transformation of Zecca's Passion," in Shepherd 2016b: 78–97.
Frye, Northrop (1982), *The Great Code*, New York: Harcourt Brace Jovanovich.
Fuller, Christopher (2004), "*UDISTE CHE FU DETTO ..., MA IO DICO CHE ...* " Pasolini as Interpreter of the Gospel of Matthew, PhD diss., Graduate Theological Union.
Fuller, Christopher (2006), "Gibson's 'Passion' in the Light of Pasolini's 'Gospel,'" *SBL Forum*. Available online: http://sbl-site.org/Article.aspx?ArticleID=508 (accessed May 31, 2020).
Gaines, Jane (n.d.), "Jeanie Macpherson," *Women Film Pioneers Project*. Available online: https://wfpp.columbia.edu/pioneer/ccp-jeanie-macpherson/ (accessed April 25, 2020).
Gallagher, Tag (1998), *The Adventures of Roberto Rossellini: His Life and Films*, Boston: Da Capo.
Gallagher, Tag (2012), *The Messiah*, *Vimeo*. Available online: https://vimeo.com/48501880 (accessed June 19, 2020).
Gaudreault, André (2016), "The Passion of Christ: A Form, a Genre, a Discourse," in Shepherd 2016b: 15–23.
Gauntier, Gene (1927), "Filming *From the Manger to the Cross*," *Flicker Alley*. Available online: https://www.flickeralley.com/wp-content/uploads/2015/03/From-the-Manger-to-the-Cross.pdf (accessed March 14, 2020).
Genette, Gérard (1997), *Paratexts: Thresholds of Interpretation*, trans. Jane E. Lewin, Cambridge: The University of Cambridge.
Giere, S. D. (2013), "'This Is My World!' *Son of Man* (Jezile) and Cross-Cultural Convergences of Bible and World," in Walsh, Staley, and Reinhartz 2013: 23–33.
Goldman, Michael (2019), "*Mary Magdalene*/Greig Fraser, ASC, ACS," *American Cinematographer. An International Publication of the ASC*, Episode #96. Available online: https://ascmag.com/podcasts/mary-magdalene-greig-fraser-asc-acs (accessed April 8, 2020).
Goodacre, Mark (1999), "Do You Think You're What They Say You Are? Reflections on *Jesus Christ Superstar*," *Journal of Religion & Film*, 3.2. Available online: https://digitalcommons.unomaha.edu/jrf/vol3/iss2/2/ (accessed June 15, 2020).
Goodacre, Mark (2004), "The Power of *The Passion*: Reacting and Over-Reacting to Gibson's Artistic Vision," in Corley and Webb 2004: 28–44.

Gospel Films Archives (n.d.). Available online: https://www.gospelfilmsarchive.com/aboutcf.html (accessed May 7, 2020).

Graybill, Rhiannon (2018), "Rock Me Sexy Jesus?: Gender and Sexuality in Biblical Films," in Walsh 2018e: 187–97.

Greene, Naomi (1990), *Pier Paolo Pasolini: Cinema as Heresy*, Princeton: Princeton University Press.

Greydanus, Steven D. (n.d.), "*The Miracle Maker* (2000)," *Decent Films*. Available online: http://decentfilms.com/reviews/miraclemaker (accessed September 26, 2020).

Greydanus, Steven D. (2003), "*The Gospel of John* (2003)," *Decent Films*. Available online: http://decentfilms.com/reviews/gospelofjohn (accessed October 14, 2020).

Greydanus, Steven D. (2021), "Through Other Eyes: Point of View and Defamiliarization in Jesus Films," in Walsh 2021c: 77–87.

Gribble, Richard E. (2003), "Anti-Communism, Patrick Peyton, CSC and the C.I.A," *Journal of Church and State*, 45.3: 535–8.

Gribble, Richard E. (2011), *American Apostle of the Family Rosary: The Life of Patrick J. Peyton, CSC*, 2nd ed., New York: Crossroad.

Griffith, David Wark ([1915] 1967), *The Rise and Fall of Free Speech in America*, Hollywood: Larry Edmunds Bookshop.

Grunes, Dennis (2007), "*The Messiah* (Roberto Rossellini, 1975)," April 20. Available online: https://grunes.wordpress.com/2007/04/20/the-messiah-roberto-rossellini-1975/ (accessed June 19, 2020).

Gunning, Tom (1986), "The Cinema of Attraction: Early Film, Its Spectator, and the Avant-Garde," *Wide Angle*, 8: 114–33.

Gunning, Tom (1994), *D. W. Griffith and the Origins of American Narrative Film: The Early Years at Biograph*, Urbana and Chicago: University of Chicago Press.

Hall, Phil (2018), "The Bootleg Files: The Lawton Story," *Cinema Crazed*, June 8. Available online: http://cinema-crazed.com/blog/2018/06/08/the-bootleg-files-the-lawton-story/ (accessed May 7, 2020).

Hardcastle, Gary L. and George A. Reisch (2006), *Monty Python and Philosophy: Nudge Nudge, Think Think!* Chicago: Open Court.

Harkness, John (1989), "The Improbable Rise of Denys Arcand," *Sight & Sound*, 58.4: 234–8.

Hasted, Nick (2018), "*Mary Magdalene* and Christian Cinema's Resurrection," *The Independent*, March 15. Available online: https://www.independent.co.uk/artsentertainment/films/features/mary-magdalene-film-rooney-mara-joaquin-hoenixreligion-a8258036.html (accessed November 10, 2020).

Haydoke, Toby (2017), "Philip Saville Obituary," *The Guardian*, January 1. Available online: https://www.theguardian.com/tv-and-radio/2017/jan/01/philip-saville-obituary (accessed October 14, 2020).

Heard, R. Christopher (2000), "They're Not Just Bad, They're Stupid and Ugly, Too: The Characterization of Baal-Worshipers in NEST Entertainment's *Animated Stories from the Bible*," in George Aichele (ed.), *Culture, Entertainment, and the Bible*, 89–103, Sheffield: Sheffield Academic Press.

Heard, R. Christopher (2016), "Drawing (on) the Text: Biblical Reception in Animated Films," in Burnette-Bletsch 2016a: 267–83.

Hebron, Carol A. (2016a), "Alice Guy Blaché and Gene Gauntier: Bringing New Perspectives to Film," in Burnette-Bletsch 2016a: 543–55.

Hebron, Carol A. (2016b), *Judas Iscariot: Damned or Redeemed: A Critical Examination of the Portrayal of Judas in Jesus Films*, London/New York: Bloomsbury.

Heetebrij, Geert (2020), "Subversive Christian Allegory *In the Heat of the Night* (1967)," *Christian Scholar's Review*, 49.3. Available online: https://christianscholars.com/subversive-christian-allegory-in-in-the-heat-of-the-night-1967/ (accessed June 17, 2020).

Henderson, Charles (1977), "Zeffirelli's Jesus: A Theological Perspective," *The Christian Century* 94 (April 20): 6.

Hewison, Robert (1981), *Monty Python: The Case Against*, New York: Grove.

Hoile, Christopher (2003), "The Mysteries—Yiimimangaliso," *Theatre World*, April 11. Available online: http://www.stage-door.com/Theatre/2003/Entries/2003/4/11_Yiimimangaliso__The_Mysteries.html (accessed November 7, 2020).

Holderness, Graham (2015), *Re-Writing Jesus: Christ in 20th-Century Fiction and Film*, London: Bloomsbury.

Hornik, Heidi J. (2019), "Mary Magdalene in the Visual Arts: Film," in Diane Apostolos-Cappadona and Katherine Marsengill (eds.), *Encyclopedia of the Bible and Its Reception*, 17, Berlin: Walter de Gruyter.

Huizinga, Johan (1949), *Homo Ludens: A Study of the Play Element in Culture*, London: Routledge & Kegan Paul.

Humphries-Brooks, Stephenson (2006), *Cinematic Savior: Hollywood's Making of the American Christ*, Westport: Praeger.

Hurley, Neil P. (1981), "Cinematic Transformations of Jesus," in John R. May and Michael Bird (eds.), *Religion in Film*, 61–78, Knoxville: University of Texas Press.

Irwin, William (2004), "Gibson's Sublime *Passion*: In Defense of the Violence," in Jorge J. E. Gracia (ed.), *Mel Gibson's Passion and Philosophy: The Cross, the Questions, the Controversy*, 51–61, Chicago: Open Court.

Jacobs, Lewis ([1939] 1967), *The Rise of the American Film: A Critical History*, New York: Harcourt, Brace.

Jameson, Fredric (1991), *Postmodernism, or, the Cultural Logic of Late Capitalism*, Durham: Duke University Press.

Jewett, Robert (1984), *The Captain America Complex*, 2nd ed., Santa Fe: Bear.

Jewett, Robert and John Shelton Lawrence (1977), *The American Monomyth*, Garden City: Anchor.

Johnson, Christine D. (2014), "'Jesus Film' Remastered to Celebrate 35th Anniversary," *Charisma News*, January 27. Available online: https://www.charismanews.com/culture/42565-jesus-film-remastered-to-celebrate-35th-anniversary (accessed July 16, 2020).

Johnson, William Bruce (2008), *Miracles and Sacrilege: Robert Rossellini, the Church, and Film Censorship in Hollywood*, Toronto: University of Toronto Press.

Kael, Pauline (1980), "*Raging Bull*," *The New Yorker*, December. Available online: https://scrapsfromtheloft.com/2017/05/08/raging-bull-religious-pulp-or-the-incredible-hulk-review-by-pauline-kael/ (accessed August 1, 2020).

Kandell, Jonathan (2019), "Franco Zeffirelli, Italian Director with Taste for Excess, Dies at 96," *The New York Times*, June 15. Available online: https://www.nytimes.com/2019/06/15/arts/music/franco-zeffirelli-dead.html (accessed July 5, 2020).

Kazantzakis, Nikos ([1955] 1988), *The Last Temptation of Christ*, trans. P. E. Bien, New York: Simon & Schuster.

Keil, Charles (1992), "*From the Manger to the Cross*: The New Testament Narrative and the Question of Stylistic Retardation," in Cosandey, Gaudreault, and Gunning 1992: 112–20.

Kelly, Mary Pat (1991), *Scorsese: A Journey*, New York: Thunder's Mouth.
Keyser, Les (1992), *Martin Scorsese*, New York: Twayne.
Kinnard, Roy and Tim Davis (1992), *Divine Images: A History of Jesus on the Screen*, New York: Citadel.
Kirk, Nicole C. (2018), *Wanamaker's Temple: The Business of Religion in an Iconic Department Store*, New York: New York University Press.
Kozlovic, Anton Karl (2004), "The Structural Characteristics of the Cinematic Christ-figure," *Journal of Religion and Popular Culture*, 8 (Fall). Available online: https://utpjournals.press/doi/abs/10.3138/jrpc.8.1.005 (accessed January 20, 2020).
Kraemer, Ross S. (2013), "*King of Kings*," in Reinhartz 2013b: 166–72.
Kramer, Fritzi (2017), "*From the Manger to the Cross* (1912): A Silent Film Review," *Movies Silently*, June 18. Available online: http://moviessilently.com/2017/06/18/from-the-manger-to-the-cross-1912-a-silent-film-review/ (accessed March 14, 2020).
Kreidel, John Francis (1977), *Nicholas Ray*, Boston: Twayne.
Kreitzer, Larry J. (1993), *The New Testament in Fiction and Film: On Reversing the Hermeneutical Flow*, Sheffield: Sheffield Academic.
Kreitzer, Larry J. (2002), *Gospel Images in Fiction and Film: On Reversing the Hermeneutical Flow*, Sheffield: Sheffield Academic.
Kreitzer, Larry J. (2018), "*Ben-Hur* (2016): Jesus Finds a Voice," in Walsh 2018e: 381–92.
Kristeva, Julia (1980), *Desire in Language: A Semiotic Approach to Literature and Art*, trans. Alice Jardine and Leon S. Roudiez, rev. ed., New York: Columbia University Press.
Kunkel, Ken (2018), "*The Greatest Story Ever Told*: The 70mm Epic Hardly Anyone Has Seen," *in70mm.com*, December 21. Available online: https://www.in70mm.com/news/2018/story/index.htm (accessed May 21, 2020).
Laird, Paul R. (2014), *The Musical Theater of Stephen Schwartz from Godspell to Wicked and Beyond*, Lanham: Rowman & Littlefield.
Lane, John Francis (2019), "Franco Zeffirelli Obituary," *The Guardian*, June 15. Available online: https://www.theguardian.com/stage/2019/jun/15/franco-zeffirelli-obituary (accessed July 5, 2020).
Lies, Elaine (2009), "Jesus Christ Goes Kabuki in Japan 'Superstar' Play," *Reuters*, February 20. Available online: https://www.reuters.com/article/us-stage-japan-idUSTRE51J1D320090220 (accessed January 3, 2021).
Linafelt, Tod (2004), "Tragically Heroic Men and the Women Who Love Them," in Timothy K. Beal and Tod Linafelt (eds.), *Mel Gibson's Bible: Religion, Popular Culture, and the Passion of the Christ*, 29–37, Chicago: University of Chicago Press.
Lindvall, Terry (2007), *Sanctuary Cinema: Origins of the Christian Film Industry*, New York: New York University Press.
Lindvall, Terry and Andrew Quicke (2011), *Celluloid Sermons: The Emergence of the Christian Film Industry, 1930–1986*, New York: New York University Press.
Loiselle, André (1995), "'I Only Know Where I Come from, Not Where I am Going,' a Conversation with Denys Arcand," in Loiselle and McIlroy 1995a: 136–61.
Loiselle, André and Brian McIlroy, eds. (1995a), *Auteur/Provocateur: The Films of Denys Arcand*, Westport: Greenwood.
Loiselle, André and Brian McIlroy (1995b), "Introduction," in Loiselle and McIlroy 1995a: 1–9.
LyricWiki: Jesus Christ Superstar (1973). Available online: https://lyrics.fandom.com/wiki/Jesus_Christ_Superstar_(1973) (accessed June 15, 2020).

Maccoby, Hyam (1977), "Jesus on the Small Screen," *Encounter*, 49.1: 42–7.
Maggi, Arnold (2009), *The Resurrection of the Body: Pier Paolo Pasolini from Saint Paul to Sade*, Chicago: University of Chicago Press.
Malone, Peter (1988), *Movie Christs and Antichrists*, New York: Crossroads.
Malone, Peter (2012), *Screen Jesus: Portrayals of Christ in Television and Film*, Lanham, MD: Scarecrow.
Marchal, Joseph A. and Robert Seesengood, eds. (2019), *Pasolini's Paul: Representation, Re-Use, Religion, Biblical Interpretation*, 27, 4–5.
Marini, Piero (n.d.), "The Way of the Cross," *Office for the Liturgical Celebrations of the Supreme Pontiff*. Available online: https://www.vatican.va/news_services/liturgy/documents/ns_lit_doc_via-crucis_en.html (accessed October 18, 2020).
Martellozzo, Nicola (2019), "The Soundscape of Pier Paolo Pasolini's *The Gospel According to St. Matthew* (1964)," *Journal for Religion, Film and Media*, 5 (1): 87–101.
McGeough, Kevin M. (2018), "Murderous Archaeologists, Doubting Priests, and Mesopotamian Demons: The Bible in Horror and Adventure Cinema," in Walsh 2018e: 60–72.
McGeough, Kevin M. (2021), "The 'False Syllogism' of Archaeological Authenticity in Jesus Movies," in Walsh 2021c: 115–25.
McKinney, Devin (1993), "Violence: The Strong and the Weak," *Film Quarterly*, 46 (4): 16–22.
McMahan, Alison (n.d.), "Alice Guy Blaché," *Women Film Pioneers Project*. Available online: https://wfpp.columbia.edu/pioneer/ccp-alice-guy-blache/ (accessed February 23, 2020).
McMahan, Alison (2002), *Alice Guy Blaché: Lost Visionary of the Cinema*, New York/London: Continuum.
Méliès, Georges (1988), "Cinematographic Views," trans. Stuart Liebman, in Richard Abel (ed.), *French Film Theory and Criticism: 1907–1939*, 1: 35–47, Princeton: Princeton University Press.
Merritt, Russell (1979), "On First Looking into Griffith's Babylon," *Wide Angle*, 3.1: 12–21.
Merritt, Russell (1990), "D.W. Griffith's *Intolerance*: Reconstructing an Unattainable Text," *Film History*, 4.4: 337–75.
Middleton, Darren J. N., ed. (2005), *Scandalizing Jesus: Kazantzakis's the Last Temptation of Christ Fifty Years On*, New York: Continuum.
Middleton, Darren J. N. and S. Brent Plate (2013), "'Who Do You *See* That I Am?' *Son of Man* and Global Perspectives on Jesus Films," in Walsh, Staley, and Reinhartz 2013: 133–48.
Miller, Scott (2016), "Inside *Jesus Christ Superstar*: Background and Analysis," *New Line Theatre*. Available online: http://www.newlinetheatre.com/jcschapter.html (accessed June 17, 2020).
Minthe, Caterina (2018), "The Most Disruptive Fashion Is Happening at a Refugee Camp in Jordan," *Vogue*, April 25. Available online: https://en.vogue.me/fashion/news/sep-jordan-refugee-camp-mary-magdalene-movie/ (accessed April 11, 2020).
Moen, Kristen (2013), *Film and Fairy Tales: The Birth of Modern Fantasy*, London: I.B. Tauris.
Mokoena, Katleho K. (2017), "Steve Biko Christ-Figure: A Black Theological Christology in the *Son of Man* Film," *HTS: Teologiese Studies/Theological Studies*, 73.3. Available online: http://www.scielo.org.za/scielo.php?script=sci_arttext&pid=S0259-94222017000300090 (accessed November 6, 2020).
Moore, Anne (2018), "Counting Errors or Understanding Filmic History: Historiophoty and Biblical Films," in Walsh 2018e: 36–48.
Morgan, David (1999), *Monty Python Speaks!* New York: Avon.
Morgan, David (2004), "Catholic Visual Piety and *The Passion of the Christ*," in Plate 2004: 85–96.

Moss, Marilyn Ann (2004), *Giant: George Stevens, a Life on Film*, Madison: University of Wisconsin Press.

Museum of Modern Art (n.d.), "Comprehensive U.S. Retrospective on Director Roberto Rossellini," November 15–December 22, 2006. Available online: https://assets.moma.org/documents/moma_press-release_387104.pdf (accessed June 25, 2020).

Nadar, Sarojini (2013), "'Wathint'Abafazi Wathint'imbokodo'!—The Son of Woman in the *Son of Man* as an Embodiment of the Struggle for Justice," in Walsh, Staley, and Reinhartz 2013: 61–8.

Nietzsche, Friedrich ([1887] 1974), *The Gay Science*, trans. Walter Kaufmann, New York: Vintage.

Nkadimeng, Thabang and Lloyd Baugh (2013), "Strategies of Sound: Revolutionary Music and Song in *Son of Man*," in Walsh, Staley, and Reinhartz 2013: 34–47.

Noll, Mark (2009). *The New Shape of World Christianity: How American Experience Reflects Global Faith*, Westmont, IL: IVP Academic.

Nowell-Smith, Geoffrey (1977), "Pasolini's Originality," in Paul Willemen (ed.), *Pier Paolo Pasolini*, 4–19, London: BFI.

O'Brien, Catherine (2016), "Women in the Cinematic Gospels," in Burnette-Bletsch 2016a: 449–62.

O'Dell, Paul (1970), with the assistance of Anthony Slide, *Griffith and the Rise of Hollywood*, New York: Castle.

Ourlser, Fulton (1950), *The Greatest Story Ever Told*, Garden City: Doubleday.

Paffenroth, Kim (2001), *Judas: Images of the Lost Disciple*. Louisville: Westminster John Knox.

Pagano, Gianmario (n.d.), "Differences between the CBS and International Version," *HollywoodJesus*. Available online: http://www.hollywoodjesus.com/jesus_series1.htm (accessed August 27, 2020).

Page, Matthew (2005), "*Golgotha* (Ecce Homo 1935)," *Bible Films Blog*, July 27. Available online: https://biblefilms.blogspot.com/2005/07/golgotha-ecce-homo-1935.html (accessed May 7, 2020).

Page, Matthew (2006a), "*The Gospel of John* (2003): A Few Thoughts," *Bible Films Blog*, August 17. Available online: https://biblefilms.blogspot.com/search?q=gospel+of+john (accessed October 14, 2020).

Page, Matthew (2006b), "*Jesus* (1999–miniseries)," *Bible Films Blog*, April 27. Available online: https://biblefilms.blogspot.com/search/label/Jesus%20%281999%29 (accessed August 27, 2020).

Page, Matthew (2006c), "*Miracle Maker* Scene Guide," *Bible Films Blog*, April 20. Available online: https://biblefilms.blogspot.com/2006/04/miracle-maker-scene-guide.html (accessed September 25, 2020).

Page, Matthew (2010), "Genesis Project: Luke Ch. 1–4," *Bible Films Blog*, November 19. Available online: https://biblefilms.blogspot.com/2010/11/genesis-project-luke-ch1-4.html (accessed July 9, 2020).

Page, Matthew (2013), "*The Bible*," *1More Film Blog*, November 30. Available online: https://www.patheos.com/blogs/1morefilmblog/the-bible/ (accessed August 29, 2020).

Page, Matthew (2016a), "Prefiguring Jesus in *Jeremiah*," *Bible Films Blog*, May 23. Available online: https://biblefilms.blogspot.com/search/label/Bible%20Collection%20%28The%29 (accessed August 28, 2020).

Page, Matthew (2016b), "Roberto Rossellini: From Spiritual Searcher to History's Documentarian," in Burnette-Bletsch 2016a: 623–34.

Page, Matthew (2017a), "*Day of Triumph* (1954)," *Bible Films Blog*, March 10. Available online: https://biblefilms.blogspot.com/2017/03/day-of-triumph-1954.html (accessed May 7, 2020).

Page, Matthew (2017b), "*La naissance, la vie et la mort du Christ*," *Bible Films Blog*, March 27. Available online: https://biblefilms.blogspot.com/2017/03/la-naissance-la-vie-et-la-mort-du.html (accessed February 23, 2020).

Page, Matthew (2018), "*Mary Magdalene 2018*," *Bible Films Blog*, March 17. Available online: https://biblefilms.blogspot.com/2018/03/mary-magdalene-2018.html (accessed November 10, 2020).

Page, Matthew (2019), "Blocking and Shot Selection in *Jesus of Nazareth* (1977)," *Bible Films Blog*, November 9. Available online: https://biblefilms.blogspot.com/search/label/Jesus%20of%20Nazareth (accessed July 3, 2020).

Page, Matthew (2021), "Jesus of Cinecittà," in Walsh 2021c: 127–39.

Papanikolaou, Eftychia (2005), "Identity and Ethnicity in Peter Gabriel's Sound Track for *The Last Temptation of Christ*," in Middleton 2005: 217–28.

Pasolini, Pier Paolo (1988), *Heretical Empiricism*, ed. Louise K. Barnett, trans. Ben Lawton and Louise K. Barnett, Bloomington and Indianapolis: Indiana University Press.

Pasolini, Pier Paolo (2014), *Saint Paul: A Screenplay*, trans. and introduced, Elizabeth Castelli, London/New York: Verso.

Pelikan, Jaroslav (1985), *Jesus through the Centuries: His Place in the History of Culture*, New Haven: Yale University Press.

Pieto, Rick (2011), "'The Devil Made Me Do It': Catholicism, Verisimilitude and the Reception of Horror Films," in Regina Hansen (ed.), *Roman Catholicism in Fantastic Film. Essays on Belief, Spectacle, Ritual and Imagery*, 52–64, Jefferson, NC: McFarland.

Pippin, Tina (2013), "*Godspell*," in Reinhartz 2013b: 103–8.

Pippin, Tina (2018), "Desert Tales: Mark and *Last Days in the Desert*," in Walsh 2018e: 335–45.

Plate, S. Brent, ed. (2004), *Reviewing the Passion: Mel Gibson's Film and Its Critics*, London: Palgrave Macmillan.

Pope Paul VI (1965), *Nostra Aetate*. Available online: https://www.vatican.va/archive/hist_councils/ii_vatican_council/documents/vat-ii_decl_19651028_nostra-aetate_en.html (accessed July 1, 2020).

Prothero, Stephen (2003), *American Jesus: How the Son of God Became a National Icon*, New York: Farrar, Straus, and Giroux.

Pucci, Giuseppe (2016), "*Christus* (Cines 1916): Italy's First Religious 'Kolossal' by Antamoro and Salvatori," in Shepherd 2016b: 200–10.

Punt, Jeremy (2013), "'Thula' ('Be Quiet'): Agency in *Son of Man*," in Walsh, Staley, and Reinhartz 2013: 48–60.

Pyper, Hugh S. (2018), "A Case Study in Translation, Postcolonialism, and Biblical Film," in Walsh 2018e: 210–22.

Reinhartz, Adele (2003), *Scripture on the Silver Screen*, Louisville: Westminster John Knox.

Reinhartz, Adele (2007), *Jesus of Hollywood*, Oxford/New York: Oxford University Press.

Reinhartz, Adele (2009), "Jesus and Christ-Figures," in John Lyden (ed.), *The Routledge Companion to Religion and Film*, 420–39, London and New York.

Reinhartz, Adele (2012), "Violence against the Jews, Anti-Judaism in the Movies," in Reinhold Zwick (ed.), *Religion und Gewalt im Bibelfilm*, 133–44, Marburg: Schüren-Verlag.

Reinhartz, Adele (2013a), *Bible and Cinema: An Introduction*, London and New York: Routledge.

Reinhartz, Adele (2015), "Hook-Nosed Heebies: Brian, Jesus and Jewish Identity," in Taylor 2015: 207–20.

Reinhartz, Adele (2016), "Judaism and Antisemitism in Bible Movies," in Burnette-Bletsch 2016a: 777–91.
Reinhartz, Adele (2021), "Failed Christ Figures in Québec Films," in Walsh 2021c: 249–60.
Reinhartz, Adele, ed. (2013b), *Bible and Cinema: Fifty Key Films*, London/New York: Routledge.
Reynolds, Herbert (1992), "From the Palette to the Screen: The Tissot Bible as Sourcebook for *From the Manger to the Cross*," in Cosandey, Gaudreault, and Gunning 1992: 275–310.
Richie, Donald (1970), *George Stevens: An American Romantic*, New York: Museum of Modern Art.
Robert, Valentine (2019), "The Resurrection of Painting: Tissot and Cinema," in Melissa E. Buron (ed.), *James Tissot*, 72–5, Munich/London/New York: Prestel.
Robinson, Thomas A. (2013), "Girl Evangelists. Uldine Utley (1912–1995)." Available online: https://girlevangelists.org/Uldine_Utley.html (accessed April 29, 2020).
Rohrer-Walsh, P. Jennifer (2002), "Coming-of-Age in *The Prince of Egypt*," in Aichele and Walsh 2002: 77–99.
Rohrer-Walsh, P. Jennifer (2018), "A Genre(s) Approach to *The Prince of Egypt*," in Walsh 2018e: 300–10.
Rohrer-Walsh, P. Jennifer and Richard Walsh (2013), "Mary and the Mothers," in Walsh, Staley, and Reinhartz 2013: 166–77.
Rosenstone, Robert A. (2006), *History on Film/Film on History*, Harlow: Pearson.
Roszak, Theodore (2005), *Flicker*, Chicago: Chicago Review.
Ruhlmann, William (2000), "*Jesus: The Epic Mini-Series [Original Television Soundtrack]*," *Allmusic*, March 28. Available online: https://www.allmusic.com/album/jesus-the-epic-mini-series-original-television-soundtrack-mw0000605728 (accessed August 27, 2020).
Runions, Erin (2003), *How Hysterical: Identification and Resistance in the Bible and Film*, New York: Palgrave Macmillan.
Runions, Erin (2010), "Tolerating Babel: The Bible, Film, and the Family in U.S. Politics," *Religious Studies and Theology*, 29.2: 143–69.
Runions, Erin (2013), "*Son of Man* and Resistance to U.S. Imperialism," in Walsh, Staley, and Reinhartz 2013: 178–91.
Ryan, Barbara and Milette Shamir (2016), *Bigger Than Ben-Hur: The Book, Its Adaptations, & Their Audiences*, Syracuse: Syracuse University Press.
Said, Edward W. ([1978] 1994), *Orientalism*, New York: Vintage.
Sanders, Julie (2006), *Film Adaptation and Appropriation*, London/New York: Routledge.
Schaberg, Jane (1996), "Fast Forwarding to the Magdalene," in Alice Bach (ed.), *Biblical Glamour and Hollywood Glitz*, Semeia, 74: 33–45.
Schechner, Richard (1985), *Between Theater and Anthropology*, Philadelphia: University of Pennsylvania Press.
Schickel, Richard (1996), *D. W. Griffith: An American Life*, New York: Limelight.
Schneidau, Herbert N. (1976), *Sacred Discontent: The Bible and Western Tradition*, Berkeley: University of California Press.
Schneider, Michael (1999), "Italians Flock to 'Jesus' Mini," *Variety*, December 28. Available online: https://variety.com/1999/tv/news/italians-flock-to-jesus-mini-1117760324/ (accessed August 28, 2020).
Scholz, Susanne (2012), "Veggies, Women, and Other Strangers in Children's Bible DVDs: Toward the Creation of Feminist Bible Films," in Caroline Vander Stichele and Hugh S. Pyper (eds.), *Text, Image, and Otherness in Children's Bibles: What Is in the Picture?* 99–120, Atlanta: SBL.

Schrader, Paul (1990), *Schrader on Schrader*, Kevin Jackson (ed.), London: Faber & Faber.
Schrader, Paul (2018), *Transcendental Style in Film: Ozu, Bresson, Dreyer, with a New Introduction*, Berkeley: University of California Press.
Schwartz, Barth David (1992), *Pasolini Requiem*, New York: Pantheon.
Scodel, Ruth and Anja Bettenworth (2009), *Whither Quo Vadis? Sienkiewicz's Novel in Film and Television*, Chichester: Wiley-Blackwell.
Seesengood, Robert Paul (2018), "Seven Stations of Affect: Religion, Affect, and Mel Gibson's *The Passion of the Christ*," in Walsh 2018e: 175–86.
Seesengood, Robert Paul (2021), "'It's Alive!': Frankenstein and His Horrible Fellows as Messianic Figures," in Walsh 2021c: 311–21.
Seesengood, Robert Paul and Richard Walsh (2018), "There's a New Messiah in Town: The Messianic in the Western," in Walsh 2018e: 248–59.
Shepherd, David J. (2013), *The Bible on Silent Film: Spectacle, Story and Scripture in the Early Cinema*, Cambridge/New York: Cambridge University Press.
Shepherd, David J. (2015), "When Brian Met Moses: *Life of Brian* (1979), *Wholly Moses* (1980) and the 'Failure' of Biblical Parody," in Taylor 2015: 43–54.
Shepherd, David J. (2016a), "*La naissance, la vie et la mort du Christ* (Gaumont, 1906): The Gospel According to Alice Guy," in Shepherd 2016b: 60–77.
Shepherd, David J. (2018), "'Blessed Are the Peacemakers': The Deployment of Jesus in American and German Cinema during and after the First World War," in Walsh 2018e: 124–38.
Shepherd, David J., ed. (2008), *Images of the Word: Hollywood's Bible and Beyond*, Atlanta: Society of Biblical Literature.
Shepherd, David J., ed. (2016b), *The Silents of Jesus in the Cinema (1897–1927)*, New York/London: Routledge.
Siciliano, Enzo (1982), *Pasolini: A Biography*, trans. John Shepley, New York: Random House.
Simon, Joan (2009a), "The Great Adventure: Alice Guy Blaché: Cinema Pioneer," in Simon 2009b: 1–24.
Simon, Joan, ed. (2009b), *Alice Guy Blaché: Cinema Pioneer*, New Haven/London: Yale University Press.
Sobchack, Vivian (2008), "Embodying Transcendence: On the Literal, the Material, and the Cinematic Sublime," *Material Religion*, 4.2: 194–203.
Stack, Oswald (1969), *Pasolini on Pasolini: Interviews with Oswald Stack*, Bloomington, Indiana University Press.
Staley, Jeffrey L. (2013a), "*From the Manger to the Cross* (1912)," in Reinhartz 2013b: 98–103.
Staley, Jeffrey L. (2013b), "What Hath New York City to Do with Khayelitsha? An Intertextual Reading of Two Jesus Films," in Walsh, Staley, and Reinhartz 2013: 95–109.
Staley, Jeffrey L. (2016), "Martin Scorsese's *Aviator* as Theological Complement to His *Last Temptation of Christ*," in Copier and Vander Stichele 2016: 233–49.
Staley, Jeffrey L. (2018), "The First Seventy Years of Jesus Films: A Canonical, Source-Critical History," in Walsh 2018e: 79–92.
Staley, Jeffrey L. (2021), "One Hundred Years of Cinematic Attempts at Raising a Stiff (Jn 11: 1–46)," in Walsh 2021c: 41–53.
Staley, Jeffrey L. and Richard Walsh (2007), *Jesus, the Gospels, and Cinematic Imagination: A Handbook to Jesus on DVD*, Louisville: Westminster John Knox.
Stern, Richard C., Clayton N. Jefford, and Guerric DeBona (1999), *Savior on the Silver Screen*, New York: Paulist.

Suit, Kenneth (2017), *James Friedrich and Cathedral Films: The Independent Religious Cinema of the Evangelist of Hollywood*, Lanham, MD: Lexington.
Swindell, Anthony C. (2010), *Reworking the Bible: The Literary Reception of Fourteen Biblical Stories*, Sheffield: Sheffield Phoenix.
Tatum, W. Barnes (2013), *Jesus at the Movies: A Guide to the First Hundred Years and Beyond*, 3rd ed., Salem: Polebridge.
Taylor, Joan (ed.) (2015), *Jesus and Brian: Exploring the Historical Jesus and His Times via Monty Python's Life of Brian*, London: Bloomsbury T&T Clark.
Taylor, Justin (2017), "The Amazing Lumo Project," *The Gospel Coalition*, August 28. Available online: https://www.thegospelcoalition.org/blogs/justin-taylor/the-amazing-lumo-project-filming-all-four-gospels-as-feature-films-using-only-the-unabridged-bible-as-the-script/ (accessed May 13, 2020).
Tebelak, John-Michael, with music and new lyrics by Stephen Schwartz (2012), *Godspell Libretto Vocal Book*, rev., New York: Music Theater International. Available online: http://michaelsewellarts.com/uploads/3/4/9/8/34986667/godspelllibretto_vocalbook[2012revival].pdf (accessed June 8, 2020).
Telford, William R. (2005), "The Two Faces of Betrayal: The Characterization of Peter and Judas in the Biblical Epic or Christ Film," in Eric S. Christianson, Peter Francis, and William R. Telford (eds.), *Cinéma Divinité: Religion, Theology, and the Bible*, 214–35, London: SCM.
Telford, William R. (2015), "*Monty Python's Life of Brian* and the Jesus Film," in Taylor 2015: 3–18.
Testa, Bart (1994), "To Film a Gospel … and Advent of the Theoretical Stranger," in Patrick Rumble and Bart Testa (eds.), *Pier Paolo Pasolini: Contemporary Perspectives*, 210–31, Toronto: University of Toronto Press.
Testa, Bart (1995), "Arcand's Double-Twist Allegory: *Jesus of Montreal*," in Loiselle and McIlroy 1995a: 90–112.
Theissen, Gerd (1987), *The Shadow of the Galilean: The Quest of the Historical Jesus in Narrative Form*, trans. John Bowden, Philadelphia: Fortress.
Tollerton, David (2015), "'Blasphemy!' On Free Speech Then and Now," in Taylor 2015: 55–67.
Turner, John G. (2008), *Bill Bright and Campus Crusade for Christ: The Renewal of Evangelicalism in Postwar America*, Chapel Hill: University of North Carolina Press.
Turner, Victor (1967), *The Forest of Symbols*, Ithaca: Cornell University Press.
Tutu, Desmond (2007), *Believe: The Words and Inspiration of Desmond Tutu*, Boulder: Blue Mountain.
Vallance, Tom (1994), "Obituary: Samuel Bronston," *Independent*, January 20. Available online: https://www.independent.co.uk/news/people/obituary-samuel-bronston-1408086.html (accessed May 12, 2020).
Van Gennep, Arnold (2019), *The Rites of Passage*, trans. Gabrielle L. Caffee and Monika B. Vizedom, 2nd ed., Chicago: University of Chicago Press.
Vander Stichele, Caroline (2016), "Reframing Jesus: Dreyer's Lifelong Passion," in Burnette-Bletsch 2016a: 587–98.
Vander Stichele, Caroline (2018), "A Deadly Daughter? Salome's Cinematic Afterlife," in Walsh 2018e: 358–68.
Vander Stichele, Caroline (2021), "From the New Testament to *The Brand New Testament*: Moving Beyond 'Jesus' Films," in Walsh 2021c: 175–85.
Vander Stichele, Caroline and Todd Penner (2006), "Passion for (the) Real: *The Passion of the Christ* and Its Critics," in J. Cheryl Exum (ed.), *The Bible in Film/The Bible and Film*, 18–36, Leiden: Brill.

Vargo, Marc E. (2003), *Infamous Gay Controversies of the Twentieth Century*, New York: Routledge.

Viano, Maurizio (1993), *A Certain Realism: Making Use of Pasolini's Film Theory and Practice*, Berkeley: University of California Press.

Wake, Oliver (n.d.), "Saville, Philip (1930–)," *BFI Screenonline*. Available online: http://www.screenonline.org.uk/people/id/1343327/ (accessed October 14, 2020).

Walsh, Frank (1996), *Sin and Censorship: The Catholic Church and the Motion Picture Industry*, New Haven/London: Yale University Press.

Walsh, Moira (1961), "Christ or Credit Card?" *America*, 106.3 (October 21): 71–4.

Walsh, Richard (2003), *Reading the Gospels in the Dark: Portrayals of Jesus in Film*, Harrisburg, PA: Trinity Press International.

Walsh, Richard (2005a), *Finding St. Paul in Film*, New York/London: T&T Clark.

Walsh, Richard (2005b), "Three Versions of ~~Judas~~ Jesus," in George Aichele and Richard Walsh (eds.), *Those Outside: Noncanonical Readings of Canonical Gospels*, 155–81. Harrisburg, PA: T&T Clark.

Walsh, Richard (2005c), "Wrestling with *The Passion of the Christ*: At the Movies with Roland Barthes and Mel Gibson," *The Bible and Critical Theory*, 1.2. Available online: https://cpb-ap-se2.wpmucdn.com/blogs.auckland.ac.nz/dist/f/375/files/2018/04/vol1-no2-2005-passion-of-the-christ-walsh-25-91-1-PB-sgx8i0.pdf (accessed October 24, 2020).

Walsh, Richard (2006), "The Gospel According to Judas: Myth and Parable," *Biblical Interpretation*, 14.1–2: 37–53.

Walsh, Richard (2008a), "*Barabbas*: The Cross That Damns," in Shepherd 2008: 113–29.

Walsh, Richard (2008b), "*The Passion* as Horror Film: St. Mel of the Cross," *The Journal of Religion and Popular Culture*, 20.1. Available online: https://utpjournals.press/doi/10.3138/jrpc.20.1.002 (accessed October 22, 2020).

Walsh, Richard (2010), *Three Versions of Judas*, London: Equinox.

Walsh, Richard (2013a), "A Beautiful Corpse: Fiction and Hagiography in *Son of Man*," in Walsh, Staley, and Reinhartz 2013: 192–205.

Walsh, Richard (2013b), "*Monty Python's Life of Brian*," in Reinhartz 2013b: 187–92.

Walsh, Richard (2016a), "*The Birth of a Nation* (D. W. Griffith, 1915) and *Intolerance* (Triangle/Wark, 1916): Griffith's Talismanic Jesus," in Shepherd 2016b: 179–99.

Walsh, Richard (2016b), "David Wark Griffith: Filming the Bible as the U.S. Story," in Burnette-Bletsch 2016a: 535–42.

Walsh, Richard (2016c), "Jesus Movies," in Timothy Beal (ed.), *Oxford Encyclopedia of the Bible and the Arts*, 497–507, Oxford: Oxford University Press.

Walsh, Richard (2016d), "On the Harmony of the (Asocial) Gospel: *Intolerance*'s Crosscut Stories," in Copier and Vander Stichele 2016: 43–78.

Walsh, Richard (2016e), "Paul and the Early Church in Film," in Burnette-Bletsch 2016a: 497–515.

Walsh, Richard (2017a), "Jesus Films," in *The Encyclopedia of the Bible and Its Reception* 14: 88–96, Berlin: Walter de Gruyter.

Walsh, Richard (2017b), "Now That Was a Nice Hanging: *The Hateful Eight* as Parable?" *Journal of Religion & Film*, 21.2 (October). Available online: http://digitalcommons.unomaha.edu/jrf/vol21/iss2/17/ (accessed November 7, 2020).

Walsh, Richard (2018a), "Cinematic Acts and the Triumph of Christianity," in Mikeal Parsons and Richard Walsh (eds.), *"A Temple Not Made with Hands": Essays in Honor of Naymond H. Keathley*, 188–201, Eugene: Pickwick.

Walsh, Richard (2018b), "Introduction: Biblical Film Studies," in Walsh 2018e: 1–18.
Walsh, Richard (2018c), "'My Kingdom Is Not of This World': Johannine Jesus Films and Christian Supersessionism," in Adele Reinhartz (ed.), *The Gospel of John and Jewish-Christian Relations*, 165–83, Lanham: Lexington Books/Fortress.
Walsh, Richard (2018d), "Never Say I Am the Christ. I Am the Son of Man," in Edwin K. Broadhead (ed.), *Let the Reader Understand: Essays in Honor of Elizabeth Struthers Malbon*, 295–311, London/New York: T&T Clark.
Walsh, Richard (2019), "Ready for His Closeup? Pasolini's *San Paolo* and *Paul, Apostle of Christ* (2018)," *Journal of the Bible and Its Reception*, 6.1: 1–37.
Walsh, Richard (2021a), "A Modest Proposal for Christ-Figure Interpretations: Explicated with Two Test Cases," in Walsh 2021c: 285–97.
Walsh, Richard (2021b), "Reading the Gospel(s) in the Dark: The Gospel Effect," in Walsh 2021c: 103–14.
Walsh, Richard, ed. (2018e), *T&T Clark Companion to the Bible and Film*, London/New York: T&T Clark.
Walsh, Richard, ed. (2021c), *T&T Clark Handbook of Jesus and Film*, London/New York: T&T Clark.
Walsh, Richard, Jeffrey L. Staley, and Adele Reinhartz, eds. (2013), *Son of Man: An African Jesus Film*, Sheffield: Sheffield Phoenix.
Warren, Meredith and Katie Edwards (2018), "*Mary Magdalene* Is yet Another Example of Hollywood Whitewashing," *The Conversation*, March 29. Available online: https://theconversation.com/mary-magdalene-is-yet-another-example-of-hollywoodwhitewashing-94134 (accessed November 15, 2020).
Webb, Robert L. (2004a), "The Flashbacks in *The Passion*: Story and Discourse as a Means of Explanation," in Corley and Webb 2004: 46–62.
Webb, Robert L. (2004b), "*The Passion* and the Influence of Emmerich's *The Dolorous Passion of Our Lord Jesus Christ*," in Corley and Webb 2004: 160–72.
West, Gerald O. (2013), "The *Son of Man* in South Africa," in Walsh, Staley, and Reinhartz 2013: 2–22.
Westbrook, Vivian (2016), "*The King of Kings* (DeMille Pictures, 1927): The Body and the Word on Film," in Shepherd 2016b: 256–70.
Wilkins, Peter (1995), "No Big Picture: Arcand and His US Critics," in Loiselle and McIlroy 1995a: 113–35.
Williams, Alan Larson (1992), *Republic of Images: A History of French Filmmaking*, Cambridge: Harvard University Press.
Williams, Alan Larson (2009), "The *Sage Femme* of Early Cinema," in Simon 2009a: 33–46.
Wilson, Eric G. (2006), *Secret Cinema: Gnostic Vision in Film*, New York: Continuum.
Wood, Michael (1989), *America in the Movies*, 2nd ed., New York: Columbus University Press.
Zeffirelli, Franco (1984), *Franco Zeffirelli's Jesus: A Spiritual Diary*, San Francisco: Harper & Row.
Zegarac, Nick (2008), "Samuel Bronston's Vanishing Empires," *The Hollywood Art*, March 2. Available online: http://thehollywoodart.blogspot.com/2008_03_01_archive.html (accessed May 12, 2020).
Ziolkowski, Theodore (1972). *Fictional Transfigurations of Jesus*, Princeton: Princeton University Press.
Zwick, Reinhold (1997), *Evangelienrezeption im Jesusfilm: Ein Beitrag zur Intermedialen Wirkungsgeschichte des Neuen Testaments*, Studien zur Theolgie und Praxis der Seelsorge 25, Würzburg: Seelsorge/Echter.

Zwick, Reinhold (2013), "Between Chester and Capetown: Transformations of the Gospel in *Son of Man*," in Walsh, Staley, and Reinhartz 2013: 110–19.

Zwick, Reinhold (2014), *Passion and Transformation: Biblische Resonanzen in Pier Paolo Pasolini's "mythischem Quartett,"* Marburg: Schüren.

Zwick, Reinhold (2016), "*Der Galiläer* (Express-Film, 1921) and *I.N.R.I.* (Neumann-Film, 1923): The Silence of Jesus in the German Cinema," in Shepherd 2016b: 211–35.

Zwick, Reinhold (2018), "German Jesus Movies," in Walsh 2018e: 139–50.

Zwick, Reinhold (2021), "Inculturation and Actualization: Rabah Ameur-Zaïmeche's *Histoire de Judas*," in Walsh (2021c): 67–76.

FILM INDEX

Atti degli apostoli 155, 161 n5, 162 n26, 163 n45
Aviator 221, 228 n59, 228 n62

Barabbas 88 n44, 218, 319 n20
Ben-Hur 2, 15 n11, 25 n19, 59, 74, 75, 86 n4, 87 n24, 88, 118 n11, 203, 255 n32, 260, 262, 266 n5, 284, 286, 288
The Bible 197, 249–50, 256 n39, 278 n5, 288
The Bible Collection 3, 249–50
The Birth of a Nation 47, 52, 53–4, 56 n5, 56 n10, 58 nn29–35
Braveheart 287, 289

Celui qui doit mourir (He Who Must Die) 1, 235
Christus 3, 46 n24
The Color of the Cross 304–5, 308 n25

Day of Triumph 85–6 n3, 87 n23
Le Déclin de l'empire américain 235, 236, 241 n45, 242 nn46–7

La Fée aux Choux 21, 25 n18
The Fiddler on the Roof 138, 206

Der Galiläer 2, 54, 58 n36, 295 n11
Godspell 2, 4, 8, 11, 16 n27, 121–32, 133, 139, 144 n9, 155, 162 n20, 181 n23, 186, 188, 195 n22, 226 n24, 233, 244, 246, 266 n9, 301, 303, 308 n21, 313
Golgotha 2, 74
The Gospel of John 2, 3, 8, 16 n26, 37, 71 n12, 183 n62, 202, 206, 268–79
Gospel Road 3, 88 n27, 121, 126, 129 n2, 197

The Greatest Story Ever Told 2, 7, 8, 9, 11, 16 n27, 16 n34, 71 n7, 72 n21, 97, 105–20, 125, 130 n14, 133, 135, 144 n11, 147, 160 n3, 162 n31, 164, 167, 168, 170, 174, 184, 195 n16, 202, 215, 219, 221, 227 n29, 233, 246, 255 n12, 256 n40, 257–8, 261, 266 n17, 284, 286, 288, 295 n18, 298, 307 n14, 311, 318 n16

Histoire de Judas 15n10, 304, 312, 313, 319 n20
Histoire d'un crime 32

I.N.R.I. 2, 56 n6
Intolerance 1, 3, 11, 16 n35, 47–58, 59, 80, 94, 145 n24, 185, 201, 235, 305

Jerusalem in the Time of Christ 42, 45 n6, 45 n12, 45 n20, 46 n26
Jesus (1999) 3, 7, 8, 9, 16 n34, 119 n15, 119 n25, 131 n26, 165, 204, 225 n6, 243–56, 257, 258, 260, 261, 266 n16, 281, 295 n9, 295 n16, 295 n20, 301, 310, 318 n15
Jesus Christ Superstar 1, 3, 4, 7, 8, 9, 11, 16 n30, 45 n14, 70 n4, 88 n29, 103 n18, 121, 126, 131 n26, 133–46, 161 n7, 174, 180 n8, 190, 203, 213, 215, 225 n6, 226 n10, 235, 236, 241 n33, 255 n11, 281, 283, 285, 296 n33, 310, 311, 314, 318 n8
Jésus de Montréal 1, 4, 7, 9, 11, 15 n14–15, 16 n27, 133, 140, 146 n43, 161 n7, 196 n27, 227 n46, 229–42, 280, 297 n49, 303
The Jesus Film 3, 7, 8, 9, 11, 16 n35, 35 n12, 37, 181 n31, 182 n52, 197–212, 226 n25, 245, 246, 258, 209, 266 n22, 274, 278 n6
Jesus of Nazareth 2, 3, 7, 8, 9, 11, 15 n22, 16 n34, 119 n25, 160 n3, 161 n9, 162 n26,

164–83, 194 n2, 197–8, 201, 202, 203, 205, 211 n7, 211 n11, 219, 226 n10, 227 n40, 229, 243, 245, 246, 247, 249, 255 n11, 255 n27, 256 nn39–41, 258, 260, 261, 266 n2, 266 n17, 277 n1, 283, 295 n18, 295 n20, 319 n22, 320 n30
Jesus Town USA 1, 85 n3, 235
Judith of Bethulia 47, 52, 53

The King of Kings 3, 7, 8, 11, 46 n28, 55, 59–73, 74, 86 n8, 87 n23, 87 n26, 89 n47, 119 n20, 131 n26, 136, 138, 144 n19, 145 n30, 162, n22, 172, 204, 213, 228 n56, 243, 245, 249, 258, 260, 272, 285–6, 287, 296 n23, 307 n14, 310, 319 n18
King of Kings 2, 7, 8, 9, 11, 16 n27, 73 n37, 73 n47, 74–89, 95, 106, 119 n17, 119 n23–5, 119 n30, 120 n36, 131 n27, 136, 138, 145 n27, 148, 161 n7, 162 nn18–19, 162 n29, 174, 195 n16, 201, 203, 225 n6, 226 n25, 243, 244, 245, 246, 247, 257, 258, 273, 286, 288, 296 n31, 296 n33, 301, 307 n14, 309, 312, 318 n15

The Last Temptation of Christ 3, 4, 7, 8, 9, 11, 70 n4, 72 n26, 78, 119 n25, 131 n26, 137, 145 n35, 161 n9, 180 n8, 181 n26, 185, 213–28, 231, 232, 243, 244, 245, 247, 249, 255 n11, 255 n18, 257, 261, 266 n16, 269, 295 n9, 295 n14, 310, 311, 312–3, 314, 318 n8, 320 n30
The Lawton Story 1, 85 n3, 235
The Lumo Gospels 11, 81–2, 206, 266 n10, 279 n24

From the Manger to the Cross 3, 7, 8, 11, 31, 35 n18, 36–46, 54, 55, 71 n11, 71 n18, 72 n26, 72 n33, 88 n29, 109, 137, 168, 198, 202, 211 n9, 213, 227 n29, 312, 318 n16
Mary Magdalene 5, 7, 8, 11, 15 n10, 25 n10, 70 n4, 182 n41, 245, 247, 309–20
Mean Streets 220, 226 n9
Il messia 3, 4, 5, 7, 8, 11, 14 n2, 15 n10, 16 n29, 25 n10, 102 n11, 147–63, 165, 172, 218, 219, 226 n10, 247, 260, 266 n9, 279 n19, 286, 301, 309, 312, 313, 314, 318 n2, 318 n9, 319 n20

The Miracle Maker 2, 3, 7, 8, 11, 257–67, 282, 310
Il miracolo 155, 161 n8, 163 n40
Monty Python's Life of Brian 2, 3, 4, 11, 15 n14, 16 n36, 146 n43, 146 n45, 161 n7, 161 n9, 184–96, 210 n3, 236, 241 n34, 256 n35, 296 n29, 297 n48

New Media Luke 197, 205–6, 279 n26

Parable 126–7, 131 n34, 155
The Passion of the Christ 1, 2, 4, 7, 8, 9, 11, 15 n24, 16 n30, 24 n2, 25 n9, 35 n14, 62, 87 n22, 103 n18, 131 n26, 145 n24, 145 n35, 150, 169, 172, 182 n52, 182 n55, 195 n24, 219, 225 n6, 244, 246, 274, 280–97, 298, 311, 314

Quo Vadis, 15 n11, 58 n28, 59, 73 n52, 74, 86 n4, 87 n24

Rebel Without a Cause 81, 89 n48
La ricotta 2, 15 n9, 18, 96–7, 103 n19, 151, 183 n59, 195 n16, 235, 286, 308 n26
Risen 88 n27, 261
The Robe 66, 74, 80, 88 n27, 203, 314
Roma città aperta 154, 163 nn41–2

The Searchers 87 n20, 119 n25, 120 n40
Seduto alla sua destra 304
Shane 113–14, 118 n6, 118 n25, 120 n35, 120 n37, 120 nn42–3
The Sign of the Cross 65, 66, 73 n52, 194 n6, 249
Silence 221
Son of God 249, 256 n39, 278 n5, 288
Son of Man 2, 4, 5, 7, 8, 11, 25 n10, 57 n13, 72 n21, 86 n11, 121, 131 n28, 162 n18, 247, 255 n12, 286, 298–308, 311, 312, 313, 314, 318 n9, 318 n16
Su re 89 n51, 162 n35, 308 n25

The Ten Commandments (1923) 56 n6, 59, 65–6, 249
The Ten Commandments (1956) 65, 86 n4, 182 n55
Le tout nouveau testament 14 n3

Il vangelo secondo Matteo 3, 4, 7, 8, 9, 11, 15 n23, 16 n30, 35 n7, 35 n14, 37, 42, 57 n12, 88 n32, 88 n42, 90–104, 119 n18, 121, 122, 125, 127, 130 n16, 131 n22, 132 n32, 134, 138, 145 n24, 153, 162 n14, 162 nn35–6, 163 n44, 172–3, 182 n47, 198, 205–6, 218, 219, 225 n3, 226 n27, 227 n29, 255 n27, 283, 295 n20, 296 n36, 301, 303, 307 n4, 307 n7, 307 n16, 314, 318 n9

La vie du Christ 1, 2, 5, 8, 15 n24, 17–26, 27–9, 31, 35 n13, 35 n16, 36, 41

La vie et passion de notre seigneur Jésus Christ 1, 7, 27–35, 36, 41

The Visual Bible: Matthew 206, 274, 279 n26

TOPIC INDEX

Andrew 86, 107, 148, 165, 244–5, 255 n15, 268–9, 271
angels 17–22, 25 n15, 27–31, 45 n11, 106, 121–2, 124, 125, 148, 184, 214, 216, 219, 225 n7, 227 n33, 227 n43, 228 n55, 268, 301, 304, 307 n8, 308 n23, 310, 313
 in infancy 20, 27–8, 30–1, 37, 91, 147, 165, 198, 201, 255 n9, 298–9, 308 n20
 in passion 18–19, 25 n11, 29, 72 n33, 94, 198, 202, 203, 217, 227 n44, 300–1, 308 n20, 319 n27
annunciation *See* Mary
anointing 134, 137, 231, 271, 311, 313
 in Bethany 38, 45 n17, 93, 271
 by Magdalene 109, 134
 by sinful woman (Lk. 7:36-50) 149, 240 n16
  sinful woman is Magdalene 7, 19, 22, 28, 38, 60, 134, 167, 170, 181 n30, 201, 214, 258, 261, 299
 waste complaint 36
 by Judas 38, 93, 134, 271, 299
antichrist 4–5, 187–90
(Herod) Antipas *See* trial of Jesus 2, 9, 75, 87 n25, 105–6, 108, 112, 119 n23, 119 n28, 145 n31, 151, 165, 167, 181 n24, 243, 255 n22, 258–9, 266 n12, 295 n16, 309
 arrest and execution of Baptist 75–6, 92, 107–8, 111, 119 n19, 119 n23, 148, 149, 150, 165, 166, 201, 255 n22, 258
anti-Semitism *See* Orientalism 8, 16 n34, 16 n35, 29, 45 n23, 46 n27, 54–5, 72 n23, 86 n8, 103 n16, 119 n32, 138, 145 n36, 162 n32, 168, 170, 275, 278 n17, 288, 289, 295 n11

apocalyptic *See* kingdom to come
Arcand, D. 11, 235–6, 240 n17, 240 n22, 240 n27, 241 nn31-2, 241 n36, 241 nn44-5, 242 nn46-8
arrest *See* Gethsemane; Judas 22, 36, 61, 73 n37, 74, 93, 131 n23, 135, 230, 232, 271, 282, 300

bad thief (Gesmas) 73 n36, 284, 285, 287
Baptism of Jesus 28, 37, 75, 91, 94, 106, 122, 148, 165, 201, 211 n9, 214–5, 244, 257, 268–9, 274, 278 n11, 299, 302, 311
 Dove 28, 148, 165, 211 n9, 257
 heavenly light 244, 257
 heavenly voice 75, 91, 95, 148, 165, 201, 257
Barabbas
 people's choice 61, 86 n3, 86 n8, 151, 169, 187, 203, 246, 255 n28, 260, 266 n19, 272, 283
 robber, thief, zealot 75, 76–8, 79, 80, 81, 88 n35, 168–9, 211 n11, 218–9, 227 n35, 245, 259, 295 n16, 296 n31
behold the lamb of god (Jn 1:29, 36) 37, 39, 40, 88 n29, 107, 148, 165, 180 n8, 215, 229, 243, 244, 255 n11, 256 n33, 257, 262, 268–9
beloved disciple *See* John, the disciple 46 n25, 170, 217, 233, 269, 270, 272, 273, 278 n13, 279 n23, 319 n25
 Baptist's disciple 268–9
 at the cross 45 n19, 72 n36, 272
 at the last supper 271
 at the trial 271
betrayal *See* Judas

Biblical epic *See* myth 1–5, 8, 21, 47, 52–4, 65–6, 73 n37, 73 n46, 74, 75, 79–81, 86 nn4–5, 90, 96–7, 102 n9, 103 n23, 105, 112–3, 121, 131 n19, 144 n7, 145 n31, 153, 165 n5, 172, 174, 180 n14, 181 n24, 184, 187, 188–9, 197, 207, 219, 226 n11, 226 n26, 227 n29, 235, 249, 257, 262, 266 n6, 288–9
biopic 80–1, 87 n22, 219–20, 228 n57, 243
blasphemy charge 103 n19, 109, 110, 135, 149, 150, 166, 168, 170, 184, 215, 259, 282, 295 n11, 295 n22
blood curse (Mt. 27:25) 29, 35 n14, 54, 61, 63, 86 n8, 93, 138, 151, 266 n19, 296 n26
Bluteau, L. 239 n1
Bosch 9, 216, 284, 289, 290, 295 n14, 295 n16
brought a sword (Mt. 10:34) 90, 91, 94, 95, 102 n7, 166, 205, 215, 218
burial 19, 62, 78, 94, 110, 131 n32, 151, 203, 233, 247, 260, 272, 300, 312

Caiaphas *See* trial, Sanhedrin 8, 16 n33, 63, 71 n6–7, 71 n12, 73 n43, 76, 77, 86 n3, 88 n38, 103 n16, 110, 134, 170, 202, 211 n13, 243, 247, 255 n29, 296 n24, 299
    Jewish trial 18–29, 61, 93, 109, 111, 135, 150, 168, 181 n38, 203, 246, 259, 282, 295 n18, 295 n22
    in ruined temple 62, 72 n23, 286
    satanic 72 n32, 282, 283, 286–7, 294 n5, 296 n34, 301
    spies and traps (*see* Sorak; Zerah) 59, 60–1, 107, 135, 150, 162 n22, 168, 245, 271, 281
    on Via Dolorosa and at the cross 61–2, 284–5, 295 n11
call of the disciples 75, 121
    Fishermen (Lk. 5–11) 28, 37–8, 91, 148, 166, 168, 198, 201, 245, 258, 269, 271, 278 n11
    John's disciples (Jn 1:35–42) 107, 131 n23, 148, 165, 244, 268–9, 272
    Matthew (Levi) 61, 95, 107, 166, 201, 245, 258, 274
    the Twelve 60, 91, 245, 299

canaanite woman *See* Syrophoenician woman
Carpenter (Artisan) 35 n13, 37, 59, 61, 63, 66, 72 n26, 149, 150, 153, 165, 213, 244, 257, 278 n11, 282
Caviezel, J. 295 n6
Centurion's confession 37, 73 n38, 77, 78, 80, 86 n3, 94, 110, 169, 187, 203, 255 n31, 260
Children *See* Manger; Nazareth childhood; slaughter of the innocents 18–19, 21–2, 25 n15, 35 n13, 37, 53, 71 n20, 91, 92, 94, 105, 111, 118 n7, 148, 151, 170, 197, 210 n3, 217, 282–3, 290, 298, 301, 307 n14, 310, 311
    Jesus among the children 3, 49, 92, 94, 107, 119 n21, 134, 144 n16, 149, 168, 201, 230, 244, 247, 248, 254 n1, 257–67, 269, 300
    of such are the kingdom 9, 59–63, 92, 112–3, 119 n21, 155, 168, 202, 257–67, 262, 312–13, 314, 318 n2
    suffer the children 48, 60, 62
    villains oppose 60, 63, 226 n24, 307 n15
    dismiss "Jesus" as "for children" 72 n21, 119n21, 214, 299–300
Christ figure *See* antichrist; Messiah; unchrist 1, 2, 3, 4–5, 10, 15 n12, 15 n18, 47, 50, 53–4, 56 n5, 89 n50, 103 n18, 146 n42, 221, 228 n62, 229, 239 n4, 242 n48, 286, 290
Claudia 9, 20, 72 n30, 74, 75, 76, 77, 87 n25, 109, 144 n17, 185, 283, 286, 294 n5, 295 n15, 296 n34
cleansing lepers 38, 66, 71 n17, 92, 144 n15, 182 n54, 184–5, 186, 187, 188
come unto me (Mt. 11:28–30) 92, 107, 149, 168, 201
cross (symbol, talisman, distinctive; *See* crucifixion; Via Dolorosa; cross foreshadowing) 2, 3, 18, 20, 25 n9, 39, 48, 49–51, 54, 55, 61, 62, 66, 72 n23, 73 n41, 74, 77, 78, 88 n40, 106, 110, 133, 136, 145 n24, 151, 182 n40, 184, 187, 195 n16, 195 n24, 202, 204, 217, 220–1, 233, 284, 296 n33, 301, 302, 305, 311

cross foreshadowing *See* passion prediction 9, 19, 35 n5, 37, 48, 60, 61, 72 n26, 119 n24, 106, 148, 164, 181 n26, 202, 213–4, 226 n10, 229, 232, 241 n36, 258, 300, 318 n16
crown of thorns 29, 61, 150, 216, 217, 272, 284
crucifixion *See* bad thief; Centurion's confession; good thief; last words; Mary; Magdalene 124–5, 231
    darkness 29, 39, 40, 62, 63, 77, 94, 203, 260, 285
    death 39, 62, 94, 110, 124, 136, 151, 203, 217, 218, 232, 233, 241 n36, 247, 260, 285, 312, 313
    earthquake 36, 39, 40, 62, 94, 247, 285–6, 287
    mockery 103 n20, 136, 169, 203, 247, 260, 285
    nailed to the cross 18, 39, 40, 93, 110, 124, 133, 136, 169, 203, 205, 216, 231, 246, 260, 272, 285, 301, 308 n26
    placard (INRI) 93, 203, 272, 285
    raising of the cross 39, 62, 77, 110, 136, 169, 203, 216, 247, 260, 272, 285, 301
    spear 169, 231, 255 n32, 286

Dafoe, W. 225 n3, 226 n23, 227 n48, 244
dark hermit 2, 8, 106–7, 108, 109–10, 111, 113, 119 n32, 120 n33, 233, 243, 247, 256 n40, 298
Deacon, B. 197, 211 n8, 211 n16
DeMille, C. 11, 64, 65–6, 70 nn1–2, 71 nn11–12, 71 nn15–16, 71 nn19–20, 72 n23, 72 n27, 73 nn36–7, 73 nn43–4, 73 nn46–50, 87 n23, 87 n26, 89 n47, 249
denial *See* Peter
deposition *See* Pietà 18, 78, 94, 96, 169, 260, 286, 295 n11
Doré illustrations 9, 28, 29, 35 n3

Ecce Homo (Jn 19:5) 17, 29, 30, 31, 39, 110, 136, 150, 169, 170, 181 n31, 216, 246, 266 n19, 284, 300
empty tomb 110, 151, 169, 203, 247, 260
epic *See* Biblical epic

Exorcism *See* Magdalene 37, 45 n10, 71 n10, 71 n19, 166, 181 n20, 198, 199, 299, 309

feeding the multitude 92, 149, 198, 255 n22, 271, 272
festival *See* passover 147, 149
foot washing (of disciples) 38, 124, 131 n23, 150, 271, 283, 319 n25

Garber, V. 130 n4, 130 n12, 132 n37
Gauntier, G. 42, 45 n3, 45 n11, 45 n13
gender *See* patriarchy 5, 8, 21–2, 25 n15, 26 n25, 29, 35 n13, 41, 46 n25, 246, 319 n21
genre 11–13, 14 n3, 16 n42, 80, 188–9
Gethsemane (garden of Olives; *See* arrest; Judas; temptation) 18, 19, 21, 22, 25 n11, 38, 62, 63, 72 n32, 73 n37, 77, 86 n7, 87 n22, 93, 109, 135, 150, 168, 208, 216, 217, 227 n47, 258, 281, 283, 288, 294 n5, 300, 307 n11, 311
Gibson, M. 4, 11, 288–90, 295 n7, 295 n11, 296 nn36–7, 297 n46
gnostic 5, 29, 35 n9, 120 n44, 221, 228 n62
for god so loved the world (Jn 3:16) 70 n5, 107, 246, 247, 249, 255 n26
good shepherd 76, 88 n29, 107, 119 n21, 149, 161 n7, 270
good thief (Dismas; Today in Paradise; Lk. 23:43) 39, 72 n 36, 93, 96, 101, 203, 216, 255 n31, 285, 295 n11
Griffith, D. W. 47, 51, 52–4, 56 n1, 56 n5–6, 56 n8, 57 nn18–22, 57 nn24–7, 58 nn28–32, 58 n34, 65
Guy, A. 21–2, 24 n5, 25 nn6–7, 25 nn17–8, 25 nn21–2, 26 nn23–5, 27–8, 31–2, 36, 38, 41, 314, 315, 319 n27

handwashing 29, 39, 74, 86 n8, 110, 136, 151, 260, 284, 300
head guard 270–2
healing the blind 28, 38, 45 n16, 71 n15, 86 n9, 108, 109, 129 n1, 186, 202, 215, 230, 310, 318 n11
    girl (DeMille) 59–60, 62, 63, 71 n10, 258
    at Jericho 36, 38

man born blind (Jn 9) 60, 109, 150, 168, 270, 271
  with mud/spittle 168, 215, 270, 310
healing the lame 28, 59–60, 92, 107, 109, 215, 245
  Jn 5:1-18, 60, 121–2, 270, 271
  paralytic lowered through roof 38, 71 n11, 166, 258, 299
Henderson-Bland, R. 38, 42, 45 n11, 45 n15
Herod (the Great) 30, 37, 38, 45 n12, 74–5, 91, 105, 112, 118 n7, 147, 151, 164, 165, 181 n24, 298–9
History 3–5, 11–13, 15 n14–15, 41, 42, 51, 52, 155, 171
Hunter, J. 75, 81, 87 n20, 89 n47

I am(s) (Johannine) 36, 38, 40, 45 n5, 63, 76, 105, 107, 108, 109, 110, 112, 149, 164, 167, 168, 171, 211 n15, 245, 246, 270, 271, 272, 275, 282, 285, 295 n17
  Jn 12:46 59–60, 64
I am with you always (Mt. 28:20) 62, 64, 94, 110, 169, 203, 260, 274
Imperialism *See* Orientalism 4, 5, 11, 12, 42, 46 n27, 51–2, 54, 80, 81–2, 188, 211 n8, 211 n18, 277 n1, 288, 299, 304–5, 307 n16, 313
Irazoqui, E. 102 n11, 162 n14, 225 n3

Jesus adjacent 2–5, 6–9, 15 nn10–12, 18–19, 25 n19, 171–2, 184, 189, 190, 237, 314–15
Jesus relocation 1–5, 13, 15 nn6–7, 131 n31, 138, 140, 235, 298, 303
Jewison, N. 11, 138–9, 144 nn5–7, 144 n10, 144 n20, 145 n23–4, 145 n27, 145 n38, 146 nn39–40
John, Gospel of 5, 11, 27, 36, 45, 60, 98–101, 103, 104 n24, 111, 112, 113–14, 134, 144 n14, 153, 170, 227, 249, 259, 262, 268–79, 296 n32, 312
John the Baptist *See* Baptism of Jesus; behold the lamb of god
  are you the one to come 76, 92, 106, 148, 201
  arrest and death 75–6, 79, 91, 92, 107–8, 111, 119 n19, 119 n23, 148, 149, 150, 165, 166, 201, 229, 233, 245, 255 n22, 258
  Jesus's destiny 8, 16 n27, 78, 90, 93, 111, 119 n24, 122, 124, 125, 130 n4, 130 n8, 131 n24, 214–5, 227 n30, 244
  preaching 45 n4, 75, 78, 92, 93, 106–7, 112, 119 n24, 122, 124, 125, 130 n11, 148, 165, 181 n20, 181 n35, 214–5, 244, 268, 309, 311
John, the disciple *See* beloved disciple 75, 98, 148, 151, 152, 166, 216, 227 n46, 281, 282, 283, 285, 286, 295 n16
  Baptist's disciple 107, 244
  at the cross 39, 93, 94, 285–6
  at the last supper 150, 168
  at the tomb 110, 247, 255 n15
  at the trial 93, 150–1, 283
  on Via Dolorosa 246, 284
Joseph 2, 7, 35 n13, 37, 41, 86 n7, 91, 94, 105, 147–8, 164–5, 170, 180 n11, 180 n15, 243–4, 254 n1, 255 n10, 255 n17, 255 n21
Joseph of Arimathea 107, 110, 119 n21, 166, 167, 168, 170, 180 n5, 181 n24, 182 n48, 198, 203, 259, 272, 282, 286, 295 n11
Judas *See* anti-Semitism; Gethsemane; Arrest 8, 16 n28, 39, 59, 62, 71 n19, 74, 81, 107, 108, 111, 119 n31, 138, 145 n28, 149–50, 151, 169, 180 n19, 181 n34, 227 n40, 233, 246, 255 n27, 261, 270, 278 n11, 295 n20, 301, 310–13
  anointing complaint (*see* anointing) 36, 38, 93, 134, 162 n21, 299
  betrayal 16 n29, 18, 45 n21
  destiny (story, tradition) 120 n33, 125, 130 n8, 131 n24, 135–6, 138, 140, 145 n29, 187, 190, 213, 216–17, 226 n10, 226 n22, 227 n37
  hanging 16 n30, 38, 62, 78, 93, 103 n18, 110, 135, 145 n21, 169, 254, 283, 312
  kiss 38, 77, 124, 135, 150, 167, 216, 245, 259, 300, 311
  money (30 pieces) 38, 39, 61, 109, 135, 145 n36, 150, 162 n27, 167, 246, 259, 271, 281
  politics 59, 61, 63, 133–4, 167–8, 170

revolution 75, 77, 78, 86 n3, 87 n23, 88 n34, 166, 213–16, 245–6, 247, 255 n25, 258–9, 261, 266 n12, 299
satanic (or dark) 38, 40, 42, 55, 60, 72 n21, 72 n32, 109, 144 n7, 168, 202, 204, 260, 271, 282–3, 286, 287, 289, 294 n5
watches passion events 62, 63, 77, 93, 94, 282–3, 300, 312

kingdom, not of this world (Jn 18:36) 61, 63, 72 n27, 77, 109, 110, 112, 136, 149, 150, 162 n17, 169, 230, 272, 297 n42
kingdom to come 50, 54, 106, 119 n14, 120 n44, 149, 153, 232, 234, 242, n49, 259, 302, 309, 310, 311, 312, 313, 318 n2
kingdom within (Lk. 17:12) 5, 76, 107, 112, 162 n17, 202, 231, 312
religious subjectivity or spirituality 88 n42, 112, 164–5, 221

last supper *See* foot washing 18–19, 20, 22, 25 n11, 27, 35 n3, 39, 61, 62, 73 n39, 74, 77, 88 n35, 93, 111, 126, 135, 137, 162 n15, 162 n25, 168, 180 n10, 198, 202, 216, 232, 246, 259, 271, 284, 285, 300, 319–20 nn16–17
last words (from the cross) 88 n40, 110, 151, 169, 203, 272, 319 n20
father, forgive (Lk. 23:34) 72 n36, 88 n40, 110, 136, 151, 154, 169, 203, 217, 247, 285
into thy hands (Lk. 23:46) 73 n36, 88 n40, 110, 136, 169, 198, 203, 247, 260, 285
my god, my god (Mk 15:34; Mt. 27:46) 73 n36, 88 n40, 94, 110, 136, 169, 217, 227 n50, 231, 234, 247, 254 n8, 285
Lazarus 227 n45, 243, 254 n1, 257–8
raising of 27, 28, 38, 60, 61, 71 n10, 105, 108–9, 112, 119 n25, 150, 153, 162 n31, 164, 167, 212 n26, 215, 227 n35, 243, 249, 254 n8, 259, 261, 262, 270–1, 299, 307 n12, 308 n20, 310–1, 307 n14, 315, 318 n13, 319 n25
Stevens's character 2, 8, 107, 108–9, 111, 112, 113, 119 n31, 120 n36

leading Pharisee 2, 71 n12, 269–72, 273
Livio 8, 243, 245, 246–7, 255 n17, 255 n22
love command *See* sermon on the mount 3, 5, 50, 76–7, 78, 122, 149, 150, 151, 153, 168, 214–5, 227 n36, 231, 234, 235, 271, 311, 312, 314
Lucius 2, 8, 9, 75–8, 79, 80, 81, 82–5, 86 nn8–9, 86 n13, 88n27, 88 n35, 88 n38, 247, 296 n31
Luke, Gospel of 7, 9, 11, 18, 22, 24 n1, 35 n2, 37, 54, 72 n33, 86 n10, 87 n13, 103 n23, 126, 153, 161 n7, 164, 171, 197–212, 257, 260, 262, 264 n4, 266 n15, 279 n20, 279 n26, 296 n25, 307 n6

Magdalene *See* anointing; woman taken in adultery 7, 16 n25, 18, 15 n14, 39, 70 nn4–5, 76, 94, 108, 134–7, 145 n26, 162 n25, 166, 182 n41, 187, 190, 198, 213, 214, 215, 217, 226 nn12–13, 226 nn18–19, 230, 242 n49, 245, 248, 269, 270, 284, 285, 286, 295 n16, 329 n23
conversion (see Exorcism) 2, 7–8, 46 n28, 59–61, 62–3, 65, 87 n26, 129 n2, 144 n19, 170, 181 n 28, 181 n30, 204, 228 n53, 286, 314–15
at the cross 39, 45 n19, 62–3, 110, 169, 272, 285, 312, 313
disciple 7–8, 108, 111, 233, 243, 246, 247, 272, 273, 279 n18, 309–20
exorcism (of Mary) 7, 60, 63, 129 n2, 134, 257–8, 261, 309–10, 314, 318 n4
at last supper, trials, or on the Via Dolorosa 72 n31, 136, 150–1, 169, 216, 246, 259, 271–2, 282–4, 311–2
resurrection appearance (announcement, empty tomb) 62, 78, 110, 111, 151, 169, 204, 231, 247, 260–1, 272, 312
Magi *See* wise men
Manger 18, 29, 30, 36, 37, 105, 184
Mark 150–1
The King of Kings character 8, 59–60, 62, 63, 71 n11–12, 71 n15, 71 n24, 260
Mark, Gospel of 11, 17, 25 n13, 36, 45 n17, 60, 71 n15, 73 n41, 103, 153, 234, 237, 278 n6, 279 n25

Mary *See* Manger; nativity; Nazareth childhood; Pietà) 7, 15 n23, 77, 145 n26, 161 nn9–10, 216, 227 n33, 254 n6, 255 n12, 318 n15
  annunciation 27, 28, 37, 165, 180 n2, 198, 211 n9, 244, 255 n21, 298, 302, 307 n6, 311
  co-sufferer (co-redeemer, intercessor) 15 n23, 60, 62, 71 n15, 73 n36, 73 n39, 92–4, 151–2, 239 n7, 282–4, 286, 287, 294 n5, 300–1
  at the cross 39, 41, 45 n19, 77, 92–4, 110, 151, 169, 246, 272, 285–6, 312
  nativity 19, 22, 25 n13, 19, 30, 35n13, 90–1, 120 n36, 164–5, 170, 180 nn2–4, 182 n39, 244, 257
  resurrection appearances (empty tomb) 62, 94, 151, 152
  teacher (mentor) 37, 45 n13, 75, 78, 87 n25, 147, 148–9, 150, 152–3, 165, 244, 245, 247, 248, 255 n21, 294 n5, 298–9, 301, 308 n20, 311
  Via Dolorosa 39, 151, 246, 284–5, 294 n5
  virgin (birth) 45 n13, 138, 147, 151, 154, 161 n8, 170, 186, 187, 201, 255 n9
Matthew, Gospel of 11, 35 n2, 26, 45 n17, 54, 72 n24, 90–104, 121–32, 164, 227 n46, 274, 298
Méliès, G. 31–3, 35 n18, 104 n26
Messiah *See* antichrist; Christ figure; unchrist
  making of 2, 17, 140, 146 n45, 161 n7, 165, 185–6, 187–90
  non-Christian 2, 4–5, 15 n18, 75, 76–7, 79, 140, 161 n7, 184, 187–90, 236–7, 242 n49, 304
myth 3–4, 11, 13, 15 n16, 16 n41, 35 nn20–1, 94, 96–7, 106, 120 n37, 133–4, 135, 140, 174, 182 n50, 188–9, 195 n15, 212 n25, 304

nativity 7, 17, 18, 22, 27–8, 29, 35 n2, 35 n17, 38, 74, 86 n10, 105, 120 n36, 147, 155, 180 n3, 257, 288
Nazareth childhood 27, 35 n13, 37, 75, 106, 164–5, 170, 180 n3, 180 n5, 244, 284, 298–9, 311

Nazareth rejection *See* synagogue 108, 148, 152, 162 n15, 164, 165, 168, 181 n32, 201, 215
Neeley, T. 136, 144 nn5–6, 145 n24, 146 n46
Nicodemus 71 n7, 107, 109, 110, 111, 119 n21, 168–9, 170, 171, 180 n8, 181 n24, 269, 270, 271, 272, 282
nonviolence (teaching of; *See* Sermon on the Mount) 3, 5, 50, 230, 299, 303

Olcott, S. 40–2, 45 n6, 45 n9, 45 n12, 45 n16, 46 n26, 54, 72 n33
Orientalism *See* anti-Semitism; Imperialism 3, 5, 9, 15 n13, 24 n4, 35 n3, 41, 42, 46 n26–8, 53, 59, 63, 74, 225 n5, 288, 296 n23, 296 n38

parable 4, 5, 13, 15 n17–18, 16 n41, 38, 86 n3, 92, 97, 122, 126–7, 131 n17, 149, 188–9, 226 n24, 235, 245, 258, 261, 304, 307 n11
  good samaritan 85 n3, 122, 149, 167, 195 n26, 198, 202, 211 n11, 259, 261, 266 n14
  mustard seed 214, 258, 309, 312, 314
  pharisee and the tax-collector 47, 48–9, 122, 201–2, 205
  prodigal son 122, 123, 125, 126, 166, 170, 181 n23, 181 n37, 217, 226 n18
  seeds (Sower) 86 n3, 201, 214
  Sheep and the Goats 122, 123, 131 n32
Pasolini, P. 11, 15 n23, 42, 57 n12, 94–7, 102 nn2–9, 103 nn13–14, 103 n16, 103 n19, 103 n23, 104 nn26–30, 153–4, 162 n34, 163 n44, 172, 219, 235
passion film 1–5, 17
passion play 1–5, 14 n4, 15 n15, 17, 18, 41, 54, 85 n3, 96, 138, 140, 160 n3, 196 n27, 229–35, 237, 240 n23, 280, 297 n49
passion prediction *See* cross foreshadowing 71 n19, 92, 93, 150, 162 n23, 167, 168, 201, 202, 240 n14, 255 n27, 259, 271, 282, 300, 307 n13, 307 n17, 311
passover *See* festivals 76, 77, 148, 150, 151, 164, 165, 167, 168, 169, 226 n10, 245, 281, 282, 309, 310

patriarchy *See* gender 5, 7, 8, 11, 21–2, 29, 35 n13, 71 n20, 312–3, 314, 315, 319 n27, 320 n30
Peter *See* call of the disciples 8, 60, 109, 119 n16, 148, 166, 170, 182 n55, 198, 204, 205, 216, 217, 227 n32, 233, 245, 246, 258, 259, 269, 270, 271, 281, 282, 295 n16, 299, 300, 301, 310, 311, 313
   confession 92, 108, 131 n32, 166–7, 181 n32, 198, 201, 205, 215, 230, 234, 245, 272, 311, 315
   denial 18, 34 n1, 61, 72 n29, 77, 93, 94, 109–10, 111, 120 n36, 135, 145 n23, 150, 164, 168–9, 170, 202, 205, 216, 227 n40, 246, 255 n27, 259, 271–2, 282, 295 n20, 300
   resurrection appearances (tomb) 110, 169, 182 n41, 182 n43, 203, 231, 247, 260, 272, 312, 314
Phoenix, J. 318 n7
Pietà *See* deposition 7, 26 n23, 78, 135, 151, 152, 154, 163 n42, 169, 217, 232, 233, 247, 286, 287, 301, 302, 312
pilate *See* Barabbas; blood curse; crown of thorns; Ecce Homo; handwashing; scourging; Trial 9, 16 n35–6, 18, 39, 42, 45 n23, 54, 61, 63, 73 n43, 73 n45, 74, 75, 76, 77, 78, 79, 86 n8, 87 n25, 88 n38, 93, 109–10, 111, 112, 119 n28, 134, 135–6, 140, 150–1, 162 n17, 162 n29, 164, 168–9, 170, 185, 187, 198, 202–3, 211 n13, 216, 230, 243, 245, 246, 247, 255 n24, 259–60, 271, 272, 280, 283–4, 285, 286, 288, 294 n5, 295 nn21–2, 296 n24, 296 n26, 296 n34, 299, 300, 301, 307 n5
Powell, R. 171, 174, 180 n16, 182 n42, 182 n51, 256 n39
prophets (prophecy) 16 n27, 75, 88 n42, 105, 106–7, 110–11, 112, 120 n33, 147, 148, 160 n3, 161 n7, 164, 165, 168, 170, 171, 185, 230, 234, 241 n36, 296 n34, 310, 311
   Hosea 6:6 106, 107, 109, 112
   Isaiah 6:9–10 94, 95
   Isaiah 40:1–3 106, 165, 166
   Isaiah 53 48, 54, 89 n51, 169, 170, 171, 180 n8, 215, 219, 228 n55, 281, 286, 288
   Isaiah 61:1–2 148, 150, 165, 201
   Micah 5:2 105, 106, 108, 110, 111, 112, 147, 164

raising of Jairus's daughter *See* Tamar 18, 19, 28, 35 n17, 230, 258
raising of Lazarus *See* Lazarus
raising of the widow's son at Nain 38, 198, 210 n3, 307 n14
Rasalingam, S. 81–2, 206, 266 n10
Ray, N. 80–1, 86 nn7–9, 88 n28, 88 n32, 88 nn41–2, 88 n46, 89 n47, 89 n59, 118 n9, 119 n24
Rembrandt 9, 62, 73 n34
resurrection (of Jesus) 24, 29, 32, 35 n3, 35 n7, 37, 40, 45 n11, 59, 62, 94, 217, 227 n51, 231, 232–3, 241 n42, 286, 301
   Roman guard 25 n13, 29, 62, 73 n38, 110, 169, 232
resurrection appearances (*see* Mary; Magdalene; Peter; Thomas) 22, 33 n7, 86 n7, 131 n32, 247, 260
   commissioning 94, 110, 203
   sea of Galilee 78, 86 n9, 272
   upper room 62, 169, 247
rich young man (ruler; *See* Lazarus) 103 n12, 111, 166, 180 n19, 202
Rossellini, R. 11, 96, 102 n8, 102 n11, 153–5, 160 nn3–4, 161 n5, 161 nn7–10, 161 n13, 162 nn14–15, 162 n19, 162 n26, 162 n28, 162 n30, 162 nn32–4, 163 nn39–41, 172, 173
Rossi, P. 162 n14

Sabbath controversies 60, 103 n12, 148–9, 202, 247, 270
Salome 7, 38, 75, 76, 78, 87 n16, 87 n26, 89 n48, 92, 93, 119 n23, 149, 166
samaritan woman 7, 18, 19, 22, 27, 28, 38, 148, 269, 310, 311, 312, 319 n25
satan *See* Dark Hermit 8, 61, 63, 72 n32, 75, 91, 92, 103 n23, 106, 124, 144 n7, 166, 167, 170, 202, 214–5, 217, 219, 227

n49, 240 n8, 244, 246, 247, 255 n26,
257, 259, 281–2, 260, 266 n10, 281–3,
284, 286, 287, 289, 290, 294 n5, 295
n11, 295 n22, 297 n42, 298–9, 300,
301, 302, 304, 306 n1, 307 n16
Snake (Gen. 3?) 199, 201, 214, 282, 287, 298
Scorsese, M. 11, 88 n46, 145 n35, 218–21, 225
nn5–6, 225 n8, 226 n9, 226 nn11–12,
226 n20, 227 n48, 227 n51, 228 n52,
228 n54, 243, 314
scourging 20, 29, 39, 62, 72 n23, 77, 88 n40,
136, 150, 170, 198, 203, 216, 231, 266
n19, 272, 283–4, 285, 287, 290, 294 n5,
295 n16, 296 n25
sermon on the mount (Mt. 5–7, Sermon on
the plain, Lk. 6:20-49) 38, 51, 76–7, 78,
79, 86 n8, 88 nn28–9, 88 n32, 88 n37,
92, 95, 106, 107, 108, 111, 119 n25,
122–3, 124, 126, 145 n27, 149, 167,
173, 184, 187, 196 n27, 201, 226 n25,
230, 231, 242, 245, 314
   golden rule 76, 122, 149, 168
   lord's prayer (Mt. 6:9-13) 61, 72 n27, 76,
108, 150, 167, 311
   love enemies (Mt. 5:44) 76, 92, 122, 131
n19, 168, 245, 284, 299
   seek kingdom first (trust God, Mt.
6:25–34) 92, 107, 110, 111, 112, 113,
118 n2, 119 n13, 122, 166, 202, 230,
231, 258, 313, 314
   turn other cheek (Mt. 5:39) 109, 122, 131
n19, 168, 214, 245
shepherds 37, 164, 201, 298, 308 n20
Simon of Cyrene 2, 8, 39, 62, 63, 73 n40, 110,
169, 187, 203, 216, 255 n31, 266 n19,
284–5, 286, 287, 290, 295 n11, 296
n29–31
Sisto, J. 244, 254 n2, 256 n42
slaughter of the innocents 18–19, 28, 30, 37,
74–5, 91, 94, 105, 119 n19, 147, 164,
165, 167, 255 n12, 298–9, 300–2, 307
n10, 308 n20
Sorak 2, 8, 107, 109, 111, 119 n21, 119 n26,
119 n32, 170, 247, 258
stations of the Cross 17, 24 n1, 229, 230–1,
233, 239 n2, 240 n9, 240 n23, 241

nn35–6, 241 n42, 280–1, 283, 294
nn1–2, 294 n4, 296 n27, 297 nn48–9
Stevens, G. 11, 112–14, 118 nn1–2, 118 n5–6,
118 n9, 119 n16, 119 n21, 119 n24–5,
120 nn34–5, 120 n37, 120 n40, 120
n42–5
Susanna 148, 149, 150, 151, 152, 161 n11,
318 n2
synagogue See Nazareth rejection 103 n16,
107, 112, 131 n32, 148, 150, 164, 165,
166, 168, 170, 201, 215, 247, 257, 262,
270, 309
Syrophoenician (or canaanite) woman 5, 7,
245–6, 248, 310

Tamar See raising of Jairus's daughter 2, 8,
257–62, 266 n4
tax controversy 60–1, 76, 86 n10, 150, 181
n37, 243–4, 245, 255 n17, 259, 260,
310
technological developments
   70mm 74, 79, 86 n6, 87 n21
   animation 184
      animation techniques 262–4, 266 n10,
266n23 267 nn24–5
      cel animation 257–9, 261–2, 264, 265
n1, 266 n9
   blue wash 28
   CGI 285–7, 295 n19, 319 n24
   Cinerama 118 n10
   crosscut 47, 51, 57 n27
   digitalizing 272–3
   dissolve 105, 108–110, 134
   Dolly and track 88 n28
   eyemo camera 71 n16
   freedive photography 318
   freeze-frame 134
   handheld camera 98, 153, 282
   huge sets 53, 57 n18
   intertitles 20, 22, 26 n26, 36–7, 44, 56 n4,
57 n20, 72 n28, 73 n42
   montage 135, 137, 145 n2
   pan Cinor zoom 160 n4
   slow motion 134, 136, 295 n19
   stencil coloring 32
   stop motion puppetry 257, 262 n4

superimposition 28–9, 32, 51–2
talkies 74, 85 n3
television 172–4, 180 n1, 180 n19, 243, 250, 256 n35, 256 n41, 257 n15
tinting 35 n19
two-strip technicolor 59, 66, 74
ultra panavision 70 118 n10
videotape 299–300
zoom 133, 171–2
temple
  cleansing 27, 38, 42, 61, 63, 72 n27, 75, 77, 86 n8, 92, 109, 112, 131 n32, 134, 148, 167–8, 202, 215–6, 231, 245, 259, 269, 311
  Jesus at twelve 28, 37, 147–8, 164–5, 211 n9, 244, 257, 259
  revolt/slaughter 74, 77–8, 109, 119 n30, 168, 202, 215–6, 243, 246, 255 n24, 270
  veil split 62, 72 n23, 203, 260, 285–6
temptation (of Jesus)
  on the cross 213, 217, 227 n50, 228 n53, 260
  in the garden (*see* Gethsemane) 124, 131 n26, 135, 136, 137, 145 n28, 246, 259, 261, 266 n16, 281–2, 287, 295
  in the temple 61, 72 n27
  in the wilderness 42, 75, 77, 91, 97, 106, 119 n13, 133–4, 180 n17, 201, 202, 214–5, 219,232, 243, 244, 247, 255 n25, 257, 261, 298
Thomas 166, 170, 230, 233, 245, 246, 258
  resurrection appearance 62, 86 n3, 169, 247, 260, 272, 286
Tissot illustrations 9, 15 n13, 17–18, 22, 24 n5, 25 n12, 28, 36, 37, 38, 39, 40, 41, 42, 44 n1–2, 45 n15, 45 n22, 46 n24, 211 n9
Torah 16 n29, 48, 54, 66, 73 n50, 92, 109, 122, 147–8, 149, 150, 165, 166, 167, 170, 180 n5, 215, 228 n58, 279 n17, 299
transfiguration 9, 18, 19, 27, 28, 29, 30, 31, 33, 35 nn11–12, 37, 61, 62, 92, 131 n32, 136, 137, 140, 170, 181 n31, 201, 202, 203–4, 205, 221, 228 n56, 228 n62, 245, 247, 286

trial (of Jesus)
  before Antipas 39, 77, 109–10, 135, 169, 198, 203, 260, 283
  before Pilate (*see* Barabbas; blood curse; crown of thorns, Ecce Homo; handwashing; scourging) 16 n34, 18, 19, 22, 39, 45 n23, 50, 61, 72 n23, 74, 77, 88 nn36–8, 93, 94, 109–10, 131 n32, 136, 143 n3, 164, 169, 216, 246, 260, 280, 283–4, 288, 295 n22, 319 n20
  Sanhedrin 16 n34, 45 n23, 61, 77, 86 n8, 92, 93, 94, 109, 111, 118 n5, 119 n32, 131 n32, 138, 150, 164, 168, 170, 181 n38, 182 n45, 203, 216, 246, 259, 266 n17, 280, 282, 295 n18, 295 n22, 304, 319 n20
triumphal entry 17–18, 22, 29, 38, 41, 61, 71 n10, 72 n27, 74, 77, 109, 131 n32, 135, 150, 152, 167–8, 202, 215, 259, 271, 284, 300

unchrist *See* antichrist; Christ figure 4–5, 187–90, 195 n24, 195 n26

Veronica 15 n24, 17–20, 22, 26 n25, 29, 30, 39, 88 n39, 169, 216, 260, 284, 286, 299, 319 n27
Via Dolorosa (carrying the cross; *See* Simon of Cyrene; stations of the cross; Veronica) 7, 17–18, 19, 20, 22, 29, 39, 48, 49, 50, 54, 61, 62, 63, 73 n40, 77, 88 n39, 93, 110, 120 n36, 136, 147, 151, 152, 169, 184, 187, 198, 203, 213, 216, 226 n13, 230–1, 246, 248, 260, 262, 272, 284–5, 287, 294 n2, 294 n5, 295 n14, 295 n16, 296 n27, 296 n30, 311, 312, 313, 314, 318 n4, 319 n27
virgin (birth, *See* Mary)
visual translation 4, 5, 11, 13, 37, 81–2, 206, 266 n10, 279 n24
Von Sydow, M. 105, 108, 118 n3, 215

walking on water 28–9, 30, 35 n18, 38, 45 n6, 92, 135, 230, 240 n11, 240 n19, 240 n29, 245, 248, 270, 271

Warner, H. B. 71 n16, 89 n47
wedding at Cana 28, 38, 41, 47–8, 50, 51, 57 n11, 215, 226 n10, 240 n21, 243
what is truth (Jn 18:38) 77, 150, 162 n16, 169, 272
wise men 19, 27, 28, 35 n17, 37, 39, 91, 105, 147, 164, 181 n24, 182 n55, 190, 298
woes against the scribes and Pharisees (Mt. 23) 8, 51, 93, 95, 109, 124, 150, 168, 231, 307 n16
woman taken in adultery 7, 38, 47, 48, 49, 54, 57 n11, 61, 72 n27, 165, 168, 180 n5, 184, 230, 233, 245, 270, 307 n12, 310

Magdalene 7, 45 n20, 75, 78, 107, 111, 134, 137, 150, 162 n22, 214, 284, 286, 299, 307 n10
women with Jesus (Lk. 8:2-3) *See* guy; Magdalene; Mary; Susanna 19, 20, 22, 152, 162, 204, 233, 314

Young, R. 249–50, 256 n42

Zecca, F. 31–2
Zeffirelli, F. 11, 172–3, 180 nn9–11, 180 n13, 180 n17, 180 n19, 181 nn21–2, 181 n24, 181 n29, 181 nn31–2, 181 n34, 182 n40, 182 n42, 182 n55, 183 nn56–8
Zerah 2, 8, 167–8, 169, 170, 181 n24, 181 n34, 247

www.ingramcontent.com/pod-product-compliance
Lightning Source LLC
Chambersburg PA
CBHW051803230426
43672CB00012B/2612